The Scale and Nature of the Late Bronze Age Economies of Egypt and Cyprus

Keith Padgham

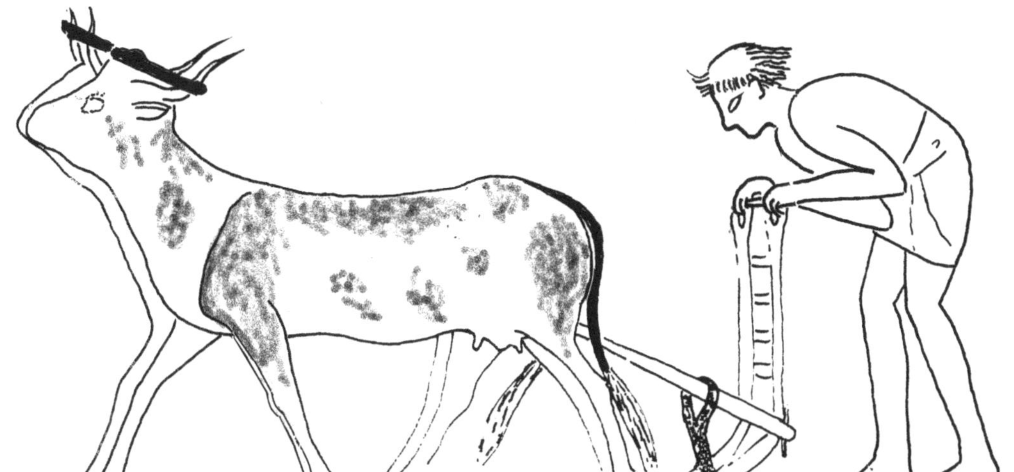

BAR International Series 2594
2014

Published in 2016 by
BAR Publishing, Oxford

BAR International Series 2594

The Scale and Nature of the Late Bronze Age Economies of Egypt and Cyprus

ISBN 978 1 4073 1222 4

BAR Publishing is the trading name of British Archaeological Reports (Oxford) Ltd. British Archaeological Reports was first incorporated in 1974 to publish the BAR Series, International and British. In 1992 Hadrian Books Ltd became part of the BAR group. This volume was originally published by Archaeopress in conjunction with British Archaeological Reports (Oxford) Ltd / Hadrian Books Ltd, the Series principal publisher, in 2014. This present volume is published by BAR Publishing, 2016.

Printed in England

BAR
PUBLISHING

BAR titles are available from:

BAR Publishing
122 Banbury Rd, Oxford, OX2 7BP, UK
EMAIL info@barpublishing.com
PHONE +44 (0)1865 310431
FAX +44 (0)1865 316916
www.barpublishing.com

For Joan

Cover illustration from the tomb of Nakht (TT 52)

The Scale and Nature of the Late Bronze Age Economies of Egypt and Cyprus

Table of Contents

Preliminaries

List of Figures

All figures have been sketched by the Author

List of Tables

Chapter 2

List of Reports in the Appendix

Acknowledgements

This study is the revised version of my doctoral dissertation. It would not have been possible to undertake and to complete this research without the encouragement of my friends and family. I am deeply grateful for the love, help and support of my wife, Joan. Without her encouragement, I would have faltered but together it has been a great adventure. During the course of my studies, I was fortunate to receive advice and help from many scholars to whom I would like to extend my appreciation and thanks. In particular, I am grateful to Professor A.B. Lloyd, who despite my age and a lifetime in industry, encouraged me to start my studies at Swansea University in Egyptology and Ancient History, which at the time was a daunting prospect. My special thanks go to my two supervisors, Professor David Gill and Dr. Kasia Szpakowska, whose enthusiasm for Ancient History inspired me to take my studies further. Finally, my thanks for the advice and the opportunity to share ideas over countless coffees with all the friends I have made at Swansea University, UCL, the Faculty of Oriental Studies at Oxford, the OEB development team, and the staff and readers at the Sackler Library.

Abbreviations

Acc. no.	Accession number
BH	Beni Hasan
BM	British Museum
DeM	Deir el-Medina
EA	El-Amarna
EK	El-Kab
FAO	Food and Agriculture Organization of the United Nations
GC/MS	Gas chromatography/mass spectrometry
ha	Hectares
Inv. no.	Invoice number
n=	Size of sample
NAA	Neutron Activity Analysis
RS	Ras Shamra
SEG	Social Economic Group
TT	Theban Tomb
UC	University College
UR	Ur
yr	Year

Abbreviations used for time periods:

EBA	Early Bronze Age
MBA	Middle Bronze Age
LBA	Late Bronze Age
EIA	Early Iron Age
OK	Old Kingdom
MK	Middle Kingdom
NK	New Kingdom
LC	Late Cypriot
LH	Late Helladic
LM	Late Minoan

Abbreviations used for cited texts:

KRI III. *Kitchen, K.A. 2000. Ramesside Inscriptions. Translated and Annotated. Translations: Ramesses II, His Contemporaries.* Vol. 3. Oxford: Blackwell Publishers.

PM 1^2/1 Bertha Porter and Rosalind Moss. 1994. *Topographical Bibliography of Ancient Egyptian Hieroglyphic Texts, Reliefs, and Paintings.* Vol. 1. *The Theban Necropolis.* Part 1, *Private Tombs*. Second Edition, revised and augmented. Oxford: Clarendon.

Wb. Adolph Erman and Hermann Grapow, eds. 1926–1953. *Wörterbuch der aegyptischen Sprache: im Auftrage der deutschen Akademien.* 7 Vols. Leipzig: J. C. Hinrich'schen Buchhandlungen.

Conversion factors

1 acre	= 4,047 m^2 = 0.4047 ha
1 aroura	= 0.2757 ha
1 ardab	= 198 litres
1 feddan	= 0.42 ha
1 ha	= 10,000 m^2
1 *heqat*	= 4.8 litres
1 MK sack (*khar*)	= 48 litres
1 MK deben	= 27.3 g
1 NK sack (*khar*)	= 76.8 litres
1 NK deben	= 91 g
1 NK *oipe*	= 19.2 litres
1 stremma	= 0.1 ha
1 US bushel	= 30.28 kg

Chronology

NK Egypt

Eighteenth Dynasty

Ahmose	1550–1525
Amenhotep I	1525–1504
Tuthmosis I	1504–1492
Tuthmosis II	1492–1479
Tuthmosis III	1479–1425
Hatshepsut	1473–1458
Amenhotep II	1427–1401
Tuthmosis IV	1401–1391
Amenhotep III	1391–1353
Amenhotep IV/Akhenaten	1353–1335
Smenkhkare	1335–1333
Tutankhamun	1333–1323
Ay	1323–1319
Horemheb	1319–1307

Nineteenth Dynasty

Ramesses I	1307–1306
Seti I	1306–1290
Ramesses II	1290–1224
Merneptah	1224–1214
Seti II	1214–1204
Siptah	1204–1198
Twosret	1198–1196

Twentieth Dynasty

Sethnakhte	1196–1194
Ramesses III	1194–1163
Ramesses IV	1163–1156
Ramesses V	1156–1151
Ramesses VI	1151–1143
Ramesses VII	1143–1136
Ramesses VIII	1136–1131
Ramesses IX	1131–1112
Ramesses X	1112–1100
Ramesses XI	1100–1070

LBA Cyprus

LCIA (ProBA I)	1650–1550
LCIB (ProBA I)	1550–1450
LCIIA (ProBA II)	1450–1375
LCIIB (ProBA II)	1375–1300
LCIIC (ProBA II)	1340/1315–1200
LCIIIA (ProBA III)	1200–1100
LCIIIB (ProBA III)	1100/1050

Conventions

All calculations in the spreadsheets and the text use SI (System International) units: kg for weight, m for length, m^3 for volume, and kg/m^3 for density. If pre-modern sources have been used, their unit terminology is given together with the SI equivalent.

Although the use of the terms 'manpower' and 'man-days' may be seen as politically incorrect, they are used in this study because by convention they are employed in discussions on labour-rates, workload, and the number of workers required to complete a task.

Chapter 1: Introduction and past scholarship

1.1 Introduction

The Late Bronze Age (LBA) economy can be defined by three core characteristics: its scale, the economic and political interaction between the ruling élites, and the degree to which the economy was central to the operations of the institutions of the state.[1] The nature of the LBA economy is strongly debated between those scholars who consider it was substantive and those who think it was formalist. Substantivists maintain that in ancient and primitive societies, the economy was 'embedded' within social relations so that it can only be studied in context as part of a local or regional cultural system.[2] Formalists believe that modern economic theory is universally applicable to ancient and modern economies because all societies have unlimited wants that can never be satisfied from the available resources such as workers, land, and capital. This means that rational choices must be made on their use to maximise satisfaction. The decisions made in this process create a supply-and-demand market.[3] The substantive/formalist debate has been ongoing for the last 120 years, and no definitive resolution has been reached between its protagonists.

The aim of this study is to interpret the scale and nature of the economy of the Eastern Mediterranean in the latter period of the LBA. It does this by using a quantitative approach that estimates the size of the workforce required to meet basic needs (food, clothing, and shelter) and state needs. The quantitative findings are used to assess the proportion of the workforce dedicated to basic and non-basic activities of LBA Cyprus and NK Egypt, based on the food required to support a worker and his dependants. This allows the assessment of the relative economic strengths of each region, the extent to which their economies were embedded within their culture, and their economic interactions with other LBA Eastern Mediterranean states.

The acquisition of copper and tin to manufacture bronze is central to our understanding of the political and economic development of the LBA Eastern Mediterranean. The desire for the ownership of bronze stimulated an interconnected trading pattern that extended from Central Asia to the Central Mediterranean. In return for copper and tin, other goods and staples were made for exchange, creating a nexus of cultures who exchanged goods and services at an unprecedented level. Technological solutions were overcoming the limitations of the past and old orders based on 'gift exchange' and 'redistribution' were being challenged. These developments question whether an embryonic market economy was evolving at this time. It is this exciting period of history that provided the stimulus to this book. I hope that the methodology employed here encourages scholars to increase their use of quantitative models in their research adding a new dimension to traditional, ethnographic, archaeo-scientific, and experimental archaeology.

Scope

This study examines Cyprus and Egypt within the time span 1400–1050 B.C., which is the later period of the Late Bronze Age and the Early Iron Age transition.[4] In Cyprus this includes LCIIA–LCIIIB (ProBA II–III) and for Egypt it includes the reigns of Tuthmosis IV to Ramesses XI in the New Kingdom. In this study Cyprus and Egypt are referred to as LBA Cyprus and NK Egypt and these two regions were selected for the quantitative studies. Cyprus was chosen as representative of dry farming regions of the north-eastern Mediterranean and because it had an important role in the interregional copper trade.[5] Egypt has been chosen because its annual rainfall was insignificant and it was reliant on the annual inundation to grow food. It produced regular food surpluses which, combined with tribute from regions under the hegemony of Egypt, made it the largest economy in the LBA Eastern Mediterranean. Discussions also include Ugarit because of its importance as a major trading centre for land and maritime trade and its strategic geographic position in the LBA.[6] Ugarit provided a buffer zone between the Egyptians and the Hittites until the end of the LBA when Ras Shamra was destroyed *c.*1190 B.C.[7] As the power of Mitanni waned, the Ugarit buffer helped protect the Eastern Mediterranean flank from the rising power of Assyria. This balance of power and relative peace led to 100 years of expanding interregional trade between the Central and Eastern Mediterranean, Mesopotamia, and Central Asia.

The Eastern Mediterranean is defined for the purposes of this study as being within the boundaries of Libya, Upper

---

[1] North 1991: 97 defines 'institutions' as, 'The humanly devised constraints that structure political, economic and social interaction. They consist of both informal constraints (sanctions, taboos, customs, traditions, and codes of conduct), and formal rules (constitutions, laws, property rights).' Hodder 1977: 199 states, 'Economic institutions are cultural traits, and analysis of them must be inductive.'

[2] Hodder 1977: 199.

[3] In this study 'market' refers to the total supply-demand process of services and goods. The physical place where goods and services are sold or exchanged is termed a 'marketplace'. Modern economic theory is also referred to as 'neoclassical economics.'

[4] For this study, references to LBA apply to this time period.

[5] By convention, dry farming areas are those that have a rainfall between 380 mm and 500 mm per annum, supplemented by some form of irrigation. Without irrigation, rainfall limits for dry farming lie between 500–750 mm. In both cases, the bulk of this rainfall must fall in spring and early summer.

[6] Yon 1994 and Yon 2006.

[7] During the reign of Amenhotep III and possibly as early as the reign of Tuthmosis IV, Ugarit was a vassal state of Egypt (Astour 1981: 15). Egypt and the Hittites had agreed to a peaceful coexistence and Ramesses II and Hattušiliš III signed a peace treaty in 1284 B.C. This re-established Ugarit's trading links with Egypt, providing an important trading route between Anatolia and Egypt (Astour 1981: 24–26).

and Lower Egypt, the northern and southern Levant, Ugarit, middle and southern Anatolia, and Cyprus.

Sources of evidence

The sources of evidence for Chapters 2–5 are provided in each chapter. Wherever possible LBA evidence has been used and supplemented by ethnographic, experimental, and modern scientific evidence. Some Egyptian tomb scenes studied are MK or early NK because later in the NK the scenes became focussed on the afterlife and not representations of daily life. However similar scenes in the book of the dead and some NK tombs show that the processes depicted were similar.

Methodology

It is not my intention to re-open the processional and post-processional arguments of the 1970–1980s as I believe both approaches complement each. This study draws upon scientific methods, particularly process modelling, to examine the nature of the economies of Cyprus and Egypt. Hopkins defined a 'model' as a simplification of a complex reality, designed to show up the logical relationships between its constituent parts.[8] Process modelling does not in itself prove how the ancients worked, but it helps us to understand how and what they could have accomplished using the tools available to them. It highlights the technological and process problems faced by ancient cultures, which are not immediately apparent from the examination of archaeological records. It allows the quantification of the size of the workforce necessary for each key process and it is within this framework of the workforce requirements for the basic and non-basic sectors of the LBA economy that the decision-making by the élite, who were responsible for prioritising society's needs, can be postulated. This study demonstrates that a process-based approach is not in conflict with post-processional archaeology. Rather, it provides an objective quantitative framework for the LBA economy defining the boundaries of what was possible with the resources available. Within this framework, post-processual interpretation can take place.

To analyse and quantify the key processes of the LBA economy in this study two analytical models have been developed. The first is the hierarchy of social needs and the second the concept of 'cost' equated to the number of workers needed to perform a task and the food consumed by them and their dependants.

The concept of the Hierarchy of Needs

The basic requirement of all societies is that its people have to be fed, clothed, and sheltered. These are the life supporting basic needs and the highest priority has to be the allocation of available workers to these processes.[9] Only when the basic needs of a society have been met can the non-basic needs be satisfied, which includes state administration, an army, non-critical state infrastructure projects, added-value production, and the desire for conspicuous consumption by the élite. The relationship between basic and non-basic processes is shown in Figure 1.1, which illustrates the concept of the 'Hierarchy of Needs'. The balance between the size of the basic and non-basic workers is central to any discussion on the scale of the LBA economy.

Basic needs are classified into two categories. The first is the primary physiological need to provide adequate food and water to maintain the population. The second category satisfies the basic needs for domestic cloth, pottery, shelter, and any critical infrastructure activities that maintain food production. In Egypt, infrastructure investments included the maintenance of dykes, canals, and basins that were critical to the success of the harvest. These basic processes had the highest priority and the ruling élite had the responsibility to ensure they were adequately supported.

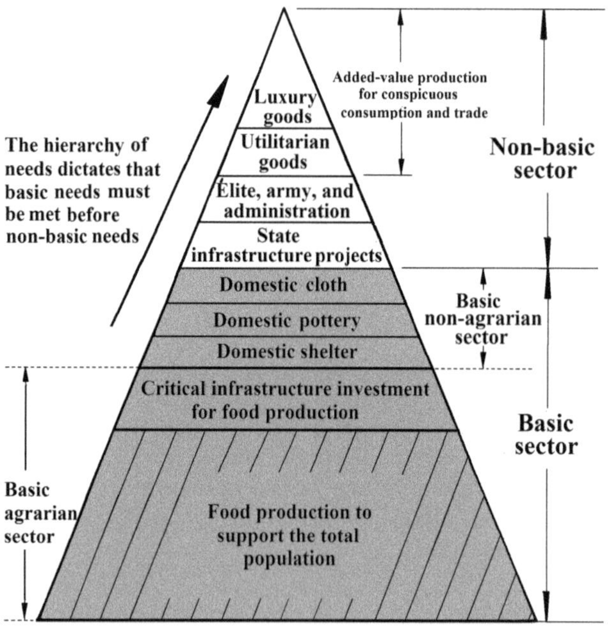

Figure 1.1: The Hierarchy of Needs.

Non-basic needs fall into two major categories. The workforce required to meet non-basic state needs and the workforce required to meet the conspicuous consumption needs of the élite. The highest priority for workers in the first category was to support state capital projects such as the provision of state granaries, a standing army, sea-going ships, and riverine boats, administration centres, and the manufacture of bronze tools and weapons.[10] The second category is the added-value workforce who produced temples, palaces, and élite goods for internal conspicuous consumption and the goods made for gift

[8] Hopkins 2002: 191.

[9] The behavioural psychologist Abraham Maslow hypothesised that human endeavour could be explained in terms of striving to fulfil a Hierarchy of Needs; the accomplishment of one need was necessary before an individual could satisfy a higher need (Maslow 1970).

[10] Although the use of the terms 'manpower' and 'man-days' may be seen as politically incorrect, they are used in this study because by convention they are employed in discussions on labour-rates, workload, and the number of workers required to complete a task.

exchange and trade at an interregional level.[11] The priorities made between state needs and conspicuous consumption needs, indicates the balance that the élite made between the maintenance of state institutions and their own personal prestige and status. How the élite prioritised these non-basic processes provides us with an insight into the nature of the LBA economy. The resource ratio of non-basic to basic workforces is also the measure used in this study to compare relative economic strength between regions.

Cost in the context of the ancient economy

Many historians believe that 'cost' is a modern economic concept and not relevant in antiquity. However, every member of society had to be fed, and cost in this study is defined as the quantity of rations required by workers and their dependants for them to be able to complete a task and does not relate in any way to the neoclassical definition.[12] In antiquity, the cost of production was predominantly worker based, as capital investment in technologically complex tools and machinery was minimal. Using this approach for calculating the cost means that any process can be compared with another. If one process involved twice the number of workers than another, and therefore twice the rations, we can say this process is twice as expensive. The assumption used in the model is that manual workers had sufficient food to maintain themselves and their dependants at an adequate subsistence level. In the context of this study slaves are treated as part of the general workforce because they too required food to work effectively.[13] Skilled workers, such as the royal tomb artisans at Deir el-Medina received rations above a subsistence level and they are discussed separately.

In order to understand how the LBA economy operated this study assesses and evaluates:

- The workforce required to produce sufficient food to feed the populations of NK Egypt and LBA Cyprus.
- The workforce required to meet the domestic demand for cloth and shelter.
- The workforce that could be dedicated to added-value activities.
- The workforce required to produce bronze.
- The workforce required to support state infrastructure projects.
- The efficiency of LBA redistribution of food rations.

Throughout this study a demographic cohort of 100,000 is used to enable normalised comparisons to be made between the workforces of Cyprus and Egypt.[14]

Process modelling

Two techniques are used in this study for quantitative process modelling: the use of a process analysis tool called *chaîne opératoire* and computational spreadsheets for the numerical calculations involved.

Chaîne opératoire

The use of *chaîne opératoire* and other scientific, mathematical, and statistical techniques became popular in the 1960–1970s with those scholars who attempted to isolate and study the different processes at work, within a society and between societies (processual archaeology).[15] One of the most influential scholars in this field was Binford who advocated the use of the 'scientific method' for archaeological studies: observation, hypothesis formulation, and testing. 'We begin with observations on the archaeological record, then move to explain the differences and similarities we observe. This means setting forth processual hypotheses that permit us to link archaeological remains to events or conditions in the past which produced them. Once hypotheses are explicitly stated, we can determine what additional observations must be made or available data collected to test the validity of our hypotheses.'[16] Binford's approach has its critics who prefer the post-processual school of archaeology.[17] Hodder believes processual archaeology is flawed because the approach cannot account for the great richness, variability, and specificity of cultural production and the individuals involved.[18] He rejects Binford and Sabloff's assertion that independent and objective scientific measurements can bridge the relationship between the material culture, and the society that produced them.[19]

In this study the ancient processes of agriculture, cloth production, domestic buildings, and bronze production, are analysed using *chaîne opératoire* sequence analysis. This analysis breaks down processes into a logical

[11] 'Added-value' is the term used for the increase in value added to a product as the result of a particular manufacturing process. Value can be a measured in both practical and intangible terms. For example, an article may have no practical value but its ownership increases the social status of the owner.

[12] The neoclassical definition of cost is those production factors, both variable and fixed, for which revenue must be used in payment to the producers of the good (Schneider 1974: 231).

[13] Meskell suggests that slavery should be viewed as a sliding scale, ranging from those captured in wars and those native Egyptians forced to become slaves because of personal economic hardship (Meskell 2002: 105).

[14] The estimates for population levels in antiquity vary widely especially for Cyprus where most of the estimates relate to settlements within a discrete geographic area of Cyprus as in the field study of Marki by Webb and Frankel 2004. The total population of LBA Cyprus is likely to be lower than 100,000 and for absolute comparisons between regions, the results can be prorated down to the estimated population.

[15] *Chaîne opératoire* was developed in France and applied to the study of prehistoric technologies. Leading exponents were Leroi-Gourhan 1965: 35, Lemonnier 1976, Edmonds 1990, Audouze 1999, and Schlanger 1990.

[16] Binford 1968: 270. See also Binford and Sabloff 1982: 144–148 and Table 1, which summarises the major differences between the processual and post-processual archaeology.

[17] For processional archaeology, see Binford 1968, Binford 1981, and Binford and Sabloff 1982. For post-processional archaeology, see Hodder 1977, Hodder 1991a, and Hodder 1991b.

[18] Hodder 1991b: 43.

[19] Hodder 1991b: 16–17.

sequence of work activities, and plots the relationship of these activities in time, where they took place, the tools and materials used, as well as the wastage involved. The time needed to complete each activity is determined by using evidence from experimental archaeology, ethnographic evidence, and the detailed depictions of ancient processes in NK Egyptian tombs. The sum of the times taken to complete each discrete activity creates a labour-rate for the process that is used to calculate the workforce needed to complete the task. Labour-rates are the man-days (man-years if more applicable to the task) per unit output of the task. A harvesting labour-rate unit would be man-days/ha, spinning wool would be man-days/kg of wool spun, and smelting copper would be man-days/kg copper produced. As humans cannot work continuously at the same labour-rate due to a range of factors (fatigue, sickness, age, gender, or skill level), the 'manpower' has to be adjusted upwards to compensate. A full description of the relationship between labour-rates, workload, and manpower is provided in Section 2.7. Throughout this study the working day is assumed to have been nine hours and that 314 days were worked each year.[20]

Spreadsheet analyses

To quantify the relevant ancient processes underpinning the economies of Cyprus and Egypt, four Excel spreadsheet models were developed.[21] Each spreadsheet calculates the labour-rates, workload, and manpower involved in the process and has a name for reference (AGCALC for the agrarian process, CLOTHCALC for cloth production, SHELTER for mud-brick production in Egypt for selected domestic and state infrastructure buildings, BRONZECALC for the production of bronze). Summary tables of the results are provided in each relevant chapter. Copies of the full spreadsheets can be obtained from the author by application to BAR.

A major benefit of process analysis, particularly when it is computer based, is the ease with which data parameters can be changed to assess the validity of some of the more speculative assumptions.[22] Replicating ancient processes using computational techniques is not a linear process but is better viewed as an iterative process, allowing the refinement of assumptions to assess their impact, which may not be possible using more traditional fields of study. It is the relative scales of the findings and the patterns of the data rather than the absolute numerical results from the model that are important. In many ways, it is the questions that arise out of the process analysis that are as valuable as the results provided by the model. The economic quantative models developed for this study are flexible and have the potential to be applied to any pre-industrial economy.

Modelling the LBA economies of Cyprus and NK Egypt to determine the theoretical optimum ratio between basic and non-basic workforces is my contribution to increasing our understanding of the scale and nature of the LBA economy. It is the priorities and choices made by the élite in directing those resources that they could control, the degree of formal planning and how they achieved their objectives, that provide a new perspective on the operation of the ancient economy.

Layout

This chapter is completed by a review of the past scholarship associated with the minimalist/primitive and the substantive/formalist debate, past and present. It identifies the main areas of divergence between the two views and their relevance to an understanding of the operation and nature of the LBA economy.

Chapters 2–5 analyse the four main production processes that made up the LBA economy: food production, domestic cloth, shelter, and the production of bronze from the mining of tin and copper ores through to alloying them. For each of these processes the manpower required in Cyprus and Egypt is calculated and compared.

Chapter 6 assesses the scale of the LBA economies by bringing together the findings of Chapters 2–5, the demand for bronze and the improvements in ship technology, which increased the level of trade. Specific case studies test Polanyi's assertion that workers' rations could be provided through a total redistribution process. Other case studies quantify the proportion of the added-value workforce that had to be dedicated to the manufacture of weapons to support a standing army, and the demand for bronze equipment by the agrarian sector, and craftsmen. Discussions follow on how Cyprus could meet the demand for copper and what options were open to it to avoid supply constraints. Chapter 6 also discusses the findings of the quantitative analyses in the context of the substantive/formalist debate. For the interpretation of the nature of the economies of Egypt and Cyprus, four conceptual constructs are considered: Marx's 'Asiatic mode of production', Diakonoff's 'two-sector' model, Weber/Schloen's 'patrimonial model', and Wallenstein's 'core/periphery world-systems.'

1.2 Past scholarship

This section reviews the minimalist/primitivist view of the ancient economy and the substantive/formalist debate that came to the fore with Polanyi's treatise, *The Great Transformation* published in 1944.

Bücher

One of the first scholars to articulate the nature of the ancient economy was Karl Bücher [1847–1930]. He identified three key development stages in the evolution

[20] It is assumed for this study that workers had one rest day every ten days (36 days/year). An average of fifteen days sickness per year has been assumed. In total it is assumed that workers were productive for 365–(36+15) = 314 days.

[21] Excel © is a registered product of The Microsoft Corporation.

[22] This approach is particularly well suited when analysing processes that have more than one variable. Modern computer applications, in particular relational databases in conjunction with statistical packages, are used to carry out regression, multivariate, and principle component analyses.

of the economy, which corresponded approximately to the three great historical epochs. Antiquity was characterised by a 'closed household economy' *(geschlossene Hauswirtschaft),* the economy of the Middle Ages as 'city economy' *(Stadtwirtschaft),* and the modern world by 'national economy' *(Volkswirtschaft).*[23] Bücher took a minimalist (small in scale) and primitivist view (low level of technology) of the ancient economy, linking its centre of gravity, scale, and organisation to production units that equated to the *oíkos* (family household).[24] In an *oíkos* economy, the various households or production units were responsible for the production of goods for their own use, storage of raw materials and goods, and the manufacture of indispensable goods for exchange. Those who subscribe to a primitive and minimalist view see the ancient economy as almost wholly agrarian, with non-agrarian production at a primitive and nominal level. Bücher [1893] ignored or dismissed as unimportant the evidence for trade and non-agrarian added-value production in the ancient economy.[25]

Weber

Max Weber [1864–1920] also took a position that the economies of antiquity were very different in scale and nature to the early European capitalist economies of fifteenth/sixteenth centuries A.D. onwards.[26] He emphasised the dominance of the labour-intensive production of staples in antiquity. He concluded that the main inhibitors to the development of a market economy in antiquity were an inefficient and uneconomic transport system, the lack of private capital to support entrepreneurial activities, and the low level of consumer demand caused by the concentration of wealth within a small ruling élite.[27] Weber also felt that ancient societies lacked effective cost accounting systems so that the relationship between the cost of production of a good, the value of the good, and its price could not be determined.[28]

Meyer and Rostovtzeff

The first to challenge these minimalist and primitive views, were Meyer [1855–1930] and Rostovtzeff [1870–1952], now commonly called the first 'modernists.'[29] Meyer concluded that, '... the later period of antiquity was in essence entirely modern.'[30] He believed that trade and added-value production was in nature the same, with similar underlying structures and processes.[31] Rostovtzeff asserted that modern development, '... differs from the ancient only in quantity and not in quality.' He suggested that the Greco-Roman world was strongly influenced by the market-orientated economies of Mesopotamia and the ancient Near East and that it moved from an *oíkos* economy to one that possessed within it all the attributes of the modern economy. However, he considered that the scale of this economy was smaller in volumetric terms.[32]

Finley

Finley [1912–1986], perhaps as a counter balance to the modernists, asserts in his influential book, *The Ancient Economy* that the ancients, '... lacked the concept of an 'economy", and, *a fortiori*, that they lacked the conceptual elements which together constitute what we call the "economy."' He continues, '... of course they farmed, traded, manufactured, mined, taxed, coined, deposited and loaned money, made profits or failed in their enterprises. And they discussed these activities in their talk and their writing. What they did not do, however, was to combine these particular activities conceptually into a unit, in Parsonian terms into "a differentiated sub-system of society."''[33]

Finley also challenged the scale of trade suggested by the modernists and considered that there was a lack of archaeological and literary evidence for trade in the ancient economy and this is, '... a silence that is explained in the simplest way, because there was effectively nothing to speak about.'[34] However, when Finley wrote *The Ancient Economy* in 1973, the application of a forensic scientific approach to archaeology, particularly in respect to marine archaeology and its links to interregional trade, was in its infancy.

Polanyi's substantivism

The debate on the nature of the ancient economy reached a new level of scholarly interest in the 1940s and 1950s stimulated by the work of the economic anthropologist Karl Polanyi [1886–1964].[35] He considered that the

[23] Möller 2000: 1.

[24] Weber 1976 [1896]: 43 citing Bücher 1893.

[25] Morley 2004: 37.

[26] Weber 1976 [1896]. He believed that the emergence of the Calvinistic 'Protestant work ethic' in Northern Europe encouraged the growth of private enterprise, trade, and the accumulation of wealth and that this was the catalyst to the development of an embryonic capitalist market economy (Weber 2009 [1904–1905]). The terms 'primitivist', 'minimalist', and 'substantive' have a considerable overlap and they differ more in emphasis than in substance (Cooney 2008: 80, Footnote. 3). For an Egyptian focus, see Janssen 1975a: 131, 137–139, and 183–184 and Bleiberg 1988, 1995, and 1996, who both define the ancient Egyptian economy as substantive, based on redistribution and reciprocity with minimal market activity.

[27] Weber 1976 [1896]: 65–66. Weber emphasised the difficulty of apportioning the costs of labour, particularly slave labour. For the purposes of this study, the difference between the rations of a slave and a normal manual worker is not significant, as both had to be fed adequately if they were to work effectively.

[28] Weber 1976 [1896]: 54, 66.

[29] Meyer 1922, Meyer 1924, and Rostovtzeff 1941. Rostovtzeff limited his analysis to the Classical Period. For a modern commentary of Meyer's and Rostovtzeff's work, see Morley 2004: 37–39.

[30] Morley 2004: 37 citing Meyer 1922: 89.

[31] Meyer 1924.

[32] Rostovtzeff 1941: 1301–1304. Rostovtzeff 1941: 1303 asserts, 'The innovations in the organisation of economic life, all of which tended towards what, with all reserve, we may call "capitalism"..., certainly did not remain confined to the Hellenistic world.'

[33] Finley 1985: 21 and Parsons and Smelser 1956. Discussed further by Renger 1994: 170–173 and Morley 2004: 33–34.

[34] Finley 1985: 136. Snodgrass 1991: 15–20 also takes the same position.

[35] The most influential was Karl Polanyi's treatise *The Great Transformation* published in 1944, which explained the rise of the market economy in substantive terms. The term 'substantive' as applied to economic anthropology was created by Polanyi himself (Schneider 1974: 2 commenting on Polanyi *et al.* 1957: 243 ff).

ancient economy was based on internal redistribution (principally of agrarian products) controlled by the élite, with reciprocity (gift exchange) and administered trade as the prime mechanisms for the exchange of goods between ruling interregional élites. Polanyi promoted the argument that only substantivism provides an analytical framework that explains the workings of the ancient economy.[36] Substantivists maintain that pre-modern and modern economies were so fundamentally different that they rendered the vocabulary of modern economics, such as maximizing, economizing, scarcity, profit, and cost, inaccurate and misleading when applied to the study of ancient and primitive tribal societies.[37] They argue that the ancient economy must be studied in its social context because economic activity has different meanings in different social contexts.[38]

The embedded economy

Polanyi built on Weber's 'primitivist' view, concluding that the ancient economy was 'embedded' in society, rather than being a distinct economic activity. Polanyi used the term 'embedded' to emphasise that the economy served to maintain the social system.[39] He proposed that an embedded economy gave ancient cultures their unity, stability, and structure, and that within this institutionalised system, there was no concept or requirement for modern economics.[40] Polanyi emphasised the importance of separating economic motives from social relations. He emphasised that an individual's motivation is not driven by economic interests but '… submerged in his social relations, as man does not aim to safeguard his individual material self-interest. He does not act so as to safeguard his individual interest in the possession of material goods; he acts so as to safeguard his social standing, his social claims, his social assets. He values material goods only in so far as they serve this end.'[41] Substantivists believe that prestige gained from the services given to the king, was the major motivational driving force. From this privileged position, the individual was provided with rewards.[42] For Polanyi, neoclassical theory was inappropriate for the study of the ancient economy because the concept of a 'market' by definition self-regulates the economy independently from the rest of society.[43] For Polanyi the formalist belief of a market in antiquity was wrong because, '… it means no less than the running of society as an adjunct to the market. Instead of economy being embedded in social relations, social relations are embedded in the economic system.'[44]

Patterns of exchange

Polanyi believed that materials 'wants' (staples, commodities, and luxury products) across all the social strata within pre-capitalist society, could be satisfied through redistribution, reciprocity, and administered trade. To understand how these processes related to each other within an embedded economy they have to be examined within a social, political, and religious context for the specific culture under study.[45]

Redistribution

Redistribution in the LBA was the primary mechanism whereby the state collected goods, mainly from the agrarian sector and rationed them back to the people according to their hierarchical position in society.[46] For the process to work effectively the state needed access to the harvest, organisational processes to collect and redistribute the harvests, and buildings for storage. The redistribution process from a practical standpoint was inefficient due to the slow methods of transport, wastage, vermin, corruption, and natural disasters.

Polanyi believed that redistribution could work effectively due to custom, law, or ad hoc decisions from the centre-maintained control of the process.[47] He referred to this centralised control as 'centricity' because the power to determine who should receive redistributed rations, which resulted in a relationship of obligation, was located at an identifiable centre.[48] Redistribution could operate in two ways, either by a collection-storage-redistribution process or by a change in the rights of appropriation without any change in the actual location of the goods.[49]

Reciprocity

Reciprocity was the means by which LBA ruling élites exchanged luxury and other goods. This is often referred to as 'gift-exchange' but as Finley commented, the term

[36] Polanyi 1957, Polanyi and Dalton 1971, Polanyi and Pearson 1977, Finley 1973, and Finley 1985.

[37] According to Dalton and Köcke 1983: 26–27 the use of neoclassical economic vocabulary is inappropriate in three ways: it overstates the similarities and understates the differences between non-market economies and industrial capitalism, it fails to describe what is important and unique about the non-market economy, and it inhibits an understanding of the operation and money usage in non-market economies.

[38] Polanyi was highly critical of unfettered market liberalism as well as a fully centralised state-economy. Van De Meiroop 2004: 56 suggests that, 'He looked thus for a 'third way' which would protect the individual in an economy embedded in the social structures. This led to a revival of his writings since 1990, and he has become an icon of the anti-globalization movement.'

[39] Schneider 1974: 7.

[40] Polanyi 1957a: 249.

[41] Polanyi 1944: 46 and 55. Also, see Polanyi 1947, Arensberg, and Pearson 1957: 242, 250, 299, and 302. For a commentary, see Morris 1994: 352.

[42] In NK Egypt, nobles who gave outstanding service to the king were rewarded publically with a necklace of gold called the 'Gold of Honour'. In addition they received many other valuable goods (Binder 2008).

[43] Polanyi 1944: 124–135.

[44] Polanyi 1944: 57.

[45] Bleiberg 1996: 8.

[46] Southern Mesopotamian UR III ration texts show that wool, clothing, and oil were also included in the redistribution process (Van De Meiroop 2004: 59).

[47] Polanyi 1957b: 253 and Polanyi 1977: 40. Polanyi 1944: 55 argues that personal gain was not a motive, 'Custom and law, magic and religion co-operated in inducing the individual to comply with rules of behaviour which, eventually, ensured his functioning in the economic system.'

[48] Polanyi 1977: 40–42. Also see the comments on 'centricity' in Pearson 1977: xxxiv.

[49] Polanyi 1977: 40. This is an important distinction as this study argues in Section 6.4 that for Egypt it made no logistical sense to move food from the agrarian sector into state/temple granaries and then redistribute it with all the associated losses within the distribution process.

'gift' can be misconstrued, 'It may be stated as a flat rule of both primitive and archaic societies that no one ever gave anything, whether goods or services or honours, without proper recompense, real or wishful, immediate or years away, to himself or to his kin. The act of giving was, therefore, in an essential sense always the first half of a reciprocal action, the other half of which was a counter-gift.'[50] Mauss [1872–1950] suggested that the purpose of gift exchange was to reinforce social relationships between different sectors of society irrespective of whether this was at a local or interregional level. One of the best examples of reciprocity between heads of states is described in the cuneiform tablets known collectively as the Amarna letters.[51] The accepted norm dictated that both parties to the exchange considered the goods were of equal value but not necessarily in terms of its equivalence in silver shekels. Liverani differentiated gift exchange from barter by defining the former as being motivated by prestige with the gift reciprocated after a lapse of time, whereas barter was motivated by economic interest, mutual agreement on the value of the goods, with the exchange taking place simultaneously.[52] Reciprocity worked effectively because it built upon long-term relationships that implied trust and confidence between all parties.[53] The process was embedded within a complex matrix of social protocols and kinship between élites that could include royal marriages.[54] The advantage of a relationship based on obligation was that it reinforced the prestige and power of the parties concerned as well as the benefit of continuing useful economic relations.[55]

There is a typology of reciprocity in ancient economies. The three forms of exchange that operated in the LBA Eastern Mediterranean were ceremonial gift exchange between ruling élites, exchange between ruling élites for goods that had a utility value, and exchange of utilitarian goods between non-royal representatives of the ruling élites.[56] In ceremonial exchange, there was a strict observance of protocols in the gift exchange process that operated at different levels. The highest level was the exchange of prestige goods (not necessarily having any commercial value) between rulers of approximate equal rank. In this form of exchange, the goods were itemised and quantified in such a way that the receiver could come to his own conclusion on their comparative value.[57] On occasions the products exchange through the institution of reciprocity appear from a modern perspective to be irrational in purely economic terms. For example in EA 40, the king of Alašia (Cyprus) sent two ivory tusks to the Egyptian king and asked for ivory in return.[58] The gift here however, is an end in itself and not a means to acquire a commodity that is scarce in the receiver's own domain.[59]

Utilitarian exchange of goods between ruling élites took place when a king required commodities that had a utilitarian value, such as copper, tin, wood, and olive oil.[60] For example, the king of Alašia exchanged copper and wood and received in return payment in silver shekels. On another occasion, he received olive oil from Ugarit in return for 1,000 silver shekels.[61] The fact that king of Alašia paid with the international unit of account namely silver shekels for the olive oil emphasises the commercial nature of the exchange.[62]

Exchange between non-royal representatives of the ruling élites took place between those of comparable rank. They were considered to be 'brothers' and able to exchange valuable but utilitarian goods such as swords, robes, animals, and garments for gold or silver but not necessarily at market rates. To complete the transaction a gift was commonly included.[63] The lowest level of exchange applied to those of unequal rank where transactions were completed using market rates. The

[50] Finley 1956: 68. Janssen, referring to ancient Egypt, prefers the term 'gift giving' rather than 'gift-exchange' (Janssen 1988: 16). He defines a framework of households linked through kinship where the receiver of the gift received what they required but in return became the debtor of the giver. In this patrimonial framework, each household was therefore a source of credit that allowed obligations to build up within an ever-changing matrix of creditors and debtors (Janssen 1988: 16–17).

[51] See Moran 1992 for an extensive commentary on the Amarna letters with translations. Hereafter each letter follows the convention EA followed by the letter number as per Moran.

[52] Liverani 1979b: 30, Footnote 53. In gift-exchange excessive delay in the return of a gift could lead to frustration (EA 35: 13–14 and EA 7: 53–60).

[53] Polanyi 1944: 61. In Janssen's study of the ostraca from Deir el-Medina that recorded debts and credits, he uses the term 'general reciprocity' to describe how the debts may not have been repaid for some time and that the maintenance of good relations was more important than any short term gain (Janssen 1994c: 136).

[54] Evans-Pritchard emphasises the 'totality' of the exchange process, which involved economic, juridical, moral, aesthetic, religious, mythological, and socio-morphological phenomena (Evans-Pritchard 1969: vii–viii. Introduction to Mauss 1969).

[55] Sahlins 1972: 155 citing Firth 1959: 421.

[56] Herskovits took the view that the last two types of exchange were closer to commercial trade than gift-exchange because the primary motive was to obtain goods with a utility value to meet the demands of everyday existence (Herskovits 1952: 180). Schneider 1974: 255 defines the 'utility' of a good as the quality of goodness or desirability inherent in a good that is not the good itself.

[57] For a typology of the value of gifts and the relative status of giver and receiver, see Sahlins 1972: 206–275 based on ethnographic evidence and Liverani 1979b: 22–30 based on Near East textual evidence. This evaluation by the receiver of the gift could lead to tensions (Liverani 1979b: 25). The Mari text (Archives royales de Mari 5.20 *c.*1810–1760 B.C.) from the king of Qatna to Ishme-Dagan, kin of Ekallate, illustrates this, 'This matter is unspeakable, yet I must speak and relieve my feelings: you are a great king: you asked me for two horses, and I sent them to you. And now you sent me (only) 20 minas of tin. Is it not a case that, without any quibbling and in full, you got (what you wanted) from me? And you dare to send me this paltry amount of tin! If you sent me nothing at all, by the gods of my fathers, I could not have been so angry.' Transcribed and translated into French by Dossin 1952: 37–39. English translation by Kuhrt 1995: 101.

[58] Liverani 1979b: 22.

[59] Liverani 1972b: 25. Gregory defines commodity as a 'socially desirable thing with a use-value and an exchange-value. The use-value of a commodity is an intrinsic property of a thing desired or discovered by society at different stages in its historical evolution. a commodity as a socially desirable thing with a use value and an exchange value' (Gregory 1982: 10).

[60] Liverani 1979b: 28–29.

[61] RS 20.168: 10–25 translated by Nougayrol 1968: 80–83.

[62] Other examples being, copper exchanged by the king of Alašia with the King of Egypt silver (EA 35, 19–22 and 43–44, EA 37, 18) and timber exchanged by the king of Alašia with the King of Egypt for silver (EA 35, 27–29).

[63] Liverani 1979b: 29–30.

value of the goods was generally calculated in copper or silver shekels.[64]

Administered trade

Polanyi held the view that in substantive economies trade was administered and the import and export trade for commodities and perhaps staples were sourced through government or government-controlled channels.[65] Ports of trade were the conduit for foreign goods to enter the state, providing a politically neutral meeting place for merchants where the goods were physically exchanged. The exchange rates were agreed between the ruling élites through formal treaties.[66] Polanyi considered that if this process was to work effectively it was vital that there was a secure supply of goods to make it worthwhile for merchants to undertake potentially hazardous trips by sea. Ports of trade were sited on a riverbank or coast but could be found inland on the border of two regions. They had facilities for disembarkation, lading, portage, grading of goods, and storage. At these sites the local controlling élite agreed equivalencies as well as providing civil protection to the foreign traders.[67] Ports of trade operated on the periphery of the state, acting as a 'buffer', both economically and politically, between the trader and the host power. In this way the host power could maintain control over external influences that might prove disruptive to society in general.[68] Ports of trade provided the convenience of collecting custom duties and taxes within a politically neutral meeting place between importers and exporters.[69]

The formalist case

The formalists consider that the ancient economy was different from a modern market economy only in its size, not its nature.[70] They consider that the operation of the ancient economy was rational and that elements of modern economic theory apply to it. A basic universal principle of formalism is that man has unlimited 'wants' but lives under circumstances of scarcity (marginal utility theory) and is unable to satisfy all of them.

Economising through rational choices

Formalists such as Firth and Herskovits argue that economic theory is universal because all cultures, old and new, have to contend with scarcity and as a result have to make rational decisions on allocating resources (labour time, land, and assets).[71] They assume that people behave rationally irrespective of where or what era they are or were living.[72] In the process of making these choices their aim will be to maximise satisfaction for the least input of labour resources and capital.

Another critic of Polanyi was Douglas North who proposed that in antiquity, transaction costs made economising behaviour necessary. However, in support of Polanyi's overall position, North did conclude that transaction costs '... would have been an insuperable barrier to price-making markets throughout most of history.'[73] He also accepted that all societies, old and modern, have elements of reciprocity, redistribution within them that work in parallel with the operation of markets.[74]

The market

An area of strong disagreement and the fundamental dividing line between formalists and substantivists was whether in antiquity there was such a concept as a 'market'. Formalists argue that the existence of a market balances supply and demand for goods through pricing mechanisms that in turn regulate the flow of goods from one interested party to another. If demand is high, prices will rise, thereby lowering the demand for the goods as they become unaffordable. Von Mises' definition of a market captures its rational nature, 'The market is not a place, a thing, or a collective entity. The market is a process, actuated by the interplay of the actions of the various individuals cooperating under the division of labour. The forces determining the continually changing state of the market are the value judgements of these individuals and their actions as directed by these value judgements.'[75] The extent to which any governing body could control or influence the market in antiquity was, as

[64] Liverani 1979b: 30.

[65] Polanyi 1977: 94–95.

[66] Polanyi 1963: 51. For ports of trade in the Eastern Mediterranean, see Revere 1957. Ugarit was both a state and a port of trade (Polanyi 1963: 53–55). In her study of Saite Naukratis in the Twenty-Fifth Dynasty, Möller concludes that it acted as a port of trade between Greek mercenaries and the Egyptian state (Möller 2000: 215).

[67] Polanyi 1963: 52.

[68] Humphreys 1969: 192. Polanyi suggests that the Hittites established ports of trade on the coast because they had no historic or cultural affinity to the sea (Polanyi 1963: 42–48). The Hittites were not a seafaring culture and pragmatically allowed goods to flow from across the Eastern Mediterranean to the Hittite heartland without the cost of defending a coastal territory away from their homeland. The Hittites gave semi-autonomy to Ugarit in the reign of Niqmadu II. For this settlement, Ugarit paid tribute that was raised from local communities, amounting to 9 kg of bullion gold and 2 kg of gold vessels. Other goods, silver, linen, and purple dyed wool, were paid to other court officials in the Hittite palace (Kuhrt 1995: 308–309).

[69] See Silver 1985: 75–77, 113 Note 3 for textual sources related to tax collection in ports of trade.

[70] See Footnote 3 for how this study differentiates a market from a marketplace.

[71] Herskovits 1952: 8 writes, 'The means by which the ends of the economizing process, however defined, are achieved, comprise universals in the human experience. They therefore provide the basis for all generalizations concerning the nature and functioning of economic systems, whatever their form and whatever the particular mechanisms they may use to convert these means into satisfying the wants that make up the socially sanctioned ends toward whose fulfilment a given economy is directed.' In a similar vein, Firth asserts, '... the logic of scarcity is operative over the whole range of economic phenomena, and that, however deep and complex may be the influence of social factors, the notions of economy and of economising are not basically separate.' (Firth 1964: 4).

[72] In economic modelling, this is called the 'rational behaviour model' (Wilke 2000: 82).

[73] North 1981: 710. Transaction costs are defined by Renger 1994: 159–160 based on North 1981: 18ff and 203ff as '... the costs of specifying and enforcing contracts and other relations upon which exchange and other forms of economic organization are based. They include resources used for obtaining and disseminating information, measuring of goods and staples, and the conclusion as well, as the enforcement of contracts and the specification and guaranteeing of property rights.'

[74] Bleiberg 2007: 11 commenting on North 1977 and North 1984.

[75] Von Mises 1949: 257.

today, limited and formalists take the position that the market is a natural law that automatically follows the dynamics of the supply and demand process. In the LBA no region had all the natural resources required to meet its needs within its own borders and to make bronze, tin would have been in demand by them all. Formalists maintain that the importance to the economy of this metal and to a lesser degree copper, across the Eastern Mediterranean, would have led to competition for supply that could not be met by Polanyi's administered trade model. Formalists consider that human nature has not changed and place strong emphasis on the natural desire of individuals for advancement, using personal enterprise to achieve their goals.[76] They propose that entrepreneurial, profit-seeking merchants would exploit opportunities leading to a true metals market, which followed the law of supply and demand.

1.3 The unresolved argument

The substantive/formalist debate revolves around two conflicting concepts concerning the nature of the ancient economy. The formalists believe that the ancient economy operated in a rational manner to prioritise unlimited wants in a world of scarce resources. The substantivists on the other hand, believe ancient ruling élites made choices based on social considerations with a form of rationality dependent on relationships, obligation, and social hierarchy, and not profit.

The substantive view is that a neoclassical market is irrelevant to our understanding of the workings of the ancient economy. Polanyi and Finley argued that there were no wide-ranging markets in antiquity, and therefore the market could not in isolation organise and direct production, distribution, and consumption.[77] Dalton asserts that exchange transactions of material goods in non-market economies are an expression of, '... social obligations which have neither mechanism nor meaning of their own apart from social ties, social obligations, and social situations.'[78] Polanyi argued that a market in antiquity was, '... no more than incidental to economic life.'[79] In his opinion, the requirement for a market to regulate supply and demand becomes redundant if the motives for production was use rather than gain, and the material needs were sufficiently met by redistribution, reciprocity, and administered trade.[80] He believed market behaviour was a late feature, and rejected the idea that money was an invention that inevitably created markets.[81] He argued against the need for a distinctive economising method of allocating insufficient means in scarcity situations, as insufficiency of means did not in itself create scarcity, 'If you have not got enough, you must go without.'[82] Polanyi proposed that equivalences rather than prices were the norm in antiquity. He defined equivalencies as money amounts (normally the silver shekel) exchanged for goods that were set by authoritative decree or by custom, not based on supply and demand.[83] Similarly, Haring uses the term 'money-barter' to facilitate the exchange of commodities in Pharaonic Egypt using units of grain, copper, and silver as value comparators. This appears from the limited textual evidence available, to have led to stable prices.[84] Substantivists also point out that the slow pace of transport would have inhibited the operation of a market in antiquity, in particular the speed of communication regarding opportunities for trade.[85] This is in direct contrast to modern markets, where merchants and traders respond instantly to the information they receive about current prices and exchange rates, adjusting theirs accordingly.

A substantive economy would be less responsive to market forces, more introspective, with a greater emphasis on maintaining social order. In contrast, a formalist economy would tend to direct resources to meet the demands of internal and external markets, prepared to take entrepreneurial risks and in so doing, maximise the return on their investment. In a formalist economy discretionary state spend would be directed towards improvements in state infrastructure projects such as harbours and transport links rather than projects that were primarily prestigious in the eyes of other ruling élites.

Formalists view the ancient economy as essentially the same as the present but different in scale, in direct contrast to substantivists who see it as being fundamentally different from the modern supply and demand market economy. Moreland is critical of those who see the past either '... as Same (a primitive version of our present, which teleologically evolves into it) or as Other (as a remote, alien, fundamentally *different*, world). Both "visions", as monolithic perceptions, impose uniformity on a variegated past and thereby obscure rather than reveal.'[86]

---

[76] Kemp in his *Anatomy of a Civilisation* discusses 'The birth of economic man' where he presents the argument that in NK Egypt, private initiative did thrive in a world without coinage (Kemp 2006: 238–260). Also, see Cooney 2007b and 2008 for evidence of private enterprise in the funerary industry at Thebes. For a contra position, see Bleiberg 1994 who uses the evidence of ancient Egyptian 'wisdom texts' and the MK pessimistic literature to demonstrate that the Egyptian attitude to success, wealth, and greed was not compatible with self interested individuals who maximised scarce resources.

[77] Polanyi 1944: 57–59, Dalton 1971, and Humphreys 1969: 180–181, 184–191. Janssen is also sceptical of neoclassical theory applied to ancient Egypt (Janssen 1975a: 131). Finley asserts that a modern market governed by supply and demand must be more that the exchange of goods over a long distance. It must show interlocking behaviour and responses over a large area (Finley 1973: 34). Bleiberg supports the emphasis that Polanyi placed on redistribution particularly with regard to the NK Egyptian economy (Bleiberg 1988 and Bleiberg 1995: 1375). See also Gelb 1965 for the ancient Mesopotamian ration system.

[78] Dalton 1971: 64. See commentary in Bleiberg 1988: 159.

[79] Polanyi, 1944: 43.

[80] Polanyi 1944: 55.

[81] Polanyi 1944: 64.

[82] Polanyi 1977: 28.

[83] Snell 1991: 131 commenting on Polanyi 1977: 77 ff. Polanyi proposed that when the harvest produced shortfalls or gluts, equivalencies were changed in whole amounts, for example two to one for a shortfall or half to one in a glut (Polanyi 1977: 95). In contrast, market prices would reflect the exact supply and demand situation.

[84] Haring 2009: 6.

[85] Morley 2007: 26 and 33.

[86] Mooreland 2000: 2.

Chapter 2: Agriculture in the Late Bronze Age

2.1 Introduction

Chapter 2 is the first of three chapters that describe the basic processes of the economies of LBA Cyprus and NK Egypt. These processes form the 'basic sector' as defined in the Hierarchy of Needs in Chapter 1. Of these, agriculture satisfied the prime physiological need for food (Figure 2.1). This chapter investigates the resources required to support agriculture in Cyprus and Egypt and calculates the number of agrarian workers needed to feed the total population. Agrarian workers were required, not only to feed themselves and their families, but also to feed the non-food producing workforce and the élite. Without a surplus of food supplies from the harvest and animal husbandry, non-agrarian activities could not have been supported.

The agro-systems of Egypt and Cyprus provide good examples of two fundamentally different types of ancient farming. Egypt is an example of a 'hydraulic civilisation', dependent on the annual inundation of the Nile and Cyprus is representative of a Mediterranean dry-farming agro-system, dependent on rainfall. The availability of water, how crops were irrigated, and the variability of the climate governed agricultural practice. Section 2.2 examines how each region exploited their water resources and the effect this had on their farming practices.

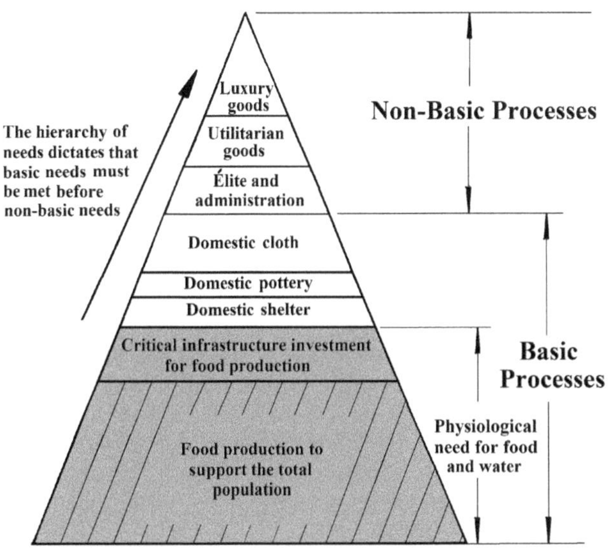

Figure 2.1: The prime physiological need for food within the framework of the Hierarchy of Needs.

Section 2.3 quantifies the total energy required (million kcals) to feed a cohort of 100,000 men, women, and children/year).[87] From this base, the diet to produce these calories is assessed (Sections 2.4–2.5). This is followed in Section 2.6 by the quantification of the weights of the food that needed to be produced and the area of land under cultivation. The labour-rates and workload for each farming activity are assessed in Section 2.7 and used to calculate the agrarian workload (man-years) to support a 100,000 cohort/yr. The chapter finishes with the calculation of the manpower needed to meet the agrarian workload in Section 2.8. The analyses in this chapter are used in Chapter 6, which determines the scale and the nature of the Cypriot and Egyptian economies.

Sources of evidence

Egyptian tomb paintings and texts are a major source of evidence and these are used to identify the sequence of the activities in the Egyptian farming cycle. Although Egyptian tomb paintings are often cited as evidence for agricultural products and processes, care has been taken in the interpretation of the scenes because they reflect the expectations of the élite. Many of the scenes are symbolic and show the deceased in an idealised afterlife. However, we can use the scenes to get some insight into what foodstuffs were cultivated and the farming processes involved. Where appropriate, texts related to farming practices from Mesopotamia, the Aegean, and the Classical Period are also used.

A multi-disciplined approach is necessary to complement the primary evidence.[88] This is especially so for LBA Cyprus because archaeological evidence is sparse. The analysis of food residues, ethnographic studies of farming and food preparation practices, experimental archaeology, skeletal and dental evidence, and contemporary dietary/nutrition requirements have all been used. Archaeobotanical evidence identifies the types of crops grown in the LBA. Infrared spectroscopy, gas chromatography/mass spectrometry and other modern scientific techniques identify food residues such as fats, oils, and honey found on the surface of ancient pots and/or the analysis of lipids absorbed within the pot fabric during cooking. Similarly, archaeozoological evidence of bone assemblages has been used for estimating the size and weight of LBA goats and sheep and to understand how meat was cooked or preserved for later consumption.[89]

Ethnographic evidence of traditional farming practices is applied extensively in this study.[90] The term 'traditional farming' refers to farming practices before the introduction of modern farming equipment and the

[87] A cohort is a group of people who share a common characteristic or experience within a defined period. By convention, demographic studies use a population cohort of 100,000 and this unit is used throughout this study. It is also the convention that demographic studies are zero-index based. The starting point of demographic studies is l_0 = 100,000 i.e. 100,000 babies that have survived childbirth and follows these 100,000 individuals throughout their lives until they are all dead (Parkin 1992: 75).

[88] Foaden and Fletcher 1908, FAO 1969, Russell 1988, Haldane 1990, Reynolds 1992, Haldane 1993, Mills and White 1994, Halstead and Jones 1997, Mattingly 1998, Reynolds 1999, Serpico and White 2000: 412–420, Clapham and Rowley-Conwy 2006, and FAO 2007.

[89] Lyman 1979, Luff 1994, Brothwell and Brothwell 1998, and Ikram 2000.

[90] Third world evidence published by the Farming and Agriculture Organisation (FAO) of the United Nations Organisation is used extensively in this study.

widespread use of fertilisers. Ethnographic studies of traditional farming demonstrate that the options for farming practices were limited and suggest that, when faced with the same climatic conditions, we can expect a similar approach to farming in antiquity. Results from experimental archaeology such as that carried out at the Butser Ancient Farm, which replicates ancient Iron Age farming practices, have been particularly useful in estimating labour-rates.[91]

2.2 The farming practices of NK Egypt and LBA Cyprus

The agro-systems of LBA Cyprus and NK Egypt followed a farming strategy of risk-minimisation common to all cultures of this period.[92] Crops were not cultivated only on the grounds of their yield but also on their suitability for the climatic condition and the type of land available. Accordingly, this study takes into account the effect on the yield of the crops cultivated on the best, average, and marginal land. Nor was it possible to make a choice between arable farming and animal production. Instead, 'a complex web of strategies was employed to minimise vulnerability and risk of loss.'[93] In the sections following, reference is made to some of these strategies such as intercropping, fallowing, cultivating drought resistant crops, and growing crops resistant to high salt levels in the soil. Agricultural activity has two peaks of workload, ploughing and harvesting/processing of crops. If more than one crop is grown it may have been necessary to delay the sowing of one beyond its optimum date to avoid simultaneous peaks in workload activity.[94] With some crops this is not possible and in Egypt the wheat harvest coincided with the flax harvest.[95] Equally important was the necessity of a balanced arable/livestock strategy to provide a suitable diet and food source in times of failed harvests. Livestock provided secondary products such as dairy products, wool, leather, and manure to fertilise the land; manure could also be burnt as fuel. Bovines were used for the cultivation of the soil; donkeys were used to transport goods, and in common with cattle, could be used to thresh the cereal crops.[96]

NK Egypt

The inundation

Egypt's climate with negligible rainfall is atypical compared with the other regions in the Eastern Mediterranean.[97] Egypt's farming was wholly dependent on the Nile and the importance of the inundation is demonstrated by the division of the year into three seasons, one of which is the *akhet,* which means 'inundation'.[98] The river rose during the months of July to September and from the middle of August onwards the water was high enough to spread to the surrounding land.[99] The large area of land that was flooded meant that the Egyptians could grow large quantities of cereal crops supplemented by horticultural crops, which were irrigated manually. The Nile inundation enabled NK Egypt to produce large food surpluses.

The Nile runs for more than 6,625 kilometres and flows almost due north.[100] It is fed by the Blue Nile that provides 83% of the flow of water, the White Nile provides 16% and the River Atbara contributes an additional 1% (Figure 2.2). The flow of the Blue Nile hardly varies because its source is Lake Tana, fed from the rainfall in the Ethiopian plateau. Each summer, monsoons fill the lake, sending water and silt down the Blue Nile and before the construction of the dams at Aswan, caused the annual inundation.

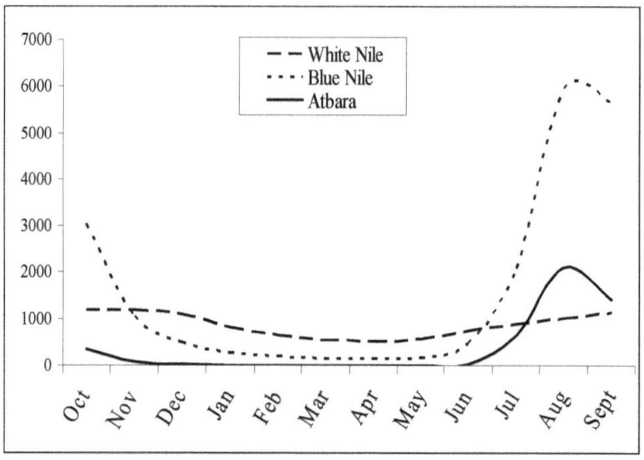

Figure 2.2: Monthly average discharge (m^3/s) from the major rivers feeding the Nile.
Beaumont 1993: Table 2.4 citing source data UNESCO 1969.

The vast capacity of Lake Tana evens out any variation in rainfall giving a consistent discharge into the Blue Nile. In contrast, fluctuations in the rainfall in Uganda, which feeds the White Nile, dictated the height of the inundation. A low inundation caused by a dry season in Uganda was also affected if the River Atbara ran dry, which occurred frequently.[101]

Management of the inundation

Egypt's method of irrigation exploited the natural inundation and the natural topography of the Nile valley,

[91] The Butser Ancient Farm in Hampshire UK, has for 25 years studied and followed British Iron Age farming practices. The work of the founder, the late Dr Peter Reynolds, is used in this study, in particular Reynolds 1981 and 1992.

[92] Butzer 1996: 142–144. See also Gallant 1991, Halstead 1993, and Halstead and Jones 1997.

[93] Butzer 1996: 143. Also, see Halstead and Jones 1997.

[94] See Halstead and Jones 1997: 287-288 for the wide range of strategies used by farmers in dry farming areas to minimise time stress at critical periods in the agricultural calendar.

[95] Allen 2002: 134.

[96] Halstead and Jones 1997: 280–283.

[97] Foaden and Fletcher 1908: 150–186. The temperature averages for Giza and Aswan were calculated over a 20 year period from 1885–1905. For a modern analysis of the mean Egyptian temperatures, particularly for the Nile Valley, see Zahran and Willis 1992: 6–7, 255–257.

[98] *Wb.* 1, 13.2. The other two seasons are *peret* (emergence; *Wb.* 1, 525.7), and *shemw* (harvest; *Wb.* 4, 481.1–11).

[99] Murray 2000a: 514.

[100] From Aswan to the Mediterranean Sea, the river bed slopes on average, about 0.08 m/km, while from the river's edge to the desert margin the Nile Valley averages 0.12 m per kilometre slope (Brewer 2007: 131–132). Willcocks 1889: 187 recorded a slope of 0.07 m/km.

[101] Brewer and Teeter 2007: 24.

which allowed the floodwater to flow by gravity across the flood plain.[102] The Egyptians took advantage of the natural shape of the Nile valley and the levees (riverbanks) that were formed from the silt and clay deposited by the inundation. These levees ran parallel to the river and they could be 3 m high when the Nile was at its lowest.[103] The combination of the levees and the lower land between the levees and the desert edge created basins that filled up to a depth of 1–2.5 m when the floodwater overflowed the levees.[104] The water soaked into the alluvial soil, increasing the water table and supporting a grain crop without the need for further irrigation.[105] In the years of low inundation, simple sluices were cut through the levees to flood the valley floor.[106] After 6–8 weeks, as the level in the main channel of the Nile water fell, surplus lying water drained back into the river through the same sluices or natural breaks in levees that it had entered. Immediately the floodwaters had receded, the crops were sown.

Dykes, built at right angles to the Nile, separated the flooded basins, each one slightly higher than the adjacent basin downstream.[107] NK scenes of the 'Fields of Reeds' show arable land surrounded by watercourses.[108] Eyre suggests they depicted controlled basin flooding that enabled farming to spread to previously uncultivated land.[109] The head of basin water upstream could be channelled through feeder canals into other basins downstream and across the valley floor to the edges of the desert. This land would not normally be reached by the floodwaters of an average or below average inundation.[110] Mays has suggested that the beds of these feeder canals were cut so that they were halfway between the lowest level of the Nile and ground level and maintained a natural downstream slope less than that of the Nile. In this way, these feeder canals could supply on average, eight basins in series.[111]

Canals such as the Bahr Yusef or natural depressions, retained water after the inundation receded. In addition, because the water table is high in the Nile Valley, wells were dug to extend the area of land for horticultural crops. Shadufs were used primarily for these crops, orchards, and gardens close to the Nile and along canals.[112] These irrigation methods are discussed in further detail in Section 2.7 when the manpower associated with managing the inundation and using the shaduf is calculated.[113]

Limitations of the inundation

The Nile inundation varied not only year on year, over time the average height of the inundation also varied. The average of the differences between the high and low levels of the annual inundation varied significantly for each century. The data for the measurements taken on the nilometer at Rhoda Island near Cairo show that over 13 centuries (A.D. 639–1904) the difference was 1.2 m.[114] For average or higher inundations, the harvest cycle would follow the same pattern that had been in place since the Predynastic Period and sufficient or surplus crops could be grown. If the inundation was low in a given year, little could be done to compensate. Land that could not be irrigated was left fallow (with no cultivated crops) and livestock pastured on the naturally occurring vegetation.

Egypt was not immune to periods of famine and a long period of famine during the OK is described on a 'Famine stele' at Aswan. Drought and famine in the OK is described in the Late Period 'Book of the Temple'.[115] Poor harvests may explain the economic instability of Egypt in the First, Second, and Third Intermediate Periods. Failed harvests are considered to be a contributory factor to the economic depression in the Near East LBA/EIA transition.[116] The major cause of famine was a succession of inundations that were too low, too high, or too late, which significantly reduced harvest yields. A particularly high or late inundation delayed ploughing and sowing (normally done in October and November) due to water remaining in the basins.[117] Consequently, the harvest was delayed to late May/early June and this increased wastage through dried out and

[102] Brewer 2007: 131. Artificial irrigation was established by the First Dynasty (Butzer, 1976).

[103] Brewer and Teeter 1999: 25 and Jeffreys 2007: 8.

[104] Foaden and Fletcher 1908: 150 and Brewer and Teeter 2007: Figure 2.4. See, Hillier *et al* 2007: 1013, Figure 2 for the NASA shuttle mission image that shows old levees across the Nile Valley at Luxor.

[105] Bowman and Rogan 1999: 2 and Butzer 2001: 184. The considerable area of the land under water is revealed by the mapping project carried out at the end of the nineteenth century A.D., sponsored by the British Government (Willcocks 1889, Willcocks 1904, and Willcocks and Beadnell 1904). It mapped Upper Egypt with a focus on the basin and canal irrigation systems. The largest basins were the Delgâwi basin in the Sohagia system and the Koshêsha basin at the tail of the Bahr Yusef system. They covered 194 and 162 km^2 of land respectively. In total there were 103 basins (covering an area of 4,751 km^2) on the east bank and 62 basins on the west bank (covering an area of 1,167 km^2). The average size of all the basins was 36 km^2. In addition there was extensive canal irrigation of 3,046 km^2 giving a grand total of land under irrigation in Upper Egypt of 8,964 km^2.

[106] Sluices in the NK would be little more than breaks in the levees filled with wood, mud-bricks, rubble and earth.

[107] Twelfth Dynasty texts show that major efforts were made to guide and restrict water flow and that by the mid Twelfth Dynasty, basin flooding was well established. Developments in basin flooding continued into the NK and up to the end of the nineteenth century A.D. (Willcocks 1889, Schenkel 1978: 29–36, Endesfelder 1979: 43–45, and Eyre 1994b: 78).

[108] These fields are imaginary, they depict the ideal land in the afterlife on which the deceased official would grow his crops but it is reasonable to consider that they reflect some reality.

[109] Eyre 1994b: 78.

[110] Foaden and Fletcher 1908: 151–152 and Brewer 2007: 133.

[111] Mays 2010: 56–57. See Lloyd 1983: 327, Figure 4.8 for a diagram of the basin system in the Late Period.

[112] Eyre 1994b: 64 and Butzer 2001: 185. The NK tomb of Ipuy (TT 217) shows workers collecting water in a shaduf for the irrigation of trees and flowers (Davies 1927: Plate XXIX).

[113] Eyre 1994b: 79, Footnotes 159–160. An Egyptian model (BM 36903) of an orchard with a central rectangular pond is illustrated in Plate VIII.

[114] Tabular data taken from Willcocks and Beadnell 1904: 51–52.

[115] Lichtheim 1976b: 95 and Quack 1997: 299 respectively.

[116] Butzer 1997, Hassan 1997a, and Weiss 1997.

[117] Foaden and Fletcher 1908: 152.

brittle grain, which was shed before the crop was harvested.[118]

If the inundation was excessively high, the natural levees eroded, causing the river to change direction violently. This happened on numerous occasions throughout Egypt's long history and washed away field systems, destroying dykes and settlements in its wake. Oxen and donkeys were also in danger from flash floods if they could not be moved in time to higher ground. The harvest was impacted because excessive floodwater could not drain away in time for planting.[119] Contemporary observations of the excessive floods in 1818 A.D. and 1878 A.D. reveal the level of devastation inflicted on agricultural communities when the Nile broke its banks during a very high inundation.[120]

Other causes of crop failure in Egypt

Another cause of harvest failure was the dry, hot dust-laden 'Khamsin', a southerly wind that lowered crop yields through desiccation. The Khamsin occurs between March and early June produced by an eastward-moving depression that tracks along the northern coastal fringe of North Africa. This draws in hot sand-laden air from the Sahara with speeds up to 140 km per hour. Temperatures overnight can rise 25 degrees to 46°C, and the relative humidity may drop to 5–10 per cent. If the wind occurs when cereal crops are maturing, the ears are damaged and seed formation ceases. If the Khamsin occurs later in the growing season, the hot dry wind causes the ears to turn white and the seeds to shrivel, significantly lowering the yield rates.[121]

A challenge common to modern farmers and their counterparts in antiquity is evapotranspiration, a function of natural evaporation of water from the soil combined with plant transpiration of water vapour from the stomata in the leaves. The evapotranspiration rate is also affected by wind speed and at Aswan in June, the evaporation rate can be as high as 19.3 mm/day with a resulting evapotranspiration rate of 7.8 mm/day.[122]

Although the annual inundation meant that there was usually sufficient water for the crops, maintaining the levees, sluices, dykes and basins, and large state irrigation projects such as maintaining the Bahr Yusef canal from the ingress of sand, involved considerable labour.

LBA Cyprus

The impact of annual rainfall on harvest yields

Cypriot farmers in the LBA were faced with more climatic issues than their counterparts in Egypt. The climate of Cyprus is typical of the Eastern Mediterranean with relatively mild, rainy winters and hot summers. October to the end of March is cold with high precipitation levels and April through to September is hot and dry. By convention, a dry farming region has a rainfall between 380 mm and 750 mm per annum.[123] Cyprus receives on average between 450–600 mm/yr annual rainfall but this is not evenly distributed. The average annual total precipitation is between 300 and 350 mm in the central plain and the flat south-eastern parts of the island. The mountains of Cyprus can have a local influence on precipitation levels when the moisture carrying air from the Central Mediterranean meets elevated ground. This increases precipitation on the south-western windward slopes of the central massif (the Troodos mountain range) from 450 mm up to nearly 1,100 millimetres at the top. The Kyrenia range, stretching 100 miles along the extreme north of the island, produces up to 550 mm of rainfall along its ridge at about 1,000 metres.[124] Wheat, barley, pulses, olives, figs, grapes, and legumes are cultivated successfully today with these levels and patterns of rainfall and the archaeobotanical record shows that they were also grown in antiquity.[125]

The management of drought in dry farming areas

Up to 75% of the variability in cereal yields across dry farming areas of the Eastern Mediterranean is a function of the distribution of rainfall rather than the seasonal total.[126] Whilst it is generally accepted that annual rainfall above 380 mm is required for successful dry farming, below average harvests are possible with precipitations as low as 250 mm following a cereal-legume-fallow strategy (discussed below).[127] At this level of annual precipitation (250 mm), yield levels vary widely. Arnon suggests that a reduction of 25 mm from this level could result in complete crop failure. However, 50 mm above the minimum requirement (300 mm) could double the yields.[128]

In Cyprus most of the rivers flowing from the Troodos mountains are seasonal and become dry in summer (with the exception of the main branches of the Ezousas and the Xeropotamos). Even in summers with rainfall greater than 300 mm, some form of irrigation is required at the height of the summer season. Some irrigation comes from natural aquifers or springs, and riverbeds filled with gravelly alluvia. The latter serve as a form of aquifer that

[118] In 1877, the inundation was two metres below average and 35% of the land was without irrigation (Butzer 1976: 53).

[119] Hassan 1997a: 10–11 and Hassan 1997b: 63. The Nile has moved 5 km across the Nile Valley at a rate of 2–3 km per 1000 years (Hillier *et al* 2007: 1012–1013, Figures 1–2).

[120] Willcocks 1889: 182–188 and Willcocks and Beadnell 1904: 70–72.

[121] Arnon 1972a: 43 and Beaumont 1993: 17–19.

[122] Beaumont 1883: 21–22 and Tables 2.2–2.3.

[123] 65% of the earth's land surface has less than 750 mm per annum (Widtsoe 1913: 28–34). The success or otherwise of dry farming is the timing of annual rainfall because the bulk must fall in the growing season between spring and early summer. For a diagram of the average rainfall in the Central and Eastern Mediterranean, see Roaf 1990: 22–23.

[124] Data from the Meteorological Service of the Republic of Cyprus.

[125] For the paleobotanical record of the area around ancient Idalion using Streuver's flotation technique see Stewart 1974.

[126] Van Oosterom, Ceccarelli and Peacock 1993: 307.

[127] Arnon 1972a: 462–463.

[128] Arnon 1972a: 30–31, 462–463. However although cereal harvests are possible with 250 mm, there is a high risk of crop failure.

can be used to irrigate localised agriculture.[129] A run of 2–3 concurrent seasons of low precipitations within the range 150–200 mm leads to a drop in the water table, with consequent drying up of the natural springs feeding rivers.[130]

The main cereal-growing area is the central Mesaoria plain, which has no perennial streams and traditional farms in the area exploited flash floods by directing the water through weirs into a maze of water channels to the cereal fields.[131] It is likely that this was also practiced in antiquity. Another method for the conservation of rainfall in LBA Cyprus may have been to build dams similar to those found on the island of Pseira near to Crete. In the Bronze Age, dams were built across the smaller ravines for irrigation, animal, and domestic purposes. The catchment area behind each dam held between 500–600 m^3 of water, which was carried up from the dam in clay pots to the upper terraces. An additional benefit to farmers was that the soil washed down from the upper levels was periodically dug out of the catchment area and put back on the upper terraces. This improved the fertility of the soil especially when mixed with animal dung.[132]

The management of above average rainfall in dry farming areas

A major problem for farmers was a sequence of above average annual rainfall. Floodwater from the rivers carried alluvial deposits to coastal plains and flat inland basins. This was a benefit if the deposits originated from nutrient-rich soils and rocks such as limestone and basalt because they provided favourable conditions for agriculture.[133] However, excessive rain causing flash floods on sloping rocky ground washes away the limited top soil to below the threshold depth of 0.3 m required for adequate root growth of cereals and pulses.[134] Even if the threshold depth is retained, successive above average, wet winters, can wash out soil fines that are less than 0.1 mm and can permanently alter the structure and fertility of the soil. In addition, trace elements and organisms essential for growth and disease resistance are leached out of the soil. The exposed stony ground encourages rain to soak away more rapidly, which in turn exacerbates the effect of the summer droughts in following years. To help to retain the top soil, fields on sloping land were terraced.

Soils that become waterlogged from flooding, lead to a reduction in cereal plant growth, impairing root formation, tillers, and fertile heads, and delaying ear emergence and plant maturation. Experiments by Watson *et al* on the impact of intermittent and continuous water logging across different soil types show reductions in yields for barley and wheat up to 39% and 46.5% respectively.[135] Ploughing in wet conditions using heavy oxen, typical of LBA Cyprus, can create an additional problem by forming a 'plough pan' below the surface. The pan prevents water drainage and if repeated in successive above average wet winters, the plough pan reaches a critical depth, making the land waterlogged every winter. At the same time the plough pan causes the limited annual rainfall to run off because the top 0.2 m is waterlogged. This progressively lowers the underlying water table, aggravating the problems of meeting the demand for water in the growing season.[136]

Dry farming practice

Our knowledge of dry-farming practices in LBA Cyprus is limited due the relative paucity of archaeological or textual evidence. This study assumes that ethnographic evidence from pre-mechanised traditional farming practices, which faced similar irregular rainfall patterns and used similar farming technology, gives an insight into the practices used in antiquity. For example, ethnographic studies show that traditional farming methods, crops, and cropping practices in the relatively recent Eastern Mediterranean are similar to those recorded in the 'Gezer Calendar'.[137] This EIA tablet from Tel Gezer in Israel (*c.*900 B.C.) has seven intact lines:

> Line 1: Two months of harvesting (olives).
> Line 1–2: Two months sowing (cereals), 2 months of late growing (legumes and vegetables).
> Line 3: One month of hoeing weeds (hay/fodder) production.
> Line 4: One month harvesting barley.
> Line 5: One month harvesting (wheat) and measuring (grain).
> Line 6: Two months cutting grapes.
> Line 7: One month collecting summer fruits.[138]

This list demonstrates the ancient practice of multi-cropping, which reduced the risk of famine from a mono-crop strategy. In addition, a multi-cropping strategy adds variety to the diet and has the advantage of spreading labour effort across the year since the crops reach maturity at different times. Planning was required to avoid crops reaching maturity at the same time in the calendar and overstretching resources for the labour-intensive activities in the agrarian cycle such as soil

[129] Rupp *et al* 1984: 136.

[130] See Halstead 1989: 74 for the impact of clusters of low annual rainfall levels on the farming communities of eastern Thessaly. He discusses the strategies of the traditional farmers to counter precipitation levels below 300 mm in three out of four growing seasons between 1931–1932 and 1934–1935. In the Larisa plain rainfall failed to reach this level eleven times (including twice below 150 mm) in the four growing seasons between 1964–5 and 1977–8.

[131] Littlejohn 1946: 123. The Mesaoria plain extends between the Troodos and Kyrenia mountain ranges and covers an area of 31,000 ha (1200 square miles).

[132] Betancourt and Simpson 1992: 52–53.

[133] Arnon 1972a: 64, Zangger 1992: 15, and Halstead 1994: 196.

[134] Ethnographic evidence from Morocco indicates that a soil depth of 0.3 m was needed for growing barley and legumes (Tiedeman *et al* 1998: 288).

[135] Reduction in wheat grain yields were 40% and 53% for intermittent and continuous water-logging regimes respectively (46.5% average across both water-logging regimes). However, there was no differential effect of the two water-logging treatments on the grain yield of barley which had a yield reduction of 39% (Watson *et al* 1976).

[136] FAO 1994.

[137] Halstead 1897 and Halstead and Jones 1997.

[138] Borowski 1987: 38; Table 2 interprets line 3 as hay/fodder production rather than weeding of crops. A photograph of this tablet is given in Borowski 1987: 35, Figure 2. Gezer is 30 miles west of Jerusalem near the coast with rainfall levels within the Cypriot rainfall range.

preparation, weeding, watering, and harvesting.[139] The farmers followed the multi-cropping strategy using traditional agricultural tools whose antecedents can be traced back to antiquity. They grew wheat, barley, pulses, and vetches for fodder. Pulses and vetches were sown in November, barley in November/December, and wheat and lentils in January/February. Depending on the weather conditions, winter ploughing was between November and February.[140]

This study supposes that farmsteads in Cyprus, as in the recent north-eastern Mediterranean studied by Halstead and Jones, were nucleated settlements with dispersed land holdings.[141] With limited labour available, farming strategies optimised the time and effort needed to tend the crops and minimise transport effort. For practical reasons, the outer regions of the farm would be sown with cereal crops in a bi-annual rotation with either leaving the land fallow, or growing fodder or nitrogen fixing legumes. Once sown, they required less human intervention than vegetables, vines, and olive crops, which were cultivated in the inner rings.[142] Livestock were kept close to the house to give them protection from predators, easy access to milk for dairy products, and to provide warmth in winter because their stalls were often located within the domestic dwelling.[143] Their proximity also allowed the convenient collection of manure used to improve the fertility of the soil.[144] This is not to say the farms were isolated; it would have made sense to concentrate them around water sources or in agricultural settlements such as Aredhiou *Vouppes* and Analiondas *Palioklichia.*[145] If a number of farmsteads existed within a socially cohesive community able to form large flocks, then transhumance became a viable practice.[146]

In summary, the problem of too little or too much rainfall can be mitigated to some extent by cultivating crops that require water at different times and there was considerable diversity in the crops grown in the Eastern Mediterranean islands. However, the variability of the supply of water inherent within a dry-farming culture such as LBA Cyprus makes the production of a reliable harvest surplus for non-basic workers significantly more difficult than Egypt. On the other hand, the need for extensive irrigation in LBA Cyprus was less than in Egypt because it had annual rainfall and as a result, it required a smaller expenditure of manpower. This topic is returned to in Section 2.7, which assesses the manpower involved in the irrigation of cultivated land in Cyprus and Egypt and in Chapter 6, which compares and contrasts the difference in scale between the Egyptian and Cypriot agricultural sectors.

Fallowing/crop rotation in Cyprus and Egypt

When crops are grown repeatedly on the same strip of land each year, three problems can occur that significantly lower crop yields: a drop in fertility, a concentration of weeds that are crop specific and which compete for water, nutrients, and light, and a lowering of resistance to diseases that are crop specific. Fallowing, allows the soil to recover and in dry farming regions it assists the farmer to manage the lack of moisture in the soil. It was of particular relevance in Cyprus, which was dependent on rainfall. Fallowing is an important factor in this study as it directly influences the number of agrarian workers needed to prepare the soil for sowing because it is significantly more difficult to plough land left fallow in the previous year.

Egyptian fallowing practice

In basin land the practice of rotational fallowing as practiced in dry farming regions would be unlikely as the annual inundation provided an adequate water table and fertile silt for the season's crop.[147] On the limited evidence available, this study considers that a policy of deliberate rotational fallowing, certainly on basin land, was not implemented because the basins were dedicated primarily to cereal cultivation. Therefore, large areas of permanent pastureland in the Nile Valley were limited.[148] A small percentage of plots of land were likely to have been left fallow for other reasons. There could be a change of ownership, crop gluts, years with a high inundation so that the land required time dry out, higher land that was only rarely covered by the inundation, shortage of workers, or shortage of seed corn for marginal land following a poor harvest. Land left fallow would allow grass, weeds, and self-seeded legumes to grow, providing an alternative to cultivated green fodder. Egyptian texts refer to plots of pastureland called *smi* and the titles 'overseer of the pasture' and 'overseer of the pastureland' attest to the use of land as pasture for livestock.[149] From the Heqanakht letters there is reference to 14 arouras (3.86 ha) of 'land that is in pasturage' (II 33).[150] Allen calculates that if this area of land was used for pasture, it could provide about half of the estimated annual fodder for all of Heqanakht's cattle, with the remainder supplied from the stalks of harvested grain and other sources.[151]

[139] As highlighted in the ethnographic study of the villages of two semi-arid Aegean islands, Karpathos and Amorgos (Halstead and Jones 1997: 44, 47, and 53).

[140] Halstead and Jones 1989: 279.

[141] Halstead and Jones 1997: 282.

[142] Butzer 1996: 142.

[143] Ethnographic evidence from Karpathos and Amorgos show that most working animals were kept in stalls in the immediate vicinity of the farm (Halstead and Jones 1997: 282–283).

[144] Halstead and Jones 1997: 273 and 284.

[145] Knapp 1997a: 50–51, Keswani and Knapp 2003: 217, Knapp 2003: 561, 571, and 573, Knapp and Given 2004: 91, and Steel and Janes 2005 have proposed that these agricultural villages stored surplus crops and redistributed them to the mining communities in the Troodos mountains.

[146] The seasonal movement of livestock between summer and winter pastures, for example seasonal pastures on rocky slopes in spring and marshy areas in late summer (Halstead 1996: 35).

[147] See further discussion relating to the benefits of silt in the section below on the fertility from inundation silt.

[148] The exception being large numbers of beef stock raised for religious and royal purposes (Kemp 1994: 138–146). Moens and Wetterstrom 1998 suggest that such herds were raised in the Delta.

[149] *Wb.* 4, 121.14, *Wb.* 2, 97. 14–15, 97.17, and 98. 1.

[150] Conversion rate 1 aroura = 0.2757 ha.

[151] Allen 2002: 162. Allen translates this as 1.4 dekarouras (dar) a unit of area equating to 14 arouras (Allen 2002: 151, Footnote 68).

The Heqanakht letters also show that plots of land previously under pasture were subsequently ploughed to grow other crops.[152]

Egyptian fallowing may have been practiced on low-lying land on the boundary edge between valley and desert where water from a high inundation collected. As it evaporated, the water would leave areas of salty stagnant water leading to the build up of salts, which are detrimental to future arable cultivation.[153] However, if such land was left fallow, the resulting growth of sparse grass, sedges, reeds, and weeds would have helped to dry out the soil, thereby preventing the salts rising.[154] The land would also allow limited grazing of livestock, although it would be necessary to supplement their feed.[155] For Egypt this study assumes 55% of marginal land was left fallow in the previous year, 25% of average land was left fallow in the previous year, and 5% of best land was left fallow in the previous year.

Cypriot fallowing practice

Ethnographic studies demonstrate that fallowing of up to 50% of the cultivated land was customary in Cypriot agriculture.[156] The most drastic practice is bare fallowing when the land is cultivated only once every two or three years. The weeds are ploughed up before they seed, which minimises the impact of weed infestation and crop disease, but it has penalties.[157] There is an increased labour cost of a ploughing cycle without a crop, there is a reduction in arable land available for cultivation, and there is still a need for deliberately grown fodder.[158] The ethnographic studies in Cyprus record that bare fallowing was deliberately practised to maximise the water content between seasons rather than use the land for pasture for meat production. Brengle's study of dry land farming practices and Wilkinson's model of rainfall patterns in Northern Mesopotamia between 1961–1990 show that fields left fallow, provided they were kept weed free, would have retained between 15–20% of water in the soil that was available for the crop grown the following year.[159]

Garnsey suggests that a satisfactory rotation system for dry farming/semi-arid conditions would be a three-year cycle. A plot of land would grow a wheat/barley crop in the first year, legumes in the second, and in third year left fallow.[160] Traditional dry farming methods practised until recently across the Eastern Mediterranean allowed livestock to graze on the post harvest stubble/weed/grass so that their dung manured the soil. However, grass covered fallowing within a multi-cropping strategy had the disadvantage that it made the land more difficult to plough the following year. To bring it back into cultivation required three ploughings between March and May to prepare the soil for sowing. Although land that had been cultivated the previous year also required three ploughings, it did not take as much time as preparing the fallow land. For Cyprus, this study assumes 75% of marginal land was left fallow in the previous year, 37% of average land was left fallow in the previous year, and 10% of best land was left fallow in the previous year.

Maintenance of soil fertility

Egypt had the benefit of the annual inundation that deposited fertile silt on flooded land. However, it needed to fertilise horticultural land irrigated with water from canals and wells, which contained little or no silt.[161] In Cyprus, the land needed to be fertilised to replace nutrients lost through plant cultivation and leaching from the soil. Before the introduction of modern fertilisers in the nineteenth century A.D., replacing the fertility of the soil was limited to the application of livestock and human waste to the soil as manure or the cultivation of nitrogen fixing plants.

Fertility from inundation silt in Egypt

Silt carried by the Nile from the Ethiopian highlands and deposited on the basin floor, maintained the fertility of the soil. Without the silt, agriculture would have been limited to those areas close to the Nile that were irrigated manually and fertilised from the application of animal dung. The crop yield of basin land depended on the amount of silt deposited and consequently basins or parts of basins, which were nearest to the source of supply, were more fertile as they received most silt.[162] Newman considers that the Nile silt laid down 21 kg/ha/yr of particulate inorganic phosphorus that would support cereal yields around 1,000 kg/yr.[163] This yield is of the same order as that used in this study for average land of 1,498 kg/ha and 1,567 kg/ha for barley and wheat respectively. For higher yields, other sources of phosphorus would have to be supplied from manure.

Manuring in Cyprus and Egypt

Manuring with excreta from livestock and humans improved crop yields by providing nutrients to the crops. In addition, it increased the humus levels, improving the texture and water retaining properties of the soil.[164] This

---

[152] Allen 2002: 160–162, 170, and Footnote 101.

[153] Gardiner 1947a: 10*56.

[154] Gibson 1974: 10–11 discusses how in basin land, grasses and legumes dried out the subsoil to a depth of two meters. This prevented the water from rising and bringing salt to the surface with the added benefits that the legumes replenished the land with nitrogen (discussed below), and retarded wind erosion of the topsoil.

[155] Fallow land could produce sufficient calories to maintain livestock in a healthy state provided they were fed supplementary rations of barley, cereal stubble, cereal straw, and/or chaff left over from the threshing process of cereals (Halstead and Jones 1997: 280–281).

[156] Todd 1979: 293.

[157] Halstead 1897: 82.

[158] Jameson 1983: 8.

[159] Brengle 1982: 73–101 and Wilkinson 1994: 499–501.

[160] Garnsey 1992: 151.

[161] In Egypt, manuring was only necessary for land not irrigated by the Nile, for those areas left dry after a low inundation, or for non-cereal summer crops irrigated by water that was not silt laden (Murray 2000a: 516).

[162] Foaden and Fletcher 1908: 151.

[163] Newman 1997: 1340.

[164] Nitrogen in the top soil decomposes rapidly on higher ground. This decomposition is particularly apparent on the levees and lands on the edges of floodplain and this land required manuring to replace nitrogen nutrients (Butzer 1976: 89). Manure also improves the moisture retention in the soil but Mediterranean traditional dry farming practices show that it was preferred to improve moisture content through bare fallowing because this allows two years' rainfall to be stored for one bi-annual crop (Halstead 1897: 81).

section estimates the annual quantity of animal and human waste produced by a small farm and identifies the choices for its use, which would have to be made by Cypriot and Egyptian farmers.[165] On farms, animals would primarily be beasts of burden and not kept for their meat.[166] It was uneconomical in terms of human effort compared with growing cereals and pulses, which produce more energy per unit area than animal protein because when animals turn plants into meat, energy is lost in the process.[167] At most, a small farm would have a pair of oxen for ploughing, two cows for breeding and dairy products, one to two donkeys for transport, and a few sheep, goats, and pigs. The estimated production of animal dung for such a farm is 57,232 kg/yr (Table 2.1).[168] To this can be added human excreta and assuming a family of six per farm, this would amount to 1,095 kg/yr of nitrogen-rich waste each per year.[169] The total volume of livestock and human manure is 270.4 m^3/yr (Table 2.1) and if spread at the rate typical for Roman agriculture calculated by Spurr, of 69.1 m^3/ha, the area covered would be 3.9 ha.[170]

In Egypt, the artistic record shows that plots dedicated to horticulture and viticulture were located near water sources on levees or along canal banks. However, water fed to the plots would not contain the nutrient rich silt of basin agriculture.[171] As horticulture plots grew more than one crop in a year and viticulture required a high organic content soil, it is likely that scarce livestock dung would be used for this type of cultivation and this has been assumed for both Egypt and Cyprus.

Dried animal manure was also used as a fuel for cooking and it would have been highly valued but limited in supply in most small farms of say 3–4 ha.[172] Animal dung is used as fuel for domestic cooking in Egypt today. Indian ethnographic evidence shows that 3,162 kg/yr of dried animal dung is needed to meet the cooking needs of a rural family of five.[173] This is equivalent to 18.4% of the total wet dung produced per year/family and would reduce the area of land that could be manured from 1.84 to 3.2 ha. Assuming small farms would have been in the range 2–4 ha, careful decisions had to be made on what crops the limited supply of dung would be used.[174]

	No. of animals	Total dung kg	Total dung m^3
Oxen	2	50	0.0566
Dairy cow	1	53.5	0.0538
Donkey	1	17.8	0.0227
Pigs	3	4.7	0.1948
Sheep/goats	12	21.4	0.0204
	Per day	147.4	0.3483
	Per year	57,232	269.3
	Human/year	1,095	1.1
	Total/year	**58,327**	**270.4**

Table 2.1: Estimated animal waste produced by a small farm 2–3 ha.

Nitrogen fixing with legumes

Legumes, in addition to their contribution to the diet and/or use as fodder for livestock, fix atmospheric nitrogen in root nodules. If they are ploughed into the soil prior to the formation of seed, they increase soil fertility and crop yields. Arnon considers that a pasture/legume fallow rotation with cereals is particularly suitable for dry farming/semi-arid conditions. This method is based on alternating periods of two or more years of annual, self-seeding legumes that are grazed by cattle or sheep, followed by one or more years of grain-crops. In a year with high rainfall, the legumes and any remaining cereal stubble from the previous crop allowed grazing all year.[175] Arnon points out that if the legumes are cropped before the seed is formed, the amount of plant nutrients removed from the soil is minimal whilst the soil is enriched in nitrogen and organic matter.[176] Trials carried out in Cyprus by the Department of Agriculture between 1934–1944 show that the mean wheat yields increases by 199% by using a wheat/legume rotation. However, contrary to expectations, wheat-bare fallowing rotation increased yield by more than 250%. The most dramatic increase in the yields was with wheat-green manure rotation, which gave an increased yield of 381%. A summary of the results is given in Table 2.2.[177]

Harvest Year	Wheat-wheat	Wheat-bare fallow	Wheat-green manure	Wheat-legume
1936	75	155	280	120
1938	255	865	1,080	560
1940	65	100	215	115
1942	280	730	1,310	655
1944	190	335	410	270
Average	**173**	**437**	**659**	**344**
% yield increase		**253**	**381**	**199**

Table 2.2: Yield of wheat grain (kg/ha) following crop rotation.

Adapted from Littlejohn 1946: 127, Table 3.

165 Arnon 1972a: 484 points out that manure from sheep/goats that have grazed on weedy areas needs to be composted at high temperatures to kill the seeds, otherwise they are transferred to the arable plots and re-grow.

166 For Classical evidence of livestock numbers on small farms, see, Garnsey 1993. For ethnographic evidence see Halstead 1993, Halstead and Jones 1993: 280–283, and Halstead and Jones 1997.

167 Garnsey 1999: 16.

168 Hermanson and Kalita 2012.

169 A family of four produces approximately 2 kg of nitrogen-rich excreta each per day (Miller 1990: 130). This study has assumed a family size of 6 and therefore uplifted the rate to 2.75 kg/day. The accepted average density of human faeces is 1 g/cm^3 therefore the annual volume for a family of 6 would be 1.1 m^3/yr (Ferreira 2005: 347).

170 Spurr 1986: 127–131.

171 Murray 2000c: 616.

172 The Egyptian Ministry of Agriculture data shows that 1 ton of manure (a mix of earth and excreta) provides approximately 2.5–3.4 kg of N_2, 1.7–3.4 kg of P_2O_5, and about 8.3 kg of K_2O (Ruf 1993: 199). One source of fertiliser used in post Medieval Egypt was crushed mud-bricks (*sebakh koufri*) from Nile settlements that had made the bricks with Nile mud laid down over millennia of inundations (Ruf 1993: 195).

173 Assumptions based on data in Mansinghka 2002: Chapter 5.

174 This has been taken into account in Section 2.6 below where it has been assumed that below average quality of land would not have been manured and would consequently produce low yields.

175 Arnon 1972a: 463.

176 Arnon 1972a: 467.

177 Littlejohn 1946. All the strips in the trials were contiguous on poor/average land, in the same field. This ensured commonality in soil types and rainfall levels.

2.3 The energy requirement to feed a 100,000 cohort/yr

Agrarian workers in the LBA had to produce sufficient food to feed themselves and the non-food producing workforce and the élite. The first stage in assessing the number of workers required to feed the total population is the quantification of the total energy required to feed a cohort of 100,000 men, women, and children/yr. This section determines the number of individuals (male and female) within specific age bands (hereafter 'demographic profile'). These age bands are multiplied by the daily calorie requirement of individuals within the bands, taking into account whether they were in active or sedentary occupations. To calculate the annual calorie requirement for the 100,000 cohort, the result is multiplied by 365.

Demographic age profile

The demographic age profile in Table 2.3 and throughout this study uses the Coale-Demeny developed life tables based on evidence from Mauritius between the years 1942–1946 A.D.[178]

Demographic-age bands	
Infants under 4 breastfed	3,240
Weaned infants under 4	11,840
Children 4–6 years	9,240
Children 7–9 years	5,600
Adolescents 10–12 years	5,410
Adolescents 13–15 years	5,330
Adults 16–19 years	6,670
Adults 20–39 years	28,090
Adults 40–49 years	10,810
Adults 50–59 years	8,200
Adults 60–69 years	4,430
Adults 70+ years	1,140
Total	**100,000**

Table 2.3: Survivors collated by demographic-age band using the Coale-Demeny Model 3 West.

Frier, Parkin, and Scheidel have also made important contributions to the estimation of the demographic-age profile of populations in antiquity.[179] Scheidel's work considers the impact of pandemic plagues on the absolute size of populations in antiquity, which he considers were much lower than the current consensus of scholars.[180]

Calorie requirements

The daily calorie recommendation (kcals/day) entered into AGCALC is that given by the FAO for manual workers using hand tools on the land, undertaking a range of agrarian activities.[181] Where necessary this information has been supplemented from other sources.[182] The study assumes that children under three years were breastfed and did not require other significant calories intake.[183] The total calorie requirement for a cohort of 100,000 has to take into account that some members have sedentary occupations and have a lower daily calorie requirement as shown in Table 2.4.[184]

Demographic age bands	Calorie requirements kcals/day			
	Active		Sedentary	
	Male	Female	Male	Female
Infants under 4 breastfed	0	0	0	0
Weaned infants under 4	1,000	1,000	1,000	1,000
Children 4–6 years	1,878	1,790	1,800	1,700
Children 7–9 years	2,190	2,110	2,000	1900
Adolescents 10–12 years	2,600	2,600	2,300	2,100
Adolescents 13–15 years	3,237	3,100	2,400	2,050
Adults 16–19 years	3,300	2,500	2,400	2,050
Adults 20–39 years	3,525	2,500	2,300	2,000
Adults 40–49 years	2,700	2,500	2,250	2,000
Adults 50–59 years	2,400	2,150	2,050	1,900
Adults 60–69 years	2,250	1,947	2,000	1,830
Adults 70+ years	2,200	1,900	1,850	1,830

Table 2.4: Summary of the daily calorie requirement in kcals/day for males and females.

The percentages by demographic age groups for the 100,000 cohort that had sedentary occupations are given in Table 2.5.

Demographic age bands	% of males with sedentary occupations	% of females with sedentary occupations
Infants under 4 years	N/A	N/A
Children 4–9 years	5	5
Adolescents 10–15 years	7	15
Adults 16–50 years	10	25
Adults 50–59 years	15	30
Adults 60+ years	60	70

Table 2.5: The percentage of males and females in sedentary occupations.

The resulting total calorie requirement for active and sedentary individuals is 84,684 million kcals/100,000 cohort/yr (Table 2.6).

Calorie requirements million kcals/100,000 cohort/yr				
	Male		Female	
Demographic age band	Active	Sedentary	Active	Sedentary
Weaned infants under 4	2,148		2,148	
Children 4–9 yrs	5,135	257	4,916	240
Adol's 10–15 yrs	5,360	325	4,713	606
Adults 16–50 yrs	25,383	2,820	15,593	4,173
Adults 50–59 yrs	3,053	539	2,252	853
Adults 60+ yrs	911	1,366	591	1,302
Totals	**41,990**	**5,307**	**30,213**	**7,174**

Table 2.6: Active and sedentary energy requirements million kcals/100,000 cohort/yr by demographic age bands.

[178] Coale, Demeny, and Vaughan 1983.

[179] For other demographic profiles in antiquity, see the work of Frier 1982, Scheidel 1982, Parkin 1992, Scheidel 1996, Frier 2000, Scheidel 2001b, and Parkin 2003.

[180] Scheidel 2001a. The factor with the greatest impact on population size is the Net Reproduction Rate of women (NRR). This is a measure of the number of daughters that a cohort of newborn girls will bear during their lifetime and the extent to which they will replace themselves (Dharmalingam 2004).

[181] FAO 1973.

[182] Allbaugh 1953: 106–135, Tables 8–9, Foxhall and Forbes 1982: 49–50, particularly Footnote 26, and Gallant 1991: 73, Table 4.5.

[183] Szpakowska 2008: 213–214 discusses the evidence for breastfeeding as a form of contraception and its impact on family size in antiquity.

[184] For comparison, see Jongman 2007: 599, Table 22.1.

2.4 *The diets of LBA Cyprus and NK Egypt*

The calories required by the populations of Cyprus and Egypt were provided by a range of foodstuffs. This section examines the diets of both LBA regions and considers which crops were grown and what animals were raised to provide the 84,684 calories to feed a cohort of 100,000/yr. This analysis of the LBA diet cannot be definitive, but this section has incorporated a wide range of evidence to make the assumptions as representative as possible.

The LBA Cypriot diet

Unlike ancient Egypt, which has extensive textual, artistic, and archaeological evidence with which to study NK farming practices, Cyprus has limited evidence of the farming methods in the LBA and the assessments of their farming practices are based on archaeobotanical and ethnographic investigations. An important source for this study is the study of pre-mechanised farming by Allbaugh, carried out immediately following the Second World War. His study was one of the first scientific studies of a rural community that used traditional farming practices.[185] Table 2.7 lists the foods in the Cretan diet identified in Allbaugh's study and the proportion of calories they contributed to the total intake required by an adult.

Food type	Allbaugh's study kg/person/yr	Energy intake kcals/day	% calorie intake
Cereals	127.7	1,162	46.7
Potatoes	38.6	76	3.1
Honey	5.4	45	1.8
Grapes	10	21	0.8
Pulses	38	133	5.3
Vegetables	32.1	22	0.9
Greens	5	3	0.1
Olives	2.4	7	0.3
Figs	5	3	0.1
Fruit in season	63.3	104	4.2
Tomatoes + citrus	28	13	0.5
Mutton/goat/game	11.1	76	3
Fish	8.9	33	1.3
Milk	27.1	62	2.5
Cheese	7.4	53	2.1
Animal fats	1.2	29	1.2
Olive oil	29.7	650	26.1
Total	**440.9**	**2,492**	**100**

Table 2.7: The percentage mix of food types for the daily diet of a Cretan adult.

It is reasonable to consider that farmers faced with the same conditions, equipment, livestock, and crops, would have followed similar agricultural practices in the LBA. The LBA Cypriot calorie requirement is based on Allbaugh's study. Different foodstuffs were consumed in the LBA and so some adjustments to Allbaugh's records need to be made.

The proportion of calories provided by the diet is based on the following assumptions:

- The agriculture was, as it is today, based around the production of cereals, grapes, and olives (Mediterranean triad diet).[186]
- Calories from potatoes would have been provided by cereals.
- The cereals grown in the LBA were barley and emmer wheat.
- The calories from tomatoes would have been provided by vegetables and fruit.
- The proportion of figs in the LBA diet is increased to reflect their wide availability and ease of drying and storing.[187]
- Protein consumption was biased to mutton, goat, and game. Fresh fish would be more available in the harbour towns along the south-western coastal fringe of Cyprus.
- Olives/olive oil were the major source of lipids.

The foodstuffs that provided the 84,684 calories in the Cypriot diet are listed in Table 2.8.

The NK Egyptian diet

Table 2.9 estimates the proportion of food types that provided the necessary 84,684/kcals/100,000 cohort/yr in NK Egypt. It is adapted from the diet of LBA Cyprus in Table 2.8 to reflect the food types available in NK Egypt. There would have been a greater proportion of cereals in the Egyptian diet and imported olive oil would have been limited to the Egyptian élite.[188] Lipids, for most of the population would have been supplied from animal fats. Compared with Cyprus, there would have been a greater intake of protein from fowl and fish from the Nile. The consumption of grapes and wine set at 3.5 kg/person/yr for NK Egypt is assumed to be by the élite. For the non-élite, dates, figs, and beer probably contributed these calories. Similarly, hive honey set at 2.5 kg/individual would have been another élite consumable. For the non-élite, additional sweet fruit or wild honey would have been consumed. The contribution of the calories by food type for a cohort of 100,000/kg/yr in LBA Cyprus and NK Egypt is compared in Table 2.10.

[185] Farming in Crete before World War 2, used traditional methods with limited capital investment in modern farming equipment or practices. Most farmers owned a wooden plough, a sickle, and a hoe. In addition, the average farmer for this post war period had a donkey, an ox or a work cow (Allbaugh 1953: 249). Only 24% of farmers had steel ploughs; 42% had wooden ploughs (Allbaugh 1953: 249, Table 44). As in antiquity, the majority of farms were small. In 1929, 45% of farms had an average size between the range 0.2–2.5 ha and 24% between the range 2.5–5 ha. By 1948, farms with an average size between 0.2–2.5 ha had only increased in number to 47% of all farms while farms in the range 2.5–5 ha had fallen to 16% of all farms (Allbaugh 1953: 251, Figure 12).

[186] Garnsey 1999: 13–17. This is supported by Allbaugh's study, which showed that in 1947–1948, 83% of Cretan farmers grew cereals, 85% cultivated wine grapes, 15% table grapes, 29% raisins, and 97% olives (Allbaugh 1953: 266, Table 47).

[187] Linear B records from Pylos (PY Ab series) show that figs were included in the rations given to palace workers (Palmer 1989).

[188] There are few finds of the type of Aegean stirrup jar that held olive oil (Hankey 1995: 117).

Food type	LBA Cyprus consumption kg/person/yr	Energy intake kcals/day	Energy intake Million kcals/yr/ 100,000 cohort	% calorie intake
Barley	112	614	17,329	20.5
Barley for beer	62	564	15,916	18.8
Emmer	90	823	23,216	27.4
Honey	2.5	21	594	0.7
Grapes/wine	8	16	464	0.5
Pulses	42.5	148	4,188	5
Vegetables	35	24	668	0.8
Greens	20	10	294	0.4
Olives	10	28	796	0.9
Figs	30	15	434	0.5
Fruit	52	85	2,413	2.8
Meat	19	130	3,673	4.3
Fish	8	30	839	1
Milk	12	28	779	0.9
Cheese	5	36	1,013	1.2
Fats	4	99	2,790	3.3
Olive oil	15	329	9,278	11
Total	**527**	**3,000**	**84,684**	**100**

Table 2.8: The percentage mix of food types for the diet of a cohort of 100,000/yr in LBA Cyprus.

Food type	NK Egyptian consumption kg/person/yr	Energy intake kcals/day adapted for Egypt	Energy intake Million kcals/yr/ 100,000 cohort	% calorie intake
Barley	118	1,070	30,207	35.7
Barley for beer	112	596	16,825	19.9
Emmer wheat	56	512	14,454	17.1
Honey	2.5	21	593	0.7
Grapes/wine	3.5	7	198	0.2
Pulses	85	223	6,286	7.4
Vegetables	115	79	2,230	2.6
Figs/palm dates	10	59	1,665	2
Mutton/goat	12	82	2,315	2.7
Fish	17	63	1,779	2.1
Duck/goose	8	55	1,553	1.8
Diary milk	9	21	593	0.7
Cheese	2	14	395	0.5
Animal fats	8	198	5,591	6.6
Total	**558**	**3,000**	**84,684**	**100**

Table 2.9: The percentage mix of food types for the diet of a cohort of 100,000/yr in NK Egypt.

Crop	Cyprus		Egypt	
	%	Million kcals/yr/ 100,000 cohort	%	Million kcals/yr/ 100,000 cohort
Barley	39.3	33,246	55.6	47,032
Emmer wheat	27.4	23,215	17.1	14,454
Honey	0.7	594	0.7	593
Wine/grapes	0.5	464	0.2	198
Pulses	4.9	4,188	7.4	6,286
Fruit/vegetables	4.5	3,809	4.6	3,895
Protein	5.3	4,512	6.7	5,647
Dairy	2.1	1,792	1.2	988
Olives/olive oil	11.9	10,074	0	0
Animal fats	3.4	2,790	6.5	5,591
Total	**100**	**84,684**	**100**	**84,684**

Table 2.10: The percentage mix of food types required to feed a 100,000 cohort/yr in LBA Cyprus and NK Egypt.

The balanced diet

The collation of the results above show that the LBA diet, though simple compared to modern diets could provide the necessary 84,684 million kcals/100,000 cohort/yr for both LBA Cyprus and NK Egypt. Equally important, the diets of both regions provided the necessary balance of carbohydrates, pulses, fruit and vegetables, fats and oils, protein, and dairy products to maintain the population (Tables 2.11–2.12).

LBA Cyprus	Consumption kg/person/yr	Energy intake Million kcals/yr/100,000 cohort	% calories intake by food type
Carbohydrates	275	57,519	67.9
Pulses/veg./fruit	190	8,793	10.5
Protein/dairy	44	6,304	7.4
Oils/fats	19	12,068	14.2
Total cereals	**528**	**84,684**	**100**

Table 2.11: The calories provided by the four basic food types of the LBA Cypriot diet.

Variety in the diet would have been achieved trough the consumption of a wide range of fruit and vegetables grown on the farms or through barter in local markets. In Egypt, different cuts of meat would have entered the diet to some sections of the population through the reversion of offerings from the temples.[189]

NK Egypt	Consumption kg/person/yr	Energy intake Million kcals/yr/100,000 cohort	% calories intake by food type
Carbohydrates	292	62,277	73.5
Pulses/veg./fruit	210	10,181	12
Protein/dairy	48	6,635	7.9
Oils/fats	8	5,591	6.6
Total cereals	**558**	**84,684**	**100**

Table 2.12: The calories provided by the four basic food types of the NK Egyptian diet.

Table 2.13 highlights the different types of fats and oil that provided the calories from lipids in Cyprus and Egypt. There was a high calorific contribution from olives/olive oil in the Cypriot diet and in NK Egypt, lipids were supplied by animal fats.

Food category	Cyprus		Egypt	
	%	Million kcals/100,000 cohort/yr	%	Million kcals/100,000 cohort/yr
Animal fats	3.3	2,790	6.6	5,591
Olives/olive oil	11.9	10,074	0	0

Table 2.13: A comparison of the calories provided by lipids in the diets of LBA Cyprus and NK Egypt.

2.5 Evidence for the diet

The evidence for the range of crops cultivated and the livestock raised in LBA Cyprus and NK Egypt is

[189] Kemp 2006: 265.

considered next. They provided the carbohydrates, pulses, fruit and vegetables, fats and oils, protein, and dairy products identified in Section 2.4.

Carbohydrates

Carbohydrate intake in antiquity was predominantly in the form of cereals, which were processed into bread and beer.[190] The alcohol in beer inhibits the growth of bacteria found in natural water supplies, which can be detrimental to health.[191] The prominence of beer in the Egyptian diet also reflects its value as a food as well an acceptable drink.[192] The diet for the élite in both regions was supplemented by limited quantities of wine and honey.

Types of cereals grown in Egypt and Cyprus

Archaeobotanical evidence from the domestic debris that accumulated in ancient settlement sites and in Egypt, funerary offerings found in tombs, show that two species, wheat (genus *Triticum*) and barley (genus *Hordeum*), were grown.[193] Seeds have been recovered that show at least two varieties of glume wheats were grown, emmer (*Triticum dicoccum*) and possibly but less certain, Einkorn (*Triticum monococcum*).[194] These wheat varieties have tough glumes (husks/hull/chaff) that tightly enclose the wheat kernel.[195] Barley was represented by two-row *(Hordeum distichum*), and six-row *(Hordeum vulgare*). Both varieties of barley are termed 'hulled' barley as they have a hull of two bracts as well as a tough fibrous outer coat, which strongly adheres to the barley kernel.[196] One advantage of hulled cereals is that the awns and cohesive glumes act as a deterrent to birds.[197]

Although there is a wide corpus of administration texts that deal with cereal rations, tax, temple offering lists, and harvest yields, the identification of the cereal is not always certain. Gardiner identified several words that he considered to be different botanical species or varieties.[198] There is some uncertainty for the translation of *bdt* as emmer wheat and *it* as barley as these words are used interchangeably in the production lists of breads, cakes, and beer.[199] Gardiner suggested that in administrative texts, scribes used black ink to denote barley and red ink for wheat.[200] However, this colour coding is not consistent because the scribes also used red ink for combinations of barley and wheat, which Gardiner calls 'corn'.[201] Four specific kinds of grain appear in the MK Heqanakht letters: *iti-nitt* (full barley), *bti* (emmer), *swt* (a kind of emmer), and *w3t* (an unidentified type of barley).[202]

Ratio of wheat to barley cultivated

A wide range of evidence suggests that the yields of wheat varieties were greater than barley and therefore they required less land and less manpower to produce a given number of calories. It would be expected therefore that more wheat would have been cultivated. However, other factors dictated a dual crop strategy in which there was widespread cultivation of both barley and wheat.

While we know the species of cereals grown, the proportions of barley to wheat grown in the LBA however is less certain. Evidence from settlement sites does not necessarily indicate the ratios for human consumption. Traces of barley and wheat could have come from burnt animal dung, fodder, temper in pottery, mud-brick, or stable litter.[203] Sites where grains have been discovered such as Deir el-Medina and Amarna in Egypt and the harbour sites along the south-west coast of Cyprus may be atypical compared with those in the Delta and the Cypriot rural hinterland.[204] For Egypt in particular, most of the evidence from the rural settlements along the Nile valley has been destroyed due to the lateral movement of the Nile across the centuries.[205]

However, there are other factors that allow reasonable assumptions to be made. Ethnographic evidence from traditional farming practices demonstrates that in areas of low rainfall or periods of prolonged drought, common across much of the Near East, barley is still grown extensively.[206] Barley also has a shorter growing season than wheat, a higher tolerance of high temperatures and

---

[190] For sources of evidence and descriptions of the Egyptian brewing process, see Geller 1992 and Samuel 2000. The proportion of calories consumed from beer is an estimate based on the rations of loaves and beer listed in the Hammamat inscriptions, these varied by rank and profession (Mueller 1975: 253).

[191] Beer production is discussed later in Section 2.7.

[192] Curtis 2001: 140 and Kemp 2006: 172.

[193] Feldman, 1986: 124–127. By selecting hybrids that stood erect and ripened at the same time, the plants were able to withstand weed competition and the time spent harvesting was minimised. Choosing seed corn from hybrids with the largest number of fertile florets, increased the yield. Choosing the seed corn from plants that had less awn (bristle-like spikelets) and husks minimised the time needed to thresh the cereal.

[194] Murray 2000a: 512. It might be that einkorn was present as a weed in the fields of other cereals and was never a crop in its own right in ancient Egypt (Murray 2003a: 513).

[195] Hillman 1984: 128–129.

[196] Modern varieties of cereals are not hulled and are termed 'free-threshing' or 'naked' grains.

[197] Reynolds 1981: 111. As discovered in the experimental archaeology at the Butser Ancient Farm.

[198] Gardiner 1941: 24, Footnote 3 and Gardiner 1947b: 221*. He speculated that one term was for spelt but this species has not been attested in the NK archaeobotanical record (Dixon 1969: 138 and Murray 2000a: 513).

[199] Kemp 1994: 145.

[200] Gardiner 1941: 26–27 and comments by Dixon 1969: 138. Janssen 2004 uses Gardiner's hypothesis in his analysis of the papyri relating to grain transport in the Ramesside Period (see his analysis of Papyrus Amiens, rt. I, Janssen 2004: 13, Footnote 9 and Papyrus Amiens, rt. II, Janssen 2004: 16, Footnote 4).

[201] Gardiner 1941: 26–27. When the scribes wanted to refer specifically to barley they wrote *it-m-it* meaning 'barley as barley', i.e. barley which really is barley (Gardiner 1941: 24, Footnote 3).

[202] Allen 2002: 142, Footnote 4.

[203] Murray 1993: 165, 167 and Murray 2000a: 513. Recent archaeobotanical research shows that the proportions within excavated seed assemblages can be as much as to 19.5% in error caused by earthworms ingesting seeds. The effect is greatest on small seeds that are less than 2 mm in diameter.

[204] The inhabitants of these sites would primarily be non-agrarian workers fed on rations sometimes in the form of loaves that were made from grain stored in state granaries. Consequently, the mix of foodstuffs may have differed from that of rural agrarian workers.

[205] Hillier *et al* 2007.

[206] Zohary and Hopf 1994: 55–64.

soil salinity.[207] Soil in hydraulic cultures, such as Egypt, whose agriculture is reliant on irrigation, is prone to build up of salt levels in the soil if the basins are not flushed out by the next inundation.[208] The accumulation of salt is detrimental to the growth of wheat. Barley had other advantages for the Egyptians; it required fewer man-days/ha to grow, and was used for beer production. It is likely therefore that a significant proportion of the cereal crop in Egypt was barley. However, barley does not have as high a yield as wheat and as wheat in NK Egypt was the cereal of choice for bread, a significant quantity of emmer would also have been cultivated.[209]

The soil in rain fed Cyprus did not have this accumulation of salt and more wheat could be grown than in Egypt, particularly on the south-western windward slopes of the central massif where the rainfall is higher. Emmer wheat grows best in areas with an annual rainfall of 600–760 mm of rainfall or in those areas that can be adequately irrigated.[210] Therefore, tolerance of salt was not an important factor and the higher yield of wheat was probably the determining factor in choice of crop. Nevertheless, growing both wheat and barley spread the risk against one crop failure and it is known from the archaeobotanical record that some barley was grown in LBA Cyprus.[211] The cultivation of both cereals had other advantages. It spread workload peaks because barley was sown in November and harvested in February avoiding a clash with emmer wheat, which was sown in January and harvested in April.

The proportion of cereals in the Eastern Mediterranean LBA diet was probably lower than in Egypt as the calorie intake was supplemented significantly by olive oil, whereas in LBA Egypt lipids in the diet were restricted to meat consumption (See Table 2.13).[212] For this study, the calorie contribution of both cereals to the diet in Cyprus and Egypt is assessed as 69.4% and 75.3% when uplifted for seed corn and wastage (see ahead to Section 2.6). Cereal grains were further processed into bread and beer and the manpower implications of this are discussed in Section 2.7.

Honey in Egypt and Cyprus

Honey played a significant part in the diet of many ancient cultures as a highly prized consumable and although it is not known when bees were first kept in hives, it is certain that hive honey and wild honey was available to LBA Near Eastern cultures. There is substantial pictorial and written evidence for the production and consumption of honey in NK Egypt but not for Cyprus until much later.[213] However, LBA evidence from other Eastern Mediterranean regions suggests that during this period Cyprus too would have kept bees for the production of honey.

Honey in Egypt

There are many ancient Egyptian written references to honey; the earliest is in the Sixth Dynasty tomb of Sebni (*c.*2200 B.C.).[214] Honey was a valuable commodity and formed part of the offerings that the king presented to the gods.[215] The king also supplied his officials with honey; in his tomb at Thebes (TT 81), Ineni boasts of how the king gave him many foodstuffs, including honey.[216] Mortuary offerings made to the deceased nobles also included it and two jars in the tomb of Tutankhamun are thought to have contained honey.[217] Its value is demonstrated by its use as an ambassadorial gift and it was received as tribute and collected as tax.[218] The depiction of honey in élite tomb scenes and in temple scenes and lists shows that in ancient Egypt, honey was valuable commodity. Large quantities were produced for the consumption of the élite as part payment for service and through redistribution from the temples. Honey was used for sweetening and added to bread, cakes, and perhaps to wine.[219] It is unlikely however that those further down the social scale had access to hive honey. It is more likely that some wild honey was available to those prepared to find and collect it. However, the quantity consumed by majority of the population would be low.[220]

From the LBA, scenes of honey production and its collection can be seen in situ in the NK Theban tombs of Rekhmire, TT 100 (Figure 2.3), and TT 73 the tomb of Amenhotep.[221] Also from the NK, a scene of honey

[207] Renfrew 1984, Samuel 1993: 278–279, and Murray 2000a: 510–513. Barley, with its greater ability to withstand drought and grow in saline soils, is cultivated today in dry farming agriculture of Iraq, Syria and Iran.

[208] Willcocks 1889: 64 and Foaden and Fletcher 1908: 24.

[209] Samuel 2000: 558.

[210] Zaccagnini 1975: 217.

[211] Seeds of hulled and naked barley, and emmer wheat have been found in Cyprus in LBA contexts (Stewart 1974: 123). Ancient texts from Nuzi indicate that the ratio of barley, emmer, and bread wheat (*Triticum vulgare*) and/or club wheat (*Triticum compactum*) grown were in the ratio, 6:2.3: 1 (Zaccagnini 1975: 216).

[212] For the consumption of olive oil see the section on vegetable oils below.

[213] The use of beeswax is also widely attested in ancient Egypt (Serpico and White 2000: 409–412).

[214] Breasted 1906a: Text 366 and Sethe 1933: 135–40. For other textual references to for honey, see the index in Breasted 1906e: 132.

[215] The Papyrus Harris lists the very large quantities of honey that Ramesses III offered to the temples during his reign (Breasted 1906d: Texts 87–206).

[216] Breasted 1906b: Text 117. Hieroglyphic text and translation in Dziobek 1992: 51 and 54.

[217] The jars were labelled 'honey of good quality' but on testing the contents, the presence of honey could not be confirmed. A large amphora in the king's tomb held material that had once been viscous and contained crystals of sugar. However, the material might have been fruit juice (Lucas and Harris 1962: 26–27).

[218] In the OK, Sebni took honey as a gift on an expedition to Nubia (Breasted 1906a: Text 366). Tuthmosis III received honey as tribute on his campaign in the Levant (Breasted 1906b: Text 462). In Papyrus Harris, Ramesses III recorded that for the temple of Re at Heliopolis, he appointed royal honey collectors accompanied by archers and tax collectors (Breasted 1906d: Texts 266 and 283).

[219] Breasted 1906d: Text 300, Darby 1977: 431 and 435, and Murray 2000b: 591. Honey in jars offered for payment of tax appears in a scene in the tomb of Rekhmire (Davies 1943b: Plate XXXIII).

[220] The greater effort required to produce honey meant that it is unlikely to have been as common a sweetener as dates, sycamore fig, and possibly, carob (Szpakowska 2008: 96).

[221] Tomb of Rekhmire, Davies 1943a: 44–45 and 1943b: Plates XLVIII–XLIX and the scene from TT 73 in Säve-Söderbergh 1957: Plate IX B. For other ancient Egyptian evidence for the use of honey, see Lucas and Harris 1962: 25–26 and 87.

offered to the king appears in TT 101, the tomb of Tjener.[222] The scenes show that the hives were cylindrical and stacked horizontally, one above the other. The blue-grey colour of the hives depicted in the tomb of Rekhmire is thought to represent that they were made of unbaked mud.[223]

Figure 2.3: Taking honeycombs from hives.
Sketch of Davies 1943b: Plate XLIX. The tomb of Rekhmire (TT 100).

The warm Egyptian climate is ideal for bee keeping and because for honey production bees need water as well as nectar from flowers, apiaries were sited along the Nile valley and in the Delta, a region which is particularly suitable for bee keeping.[224] Placed on land that was not under cultivation, the hives were moved when necessary to protect them from the Nile inundation.[225] In the early twentieth century, harvesting the honey took place in April/May and the main harvest in November, however in Upper Egypt there was only one collection, which took place in September.[226] Today, as in ancient Egypt, smoke was blown into the hive to calm the bees so that the combs could be removed safely.[227] The ethnographic study of traditional beekeeping suggests how the honey in the NK may have been extracted. The combs were placed in a 'sack' made of cow or water buffalo hide with a large and small opening. The combs were placed in the skin through the large opening with the smaller hole tied off. The large opening was then tied and the sealed sack was stamped on to release the honey. The clear honey was poured from the small opening into jars. The remaining contents with wax and other debris, was mixed with water, ten parts of honey to one and a half parts of water. This mixture was tipped into a large pottery vessel (*zir*) with a small hole in the base. A sieve of twigs and halfa grass over the hole trapped the dirt and dust and the honey was collected in a container below.[228]

Honey in Cyprus

Cyprus had direct contact with LBA Near Eastern cultures where beekeeping for honey was practised and although there is no physical or written evidence of beekeeping on the island in the LBA it would be surprising if they did not do so.[229] Certainly, throughout the later centuries there is evidence for large-scale beekeeping in Cyprus.[230] The traditional hive now found in Cyprus is a horizontal (slightly flared) cylinder of clay. As in Egypt, the flight entrance is at the front and the honey collected from the rear.[231]

Attestation for beekeeping and honey in the ancient Near East comes from several items of written evidence that highlight the value of honey. Among the laws regulating prices in the Hittite Law Code (*c.*1500 B.C.), one clause refers to honey, 'One tub (*zi-pid-da-ni* [value unknown]) of honey costs one shekel of silver'. A tub of butter and a sheep had the same price, indicating the high value of the honey. Two other clauses describe the punishment for stealing a bee swarm and bee-houses (hives).[232] Evidence of honey production in the Levant comes from the annals of Tuthmosis III (1479–1425 B.C.) who received 470 (*mn-*) jars of honey as part of the tribute on his fifth campaign in Zahi.[233]

Viticulture

The cultivation of grapes also contributed carbohydrate in the diets of LBA Cyprus and NK Egypt. Apart from their use in making wine, fresh grapes or dried grapes can be consumed as food. The wild grape is found around the Mediterranean basin with the exception of Egypt and Libya.[234] The domesticated grape vine (*Vitis vinifera*) is a perennial climber and different varieties produce purple, red, green, and white grapes, which can be sweet or sour. Egyptian tomb scenes of viticulture also show the vines supported over a trellis or poles or over trees and arbours (Figure 2.14).[235] Grapes grow well in areas that have between 400 and 800 mm of rainfall. The ideal average yearly temperature for viticulture is 15° C with a maximum in summer of 22°C and in winter, a minimum of 3°C. The regions best suited to growing grapes are in

[222] Davies and Gardiner 1936: Plate XXXIV. For other tomb scenes associated with beekeeping, see TT 92, TT 93, TT 131, TT 155, TT 277, TT 305, and A5 (PM 1^2/1: 467 (d)).
[223] Crane and Graham 1985: 4–5.
[224] The bee was the symbol for Lower Egypt and from the beginning of the OK, the king of Egypt included the title *nswt-bity* meaning 'He of the Bee' in his throne name. This stated his rule over Lower Egypt as well as Upper Egypt (Allen 2000: 65).
[225] Ransom 1937: 27. A Ptolemaic petition (*c.*250 B.C.) asking for help with transporting the hives.
[226] Mellor 1928: 26.
[227] The scenes in TT 100 and TT 73 show this method of harvesting the honeycomb.
[228] Mellor 1928: 26, Crane and Graham 1985: 4–5, and Serpico and White 2000: 410–411. In Egypt in 1950, three grades of honey were produced: virgin grade, second grade from pressing the honeycombs and third grade by crushing the residue (Darby 1977: 433).
[229] The earliest known reference to bees in Cyprus is by Herodotus (*c.*400 B.C.) who reported that a swarm had occupied a human skull hanging in front of the temple of Aphrodite (Herodotus, *Histories* 5. 114).
[230] Pliny, *Naturalis historia* 11.14.33 records abundant honey in Cyprus. In 1894, there were about 520,000 traditional hives.
[231] Crane 1999: 184–186.
[232] Pritchard 1955: 193, clauses 91–92 and 196, clause 181 and Crane 1985: 9–10.
[233] Breasted 1906b: Text 462.
[234] See Zohary and Hopf 1994: 146, Map 16 for the distribution of the wild grape vine, *Vitis vinifer L. subsp. sylvestris* around the Mediterranean.
[235] Murray 2000b: 583–584.

the temperate zones and this includes Cyprus but not Egypt.

Ancient Egypt

Evidence for LBA viticulture comes from NK tomb scenes, and written, archaeobotanical and archaeological evidence.[236] It seems that the domesticated grape was introduced into Egypt from the Levant as early as the Predynastic Period.[237] Grape seeds have been found in Predynastic settlements and in First Dynasty graves.[238] Several NK sites have grape remains including Deir el-Medina, Amarna, and Memphis.[239] Imported wine amphorae from Palestine have been discovered, the earliest being at Abydos (3150 B.C.).[240] Wine is thought to have been mainly red in ancient Egypt and no texts have been found that refer to white wines in the Pharaonic Period (3150–332 B.C.). However, the testing of labelled wine amphorae in Tutankhamun's tomb shows that some contained white wine and demonstrates that white wine was produced in Egypt towards the end of the Eighteenth Dynasty.[241]

In Egypt, vines needed manual irrigation with the use of the shaduf.[242] They are often represented as growing on raised land and enclosed by a wall.[243] The ancient Egyptian term for vineyard *k3nw/k3mw* means orchard or garden and tomb scenes show them in the same context. Wine was produced in the Nile Valley itself, mostly on the west bank, which would have maximised the hours of sunlight. The production of wine seems to have been more widespread in the NK when considerable investment was made in temple viticulture. The Ramesseum alone owned 18 vineyards in Lower Egypt and the Delta. Ramesside labels on wine amphorae show that at least 36 estates produced wine, mostly located in the north-eastern Delta.[244] Apart from the temples, the king and his family owned vineyards and wine making facilities and its consumption is unlikely to have spread to the majority of the population. There is however, textual evidence that wine was provided for non-royal officials and lower levels of society on special festival occasions. Even so, it is unlikely that wine played a significant part in the diet of general populace of NK Egypt.[245] AGCALC assumes that a mix of wine and grapes formed 0.2% of the diets of the Egyptian élite.

LBA Cyprus

The consumption of wine signified power and status in the LBA and it was drunk in élite festivities across the Near East and the Mediterranean.[246] Winemaking in the Eastern Mediterranean is attested by the remains of pressed grape skins with grape pips and stalks in pithoi, which were discovered at Myrtos as early as the closing century of the Early Helladic Period (2800–2500 B.C.).[247] At the Cypriot LBA settlement of Aredhiou *Vouppes*, located at the edge of the northern foothills of the Troodos mountains, fragments of kraters for mixing wine and other ware associated with drinking wine have been found.[248] Steel writes that for the LBA, 'there is unequivocal evidence for the introduction of orchard husbandry to Cyprus, specifically the cultivation of olives and grapes.'[249] However, this has not been confirmed by evidence of wine residue in the fabric of pots. Nevertheless, the evidence of wine production in the Aegean and Levant in the same period makes it almost certain that LBA Cyprus also produced wine.[250]

Vines are deep-rooted and perennial; they can grow in marginal soils and exploit seasonal labour not needed for cereals.[251] The Mediterranean climate of Cyprus was ideal for grape cultivation and normal rainfall patterns ensured that the vines would have received sufficient water without the need for the extensive manual irrigation. Ethnographic evidence from Cypriot traditional farming shows that the majority of the farmers grew vines and it is very probable that they did so in the LBA.[252] The model assumes that a mix of wine and grapes formed 0.5% of the diets of the Cypriot élite. It is assumed that these calories would be supplied by beer for the non-élite.

Horticulture

The LBA diet included a variety of vegetables, which provided essential vitamins and mineral salts. Grown according to their season, they could be intercropped with other plants.

NK Egypt

The arid climate of Egypt has ensured that fruits and vegetables eaten in NK Egypt have survived through

[236] Archaeobotanical evidence for the grape vine in Egypt includes charred and desiccated fruit, seeds, stem, leaves and wood and wine jars, seals, labels and presses. For a full description and bibliography of archaeological evidence and the scientific analysis of wine residues, see Murray 2000b.

[237] Murray 2000b: 581.

[238] Trade in wine was for the élite who considered it was important for the afterlife; amphorae of wine were placed in élite and royal tombs (Curtis 2001: 144). For other evidence of Predynastic wine consumption, see Sievertsen 2007: 13.

[239] Renfrew 1985: 177–178, Murray 1993: 166, and Schiaparelli 2008: 49.

[240] More than 200 Syro-Palestinian jars were found intact and in situ in an early dynastic royal tomb at Abydos (McGovern 1997: 90, Footnote 81). NAA and organic analyses show that wine, with tree resin, grapes and figs as additives, were imported from the southern Hill Country of Palestine, and the Jordan Valley (McGovern *et al*: 1997).

[241] Guasch-Jané *et al* 2006. Some amphorae were labelled with the name of the Egyptian estate on which they were produced.

[242] Murray 2000b: 583–584.

[243] While vines grown in containers require less irrigation, the roots soon become cramped to the detriment of the plant (Murray 2000b: 583).

[244] Wine labels found at the Ramesseum show that estates on the west bank at Thebes produced wine. At Amarna, 165 wine labels indicate that the wine was produced in quantity from the 'Western River' estates owned by the royal family (Kitchen 1992: 116–120, Figure 1 and Tables 1–2, Lesko 1995: 226–227, and McGovern 2003: 141–147 and 143).

[245] Murray 2000b: 578.

[246] Curtis 2001: 144 and Jennings *et al* 2005.

[247] Mylonas 1959: 39 and Renfrew 1995.

[248] Steel 1998: 289–292.

[249] Steel 2004: 169–170.

[250] The evidence of imported Mycenaean feasting paraphernalia excavated in the settlement at Kalavasos indicates the importance of wine consumption by the élite (Steel 2004: 170).

[251] Halstead 1992: 106. Vine roots grow deeply (4–15 m) and in land where there is a high water table, aeration is reduced to the detriment of the vine (Murray 2000b: 583).

[252] Allen 1989: 433.

desiccation. Evidence from tomb scenes, textual references, archaeobotanical, and archaeological investigations show that a wide range of pulses, vegetables, and fruits formed a significant part of the Egyptian diet in the NK.[253] Vegetables including the onion, garlic, watermelon, melon, and chufa nuts are all attested and the most common type of pulse found is the lentil (*Les culinaris*).[254] The fruits: sycamore figs, common figs, grapes, dates, dom palm nuts, and pomegranates have also been found in NK contexts.[255] Unlike cereals, farming of fruits and vegetables requires a constant supply of water and careful tending. They would have been planted close to the river or canals where the water could be lifted by shaduf or collected manually in vessels.[256]

Cyprus

Allbaugh's 1953 ethnographic study of Crete reports that the diet included large quantities of vegetables and fruit.[257] Pulses such as white beans, fava, and broad beans, were a major food type, consumed mostly in the winter.[258] In autumn, the diet was dominated by green vegetables, which included radikia, mustard greens, spinach, and cabbages. Grapes were the most common fruit and other fruits consumed were melons, apples, and pomegranates. Not all these fruits and vegetables were available in the LBA but it is likely that the diet would still have included significant quantities of lentils, green leaf vegetables, grapes, melons and pomegranates, which are known to have been consumed around the Mediterranean basin at that time.[259] It has been assumed that pulses, fruit, and vegetables in the Cypriot diet provided 10.5% of the daily calorie requirement in line with the Allbaugh's 1953 study of 11.4%. For Egypt, a slightly higher percentage of 12% has been allocated in AGCALC because, as discussed next, fewer calories were supplied from vegetable oils.

Vegetable oils

Olive oil

Oils and fats (lipids) are a key ingredient of a well balanced diet because they carry vitamins and play a part in cell renewal. The high calorific value of the olive and its oil provides a relatively low labour-rate crop to supplement cereals and pulses.[260] Wild olives grow well in the right conditions and archaeobotanical evidence shows that olives were indigenous around most of the Mediterranean.[261] The ideal conditions for olive trees are on the slopes of hills between 300 m and 1200 m. They flourish in those areas where the average annual temperature is within the range 16–22ºC and winter temperatures do not to fall below minus 10°C.[262] Olive trees can grow on poor soil and are drought resistant, surviving on as little as 150 mm of rain. This makes them suitable for marginal grazing land above the plains and lower slopes dedicated to cereals and pulses.[263]

Olive cultivation in LBA Cyprus

There is archaeological, archaeobotanical, and ethnographic evidence for olive and olive oil consumption in LBA Cyprus where wild and domesticated varieties of the olive have been found in the archaeological record. The earliest stratified evidence (Cypriot IIC Period *c.*1300 B.C.) of olive oil production in Cyprus is at Maroni.[264]

Intense cultivation of the olive took place towards the end of the LBA.[265] The archaeological record reveals that large volumes of olive oil were processed in LBA Cyprus. A large complex, still under excavation at Kalavasos-Ayios Dhimitrios in the Vasilikos Valley has evidence of extensive olive oil processing. The large pillared hall called Building X held *c.*50 pithoi ranging in height from 1.6 m–2 m and holding *c.*580 and 1200 litres respectively. In total the pithoi are estimated to have a capacity of 50,000 litres.[266] Twenty samples taken from the lower bodies of the pithoi in Building X have been GC/MS tested and the majority shown to have held olive oil.[267] The building is thought to have had a footprint of 1000 m^2 and the entire oil producing complex exceeded 5000 m^2.[268] The adjacent building, Building XI, housed crushing equipment, a stone weight, and a ceramic basin with a hole in it. The pebble floor was ridged, probably to enable olive oil to flow into a large stone rectangular block. This weighed 3.5 tons and was hollowed out to

[253] Murray 2000c: 610, Table 24.1 lists the fruits and vegetables and the NK sites in which they have been found.

[254] Murray 2000c: 609–614, particularly Tables 24.2, 24.3, and 24.4.

[255] In spite of its frequent depiction in tomb scenes and textual references, fewer date stones have been found in the archaeological record than expected (Murray 2000c: 619).

[256] Brewer 2007: 137 and Murray 2000c: 614.

[257] Allbaugh 1953: 108–109.

[258] Pulses require significant cooking time and when eaten in winter, the hearth served to heat the home as well (Allbaugh 1953: 108).

[259] On the Ulu Burun shipwreck were grape pips (from either raisins or wine), pomegranate seeds and fruit fragments, whole pomegranates, olive stones, and charred barley and wheat (Pulak 1998: 210 and Pulak 2001: 37). Sarpaki 1992: 61–76 examines the paleobotanical evidence for common food types in the LBA Mediterranean and suggests that the consumption of lentils expanded significantly in this period. They required less manpower to grow and harvest and also improved the soil.

[260] The nutritional value of 0.1 kg of olives is equivalent to 1.5 litres of full cream milk (Mattingly 1996: 222–223).

[261] Zohary and Hopf 1994: Map 15.

[262] In Spain, cultivation has been registered at 1500 m, 1200–1300 m in the Atlas Mountains of Morocco, 850 m in the Mount of Olives Jerusalem, 800 m in Southern Anatolia, and 650 m in Syria and Cilicia (Mattingly 1996: 214–215).

[263] Aschenbrenner 1972: 53–54 and Mattingly 1996: 215.

[264] Knossos Linear B tablets and Greek texts show that wild and domesticated olives were collected (Melena 1983: 97–99,100–103). The lack of evidence from the EBA–MBA may be because the context of the excavations was funerary and not domestic (Hadjisavvas 1996: 64 ff).

[265] For a review of the Aegean textual, archaeobotanical and archaeological evidence see Melena 1983, Runnels and Hansen 1986, and Riley 2002. For the dendro-archaeological evidence of olive trees and olive stones across the Southern Levant, see Lipschitz 1996, Table 1.

[266] South 1997: 30–31, Figures 9–11. For a site report of Building X, see South 1992.

[267] Multiple methyl esters associated with olive oil have been identified in 15 of 19 samples of pithoi from the pithos hall, suggesting that olive oil may have been the main commodity stored there (Keswani 1993: 76).

[268] South 1995: Figures 2–3.

hold 2,000 litres of oil.[269] The total complex demonstrates that olive oil production in the LBA Cyprus had reached an industrial scale.[270]

Approximately 2,500 olive stones were found on the Ulu Burun shipwreck (*c.*1300 B.C.) in a Canaanite jar.[271] They had a mean size of 15.3 by 8 mm and are larger than typical olive stones from most Near Eastern Mediterranean Bronze Age sites. It is possible that they were a luxury export.[272] This would suggest that the quality of olives and its oil varied around the Mediterranean as it does today, providing a niche market to satisfy élite demand.[273]

Allbaugh's ethnographic study of the Cretan diet in 1940–1950 A.D. shows that 26.1% of the calories required in the diet were met by the consumption of olive oil and a further 0.3% by fresh olives (Table 2.7).[274] This study has modified Allbaugh's results (Table 2.8) down to 11.0% and fresh olives to 0.9% reflecting the probability that in antiquity less olive oil was consumed as a result of a lower scale of production.[275] The consumption of fresh olives may have been greater in the LBA as they were nutritious in their own right but avoided the additional workload processing them to make oil. This has been reflected in AGCALC.

Based on ethnographic evidence of multi-crop terrace production in the Greek Islands, this study has assumed an average of 100 olive trees per ha.[276] In cultivating olive trees, farmers needed to take into account that it takes 15 years before a newly planted olive tree reaches maturity and the fruiting pattern of olive trees is bimodal. This affects olive oil production as illustrated in Table 2.14.[277] It would have been necessary either to store enough oil for the low yield years or to import olives and oil.

Year	Thousands of metric tons of olive oil
1946	80
1947	145
1948	46.7
1949	224.6
1950	38
1951	140
1952	70

Table 2.14: Olive oil production in Greece.
Aschenbrenner 1972: 53 citing Sweet-Escott: 1954.

Olives in NK Egypt

The climatic and topographic conditions in Egypt are not favourable for the widespread cultivation of olive trees unless they are constantly irrigated, as they are today.[278] Charred archaeobotanical evidence from Kom Rabʿa at Memphis indicates that the olive had arrived in Egypt and entered the archaeological record by the Thirteenth Dynasty in the MK, although finds of stones become increasingly common from the NK onwards.[279] However, the lack of significant quantities of olive stones suggests that even during the NK, olives and olive oil were an import. As such, they would have been a luxury in the élite diet.[280] The Egyptian word *b3ḳ* has been translated as olive oil though some scholars consider it is the word for moringa oil.[281]

Other oil producing vegetables were available in Pharaonic Egypt. Serpico and White list castor, balanos, safflower, linseed, moringa, almond, and tiger nut oil (chufa).[282] Of these, castor, safflower, and linseed oils are unlikely to have played any significant part the diet.[283] Moringa, almond, and tiger nut oils are edible but almond oil would have been scarce as almond trees grow best in Mediterranean maquis vegetation and are not easily grown in the Egyptian climate.[284] It would therefore be expensive and exclusive to the élite.[285] Sesame seed can be pressed to produce oil but it is possible that it only reached Syria-Palestine at the earliest in the Iron Age and Egypt in the Ptolemaic Period and therefore sesame oil has been excluded from this study.[286]

[269] South 1997: 31.

[270] Large pithoi in LC III contexts have been found in urban sites of Kition, Enkomi, Hala Sultan Tekke, Myrtou-*Pigadhes*, Kourion, and Kouklin (Pilides 1996). See also Keswani 1993: 76.

[271] Haldane 1993: 352–356, Pulak 1998: 201 and 210, and Pulak 2001: 37.

[272] Haldane 1993: 353–355, and Table 1 and Figure 3 in particular.

[273] There is evidence of large-scale olive oil production in LBA Ugarit where a large deposit of amphorae was found in a storage depot at Ras Shamra's port of Minet el-Beida. An olive oil press excavated in 1959 at Ras Shamra (tentatively dated to the end of the third millennium B.C.) was of sufficient size to be considered as an industrial installation rather than a domestic press (Callot 1994: 191–196 and Figures 303–307). It has been cautiously estimated from Ugaritic tax texts that the total annual production from one village alone was 15 metric tons and the average across nine villages was 27.5 metric tons. This indicates that the production of olive oil in Ugarit was an important contributor to its economy in the LBA (Heltzer 1996a: 80–89).

[274] Allbaugh 1953: 107, Table 15 and A51. This equates to a daily consumption of 80 g/individual of olive oil in rural Crete (Riley 2002: 64).

[275] Olive oil presses were smaller in the LBA/EIA than those used in the time of Allbaugh's study.

[276] For example in Messenia over 15,000 oil olives trees covered 130 ha that equates to 115 trees/ha (Aschenbrenner 1972: 53). For the assumptions used by the authorities on olive tree densities for the assessment of tax in the time of Diocletian, see Mitchell 2005: 94.

[277] Aschenbrenner 1972: 53, Mattingly 1996: 219–220, and Mitchell 2005: 94. The effect on the output of the biannual habit of Tunisian olive oil production 1950–1977 is illustrated in Mattingly 1996: 220, Figure 9.4.

[278] In modern Egypt olives form an important crop around the Siwa Oasis. (Zohary and Hopf 1994: 139, map 15).

[279] Murray 2000c: 610, Table 24.1 and Serpico and White 2000: 398–399.

[280] Evidence of olives in the NK has been found at Amarna (Renfrew 1985: 188). Ramesses III attempted to grow olive trees at Heliopolis (Breasted 1906d: Text 145). Otherwise, attestation to the olive is from linguistic evidence, which has to be treated with caution (Brewer *et al* 1994: 42–43 and Serpico and White 2000: 399).

[281] Koura 1995 and Serpico and White 2000: 399.

[282] In Egypt, local oil production was not sufficient and oil was imported and taken as tribute from the Near East where olives were plentiful (Brewer *et al* 1994: 42). See also Serpico and White 2000: 391–405.

[283] Castor oil has an unpleasant taste, and contains poisonous ricin if incorrectly processed and safflower oil has an unpleasant odour. Although used in some regions for cooking today, linseed oil quickly turns rancid (Serpico and White. 2000: 392–397).

[284] Serpico and White. 2000: 395–396, 401–402. For Egyptian ethnographic evidence of the extraction of oil from moringa seeds, see Osborn 1968: 173.

[285] Hepper 1992: 62.

[286] The finds of sesame in the archaeological record are rare. It is also unlikely that sesame was grown in the NK to any significant extent because the annual inundation coincides with the sowing season of

The manufacturing process of oil extraction from indigenous Egyptian plants was laborious and time-consuming (removal of foreign material, grinding, probably de-hulling, boiling, and pressing) compared with the fleshy high oil contents of olives.[287] It is probable that most vegetable oils were not used for general consumption but were used instead for the base of unguents and perfumes for the élite.[288] Therefore, for the model it has been assumed that NK Egyptians received their lipid requirements from fat rendered from the meat of the wildfowl and ruminants that formed the protein element of their diet.

Protein, animal fats, and dairy products

Protein is necessary to repair body cells and make new ones. Fats, a subgroup of lipids, provide a means of storing energy and are a structural component of cell membranes that control and protect the movement of substances in and out of body cells. Milk and dairy products contain many nutrients such as calcium, magnesium, phosphorous, zinc, iodine, folic acid, and vitamins A, B12, and C. This section estimates the percentage of calories in the diets of Cyprus and Egypt from protein, animal fats, and dairy products.

Protein

Pulses provide a source of protein in the diet but the most effective supply is meat. However, raising livestock is relatively expensive in manpower terms because animals need fodder and pasturage. The evidence suggests that for the LBA non-élite, meat did not form the major part of the diet. When protein was consumed, it would have been predominantly mutton, goat, fish, and wildfowl.[289]

LBA Cyprus

Bone assemblages of domesticated long and short horned cattle, sheep, goats, and pigs, dating to before the LBA, have been found across the Eastern Mediterranean. In his ethnographic Cretan study, Allbaugh records that goat and kid, followed by mutton were the meats chiefly consumed and the consumption of beef, pork game, and poultry was low. On average 0.213 kg per individual of meat and meat products were eaten per week, 0.171 kg per individual each week of fresh or preserved fish, 0.048 kg of snails, and perhaps one egg a week.[290]

This study assumes that the total protein intake of meat (mutton/goat, fish, and wildfowl) was 27 kg/individual/yr (Table 2.15) of which 14 kg/adult/yr was provided from sheep and goats. The average sheep had 18 kg of useable off-the-bone meat.[291] To provide 14 kg/adult/yr would have require a maximum culling of 62,400 animals per year, which on average equates to four animals per family per year.[292] This would not have had a detrimental effect on maintaining a viable breeding flock.

NK Egypt

The Nile valley with its annual inundation favours arable farming, leaving land on the edges of the desert suitable for rough pasture.[293] Beef was an important offering made by the king to the gods in the temples and then shared out amongst the élite priests and their families.[294] Multidisciplinary investigations of mummified remains have shown the presence of atherosclerosis among élite groups in Egyptian society, in particular those with priestly status and their families. Atherosclerosis in the general population of ancient Egypt was not common. This could reflect a significant difference in the diet of the élite and the majority of the population whose diet was largely vegetarian, supplemented by fish and fowl, and only the occasional consumption of red meat.[295] The butchery marks on bones excavated from the middens in the Workmen's Village and residential districts of Amarna indicate that goats, pigs, and a small number of cows were kept by this group of the population and this meat would have entered the diet.[296]

Not all meat was consumed immediately; in Egypt, to prevent spoilage there were several methods of preserving it such as wet and dry salting and curing with fat, beer, or honey. There are tomb scenes that show meat hung on a line to dry, which would have resulted in a meat product similar to biltong.[297]

sesame in mid June–July. This would have made its cultivation almost impossible except perhaps on a small scale in the Fayum and the Delta (Zohary and Hopf 1994: 132–133, Serpico and White 2000: 397–398, and Serpico 2004: 101).

[287] Serpico and White 2000: 405–407.

[288] Manniche 1999.

[289] Brewer 2007: 140–142.

[290] Allbaugh 1953: 110.

[291] Lyman 1979: 542, Table 4. It is assumed here that a goat would provide approximately the same useable off-the-bone weight of meat.

[292] The calorific value for mutton is 2,500 kcals/kg. This value is normally applied to lean meat and mutton has a high fat content. The reason for using the lower value is that in antiquity fat was a useful commodity and would have been cut off for cooking, lighting or as a base for perfumed unguents (Manniche 1999: 83, 85 and Serpico and White 2000: 407–408). Also, any attached fat on the meat would melt into the fire during roasting.

[293] On the other hand, it is thought that large herds of cattle were raised in the Delta (Moens and Wetterstrom 1998).

[294] For the records of the large quantities of meat supplied by Ramesses III to the temples listed in the Harris Papyrus, see Breasted 1906d: Texts 87–191. The king also donated large quantities of waterfowl and geese.

[295] David *et al* 2010: 718.

[296] Kemp 1994: 143 and Luff 1994. A pig farm with a series of pens attached to a workman's house (building 300) has been excavated by Hulin 1986. The limited size of the pens suggests they were a holding point for pigs before they were processed, salted, and preserved in pots with a white gypsum topping to protect the contents from bacteria and contamination. Kemp suggests that keeping the pigs may represent a private initiative to increase the villagers' income, who could sell them in the main city as well as supplying themselves. The pigs were fed on grain and their bone assemblages show they were slaughtered between one and two years old (Kemp 1994: 143, Luff 1994, and Kemp: 2006: 331–332, Plate 10).

[297] Raw meat remains safe for consumption in the Egyptian climate for 8 hours in summer and 12 hours if kept in the shade. See Ikram 2000: 659–669 and Luff 1994: 162 for methods of meat preservation. A scene of butchery, the hanging of meat, and the processing of meat appears in the Twelfth Dynasty tomb of Antefoker (TT 60) at Thebes (Davies and Gardiner 1920: Plate VIII–IX). At Amarna, the Aten temples stored meat from sacrifices in large pots (0.64 m high with a 0.25 m rim). Ink labels provided information relating to the jars' contents, the date, and the name

To supplement the supply of meat, additional supplies of protein would have entered the diet through hunting and fishing.[298] The migrations of geese and ducks provided an additional source of meat for all social classes and textual evidence from MK Lahun suggests that large quantities of fish were consumed. A late MK papyrus lists catches of fish of 2,000 and another of 1,400, of which 1,000 were gutted.[299] One ostracon from Deir el-Medina shows that one fisherman supplied on average 147 kg per month, over a 6 month period.[300] Two other ostraca record that the monthly ration of fish to the tomb workers and their families at Deir el-Medina ranged from 8.4–10.92 kg/month.[301] Large quantities of fish that had been offered to the gods in the temples would have been shared out amongst the élite priests.[302] This study assumes that the total protein intake of meat: mutton/goat, fish, and wildfowl, was 37 kg/individual/yr (Table 2.15). This reflects the availability of fish and wildfowl for most of the population in close proximity to the Nile.

	Allbaugh's study kg/yr	LBA Cyprus kg/yr	NK Egypt kg/yr
Meat goats/sheep	11.1	14	12
Fish	8.9	8	17
Wildfowl	0	5	8
Other	8.2	0	0
Total cereals	**28.2**	**27**	**37**

Table 2.15: Protein consumption estimated for the study compared with Allbaugh's study.

Animal fats in the Egyptian and Cypriot diet

Fats provide more than twice the calories of the equivalent weight of proteins and carbohydrates, providing high energy with low bulk.[303] Typically, 20% of meat is fatty tissue although some animals, such as duck, goose, and fat-tailed sheep have a higher proportion of fat. Fat tailed sheep were the dominant breed in the NK Egypt and their tail can weigh as much as 20 pounds.[304] Fat would therefore have been consumed when cooked meat was eaten. The meat itself could also be preserved in fat-filled amphorae similar in concept to confit of duck, and this would have added to the intake of fat.[305] Excavations at the palace site of Amenhotep III at Malkata at Thebes, have found labels and sealings from amphorae identifying the contents as dressed meat and fat from sheep and fowl.[306] Allbaugh reported that the consumption of lipids in the Cretan diet was high and came mainly from olive oil.[307] This study assumes that the calories provided by animal fats represent 3.3% and 6.6% of the diet for Cyprus and Egypt. The lower percentage for Cyprus reflects the ease of growing olive oil and its widespread consumption discussed previously.

Dairy products in Cyprus and Egypt

Milk (*irṯt*) formed a part in the Egyptian diet and was consumed by children, the sick, and possibly by adults.[308] Kings were depicted being suckled by the goddess Hathor in her human and cow form.[309] Milk was also included in the offerings to the gods in religious rituals and the king is shown offering milk to Ra-Harakhte in TT 279 the Theban tomb of Pabasa.[310] Tomb scenes of milking appear throughout the Pharaonic Period and a sunken relief on the Eleventh Dynasty sarcophagus of Queen Kawit shows a cow being milked.[311] Cheese and curds formed part of the diet and a type of cheese was included in a funerary meal, found in an élite tomb (Tomb 3477) at Saqqara.[312] The milk production of Egyptian cattle is likely to have been low, perhaps only one litre a day, from lactating cows who had to feed their calves.

Allbaugh's study of Crete shows that 2.5% and 2.1% of the annual total energy requirement was provided by milk and cheese respectively. It is likely that because natural pasturage was limited in LBA Cyprus and Egypt, the consumption of dairy products was lower than Allbaugh's figures. For Cyprus and Egypt, a consumption of 17 and 11 kg/yr/individual respectively has been used (Table 2.16). This represents 2.1% and 1.2% of the total calories consumed/year in Cyprus and Egypt (Table 2.10). This reflects the greater availability of pasture in Cyprus than in Egypt.

	Allbaugh's study kg/yr	LBA Cyprus kg/yr	NK Egypt kg/yr
Milk	27.1	12	9
Cheese	7.4	5	2
Total	**34.5**	**17**	**11**

Table 2.16: Estimates of the consumption of dairy products in the Cypriot and Egyptian diets.

of the butcher, 'Regnal year 7, 3rd month of summer. The depot "Soul of 'Ra lives".' Preserved meat: intestines, of the daily offerings, provided by the butcher Wepet.' (Kemp 1994: 139–143, and Figure 14.3). Also, see Pendlebury 1951a: 174 and Pendlebury 1951b: Plate XCII, nos. 204–6. For a full analysis of Egyptian meat processing from slaughter to consumption, see Ikram 1995 and Ikram 2000.

298 Brewer and Friedman 1989: 11 have identified from tomb scenes 14 families of fish representing 20 different sub families, all of which could have entered the Egyptian diet.

299 Collier and Quirke 2006: 152–153, 172–173 citing papyri UC 32097B and UC 32142B and Szpakowska 2008: 97–98. These two examples are part of a large number of accounting lists of fish caught and gutted.

300 Brewer and Friedman 1989: 16 citing Christophe 1967: 193–194.

301 Janssen 1975b: 418 (Ostracon Deir el-Medina 142) and Janssen 1997: 46 (Ostracon Gardiner 192). Assuming the rations were within the range given, the monthly fish intake equates to 15 kg/person/yr for an average family of 6 individuals.

302 The Harris Papyrus records that over a period of 31 years, Ramesses III donated some 474,640 gutted, fresh and pickled fish for the festivals in honour of Amun at Thebes. Another 19,600 fish was given to smaller temples throughout Egypt (Brewer and Friedman 1989: 16).

303 Brewer *et al* 1994: 41.

304 Ikram 2000: 656. It has been suggested that the *Bos indicus* cattle with a fatty hump behind the neck was introduced during the NK but this is disputed (Serpico and White 2000: 407).

305 A similar amphora was found in the tomb of Kha at Thebes (TT 8).

306 Kemp 1994: 139.

307 Allbaugh 1953: 111–112.

308 Darby *et al* 1997: 758 and 760–722. A letter from the mayor Sennefer (Papyrus Berlin 10463) orders that fresh milk should be ready for his return home (Caminos 1963: 31).

309 Hatshepsut suckles from the udder of Hathor in her cow form in the temple at Deir el-Bahri (Bleeker 1973: 52).

310 PM $1^2/1$: 358, (12).

311 Brewer *et al* 1994: 85, Figure 7.5. Cairo Museum. Inv. no. JE 47397.

312 Zaky 1942. However, this identification is not certain.

2.6 Area of land required

Table 2.6 and Tables 2.8–2.12 show that to feed a 100,000 cohort, 84,684 million kcals/yr were required. The portion of these calories satisfied by cultivated crops (cereals, pulses, vegetables, grapes, wine, olives, and olive oil) is given in (Table 2.17). The rest of the calories come from protein, fats, and oils, small quantities of honey, and dairy products.

Food category	LBA Cyprus		NK Egypt	
	%	Million kcals/100,000 cohort/yr	%	Million kcals/100,000 cohort/yr
Cultivated crops	88.6	74,996	84.9	71,866
Protein/dairy	7.4	6,304	7.8	6,635
Animal fats	3.3	2,790	6.6	5,591
Honey	0.7	594	0.7	593
Total	**100**	**84,684**	**100**	**84,684**

Table 2.17: Total million kcals calories to feed a 100,000 cohort/yr for each major food category.

The calculation of the area of land needed to grow the crops to provide the 74,996 and 71,866 million kcals/100,000 cohort/yr for Cyprus and Egypt (Table 2.17) requires five discrete analytical stages:

Stage 1: The need for seed corn

The energy provided by the cultivated crops has been uplifted to provide the seed corn for next year.[313] It is assumed that for other cultivated crops the area required for seed is negligible and can be ignored. Allen and Baer's analysis of the MK Heqanakht letters points to a 1:10 seed to yield ratio, which is used for this study (Row B in Table 2.18).[314]

Stage 2: Loss from wastage

Similarly, there would be a need for an additional 15% of land to compensate for wastage incurred through pests, birds, and process losses in harvesting, transport, milling of cereals, and storage (Row C in Table 2.18).[315] A major factor affecting crop yields and therefore the calories obtained is the variation in the quality of the land on which they are cultivated. This study allocates land for cultivation into marginal, average, and best land and the percentage calories from crops grown on each type of land is given in Table 2.19. The percentages used in AGCALC are based on a range of factors such as the crop's resistance to drought, soil salinity, and access to water for irrigation. The resulting calories required to be grown by cultivated crop are given in Table 2.20 and Table 2.21 for Cyprus and Egypt respectively.

Total energy requirement to support a cohort of 100,000/yr	Energy produced by cultivated crops (Million kcals/100,000 cohort/yr)	
	Cyprus	NK Egypt
Row A: Energy required by a 100,000 cohort/yr for cultivated crops	74,996	71,866
Row B: Cereals and pulses uplifted by 10% for next year's seed corn	6,065	6,777
Row C: Cultivated crops and seed corn uplifted by 15% for wastage	12,159	11,796
Total for cultivated crops	**93,220**	**90,439**
Protein/dairy	6,304	6,635
Animal fats	2,790	5,591
Honey	594	593
Total	**102,908**	**103,259**

Table 2.18: Total million kcals calories to feed a 100,000 cohort/yr uplifted for wastage and seed corn.

Cyprus	%	%	%	Total
Barley	35	55	10	100
Emmer	15	65	20	100
Pulses	25	55	20	100
Vegetables/fruit	5	25	70	100
Olives/oil	20	70	10	100
Grapes	5	55	40	100
Fodder	60	35	5	100
Egypt	**%**	**%**	**%**	**Total**
Barley	35	55	10	100
Emmer	15	65	20	100
Pulses	25	55	20	100
Vegetables/fruit	5	20	75	100
Grapes	5	50	45	100
Fodder	60	35	5	100

Table 2.19: Proportions (%) of crops grown on marginal, average, and best land in Cyprus and Egypt.

Crop	Marginal land	Average land	Best land	Total calories
Barley	14,720	23,131	4,206	42,057
Emmer	4,405	19,089	5,874	29,368
Pulses	1,324	2,913	1,059	5,296
Vegetables/fruit	219	1,095	3,066	4,380
Olives/oil	2,317	8,110	1,159	11,586
Grapes	27	293	213	533
Total	**23,012**	**54,631**	**15,577**	**93,220**

Table 2.20: Calories provided by each food type of cultivated crops for Cyprus (million kcals/100,000 cohort/yr).

Crop	Marginal land	Average land	Best land	Total calories
Barley	20,823	32,723	5,951	59,497
Emmer	2,743	11,885	3,657	18,285
Pulses	1,988	4,373	1,590	7,951
Vegetables/fruit	224	896	3,359	4,479
Grapes	11	114	102	227
Total	**25,789**	**49,991**	**14,659**	**90,439**

Table 2.21: Calories provided by each food type of cultivated crops for NK Egypt (million kcals/ 100,000 cohort/yr).

Stage 3: Weight of crops grown

The weight of crops required to satisfy the calorie requirement (Table 2.23) is calculated by multiplying the calories for each food type from Stage 3 (million kcals/yr/100,000 cohort/yr) x 1,000,000 ÷ the calorific

[313] It is also assumed that the area of land required for non-cereal crop seed reserves is not significant and can be ignored.

[314] Allen 2002: 160–161 suggests a sowing rate of 1.5 sacks/aroura with an expected yield of 15 sacks/aroura. Baer arrives at the same conclusion (Baer 1962: 31–33 and Baer 1963: 14–15).

[315] Modern ethnographic evidence shows that the average weight loss in eastern and southern Africa grain production ranges from 10–20%. The principle causes of wastage are the shattering of grain heads when harvesting, spillage at each stage of the process from harvesting through to consumption, grain left in the ears of corn in the threshing process, and losses when stored due to insects, rodents, and birds (World Bank, FAO, and IFAD 2008: 7–16).

value of each food type in Table 2.22 (kcals/kg).[316] At this point in the calculation the weight of crops excludes seed corn and wastage, which is included later in Stage 5.

Calorific value of foodstuffs (kg/ha)			
Foodstuff	**kcals/kg**	**Foodstuff**	**kcals/kg**
Barley Emmer	3,320 3,340	Figs Fruit	187 600
Potatoes	720	Tomatoes/citrus	170
Honey Grapes/wine	3,072 750	Mutton/goat/game Fish	2,500 1,356
Pulses	1,281	Milk	840
Vegetables and fruits	190–247	Cheese	2,620
		Animal fats	9,019
Fresh olives	1,030	Olive oil	7,999

Table 2.22: Calorific value of foodstuffs included in this study (kcals/kg).

Crop	Calorific value kcals/kg	Cyprus kg/100,000 cohort/yr	Egypt kg/100,000 cohort/yr
Barley	3,320	12,667,771	17,920,783
Emmer	3,340	8,792,814	9,376,924
Sub total cereals		21,460,585	27,297,707
Pulses	1,281	4,135,799	3,961,076
Vegetables/fruit	468	9,352,919	2,083,256
Olives/oil	7,999	1,448,431	0
Grapes	750	710,667	305,108
Total		**37,108,401**	**33,647,147**

Table 2.23: Weight of crops grown (kg) in both regions.

Stage 4: Yield rates

The ethnographic evidence for yield rates using traditional farming methods for Egypt and Cyprus is given in Reports 2.1–2.2 and 2.4–2.6 in the Appendix and is summarised in Tables 2.24–2.25.[317] The ethnographic evidence for Egypt is from a period when fertilisers had been introduced on land irrigated by mechanical pumps, which boosted crop yields. When farming practices relied solely on the Nile silt and manure from animals, crop yields would have been less.[318] The yields in the first half of the twentieth century typically used sulphate of ammonia fertilisers at a rate of 75–150 kg/feddan (178.5–357 kg/ha).[319] In NK basin agriculture, the Nile inundation carrying nutritious silt would only reach the marginal land in exceptionally high floods and in years of low inundations some of the average land would not be flooded. To compensate for this, the Egyptian ethnographic data has been adjusted downwards for marginal and average land by 15% and 5% respectively (Table 2.24). The averages of the ethnographic yield data determined for cereals and pulses grown in the dry farming regions representative of Cyprus are summarised in Table 2.25. Reports 2.1–2.2 and 2.4–2.5 in the Appendix support Grigg's conclusion that cereal yield rates in the Eastern Mediterranean rarely exceeded 650 kg/ha except on very good soils.[320] The yields for olive oil production (Report 2.6 in the Appendix) are low compared with recent olive oil production in Cyprus (an average of 1,621 kg/ha in 1998).[321] The ethnographic production rates used for Cyprus reflect small farms and local consumption rather than modern industrial scale commercial production for export.

Egypt	Crop yield kg/ha		
With fertiliser	**Marginal**	**Average**	**Best**
Barley	1,426	1,577	1,728
Wheat	1,507	1,650	1,793
Pulses	1,579	1,634	1,689
Without fertiliser	**Marginal**	**Average**	**Best**
Barley	1,212	1,498	1,728
Wheat	1,281	1,567	1,793
Pulses	1,342	1,553	1,689
Grapes[322]	1,753	2,921	4,382

Table 2.24: Egyptian crop yields adjusted to reflect the period prior to chemical fertilisers.

Cyprus	Crop yield kg/ha		
	Marginal land	**Average land**	**Best land**
Barley	407	660	1,072
Wheat	399	714	1,454
Pulses	455	562	802
Olives[323]	180	272	398
Grapes	1,753	2,921	4,382

Table 2.25: Cypriot crop yields.

Stage 5: Area of land needed to grow crops

The total area required for cultivated crops = weight of crops derived from Stage 4 (kg) ÷ the harvest yield from Stage 5 (kg/ha). This area is uplifted by 10% for seed corn and 15% for wastage. A summary of the total area required for cultivation crops is given in Table 2.26.

Cultivated crops	LBA Cyprus		NK Egypt	
	Area uplifted for seed corn and wastage	**%**	**Area uplifted for seed corn and wastage**	**%**
Cereals	38,134	65.6	20,376	65.7
Pulses	7,352	12.6	5,479	17.6
Vegetables/fruit	1,667	2.9	1,667	5.4
Grapes	220	0.4	91	0.3
Olives/oil	5,699	9.8	0	0
Fodder	5,083	8.7	3,417	11.0
Total	**58,155**	**100**	**31,030**	**100**

Table 2.26: Area of land (ha) required to grow the crops to feed a cohort of 100,000/yr.

The results clearly demonstrate the need for a large area of land to be dedicated to cereal production for the ancient diet. In LBA Cyprus, some alleviation for the demand for land for cereals may have come from

[316] The weight of barley for Egypt includes that required for the production of beer.

[317] Report 2.3 in the Appendix identifies the source of ancient Egyptian textual evidence and summarises the yield rates. These are for reference only as it is not certain that they are fully representative.

[318] See Ruf's comments above in the section on fertility from inundation silt in Egypt.

[319] Foaden and Fletcher 1908: 292–293.

[320] Grigg 1974: 135.

[321] Source data Agricultural Statistics, 1985–1999. Department of Statistics and Research, Ministry of Finance, Cyprus.

[322] This study has used for both regions the ethnographic evidence from Crete (Allbaugh 1953: 277, Table 50) for the wine grape yield on unfertilised average land = 23.5 cwt/acre (2,921 kg/ha).

[323] One kg/ha of oil = 1.16 litres/ha.

growing grain in olive groves, widely practiced today in Cyprus and Crete.[324]

2.7 The labour-rates, workload, and manpower required to support the agrarian cycle

In this section the evidence from texts, tomb paintings, ethnographic and experimental archaeology is used to estimate the labour-rates (man-days required to complete the task per hectare of land) for the cultivation of grain crops. The workload (man-years) using labour-rates (man-days/ha) for each activity in the agrarian cycle (tilling, weeding, irrigation, harvesting, threshing, and winnowing) is also quantified. The labour-rates for milling grain, cultivating vegetables, fruit, grapes, olives, making wine and beer, raising animals for protein and dairy products, and the production of fodder have different labour-rate algorithms and are calculated separately. The need for fodder is an important consideration as its provision carries additional workload implications and it is also included. This section begins by explaining the difference between labour-rate, workload, and manpower but the agrarian manpower is calculated in Section 2.8.

The interrelationship of labour-rate, workload, and manpower

The term workload (man-days) and the number of workers required to complete a task (commonly referred to as manpower) are not the same. The manpower required to complete a task is always higher than the workload because not all the workers work at the same rate and invariably delays occur when carrying out any task other than the simplest. The agricultural cycle had many peak loads of activity when there might have been conflicting demands on the available labour or equipment. In carrying out the varied tasks the workers needed to move from one activity to another and this took time, particularly if they had to travel any appreciable distance. Ethnographic evidence suggests that farmland fragmentation into small non-contiguous plots caused labour productivity to decrease by 50%.[325] At times, workers can be sick and other agricultural workers may have replaced them `whose physical strength or skill level were below the optimum required to complete the task. In Cyprus, rainfall could delay the start of agricultural activities or interrupt them and in Egypt, a late inundation delayed the start of tilling the soil, a delay that continued throughout the ensuing agricultural cycle. The number of possible delays within the agrarian cycle means that the estimates of manpower given in this study should be considered as a minimum.

Labour-rate

The labour-rate is the time it takes to complete a unit of activity and it is used to calculate the workload. If it takes 1,000 man-hours to weed 2 ha of land, the labour-rate is 500 man-hours/ha. The most common unit used in this study is man-days/ha and assumes a productive agricultural working day was nine hours unless otherwise stated. The number of productive hours is always less than the hours of daylight available as time is taken for eating, resting, and other factors (average 11.8 daylight hours across the year in Egypt). In the weeding example above the labour-rate would be = 500/9 = 56 man-days/ha.

Workload

The workload is the number of man-days or man-years, whichever is more applicable, to complete an activity. In all the workload calculations in this study it has been assumed that agrarian manual workers worked 314 days out of 365.[326] The formula for workload (man-days) = man-days/ha (labour-rate) × number of ha. Generally, if the workload exceeds 314 days then it is more convenient to use units of man-years. In this example workload (man-years) = man-days/ha (labour-rate) × number of ha ÷ 314.

Manpower

Manpower is equivalent to the number of workers required to complete a task. It takes into account the productivity of the worker, adjusted by a competency index, which is explained below. If the workload is stated in man-days then manpower = workload × competency index ÷ days worked per year (314). Adolescents and women could not expend as much effort in hard labour activities as a mature man. Other factors that influence the productivity of the worker are their health, age, and skill level. Using a standard index of 1 for a healthy male, the competency indices used in this study for males and females of different ages are given in column B in Table 2.27.[327] For any given age group (for example males aged 10–12 in Table 2.27) the equivalent number of adult and fully skilled workers (column C) would be equivalent to 2,705 × 0.65 = 1,758 male workers.[328] The overall resulting age and competency index for the male and female working population is calculated by dividing the sum of column B by the sum of column C = 70,110 ÷ 53,900 = 1.3.

To illustrate, if an Egyptian estate had 100 ha of land requiring weeding carried out by men and women the

[324] Personal observation in 2004.

[325] Dovring 1967: 169.

[326] It is assumed for this study that workers had one rest day every ten days (36 days/year). An average of fifteen days sickness per year has been assumed. In total it is assumed that workers were productive for 365–(36+15) = 314 days.

[327] For a similar ethnographic approach see McMillan 1988: 104, Sokona 1988, and Brun 1992). Janssen's analysis of absence from work of the necropolis workers at Deir el-Medina in year 40 of Ramesses II (Ostracon BM 5634) provides additional insight to days lost in NK Egypt (Janssen 1980b). Of particular interest was the frequent occurrence of the word *mr* meaning 'to be ill and to suffer', which occurs almost a hundred times (Janssen 1980b: 128). Other reasons for absence were free days, feast days, as well as absence for second jobs such as brewing and house building, in addition to their regular employment (Janssen 1980b: 143ff).

[328] For the demographic age profile of individuals within age bands see Table 2.3.

workload would be = 100 (area ha) × 56 (weeding labour-rate man-days/ha) = 5,600 man-days = 5,600 ÷ 314 (days worked/yr) = 18 man-years. The competency index of 1.3 means that the number of workers required would be 30% greater and the workload has to be increased. The resulting number of male and female workers required would be = 5,600 (workload man-days) × 1.3 ÷ 314 (days worked/yr) = 23 workers. If the weeding task was completed only by males then the number of male workers = 5,600 (workload man-days) × 1.17 (competency index for males) ÷ 314 (days worked/year) = 21 workers.

Age bands	A. Male survivors in age band	B. Male competency indices	C. Equivalent no. of male workers
7–9	2,800	0.3	840
10–12	2,705	0.65	1,758
13–15	2,665	.9	2,399
16–19	3,335	1	3,335
20–39	14,045	1	14,045
40–49	5,405	.85	4,594
50–59	4,100	.7	2,870
Age bands	**A. Female survivors in age band**	**B. Female competency indices**	**C. Equivalent no. of female workers**
7–9	2,800	.25	700
10–12	2,705	.6	1,623
13–15	2,665	.75	1,999
16–19	3,335	.8	2,668
20–39	14,045	.8	11,236
40–49	5,405	.7	3,784
50–59	4,100	.5	2,050
Totals male and female	**70,110**		**53,901**
Competency index (males)			1.17
Competency index (females)			1.46
Competency index (males & females combined)			1.3
Percentage uplift in workers required			30

Table 2.27: Competency indices collated by age band and gender.

To calculate the workload required for the total agrarian cycle, it is necessary to estimate the labour-rate for each of the activities in the agrarian year. Each activity is now taken in turn to examine the tools used and how they were used. From these considerations, the labour-rates and workloads are calculated. The calculation of manpower is completed in Section 2.8

Preparing the land, ploughing, hoeing, and sowing

The labour-rate (man-days/ha) for preparing the land for sowing and planting includes ploughing, hoeing, clod breaking, and covering the seeds.[329] The time taken in LBA Egypt and Cyprus to plough one hectare of land, to sow it, and to cover the seed with soil is derived (labour-rate) and the workload associated with the activities is calculated in this section.

The ard plough and hoe

Since *c.*4000 B.C. the symmetrical ard has been in use in the Near East and this type of plough had changed little by the LBA. Most of the designs that have been found are capable of ploughing a furrow between 100 mm and 250 mm (Figures 2.4 and 2.5).[330] The plough's handle and crossbar were made of wood and in NK Egypt, plough-points made of bronze began to be used. The top of these plough points were hollow and 8–10 cms wide where they were attached to the plough shaft. The other end was forged into a point for ploughing the soil.[331]

The ard used for soil preparation is attested in Egypt from the OK. The 'Beladi' plough used in Egypt at the end of the nineteenth century A.D. closely followed the design of the ploughing ard shown in tomb paintings from Pharaonic Egypt.[332]

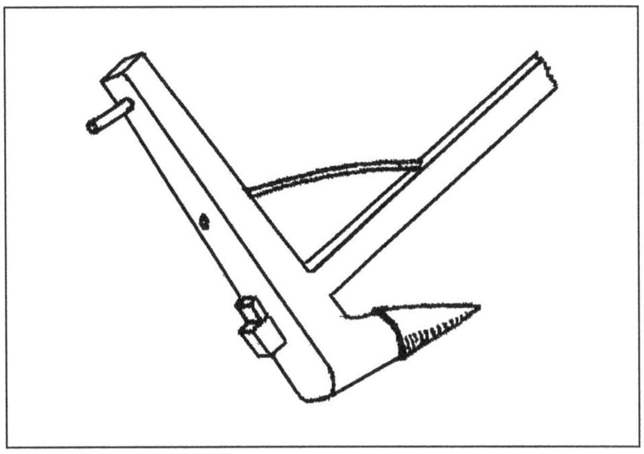

Figure 2.4: Symmetrical ard.
Sketch of Russell 1988: 118, Figure 15.

Similar wooden ard ploughs are still used in Egypt today with cattle harnessed to a wooden yoke.[333] Third millennium models of ploughing from Vounous in Cyprus and Nemea in Greece show that they too were pulled by oxen controlled by yokes.[334]

Figure 2.5: Ploughing using an ard plough.
Sketch of Davies 1917: Plate XXI. The tomb of Nakht (TT 52).

[329] Clod breaking is the term for breaking up lumps of dried soil.

[330] Reynolds 1981: 99–100, Varisco 1982, and Russell 1988: 118–121 Figure 15. For the development of the ard see FAO 1969: 44–63.

[331] Borowski 1987: 49–51, Figure 4.

[332] Foaden and Fletcher 1908: 111, Figures 9a and 9b.

[333] These modern ploughs are almost identical in design to those portrayed in the NK tomb of Duauneḥeḥ (TT 125) (Bartosiewicz *et al* 1997: 24–25, cover photograph and Figures 10–12).

[334] For details and published photograph see Karageorghis 1981: 44, Catalogue no. 30 and Pullen 1992: 49–50, Figure 1.

Hoes were made of wood and used to cultivate small areas of land, removing weeds, and clod breaking (Figure 2.6). The Gelidonya wreck had a large number of bronze socketed heads thought to be fitted to hoes to improve their effectiveness.[335]

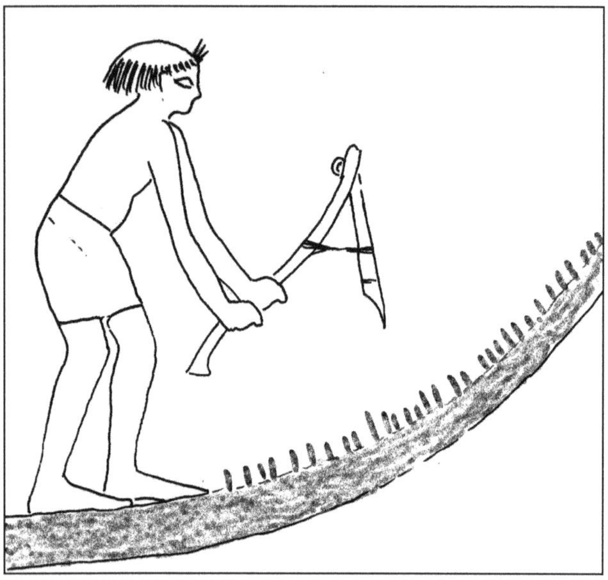

Figure 2.6: Hoeing with a wooden hoe.
Sketch of Davies 1917: Plate XXI. The tomb of Nakht (TT 52).

Factors affecting the labour-rate for preparing the land

Three factors influence the labour-rate for preparing the land for sowing and planting:

- The area of the land ploughed and hoed.
- The quality of the land.
- The area of land cultivated or left fallow in the previous year.

Area of land ploughed and hoed

The most likely method of soil preparation for cereals was the use of the plough followed by the hoe for clod breaking to obtain a fine tilth.[336] This study assumes that land dedicated to horticulture, viticulture, oleoculture, and green fodder would be prepared by hoes. It has also been assumed that due to the variability of the timing of the inundation in Egypt and uncertain rainfall patterns in Cyprus, farmers could not always follow the ideal timetable for the agrarian cycle. Therefore, some small tracts of land may have been left as fallow or brought into cultivation later in the agrarian cycle. In these cases, it would probably be more convenient to prepare the soil with hoes rather than move the plough and oxen to the small, dispersed tracts of land. To cater for this variability it is assumed that the percentage of land ploughed and hoed in Cyprus and Egypt, is as given in Table 2.28.

Cultivated crops	LBA Cyprus		NK Egypt	
	Area of land ploughed	Area of land hoed	Area of land ploughed	Area of land hoed
Cereals	30,508	7,627	16,301	4,076
Pulses	5,882	1,470	4,384	1,095
Vegetables/fruit	0	1,887	0	1,758
Olives/oil	0	5,699	0	0
Fodder	4,066	1,017	2,734	683
Sub total	**40,456**	**17,700**	**23,419**	**7,612**
Total area	**58,156**		**31,031**	
% ploughed/hoed	**70**	**30**	**75**	**25**

Table 2.28: Area of land (ha) collated by areas ploughed and hoed.

Quality of land ploughed or hoed

Table 2.29 and Table 2.30 indentify the areas of best, average, and marginal land, which would have been ploughed and hoed for Cyprus and Egypt respectively. With regard to the crops grown on these types of land, more barley than wheat has been allocated to marginal land because of its tolerance to drought and salinity. Green fodder and vetches are also assumed to have been grown mainly on marginal land because they would grow on this quality of land and their nitrogen fixing properties improved the soil.

Area (ha) under cultivation	Cyprus			
	Marginal	Average	Best	Total
Barley	11,544	11,191	1,252	23,987
Emmer wheat	3,735	9,046	1,366	14,147
Pulses	2,273	4,047	1,032	7,352
Olives	1,606	3,729	364	5,699
Fodder	3,050	1,779	254	5,083
Vegetable/fruit	83	417	1,167	1,667
Grapes	21	134	65	220
Total area	**22,312**	**30,340**	**5,500**	**58,155**

Table 2.29: Area of land (ha) under cultivation collated by area and quality of land in LBA Cyprus.

Area (ha) under cultivation	Egypt			
	Marginal	Average	Best	Total
Barley	5,485	6,974	1,099	13,558
Emmer wheat	1,241	4,395	1,182	6,818
Pulses	1,549	2,946	984	5,479
Fodder	2,050	1,196	171	3,417
Vegetable/fruit	83	417	1,167	1,667
Grapes	8	52	31	91
Total area	**10,416**	**15,980**	**4,634**	**31,030**

Table 2.30: Area of land (ha) under cultivation collated by area and quality of land in NK Egypt.

Egyptian tomb paintings show that horticultural crops and grapes were grown on best land close to water sources as shown in the tomb of Ipuy (TT 217); this was probably the same in Cyprus.[337] Ethnographic evidence shows that olive groves provide adequate yields on average or marginal land and this assumption is applied to Cyprus.

Area of land cultivated or left fallow in the previous year

The areas of land for Cyprus and Egypt left fallow or cultivated in the previous year are given in Table 2.31.

[335] Bass 1967c: Figure 102.
[336] Takács 1982. It is possible that on land which was too swampy to plough, pigs were used to grub up the land allowing it to dry out so that conventional tilling could follow.

[337] Davies 1927: Plate XXIX.

	LBA Cyprus		NK Egypt	
Cultivated crops	Land left fallow	Land cultivated	Land left fallow	Land cultivated
Cereals	19,209	18,925	6,655	13,720
Pulses	3,305	4,047	1,638	3,842
Vegetables/fruit	405	1,482	352	1,406
Olives/oil	2,621	3,078	0	0
Fodder	2,971	2,112	1,435	1,982
Sub total	**28,511**	**29,644**	**10,080**	**20,950**
Total area	**58,155**		**31,030**	

Table 2.31: Summary of land (ha) collated by land left fallow or cultivated in previous year.

Tillage

Ploughing labour-rates

Columella, writing in the first century A.D. records two examples of preparing fallow land suitable for sowing grain, using a Roman symmetrical ard with one yoke, and two oxen. The first was completed with four ploughings and at a rate of 40 hrs/iugerum (159 hrs/ha).[338] The second was completed with three ploughing and a total ploughing rate of 45 hrs/iugerum (183 hrs/ha).[339] The resulting ploughing rates are given in Table 2.33 and Table 2.36. It is assumed in this study that two workers were required for ploughing. One would have controlled the oxen and plough and the other would help turning the plough and oxen at the end of the field as well as giving general assistance with feeding and watering the two oxen.

The type of land affects the ploughing rate and marginal land is harder to plough than best and average land. Land left fallow in the previous year is also harder to plough than land cultivated in the previous year. Table 2.32 shows the percentage increase in ploughing rates for marginal and best land compared with average land and whether the land had been left fallow or cultivated in the previous year. These calculations assume that the ploughing rates of Egyptian average land are 75% that of Cypriot average land.

Marginal land: % increase in ploughing rate compared with average land	Cyprus %	Egypt %
Land left fallow in previous year	145	135
Land cultivated in previous year	135	125
Best land: % decrease in ploughing rate compared with average land	**Cyprus %**	**Egypt %**
Land left fallow in previous year	–5	–5
Land cultivated in previous year	–7	–5

Table 2.32: Summary of adjusted ploughing labour-rates for land left fallow or cultivated the previous year.

[338] Russell 1988: 122, Table 25, the interpretation of Columella, *De re rustica* 2.4.8. Conversion units used: 1 iugera = 2,522 m^2 = 0.2522 hectares. Russell has assumed that the labour-rate for breaking fallow land reflects the additional time required to till a unit of land when cutting consecutive furrows with the ard in alternately upright and sloping positions (Russell 1988: 121–122, particularly Figure 16b).

[339] Russell 1988: 122, Table 26, the interpretation of Columella, *De re rustica* 2.12.8.

Broadcasting the seed and covering with soil labour-rates

The final stage of tillage and sowing is hand broadcasting or sowing directly into seed drills followed by covering the seed with a fine tilth of soil, by using hoes or an ard.[340] This activity is equivalent in modern terms to harrowing and ensures that the seed is covered sufficiently with soil to protect it from birds and vermin.[341]

Ethnographic evidence suggests that rakes, hoes, logs, or bundles of brush were used in the harrowing process.[342] Egyptian tomb scenes show farmers broadcasting seed, followed by the ard pulled by oxen (Figure 2.7).[343] The use of sheep and pigs to cover the seeds by trampling is also depicted in Egyptian tomb scenes.[344] Using animals would have been particularly well suited in the softer soils of the Delta.[345] Ploughing in the seed has a nominal labour-rate up to one man-day/ha maximum. American nineteenth century ethnographic evidence shows that the labour-rate for broadcast sowing was an average 0.367 man-days/ha.[346] The resulting combined labour-rates for tillage and broadcast sowing the seed for Cyprus and Egypt are given in Tables 2.33–2.36.

Figure 2.7: Broadcast sowing.
Sketch of Tylor et al 1895: Plate IV. The tomb of Paheri (EK 3).

[340] Reynolds 1981: 108.

[341] In dry farming regions, 0.1 m of soil cover is necessary to ensure sufficient moisture content for germination. In post inundation wet land such as in Egypt 0.05 m would be sufficient (Steensberg 1976: 272). Foaden and Fletcher 1908: 107 point out that if seeds are covered too deeply there would be too much moisture and too little air.

[342] Hillman 1984: 116.

[343] See also the scene in the MK tomb of Urarna, which shows the seed broadcast by a man ahead of the oxen (Vogelsang-Eastwood 2000: 270, Figure 11.2). Inscriptions with the tomb scenes at Meidum also attest to the plough used to cover the seed after sowing (Harpur 1987: 161).

[344] The MK tomb of Djehuty-Hetep at Bersheh shows two men sowing with a flock of sheep to trample in the seed (Stevenson Smith 1951: 324–325 and Figure 2). The NK tomb of Nebamun (TT 24) shows pigs trampling the seed (Newberry 1928: Plate XIX, Figure 2).

[345] The soft waterlogged soils were suitable for trampling (Lloyd 1976: 77) and the plough was probably more common in Upper Egypt (Murray 2000a: 519).

[346] Russell 1988: 115.

Land left fallow in previous year–man-days/ha	Marginal land	Average land	Best land
First ploughing breaking fallow land	15.8	11.3	10.7
Second ploughing	8	5.7	5.4
Cross plough to break up ridges	6	4.3	4.1
Fourth ploughing	2	1.4	1.4
Sowing	0.37	0.37	0.37
Ploughing in the seed	1	0.73	0.7
Total	**33.17**	**23.8**	**22.67**

Table 2.33: Cypriot tillage and sowing labour-rates (man-days/ha) for land left fallow in previous year.
Adapted from Russell 1988: 122–124.

Land left cultivated in the previous year–man-days/ha	Marginal land	Average land	Best land
First ploughing	7.4	5.7	5.1
Second ploughing	5.6	4.3	3.9
Cross ploughing	1.9	1.4	1.3
Sowing	0.37	0.37	0.37
Ploughing in the seed	0.9	0.73	0.7
Total	**16.17**	**12.5**	**11.37**

Table 2.34: Cypriot ploughing and sowing labour-rates (man-days/ha) for land cultivated in the previous year.
Adapted from Russell 1988: 122–124.

Land left fallow in previous year–man-days/ha	Marginal land	Average land	Best land
First ploughing	11.7	9.0	8.6
Cross ploughing	4.5	3.4	3.3
Third ploughing	1.5	1.1	1.1
Sowing	0.37	0.37	0.37
Ploughing in the seed	0.4	0.37	0.3
Total	**18.47**	**14.24**	**13.67**

Table 2.35: NK Egyptian ploughing and sowing labour-rates (man-days/ha) for land left fallow in previous year.

Land left cultivated in the previous year–man-days/ha	Marginal land	Average land	Best land
First ploughing	5.49	4.57	4.34
Sowing	0.37	0.37	0.37
Ploughing in the seed	0.44	0.37	0.35
Total	**6.3**	**5.31**	**5.06**

Table 2.36: NK Egyptian ploughing and sowing labour-rates (man-days/ha) for land cultivated in the previous year.

Hoeing and clod breaking labour-rates

An additional activity in preparing the land for cultivation is hoeing and clod breaking. To my knowledge there is no experimental archaeological on the labour-rates for the use of wooden hoes as used by the NK Egyptians (Figure 2.6) so my estimates of hoeing labour-rates are based on two ethnographic studies. Lewis's study of the mountainous Tepoztlán district in Mexico shows that bush land could be prepared for sowing at a labour-rate of 60 man-days/ha.[347] However, Lewis's findings were based on the use of steel hoes and these would be significantly more productive than the wooden hoes used in NK Egypt.

The FAO 2007 hoeing study with metal bladed hoes on good farmland suggests a hoeing labour-rate of 300 hrs/man/ha (33.3 man-days/ha assuming a 9 hour day).

For Cyprus, hoeing land for growing cereals or pulses, I have chosen 45 man-days/ha for average land left fallow the previous year. This based on reasonableness rather than experimental or ethnographic evidence. Lewis's study (60 man-days/ha) is reduced by 25 man-days/ha. This takes into account hoeing land on less difficult terrain but this labour-rate is increased in turn by 10 man-days to reflect the less efficient wooden hoe used in LBA Cyprus, compared with metal hoes used in Lewis's study. This results in a labour-rate = (60–25) + 10 = 45 man-days/ha for average land.

For Egypt, with mainly alluvial basin land, I have used as a starting point the FAO hoeing rate of 33.3 man-days/ha. However, the Egyptian alluvial soil within the basins would probably make hoeing easier than the FAO example and I have reduced it to 20 man-days/ha. To this, I have added 10 man-days/ha to compensate for the less efficient wooden hoes compared to the metal hoes used in the FAO example. This results in a labour-rate of 30 man-days/ha for average land left fallow the previous year. For both Cyprus and Egypt, the percentage increase and decrease in ploughing labour-rates for marginal and best land compared with average land that had been left fallow or cultivated the previous year are the same as the ratios used for ploughing in Table 2.32.

Ploughing with an ard causes the formation of hard segments of soil. The soil particles become closely packed together and on drying, the soil cracks to form clods.[348] If irrigated basin land is ploughed before the soil has dried out sufficiently after the inundation, the hot sun bakes the clods into hard lumps. If left, clods exacerbate the loss of water by evaporation from the sides of the large cracks that separate the clods. In addition, large clods act as isolated pockets of soil limiting root growth of young plants.[349] Land that is not level due to large clods also increases the evaporation of water following irrigation.[350] To improve seed germination the clods have to be broken down to a fine tilth.[351] Egyptian tomb paintings show workers using hoes in scenes that also depict ploughing and sowing.[352] It is possible that they are not hoeing but clod breaking instead.[353]

[347] Lewis 1951: 154–157, Table 38. Although the Tepoztlán district in Mexico is a temperate zone, Lewis's hoeing measurements were made on the slopes of the Cerros Colorados and on areas of black volcanic rocky ground where ploughing is not feasible. The land is characterised by rocky outcrops and semi-deciduous scrub forest.

[348] Foaden and Fletcher 1908: 91. Early nineteenth century study of agriculture in Egypt.

[349] Foaden and Fletcher 1908: 102–103.

[350] Foaden and Fletcher 1908: 103.

[351] One of the benefits of bare fallowing is that atmospheric conditions bring about a better tilth (Foaden and Fletcher 1908: 89). Variation in night and day temperature and in Cyprus, rainfall in winter, causes clods of soil to break down.

[352] Shore 1990: 164–166 suggests that the phrase *nḳrw m nḳr* in Heqanakht II, rt. 30 should be translated as 'smash the clods with a smashing.' He suggests that the long handled hoe in the tomb of Nakht in association with broadcasting seed, is a clod breaker.

[353] In the Yemeni a pick is used for breaking up clods turned up by the ard (Varisco 1982: 159). Scrapped pick heads were found on the Gelidonya wreck (Bass 1967c: 84, Figure 99).

Clod breaking would have been necessary in both LBA Cyprus and NK Egypt.[354] The labour-rate for clod breaking is a function of the area of land covered in clods and the human effort to break them up. A cautious estimate for the labour-rate for clod breaking is to assume that 15% of land area in Cyprus and 25% in Egypt required this preparation. The area is higher for Egypt than Cyprus because the saturated basin land, after the inundation, is more prone to clod formation as it dries out.

Workload for preparing the land

Ploughing and hoeing

Using the labour-rates derived above, the workload required for tillage (ploughing, hoeing, clod breaking, and covering the seed) can be calculated (Table 2.37). The results clearly show that tillage workload costs in terms of man-years of effort were significantly lower for Egypt than for Cyprus. This is due to the lower area of land required (as shown in Table 2.26) to be cultivated in NK Egypt as a result of the higher crop yields (Table 2.25) from the arable crops grown under basin agriculture.

Activity	Cyprus	Egypt
Ploughing	3,446	814
Hoeing	1,464	435
Clod breaking	1,256	433
Sowing	59	35
Covering seed	124	37
Total man-years	**6,349**	**1,754**

Table 2.37: Summary of workload for tillage and sowing of cereals, pulses, and fodder (man-years/100,000 cohort/yr).

Sowing

Table 2.38 provides the sowing workload associated with each type of crop. Because Egypt has a lower proportion of land classified as marginal, the workload is lower.

Crop	Cyprus	Egypt
Barley	27	16
Emmer wheat	16	8
Pulses	9	7
Vegetables and fruit	1	1
Fodder	6	3
Total man-years	**59**	**35**

Table 2.38: Sowing workload for both regions (man-years/100,000 cohort/yr).

Weeding

Weeds compete with crop plants for moisture, sunlight, and nutrients and contaminate the crop when it is harvested.[355] The ancient varieties of cereal varied considerably in standing height and short spikelets close to the ground could be covered by weeds and remain un-harvested.[356] Consequently, weeding was important to improve ancient crop yields and removing the weeds had an associated workload. Once a crop is established then ongoing weeding serves no additional benefit and can be a disadvantage, loosening the root system of the prime crop.[357] Basler demonstrates the importance of weeding in lentil production, particularly in the early part of the growing season before the lentil plants build up a protective canopy from weed infestation (Table 2.39).[358]

Sowing rate of lentils (kg/ha)	Yield from lentil fields that have been left un-weeded (kg/ha)	Yield from lentil fields following biannual weeding in the growing season (kg/ha)
100	59.8	642.3
150	89.9	586.8
200	61.9	440.5

Table 2.39: Ethnographic evidence for the influence of biannual weeding on lentil yield rates.

For the purposes of this study, it is assumed that in the LBA weeding was carried out using wooden hoes.[359] This study uses the FAO ethnographic study of weeding practices in Zimbabwe.[360] Weeding with a hoe varied from 15.6–7.2 man-days/ha with the labour-rate effort decreasing after each weeding cycle. This study assumes the crops were weeded three times before they became established. The Egyptian labour-rate has been reduced by 10% to reflect that the soil in the Egyptian basin field would be easier to weed than Zimbabwe land but Cyprus has similar conditions to Zimbabwe and the labour-rate is assumed to be the same. For each analysis there is a 10% uplift for weeding with less efficient wooden hoes rather than the metal hoes used in the ethnographic study (Table 2.40).[361]

Weeding	FAO 2007 man-days/ha	Cyprus man-days/ha	Egypt man-days/ha
First	15.6	17.1	15.4
Second (interpolated)	11.4	12.5	11.4
Third	7.2	8.3	7.2
Labour-rate	**34.2**	**37.9**	**34**

Table 2.40: Weeding labour-rate (man-days/ha) used in this study for cereal crops.

For cereals grown in Egypt, the archaeobotanical record suggests that minimal weeding was performed and the Egyptian weeding labour-rate for cereals is further reduced by 66%.[362] For the weeding of pulses a higher labour-rate is used. Basler's ethnographic study shows that to maximise lentil yields by traditional manual hand weeding required a labour-rate of 56 man-days/ha. A summary of the weeding labour rates is given in Table 2.41.[363]

[354] Goe 1982: 146. Ethnographic evidence from South Arabia shows that a 'sort of mallet' was used to break up clods of earth in the fields (Doe and Serjeant 1975: 7).

[355] See Arnon 1972a: 479 and Foaden and Fletcher 1908: 104–105.

[356] Reynolds 1981: 115, Figure 2.

[357] Reynolds 1981: 115.

[358] Basler 1981: 145, Table 1.

[359] Murray 2000a: 517.

[360] FAO 2007.

[361] If seeds were sown in rows then a light ard could have been used for weeding between the rows. Ethnographic evidence from Zimbabwe shows that the use of a donkey drawn cultivator can give a dramatic increase in productivity and the workload is reduced by 85% (Carr and Hartl 2010: 27).

[362] Murray 2000a: 520.

[363] Basler 1981: 147, Table 6. The early weeding operation by hand hoeing is 38.9 man-days/ha and the second weeding operation by hand pulling is 17.1 man-days/ha giving, a total of 56 man-days/ha.

Labour-rates man-days/ha	Cyprus man-days/ha	Egypt man-days/ha
Barley	37.9	22.7
Emmer wheat	37.9	22.7
Pulses	56	56
Fodder	37.9	34.4
Vegetables/fruit	37.9	34.4
Grapes	37.9	34.4

Table 2.41: Summary of the labour-rates for weeding by crop.

Weeding workload

The resultant workload for Cyprus and Egypt using the above labour-rates and the area of land under cultivation are 6,770 and 3,013 man-years respectively. The workload collated by crop is given in Table 2.42.

Weeding workload	Cyprus man-years	Egypt man-years
Barley	2,901	979
Emmer wheat	1,712	491
Pulses	1,311	977
Fodder	616	375
Vegetables/fruit	203	183
Grapes	27	8
Workload (man-years)	**6,770**	**3013**

Table 2.42: Summary of the weeding workload required for Cyprus and Egypt (man-years/100,000 cohort/yr).

Irrigation

Labour-rate for Egyptian basin irrigation

A key activity in the agrarian cycle was the maintenance of the basin infrastructure that controlled the inundation. We can get some perspective of the importance and scale of the activities involved, from the ethnographic studies in the nineteenth and early twentieth century by Willcocks.[364] He emphasises the importance of maintaining dykes, sluices, and the clearance of channels and canals. Effort was also required to control the flow of the inundation particularly when the inundation was above or below average. The heaviest particles of alluvial silt and sand in the floodwater were deposited first. This led to build up of deposits close to the water entry points to the basin, which had to be spread more evenly across the basin. The most common entry points were cuts in the dykes that had to be repaired following the inundation.[365] These time consuming activities would be necessary throughout the NK and this study has assumed a labour-rate of 95.6 man-days/inundation/farm. The number of farms/100,000 cohort was 8,723 and the resulting workload would be 2,656 man-years/100,000 cohort.[366]

Labour-rate for shaduf irrigation

The use of the shaduf was an innovation of the NK and the earliest evidence for its use is in an Eighteenth Dynasty tomb scene.[367] It comprised a container on a pole and lever device that lifted water from the river or canal. The water was then fed by a pipe to temporary channels in the soil that directed the water to where it was required (Figure 2.8).

Figure 2.8: Raising water with a shaduf.
Sketch of Davies 1933: Plate XLVI. The tomb of Neferhotep (TT 49).

The shaduf could only effectively raise water 1.5 m above the river and only irrigate an area up to 1.5 ha.[368] To raise water up to higher field systems (up to a maximum of 3–4 m) required three shadufs in series. Spillage between the three shadufs in series reduced the area that could be irrigated to a maximum of one ha.[369] This means that shadufs could only be a viable method of irrigation for horticultural plots close to sources of water. Because water collected by the shaduf did not carry silt, land irrigated by this method needed the application of animal dung and night soil.[370] This method of irrigation can be observed in modern Egypt today. Petrol/diesel driven pumps have replaced the shaduf but the same process of creating temporary earth channels and earth dams to direct and control the supply of the right amount water to the where it is needed, is still practiced.

The labour-rate estimates for Egypt are based on ethnographic evidence and NK tomb paintings, which depict the use of the shaduf. As Foaden and Fletcher point out, a single worker could not operate a shaduf continuously, so the following analysis assumes a team of three men was necessary. The three men would alternate tasks, sharing the effort of lifting the water and directing it along temporary earth channels made with a hoe, to the plants. Alternatively, the lifted water could be carried where it was needed in large pots on a shoulder yolk.[371]

The labour-rate (man-days/ha) to operate the shaduf is dependant on the average water requirement of crops and the discharge rate of a shaduf. Macdonald's 1920 study of

[364] Willcocks 1889 and Willcocks 1904.
[365] Willcocks 1889: 58.
[366] The calculation of basin irrigation workload is an iterative process as the total agrarian workload is also a function of the basin irrigation workload. The key steps from AGCALC are summarised in Report 2.8 in the Appendix.
[367] Murray 2000a: 515.
[368] Butzer 2001: 185 and Forbes 1993: Table IV, 38–39.
[369] Forbes 1993: Table IV, 38–39.
[370] Butzer 1976: 89–90.
[371] Eyre 1994b: 63.

the volume of water needed for second crops grown without the benefit of flood water, was 1,510 m^3/feddan for wheat, 1,575 m^3/feddan for barley, 1,340 m^3/feddan for beans, 3.560 m^3/feddan, and 2,000 m^3/feddan for onions. Taking an average of the beans and onions as typical for LBA horticulture, AGCALC uses a water volume requirement of 1,670 m^3/feddan/yr (701 m^3/ha/yr) for land that has not received flood water.[372] Foaden and Fletcher's measurements of the discharge rate of shadufs made in the early twentieth century was 5.88 m^3/hr.[373] The shaduf labour-rate would be 701 (water requirement m^3/ha/yr) × 3 (no of men in team) ÷ (5.88 (discharge rate of a shaduf m^3/hr) × 9 (hrs worked/day)) = 40 man-days/ha/yr.

Manual irrigation in Cyprus

In modern Cyprus today only 16.2% (35,000 ha) of the total agricultural land is artificially irrigated.[374] It is assumed that because the annual rainfall in Cyprus ranges from 350 to 400 mm, the demand for irrigation would be significantly lower than Egypt. However, rainfall patterns are variable and at times some irrigation would be necessary.[375] This study has assumed that for Cyprus the demand for irrigation is 20% that of Egypt and equal to 140 m^3/ha/yr. There is no evidence in the archaeological record that shadufs were in use in Cyprus. Water could have been carried to the crops perhaps in pots fitted to a yoke across the shoulders as practiced in NK Egypt. It is reasonable to assume that without the mechanical advantage from the fulcrum of a shaduf, the labour effort of lifting pots out of a water source and carrying full pots to the crops would be greater and this study assumes an increase in labour-rate of 2.5 times that of Egypt.[376] The resulting Cypriot irrigation labour-rate = water requirement (140 m^3/ha/yr) × increase in labour-rate due to use of pots verses shadufs (2.5 × 2 workers/team ÷ 5.88 (discharge of shaduf (m^3/hr) × 9 hours/working day) = 13.2 man-days/ha.

Workload for manual irrigation in Cyprus and Egypt

This study assumes that all the cereals, and half the pulses and green fodder cultivated, were sustained by the annual rainfall in Cyprus and by basin irrigation in the NK and therefore did not require manual irrigation. It is also supposed that all the horticultural and viticultural requirements were sustained by manual irrigation. The irrigation required for oleoculture is limited to supporting young olive trees. The resulting workload by crop is given in Table 2.43.

Irrigation workload	Cyprus man-years	Egypt man-years
Barley	13	26
Emmer wheat	14	22
Pulses	21	43
Fodder	0	7
Vegetables and fruit	46	90
Grapes	3	4
Olives	8	0
	105	**192**
Inundation control	-	2,656
Total workload	**105**	**2,848**

Table 2.43: Summary of the irrigation workload for Cyprus and Egypt (man-years/100,000 cohort/yr).

Harvesting

Harvesting of wheat and barley has four stages: reaping, collecting, binding, and transportation to the threshing area. All four stages appear in Egyptian tomb paintings from the OK to the NK.[377] Timing is critical as Halstead and Jones observed that even a few days delay in the harvesting of ripe crops can lead to severe losses from birds.[378]

Reaping

To reap the crop the Egyptians used curved sickles made of wood with sharp, flaked stones inserted within a groove in the wood. Although copper and bronze blades were used later, the stone sickles remained in use throughout the Pharaonic Period.[379] Scenes of reaping in the NK appear in the tombs of Paheri (Figure 2.9) Sennedgem, and Nakht. They show that grain was harvested by holding the ears of grain in one hand and cutting below it with the sickle.[380]

The studies of Steensberg and Korobkova have been used here to estimate the labour-rates for reaping standing grain, using sickles with flaked stone inserts. The two studies show that these sickles could achieve a harvesting rate of 24.6 ± 3.1 man-days/ha at the 95% confidence limit.[381] This compares favourably with the experimental

[372] Macdonald 1920: 18. Note Macdonald 1920: 19 emphasises the losses incurred through evaporation, which is included in the volume given.

[373] Foaden and Fletcher 1908: 173.

[374] Papadopoulos *et al* 2005: 80.

[375] Cereals require a minimum rainfall *c*.200 mm per annum (Murray 2000a: 513). It is reasonable to assume that some irrigation was required in the drier parts of Cyprus during the early growing period of cereals. It is also likely that for farming to be sustainable, irrigated cereal productions would require alternate seasons of leaving the land fallow and crop rotation.

[376] This also includes the workload required to dig ponds near to orchards, down to below the water table to create accessible sources of water (Eyre 1994b: 66).

[377] The NK tomb of the nomarch Paheri (Tylor 1895: Plates III–V) has a comprehensive scene of agriculture. See also the tombs of Sennedgem (TT 1) in Hodel-Hoenes 2000: Figures 181–183, Nakht (TT 52) in Hodel-Hoenes 2000: Figures 11 and the tomb of Menna (TT 69) in Murray 2000a: Figure 21.10).

[378] Halstead and Jones 1997: 282 ethnographic study of the agricultural year in the Greek islands of Karpathos and Amorgos.

[379] An example is shown in Murray 2000a: Figure 21.8. For a summary of the different designs of sickles and the problem of interpreting what plant was reaped or how the crop was reaped from the patterns of wear of the stone inserts, see Murray 2000a: 520–521 and an Egyptian example in Figure 21.8.

[380] Hodel-Hoenes 2000: Figure 182. It is possible that this tomb scene is representing the afterlife ideal where the corn was abundant and grew to a great height. In contrast, the Sixth Dynasty tomb of Hesi at Saqqara, depicts the cutting of the cereal crop closer to the ground (Kanawati 2001: 88: Figure 90).

[381] Steensberg 1943: 23 and Korobkova 1981: 340. Experimental evidence shows that reaping tool with flints for the cutting edge was inferior to modern ones by a factor of 1.7 (Korobkova 1981: 341).

results of 23.2 man-days/ha.[382] Similarly, ethnographic evidence from the semi-arid Greek Islands of Amorgos demonstrates that harvesting of barley and wheat took 1.5 man-days per stremma (15 man-days/ha).[383]

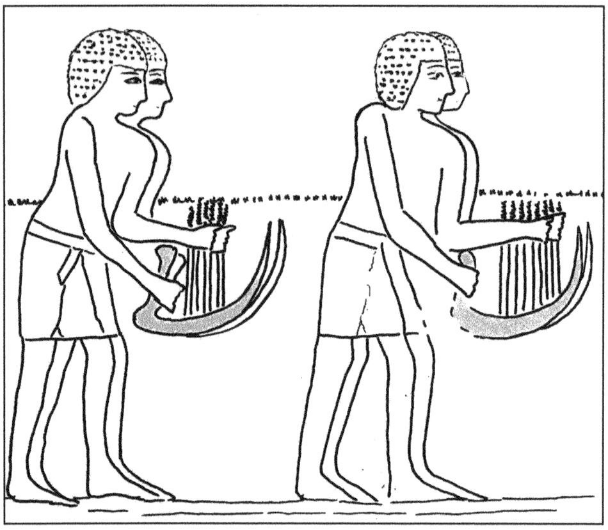

Figure 2.9: Reaping grain.
Sketch of Tylor et al 1895: Plate IV. The tomb of Paheri (EK 3).

On the island of Karpathos, a harvesting labour-rate of 30 man-days/ha was recorded for wheat. However, most of the harvesters were elderly women, which increased the length of time taken, contract labour only took 10 man-years/ha.[384] All of these labour-rates are in the range of Steensberg's and Korobkova's studies (10–30 man-days/ha). In addition, these labour-rates are within the range of reaping rates in Anderson's experiments using replicas of Neolithic one-bladed harvested knives, which incorporated a stone flake cutting edge.[385] A number of 25 m^2 plots of wild einkorn wheat ears were harvested taking between 45 and 120 minutes to complete (3.3–8.9 man-days/ha). It is probable that as many people as possible, irrespective of gender, age, and skill, would have joined in the harvest. This would have the effect of increasing the overall labour-rate for harvest and a labour-rate of 24.6 man-days/ha has been used in this study for reaping cereals. This is within the upper end of the experimental and ethnographic evidence.

Ethnographic evidence from the Greek islands, northern Africa, the Middle East, Ethiopia, and the Indian subcontinent, demonstrates that the lentil and other pod pulses were harvested by hand, pulling up the plants. They were left in piles in the field for drying before being collected and taken to a central threshing facility.[386] The only published labour-rate for this operation is from the island of Amorgos where pulling up pulses had a lower labour-rate than grain, of one man-day/stremma (10 man-days/ha).[387] This labour-rate has been used as in input parameter in AGCALC for Cypriot pulse harvesting.

Binding and transporting the harvest

The harvested cereal was bound together in sheaves, transported by foot or donkey, and stacked into heaps to await threshing.[388] This study calculates the time taken to bind the sheaves, load and unload the donkey, and transport the sheaves to the threshing shed. Ethnographic evidence from Greece shows that 7–12 donkey loads were required to clear the harvest from an area of one stremma.

Parameters	Assumption
Average farm area ha	3
Average farm area km^2	0.03
Speed of donkey km/hr	3.2
Average distance travelled to and from field km	0.16
Total distance travelled per return journey km	13.6
Hours in transit from the field to the threshing floor	4.3
Binding, loading and unloading time hrs	2.5
Loading and unloading time hrs	212.5
Total transport time plus loading/unloading hrs	219.3
Hours worked/day	9
Cypriot transport labour-rate (man-days/ha)	**24.4**
% uplift for Egypt compared with Cyprus due to dispersed field systems	30
Egyptian transport labour-rate (man-days/ha)	**31.7**

Table 2.44: Assumptions used to estimate the transport labour-rate (man-days/ha).

Using this labour-rate and assuming that the threshing shed is in the centre of the farm, the man-day requirement for transport is 24.4 man-days/ha.[389] The assumptions used in AGCALC are given in Table 2.44 and based on a farm of 3 ha. This simplified model assumes that the farmland was distributed evenly around a central farmhouse, which is more characteristic of the traditional farms of the north-eastern Mediterranean. It is clear from the letters of Heqanakht that in Egyptian farms, the fields were not contiguous. To compensate for this, the transport labour-rate for Egypt has been uplifted by 30% to 31.7 man-days/ha.

Figure 2.10 shows harvested grain transported by men in NK Egypt, other tomb scenes show that donkeys were also used.[390] The resulting workload for harvesting, binding, and loading of crops into panniers, and transport of crops for further processing for threshing and winnowing or directly into storage is summarised in Table 2.45.

[382] Russell 1988: 115–118 and Simms and Russell 1997: 699.
[383] One stremma = 0.1 ha.
[384] Halstead and Jones 1997: 279.
[385] Anderson 1999: 126, Figure 12.8.
[386] Halstead and Jones 1997: 279 and Muehlbauer *et al* 2002.
[387] Halstead and Jones 1997: 279.
[388] Modern ethnographic studies show that sheaves were transported at night or early morning when the moisture content was high, because this inhibited shedding of grain seed (Hillman 1984: 121).
[389] This assumes that 7–12 donkey loads/stremma (70–120 donkey loads/ha) were required to transport loads of straw and grain to the threshing floor (Halstead and Jones 1997: 279).
[390] The transport of harvested sheaves carried in a pannier strung below a pole by two workers is also depicted in the tomb of Menna (TT 69) (Murray 2000a: Figure 21.10). For a scene of sheaves transported by donkey, see the tomb of Pepyankh-heryib at Meir (Kanawati 2001: 88: Figure 91).

Weeding workload	Cyprus man-years	Egypt man-years
Barley	3,743	2,432
Emmer wheat	2,207	1,222
Pulses	805	729
Fodder	794	613
Vegetables/fruit	260	299
Grapes	34	16
Total man-years	**7,843**	**5,311**

Table 2.45: Workload (man-years/100,000 cohort/yr) for harvesting and transport of the crop.

Figure 2.10: Transporting harvested grain.
Sketch of Tylor et al 1895: Plate V. The tomb of Paheri (EK 3).

Threshing and winnowing grain and pulses

Harvested wheat and barley has to be threshed and winnowed to separate the spikelets of wheat and the ears of barley from the straw and chaff. Evidence for threshing and winnowing in NK Egypt comes from tomb scenes, archaeobotanical and archaeological remains, and the experimental archaeology of Samuel.[391] Evidence for the likely practice in LBA Cyprus comes from the ethnographic studies of Halstead and Jones who observed the threshing and winnowing processes in Amorgos and Karpathos and from Hillman who studied traditional farming in Turkey.[392]

NK Egypt

Cattle or donkeys were used to thresh the harvested cereal by trampling it as they moved round a shallow circular pit (Figure 2.11).[393] For smaller quantities, men might trample the cereal and beat it with sticks.[394] The hot dry climate in Egypt provided the ideal conditions for threshing because cereal crops are more brittle when dry and break up more easily.

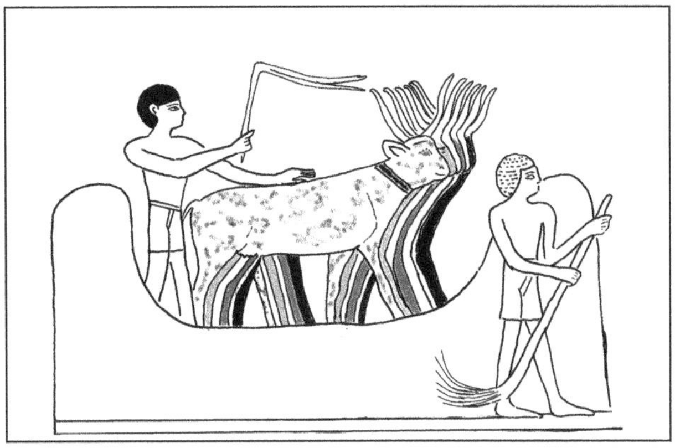

Figure 2.11: Threshing grain by oxen.
Sketch of Tylor et al 1895: Plate IV. The tomb of Paheri (EK 3).

When threshed, the ears of wheat separate into spikelets, which still have the glume attached to each grain, and the barley grains retain their hulls.[395] The threshed grain was then winnowed (Figure 2.12) to remove large fragments of straw, chaff that had separated, and any stones or other debris. When the bulk of the straw was removed, the pile of grain was winnowed again using shovels designed to fit in each hand.[396] At this point, the spikelets of wheat and hulled barley were stored until they were further processed.[397]

The grains of emmer wheat and barley that were grown in the LBA are enclosed in a bract called a glume (also termed chaff, hull, and husk) that tightly encases the grain. Indigestible to humans, this has to be removed and the process for doing this is the same for wheat and barley.[398]

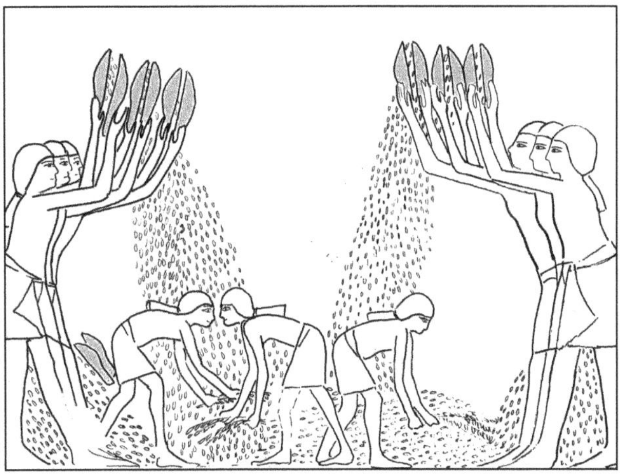

Figure 2.12: Winnowing grain with hand shovels.
Sketch of Davies and Gardiner 1936: Plate LI. The tomb of Menna (TT 69).

[391] Samuel 1993, 2000, and 2010.
[392] Hillman 1984 and Halstead and Jones 1997: 275—278.
[393] Kanawati 2001: 88: Figure 92 shows donkeys moving around a central point treading on the grain spread on the ground (Sixth Dynasty tomb of Ankhmahor at Saqqara).
[394] Eighteenth Dynasty tomb paintings of threshing in the tombs of Djeserkaraseneb (TT 38), Menna (TT 69), and Paheri (EK 3), show oxen trampling harvested ears of grain (see Murray 2000a for references for tomb paintings). Both methods of threshing are depicted in TT 69.

[395] Samuel 2000: 541, Figure 22.3 provides a flow diagram of all the stages in the process described here.
[396] Murray 2000a: 525.
[397] Samuel 1993: 278–279.
[398] These cereals are found widely in the archaeological record (Samuel 1993: 278). Chaff in the human diet also inhibits the absorption of nutrients (Samuel 2000: 545). Once removed from the grain the chaff could be fed to livestock.

The cereal was pounded in a granite or quartzite mortar, with a long wooden pestle. Carried out by a person standing, it required vigorous effort (Figure 2.13). The pounding separated the whole grain from the chaff and left some large cracked grain fragments, spikelets without the grain, and chaff.[399] In her experiments, Samuel found that dampening the cereal meant that the chaff could be more easily separated and the grain was not overly crushed. However, if this was done then the cereal would need to be dried before the next stage, which was further winnowing and sieving. Each activity had to be repeated several times to remove the separated spikelets and chaff and it took considerable effort to produce clean grains of wheat and barley that were finally picked over by hand.[400] Samuel considers that the sieving shown in Figure 2.13 depicts the sieving of the pounded mass and not as sometimes suggested, the sieving of flour.[401]

LBA Cyprus

As in NK Egypt, LBA Cyprus grew emmer wheat and hulled barley.[402] The ethnographic evidence from the Greek islands and Turkey show that a similar process to that suggested for Egypt was followed: threshing by trampling, winnowing, pounding with a mortar and pestle, winnowing again, course and fine sieving, and hand sorting, resulting in clean grain.[403] These activities were affected by the weather and each stage could vary in the time necessary depending on the conditions, taking from hours to days.[404] Hot dry conditions were ideal, cool damp conditions slowed each stage considerably.[405] The time required to complete the winnowing was directly proportional to wind strength and could take between a couple of hours up to several days.[406] In addition, it was sometimes necessary to thresh, winnow, and sieve the grain a second time or third time.[407]

There were some differences in regional practice; in Karpathos and Amorgos, Halstead did not observe the process of pounding after threshing and winnowing. In Turkey, the spikelets might be parched to make the chaff brittle before pounding and the semi-clean grain might be washed before drying and storing.[408] In both regions, a sledge with sharp, knapped, flints was sometimes used for threshing instead of trampling.[409] For small quantities of cereal, threshing could be done by beating with a stick or lashing the sheaves against a frame or stones.[410] In Turkey, the stored grain was semi-clean and in the Greek Islands, clean grain was stored.

The ethnographic studies of Halstead and Jones, Hillman, and Muehlbauer *et al* and the experimental archaeology of Samuel, demonstrate that there could be variation in the process used to separate clean grain from straw and chaff.[411] However, it has been assumed that each region employed a methodology appropriate to their type of cereal and climate and that the total labour demands for all traditional farming overall would be comparable.

Threshing and winnowing labour-rates and workload for Cyprus and Egypt

Historical data from U.S. Department of Labour (1899) suggests that the total threshing and winnowing took between 30.66–33.33 hrs/20 bushel, which equates to 0.056–0.061 hrs/ha.[412] Ethnographic evidence from Iran where oxen were used to trample over harvested grain ears and stalks, fork winnowing, and sieve winnowing has similar labour-rates of 0.055–0.070 hrs/kg. These labour-rates include fork winnowing followed by sieving with a combined labour-rate of 0.015–0.02 hrs/kg.[413]

This study uses the maximum value from the Iranian evidence = 0.07 hrs/kg and assumes a 9 hr working day. This rate has to be converted to man-days/ha to determine the workload for threshing and winnowing of grain. As the average yield of wheat/ha is greater than for barley, the equivalent labour-rates for barley and wheat are 5.13 and 5.55 man-days/ha respectively.[414] A lower labour-rate of 2.5 man-days/ha seems reasonable for threshing and winnowing of pulses as they are more loosely attached to

399 Samuel 1993: 278. Finds of mortars are common in the domestic housing at the Workmen's villages of Amarna and Deir el-Medina.

400 This cleaning phase in Samuel's experiments was time consuming but in ancient times it would have been done more efficiently by experienced workers. In large-scale operations such as large households and temple bakeries, a team of people might have carried out each step making the whole process quicker (Samuel 2000: 562).

401 Samuel 1993: 276–283–282.

402 Stewart 1974: 125–129.

403 Oxen or donkeys were tethered to a central post and driven round on a hard, circular, floor (Halstead and Jones 1997: 275).

404 Halstead and Jones 1997: 275. On a still day, course sieving could replace winnowing for small quantities of grain (Halstead and Jones 1997: 277).

405 Halstead and Jones 1997: 275. Threshing was carried out when the sun was at its highest. This facilitated the shedding of seed when the ears were at their driest.

406 Halstead and Jones 1997: 275. A breeze of dry air facilitated the separation of chaff and straw during the winnowing.

407 This was done when the grain was barley or the harvest was too large to process in one threshing (Halstead and Jones 1997: 276). Hillman 1984: 124 observed the use of shovels and baskets and other objects for additional winnowing. Repeated sieving could take place during winnowing and two to four people might be employed at a time (Halstead and Jones 1997: 277).

408 Hillman 1984: 129. The Turkish farmers parched the spikelets by leaving them on plates or drying platforms. In colder areas, kilns and hot stones were used to parch the wheat spikelets. Samuel 2000: 562 considers that parching was not necessary in Egypt.

409 Hillman 1984: 122–123 and Halstead and Jones 1997: 275. For ethnographic and experimental archaeology evidence for threshing sledges, see Skakun 1999: 203–207. For evidence of this type of sledge in the archaeological record, see Ataman 1999. Threshing sledges have been found across in all areas of the north-eastern Mediterranean and Whittaker 2003: 376 suggests they could have been used in the Bronze age if not earlier. It has been assumed that they were used in Cyprus in the LBA. Also, see Hornell 1930, Myres 1931: 32, and Whittaker 2000 for additional ethnographic evidence.

410 Samuel 1993: 276-283, 282.

411 Hillman 1984, Halstead and Jones 1997, and Muehlbauer *et al* 2002.

412 Russell 1988: 125, Table 31. The unit of 20 US bushels of cereals is a customary unit of volume used in the US cereal industry and equates to 544.32 kg. The bushel takes into account humidity and air gap interstices.

413 To thresh 100 *mann* (300 kg) of wheat using oxen took between 12–15 hrs. To winnow 300 kg of wheat took 3–4 hrs and the final winnowing using a sieve basket took 1.5–2 hrs (Watson 1979: 82).

414 This small difference between wheat and barley is explained by the higher yield of wheat compared with barley and the difference in dry densities of the two cereals.

the pod than grain kernels are to the husk. The resulting workload for combined threshing and winnowing is given in Table 2.46.[415]

Crops	Cyprus man-years	Egypt man-years
Barley	391	220
Emmer wheat	251	120
Pulses	93	44
Total	**735**	**384**

Table 2.46: Workload for threshing and winnowing wheat, barley, and pulses (man-years/100,000 cohort/yr).

Milling cereals in Cyprus and Egypt

In the LBA Eastern Mediterranean, the cleaned cereal grains were milled into flour on a saddle quern.[416] In modern traditional farming, this technology has been replaced by a rotary hand mill and so the evidence for milling relates to archaeological finds in NK Egypt and recent experimental archaeology. It is assumed that the process of milling was similar in LBA Cyprus.[417]

Milling was carried out by grinding the cleaned grain on a rectangular base stone. In NK Egypt, a round or cylindrical shaped hand-stone with a flattened grinding base was pushed over the grain to crush it.[418] A base quern stone found at Amarna measures about 400 mm by 180 mm and although no ancient Egyptian hand-stones have been identified, artistic representations suggest they were elongated domes, longer than the width of the base stone.[419] The base stone was supported on a frame that tilted it away from the miller (Figure 2.13).

Figure 2.13: Grinding and sieving grain.
Sketch of Davies et al 1920: Plate VI. The tomb of Antefoker (TT 60).

This allowed the flour to fall into a basket at the lower end and reduced to effort required to push the stone over the grain. Sloping querns have been found across Near East and in Asia Minor.[420] The tomb scenes and models show that women milled the grain and Samuel considers that the adoption of a sloping quern stone meant that they could either mill for longer periods or that older women could have been employed, freeing up younger women for other tasks.[421]

Milling labour-rates and workload

This study bases the labour-rate for milling on the experimental archaeology of Samuel.[422] She tested five different types of emmer wheat with a range of hardness and found it was possible to grind course and fine flour on the same quern.[423] Course flour was produced by taking batches of grain and making 10 passes of the hand-stone across and back the length of the stone. This flour could be re-ground with a further 20 passes to produce fine flour or 30 passes to make extra fine flour. Samuel suggests from her and other's experimental results that to grind flour for domestic daily consumption would take approximately 3 hours.[424] This study has used her results for grinding emmer Zimmerhackl, a very hard type of emmer wheat representative of those found in NK Egypt (Table 2.47).[425] Certain assumptions have to be made on the type of flour generally consumed and this study has allocated 55%, 35%, and 10% for coarse, average, and fine flour respectively.[426]

Milling very hard emmer wheat	Coarse flour	Average flour	Fine flour
Av. secs to mill 1 kg	1,830	2,770	4,600
Time hrs to grind 1 kg	0.51	0.77	1.28
Labour-rate man-days/kg	0.056	0.085	0.142

Table 2.47: Labour-rate to mill hard emmer wheat using a reproduction of an Egyptian saddle quern.
Adapted from Samuel 2010: 474, Table 4.

To convert the labour-rate to mill one kg of grain (man-days/kg) to the labour-rate to mill cereals from one ha of land, the following formula is used. Labour-rate (man-days/ha) = time to mill one kg of grain (man-days/kg) × average yield of barley or wheat (kg/ha). For Egypt, average yields for barley and wheat are 1,498 and 1,567 kg/ha and for Cyprus, the average yields for barley and wheat are 660 and 714 kg/ha (See again Tables 2.24–2.25). The resulting labour-rates are given in Table 2.48. To calculate the workload for milling sufficient barley and wheat for a 100,000 cohort/yr, the following formula is used, workload (man-years/100,000 cohort/yr) = milling labour-rates (man-days/ha) from Table 2.48 ×

[415] Workload is the labour-rate × area of land (Table 2.28 and Table 2.32) ÷ 314 (days worked/year).

[416] Curtis 2001: 201. Querns have been found in LBA contexts in Cyprus (Williams-Thorpe *et al* 1991: 28–29, Figure 1). Numerous saddle querns have been found at Deir el-Medina (Bruyère 1939: 250 and 328) and at Amarna (Peet and Woolley 1923: 78–79, 88–89).

[417] The rotary quern was invented later in the Western Mediterranean in the fifth to third centuries B.C. (Samuel 2000: 560).

[418] For examples of Egyptian saddle querns, see Darby *et al* 1976: 506, Figure 12.3 and Samuel 2000: 560. A model bakery, from the tomb of Meketre, Thebes, early Twelfth Dynasty (Metropolitan Museum of Art 20.3.12), shows three workers using stone saddle querns (Samuel 2010: 447, Figure 7).

[419] A saddle quern found at Amarna was used in the archaeological experiments on milling (Samuel 1993: 279, Figure 4).

[420] Grégoire 1999: 251.

[421] Samuel 2010: 458–459 and 467–468. The conclusion that women milled grain comes from tomb scenes and models that do not show men performing this task (Roehrig 1996: 15).

[422] In particular Samuel 2010.

[423] Samuel 2010: 489. The grain was ground and reground in 10g batches.

[424] Samuel 2010: 464.

[425] Samuel 2010: 473, Table 4.

[426] As Samuel points out, the widespread examples of bread made of coarse flour found in the archaeological record may be a taste preference for textured bread (Samuel 2010: 467). The majority of particles produced on the experimental quern were coarser, and Samuel mostly uses the term 'meal' for them. I consider that the time available for the wives of agrarian workers to produce fine flour would be limited.

area of land under cultivation (ha) from Table 2.30 ÷ 314 days worked per year.

Cypriot milling labour-rates man-days/ha	Coarse flour	Average flour	Fine flour
Barley	37.3	56.4	93.7
Emmer wheat	40.3	61.0	101.4
Egyptian milling labour-rates man-days/ha	**Coarse flour**	**Average flour**	**Fine flour**
Barley	84.6	128.1	212.7
Emmer wheat	88.5	134.0	222.5

Table 2.48: Labour-rates to mill barley and wheat for Cyprus and Egypt.

A summary of the results is given in Table 2.49 and demonstrates the considerable workload penalty for Egypt compared with Cyprus. This higher workload has two main causes; the most significant is the higher yields that increased the labour-rates/ha as shown in Table 2.48. Also, the total percentage of calories obtained from cereals in the Cypriot diet was lower than that of Egypt, 66.7% and 72.7% respectively (Tables 2.8 and 2.9).

Crops	Cyprus man-years	Egypt man-years
Barley	3,791	4,864
Emmer wheat	2,418	2,558
Total	**6,209**	**7,422**

Table 2.49: Workload (man-years) required to mill cereals in Cyprus and Egypt to feed a cohort of 100,000/yr.

Bakeries and brewing

Barley and emmer wheat grains were used for making beer and bread, the main staples of the LBA diet. The importance of both is attested in the ancient Egyptian archaeological record and administrative documents. They demonstrate that everyone, from the highest to the most humble, consumed these items every day and desired to consume them in their afterlife.[427] Previous interpretations of the methods for making bread and beer were based on the scenes and models in Egyptian tombs.[428] Recent archaeological and archaeobotanical evidence has provided a greater understand of how these foodstuffs were processed. This section considers the labour-rate and workload implications of the production of bread and beer on a domestic scale by the general population.

Bread

Tomb scenes, temple lists, and actual finds of loaves demonstrate that many different kinds of bread were baked. The majority of the surviving ancient Egyptian loaves are made from emmer and barley was rarely used.[429] The milled grain was mixed with water and other desired additives and then kneaded into a bread dough.[430] Flat unleavened breads could be baked immediately and if leavened bread was required then yeast could be added and the bread left to rise before baking.[431] Many querns and circular (round) ovens have been found in domestic contexts at Amarna and Deir el-Medina.[432] It is thought that these households were supplied with rations of unprocessed grain and were responsible for making their own bread.[433] Although at Amarna large bakeries have been found capable of the production of considerable quantities of loaves, it is not certain whether this was only for religious festival days and whether all or some of the population were provided with the bread.[434] In terms of workload, bread produced in the home would require less effort compared with the workload of milling the grain into flour. In the domestic setting it was an activity carried out by the women of the family and it was necessary to bake bread every day of the year.

Beer production

Beer is made from complex starches in the grain that are broken down into simple sugars and then fermented into alcohol by yeast.[435] NK Egyptian archaeobotanical evidence of whole grains, cereal chaff, and the shreds of cereal tissues show that beer was made from emmer wheat, barley, and sometimes a combination of the two.[436]

The finds of large vats, firebricks, and charcoal from Abydos and Hierakonpolis suggest that beer production, even in the Predynastic Period, could be a large scale, batch production process.[437] Similarly in Cyprus, installations dated to *c.*2300–1650 B.C. thought to be ovens, have been excavated at Kissonerga-Skalia in the south-west of the island.[438] Two pithoi (*c.*2200 B.C.) from Myrtos have residues that indicate barley or a barley product had been added to wine.[439] Organic residues from tripod cooking pots from the Middle Minoan site of Apodoulou in south-west Crete show that beer or beer/wine mixtures were produced.[440]

[427] Samuel 2000: 537.

[428] A MK tomb model of baking and brewing is given in Kemp 1991: 121, Figure 42.

[429] For detailed descriptions of the baking of bread and loaves at Amarna, see Kemp 1994: 145–151, Samuel 2000: 563–569, and Curtis 2001: 124–131.

[430] Samuel 1999: Figure 2 for a diagram of the ancient process from grain to loaves.

[431] All the bread samples found at Amarna contained yeast cells (Curtis 2000: 138). The source of the yeast is not known and although some scholars have proposed that it was from the froth from fermenting beer, yeast from this source does not always flourish in bread dough (Samuel 2000: 546). Amarna tomb scenes show two types of bread, flat bread and conical loaves made in a clay mould. It is possible that the shaped breads were for religious offerings (Curtis 2001: 131).

[432] Curtis 2001: 124–125 and Meskell 2002: 122–124.

[433] At Amarna, many households had their own mortars and querns and it is possible that those that did not shared communal facilities or those of a neighbour. About half the houses had a cylindrical oven at the rear of the house but it is possible that some ovens were located on the roof (Samuel 1999: 139).

[434] Kemp suggests that several hundred workers could have produced 20,000 loaves (Kemp 1994: 148–149).

[435] Samuel 2000: 550.

[436] Samuel 1996: 5.

[437] Samuel 2000: 539–544.

[438] It is possible that they were drying-kilns used for drying or curing malt or malt cakes used in the production of beer (Crewe and Hill 2012).

[439] Martlew 1999: 159.

[440] Martlew 1999: 162, 166, 172 and Martlew 2004: 140–143. Pots from Late Minoan IA and IIIA2 ritual contexts indicate that a cocktail of

Egyptian tomb scenes and models show different stages of beer making but they do not show the whole process or the sequence of the activities.[441] From these sources, some scholars suggest that lightly baked, richly yeasted bread was crumbled into a sieve with water, and the liquid was then left to ferment. There is disagreement on whether grain was malted and whether dates were added to the brew.[442] From the microscopic examination of starch grains in beer residues, Samuel suggests that the processing of the grain for making beer was a two-stage process, each having a different effect on the breaking down of starch into maltose sugar.[443] She suggests that a proportion of the total volume of grain was moistened and left to sprout, producing maltose sugars.[444] The sprouted, malted grain was dried, ground, and made into dough with water.[445] The dough was baked lightly and then crumbled into water (mashing). The remaining portion of grain was coarsely ground, mixed with water, and heated. The two parts were then added together and sieved to collect the maltose rich and flavoursome liquid called wort. Yeast may have been added from a previous brew of beer, from yeast rich skins of fruit, or the same vessel with yeasty residues might have been used again. Finally the wort was left to ferment.[446] The beer could vary in strength depending on the amount of water added in the process, the length of time allowed for fermentation, whether sugars from honey or dates were added, and whether the strained ground mass was reused for a weaker brew.[447] Scottish Courage Brewers in 1996 brewed a beer with 6% alcohol content by volume using NK Egyptian production practices. The beer was made from a 1:1 mix of emmer malt and un-malted emmer.[448] The remaining sweet mass of malted solids is thought to have been eaten, providing a valuable food source.[449] The beer was either drunk immediately or decanted into jars and sealed for storage or transport.[450]

The method for ancient brewing proposed by Samuel bears similarities with the production of a beer called *bouza* brewed by Coptic and Nubian populations in modern Egypt.[451] Approximately 75% of the grain is coarsely ground, mixed with water and kneaded into a dough, which is lightly baked into loaves. The remaining ground wheat grains are moistened with water and allowed to germinate for 3–5 days producing a malt mix that is dried in the sun before grinding and mixing with the loaves of bread. The bread is added to water and the fermentation process is started using *bouza* from a previous brew and the mixture allowed to ferment at room temperature for a 24-hour period. The wort is sieved to remove large particles and diluted with water before bottling.[452] Lucas measured the alcohol content of 16 samples of bouza from Cairo that ranged from 6.2–8.1%. Unlike most modern beers, bouza has a consistency of thin gruel, yellow in colour, with a yeasty taste showing the beer is still fermenting.[453]

The grain used for making beer was only lightly milled leaving the husk in place and so the most labour demanding aspect of brewing beer was in keeping the grain moist to allow it sufficient time to sprout, perhaps 5–7 days.[454] The brewing elapse time to produce a batch of beer was around 8–14 days and it had a shelf life of seven days. The daily consumption of beer by each family meant that beer making was a frequent activity.[455]

Bread and beer labour-rate and workload

To estimate the workload required to supply a family of six individuals with bread and beer, an average of one hour/day/family seems realistic.[456] Only the workload for the domestic production of bread and beer within a family home is estimated. It is assumed that for non-agrarian workers residing in urban or military complexes, bread and beer was produced in large bakeries and breweries. Bread and beer production in large state bakeries is an added-value process and excluded from this analysis.[457] Ethnographic evidence demonstrates that in the household, females carried out this operation and it would have formed a part of other daily activities. It is estimated here that on average one hour every day was spent baking and brewing beer. The resulting workload /100,000 cohort for Egypt and Cyprus was 1,852 man-years (Table 2.50).[458]

Number of families/100,000 cohort	16,667
Number of man-days	675,939
Total workload (man-years)	**1,852**

Table 2.50: Workload (man-years/100,000 cohort/yr) to make bread and beer.

wine, resinated wine, beer, and mead was produced. Testing of beer brewing vats at Hierakonpolis attest to the production of beer (Tzedakis and Martlew 1999: 192).

[441] Samuel 1996: 3. See Kemp 1991: Figure 42 for the tomb model of brewing from the MK tomb of Meketre.

[442] Samuel 2000: 549–550 considers that the archaeobotanical evidence does not support a routine addition of dates to beer.

[443] For the detailed explanation for her findings, see Samuel 1996 and Samuel 2000: 550–557. See also the comments of Curtis 2001: 131–141 and Jennings *et al* 2005 with some reservations on the process proposed by Samuel.

[444] Grains were sprouted with their husk because removing it would have damaged the viability of the seed. However there is little husk found in beer residues, suggesting the malted ground mass was sieved (Samuel 1996: 7–8).

[445] Samuel 2000: 551–555, Figure 22.2. Sprouted grains have been recovered from rubbish pits at the Workmen's Village at Amarna where the pitting and channelling formed when the grain was germinating matches exactly the pattern observed in modern malt and malt-based products.

[446] Samuel 2000: 555–556. Many different types of beer are named in ancient Egyptian medical texts but it is not known how they differed.

[447] Curtis 2001: 137–139.

[448] Samuel 2000: 553.

[449] Samuel 2000: 554–555.

[450] Curtis 2001: 134–137.

[451] Curtis 2001: 132–134.

[452] FAO 1999: 7.

[453] Lucas and Harris 1962: 11.

[454] Samuel 2001: 552–553.

[455] Jennings *et al* 2005: 286, Table 1.

[456] This is not the elapse time as beer takes approximately 5–6 days to complete the brewing process. Instead, the one hour assumption is sum of the activities and averaged over 5 days.

[457] Spalinger 1986 describes the baking process and analyses the quantity of ingredients used by large granaries in the reign of Seti 1.

[458] Bread was baked daily, therefore in the conversion from man-days to man-years, the divisor is 365 and not 314 as discussed in Footnote 20.

Horticulture

The types of vegetables, fruit and olives cultivated and consumed in LBA Cyprus and NK Egypt were discussed previously in Section 2.5. Ethnographic evidence from the Vasilikos Valley Project in Cyprus shows that the time required to grow horticultural crops was on average 2673.8 hrs/ha (297 man-days/ha assuming a 9 hr working day) and this labour-rate has been used for LBA horticulture in this study.[459] The area under cultivation for horticulture in Cyprus and Egypt is 1,667 ha/100,000 cohort (Table 2.29). This gives a workload for Cyprus and Egypt of 2,232 and 2,504 man-years/100,000 cohort/yr. The higher Egyptian workload is due to irrigation with shadufs and the overhead of controlling the inundation in the basins.

Oleoculture

The labour-rates and workload involved in tending olive groves are based on an ethnographic study of the Messenian community of Karpofora, 2.5 km inland from the gulf of Messina (Sicily).[460] At the time of the study (1960s) this area was still using traditional farming methods typical of the Central and Eastern Mediterranean. The land was ploughed to control the growth of weeds and grass that are most vigorous from October–March.[461] A team, typically of one man and two or three women harvested olives by hand. The man climbed the tree and with a hatchet and saw, pruned off branches laden with olives. The branches fell onto sheets laid under the tree and the women picked these up and beat them with a stick, causing the olives to fall off. Once all the branches that required pruning had been cut, the man used a long stick to knock off the higher central olives.[462]

The area of land in Cyprus dedicated to oleoculture was 5,699 ha (Table 2.26). Table 2.51 shows that olive trees on this area of land would produce 1,448,431 kg of olives to provide the 9,278 million kcals/100,000 cohort/yr for the production of olive oil and 796 million kcals/100,000 cohort/yr of fresh olives making up the Cypriot diet. The workload for ploughing between trees to keep weeds down and growing a secondary crop of cereals is assumed to be a ploughing rate between that used for marginal and average land, set at 25 man-days/ha (Table 2.33).[463] Aschenbrenner's ethnographic evidence is used for the harvesting and processing of the olives to make olive oil.[464] Report 2.6 in the Appendix gives the yield rates for the traditional production of olives and oil. Report 2.7 gives the olive oil production in Cyprus from 1985–1988 and the percentage extraction rates.

Area (ha) dedicated to oleoculture	5,669
Ploughing labour-rate man-days/ha	25
Ploughing workload (man-years)	454
Weight (kg) of olives harvested	1,448,431
Weight (kg) of fresh olives for eating	114,509
Net weight (kg) of olives used to produce olive oil	1,333,922
Harvesting labour-rate (man-days/kg)	0.05
Total harvesting workload (man-years)	231
Weight (kg) of olives to make 1 kg of olive oil	5
Total weight (kg) of olive oil produced	266,784
Processing labour-rate @ 1 man-day/70 kg oil	3,811
% uplift in processing time for refining/storage	25
Olive oil production workload (man-years)	15
Irrigation workload (man-years)	8
Total workload (man-years)	**708**

Table 2.51: The labour-rates and workload associated with growing olives and processing olive oil.

Viticulture

The consumption of grapes and wine was discussed in Section 2.5. This section formulates the labour-rates and workload associated with growing the grapes and wine production. The techniques used to make wine in the LBA were similar to the methods employed today. Making the wine involved several stages and no single Egyptian tomb shows them all although many show more than one.[465] The stages depicted include picking grapes, transporting the grapes, the pressing vat, the use of a sack press, filling wine jars, blending the wine, and sealing the jars.[466]

Grape juice ferments with natural yeasts on the skin and once the skin is broken fermentation starts. When ripe, the grape bunches were cut from the vine and taken to the area where the juice could be extracted. The grapes were traditional crushed by treading and this stage is depicted in several ancient Egyptian tomb scenes. They also show that in the NK the grape juice flowed out through a spout into pottery containers (Figure 2.14).[467] Approximately two thirds of the juice can be extracted by treading, to extract the remaining juice, the crushed grapes, with stems, seeds and skins were pressed in a sack, the ends of which were twisted around poles. Twisting the poles tightened the sack and the increased pressure forced out more juice. This juice could be either added to juice from the treading or fermented separately.[468] As skins left in the fermenting juice degrade the wine, it is possible that the juice from treading was strained to remove them.

The primary fermentation took place in wide necked pottery jars and could take up to a few weeks, depending on the temperature and the type of wine wanted. In warm conditions, it was possible this stage only took three–four

[459] Todd 1979: 292.

[460] Aschenbrenner 1972.

[461] Aschenbrenner 1972: 54.

[462] Aschenbrenner 1972: 54.

[463] Personal observation in Crete (2004) of cereals and cash crops grown in olive groves.

[464] Aschenbrenner 1972: Table 4–2. Also see Warnock's experimental archaeology based on olive remains, to determine possible processes for making olive oil in antiquity (Warnock 2007).

[465] Murray 2000b: 578–579. Sequences of wine production appear in 42 NK tombs.

[466] For all the stages, see Murray 2000b: 582–600.

[467] Murray 2000b: 586–588 and Figure 23.8 with scenes from the Theban tombs: TT 39, TT 52, and TT 90. See also Curtis 2001: 150–154.

[468] Various methods of twisting were employed (Murray 2000b: 588–590 and Figures 23.11 and 23.12 of the pressing scenes in the NK tomb of Intef (TT 155).

days.[469] Once fermented the wine was either left in the large jars or transferred to smaller jars. In the NK tomb of Kynebu (TT 113) various wines are shown being blended.[470] The jars were sealed with reeds, papyrus, and mud. Pottery jars and their seals were not airtight and this may have been desirable because if further fermentation took place, the carbon dioxide could escape.[471] Storage in such porous jars meant that the wine could not be stored for longer than five years.[472]

Figure 2.14: Harvesting and pressing grapes.
Sketch of Davies 1917: Plate XXII. The tomb of Nakht (TT 52).

The production process for wine was an annual event over a relative short period because grapes, whether on the vine or freshly picked, soon deteriorate. The production cycle is therefore characterised by the need for a large number of workers for over a short period, requiring careful planning and organisation.[473]

Labour-rates and workload

Tending vines and making wine are labour-intensive and in Egypt the need to irrigate vines with water from a shaduf added significantly to the workload.[474]

Work activity	Cyprus	Egypt
Hoeing	22	4
Irrigation	4	9
Weeding	27	10
Transport	34	16
Total	**87**	**39**
Making wine	14	6
Total workload	**101**	**45**

Table 2.52: Workload (man-years/100,000 cohort/yr) associated with viticulture.

Aschenbrenner's personal observations of viticulture and wine making using traditional methods at Karpofora close to the Messenian Gulf (south-western part of the Peloponnese) record that the total workload to make wine was 2 man-days/stremma (20 man-days/ha).[475] The area of land for the cultivation of the vine in Cyprus and Egypt was 220 and 91 ha respectively (Section 2.6). The total workload associated with viticulture is given in Table 2.52.

Dairy and protein production

The consumption of protein and dairy products was discussed in Section 2.5. This section calculates the labour-rate and workload associated with dairy and protein production. The model assumes that children up to their third birthday were breastfed and did not require dairy or protein products. This leaves a population of 96,690/100,000 cohort that needed to be supplied with milk, cheese, and meat.[476]

Dairy production

In antiquity, dairy products were predominantly sourced from sheep and goats. The volume and weight of milk is dependent on the animal's breed, its age, and the length of the lactation period. The quantity of milk is also dependent on the quality of the pasturage. As the ratio of sheep to goats is not known, for this study all milk production is assumed to have been obtained from sheep.

Generally, the ewes nurse their lambs for the first 100 days and are then milked for 150 days.[477] The Awasssi breed of sheep found across the LBA Eastern Mediterranean produces 40–60 kg of milk per lactation cycle (250 days).[478] Taking an average (50 kg) this production rate equates to a daily 0.2 kg/day or 0.194 litres/day.[479] To make one kg of feta cheese requires 5.9 kg of milk.[480] Ethnographic evidence from the Negev shows that two women could milk 176 sheep/day. If they worked a 9 hour day, one sheep could be milked in $9 \times 60 \div (2 \times 176) = 2$ minutes/animal (rounded to nearest minute).

The average time to make one kg of cheese is assumed to be 0.75 hr.[481] The annual requirement/adult for milk and cheese for Cyprus was 12 and 5 kg/yr respectively and Egypt was 9 and 2 kg/yr. These quantities are adjusted to reflect the demographic age profile (Tables 2.53–2.54). The sum of the multiplication of the demographic age profile by the milk and cheese demand results in an annual demand for Cyprus of 1,048,880 and 385,330 kg/100,000 cohort/yr respectively. Similarly, the total milk and cheese consumed in Egypt is 760,320 and 161,885 kg/100,000 cohort/yr respectively.

[469] In the NK the quality of the wine was assessed at this stage and labelled appropriately for example as 'good', 'double good', or 'triple good' (Murray 2000b: 590–591).
[470] Murray 2000b: Figure 23.13.
[471] Other suggested ancient methods of managing secondary fermentation are discussed in Curtis 2001: 161.
[472] Murray 2000b: 591, Figure 23.14. There is no evidence that NK Egyptian wine jars were coated inside with resin (Murray 2000b: 593–594).
[473] Jennings *et al* 2005: 287–288.
[474] Murray 2000b: 582–589. A papyrus (*c*.280 A.D.) lists the tasks associated with tending vines, '... layering as many vine shoots as are necessary, digging, scooping hollows around the vines, trenching ... keeping the vines well tended, giving space to growths, cutting back ... thinning of foliage.' (Darby *et al* 1977: 713). See McGovern 2003: Figure 6.6 showing the labour-intensive Egyptian wine making process portrayed in the Eighteenth Dynasty tomb of Intef (TT 155).
[475] Aschenbrenner 1972: 55, Table 4.3.
[476] For demographic age profile see again Table 2.3.
[477] Degen 2007: 10.
[478] Degen 2007: 10.
[479] All calculations in this section assume a milk density of 1.03 kg/litre.
[480] Meunier-Goddick and Nashnush 2006: 1.
[481] This is not the elapse time but the sum of the individual activities required to make cheese.

Age bands	Demographic age profile	Milk demand/ individual/ kg/yr	Cheese demand/ individual/ kg/yr
Infants under 4 breastfed	3,240	0	0
Weaned infants under 4	11,840	6	1
4 to 6	9,240	9	2
7 to 9	5,600	10	3
10 to 12	5,410	12	4
13 to 15	5,330	12	5
16 to 19	6,670	12	5
20 to 39	28,090	12	5
40 to 49	10,810	12	5
50 to 59	8,200	12	5
60 to 69	4,430	12	4
70+	1,140	10	3
Total	**100,000**	**119**	**42**

Table 2.53: LBA Cypriot dairy demand (kg/100,000 cohort/yr).

Age bands	Demographic age profile	Milk demand/ individual/ kg/yr	Cheese demand/ individual/ kg/yr
Infants under 4 breastfed	3,240	0	0
Weaned infants under 4	11,840	5	1
4 to 6	9,240	6	1.5
7 to 9	5,600	7	1.5
10 to 12	5,410	7	1.5
13 to 15	5,330	9	2
16 to 19	6,670	9	2
20 to 39	28,090	9	2
40 to 49	10,810	9	2
50 to 59	8,200	9	1.5
60 to 69	4,430	7	1
70+	1,140	5	1
Total	**100,000**	**82**	**17**

Table 2.54: NK Egyptian dairy demand (kg/100,000 cohort/yr).

The workload involved in the production of these dairy products for Cyprus and Egypt is 298 and 144 man-years/100,000 cohort/yr respectively is given in Table 2.55.

Age bands	Demographic age profile	Cypriot workload 100,000 cohort/yr	Egyptian workload 100,000 cohort/yr
Infants under 4 breastfed	3,240	0	0
Weaned infants under 4	11,840	11	11
4 to 6	9,240	16	12
7 to 9	5,600	14	7
10 to 12	5,410	17	7
13 to 15	5,330	20	9
16 to 19	6,670	25	12
20 to 39	28,090	106	49
40 to 49	10,810	41	19
50 to 59	8,200	31	12
60 to 69	4,430	14	5
70+	1,140	3	1
Total	**100,000**	**298**	**144**

Table 2.55: Workload (man-years) to satisfy the annual demand for dairy products in LBA Cyprus and NK Egypt.

Protein production

Previously, the source and annual dietary requirement per adult for meat and fish in Cyprus and Egypt was discussed in Section 2.5 and its findings are summarised here in Table 2.56.

Consumption per individual	Cyprus kg/yr	Egypt Kg/yr
Goat/mutton	14.2	12
Fish	8	17
Wildfowl	5	8
Total	**27.2**	**37**

Table 2.56: Average protein requirements for LBA Cyprus and NK Egypt (kg/yr/individual).

Using similar algorithms to those employed to calculate the demand for dairy products, AGCALC adjusts the protein consumed for each demographic age group.[482] The resulting annual Cypriot and Egyptian requirements for meat, fish, and wildfowl are given in Table 2.57.

Annual consumption	Cyprus kg/yr	Egypt kg/yr
Goat/mutton	1,123,214	949,195
Fish	609,330	1,294,826
Wildfowl	402,375	643,800
Total	**2,134,919**	**2,887,821**

Table 2.57: Total annual requirement (kg/100,000 cohort/yr) for protein for Cyprus and Egypt.

The parameters used to estimate the workload required to meet the protein requirements of Cyprus and Egypt for a 100,000 cohort/yr are summarised in Table 2.58 and the workload in Table 2.59.

Parameters	
Time (mins) to skin/butcher goat or sheep	45
Average size of flock	50
Weight (kg) off the bone	18
Weight (kg) of edible flesh from average fish	0.3
Time (secs) to gut fish	6
Time (secs) hanging/skewing fish	15
Weight (kg) of fish caught per basket	15
Fishing rate (days) to fill one basket	1
Weight (kg) of edible meat on an average duck	0.24
Number of ducks caught/net	10
Time (mins)/clap netting operation	30
Number of wildfowl hunters in a team	3
Time (mins) to pluck and gut/duck	5

Table 2.58: Assumptions to estimate the workload to provide the protein in the diet of Cyprus and Egypt.

Workload	Cyprus man-years	Egypt man-years
Shepherding	1,248	1,055
Butchery	17	14
Fishing	61	129
Fish gutting	1	3
Fish drying	3	6
Netting wildfowl	89	142
Butchery	49	79
Total	**1,468**	**1,428**

Table 2.59: Workload needed to supply the protein requirements for Cyprus and Egypt for a cohort of 100,000/yr.

[482] It is assumed that took 45 minutes to skin and butcher a goat or a sheep. The average flock size was 50 and the usable weight of meat for human consumption was 18 kg/animal. For fish, it is assumed that the usable weight of fish was 0.3 kg/fish, and it took 22 seconds to gut/skew was 22 seconds.

Fodder

Fodder was necessary to feed the livestock that provided meat and diary products and although not part of the LBA human diet, the workload involved in providing fodder needs to be taken into consideration. The farmers in antiquity, like their modern counterparts, would have had a variety of means for providing fodder. A balance had to be maintained between using land to grow food and land to supply fodder. The capital cost of keeping animals was significant; in the Roman Classical Period a cultivated area, if worked by hand, required 2 ha to support a family but 5 ha was required if work animals were kept.[483] Reliance on cultivating fodder crops in parallel with cereal crops would create a conflict in manpower requirements in the peak harvest period.[484] It is likely that most workload effective solutions would be employed and that livestock was fed largely on fallow land, grazing on cereal stubble and pulse fields, and by-products of cereal processing.[485] Green fodder could have been grown when practicable or when extra nutrition was needed.[486] However, planting fodder crops in place of the traditional fallow would have significantly increased the workload.[487] In times of cereal glut, the less valued crops could be used as fodder and cereals, fruit, and vegetables spoilt during cultivation or storage could also have been used.[488]

It is not known how much land was used in the LBA for the cultivation of fodder but the importance of supplying livestock with an adequate supply of feed was unquestionably vital for the ancient farmer. The evidence for the foodstuffs used as fodder for livestock in ancient Egypt and LBA Cyprus is discussed next using textual, archaeological, and archaeobotanical evidence but in the main, ethnographic evidence.

Egypt

Textual evidence

In the letters of Heqanakht, reference is made to 4 sacks of barley and 10.5 sacks of emmer set aside as 'grain produce for cattle'.[489] According to the Ptolemaic, Papyrus Tebtunis 53.7, the fodder crops include some emmer wheat, vetches, grasses and fenugreek for rapid fattening, and they accounted for 17% of the land.[490] At Amarna, it is possible that the cattle were kept in byres, which would have created a demand for regular supplies of fodder.[491]

Archaeobotanical evidence

Undigested seeds and plant remains are excreted in animal dung and when the dung is burnt for fuel, charred seeds become preserved in the archaeobotanical record and it is possible to see what plants may have been used for animal fodder.[492] The remains show that hulled barley was an important animal feed as was the straw from emmer, as it is today.[493] Wheat and barley can be harvested by cutting the stalk low down or by removing the heads. The latter method means there is less straw to thresh and fewer weeds to remove. However, if the remaining straw was intended for fodder it would need a second cutting. Cutting the stem low left stubble in the fields on which livestock could feed. Separated straw and chaff from winnowing and fragments of straw, un-threshed ears and large seeds from sieving could be stored and used as fodder in the spring and winter seasons.[494]

In Egypt in the Greco-Roman Period, the legume, berseem clover, grass pea, and bitter vetch were grown deliberately as animal fodder and may have been cultivated as fodder in the NK. Small-seeded wild legumes make good fodder and are sometimes found in archaeobotanical samples.[495] It is not known if they were deliberately cultivated for fodder as these plants also grow spontaneously on fallow land.[496] There is an upper limit to the amount of straw that cattle and donkeys can be fed. They can only digest 41% of barley straw and therefore green fodder or vegetable matter to supply the remaining calories and nutrients would have been necessary.[497] Assuming each farm had one donkey, the area of land dedicated to growing green fodder/donkey would be 0.21 ha.

Cyprus

It is very likely that fodder was grown in LBA Cyprus because of the need for work animals particularly in the farms with rocky soil. The lower slopes of the Cypriot Troodos mountain range provide some natural pasture but it is sparse and seasonal, and grazed in winter. Fallow fields are grazed until they are ploughed in spring. However, the evidence for the area of land set aside to grow fodder is limited. Surplus land might be sown with fodder crops of common vetch, bitter vetch, grass pea, and barley.[498] An ethnographic study of Messenia (south-west Peloponnese) showed that the fodder crops: vetch, clover, alfalfa, and grass fallow areas, occupied 7.1% of

[483] Halstead 1897: 84. The cultivated land area to feed a family that owned oxen could be as high as 10 ha (Halstead 1897: Footnote 49 and Halstead 1995: 15).

[484] Halstead and Jones 1989: 50.

[485] Halstead and Jones 1989: 48.

[486] As for example at the OK site at Kom el-Hisn in the Delta (Moens and Wetterstrom 1988: 163) where legumes were dominant in the diet. The authors suggest that the cattle were stall fed and fattened, feeding them on berseem clover grown and harvested several times a year.

[487] For example, additional transport would be necessary. One farmer on Amorgos estimated that, to feed two oxen, a calf and two donkeys over winter, he needed 25 donkey loads of threshed and winnowed chaff (Halstead and Jones 1989: 48 and Halstead and Jones 1997: 281).

[488] Halstead 1993: 64.

[489] Allen 2002: 161–162. It is possible that this refers to grain set aside to pay the tax on his cattle and not to fodder.

[490] Crawford 1979: 142.

[491] Kemp 1994: 145.

[492] Murray 1993: 165–168.

[493] Moens and Wetterstrom 1988 and Murray 1993: 165. Both these cereals have been found in cattle dung.

[494] Murray 2000a: 521–526.

[495] Moens and Wetterstrom 1988 and Murray 2000c: 638.

[496] Brewer *et al* 1994: 74.

[497] Brownson 2000: Table 1.

[498] Halstead and Jones 1989: 48, Halstead 1993: 63, and Halstead and Jones 1997: 272. Barley was grown for human consumption and fodder.

the available arable land.[499] Traditional farmers in northern Greece cultivated between 0.5 and 2 ha of bitter vetch for the plough oxen.[500] Common vetch and grass pea on Amorgos was grazed in situ by breeding and milking livestock in April and March. Stubble fields provided grazing from June to October and harvested pulse crop was preferred to cereal stubble. If the latter is grazed first by cattle and donkeys, they leave seeds and weeds for sheep and goats.

In August and September, pasture is insufficient in quantity and quality and livestock were fed considerable quantities of sown pasture and stall fodder. Threshed chaff, hay, and straw was used as winter stall fodder. In addition, the winnowed straw and chaff of nearly all the cereals and pulses were stored as winter fodder. On Karpathos, considerable quantities of hay were stored for stall-feeding.[501] Riley has speculated that pressed olive pulp and crushed stones may have been used as fodder in ancient Crete; this could have been done in LBA Cyprus.[502] The wide variety of fodder sources, the time constraints on ancient farmers, and their opportunist approach to the production of fodder suggests that the area of available land dedicated to deliberately growing animal feed would be kept to a minimum (Table 2.60).

	Total area (ha) under cultivation	
	Cyprus	Egypt
Total area	58,155	31,030
% fodder	8.7	11.0

Table 2.60: Area dedicated to growing fodder in LBA Cyprus and NK Egypt.

Table 2.61 presents the calculated workload for the production of fodder in Cyprus and Egypt.

Activity	Cyprus	Egypt
Ploughing	312	109
Hoeing	120	40
Clod breaking	117	49
Sowing/weeding/harvesting/transport	1,414	990
Irrigation	0	7
Total workload (man-years)	**1,963**	**1,195**

Table 2.61: The workload required to grow fodder in LBA Cyprus and NK Egypt (man-years/100,000 cohort/yr).

2.8 Workload and manpower

Taking the calculated workload for each activity discussed in this chapter it is possible to consolidate them to give the total agrarian workload as shown in Tables 2.62–2.63. To convert workload into manpower, the workload is adjusted by a competency index of 1.3, which means increasing the workload by an additional 30% to take into account skill levels, gender, and age.[503]

The sum of all the agrarian workloads required per year for Cyprus and Egypt is 33,361 and 25,902 man-years/100,000 cohort respectively (Column A in Table 2.62 and 2.63).

In Table 2.63 the Egyptian workload associated with managing and controlling the inundation (2,656 man-years) has been prorated across all activities as an overhead.

Cypriot agrarian sector	A. Workload man-years/ 100,000 cohort	B. Manpower/ 100,000 cohort
Ploughing	3,215	4,182
Hoeing	1,463	1,903
Clod breaking	1,256	1,634
Irrigation	105	137
Sowing	59	77
Weeding	6,770	8,806
Transport	8,074	10,502
Harvesting	735	956
Tending vegetables/fruit/grapes/olives	1,577	2,051
Refining olive oil	15	20
Milling	6,209	8,076
Making bread, beer, and wine	1,866	2,427
Production protein	1,468	1,909
Production dairy products	298	388
Honey	250	325
Total	**33,360**	**43,393**

Table 2.62: Cypriot workload and manpower required to feed a cohort of 100,000/yr, collated by agrarian activity.

Egyptian agrarian sector	A. Workload man-years/ 100,000 cohort	Workload with inundation prorated as an overhead	B. Manpower/ 100,000 cohort
Ploughing	758	845	1,099
Hoeing	435	485	630
Clod breaking	433	482	628
Irrigation	192	214	278
Sowing	35	39	51
Weeding	3,013	3,357	4,367
Transport	5,311	5,918	7,698
Harvesting	384	428	557
Tending vegetables/fruit/grapes	1,577	1,757	2,286
Milling	7,423	8,271	10,759
Making bread, beer, and wine	1,862	2,074	2,698
Prod'n protein	1,429	1,592	2,070
Production dairy	144	161	210
Honey	250	279	362
Inundation control	2,656	0	0
Total	**25,902**	**25,902**	**33,693**

Table 2.63: Egyptian workload and manpower required to feed a cohort of 100,000/yr, collated by agrarian activity.

Tables 2.64–2.65 collate the workload and manpower to feed a cohort of 100,000/yr by crop. The granary distribution workload and manpower have been prorated as an overhead across the respective workloads and manpower requirements to determine the full crop cost.

---

[499] Van Wersh 1972: 178. Table 2.26 shows that the area of cultivated land calculated in AGCALC to grow green fodder is 8.7% and 11.0% for Cyprus and Egypt respectively.

[500] Halstead 1995: 12.

[501] Halstead and Jones 1989: 48 and Halstead and Jones 1997: 280–281.

[502] Riley 1999: 37.

[503] See Table 2.27.

Cypriot agrarian sector	A. Workload man-years/ 100,000 cohort	B. Manpower/ 100,000 cohort
Barley	13,909	18,094
Emmer wheat	9,465	12,311
Pulses	2,965	3,856
Fodder	1,965	2,556
Vegetables/fruit	2,232	2,903
Olives/olive oil	708	921
Grapes/wine	100	130
Protein	1,468	1,909
Dairy	298	388
Honey	250	325
Total	**33,360**	**43,393**

Table 2.64: Cypriot workload and manpower required to feed a cohort of 100,000/yr, collated by food type.

Egyptian agrarian sector	A. Workload man-years/ 100,000 cohort	B. Manpower/ 100,000 cohort
Barley	10,867	14,135
Emmer wheat	6,986	9,087
Pulses	2,330	3,032
Fodder	1,344	1,749
Vegetables/fruit	2,504	3,258
Grapes/wine	42	54
Protein	1,435	1,866
Dairy	144	187
Honey	250	325
Total	**25,902**	**33,693**

Table 2.65: Egyptian workload and manpower required to feed a cohort of 100,000/yr, collated by food type.

2.9 Observations

The size of the agrarian workforce calculated in this study should be considered a theoretical minimum. The extent of the agricultural labour force in antiquity, as it is today in the third world using traditional farming practices, is driven by the demographic growth of families and not by state economic targets.[504] As the family size increases, more land is brought into production to feed new mouths. The proportion of the surplus to total harvest remains the same and the proportion of the non-basic workforce to basic also remains the same. Indeed this relationship remained until productivity increased with the use of mechanised farming equipment following the industrial revolution.

My approach quantifies the size of the agrarian workforce that could provide sufficient harvest surplus to maximise the size of a non-basic workforce. It provides an objective reference point in determining the options open to the élites in antiquity when managing their economies. While fundamental changes to the ratio of basic to non-basic was outside of their full control because they could not control the demographic birth or death rate, the evidence shows the élite did invest in major irrigation projects to maximise farming output. It is clear from the extensive and impressive array of these projects in Ancient Egypt that the élite did intervene directly through taxation to support and direct non-basic labour resources into the priorities that they had chosen.

The alternative approach of determining the theoretical maximum size of the agrarian sector based on agrarian families expanding in number until all suitable land was under cultivation is invalid, though the approach is useful in quantifying the theoretical upper limit.[505] This upper limit could never be reached due to the failed harvests and pandemics that naturally controlled population rates. The latter in particular would change the ratio between the basic and non-basic workforces and would have had a direct impact on the size of the harvest surplus.

This chapter has also shown that process analysis provides an objective assessment of the proportion of the population that can be supported from the harvest surplus.

[504] Dovring 1967: 163.

[505] Butzer 1976: 81–98.

Chapter 3: Cloth Production in LBA Cyprus and NK Egypt

3.1 Introduction

In Chapter 2, discussion centred on the manpower resources required to feed the population of LBA Cyprus and NK Egypt. This chapter assesses the manpower required to support another critical requirement for daily life, namely the cloth for clothing. Clothing was one of the three basic needs that had to be met across all socio-economic groups before the élite could allocate any surplus to support non-basic activities (Figure 1.1). This chapter excludes the production of cloth for external trade, mummification and funerary shrouds, and furnishing fabrics because the production of these materials, manufactured principally for the élite, came from non-basic labour.[506] It is assumed that the major cloth production of Cyprus was with wool and for Egypt, linen.

The methodology for the analyses and calculations closely follows the approach used in the analysis of food production in Chapter 2. The end-to-end cloth production process in the LBA is identified and broken down into discrete activities that follow each other in a logical sequence. The time taken to complete each activity is assessed and this enables the workload and the number of workers required to produce the cloth to be calculated. It is also necessary to estimate the demand for cloth across all socio-economic groups making up LBA society. From this estimation, the total area of cloth needed for a cohort of 100,000/yr can be determined by multiplying the number of garments required per year by the area of cloth required to make each type of garment. The evidence relating to cloth is examined and quantified in the following categories:

- The number individuals per 100,000 cohort in each socio-economic group (SEG) in LBA society (Section 3.4).
- The types and number of garments worn by the individuals, collated by socio-economic group (Section 3.4).
- The total area of cloth required to clothe a 100,000 cohort (Section 3.4).
- The amortised annual area of cloth required to satisfy the domestic clothing needs, taking into account different rates of wear and tear across the socio-economic groups (Section 3.4).
- The weight of flax or wool fibre required to make this area of cloth (Section 3.5).
- The workload required to grow the weight of flax fibre for Egypt to meet this requirement and the equivalent weight of wool for Cyprus (Section 3.6).
- The workload needed to prepare yarn, spin, and weave the required area of linen and woollen cloth (Sections 3.7–3.9).
- The manpower needed to provide Egypt and Cyprus with cloth for clothes (Section 3.10).

3.2 Sources of evidence

The hot, dry climate of Egypt has provided a wide range of yarns, cloth samples, and garments that have survived across the Pharaonic Period, which are helpful to this study. Linen (*šs*) yarn is attested in burials as early as the Predynastic Naqada I Period (*c.*4000–3500 B.C.) and woven linen is found, dating to soon after.[507] The survival or otherwise of a piece of cloth in the archaeological record also depends on the pH of the soil surrounding it. Linen and other cellulose fibres are better preserved in alkaline conditions, whereas animal protein fibres such as wool survive better in slightly acidic environments.[508] Many cloth remains are from the Workmen's Village at Amarna, where 4,962 fragments of linen and woollen cloth have been found in an area of 0.49 ha.[509]

Yarn and cloth from the regions outside of Egypt are termed 'invisibles' because organic materials in most regions do not survive the combined effects of moisture, bacteria, insects, and rodents. Evidence of Cypriot cloth and styles of clothing is limited but the loom weights and whorls in the archaeological record indicate that weaving of cloth is likely to be similar for woollen and linen production across the Eastern Mediterranean. The production processes and workload for linen and woollen cloth in this study are based principally on ethnographic evidence of weavers who use traditional craft skills. This pre-supposes that the level of technology they employed was similar in the LBA.

In addition to archaeological finds relating to cloth production, Egyptian, Mesopotamian, Ugaritic, and Aegean Linear B texts have been used to identity methods of cloth production. Steinkeller explains the terminology used in UR III texts relating to woollen textiles and the husbandry of sheep and goats.[510] Waetzoldt has identified the organisation, processes, and compensation rates of Mesopotamian cloth production.[511] His analysis of Sumerian UR III texts provides valuable information on the spinning and weaving processes, especially spinning and weaving rates at the end of the third millennium B.C.[512] Heltzer and Stieglitz demonstrate the value of cloth and garments in relation to other goods in Ugarit.[513] Halstead analyses the Aegean wool industry by combining the textual and archaeological evidence with ethnographic evidence.[514] Another useful source is

[506] An Eleventh Dynasty mummy of a nobleman called Wah, was wrapped in the equivalent of 375 m^2 of linen (Spencer 1982: 115).

[507] Landi and Hall 1979: 142 and *Wb.* 4, 539.12–540.8.

[508] Good 2001: 211.

[509] Kemp and Vogelsang-Eastwood 2001: 13–21.

[510] Steinkeller 1995.

[511] Waetzoldt 1972, Waetzoldt 1980–1983a, Waetzoldt 1980–1983b, and Waetzoldt 1987: 117–142.

[512] Waetzoldt 1972: 91–141.

[513] Heltzer 1978: 23–36, 40–51 and Stieglitz 1979.

[514] Halstead 1897: 79–81, Halstead 1996, and Halstead and Jones 1989.

Janssen's analysis of the types of garments worn used by the artisans from Deir el-Medina. The works of Barber, Kemp, Roth, and Vogelsang-Eastwood contribute to our knowledge of the tools used and the *chaîne opératoire* of cloth production.[515] Ethnographic evidence of Egyptian and Sudanese spinning and weaving has been provided by Crowfoot.[516] The work of Barber, Hall, and Vogelsang-Eastwood has been consulted to determine the area of cloth required to make Egyptian garments worn in daily life.[517] The estimated dimensions of garments from these studies are incorporated in Table 3.3 below.

3.3 The properties of linen and wool

Flax and wool provided hardwearing cloth but the characteristics of both materials influence how the respective fibres were prepared for spinning and the effort required to produce them. In antiquity, the most common type of flax was the blue-flowered *Linum usitatissimum* which grew 0.8 to 1 m high.[518] It belongs to the family of plants whose fibres are contained in bast bundles.[519] These bundles are elongated cells that reinforce the flax stem against bending moments from the wind.[520] The fibrous bast bundle structure of the flax stem is the key to its suitability for spinning and weaving. Each fibre of the plant is composed of thousands of fibrils that are arranged in a left-handed spiral similar to the fibres in twisted thread and this helps linen to resist wear.[521]

The earliest attested sample of linen weaving in Egypt is from a fifth millennium B.C. deposit in the Fayum.[522] The oldest, most complete ancient garment is a First Dynasty pleated and fringed dress from Tarkhan.[523] It has a light lacy texture due to the weave having only six wefts per inch compared with a warp count of 72 warps per inch.[524] An innovation in the MK was to loop the weft above the surface to give a noticeable texture as shown in the Eleventh Dynasty sheet from Deir el-Bahri.[525]

Dyes available to Egyptian cloth producers in the LBA were restricted to blues, red and yellow ochres, iron oxides and some plant dyes. However, flax is not an easy material to dye due to the hardness of the fibre surface and this may explain why the vast majority of Egyptian linen was left in its natural colour.[526] This study has assumed that dyed linen was an added-value process and it is excluded from the analysis of basic cloth production.

For most regions in the Eastern Mediterranean, wool rather than flax dominated the LBA cloth industry.[527] Wool is a protein fibre chiefly composed of keratin. The fibre has overlapping cuticle scales and an inner cortex. Both the cortex and the cuticle influence the fibre properties of the wool and the fibre is slightly elliptical, unlike other animal fibres.[528] Primitive sheep had a complex coat made up of kemps, hair, and wool fibre.[529] Wool can be easily coloured with a range of dyes; the most prestigious in antiquity was the purple dye made from murex shells, found in large quantities at the Cypriot LBA settlement of Hala Sultan Tekke.[530]

3.4 The area of cloth required for clothing

The area of cloth made per annum for any culture is a function of several factors:

- The socio-economic profile of the society and the proportion of the population within each of the socio-economic groups (SEG).
- The range of garments worn by each socio-economic group by gender and age.
- The number of garments owned within each socio-economic group by gender and age.
- The unit area of cloth required to make up each type of garment by gender and age.
- The rate at which garments have to be replaced due to wear-and-tear.

The demand for cloth varied by the quality and the number of garments owned by the individual. This differed by social status and reflected the hierarchical nature of LBA society. This section calculates the annual area of cloth required to clothe a cohort of 100,000 individuals across five socio-economic groups that are

[515] Roth 1913, Barber 1991, Vogelsang-Eastwood 2000, and Kemp and Vogelsang-Eastwood 2001.

[516] Crowfoot 1931 and Crowfoot 1954.

[517] Hall 1981, Barber 1982, Eastwood 1985, Hall 1986, Barber 1991, Vogelsang-Eastwood 1992a, Vogelsang-Eastwood 1993, Vogelsang-Eastwood 2000, and Kemp and Vogelsang-Eastwood 2001.

[518] See Helbaek 1960: 115–116 for the archaeobotany of the flax plant in the Near East.

[519] The cross-section of the flax stem is represented in Kemp and Vogelsang-Eastwood 2001: 26, Figure 2.1.

[520] Flax consists of three main parts: a woody core with a hollow centre, the flax fibre itself, and an outer woody cortex.

[521] Caldwell 1931: 5–6.

[522] Caton-Thompson and Gardner 1934: 46 and Plate 28.3.

[523] For a photograph and pattern of the combined bodice and sleeve, see Landi and Hall 1979: 143–144, Figures 1–2.

[524] Barber 1991: 146.

[525] The sheet is now in the Egyptian Museum in Cairo (Acc. no. 813). Later NK examples are the weft looped towels and a weft looped blanket on Merit's bed in the Eighteenth Dynasty tomb of Kha and Merit at Deir el-Medina (Schiaparelli 1927: 16, Plate 105).

[526] Caldwell 1931: 5. Kemp and Vogelsang-Eastwood 2001: 152–154 record that only 2.6% of the linen samples found at Amarna were coloured. For archaeological samples of linen and the dyes used, see Germer 1992, Schick 1998: 63–64, and Vogelsang-Eastwood 2000: 278. For an analysis of the textual evidence for the use of dyes in Ugarit, see van Soldt 1990.

[527] Waetzoldt 1980–1983b: 583.

[528] FAO 1995, Agricultural Service Bulletin, No. 122, Section 1.1.3.

[529] Kemps are coarse, bristle-like hairs that are brittle and unsuitable for spinning but the process of plucking wool conveniently left most of the coarser kemp and hair on the animal (Wild 2002: 5). Wool fibres are classified into three groups with some overlap, 'hairs and kemps' with diameter ranges 50–100 micron, and wool itself classified as 'medium' with a diameter range of 30–60 microns, and 'fine' with diameters under 30 microns (Barber 1991: 21).

[530] Karageorghis 1996: 64.

represented in the textual, artistic, and archaeological evidence of LBA society:

1. Royalty, nobles, and high élite who controlled the major offices of state.
2. Senior officials working for these state offices.
3. Professional class (scribes, architects, army officers).
4. Lower level administrators, scribes, and skilled workers.
5. The agrarian workforce and other non-skilled manual workers.

Socio-economic profiles

Socio-economic groups 1–3

In this study the term 'élite' refers to socio-economic groups 1–3. In any ancient society the size of the élite was a small proportion of the total population. Baines suggests tentatively that for Egypt, literacy levels approximated to the proportion of the total population that can be considered members of the élite.[531] Baines and Eyre estimated that the OK literacy levels for males was no higher than 1% and may have been as low as 0.33%.[532] This study uses the higher literacy rate for the élite population of 297 males and 297 females. Assuming an average family size of six, the size of the élite would be = 297 × 6 = 1,782 individuals/100,000 cohort (Table 3.1). The level of literacy in LBA Cyprus is not known but the size of the élite in is likely to have been similar in proportion to that of NK Egypt and it is assumed in this study that the size of élite/100,000 cohort would be the same. This study applies the 1% literacy estimate to represent the élite (socio-economic groups 1–3).[533] Table 3.1 shows the allocation of the élite, senior officials, and professionals (1,782 individuals/100,000 cohort) across socio-economic groups 1–3. These groups have a hierarchical structure with socio-economic group 1 owning the most clothes per individual but they were few in number, down to socio-economic group 3 which was a larger group but who owned fewer garments (Table 3.2 and Table 3.4).

Literacy and population levels/100,000 cohort	
Assumed % literacy	1
Adults aged 16 or above	59,340
Number of literate males and females	593
No. of élite male adults (a)	297
Size of average family (b)	6
Élite population (a × b)	1,782
Egyptian élite (assumed population 2,200,000)	39,204
Cypriot élite (100,000 cohort)	1,782

Table 3.1: Social Economic Groups 1–3 (élite).

Socio-economic groups 4–5

The rest of the 100,000 cohort can be allocated to socio-economic groups 4–5, which totals 98,218 individuals/100,000 cohort. Of these, I have assumed that there were 10,000 individuals comprising skilled craftsmen and their families, leaving 88,218 individuals/100,000 cohort in socio-economic group 5. Table 3.2 shows the resulting distribution across socio-economic groups 1–5 of a 100,000 cohort.

Socio-economic group	No. of individuals
SEG 1 (Royalty and nobles)	78
SEG 2 (Senior official)	186
SEG 3 (Professionals)	1,518
SEG 4 (Skilled workers)	10,000
SEG 5 (Workers)	88,218
Total	**100,000**

Table 3.2: Estimate of the number of individuals collated by socio-economic group in a 100,000 cohort.

The range and designs of LBA garments

Having estimated the number of individuals within each socio-economic group above, the next stage is to estimate the area of cloth required to make each of the most common designs and types of garments worn in the LBA Eastern Mediterranean. By far, Egypt has the most extensive evidence from both archaeological evidence and from pictorial depictions on tomb walls. However, the appearance of garments, particularly those that wrapped around the body varied, depending on how the artist depicted the different combinations of folding and tying.[534]

While cultural factors do influence garment design, ethnographic evidence from rural communities shows that different societies wear similar garments to suit the climate and their work activity. The maxim that 'form follows function' seems as applicable to clothes from ancient agricultural societies as it does to modern industrial design.[535]

Due to the random survival of organic, textual, and artistic evidence, the date of some evidence extends beyond the LBA. However, although garments have minor differences in style over time, in terms of the areas of cloth required they are comparable. For the calculations of the area of fabric required to clothe a 100,000 cohort this chapter assumes that outside of the high élite, the high cost of cloth would tend to minimise the area of cloth per garment. Also, that the commonality of the manual processes described in this study means that for practical reasons garments would be similar in design.

[531] Baines and Eyre 1983: 65–77, 81–91, Baines 1983: 572–599. Haring notes that documents found at Deir el-Medina up to the Nineteenth Dynasty indicate an oral village culture with literacy limited to the necropolis administrators. Writing spread to the wider village population in the private and judicial domains at the end of the Nineteenth and in the first half of the Twentieth Dynasties. Initially they were *aides-memoires* but increasingly they were used to supplement traditional oral modes of conducting business (Haring 2003: 266).

[532] Baines and Eyre 1983: 67 and Baines 2007: 64–68.

[533] As the size of the élite sector was so small in antiquity, the difference between a 1% or a 0.33% literacy level makes very little difference to the number of workers required to make day to day cloth for this group.

[534] See the typology of 20 Ramesside wrap-around designs Hofmann and Hofmann 2004: 167–169. Vogelsang-Eastward proposes that sash kilts and dresses were produced from simple rectangles of cloth wrapped around the body (Vogelsang-Eastwood: 1992a: 19).

[535] Sullivan 1896 introduced the concept of 'form follows function'. This concept was further developed by Greenough 1947 relating this principle to twentieth century architecture and industrial design.

The number of garments owned

The area of cloth needed to clothe the cohort is directly proportional to the total number of garments owned. Three sources of evidence have been used to quantify these numbers for the socio-economic groups 1–5 that made up NK Egyptian society:

- The archaeological evidence from élite intact tombs for socio-economic groups 1–2.
- The NK designs by Vogelsang-Eastwood and R. Janssen, and the textual study of Deir el-Medina by J. J. Janssen for socio-economic groups 3–4.[536]
- Agriculture scenes in Egyptian tombs for socio-economic group 5.

Wardrobe of socio-economic groups 1–2

Only a very small percentage of élite tombs have survived with an intact burial assemblage and of these, only the Eighteenth Dynasty tomb of Kha and his wife Merit in Deir el-Medina has an almost complete wardrobe of garments. This evidence is combined with other Eighteenth Dynasty tomb clothing assemblages and the garments found in a tomb from the Nineteenth Dynasty. It is used to estimate the number of garments owned by socio-economic group 2.[537] Meskell points out that although the burial artefacts in the tomb of Kha and Merit may not reflect those owned and worn in daily life '... given the particular nature of Egyptian mortuary practice, some measure of overlap with the living sphere can be inferred — especially in the Eighteenth Dynasty.'[538] Most of the loincloths in Kha's tomb had laundry marks showing that they had been worn at least once and were not produced just for mortuary purposes.[539] Although Kha was not a member of the Royal family nor a noble (socio-economic-group 1) he did have considerable social interaction with the highest levels of élite society.[540] In addition, the wardrobe found in his tomb is similar to tomb depictions of members of socio-economic group 2. As a result, this evidence has been chosen as the main source of evidence to estimate the number of garments representative of those owned by socio-economic group 2.

Kha's wardrobe consisted of 50 triangular loincloths, 26 knee-length garments that wrapped around the hips, and 17 sleeveless tunics.[541] In addition, there were at least 22 fringed pieces of linen.[542] Many of the garments examined have the name of Kha printed or embroidered on them.[543] However, it is not obvious from the total garment assemblage found in Kha's tomb how they were divided between him and his wife. Merit did have clothes in her own right; a folded dressing gown with additional side sections of fringed linen with Merit's own ink laundry mark was found in her personal basket.[544] Warm bedcovers and folded sheets were placed on her bed.[545]

Meskell itemised and valued the tomb goods in relation to the copper *deben*. Kha had 196 items attributed to him by name, worth 3,919 deben, compared with Merit who had 39 objects worth 787 deben.[546] The ratio in terms of deben value is 5:1 (3,919 deben for Kha and 787 deben for Merit).[547] The area of linen cloth to make up the total wardrobe of Kha is 223.7 m^2 and 105.3 m^2 for Merit, a ratio of 2.1: 1 in the husband's favour and this study uses this ratio for assessing the wardrobe for élite women.[548]

An ostracon from Deir el-Medina lists the items of clothing belonging to another NK village resident. This householder had three cloaks, ten kilts, and fifteen loincloths. His wife had two pairs of pants (?), one tunic, and one sash, a pair of sleeves and two sheets.[549] These clothes were owned by relatively wealthy members of socio-economic group 2, but not as well positioned as Kha. The combination of these two examples formed the basis from which to estimate the wardrobe across socio-economic groups 1–2.

Wardrobe of socio-economic group 3

Socio-economic group 3 incorporates professions such as senior scribes, architects, army officers, and medium ranked officials. Vogelsang-Eastwood has assessed the wardrobe of the lower professional class of the élite, which belongs to socio-economic group 3, based on tomb depictions, tomb goods, and textual evidence. Her findings suggest that a male member of this group in the NK would own two loincloths, two aprons, two knee-length kilts, one long kilt, two sash kilts, two long bag-tunics, two short bag-tunics, and two cloaks. His wife would own five loincloths, two wrap-around skirts, one simple wrap-around dress, two complex wrap-around dresses, six sashes, and two cloaks.[550]

[536] Janssen 1975b: 249–298, Vogelsang-Eastwood 1993, and Vogelsang-Eastwood 1994.

[537] See Meskell 1998: 364–366 and Meskell 1999: 176–212, 214 for a study of other Eighteenth Dynasty tombs and their tomb goods.

[538] Meskell 1998: 364. The estimates of garments owned by socio-economic group 2 should be considered as an upper limit.

[539] Hall 1986: Figures 24 and 27.

[540] Kha's burial assemblage shows that he was awarded prestigious gifts by three Pharaohs. His last appointments were for Amenhotep III as Chief in the Great Palace and Director of Public Works in the Royal Palace.

[541] Schiaparelli 1927: 91–93, Figures 63–69.

[542] Schiaparelli 1927: 98–100, Figure 66 and 70. Schiaparelli called them 'table cloths' but they are more likely to be cloth for items such as blankets, wrap-around cloaks, kilts, skirts, or shawls.

[543] Source Schiaparelli 1927: 98, Figure 71.

[544] Hall 1986: 38, Figure 27.

[545] Schiaparelli 1927: 105–106, Figures 78, 80, 129, Figure 105 and Hall 1986: 38.

[546] Meskell 1999: 185.

[547] Source data from Meskell 1999: 374, Table 1. Meskell has used the copper *deben* prices proposed by Janssen 1975b: 510–538.

[548] This is calculated from the clothing inventory in Schiaparelli 1927 and the unit area of cloth/garment in Table 3.6.

[549] Hall 1986: 62.

[550] Vogelsang-Eastwood 1992a and Vogelsang-Eastwood 1993: 181–182 lists the length and width of a range of NK garments, as well as the length of woven cloth required to make them. She has used the measurements of surviving Egyptian garments from museums to assess the method of construction of the garments and the area of cloth used in manufacture. From her reproductions of the garments she has been able to interpret the practicalities of how the more complex kilts, tunics, cloaks and dresses were wrapped around the body. For élite shawls see Schiaparelli 1927: 93 and Vogelsang-Eastwood 1992a: 37, for élite kerchiefs see Vogelsang-Eastwood 1992a: 44–46 and Vogelsang-

Wardrobe of socio-economic group 4

Ostraca from Deir el-Medina show lists of garments that are thought to be laundry lists. They attest to craftsmen and their families having loincloths, sanitary cloths, tunics, bag-tunics, draped dresses, sleeves, kerchiefs for the head as protection from the sun, and sashes worn around the waist and crosswise around the body to absorb sweat.[551] From archaeological finds, it is clear that clothes were worn extensively in daily life and recycled.[552] Re-use of clothes has been included in the calculation of the annual replacement rates of garments due to wear and tear.

Wardrobe for socio-economic group 5

The number of garments owned by members of socio-economic group 5, who were predominantly farm workers and labourers, is the more difficult to assess. There is no archaeological evidence of the clothes worn by this group and it is assumed that the number of garments owned by them were the basic minimum. Vogelsang-Eastwood has proposed garment designs from tomb scenes of workers in the fields.[553] Some workers are shown wearing kerchiefs that protected them from the hot sun.[554] Loincloths, kilts, and short skirts with sashes are commonly represented.[555] Wrap-around cloaks made from coarse cloth were worn that would have given protection from wind-blown dust and warmth at night.[556]

Total numbers of garments owned

The total numbers of garments owned by a member of any of the socio-economic groups 1–5, based on their age and gender, are given in Table 3.4. Some interpolation is required to fill the gaps in evidence for garments across all socio-economic groups. Table 3.5 presents the total number of garments owned by each socio-economic group and is used later to calculate the total area of fabric to clothe a cohort of 100,000.[557] For example in Table 3.4, the total number of loin clothes of males aged 10 and over in socio-economic group 1 is 35 (column 5). The number of individuals from this demographic group is 27 (column 4). The total number of garments = 35 x 27 = 945 (column 5 in Table 3.5).

The total area of cloth required to clothe 100,000 cohort

The total area of cloth for the cohort of 100,000 is calculated by multiplying the number of garments owned by each socio-economic group (Table 3.5) by the matrix of the unit areas of each type of garment (Table 3.6). Allowances are made for gender; reducing the area for adult females by multiplying the male unit area by the factor 0.92 and for infants aged 0–3 and 4–9 by the factors 0.56 and 0.7 respectively. The total area of cloth required to make sufficient cloth in Egypt for all socio-economic groups is estimated to be 583,557 m^2/100,000 cohort (Table 3.7). The climate of Cyprus is colder than Egypt in winter and less hot in summer and so the area of cloth for cloaks, blankets, and kerchiefs have been increased by multiplying their unit areas by the ratios 1.2, 1.2, and 0.7 respectively.[558] The cumulative total area of cloth required in Cyprus to make sufficient cloth for all socio-economic groups is 593,348 m^2/100,000 cohort.

Annual cloth requirement

During a lifetime the garments would need replacing, usually when they wore out. This section calculates the annual demand for cloth taking into account four factors:

- The minimum number of garments needed to carry out the duties of the individual.
- The number of garments acquired.
- The garment wear, depending on the owner's socio-economic group.
- The accumulation of garments by the Socio-economic groups 1–2 over their lifetime.

This evaluation provides an amortised annual requirement for cloth necessary to supply each socio-economic group with their clothing needs.

Due to the cost of cloth it is assumed that manual workers (socio-economic groups 4–5) owned the minimum number of garments to carry out their manual duties. At the other end of the social scale, socio-economic groups 1–2 had more clothes than would be expected to carry out their duties. This is because their garments would not wear out to the same degree as manual workers and they desired to reinforce their status through conspicuous display. Wear-and-tear of textiles depended on the frequency of wear, the type of work carried out when worn, and gradual deterioration through laundering.[559]

Eastwood 1993: 171–178. For farm workers' sashes and straps see Janssen 1975b: 286, Vogelsang-Eastwood 1992a: 20–21, and Vogelsang-Eastwood 1993: 73–87 and for workers' kerchiefs see Vogelsang-Eastwood 1992a: 44.

[551] Janssen 2008: 77–93, Tables III–IV and McDowell 1999: 59–61. Some of these lists were sketches of garments with dots to represent the number of each particular garment (McDowell 1999: Figure 10). For the depiction of the laundry process shown in Khnumhotep's tomb at Beni Hasan, see Newberry 1893: Plate XXIX.

[552] Petrie found that garments in funerary contexts at Deshasheh were worn and frequently darned (Petrie 1898: 47–50 and Hall 1985: 239).

[553] Volgelsang-Eastwood 1992a, 1992b, 1993, 1994, and 2000.

[554] Volgelsang-Eastwood 1993: 176, Figure 10.7.

[555] Volgelsang-Eastwood 1993: 10–31 and 53–71, Figures 2.1–2.17 and 4.1–4.25.

[556] For a wide range of depictions of NK cloaks, see Vogelsang-Eastwood 1993: 159–168, Figures 9.4–9.15. For an artist's representation of the cloaks worn at Amarna, see Kemp and Vogelsang-Eastwood 2001: 237, Figure 6.70.

[557] It is assumed that children aged nine and younger in socio-economic group 5 had no new garments and were naked or clothed in second-hand garments.

[558] The average temperature of Nicosia in January for example is 10.6°C compared with 16.1°C at Luxor.

[559] Thirty-two samples of flax textiles from the Workmen's Village at Amarna were examined for wear by the Textile Department at the University of Manchester. Thirteen samples, four unbleached and seven bleached, showed considerable evidence of wear (Kemp and Vogelsang-Eastwood 2001: 232–234, particularly Table 6.8).

Dimensions (m) and unit areas of cloth (m^2) required to make Egyptian garments plus associated references.

BAG-TUNICS

Reference for full length bag-tunics Vogelsang-Eastwood 1993: 139, Table 2.

Length m	1.28	1.2	1.135	1.37	1.38	1.35	1.21	1.28	1.27	1.24	1.18	1.18	1.4
Width m	0.88	0.7	0.95	0.85	1.03	0.88	1.09	1.01	1.25	1.255	1.17	1.1	1.15

Average		
1.27	**Area m^2 (front and back)**	**2.55**
1.02		

SHORT BAG-TUNICS

Ref. for short bag-tunics - Vogelsang-Eastwood 1993: 151					Average	Area m^2
Length m	0.7	0.92	0.91	0.93	0.87	**1.48**
Width m	0.88	0.7	0.95	0.85	0.85	

APRONS Ref. for apron - Vogelsang-Eastwood 1992a: 12-13

Semi-circle lower part		Area m^2
length m = 0.52	width m = 0.45	**0.23**
Waistband		
length m = 0.36	width m = 0.12	**0.04**
First tie		
length m = 0.9	width m = 0.08	**0.07**
Second tie		
length m = 0.9	width m = 0.08	**0.07**
	Total area of apron	**0.41**

KILTS

Reference	length m =	width m =	area m^2 =	Average
Ref. for workman's short kilt - Vogelsang-Eastwood 1993: 181.	1.2	0.6	**0.72**	**Average 0.75**
Ref Digital Eg't. Deshasheh kilt (3rd IP), Acc. no.UC 31173	1.03	0.75	**0.77**	
Ref. for official's short kilt - Vogelsang-Eastwood 1992a: 14.	1.2	0.6	**0.72**	**Average 0.81**
Ref. for official's short kilt - Schiaparelli 1927: 92.	1.6	0.56	**0.9**	
Ref. for official's long kilt - Vogelsang-Eastwood 1993: 181.	3	1	**3**	
Ref. for sash kilt (kilt only) Metropoltitan Museum, Acc. no. 36.3.176	1.88	0.55	**1.03**	**Average 1.27**
Ref. for sash kilt (kilt only) - Vogelsang-Eastwood 1993: 181.	2.5	0.6	**1.5**	

LOIN CLOTHS

	length m	width m	Area m^2
Loin cloths estimated from Amarna samples. Ref. - Kemp and Vogesang-Eastwood 2001: 186, Figure 6.17. Assume loin cloth can be made from two triangles made from a square of cloth and sown together	1	0.45	**0.45**

SASHES

Reference	length m =	width m =	area m^2 =	Average
Typical simple sash Ref. - Vogelsang-Eastwood 1992a:	3	0.15	**0.45**	
Ref for sashes - Vogelsang-Eastwood 1993: 73-76.	1.07	0.2	**0.21**	**Average 0.39**
	3	0.165	**0.5**	
Ref for large sash - Janssen 1975b: 286.	1.8	0.375	**0.68**	

KERCHIEFS

Reference	length m =	width m =	area m^2 =	Average
Ref. for kerchiefs - Winlock 1941: 10.	0.48	0.63	**0.3**	**Average 0.32**
Ref. for kerchiefs - Vogelsang-Eastwood 1992a: 46	0.65	0.5	**0.33**	
Worker's kerchiefs - Vogelsang-Eastwood 1992a: 45	0.95	0.95	**0.9**	

DRESSES

Reference	length m =	width m =	area m^2 =	
Ref. V necked dress sleeves - Vogelsang-Eastwood 1992a: 30-31.	1.36	0.8	**1.09**	**Combined 2.29**
Ref. V necked dress wrap-around skirt - Vogelsang-Eastwood 1992a: 30-31.	1.2	1	**1.2**	
Ref. for long wrap-around dress - Vogelsang-Eastwood 1993: 101.	3.05	1.075	**3.28**	
Ref. for complex wrap-around dress - Vogelsang-Eastwood 1993: 181.	4	1	**4**	**Average 3.15**
Ref. for complex wrap-around dress - Bruyère 1937: Figure 30.	1.68	1.37	**2.3**	

SHAWLS

Reference	length m =	width m =	area m^2 =	Average
Ref. for short shawl - Vogelsang-Eastwood 1992a: 37.	0.75	0.75	**0.56**	
Ref. for medium shawl - Brunton 1940: 522, 527.	1.4	0.9	**1.26**	**Average 1.79**
Ref. for med. Shawl - Vogelsang-Eastwood 1993: 101,181.	1.28	1.2	**1.54**	
Ref. for Kha's long shawls - Schiaparelli 1927: 93.	4.3	0.6	**2.58**	

SKIRTS

Reference	length m =	width m =	area m^2 =
Ref. for woman's long skirt - Vogelsang-Eastwood 1992a: 15.	1.3	0.6	**0.78**
Ref. for woman's long skirt - Vogelsang-Eastwood 1993: 181.	3	0.8	**2.4**

CLOAKS

Reference	length m =	width m =	area m^2 =	Average
Simple wrap-around cloak - Vogelsang-Eastwood 1992a: 40.	1.4	1.2	**1.68**	**Average 2.24**
Knotted wrap-around cloak - Vogelsang-Eastwood 1992a: 40.	1.4	2	**2.8**	
Complex long wrap-around cloak - Vogelsang-Eastwood 1993: 181.	3	1.2	**3.6**	**Average 3.21**
Complex long wrap-around cloak - Vogelsang-Eastwood 1992a: 42.	2.1	1.15	**2.42**	
Typical long wrap-around cloak - Vogelsang-Eastwood 1992a: 40.	3	1.2	**3.6**	

Table 3.3: Dimensions (m) and unit areas of cloth (m^2) required to make Egyptian garments.

1	2	3	4	5	6	7	8	9	10	11	12	13	14	15	16	17	18	19	20	21	22	23	24
Socio-economic group	No. within group	Gender	Pop.	Loin cloths	Kilts			Δ apron	Long bag-tunic	Sashes	Short bag-tunic	Shawls		Wrap-around cloaks		Female skirt		V neck dress	Wrap-around dress		Ker-chiefs	Blankets	Total
					Long	Short	Sash					Med/long	Short	Simple	Complex	Long	Short		Long	Complex			
1. Royalty, nobles and high élite	78	Male 10+	27	35	15	6	5	12	10	10	7	8	12	8	6						8	15	157
		Female 10+	27	15						8		4	5	3	3			8	8	4	3	6	67
		Child 4-9	12	5		2		4	2	2	4	1	1	1				3	5		2	4	36
		Child 0-3	12	2									2									2	6
2. Senior officials	186	Male 10+	65	8	5	3	2	6	6	4	4	4	5	4	2	0	0	0	0	0	6	8	67
		Female 10+	65	4	0	0	0	0	0	2		2	3	2	1	0	0	4	4	2	2	5	31
		Child 4-9	28	2	0	0	0	3	0	1	3	2	3	1	0	0	0	1	3	0	2	2	23
		Child 0-3	28	1	0	0	0	0	0	0			1		0	0	0	0	0	0	0	1	3
3. Army officers, med. rank scribes/officials	1518	Male 10+	532	3	1	3	3	2	2	2	3	1	2	1	1						2	5	31
		Female 10+	532	3						1		1	2	1	1			1	1	2	1	3	17
		Child 4-9	225	1				1			1	1	1	1				1	1		1	1	10
		Child 0-3	229																				0
4. Lower professionals, skilled workers	10000	Male 10+	3,504	2	1	2		1	1	1	1	1	1	1	1						1	2	16
		Female 10+	3,504	2						1		1	1	1		1	1	1	1	1	1	1	13
		Child 4-9	1,484											1					1		1	1	4
		Child 0-3	1,508																				0
5. Farm workers + manual labourers	88218	Male 10+	30,912	1		1			1	1	1			1							1	1	8
		Female 10+	30,912	1						1				1			1				1	1	6
		Child 4-9	13,092																				0
		Child 0-3	13,302																				0
Total	100,000		100,000	85	22	17	10	29	22	34	24	26	39	27	15	1	2	19	24	9	32	58	495

Table 3.4: Number of garments owned/individual in SEG 1–5, collated by type, age, and gender.

1	2	3	4	5	6	7	8	9	10	11	12	13	14	15	16	17	18	19	20	21	22	23	24
Socio-economic group	No.	Gender	Pop.	Loin cloths	Kilts			Δ apron	Long bag-tunic	Sashes	Short bag-tunic	Shawls		Wrap-around cloaks		Female skirt		V neck dress	Wrap-around dress		Ker-chiefs	Blankets	Total
					Long	Short	Sash					Med/long	Short	Simple	Complex	Long	Short		Long	Complex			
1. Royalty, nobles and high élite	78	Male 10+	27	945	405	162	135	324	270	270	189	216	324	216	162						216	405	4,239
		Female 10+	27	405						216		108	135	81	81			216	216	108	81	162	1,809
		Child 4-9	12	60		24		48	24	24	48	12	12	12				36	60		24	48	432
		Child 0-3	12	24									24									24	72
2. Senior officials	186	Male 10+	65	520	325	195	130	390	390	260	260	260	325	260	130						390	520	4,355
		Female 10+	65	260						130		130	195	130	65			260	260	130	130	325	2,015
		Child 4-9	28	56				84		28	84	56	84	28				28	84		56	56	644
		Child 0-3	28	28									28									28	84
3. Army officers, med. rank scribes/officials	1518	Male 10+	532	1,596	532	1,596	1,596	1,064	1,064	1,064	1,596	532	1,064	532	532						1,064	2,660	16,492
		Female 10+	532	1,596						532		532	1,064	532	532			532	532	1,064	532	1,596	9,044
		Child 4-9	225	225				225			225	225	225	225				225	225		225	225	2,250
		Child 0-3	229																				
4. Lower professionals, skilled workers	10000	Male 10+	3,504	7,008	3,504	7,008		3,504	3,504	3,504	3,504	3,504	3,504	3,504	3,504						3,504	7,008	56,064
		Female 10+	3,504	7,008						3,504		3,504	3,504	3,504		3,504	3,504	3,504	3,504	3,504	3,504	3,504	45,552
		Child 4-9	1,484											1,484					1,484		1,484	1,484	5,936
		Child 0-3	1,508																				
5. Farm workers + manual labourers	88218	Male 10+	30,912	30,912		30,912			30,912	30,912	30,912			30,912							30,912	30,912	247,296
		Female 10+	30,912	30,912						30,912				30,912			30,912				30,912	30,912	185,472
		Child 4-9	13,092																				
		Child 0-3	13,302																				
Total	100,000		100,000	81,555	4,766	39,897	1,861	5,639	36,164	71,356	36,818	9,079	10,488	72,332	5,006	3,504	34,416	4,801	6,365	4,806	73,034	79,869	581,756

Table 3.5: Number of garments owned by SEG 1–5 for 100,000 cohort, collated by type, age, and gender.

1	2	3	4	5	6	7	8	9	10	11	12	13	14	15	16	17	18	19	20	21	22	23	24
Socio-economic group	No. within group	Gender	Pop.	Loin cloths	Kilts			Δ apron	Long bag-tunic	Sashes	Short bag-tunic	Shawls		Wrap-around cloaks		Female skirt		V neck dress	Wrap-around dress		Ker-chiefs	Blankets	Total
					Long	Short	Sash					Med/long	Short	Simple	Complex	Long	Short		Long	Complex			
1. Royalty, nobles and high élite	78	Male 10+	27	0.45	3	0.81	1.27	0.41	2.55	0.39	1.48	1.79	1.79	2.24	3.21						0.32	2.1	21.81
		Female 10+	27	0.41						0.36		1.65	1.65	1.55	2.23	2.4	0.78	2.29	3.28	3.15	0.29	2	22.04
		Child 4-9	12	0.32		0.567	1	0.287	1.79	0.27	1.04	1.25	1.25	1.176	1.69			1.603	2.3	1.61	0.224	1.2	17.577
		Child 0-3	12	0.252									1									1	2.252
2. Senior officials	186	Male 10+	65	0.45	3	0.81	1.27	0.41	2.55	0.39	1.48	1.79	1.79	1.68	3.21						0.32	2.1	21.25
		Female 10+	65	0.41						0.36		1.65	1.65	1.55	2.23	2.4	0.78	2.29	3.28	3.15	0.29	2	22.04
		Child 4-9	28	0.32		0.567		0.287	1.79	0.27	1.04	1.25	1.25	1.176				1.603	2.3	1.61	0.224	1.2	14.887
		Child 0-3	28	0.252									1									1	2.252
3. Army officers, medium rank scribes/officials	1,518	Male 10+	532	0.45	3	0.81	1.27	0.41	2.55	0.39	1.48	1.79	1.79	1.68	3.21						0.32	2.1	21.25
		Female 10+	532	0.41						0.36		1.65	1.65	1.55	2.23	2.4	0.78	2.29	3.28	3.15	0.29	2	22.04
		Child 4-9	225	0.32				0.287	1.79	0.27	1.04	1.25	1.25	1.176				1.603	2.3	1.61	0.224	1.2	14.32
		Child 0-3	229	0.252									1									1	2.252
4. Lower professionals, skilled workers	10,000	Male 10+	3,504	0.45	3	0.75	1.27	0.41	2.55	0.39	1.48	1.79	1.79	1.68	3.21						0.9	2.1	21.77
		Female 10+	3,504	0.41						0.36		1.65	1.65	1.55		2.4	0.78	2.29	3.28	3.15	0.83	2	20.35
		Child 4-9	1,484	0.32								1.25	1.25	1.176					2.3			1.2	7.496
		Child 0-3	1,508	0.252									1									1	2.252
5. Farm workers + manual labourers	88,218	Male 10+	30,912	0.45		0.75			2.55	0.39	1.48	1.79	1.79	1.68							0.9	2.1	13.88
		Female 10+	30,911	0.41						0.36		1.65	1.65	1.55		2.4	0.78		3.28		0.83	2	14.91
		Child 4-9	13,092	0.32									1.25	1.176					2.3			1.2	6.246
		Child 0-3	13,303	0.252																		1	1.252
	100,000		100,000	7.16	12.00	5.06	6.08	2.50	18.12	4.56	10.52	22.20	27.45	22.59	21.22	12.00	3.90	13.97	27.90	17.43	5.96	31.50	272.13

Table 3.6: Unit areas (m^2) of cloth required to make the different types of garments.

1	2	3	4	5	6	7	8	9	10	11	12	13	14	15	16	17	18	19	20	21	22	23	24
Socio-economic group	No.	Gender	Pop.	Loin cloths	Kilts			Δ apron	Long bag-tunic	Sashes	Short bag-tunic	Shawls		Wrap-around cloaks		Female skirt		V neck dress	Wrap-around dress		Ker-chiefs	Blankets	Total
					Long	Short	Sash					Med/long	Short	Simple	Complex	Long	Short		Long	Complex			
1. Royalty, nobles and high elite	78	Male 10+	27	425	1,215	131	171	133	689	105	280	387	580	484	520						69	851	6,040
		Female 10+	27	405						216		108	135	81	81			216	216	108	81	162	1,809
		Child 4-9	12	60		24		48	24	24	48	12	12	12				36	60		24	48	432
		Child 0-3	12	24									24									24	72
2. Senior officials	186	Male 10+	65	520	325	195	130	390	390	260	260	260	325	260	130						390	520	4,355
		Female 10+	65	260						130		130	195	130	65			260	260	130	130	325	2,015
		Child 4-9	28	56				84		28	84	56	84	28				28	84		56	56	644
		Child 0-3	28	28									28									28	84
3. Army officers, med. rank scribes/officials	1,518	Male 10+	532	1,596	532	1,596	1,596	1,064	1,064	1,064	1,596	532	1,064	532	532						1,064	2,660	16,492
		Female 10+	532	1,596						532		532	1,064	532	532			532	532	1,064	532	1,596	9,044
		Child 4-9	225	225				225			225	225	225	225				225	225		225	225	2,250
		Child 0-3	229																				
4. Lower professionals, skilled workers	10,000	Male 10+	3,504	7,008	3,504	7,008		3,504	3,504	3,504	3,504	3,504	3,504	3,504	3,504						3,504	7,008	56,064
		Female 10+	3,504	7,008						3,504		3,504	3,504	3,504		3,504	3,504	3,504	3,504	3,504	3,504	3,504	45,552
		Child 4-9	1,484											1,484					1,484		1,484	1,484	5,936
		Child 0-3	1,508																				
5. Farm workers + manual labourers	88,218	Male 10+	30,912	30,912		30,912			30,912	30,912	30,912			30,912							30,912	30,912	247,296
		Female 10+	30,912	30,912						30,912				30,912			30,912				30,912	30,912	185,472
		Child 4-9	13,092																				
		Child 0-3	13,302																				
	100,000		100,000	81,035	5,576	39,866	1,897	5,448	36,583	71,191	36,909	9,250	10,744	72,600	5,364	3,504	34,416	4,801	6,365	4,806	72,887	80,315	583,557

Column	1	2	3	4	5	6	7	8	9	10	11	12	13	14	15	16	17	18	19	20	21	22	23	24	25	26	27	28	29	30	31	32	33	34	35	36	
Age	5	6	7	8	9	10	11	12	13	14	15	16	17	18	19	20	21	22	23	24	25	26	27	28	29	30	31	32	33	34	35	36	37	38	39	40	Total
Accumulation profile	1	0	0	0	0	0	0	0	0	0	0	0	0	0	0	0	0	0	0	0	0	0	0	0	0	0	0	0	0	0	0	0	0	0	0	0	1
Replacement/3 yrs					1	0	0	0	0	0	0	0	0	0	0	0	0	0	0	0	0	0	0	0	0	0	0	0	0	0	0	0	0	0	0	0	1
Replacement/3 yrs								1	0	0	0	0	0	0	0	0	0	0	0	0	0	0	0	0	0	0	0	0	0	0	0	0	0	0	0	0	1
Replacement/3 yrs											1	0	0	0	0	0	0	0	0	0	0	0	0	0	0	0	0	0	0	0	0	0	0	0	0	0	1
Replacement/3 yrs														1	0	0	0	0	0	0	0	0	0	0	0	0	0	0	0	0	0	0	0	0	0	0	1
Replacement/3 yrs																	1	0	0	0	0	0	0	0	0	0	0	0	0	0	0	0	0	0	0	0	1
Replacement/3 yrs																				1	0	0	0	0	0	0	0	0	0	0	0	0	0	0	0	0	1
Replacement/3 yrs																							1	0	0	0	0	0	0	0	0	0	0	0	0	0	1
Replacement/3 yrs																										1	0	0	0	0	0	0	0	0	0	0	1
Replacement/3 yrs																													1		0	0	0	0	0	0	1
Replacement/3 yrs																																1	0	0	0	0	1
Replacement/3 yrs																																			1	0	1
Grand total	1	0	0	0	1	0	0	1	0	0	1	0	0	1	0	0	1	0	0	1	0	0	1	0	0	1	0	0	1	0	0	1	0	0	1	0	12

Table 3.8: Accumulation/amortised replacement rate for loincloths = 3.5 yrs over the life of an adult male in SEG 5.

Column	1	2	3	4	5	6	7	8	9	10	11	12	13	14	15	16	17	18	19	20	21	22	23	24	25	26	27	28	29	30	31	32	33	34	35	36	
Age	5	6	7	8	9	10	11	12	13	14	15	16	17	18	19	20	21	22	23	24	25	26	27	28	29	30	31	32	33	34	35	36	37	38	39	40	Total
Accumulation profile	1	0	1	1	1	1	1	1	1	1	1	1	1	1	1	1	1	1	1	1	1	1	1	1	1	1	1	1	1	1	1	1	1	1	1	1	35
Replacement/7.5 yrs							1	0	1	1	1	1	1	1	1	1	1	1	1	1	1	1	1	1	1	1	1	1	1	1	1	1	1	1	1	1	29
Replacement/7.5 yrs														1	0	1	1	1	1	1	1	1	1	1	1	1	1	1	1	1	1	1	1	1	1	1	22
Replacement/7.5 yrs																				1	0	1	1	1	1	1	1	1	1	1	1	1	1	1	1	1	16
Replacement/7.5 yrs																											1	0	1	1	1	1	1	1	1	1	9
Replacement/7.5 yrs																																			1	1	2
Grand total	1	0	1	1	1	1	2	1	2	2	2	2	2	3	2	3	3	3	3	4	3	4	4	4	4	4	5	4	5	5	5	5	5	5	6	6	113

Table 3.9: Accumulation/amortised replacement rate for loincloths = 7.5 yrs over the life of an adult male in SEG 1.

1	2	3	4	5	6	7	8	9	10	11	12	13	14	15	16	17	18	19	20	21	22	23	24
Socio-economic group	No.	Gender	Pop.	Loin cloths	Kilts			Δ apron	Long bag-tunic	Sashes	Short bag-tunic	Shawls		Wrap-ar. cloaks		Female skirt		V neck dress	Wrap-around dress		Ker-chiefs	Blankets	Total
					Long	Short	Sash					Med/long	Short	Simple	Complex	Long	Short		Long	Complex			
1. Royalty, nobles and high elite	78	Male 10+	27	38	105	13	17	11	62	9	25	35	48	44	52						6	74	539
		Female 10+	27	14						7		18	22	14	20			45	65	34	3	32	274
		Child 4-9	12	2		2		1	6	1	5	3	3	2				6	14		1	6	52
		Child 0-3	12	1									3									3	7
2. Senior officials	186	Male 10+	65	21	98	17	22	16	99	10	38	47	58	44	56						12	100	638
		Female 10+	65	11						6		29	35	27	24			60	85	55	5	65	402
		Child 4-9	28	2				3		1	10	9	12	5				7	21		2	9	81
		Child 0-3	28	1									5									5	11
3. Army officers, med. rank scribes/officials	1,518	Male 10+	532	96	319	172	270	72	448	68	315	190	314	179	342						56	749	3,590
		Female 10+	532	87						38		176	290	165	237			244	349	553	31	426	2,596
		Child 4-9	225	14				13			47	56	56	53				72	104		10	54	479
		Child 0-3	229																				
4. Lower professionals, skilled workers	10,000	Male 10+	3,504	836	3,469	1,393		474	2,949	451	1,711	2,070	2,070	1,943	3,712						1,041	3,900	26,019
		Female 10+	3,504	761						416		1,908	1,908	1,792		2,775	902	2,648	3,793	3,642	960	2,313	23,818
		Child 4-9	1,484											576					1,126			588	2,290
		Child 0-3	1,508																				
5. Farm workers + manual labourers	88,218	Male 10+	30,912	4,590		7,651			26,012	3,978	15,097			17,138							9,181	21,422	105,069
		Female 10+	30,912	4,182						3,672				15,811			7,957				8,467	20,402	60,491
		Child 4-9	13,092																				
		Child 0-3	13,302																				
Total	100,000		100,000	10,656	3,991	9,248	309	590	29,576	8,657	17,248	4,541	4,824	37,793	4,443	2,775	8,859	3,082	5,557	4,284	19,775	50,148	226,356

Table 3.10: The Egyptian amortised area of cloth required to clothe a cohort of 100,000/yr.

The Egyptians may have used natron to whiten flax cloth and combined with destructive ultra-violet light, this would have weakened the linen fibres.[560] This study has made the following assumption for the average useful life of garments collated by socio-economic group (Table 3.11).

Socio-economic group	Average useful life of a garment (yrs)
1–2	7.5
3	5.5
4–5	3.5

Table 3.11: Useful life of garments collated by socio-economic group.

The amortised annual rate of cloth production

The loincloth has been chosen for socio-economic groups 1 and 5 to explain how the amortised area of cloth (m^2/yr) is calculated. The full analysis for all the socio-groups and their wardrobes are given in Table 3.4 and Table 3.5.

Starting with the socio-economic group 5, it has been assumed that each loincloth wore out every 3.5 years and no garments were retained after they were worn out. At this rate of replacement, and assuming a life expectancy of 40 years, a man would require 12 loincloths to be made over this period assuming his first loincloth was received at the age of five (Table 3.8).[561] The amortised rate per annum would be 12 ÷ 35 = 0.33 loincloths per annum.[562] The total amortised annual area of cloth required for loincloths across all adult males and females in this group = the number of male and female in socio-economic group 5 × unit area of loincloth × amortised rate = (30,912 × 0.45 × 0.33) + (30,912 × 0.41 × 0.33) = 8,772 m^2 of cloth.

For the high élite socio-economic group 1, wear-and-tear would have been significantly lower, their wardrobe would accumulate over and above that required to replace worn out garments and they had the wealth to purchase surplus garments. For this group, it is assumed that their garments only required replacement every 7.5 years. Taking the adult male as an example, the accumulated number of new loincloths over his life would be 35, the first aged 5, the second age 7, followed thereafter by one new loincloth per year until his death. As stated above after 7.5 years each loincloth will wear out and requires replacing therefore the total number of loincloths required to be made to ensure that at the end of his life for the deceased male would have owned 35 loincloths (column 5 in Table 3.4), would be 113 (Table 3.9). This results in a combined amortised accumulation and wear-and-tear rate over 35 years equal to 113 ÷ 36 (years clothed from 5 to 40) = 3.14 loincloths per annum. A similar analysis applies to a female who owned 15 loincloths when she died. The total amortised annual area (m^2) of cloth required for socio-economic group 1 males to be made each year equals the number of mature males in socio-economic group 1 × unit area of loincloth × amortised rate m^2 = 27 × 0.45 × 3.14 = 38.2 m^2 of cloth per annum. Using the same methodology for females the total annual area of cloth required for loincloths across all members of socio-economic group 1 is 55 m^2 (Table 3.10, SEG 1, column 5).

The amortised annual cloth requirement collated by garment type and social economic groups

The amortised area of cloth to be made each year to ensure sufficient fabric to clothe a sample 100,000 cohort for Egypt is 226,356 m^2 of cloth (Table 3.10). The Cypriot requirement has been increased to compensate for colder winters than Egypt. The amortised annual area of cloth required to be made each year to ensure sufficient fabric to clothe a sample 100,000 cohort for Cyprus was 238,901 m^2 of cloth. The amortised annual area of cloth required (m^2)/100,000 cohort/yr by socio-economic group for both regions is summarised in Table 3.12. From these distributions, the length of yarn required and the weight of flax to be grown each year can be determined.

Socio-economic groupings	Egypt	Cyprus
	Area of cloth m^2	
1	872	918
2	1,132	1,193
3	6,665	7,077
4	52,127	54,492
5	165,560	175,221
Total area	**226,356**	**238,901**

Table 3.12: Estimated area of fabric to clothe a 100,000 cohort/yr collated by socio-economic group.

3.5 Weight of flax fibre required

The weight of flax needed to make the cloth is used later to calculate the manpower to grow the flax and prepare it for spinning, plying, and weaving. This section calculates the weight (kg) of flax required to support the clothing needs of a population cohort of 100,000/yr for Egypt and Cyprus. This analysis is carried out in four stages:

- Estimation of the quality of the cloth used to make the garments across socio-economic groups 1–5.
- The determination of the type of yarn used to make these garments.
- The calculation of the length of yarn required.
- The calculation of the weight of flax required (kg) to produce the yarn.

[560] Natron breaks down the cement that binds the linen fibres together. This would have weakened the fibres, especially if natron was used frequently to launder the garments (Kemp and Vogelsang-Eastwood 2001: 232–234).

[561] In antiquity life expectancy from birth is not applicable for this calculation due to the high mortality rate up to the age of 5. For cloth requirements, life expectancy starts with individuals at 5 years as prior this they probably did not have clothing. For this reason it is assumed that the average life expectancy for those who have survived to the age of 5 will on average, be 40 years. It is assumed that for SEG 5, children started to help in the fields at the age of 5. However, the wear would be less for this age group and the first replacement was after 4 years followed by every 3 years for the rest of his life.

[562] This means a manual worker's loincloth would be replaced every 3 years.

Quality of cloth

The combination of the relative density of the warp and weft yarns, and the yarn diameter defines the quality of a piece of cloth.[563] The web-based database provided by the Amarna textile research team has been used to estimate the range of cloth qualities in the garments owned by socio-economic groups 1–5.[564] The database provides the yarn diameters and warp and weft counts of 3,385 textile samples found in the Workmen's Village at Amarna.[565] Yarn diameter ranged from 1: very fine (less than 0.2 mm), 2: fine (0.2–0.3 mm), 3: medium (0.4–0.6 mm), 4: coarse (0.6–0.9 mm), to 5: very coarse (greater than 0.9 mm). A summary of these diameter ranges collated by social economic group have been collated in Table 3.13.

SEG	Range of yarn diameters (n= 3,385)	Average yarn diameter mm	Sample count	%
1	Less than 0.2	0.15	503	14.9
2	0.2–0.3	0.25	2,407	71
3	0.4–0.6	0.5	435	12.9
4	0.7–0.9	0.75	34	1
5	Greater than 0.9	1	6	0.2
			3,385	**100**

Table 3.13: Yarn diameters measured from 3,385 samples from the Amarna Workmen's Village.

It is necessary to make some assumptions regarding the quality of cloth worn by each socio-economic group. They are biased towards Egyptian evidence, which is considered representative for other Eastern Mediterranean regions that had similar socio-economic hierarchies and technology of cloth production. The Amarna database shows that the majority of yarns had a weft count per cm that ranged between four and twenty-five and the majority of the warp counts per cm ranged between five and forty.[566] The Amarna database also includes twenty samples that can be classified as fine or ultra fine cloth.[567] Two scatter plot diagrams of weft/warp counts of textile samples in museums are a good fit to the envelope of the Amarna database.[568] This study assumes that the Amarna data is representative of NK textile production and that there were five main qualities of cloth worn as defined in Table 3.13. It is assumed that in general, the higher up the social scale of the owner, the finer the linen cloth.[569] However, it is likely that within any socio-economic group, a range of yarn diameters would have been used and the estimated percentage spread based on the yarn diameters measured in the Amarna database is given in Table 3.14.

	Percentage average yarn diameter mm					
	0.15	**0.25**	**0.5**	**0.75**	**1.0**	**Total**
SEG 1	35	55	9	1	0	100
SEG 2	29	60	10	1	0	100
SEG 3	16	72	11	1	0	100
SEG 4	14.9	71	12.9	1	0.2	100
SEG 5	0	10	30	45	15	100

Table 3.14: Estimated percentage distribution of yarn diameters collated by socio-economic group.

Applying these percentages to the amortised annual requirement of cloth, the area of five qualities of cloth is collated by their respective socio-economic groups (Table 3.15).

Egypt	Yarn diameters mm					Area of cloth m^2
	0.15	**0.25**	**0.50**	**0.75**	**1.00**	
SEG 1	305	480	78	9	0	872
SEG 2	328	679	113	11	0	1,131
SEG 3	1,066	4,799	733	67	0	6,665
SEG 4	7,746	37,068	6,698	521	94	52,127
SEG 5	0	16,556	49,668	74,503	24,834	165,561
	9,445	**59,582**	**57,290**	**75,111**	**24,928**	**226,356**

Cyprus	Yarn diameters mm					Area of cloth m^2
	0.15	**0.25**	**0.50**	**0.75**	**1.00**	
SEG 1	321	505	83	9	0	918
SEG 2	346	716	119	12	0	1,193
SEG 3	1,132	5,095	778	71	0	7,076
SEG 4	8,098	38,749	7,002	545	98	54,492
SEG 5	0	17,522	52,567	78,849	26,284	175,222
	9,897	**62,587**	**60,549**	**79,486**	**26,382**	**238,901**

Table 3.15: The area of cloth (m^2/100,000/yr) for Egypt and Cyprus collated by yarn diameter and SEG.

Length of yarn required to make one metre of cloth

To estimate the length of yarn required to make one square metre of cloth for the five qualities of cloth in Table 3.15, the warp and weft counts in the Amarna database are used. The distribution within each diameter band is not normal, so the median is used rather than a simple average. The warp and weft counts per metre for the 1 mm diameter yarn are extrapolated from the others, as only two samples greater than 0.9 mm were in a good enough state of preservation to be measured. The results are tabulated for 3,385 samples in Table 3.16.

Average yarn diameter mm (n= 3,385)	Median warps/m	Median wefts/m
0.15	2,940	1,690
0.25	2,260	1,230
0.5	1,760	950
0.8	1,010	810
1	800	500

Table 3.16: Average warp and weft counts in 3,385 samples collated by yarn diameter.

[563] Kemp and Vogelsang-Eastwood 2001: 99.

[564] Kemp 2013.

[565] The number of samples found in Amarna total 4,962 but not all samples were in a sufficient state of preservation for measurements to be made. When I analysed the database there were 3,385 measurable samples but the later analysis by Kemp and Volgelsang Eastwood 2001: Figure 4.11 is based on 3,687 weft/warp counts.

[566] Kemp and Vogelsang-Eastwood 2001: 99–100, Figure 4.11.

[567] Kemp and Volgelsang Eastwood 2001: 100–102 and Table 4.2.

[568] Kemp and Volgelsang Eastwood 2001: Figures 4.12b–c.

[569] Kemp and Vogelsang-Eastwood 2001: 99–103 analysed warp and weft densities and yarn diameters from textile samples excavated from the Amarna Workmen's village. They used this data to define the cloth quality and character of the weave. Ultra-fine cloth would have warp counts greater than 80 per cm, fine 60 per cm, down to 5 per cm for coarse cloth.

When estimating the length of yarn required to weave a given area of cloth, allowance must be made for the reduction in the area of woven cloth through 'take up' and 'shrinkage'. During the weaving process, the weft goes over and under the warps drawing them closer together. This is called the take-up and it could reduce the weft by as much as 10% and the warp by 8%. In addition, when the cloth is washed, shrinkage occurs. For flax and wool, this is typically 6% in the weft and 8% in the warp. Therefore, to produce a finished piece of cloth one metre square, the weft and the warp on the loom must both be set to lengths of 1.16 m. A length of 0.8 m must be added to the warp for tying off, making a length of 1.96 m for each warp.[570]

Knowing the median of the weft and warp counts, and multiplying them by the lengths of a single weft and warp identified above (0.8 m and 1.96 m respectively), the total length of yarn required to make one m^2 of cloth can be calculated. For example for the cloth using yarn with an average of 0.15 mm diameter, the average values for the weft and warp counts were 2,940/m and 1,690/m respectively. The length of yarn to make one square metre of cloth would be (2,940 × 1.96) + (1,690 × 1.16) = 7,722 m. For the full range of yarn diameter bands see Table 3.17.

Yarn diameters mm	0.15	0.25	0.5	0.75	1
Average warp count/m	2,940	2,260	1,760	1,010	800
Average weft count/m	1,690	1,230	950	810	500
Warp thread length/m^2	5,762	4,430	3,450	1,980	1,568
Weft thread length/m^2	1,960	1,427	1,102	940	580
Total	**7,722**	**5,857**	**4,552**	**2,920**	**2,148**

Table 3.17: Total length of yarn required to make one m^2 of cloth collated by Amarna yarn diameters (mm).

Total length of yarn required collated by socio-economic group

Multiplying the square metres of cloth required by each socio-economic class (Table 3.15) by its respective length of yarn (Table 3.17), the total length of yarn for all socio-economic groups can be calculated.[571] A summary for all the socio-economic groups collated by yarn diameter is given in Table 3.18. The sum of all the lengths needed to provide sufficient yarn to clothe a cohort of 100,000/yr comes to an astounding length of yarn: 955,556 km and 1,007,381 km for Egypt and Cyprus respectively. These figures demonstrate that the cloth-making industry was very labour-intensive, and explains why cloth was so highly valued.

Yarn diam.	0.15 mm	0.25 mm	0.5 mm	0.75 mm	1 mm	Total
SEG1	2,355	2,811	355	26	0	5,547
SEG2	2,533	3,977	514	32	0	7,056
SEG3	8,232	28,108	3,337	196	0	39,873
SEG4	59,815	217,107	30,489	1,521	202	309,134
SEG5	0	96,968	226,089	217,546	53,343	593,946
Total	**72,935**	**348,971**	**260,784**	**219,321**	**53,545**	**955,556**

Yarn diam.	0.15 mm	0.25 mm	0.5 mm	0.75 mm	1 mm	Total
SEG1	2,479	2,958	378	26	0	5,841
SEG2	2,672	4,194	542	35	0	7,443
SEG3	8,741	29,841	3,541	207	0	42,330
SEG4	62,533	226,953	31,873	1,591	211	323,161
SEG5	0	102,626	239,285	230,239	56,456	628,606
Total	**76,425**	**366,572**	**275,619**	**232,098**	**56,667**	**1,007,381**

Table 3.18: Length of yarn (m) required to meet the annual demand for clothing in Egypt and Cyprus.

Weight of yarn required to clothe a cohort of 100,000/yr

To calculate the weight of flax that had to be cultivated it is necessary to calculate the weight of yarn required. No data is available for the weight of extant yarns from antiquity, so estimates have been made using modern published data. The nearest modern equivalent to the 0.5 mm diameter band yarns from Amarna are Londonderry 50/3 yarns.[572] The weight (kg) of one metre of yarn is collated by yarn diameter in Table 3.19.

Av. yarn diameters mm	0.15	0.25	0.5	0.75	1
Nearest modern equivalent	160/3	130/3	50/3	20/3	18/3
Length of yarn to make 1 kg of yarn	32,280	26,228	10,088	4,035	3,632
Weight kg/m	**0.00003098**	**0.0000381**	**0.0000991**	**0.000248**	**0.000275**

Table 3.19: Estimated weight (kg) of one metre of 3 ply yarn collated by yarn diameter (mm).

Egypt	Weight of yarn collated by yarn diameter					Weight kg
	0.15 mm	0.25 mm	0.5 mm	0.75 mm	1 mm	
SEG 1	73	107	35	6	0	221
SEG 2	78	152	51	8	0	289
SEG 3	255	1,072	331	49	0	1,707
SEG 4	1,853	8,278	3,022	377	56	13,586
SEG 5		3,697	22,412	53,915	14,687	94,711
Total	**2,259**	**13,306**	**25,851**	**54,355**	**14,743**	**110,514**

Cyprus	Weight of yarn collated by yarn diameter					Weight kg
	0.15 mm	0.25 mm	0.5 mm	0.75 mm	1 mm	
SEG 1	77	113	37	6	0	233
SEG 2	83	160	54	9	0	306
SEG 3	271	1,138	351	51	0	1,811
SEG 4	1,937	8,653	3,159	394	58	14,201
SEG 5		13,976	27,321	57,521	15,603	114,421
Total	**2,368**	**24,040**	**30,922**	**57,981**	**15,661**	**130,972**

Table 3.20: Weight (kg) of yarn (dry flax fibre or wool) to clothe a cohort of 100,000/yr in Egypt and Cyprus.

[570] Length of weft required = 1 + (1 × 10/100) + (1 × 6/100) = 1.16 m. Length of warp required = 1 + (1 × 8/100) + (1 × 8/100) + 0.8 = 1.96 m (Petrini 2012).

[571] Taking as an example Egyptian cloth made with the yarn diameter 0.15 mm, the area of cloth required for socio-economic group 4 is 7,746 m^2 (Table 3.15). The length of yarn required to make one m^2 of cloth using yarn of 0.15 mm diameter equals 7,722 m (Table 3.17). Multiplying these two together gives the total length of 0.15 mm yarn used by socio-economic group 4 as 7,746 × 7,722 ÷ 1000 = 59,815 km of yarn.

[572] By convention the first number is an indicator of weight and the lower this number, the greater the weight of yarn per unit length. The second number indicates the number of threads in a plied yarn.

The total weight of yarn required to clothe a cohort of 100,000/yr is calculated by multiplying the total length of yarn required to meet the annual demand for cloth (Table 3.18) by the weight of one m of yarn (Table 3.19).

3.6 Growing flax in ancient Egypt

Cultivation of flax

Linseed was sown by broadcasting from late October to mid November and the plant was harvested in March–mid April.[573] The optimum time to harvest the flax is when the stems are half-ripe with fine fibres and this flax is termed 'green flax'. A delay in harvesting allows the fibres to coarsen, making them unsuitable for spinning, although they still have economic value as a material to make ropes and matting.[574] Flax requires prime land that readily drains as it cannot be grown in waterlogged soil but in the growing season it requires frequent watering.[575] The wall painting in the MK tomb of Urarna shows the ploughing and sowing cycle of flax, with a flock of sheep used to trample in the seed.[576] Flax germinates within 8–15 days and full growth takes up to 100 days. The harvest can start after the flower heads have died away and the seed heads have formed.[577] Flax today is grown thickly to prevent the plant branching and encourage the growth of long fibres and it is reasonable to assume the same practice was carried out in antiquity.[578] Before the advent of herbicides, weeding was imperative when the plants reached a height of 0.08 m. This prevented them from smothering the tender flax plants, taking away sunlight and nutrients. Weeds also contaminate the water during the retting process, which can damage the bast fibres.[579] The plant takes about three months to mature and the time of harvesting is important. Young plants provide fine fibres and if too old, the fibres can only be used for utilitarian cloth.[580]

Flax grows to approximately one metre, and it is harvested by pulling rather than cutting the stems, to maximise the fibre length.[581] Approximately a handful of stalks were pulled at a time as root resistance prevented removal of larger quantities (Figure 3.1).[582]

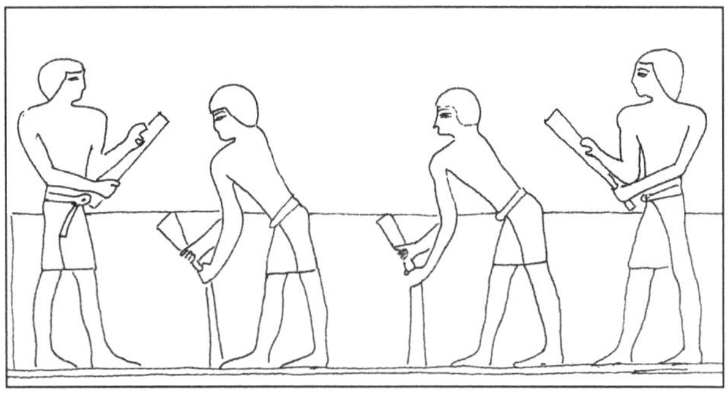

Figure 3.1: Pulling flax.
Sketch from Davies 1901: Plate XVI. The MK tomb of Urarna at Sheikh Said (Tomb 25 J).

Workload requirements for the cultivation of flax for a cohort of 100,000

The workload to grow sufficient green flax to produce the dry fibre that was required to meet demand for cloth in NK Egypt is calculated in the following steps:

- The calculation of the weight (kg) of green flax.
- The calculation of the area (m^2) needed to grow the green flax.
- The calculation of the workload (man-years/100,000 cohort) and manpower.

Weight of green flax required

Knowing the weight of dry fibre required (110,514 kg/100,000 cohort (Table 3.20), the weight of green flax needed to produce the dry fibre can be estimated. The harvested green flax passes through a number of stages during processing to produce dry fibre for spinning: rippling, retting, scutching, and hackling.[583] At each stage, water and vegetable matter are lost which results in a final yield of dry fibre of 534 kg/ha (34 stones/acre) of dry fibre/acre from a green flax yield from the field of 10,035 kg/ha (80 cwt/acre).[584] This dry fibre yield is 5.26% of the original green flax yield from the field. The ratio of dry fibre to green flax is 1:19. Using this ratio the weight of green flax that needed to be harvested to produce 110,514 kg of dry fibre suitable for spinning = 110,514 × 19 = 2,099,766 kg.

Area required to grow sufficient green flax

As stated above the yield of green flax from good soil was 10,035 kg/ha. The yield reported by Caldwell in 1931 has to be adjusted downwards to take into account the effects of chemical fertilisers introduced in the latter part of the nineteenth century A.D.[585] McCorriston estimates that the yield of dry flax fibre in ancient Mesopotamia was 335 kg/ha. To supply 2 kg/person/yr of linen ration, as recorded in UR III accounts, required 60 m^2 of land under flax cultivation.[586] Taking this rate, an

[573] Foaden and Fletcher 1910: 424–425. Sowing the flax seeds took place after the annual inundation (Vogelsang-Eastwood 1992b: 5).
[574] Allgrove-McDowell 2003: 32.
[575] Bradbury 1920: 22–23.
[576] Davies 1901: Plate XVI. Tomb 25 J at Sheikh Said.
[577] Vogelsang-Eastwood 2000: 270.
[578] Leadbeater 1976: 55. Seed rates in New Zealand between 1940–1952 ranged between 75–100 lbs/acre and in Belgium, for the same period, ranged between 120–140 lbs/acre (Hadfield 1953: 64). MacAdams 1847: 13 notes that the seed rate in Ireland in the nineteenth century A.D. was 126 lbs/acre (141 kg/ha) and the yield rate of flax seed was 557 kg/ha. Any surplus over and above that required for sowing can be used to extract linseed oil.
[579] McCorriston 1997: 522–523. Retting is discussed in Section 3.7.
[580] Vogelsang-Eastwood 2000: 270.
[581] Vogelsang-Eastwood 2000: 270. Pliny, *Naturalis historia* 19. 16–18. 19–3 describes the harvesting of flax as 'plucked up and tied together in little bundles each about the size of a handful' (cited by Forbes 1964: 29). For evidence from tomb scenes, see the portrayal of harvesting of flax in the TT 1, the NK tomb of Sennedgem at Deir el-Medina in Wilkinson 1979: 53, Figure 64.
[582] Allen 2002: Footnote 155.
[583] The general term for this waste is called tow. It could be used for other purposes such as fuel, thatch, and fodder (Hadfield 1953: 7).
[584] Caldwell 1931: 16.
[585] Richards 1982: 129–131, Table 4.9 and McCorriston 1997: 524.
[586] McCorriston 1997: 524, Table 2.

area of 381 ha under flax cultivation would be required to clothe a 100,000 cohort/yr.

Agricultural workload

The evaluations of the workload and manpower required for cultivating flax are based on the labour-rates to grow cereals in Section 2.7. Flax requires good quality soil and it is assumed that 70% of flax production was on best land and 30% on average land. To grow 2,099,766 kg of green flax would require an agrarian workload of 437 man-years (Table 3.21).

Agrarian activities	Average labour-rate man-days/ha	Workload man-years/ 100,000 cohort
Ploughing	4.8	1.9
Hoeing	10.3	8.9
Sowing	0.4	0.6
Harvesting	100	122.4
Weeding	56	69.3
Irrigation	192	233.9
Total		**437**

Table 3.21: Workload (man-years) and manpower to grow green flax for dry fibre to clothe a cohort of 100,000/yr.

3.7 Preparation of flax for spinning

Green flax has to be processed into flax fibre suitable for spinning. The process can be broken down into four discrete operations: rippling, retting, scutching, and hackling. In this section, the workload for each activity is quantified. Egyptian tomb paintings rarely depict these stages of linen production and so in the main, ethnographic, and experimental archaeology have identified the processes that were employed.

Without published data of the time taken to prepare the harvested flax for spinning using pre-industrialised methods, it was necessary to replicate the process of rippling, retting, scutching, and hackling. From this experiment, it was possible to estimate the time taken to complete each operation. Access to ripe green flax was limited, so the initial trials (seven samples) used alternative bast grasses and nettles because they replicate the main characteristics of flax. They are fibrous in nature, with a hard outer shell and an approximate standing height of 0.8–1 m. Later, after the UK flax harvest, an additional three samples of recently harvested flax were tested and no significant difference in weights/unit length was observed.

Rippling workload

The first operation was the removal of the seed heads from the flax with a wooden comb, a process called 'rippling' (Figure 3.2) before gathering into bales.[587] The ancient Egyptian word for bale of flax was *nwyt*, and comprised 60 *š3rw* (sheaves), assuming that the two bales on display in the Cairo Agricultural Museum of Dokki are representative of Ramesside practice. They measured 0.25 m in diameter and 1 m in length.[588] An individual flax stalk was called *š3j* and its diameter measured on average 3.2 mm. Each sheaf was equivalent to the quantity that could be held in an adult male hand when pulling the flax, approximately 25–30 stalks. This is also the practical limit per pull due to the root resistance of the plant.[589]

The author's own experimental results show that the average weight of a handful of flax was 0.25 kg. The total number of handfuls would be equal to 2,099,766 (weight kg of green flax required to clothe a cohort of 100,000) ÷ 0.25 (weight kg of a hand full of flax) = 8,399,064 handfuls. A process time of 60 seconds to pick up a handful of harvested flax, remove the seed heads and place it in a pile ready to be tied up into a bale is a realistic estimate and gives a rippling workload = 8,399,064 × 60 ÷ (3600 × 9 × 314) = 50 man-years.

Figure 3.2: Rippling, tying into bundles, and carrying bales to the river for retting.
Sketch of Tylor 1895: Plate III. The tomb of Paheri (EK 3).

Retting workload

The tied bales of flax were immersed in water to rot the adhesive substances that bind the bast fibres to each other in the cortex and the woody inner core, in a process called 'retting'. Retting can be carried out in running water that rots the cortical tissue of the plant within a period of 10–14 days.[590] Retting in stagnant water is faster because the bacteria present aid the decomposition.[591] It was necessary to monitor the process because more than a 50% decomposition caused the bundles of fibres to

[587] For example the NK tomb of Paheri at El-Kab (Tylor 1895: Plate III). A wooden comb from MK Kahun and thought to have been used for rippling is in Manchester University Museum (Acc. 6859). Volgelsang-Eastwood 1994: 19 has a photograph of this comb.

[588] Allen 2002: Footnote 153. There is a published photograph of the two Dokki bales in Brewer and Redford 1994: 37, Figure 4.2. A man's hand can hold a roll of flax stems of an approximate area of 0.00101801 m^2 (0.036 m diameter), and, when tied tightly in a bale, this area is reduced to 0.000804 m^2. Using the Dokki example, the cross-sectional area of a bale is 0.0491 m^2. Dividing the area of the bale by the area of a compressed handful provides a close approximation of 60–61 sheaves per bale. This may have been a base accounting unit of taxation in the time of Heqanakht (MK).

[589] Allen 2002: Footnote 154–155.

[590] Forbes 1964: 28 estimates 5–15 days for retting.

[591] Leadbeater 1976: 59.

disintegrate.[592] It has been suggested that the ancient Egyptians may not have not practise retting, Vogelsang-Eastwood considers that the scene in the tomb of Amenemhat at Beni Hasan does not, as commonly supposed, show retting taking place and that it depicts vegetables in a raised bed.[593] However, proximity to the Nile linked to still water canals, would have made retting a likely practice and the workload rates have been based on this process.

The workload for retting comprises four operations, tying green flax into bales, carrying the bales after rippling to the water for retting, lifting them from the water post-retting, and finally splitting open the bale and spreading the sodden retted flax to dry in the sun. The experimental results discussed previously show that the average weight of a tight handful of bast material (sheaf), each with an average length of 0.8 m, is 0.25 kg. This would mean that a bale of 60 sheaves would have a dry weight of 15 kg. As stated, the weight of green flax required was 2,099,766 kg so the number of bales would be 2,099,766 ÷ 15 = 139,984.

It is assumed one man could tie up the bale and carry it from the field to the river. Lifting the bale of retted flax out of the water would have taken significant manual effort, and a wet bale would weigh significantly more than its dry weight. For the purposes of this study, it has been estimated that two workers lifted the sodden bale out of the Nile or canal onto the bank. Before the next stage of the process, the retted flax had to be carefully spread out and repeatedly turned over in the sun to dry.[594] It was important to do this carefully to ensure the fibres were not damaged and has been estimated have taken three men/bale/hr.

The workload for the total retting process is 97 man-years and the assumptions used in the calculation are outlined and summarised in Table 3.22.

No. of bales/100,000 cohort	139,984
No. of bales carried/day	60
No. of retted bales lifted from river/day	30
No. of men required carrying a bale of green flax	1
No. of trips carrying bales to river/day	2,333
No. of man-days carrying bales to river/day	2,333
No. of men carrying bales	3
No. of retted bales lifted/out of the river/day	4,666
Total man-days lifting retted bales from the river	13,998
No. of men/retted bale laying out retted flax in the sun	3
Total man-days laying out retted flax in the sun	13,998
Total man-days	**30,329**
Total man-years	**96**

Table 3.22: Parameters used to calculate the workload to ret sufficient flax to clothe a cohort of 100,000/yr.

[592] Brewer *et al* 1994: 35.

[593] Kemp and Vogelsang-Eastwood 2001: 29–30.

[594] Brewer and Redford 1994: 36.

Workload to prepare the retted flax for spinning

The dried, retted flax fibres were prepared for spinning by crushing and pulling the stem simultaneously.[595] The first action termed 'breaking', beat and bruised the stalks with a blunt instrument on a stone slab to separate the fibres from any remaining woody centre and outer layers of the stem. A pre-1930 A.D. photograph shows an Egyptian worker beating flax with a wooden mallet in a similar manner.[596] Although wooden mallets have been found in the archaeological record, this stage is not depicted in tomb scenes.[597] The fibres of linen were then separated from the woody outer stem in a process called scutching, by scraping the stems. I found that for breaking and scutching it was better to process one handful of mast material at a time.[598] We do not know with certainty the tool used in antiquity used to scutch the bast material. One MK tomb scene shows women passing the fibres through two pieces of wood (Figure 3.3), which may represent scutching. Modern traditional methods use a scutching knife or a small metal scraper. The combined beating and scutching took 4 minutes per handful of dried, retted bast material.

Figure 3.3: Woman scutching (left) and splicing on the thigh (right).
Sketch of Davies 1913: Plate XXXVIII. The tomb of Dagi (TT 103).

The third stage was 'hackling', in which the fibres were pulled though a wooden or bone comb to remove the last small fragments of woody matter, to straighten and separate the flax fibres and to align the long fibres parallel to each other ready for the production of linen thread.[599] This was done at least three times with the teeth of the combs becoming finer. Heckling organises the flax bast fibres into parallel but separated long fibres as well as removing any remaining straw or shorter tow fibres.

[595] For descriptions of these stages with references to archaeological and pictorial evidence, see Vogelsang-Eastwood 1992b: 11–12, Vogelsang-Eastwood 2000: 271, and Kemp and Vogelsang-Eastwood 2001: 28–30.

[596] Crowfoot 1931: Plate 19.

[597] A photograph of a wooden mallet from the Dokki Agricultural Museum, thought to be used for beating the retted flax, is provided in Brewer and Redford 1994: Figures 4.4. The design and weight would have made it an ideal tool for breaking the flax stems.

[598] See the experiments of Leadbeater 1976: 60–61, Figures 4.16–4.17.

[599] Kemp and Vogelsang-Eastwood 2002: 28. A photograph of a wooden comb from the Agricultural Museum, Dokki that may have been used for hackling, is provided in Brewer and Redford 1994: Figure 4.6.

Modern traditional hackling uses between three to five sizes of heckling combs depending on the quality of cloth required. Leadbeater's experiments obtained satisfactory results using a comb made from wood and nails.[600] Personal discussion with practised weavers, suggests that it would take three minutes to hackle a handful of bast material so that it is ready for spinning.[601] The equivalent time to scutch and hackle the 110,514 kg of flax required to clothe a cohort of 100,000 (Table 3.20) would be = 110,514 × 9.44 (Table 3.24) ÷ (9 × 314) = 369 man-years.

Average weight (kg) of a sample of 11 handfuls	0.25
% by weight of useable fibre for cloth production	5.3
Weight (kg) of suitable bast material fibre	0.0133
Number of handfuls to make 1 kg fibre	75.2
Av. time (mins) to beat and scutch one handful of bast	4
Av. time (mins) to hackle one handful of bast material	3.5
Total time (mins) to prepare one handful of bast material	7.5
Equivalent time (hours) to prepare one kg of bast material	9.44

Table 3.23: Experimental results to beat, scutch, and hackle bast material.

Using the estimates for the labour-rates for rippling and retting operations together with the experimental data in Table 3.23, the workload to ripple, ret, scutch, and hackle the 110,514 kg of flax required to clothe a cohort of 100,000 (Table 3.20) would be 515 man-years (Table 3.24).

Operation	Man-years
Rippling	50
Binding flax and retting	96
Scutching and hackling	369
Total	**515**

Table 3.24: Summary of the workload (man-years) required to prepare flax fibre to clothe a 100,000 cohort.

Production of linen yarn

Producing yarn for weaving linen was a three-stage process in NK Egypt.[602] It consisted of twisting filaments into a long single thread, spinning these threads to make a plied yarn, and if desired, spinning the plied yarn into thicker multiple plied yarn. The analysis of the textiles found in the Workmen's village at Amarna, showed that 98% of the thirty-two types of yarn were plied.[603]

Splicing flax filaments

The first stage involved lightly twisting the fibres and splicing (joining) them into long lengths. The bundles of fibres were rolled over the thigh to produce a lightly twisted single yarn, which was rolled into a ball (Figure 3.3).[604] To produce a continuous thread, the lengths of fibres were lapped by 0.05–0.08 m, and the joint twisted more tightly.

Spinning single yarns

The loosely twisted and spliced yarns were fed through a bowl of water to wet them, strengthen the splices, and to keep them pliable for the final stage of the process.[605] These terracotta bowls are commonly called 'wetting-bowls' made with upright loops in the bottom of the pot (Figure 3.4) to guide the yarn at an oblique angle through the bowl. The loops and bowl rim often show wear from the yarn that passed through them under tension.[606]

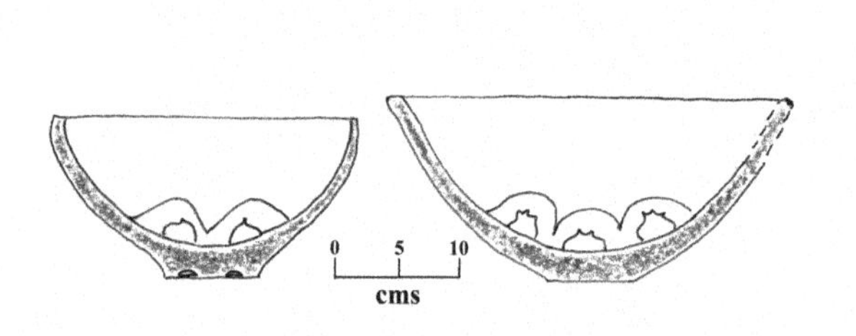

Figure 3.4: Two and three looped 'wetting bowls' found at Amarna (left) and Deir el-Medina (right).
Redrawn by author from Dothan 1963: 102, Figure 3.

The twisted thread was spun using a drop spindle to produce a tightly spun single thread yarn.[607] The spinner rolled the spindle on the thigh to provide the spinning torque as shown by spinners 2 and 3 in Figure 3.6.

Spinning and plying yarn

The threads were drawn up under tension to stop the twist from unrolling and this required an assistant, as shown in Figure 3.6. Tomb scenes show that two or more spindles could be spun at the same time, speeding up the process (Figure 3.6, spinner 2).[608] Some tomb scenes show the single yarns spun together to make a multi-ply yarn.[609] If the single yarn was twisted around another to form a 2 ply yarn, the splices were offset to ensure that no two spliced joints occurred in parallel within the twisted yarns and this increased the strength of the finished plied yarn, compensating for the weak spliced joints (Figure 3.5).[610] Egyptian tomb paintings and models show that women

600 Leadbeater 1976: 61, Figure 4.2 and Hood 2003.
601 Personal discussion with traditional weavers at a demonstration of spinning and weaving at The Weald and Downland Open Air Museum, Easter 2007.
602 Kemp and Vogelsang-Eastwood 2001: 58–60.
603 Kemp and Vogelsang-Eastwood 2001: 59.
604 Kemp and Vogelsang-Eastwood 2001: 70–73. It is also possible that this first twisting process was accomplished using two hands.
605 Dothan 1963: Figure 3 and Barber 1991: 70–72. It is possible that the bowl contained size to strengthen the spliced yarn (Kemp and Vogelsang-Eastwood 2001: 74).
606 Dothan 1963: 107 and Allgrove-McDowell 2003: 33.
607 Kemp and Vogelsang-Eastwood 2001: Figure 8.1 a spindle with its whorl from Amarna.
608 Tomb scenes are not consistent and some can be interpreted as the spinning of several single threads simultaneously or the production of plied yarn. In the tomb of Khety at Beni Hasan (Figure 3.6), spinner 1 shows a single thread spun from one wetting bowl, the second spinner appears to spin four threads from four bowls and the third spinner, two threads from two bowls (Kemp and Vogelsang-Eastwood 2001: 74–76, Figures 3.13–3.15).
609 The convention is to define yarn as s-spun if it is spun in an anti-clockwise direction and z-spun in a clockwise direction and called s and z threads. Yarn rolled and twisted on the thigh as shown, would have produced an s twist (Kemp and Vogelsang-Eastwood 2001: 57, Figure 3.1). There were 32 different types of yarn in the 3565 samples of Amarna fabric, 98% were from 3 types of plied yarn s/s, s,S2s/s, and, s,S2s/s,S2s (s=single thread, and S=two or more threads spun together Kemp and Vogelsang-Eastwood 2001: 57–59).
610 Sweeney 2006: 143.

removed (skeined) the thread off their spindles into loose coils ready for weaving.[611]

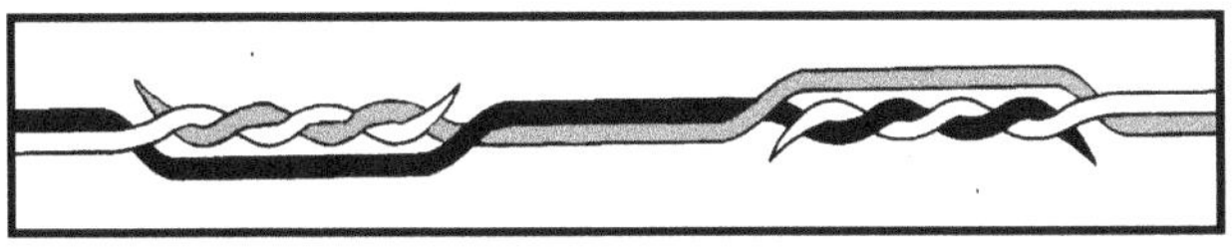

Figure 3.5: Diagram of 2 ply yarn showing how the spliced joints do not coincide.
Redrawn from Barber 1991: 47, Figure 2.9.

There is a lack of experimental and ethnographic evidence for the time taken to splice flax fibres as practiced by the ancient Egyptians and the spinning rates are a factor of the quality of fibre, variations in technique, and skill levels.[612] The author's experiments for splicing rates were 0.21 m/min.[613] Tiedemann and Jakes report that a skilled operative could spin a single flax thread at a rate of 4.73 m/min (R_s).[614] The rate to spin two threads into 2 ply yarn is 2 m/min (R_p).[615] The average total plying rate to make 2 ply yarn (i.e. spinning two individual threads and then spinning the two threads together on a spindle to make a single 2 ply yarn) is given in the relationship below.[616]

$$R_{2\ ply} = 1 \div ((1 \div R_s) + (1 \div R_s) + (1 \div R_p))\ \text{m/min}$$

Using the values for R_s and R_p given above the total combined rate to make 2 ply yarn ($R_{2\ ply}$) is 1.08 m/min. The number of minutes to produce one m of 2 ply yarn is the inverse of this relationship = 0.93 mins/m. To this must be added the splicing rate 0.21 mins/m resulting in a total spinning and splicing rate for flax of 1.14 mins/m. The Amarna textile database records that 2 ply yarn was the most common and CLOTHCALC assumes that all cloth was 2 ply.[617] Using this rate, the Egyptian workload for splicing and spinning flax was 9,565 man-years to spin sufficient yarn to make 226,356 m^2 of fabric required to clothe a cohort of 100,000.

3.8 Production of woollen yarn in LBA Cyprus

In order to identify the manpower requirements associated with the husbandry of sheep and the production of woollen cloth compared with the processes involved in making linen, this section analyses:

- The weight of wool that can be taken from a sheep in one season.
- The size of the flocks and the number of shepherds required for their husbandry.
- The weight wool required to make one m^2 of cloth.
- The time required to comb out sufficient wool to make one m^2 of cloth.

Evidence of wool yields in antiquity

The fat-tailed (*uli-gi*) sheep at Ur (UR III Period) produced on average an off-the-animal wool weight of 0.715 kg.[618] Wool from black sheep could produce higher wool yields, but the quality was poor and used mainly for coarse cloth.[619] Liverani's review of Mesopotamian and Aegean textual evidence suggests that 0.7 to 1.22 kg of wool could be obtained from one sheep. This study uses the average of this range, equal to 0.95 kg/animal.[620] It is assumed that 10% of the woollen fleece was too matted or coarse to be combed out for drop spinning and CLOTHCALC, reduces the wool yield of LBA Cyprus by 10% to 0.86 kg wool/sheep that can be used for textile production.

Number of shepherds, size of flocks, and area of grazing land

It has been demonstrated in Section 3.5 that the weight of fibre required to clothe a cohort of 100,000 in Cyprus would have been 130,972 kg. With the average yield of useful wool equal to 0.86 kg, the number of sheep 130,972 ÷ 0.86 = 152,293 sheep. Estimates of the size of flocks in antiquity vary. The Knossian D tablets suggest that flock sizes were in the range of 50–120, the variation being due to the mix of ewes, wethers and rams.[621] It has been assumed that the average flock size was 125 with each flock managed by one shepherd. The number of shepherds = 1,220 (rounded to nearest 10). Sheep and goats require between 1–4.5 ha per animal depending on the quality of the land and whether they were allowed to graze on post harvest stubble.[622] Assuming that the area required for Cyprus was 2 ha/animal/yr and the total area required for grazing would be 304,586 ha/100,000 cohort. This represents 33% of the land area (Table 3.25).

Cypriot land area ha	925,000
Number of sheep required	152,293
Assume grazing area/animal ha	2
Total grazing area required ha	**304,586**

Table 3.25: Area (ha) required for grazing sheep in LBA Cyprus.

[611] Barber 1991: 305. Thick twisted skeins of prepared yarn are on display in the Egyptian Museum, Cairo (Kemp and Vogelsang 2001: 451).
[612] Tiedemann and Jakes 2006: 301–302.
[613] Flax grew to 0.8-1 m but with the splicing overlap at each end of a minimum of 0.05 m, it is assumed for the study each splice was spaced on average at 0.8 m. The experiments took on average 10 seconds to splice two bast filaments together but with practise I suspect this could be significantly reduced. Using these conservative results, the number of splices/km = 1,000 ÷ 0.8 = 1,250. Total time to splice 1 km of bast material = 1,250 × 10 (time (secs)/splice) = 12,500 secs/km = 208.33 mins/km. This equates to a splicing rate = 208.33/1000 = 0.21 mins/m.
[614] Tiedemann and Jakes 2006: 303.
[615] Tiedemann and Jakes 2006: 303 assume a minimum plying rate (spinning two threads to make a single 2 ply yarn) of 2 m/min.
[616] Tiedemann and Jakes 2006: 300–301.
[617] Kemp 2013.

[618] Waetzoldt 1972: 18. Fat-tailed sheep are an ancient breed found across the Eastern Mediterranean and assumed to have also been bred in LBA Cyprus. For details of all sheep breeds of this period and the quality grades of the wool, see Steinkeller 1995: 51–57.
[619] Jacobsen 1970: 423, endnote 10 and Waetzoldt 1972: 51.
[620] Liverani 1979a: 70, Note 69. Killen suggests that an average weight of 0.75 kg/animal is representative of yields in antiquity (Killen 2007: 51).
[621] Killen 1964: 8–9, Footnote 49. See also Ventris and Chadwick 1973: 204 analysis of tablets Dk1070–1074 and Dl933, 938, 943, 946 and 947 (n= 10) result in an average flock size of 110 sheep.
[622] The grazing requirement is based on estimates from the Jezireh steppe in modern north-eastern Syria (McCorriston 1997: 524).

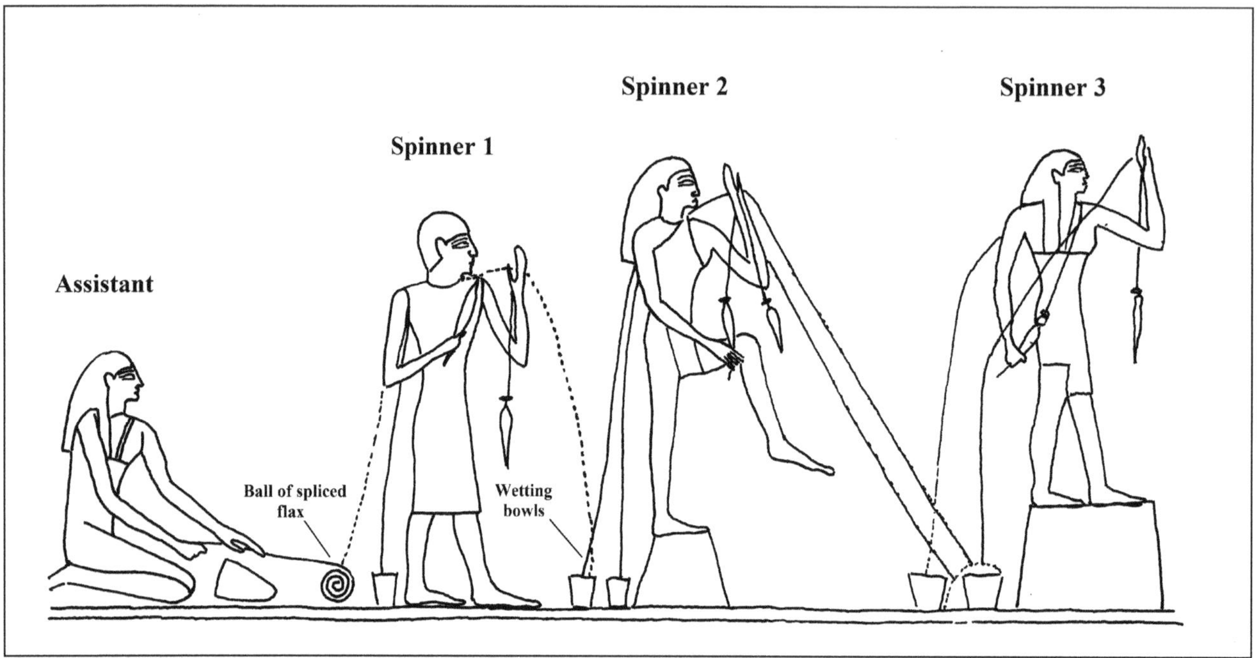

Figure 3.6: Scene of spinning in the MK tomb of Khety at Beni Hasan (BH 17).
Sketch from Kemp and Vogelsang-Eastwood 2001: 69, Figure 3.13.

Time taken to gather wool

Washing sheep

The process of gathering wool started with washing the sheep, probably in the local river to remove dirt, impurities, and parasites. The suint, a phosphate-rich residue from sheep perspiration acts as a natural detergent.[623] To wash a sheep in running water is likely to have required three people, with one washing and two holding the sheep. The number of sheep that could be washed in this manner is 12 per hour. To wash 152,293 sheep would require an annual workload of 14 man-years (Table 3.26).

Weight of fibre required to cloth 100,000 population kg	130,972
Average weight of useful raw wool/animal kg	0.86
Number of sheep required	= 130,972 ÷ 0.86 = 152,293
No. of sheep washed/hour	12
Workers required to wash and constrain a sheep	3
Total man-hours required for washing	= 152,293 × 3 ÷ 12 = 38,073
Number of hours worked/day	9
Days/yr worked in a 9 hr day	314
Workload man-years	**= 38,073 ÷ (9 × 314) = 14**

Table 3.26: Workload required for washing sheep prior to plucking (man-years/100,000 cohort/yr).

Gathering wool

The removal of wool prior to the practice of shearing is known as plucking. The bulk of the wool was removed by using a comb rather than by hand plucking and the wool was plucked in spring when the sheep were moulting.[624] Gathering wool in this way conveniently left behind the coarser kemp and hair.[625] Although the wool yield from plucking was lower than from shearing, the quality of the wool was higher because it had a greater proportion of fine woollen fibres.[626] No bronze shears have been found in archaeological record, possibly because to shear effectively, the blades must have some form of springing action. This was not possible until *c.*1000 B.C. with the introduction of iron shears that consisted of two knives joined by a spring.[627]

Unlike modern shearing methods that remove the complete fleece by a single shearer, two additional workers were required to restrain the animals. The number of sheep required to provide wool cloth for a cohort of 100,000 was 152,293 and assuming that the wool-gathering team of could shear 20 animals/day the total workload = 152,293 × 3 ÷ (20 × 314) = 73 man-years.

Combing wool

The final process in preparing wool for spinning was removing the natural tangles and kinks in the wool fibres by combing to align the fibres. From these, bundles of processed wool fibre (called roves or rolags) were spun into threads.[628] Modern fleece are generally carded and combed by traditional methods and takes on average approximately 20 hours/fleece depending on the state of the fleece and the skill level of the carder.

[623] Suint is a complex mixture of the salts of organic acids, polypeptide material, and urea (Stewart 1962: 907).

[624] Ryder 1983: 49.
[625] Wild 2002: 5.
[626] Springy iron combs are still used today for gathering wool from cashmere goats.
[627] Forbes 1964: 7.
[628] Barber 1991: 261–262.

Three factors require this labour-rate to be adjusted for wool combing in antiquity. In the LBA fleeces were only combed and not carded and less time would be expended combing each fleece because there is less usable wool from a smaller ancient sheep compared with modern breeds (0.86 kg compared with 2–2.5 kg from a modern Downland sheep).[629] However, more effort was required in antiquity due to less effective tools and this study has assumed an increase in labour-rate of 2.5 times compared with modern breeds.[630] Overall, taking these factors into account reduces this process from 20 hrs (traditional carding and combing rate) to the LBA combing workload of 17.2 hours (combing only).[631]

The number of days required to prepare the wool gathered from the sheep = the number of sheep (152,293) × combing rate of hrs/sheep (17.2) ÷ available hours worked per day (9) = 291,049 man-days (928 man-years). The resulting workload for washing, plucking, and combing the wool to produce sufficient weight (130,972 kg) of unspun wool to clothe a cohort of 100,000/yr, would have been 1,015 man-years (Table 3.27).

Preparation of woollen fibre for spinning	
Washing sheep	14
Plucking wool off the sheep	73
Combing/carding the wool for spinning	928
Total workload (man-years)	**1,015**

Table 3.27: Total workload (man-years) to prepare wool for spinning yarn to clothe 100,000 cohort/yr.

This analysis is based on the estimates of amateur and semi-professional practitioners who gave a wide variation in their estimates of the time they took to prepare the fleece for spinning. However, discussions with these practitioners were helpful in demonstrating the techniques used and the appreciation of the time taken in antiquity in preparing wool for spinning in antiquity. A recent paper by Strand gives the results of the Danish National Research Foundation's Centre for Textile Research looking at Iron Age textile technology.[632]

The Danish study results in a higher preparation time for wool taken directly from the fleece. Strand quotes time-study measurements which demonstrate that two technicians altogether took 6 hours (12 man-hours), to prepare 0.17 kg of wool ready for spinning.[633]

Spinning wool yarn

When wool is being spun the revolving spindle draws out small quantities of wool fibre (drafting), imposing a twist up the length of the thread.[634] It is the twisting that gives elasticity and strength to spun yarn.[635] Ethnographic and archaeological evidence suggests that the draft wool was spun using drop spindles and the spun yarn was then removed from the spindle ready for weaving. Barber argues that the large number of spindles found in the archaeological record could demonstrate that the spinning process was made more efficient if the spinner had on hand a large number of spindles. They could be filled, one after the other, avoiding stopping and starting and breaking the rhythm. Unwinding the spun thread is not necessary if the spindle is modified so that it can be used as a shuttle when weaving. The length of thread that can be spun from 1 kg of wool varies according to the quality of the wool fibre, the thickness the finished thread, and the weight of the spindle whorl. Tiedemann and Jakes record that a skilled operative could spin draft wool at a rate of 4.4 m/min (R_s).[636] The rate to spin two woollen threads into 2 ply yarn is 2 m/min (R_p). Using the values for R_s and R_p given above the total combined rate using the same formula in Section 3.7, the spinning labour-rate to make 2 ply yarn ($R_{2\ ply}$) is 1.05 m/min. The number of minutes to produce one m of 2 ply yarn is the inverse of this relationship = 0.95 mins/m. Taking this rate, the Cypriot workload for spinning wool was 8,209 man-years to spin sufficient yarn to make the 238,901 m^2 of cloth required to clothe a cohort of 100,000/yr.[637]

3.9 *Weaving flax and wool*

The description of weaving practices in the LBA starts with a short review of the design of vertical and horizontal looms. The key activities of the weaving process are also examined to estimate the time taken to produce one m^2 of cloth and from this the time to weave sufficient cloth to clothe a population cohort of 100,000/yr in Egypt and Cyprus. At its simplest, weaving cloth in a loom is passing a weft (crosswise) thread over and under the warp (lengthwise) threads. To do this there are three basic operations: ‘shedding’, ‘picking’, and ‘beating in’. Shedding is separating the warp threads into two layers by raising or lowering heddles to form a tunnel (the shed) that the shuttle and attached weft thread (pick) can pass through. Beating-in is pushing the inserted yarn down onto the already woven fabric with a smooth flat stick (sword) to give a tight weave.[638]

Looms and associated equipment

NK Egyptian tomb paintings show the weaving process on horizontal and vertical looms and MK models provide a three-dimensional portrayal of the spinning and

[629] Strand 2010: 12, Footnote 15.

[630] Finds from the Bronze Age sites in the Caspian Sea area suggest that combs were made of wood (Strand 2010: Footnote 15).

[631] The time taken by traditional workers to comb and card the fleece of a Downland sheep is *c.*20 hrs. It is assumed that ancient combing tools took 2.5 times longer to prepare the wool for spinning than the carding tools used today. The ratio of the weights of usable wool from an ancient breed and modern breeds = 0.86 ÷ 2.5 = 0.344. The time taken to prepare wool = 20 × 2.5 × 0.344 = 17.2 hrs/sheep.

[632] Strand 2010.

[633] It was too late to include her results in this analysis.

[634] Tiedemann and Jakes 2006: 296, Figure 2. Egypt's splicing method was probably unique in the Eastern Mediterranean. Most Near Eastern cultures used draft spinning for all fibre spinning, irrespective whether the source was flax, wool or goat hair (Barber 1991: 42–44).

[635] Crowfoot 1954: 424.

[636] Tiedemann and Jakes 2006: 303.

[637] It is generally accept that the bulk of spinning was carried out by women. However this workload could be lower if Cypriot shepherds spun wool when tending the flocks.

[638] Barber 1991: 86.

weaving process on the horizontal loom.[639] Artefacts in the archaeological record add to our knowledge of loom development from the survival of fragments of looms, weights and their associated tools.[640] From the archaeological evidence, replicas have been built and tested, providing greater understanding of weaving practices in the LBA. These experimental archaeology studies supplemented with ethnographic evidence, help determine the weaving production rates in antiquity.[641]

Horizontal or 'ground looms' have the warp stretched between two beams pegged to the ground. An ancient Egyptian horizontal loom is depicted in a painting on a dish from a Badari tomb (*c.*3600) now in the Petrie collection.[642] One of the best representations of the horizontal loom is from the MK tomb of Khnumhotep at Beni Hasan (BH 3) Twelfth Dynasty (Figure 3.7).[643]

Figure 3.7: MK Horizontal loom.
Sketch of Newberry 1893: Plate XXIX. The tomb of Khnumhotep at Beni Hasan (BH 3).

A characteristic of cloth made on a horizontal loom is for the weft to be more tightly woven on one side due to differential force of a weaver beating in with the sword from one side of the loom. To ensure the two selvedge sides of the fabric on the loom remain in line, Bellinger suggests that a fringe was added to space out the closer weft threads, keeping the selvedge even.[644] However, this is not certain and the production of fringed cloth may have been an aesthetic preference and it continued even with the use of vertical looms.[645]

The tomb of Thutnefer at Thebes (TT 104) *c.*1478–1479 B.C. has a detailed tomb painting of a vertical loom (Figure 3.8).[646] It has been suggested that from the NK onwards, vertical looms were operated by men and horizontal looms by women although other contemporary evidence suggests that women were always involved in weaving, including weaving with vertical looms.[647] Vertical looms are sometimes shown at an angle to a wall. The warp threads are not stretched between two beams, instead, they are attached to a top beam and stretched using weights, commonly made of clay or stone, which have holes in the centre to facilitate tying. Numerous weights have been found in the archaeological record and provide dating criteria for the introduction of vertical looms.[648]

Kemp and Volgelsang discuss the experimental archaeology in which four possible designs of vertical looms were reconstructed.[649] A specific aim of the experiments was to test the possible methods used by the Egyptians to slacken and then re-tension the loom to enable the warp and woven cloth to be moved down the loom during the weaving process. The most practical solution was to use a cross-beam fixed to the top of the loom frame by means of a harness, and cords. The cords enabled the movable beam to be raised, thus tensioning the warp with wooden cleats on the side loom members.

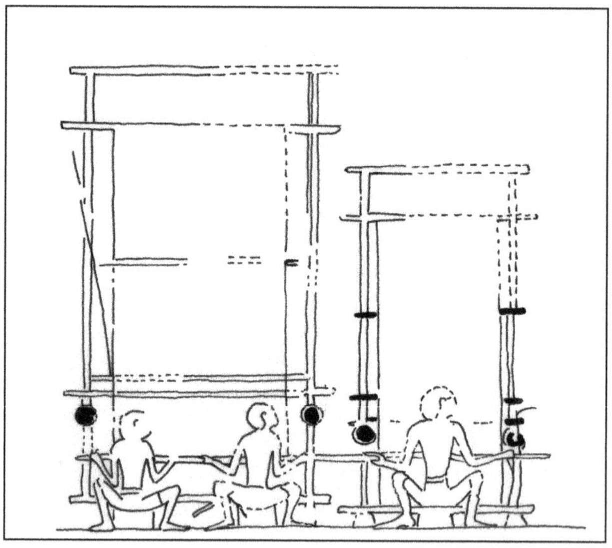

Figure 3.8: NK vertical loom.
Sketch from Davies 1929: Figure 1. The tomb of Thutnefer (TT 104).

Vertical looms produced a cloth that was close-set with evenly-spaced warp yarns and no need for a fringe on the

639 The Egyptian funerary model from the Eleventh Dynasty MK tomb of Meketre (Egyptian Museum Cairo, JE 46723) shows textile workers using horizontal looms (Hall 1986: 17, Figure 7).

640 For Egyptian finds from Gurob, see Petrie 1917: 133–136. Plate 66 and Thomas 1981: Plate 45 no. 98, Plate 5 no. 99). For Amarna finds, see Peet *et al* 1923: Plates 20.3. Heddle jacks from Kahun are in the Petrie museum UC 7278–7282 and UC 7291 (Barber 1991: 87, Figure 3.7). See also Petrie, Griffith and Newberry 1890: Plate 9, no. 12. Vogelsang-Eastwood 1994: Figures 41–44, 46 has photographs of extant parts of Egyptian looms ranging from Predynastic to Roman Egypt.

641 Barber 1991: 325–326, 370, Footnote 10, Kemp and Vogelsang-Eastwood. 2001: 405–426, and Strand 2010. Tiedemann and Jakes 2006: 295–307 give details of how fibre characteristics, fibre preparation, and spinning techniques influence production rates.

642 Acc. no. UC 9547.

643 Egyptian artists portrayed an object in the orientation that best captured its form and function. The plan view of the horizontal loom is drawn vertically to show both its design and the two operators weaving.

644 Bellinger 1959: 3.

645 Kemp and Vogelsang 2001: 133.

646 Davies 1929: 234, Figure 1.

647 Roehrig 1996: 21. The tomb owner of TT 133 was chief of weavers in the Ramesseum. A tomb scene shows four vertical looms and one of the five weavers depicted is a woman.

648 Ellis 1976.

649 Kemp and Vogelsang 2001: 405–426.

one side.[650] Uneven tension was overcome with the introduction of the double-beamed vertical loom, assisted by gravity one or two weavers could push down the sword from above with equal force.[651] Greater widths could be woven on a vertical loom as one weaver could move from side to side, or two could weave simultaneously, and they took up less floor space than horizontal looms.[652]

The width of cloth used to make garments found in ancient Egypt, ranged from approximately 0.5 m (1 cubit) for cloth from the horizontal loom up to 1.5 m (3 cubits) for cloth woven on a vertical loom.[653] Ethnographic evidence from Hebron shows that the larger horizontal looms require at least three operators if not four to maintain the correct tension in textiles with long warps. They worked sitting side-by-side working with long shed, heddle rods, and a sword beater. Weavers wove a width of 0.5–0.67 m, before passing on the shuttle to the operator sitting beside them. The outside weaver seated on the left side of the loom had an additional responsibility for fixing the weft fringe.[654] Kemp and Vogelsang-Eastwood show that the rooms where looms might have been situated in Amarna were 2.6 m wide. Allowing for elbow room, they suggest that 1.00–1.30 m is likely to have been the average width of normal cloth.[655] To achieve the finished cloth width of 1 m, the cloth width on the loom would be 1.15 m. This takes into account take up and subsequent shrinkage, leaving cloth 1 m in width.

Setting up the looms

Warping (setting up the lengthwise yarns) was a time-consuming task. According to an UR III text, it took three women three days to warp looms to produce a cloth 3.5 m x 3.5 m.[656] The workload for setting up the looms to produce sufficient cloth to clothe 100,000 cohort/yr for Egypt and Cyprus is given in Table 3.28.

	Egypt	Cyprus
Area of cloth to be produced m^2	226,356	238,901
Width of cloth produced on loom after shrinkage m	1	1
Total length of cloth m	226,356	238,901
Length of cloth produced per loom m	2	2
Area of cloth made between each warping m^2	2	2
No. of times the looms have to be re-warped	113,178	119,451
Time (days) taken to re-warp the loom	1	1
Available days/yr for production	314	314
Workload (man-years) to warp loom	**360**	**380**

Table 3.28: Workload (man-years) to warp the looms for the cloth required by a cohort of 100,000/yr.

Weaving rates

It is assumed that the weaving rates for flax and wool were the same, as the looms would have been similar and the physical sequence of weaving operations remains the same irrespective of the fibre used. Weaving rates were a function of the size of the loom, the quality of the yarn woven and the weft count (the number of transverse yarns). The greater the weft count, the greater the workload, not just because the number of shuttle operations per unit length increases, but also because as the weft count increases, more time is spent beating down.[657]

Waetzoldt's analysis of the UR III text reveals that in one day, three women could weave 0.25 m^2 of third class cloth or two women could weave 0.333 m^2 of fourth class cloth at a rate of 0.5 m^2 per day.[658] These labour-rates are used in this study for the weaving labour-rates for socio-economic groups 3–4. Weaving rates in this study assume that the loom produced a finished cloth measurement of 1 m.

Following discussions with traditional weavers at the Weald and Downland Open Air Museum at Singleton and the Fishbourne Roman Palace the estimated weaving rates/day for the fine cloth (used for socio economic groups 1–2) and artisan quality cloth (used for socio economic group 5) are given in Table 3.29. The rates for socio economic groups 3–4 are interpolated.

SEG	Area of cloth woven m^2/day	No. of days/m^2	No. of weavers	Weaving labour-rates man-days/m^2
1/2	0.08	12.5	3	37.5
3	0.277	3.61	3	10.82
4	0.333	3	2	6
5	0.5	2	2	4

Table 3.29: Number of days required to weave one m^2 of cloth.

Workload to weave the annual cloth requirement

The total weaving workload required to clothe a 100,000 cohort/yr is calculated by multiplying the annual area of cloth (226,356 and 238,901) m^2 for Egypt and Cyprus respectively) by the weaving rates (Table 3.29). The higher quality of cloth with finer yarn and close weaving has a greater workload than low quality cloth. First class cloth of the highest quality would be only have been owned by very few people (principally royalty) and has been excluded from this analysis. The resulting workloads are given in Table 3.30.

If, after taking out days lost due to sickness and other reasons, we can assume 314 working days/year, then the weaving workload required for Egypt and Cyprus is 3,769 and 3,574 man-years respectively.

[650] Lloyd 1976: 148.
[651] Bellinger 1959: 4. See Lloyd 1976: 149 for the operation of double-beamed vertical looms.
[652] Barber 1991: 82 and Capel and Markoe 2996: 21.
[653] Eyre 1998: 179, Footnote 31 and Kemp and Vogelsang-Eastwood 2001: 386.
[654] Schick 1998: 20, Colour Plate 3.12. Schick considers that at least three workers would be necessary for each vertical loom.
[655] Kemp and Vogelsang-Eastwood 2001: 386.
[656] Waetzoldt 1972: 129 translation of text ITT V 9996 (T.32) Rs I 1–3. For warping, weaving rates, and dimensions of cloth, see Petzel 1987: 22.
[657] Kemp and Vogelsang-Eastwood 2001: 108.
[658] Waetzoldt 1972: 138–139.

Quality of cloth	Egypt		
	Area of cloth m²	**Total man-days/m² of cloth**	**Total weaving workload man-days**
Second	2,004	37.5	75,150
Third	6,665	10.82	72,115
Fourth	52,127	6	312,762
Ration quality cloth	165,560	4	662,240
Total	**226,356**		**1,122,267**
Quality of cloth	**Cyprus**		
	Area of cloth m²	**Total man-days/m² of cloth**	**Total weaving workload man-days**
Second	2,111	37.5	79,163
Third	7,077	10.82	76,573
Fourth	54,492	6	326,952
Ration quality cloth	175,221	4	700,884
Total	**238,901**		**1,183,572**

Table 3.30: Total weavers' workload (man-days) to produce the cloth to clothe 100,000 cohort/yr.

3.10 Manpower requirements

Tables 3.31–3.32 show the total workload and manpower requirements to produce cloth in LBA Cyprus and NK Egypt. The competency index assumed for each process is given in column 3 of both Tables.[659]

Process	Workload	Competency index	Manpower
Husbandry of flocks	1,220	1.0	1,220
Prep'n of wool fibre	1,015	1.08	1,096
Spinning	8,209	1.1	9,030
Weaving	3,769	1.2	4,523
Total	**14,213**		**15,869**

Table 3.31: Cypriot manpower required to produce sufficient woollen cloth for a 100,000 cohort/yr.

Process	Workload	Competency index	Manpower
Cultivation	437	1.3	568
Prep'n of flax fibre	515	1.25	644
Spinning	9,565	1.1	10,522
Weaving	3,574	1.2	4,289
Total	**14,091**		**16,023**

Table 3.32: Egyptian manpower required to produce sufficient linen cloth for a 100,000 cohort/yr.

The competency indices for Egypt are higher than Cyprus to reflect that the cultivation of flax was more physically demanding than husbandry of sheep, and the process of retting and scutching, splicing flax fibres, spinning, and weaving was more complex and skilful than the production of woollen cloth. It is assumed that The resulting manpower requirements to support the basic process of producing sufficient cloth to clothe a cohort of 100,000 for LBA Cyprus and NK Egypt is 15,869 and 16,023 respectively.[660]

The competency indices in Table 3.31 and Table 3.32 may be understated as it is generally accepted, but not proven, that females carried out the bulk of the spinning and weaving. Ethnographic evidence suggests spinning and weaving for domestic cloth was fitted in between other family activities and was therefore less productive than if it had been carried out as a continuous activity.

This study has not estimated the time for sewing up the garments and further work is required on this activity to obtain the full workload and manpower requirements for the textile industry.

3.11 Observations

The cloth-producing workforce and manpower for Cyprus and Egypt are comparable in scale but the individual elements of workload and manpower are different. The most significant difference is that the cultivation workload of flax is 42% that of the husbandry of sheep. Table 3.25 shows that to clothe a Cypriot cohort of 100,000/yr, 152,293 sheep were needed, requiring 304,586 ha (3,046 km^2) of grazing land. This is a marked contrast to Egypt where to produce sufficient flax, only 381 ha/100,000 cohort/yr was required.

For both Egypt and Cyprus, the production of cloth for domestic clothing involved a significant proportion of the working population. Cyprus and Egypt required 15,869 and 16,023 workers/100,000 cohort/yr respectively. The Coale-Demeny Model 3 West demographic study described in Section 2.3 indicates that there were 29,890 individuals aged six or under and aged 60 and over (Table 2.3). The working population was therefore 70,110 per 100,000 cohort/yr for both Cyprus and Egypt. The cloth workers comprised 22.6% and 22.9 % of the working population respectively, which explains the high value of domestic cloth.

[659] The competency index for cultivation of flax uses the combined rate for men and women of 1.3 as discussed in Section 2.7. The competency indices for cloth production are lower (column 3 in Tables 3.31-3.32 as the associated activities are less physically demanding.

[660] It is important to remember that the 15,459 and. 16,024 workers for Cyprus and Egypt were not necessarily working full time on cloth production. It is probable that all women and some men were involved in some cloth activities. The manpower numbers are the sum of all the processes and equated to the number of full time workers necessary to satisfy the workload.

Chapter 4: Shelter

4.1 Introduction

The third basic need after food and clothing is shelter and this chapter considers the manpower implications of providing domestic buildings for a 100,000 cohort/yr in NK Egypt. In addition, the manpower needed for the construction of state buildings is assessed. The use of sun-baked mud-bricks was particularly suited for regions with low annual rainfall.[661] In Egypt with a climate that has negligible rainfall, large buildings were constructed using sun-baked mud-bricks that have survived to the modern day in a remarkable state of preservation, providing information on their manufacture and how they were used. To illustrate the demand for mud-bricks this chapter analyses the manpower requirements to meet the need for new buildings in three case studies.

- Case Study A: To provide shelter for the growing population in the NK Egypt.
- Case Study B: To build the domestic housing in Akhenaten's new capital city of Amarna.
- Case Study C: The construction of Egyptian state building projects such as forts and granaries.[662]

The archaeological evidence for mud-brick buildings in Cyprus is limited but across the Central and Eastern Mediterranean, mud-brick buildings with stone foundations were common for both domestic and state structures and it has been assumed that Cyprus in the LBA followed the same practice.[663] The case studies are based on Egyptian evidence drawn from tomb paintings, textual and archaeological sources, and modern Egyptian ethnographic studies. Modern studies have shown that in ancient Egypt mud-bricks made were made in a similar fashion to those made today and therefore ethnographic evidence is particularly helpful for this study.[664] The detailed scenes from the tomb of Rekhmire (TT 100) also show that the process to make mud-bricks in the NK is the same as that used in Egypt today.

4.2 The process to make mud-bricks

Mud-bricks have many benefits over other building materials. They have better insulation qualities than stone or fired baked bricks and are more versatile for construction purposes as they can be 'readily cut and shaped. Secondary changes of plan such as the insertion of a new doorway, niche, or window are easily accomplished and constructing mud-brick buildings required a lower level of skill than a stone structure.'[665] Mud-bricks are also suitable for making vaulted ceilings, as demonstrated by the NK granary in the Ramesseum (Figure 4.1).[666]

Figure 4.1: Ramesseum granary with a vaulted ceiling.
Author's photograph.

The Egyptian word for making a brick was *sḫt ḏbt*, meaning 'moulding' or 'striking a brick.'[667] The production of mud-bricks was a labour-intensive, repetitive, task. Wet mud was mixed with sand, chopped straw (*tibn*), and sometimes chaff, using an agricultural hoe or mixing the components with feet. Sand was added to provide strength to the brick by acting as a binder 'gluing' the mud and straw together.[668] The use of chaff or straw depended on availability but both materials are subject to insect infestations, which are detrimental to the structural integrity of the mud-brick.[669] Having filled the wooden mould with the mud/straw/sand mixture, the brick maker scraped off the surplus and removed the mould, leaving a mud-brick that was strong enough even at this stage to retain its shape (Figures 4.2 and 4.3).

Ethnographic evidence from mid–twentieth century Gourna in Egypt shows that a minimum of 45 kg of straw or chaff were mixed with one m^3 of mud and 0.33 m^3 of sand to make 660 bricks measuring 0.23 m in length x 0.11 m in width x 0.07 m in depth. Each brick had a volume of 0.001771 m^3.[670] The bricks had to be turned onto their side after three days to minimise cracking due to differential drying and after six days the bricks were stacked ready for use.[671]

[661] Kemp 2000.
[662] For the analyses in this chapter the spreadsheet SHELTER was developed.
[663] Wright 1992.
[664] Fathy 1973, Spencer 1979, and Kemp 2000. These authors stress that the processes for mud-brick making in Egypt today has not changed significantly since antiquity. Kemp outlines the ethnographic, textual, and archaeological evidence for Egyptian mud-brick production.

[665] Oates 1990: 389.
[666] Fathy 1973: 5–12, 211–213 describes the method for making vaulted roofs based on Nubian ethnographic evidence.
[667] Badawy 1956: 63–64, Simpson 1963: 77–78, and Spencer 1979: 3–4.
[668] Kemp 2000: 80.
[669] Kemp 2000; 82–83.
[670] Fathy 1973: 198.
[671] As Egyptian mud-bricks in antiquity were structurally the same, this action of standing the bricks on edge has been included as an activity in SHELTER.

The moulds were made from pieces of wood joined together with mortise and tenon joints, and a mould excavated in the MK town of Kahun produced bricks that were 0.284 m in length, 0.142 m in width, and 0.0864 m in depth, with a volume of 0.003484 m^3.[672]

Figure 4.2: Mixing mud with water to make mud-bricks.
Sketch of Davies 1953: Plate LIX. The tomb of Rekhmire (TT 100).

Figure 4.3: Mud mixed with straw and put in brick moulds.
Sketch from Davies 1953: Plate LVIII). The tomb of Rekhmire (TT 100).

Brick sizes did change over time and they were also adapted for the type of structure being built.[673] For most periods, they ranged between 0.30 and 0.45 m in length, 0.15–0.22 m in depth, and 0.075–0.15 m in height. Some of the largest used for the MK Fortress of Buhen, measured 0.37 in length, 0.18 m in width, and 0.12 m in height.[674] Kemp suggests that this size was probably the upper practical limit for mud-bricks as their low tensile strength makes them vulnerable to breakage when lifted by hand.[675] Figure 4.4 follows the process for making mud-bricks.[676]

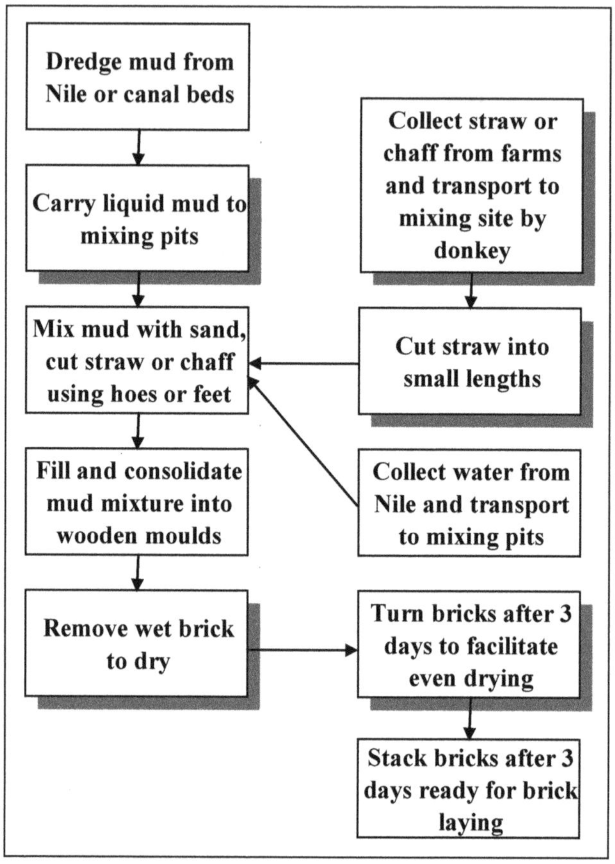

Figure 4.4: Flow diagram of the mud-brick production process.

Ethnographic Egyptian evidence demonstrates that four men can make 3,000 mud-bricks per day, a labour-rate of 1.33 man-days per 1,000 bricks.[677] However, mechanical transport and modern tools were used to dig and bring mud and sand to the site, cut the chaff and straw to a convenient size, and to mix the brick constituents. These methods were not available to the ancient Egyptians and the ancient manual process outlined in Figure 4.4 would increase the workload to 9.75 man-days/1,000 bricks as summarised in Table 4.1.[678]

Man-days required to transport straw from farms to site	0.51
Man-days to dredge silt from the Nile ready for transport	1.21
Man-days to dig sand	0.2
Man-days to transport sand & silt from the Nile/canals	5.0
Man-days to cut straw suitable for brick making	1.0
Man-days to make 1000 bricks	1.33
Stacking mud-bricks on edge	0.50
Labour-rate (man-days/1000 bricks)	**9.75**

Table 4.1: Number of man-days to make 1,000 NK mud-bricks.

[672] The brick-mould is in the Manchester Museum: Acc. no. 51.

[673] A scatter plot diagram of sample brick sizes is given in Kemp 2000: 87, Figure 4.3 using data from Spencer 1979: Plate 41–43.

[674] Emery *et al* 1979: 39.

[675] Kemp 2000: 87.

[676] Davies 1953: Plates LVIII, LIX, and LX. The artist has painted the bricks a pink-grey colour, when drying in the sun, and white when used by the builder (Kemp 2000: 83).

[677] Two brick makers supported by two labourers were required to make 3000 bricks/day (Fathy 1973: 200). Fathy shows that three men took one day to turn and stack 6,000 bricks. This equates to 0.5 man-days per 1,000 bricks. For more details of the production process using ethnographic evidence, see Clarke and Engelbach 1990: 208–209, and Kemp 2000: 79–84.

[678] Kemp notes that the majority of mud-bricks in Amarna used sand and small quantities of gravel as a binder rather than straw (Kemp 2000: 82).

The size of a brick had an impact on the time taken to make them. If the mix of mud, sand, and straw or chaff remained approximately the same, the workload for brick production is proportional to the volume. The average NK brick had a volume of 0.003438 m^3 compared to the area of a modern Egyptian mud-brick of 0.001771 m^3 (1.94 times greater in volume).[679] The time taken to make 1,000 bricks would therefore increase from 9.75 to 18.9 man-days per 1,000 bricks. Similarly, the time to make 1,000 MK Buhen bricks that were 4.51 times greater in volume than a modern Egyptian mud-brick, would increase the labour-rate from 9.75 to 44.0 man-days/1000 bricks.

Workload required to build mud-brick walls

In NK Egypt, bricks were laid with alternate header and stretcher brick courses. Soil mixed with water to form a paste was used as mortar, which when dry, formed a strong bond between the brick courses.[680] However, in the construction of large brick walls such as those found at Karnak, it was important to ensure that water in the mud mortar dried out evenly whether it was in the centre or the outside of the wall. Failure to do so caused differential contraction in the mud mortar resulting in longitudinal cracks between the brick courses, weakening the structural integrity of the wall. To facilitate drying and minimise this problem, at every thirteenth course of bricks, air passages two bricks high and half a brick wide were incorporated within the wall. In addition, some mud-brick walls used mats of rushes, reeds, and halfa grass every three to seven courses to strengthen the wall in the longitudinal plane.[681]

Modern ethnographic evidence from Gourna in Egypt shows that one bricklayer can lay a 2.5 m^3 vertical brick wall in a day.[682] Each cubic metre of wall had 400 bricks giving a mud-brick laying rate of 1,000 bricks per day. The Gourna evidence shows that up to an additional four men were required to mix and carry the mud mortar and mud-bricks to the bricklayer.[683] In the NK bricks were laid on small lumps of the mud mortar and the weight of the new brick itself would spread the mortar into circular pats. The bricks were laid close together with minimal or no mortar between them on the vertical surface.[684]

The size of the brick and the height of the structure under construction dictate the number of bricks that could be laid in a day. A modern Egyptian mud-brick layer can lay 1,000 bricks/day and the calculations in Table 4.2 have been based on this labour-rate. Like the labour-rate to make ancient Egyptian bricks of differing sizes, the labour-rate for laying the bricks is also proportional to the volume of the brick.

	Lgth. m	Wdth. m	Hgt. m	Vol. m^3	Man-days to make 1000 bricks	No. of bricks laid per day
Modern Gourna Egyptian brick	0.23	0.11	0.07	0.00177	9.75	1,000
MK Buhen fortress	0.37	0.18	0.12	0.00799	44	222
NK brick	0.25	0.125	0.11	0.00344	18.9	515
Ramesseum granary walls	0.4	0.12	0.13	0.00624	34.4	284
Ramesseum vault ceiling	0.35	0.21	0.065	0.00478	26.3	371
Amarna domestic North Suburb	0.345	0.155	0.09	0.00481	26.5	368

Table 4.2: The labour-rates to lay a range of brick sizes (man-days/1,000 bricks/day).

Another factor influencing the bricklaying rate is the height of the wall. To reflect the need for scaffolding and/or ramps in higher structures and the additional effort of lifting mortar and bricks as the structure is built, the workload requirements are uplifted by ratios on a sliding scale from 1–3 based on the height of the structure as given in Table 4.3. As shown in Table 4.2 a low wall built in the NK that did not need scaffolding or ramps only needed a team of five men working at a rate of 515 bricks per day.[685] For a wall between 2.5–6 m high, the number of men required to lay the same number of bricks would equal 5 × 2 (uplift ratio from Table 4.3) = 10 workers. If the team was restricted to five men to build a wall 2.5–6 m high then the time taken for brick laying would double and the number of bricks laid = 515 ÷ 2 (uplift ratio from Table 4.3) = 257 bricks per day.

Height of structure m	Uplift ratio
Walls under 1.25 m	1
Walls between 10.25–2.5 m	1.5
Walls between 2.5–6 m	2
Walls over 6 m	3

Table 4.3: Ratios applied to brick laying workload for high walls.

4.3 Demand for mud-bricks in ancient Egypt

Three case studies follow to illustrate the demand for mud-bricks in Egypt and the associated material and

[679] Spencer 1979 gives the measurements of representative brick sizes by time period. See also Petrie 1938: 5 and Kemp 2000: 84–88.

[680] Mud-bricks adjacent to stonework sometimes used gypsum mortar (Kemp 2000: 92). Modern Egyptian ethnographic evidence shows that mortar was mixed in the ratio of 1:2 of sand and sieved mud (Fathy 1973: 206).

[681] Clarke and Engelbach 1990: 210.

[682] Fathy 1973: 208.

[683] The high ratio of four labourers to one bricklayer is necessary because mortar dries out quickly in high ambient temperatures and therefore it must be supplied to the bricklayer in small quantities. To provide a good bond, the mud mortar must be wet and of the right consistency, because the bricks soak up the water in the mortar. This raises the possibility that it was necessary to mix up the mortar on the scaffolding of high walls such as the temenos walls of temples. This would have resulted in an increase in workload as two journeys would be required for the soil and the water.

[684] Kemp 2000: 92 and Figure 3.4a.

[685] The volume of a modern Egyptian mud-brick and a NK mud-brick is 0.001771 and 0.00344 m^3 respectively. The number of mud-bricks laid per day therefore in the NK = 1,000 × 0.001771 ÷ 0.00344 = 515.

manpower necessary to support domestic and state infrastructure mud-brick buildings. Case Study A examines the resources required to satisfy the demand for additional domestic houses for the annual increase in population by the end of the NK. However, the demand for bricks to build new houses was low compared with the large scale demand for mud-bricks for the state building programs. To appreciate the scale of these projects, two further case studies evaluate the demand for bricks. Case Study B estimates the resources required in the construction of the domestic housing for the Eighteenth Dynasty capital city, Amarna. Case Study C illustrates the resources needed to build representative state infrastructure mud-brick buildings such as granaries and forts. Each case study estimates the number of mud-bricks involved and assesses the associated workload and manpower.

Case studies A–B use Tietze's typology of Amarna domestic housing (Figure 4.5) as representative of NK domestic housing.[686] The workload required to build a house was dependent on the size of the building, and this in turn reflected the owners' socio-economic standing. Tietze's typological study of Amarna categorised domestic housing into three main classifications.[687] His statistical analysis allocated the different designs to three different classes of Amarna inhabitants and assessed the proportion of the population for each class as following: the urban workers between 54–59%, state officials between 34–37%, and the city élite between 7–9% of the total.[688] For consistency, this study uses the same five socio-economic profiles as used in the previous chapter on cloth production (Section 3.4). The relationship of Tietze's typological design categories to the five socio-economic groups used in this study is given in Table 4.4.

Socio-economic group	Tietze's categories
Socio-economic group 1	3e
Socio-economic group 2	2e
Socio-economic group 3	2c and 2d
Socio-economic group 4	1c and 1d
Socio-economic group 5	1a and 1b

Table 4.4: Relationship of Tietze's design categories to the five socio-economic groups used in this study.

The size of the dwelling determined the number of mud-bricks required and the workload required to make and lay them. The majority of Amarna workers would have lived in house design 1a. Even in modern Egypt the poorest agricultural workers live in mud-brick houses similar in design to buildings 1a–1b.

In the NK a few private farmers who owned land on the west bank of the Nile at Amarna, given to them by the king, would probably have aspired to larger houses of the 2c and 2d design. It has been assumed that houses of 2e design would have been suitable for senior officials in the state bureaucracy and that design 3e, was occupied by the high élite.

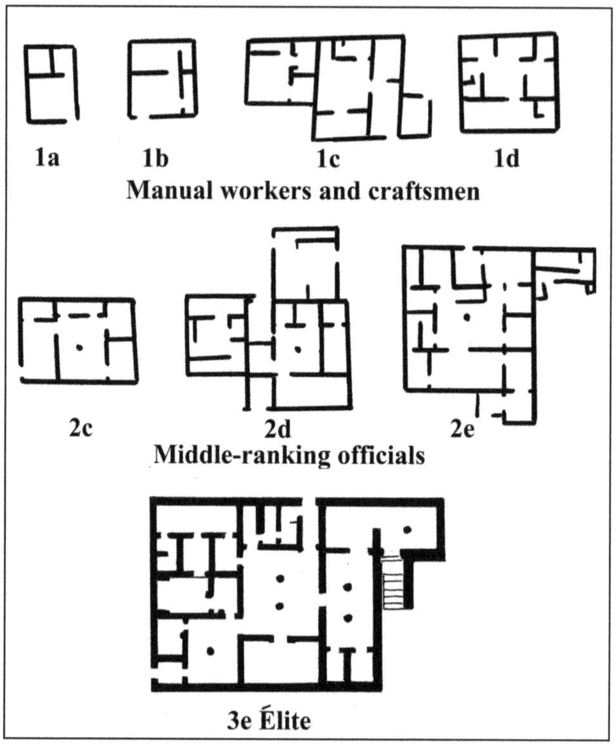

Figure 4.5: Tietze's typology of Amarna domestic housing.

Case Study A

The demand for domestic housing due to population growth in the NK

This study has used Hassan's estimates for population growth in ancient Egypt.[689] In the NK (1550–1070 B.C.) the estimated population increased from 1.25 to 2.2 million.[690] This represents an annual compound growth of 0.118% per year. With this compound growth rate, by the end of the NK the increase in the total population would have been 2,589 individuals. With an average family size of six individuals in the NK, the annual compound growth (0.118%) could be satisfied with as few as 434 additional houses built each year.[691] The distribution of house types to meet the annual population growth is given in columns 7–8 of Report 4.3 in the Appendix. Using this distribution and the dimensions from Tietze's designs the number of bricks required, man-days to make them, and man-days to

[686] Tietze 1985.

[687] These designs were identified by calculating the floor area of the house and superimposing them on the histogram of the frequencies of houses collated by floor area and volume, as excavated in central Amarna (Tietze 1985: 56–59, Figures 1 and 2).

[688] Tietze 1985: 83–84. For this study, the average of each range is taken.

[689] Hassan 1994.

[690] The opinions of scholars vary on the population of NK Egypt. In Section 2.3 the impact of pandemics on population growth is taken into account. This study considers 2.2 million as more representative than higher estimates.

[691] Kemp 1991: 157 comments that an average of 6 individuals is often used to calculate ancient populations. The number of houses required to satisfy population growth = 2,589 ÷ 6 = 431.5. As houses can only be built in complete units, the number has been rounded to 434 (Report 4.3 in the Appendix). Szpakowska 2008: 37–38 and footnotes 93–94 suggests an average family size of four to five, based on the fertility cycle of non-élite women. To this number should be added at least one adult relative, as the demographic analysis Section 2.3 shows that 24.58% were age 40 or over, and 13.77% were age 50 or over.

mix mortar and lay bricks are calculated and the results given in Report 4.4 in the Appendix. To make the mud-bricks (1,486,493 in total) and build the houses, the total workload would only be 230 man-years and manpower would be 269 workers with a competency index of 1.17.[692] This manpower requirement is for the total population of NK Egypt and equates to only 13 workers/100,000 cohort/yr.[693] This number is negligible and demonstrates that mud-brick production to satisfy population growth was only minor part of the NK mud-brick industry.

Case Study B

Domestic housing in Amarna

Amarna provides a clearly defined time capsule of NK Egyptian architecture and urban planning because it was built and then abandoned over a relatively short period of twenty to thirty years.[694] Despite the fact that much building material was recycled after the city was abandoned, the foundations and lower brick courses of the domestic and public buildings, together with their associated artefacts, provide a remarkable archaeological record of domestic and civic building in late Eighteenth Dynasty Egypt.[695]

This section estimates the workload and manpower required to build the domestic housing for this city. The number of mud-bricks needed per dwelling and the workload required to make the bricks and build the dwelling for each of the house designs are summarised in Tables 4.5–4.6 and Reports 4.1–4.2 and 4.5 in the Appendix.

House designs of Tietze's typology	1a	1b	1c	1d
No. of bricks required/house	2,161	2,743	5,298	7,605
Man-days to make bricks	57	73	140	201
Man-days to lay bricks	42	54	109	160
Total man-days/ dwelling	**99**	**127**	**249**	**362**
Total man-years/ dwelling	**0.32**	**0.41**	**0.8**	**1.2**

Table 4.5: Number of mud-bricks required, and the workload required to build each of Tietze's designs 1a–1d.

House designs of Tietze's typology	2c	2d	2e	3e
No. of bricks required	10,597	20,737	37,904	220,020
Man-days to make bricks	281	549	716	5,830
Man-days to lay bricks	233	475	904	6,256
Total man-days/dwelling	**514**	**1,025**	**1,620**	**12,085**
Total man-yrs/dwelling	**1.6**	**3.27**	**5.2**	**38.49**

Table 4.6: Number of mud-bricks required, and the workload required to build each of Tietze's designs 2c–3e.

The city of Amarna makes a particularly interesting example of large-scale domestic housing development because it is unique in its scale and speed of construction. Kemp's latest estimate for the number of domestic houses is 3,040. Using the family size of six gives a population of 18,240 for the 3,040 dwellings (estimate 1 in Table 4.7). Kemp suggests that there is evidence that slaves or hired servants also lived in the houses and the average number of residents/house could be 10 (estimate 2 in Table 4.7) giving a population *c.*30,000. Kemp emphasises the uncertainty of his estimates as some areas in the North Suburb and Main City/South Suburb are now lost beneath fields and may have had domestic housing. If so, the population could have been as high as 50,000 (Table 4.7).[696] All three of his population estimates have been collated using Tietze's typology and summarised in Table 4.7. For further detail, see Report 4.5 in the Appendix.

Urban groupings collated by Tietze's typology	%	Kemp 2008 Estimate 1	Kemp 2008 Estimate 2	Kemp 2008 Estimate 3
Élite (2e–3e)	8	1,459	2,400	4,000
Professional (2c–d)	35.5	6,475	10,650	17,750
Workers (1a–d)	56.5	10,306	16,950	28,250
Total population	**100**	**18,240**	**30,000**	**50,000**

Table 4.7: Kemp's estimates of the socio-economic mix at Amarna.

The total number of mud-bricks, the workload to make and lay them to build the houses required for the urban working class, professional class, and the city élite are given in Table 4.8.[697] To convert the workload to manpower, these assessments are increased by the same competency index of 1.17.

Urban groupings collated by Tietze's typology	Kemp 2008 Estimate 1	Kemp 1991 Estimate 2	Kemp 2008 Estimate 3 High case
Population	18,240	30,000	50,000
Élite (2e–3e)	20,319,666	33,373,065	55,621,775
Professional (2c–d)	14,171,731	23,308,919	38,848,198
Workers (1c–d)	5,757,914	9,465,093	15,775,155
No. of bricks	**40,249,311**	**66,147,077**	**110,245,128**
Workload man-yrs	**6,347**	**10,430**	**17,383**
Total manpower	**7,426**	**10,430**	**20,338**

Table 4.8: Number of mud-bricks, workload, and manpower required to build the domestic housing in Amarna.

Even for the lowest estimate, with a manpower requirement of 7,426 mud-brick makers and builders, the logistics to organise and control the movement of the capital city from Thebes to Amarna would have been immense, especially so because the actual building program may have been as short as 15 years. If the mud-brick workers brought their families with them then the number of individuals that had to be fed would be even greater. The workload and manpower identified in Table

[692] See Table 2.27.

[693] The population of Cyprus is assumed to be 100,000. Therefore 13 workers will satisfy its demand for bricks needed to meet the annual growth in population.

[694] Akhenaten (at first named Amenhotep IV) reigned from 1353 to *c.*1332 B.C. and was the creator of a religious, artistic and political revolution that led to the capital of ancient Egypt moving from Thebes to a virgin site at Amarna in Middle Egypt.

[695] The capital of Amarna moved back to Thebes shortly after the death of Akhenaten *c.*1332 B.C.

[696] Kemp 2008: 34.

[697] The Ramesseum is used as a reference granary in a discussion of Polanyi's concept of universal redistribution, in Section 6.4 and further details of this building are given in Report 4.4 in the Appendix.

4.8 only relates to the domestic housing requirements so the achievement becomes even more remarkable when taking into account the additional manpower resources needed for building the three Aten temples, the palaces, temple bakeries, workshops, military barracks, and all the other commercial and administrative buildings associated with this large capital city. Large bakeries have been excavated in Amarna that demonstrate the scale of the operation.[698]

Case Study C

State building projects

Towns and fortresses supported Egypt's economic and military interests, and new towns were created to provide labour and services for the building of major temples and royal tombs. New cities such as Amarna and Piramesses were built on virgin land, for political and religious reasons. Unlike domestic building, state building projects required vast numbers of mud-bricks. To demonstrate the scale of the mud-brick building industry needed to support state projects, five examples have been considered. These have been chosen because they are representative of Egypt's need for city walls, fortresses, and granaries in the MK and NK.

The same basic building methods and materials were used as those for domestic houses but the sheer size and height of state buildings meant a significant complexity in construction, the use of scaffolding or ramps, and carrying the mud-bricks and mortar to the bricklayer. The additional need for strength and stability of these larger state buildings such as the Buhen fortress (0.007992 m^3) required larger bricks rather than the standard NK bricks used in the Amarna North Suburb (average 0.004813 m^3).[699] However, the larger bricks required more time to make, transport, and lay.[700] A summary of four examples of mud-brick state buildings is given in Table 4.9. See further detail of the Ramesseum granary in Report 4.6 in the Appendix.

Egyptian state projects	No of bricks	Workload (man-yrs) to make and lay bricks	Manpower required
Enclosure wall for MK town of Lahun	10,035,705	1,212	1,418
Nubian fortress of Mirgissa	9,307,055	2,576	3,014
Enclosure wall for the MK fortress at Buhen	13,318,057	4,595	5,376
Granary at the Ramesseum	5,196,178	1,656	1,938

Table 4.9: The numbers of bricks, workload, and manpower to build representative state building projects.

Each example estimates the number of mud-bricks required and the workload and manpower resources required to build them. The results show that the scale of these mud-brick buildings was enormous and their construction would have had similar logistical challenges to those in Amarna.

4.4 Observations

The archaeological record of Egypt demonstrates the versatility and longevity of mud-bricks for architectural purposes. The simplicity of their manufacture and the use of readily available materials: mud, sand, water, straw, chaff, and water, provided Egypt with a cost-effective solution to the basic need for shelter and the state's need for civic, military, and economic structures. Mud-bricks enabled complex architectural designs to be built that were strong and stable, with minimal effort needed for maintenance. The innovation of vaulted ceilings added further practical opportunities for state building programmes. The cost-effectiveness of mud-brick construction is demonstrated by the fact that only 269 workers/annum would have been required to keep up with the housing demands to satisfy Egypt's population growth in the NK. The versatility of mud-bricks and their low cost as a building material meant that they satisfied all non-religious state building requirements. Because of these two factors, huge building projects could be undertaken to satisfy state needs, some with very complex designs, such as the Ramesseum granary in the NK and the Buhen fortress in the MK. The success of mud-brick construction is demonstrated by the fact that it is still one of the primary methods for building construction used today in Egypt.

[698] The bakeries would also required significant resources to move the grain from the farms to the bakeries. For evidence of large state bakeries at Amarna see Kemp 1991: 289.

[699] For detailed drawings of the MK fortress at Buhen, see Emery *et al* 1979. For the mud-brick granary at the Ramesseum see Figure 4.1.

[700] Emery *et al* 1979: 39 and Spencer 1979: 95.

Chapter 5: Bronze Production in the LBA

5.1 Introduction

This study has so far examined the basic processes that fed, clothed, and sheltered the LBA societies of Egypt and Cyprus. The production of bronze is a non-basic activity but it was fundamental to the economy of the LBA and it is necessary to understand the materials and processes involved in its production to be able to assess the scale of LBA economy. The possession of bronze was a high priority for those states that wished to maintain or increase their relative politico-economic status in the wider Eastern Mediterranean arena. Another important factor during the Ramesside Period was the investment in weapons and equipment for the standing army, which would have increased the demand for bronze in NK Egypt.[701]

This chapter provides an overview of LBA bronze production and calculates the labour-rates, workload, and manpower for each stage of the bronze production process. Section 5.2 examines the end-to-end processes involved in the production of copper, tin, and bronze and calculates the associated labour-rates. Section 5.3 calculates the labour-rates involved in the production of charcoal, which was used for smelting, refining, and alloying copper and tin. The cost of land and sea transport in the acquisition of metals in the Eastern Mediterranean is quantified in Section 5.4. The final section uses the preceding analyses to compare the cost of producing bronze in NK Egypt and LBA Cyprus. The findings of this chapter are discussed in Chapter 6 to illustrate the scale of the metals industry and the 'globalised' nature of trade in this period.

The spreadsheet BRONZECALC is used to calculate the labour-rates workload, and manpower associated with each activity, summary tables and key assumptions are provided in this chapter.

Copper, tin and bronze

NK Egypt and LBA Cyprus did not have exploitable deposits of tin, which had to be imported.[702] Textual and archaeological evidence suggests that by the LBA most, if not all, of the tin that entered the Eastern Mediterranean trading network had been transported overland from tin mined in Uzbekistan, Tajikistan or Afghanistan.[703] Ugarit may well have been the main distribution centre for the tin, utilising the harbour at Mahadu, close to Ras Shamra.[704] As the tin had to be sourced outside the Eastern Mediterranean, an international metals market developed in which the Eastern Mediterranean regions produced and exchanged added-value goods and/or other valuable raw materials for tin. In the OK and MK, Egypt had a sufficiently wide range of natural resources, including copper, which enabled it to remain relatively economically and politically isolated. However, NK Egypt was forced to trade for tin outside its borders.

The term 'bronze' can be employed differently, some scholars refer to the alloy of copper and tin as bronze and it is this alloy which is examined in this study. Others include ternary alloys found naturally, such as copper-tin-arsenic (arsenical bronze) and copper-tin-lead (lead bronze).[705] In Egypt, arsenical copper took precedence over tin bronze until the NK Ramesside Period when tin became the alloying metal of choice.[706] The mix of copper and tin varies considerably in ancient bronzes, but in the LBA the most common ratio found in tools and weapons was 90–95% by weight of copper alloyed with 5–10% of tin by weight.[707]

Mining copper and tin

Ancient mining practices are difficult to understand fully because excavating a mine is unlike traditional archaeological excavations that can assess the stratified accumulation of material over time. With mining, the reverse occurs and the evidence of early activity is destroyed by later mining activity.[708] Nowhere is this more evident than in the Cypriot mines around the Troodos mountains where much evidence has been destroyed by Roman and Medieval mining operations as well as modern open-cast mining. This problem is compounded by the use in modern times of ancient slag heaps for road construction.[709] It is fortunate that the ancient mines at Timna in the Arabah Sinai copper fields have largely escaped destruction from continued mining. In Cyprus, a few preserved parts of Bronze Age mines at Ambelikou-*Aletri,* Politico Phorades, and Apliki give some indication of the techniques used to mine and smelt sulphide ores. These mines have been chosen for the analysis of Cypriot copper production in this quantitative study.[710] The relatively easy access to the copper sulphide ores on the edges of the Cypriot Troodos mountain range, using adit or open-cast methods made mining a low-cost operation in terms of workload. This type of mining is in

701 Spalinger 2005: 202–205, 214–230, Footnote 16.

702 Cassiterite (tin oxide SnO_2) was the most common tin ore mined in antiquity. Improved modern mining techniques enable deposits of cassiterite tin ore in the Eastern Desert to be mined today (Sabet *et al* 1976). There are no textual references to tin mining in Pharaonic Egypt though a few tin objects appear in funerary contexts (Ogden 2000: 171).

703 Maddin *et al* 1977, Muhly 1985, Muhly *et al* 1991, Muhly 1993, Yener and Vandiver 1993, Yener *et al* 1993, Weisgerber and Cierny 2002, Cierny and Weisgerber 2003, Gillis *et al* 2003, Kassianidou 2003, and Pigott 2011.

704 Heltzer 1977 and Astour 1981: 8, 24.

705 Pare 2000: 13.

706 Ogden 2000: 153. See Pare 2000: Figure 1.3 for the distribution of tin bronze in Egyptian artefacts for the period 2200–1800 B.C.

707 The majority of Egyptian artefacts have up to 10% tin by weight though a few bronze artefacts have levels of 16% (Ogden 2000: 154).

708 Weisgerber 2006: 2.

709 See Koucky and Steinberg 1982a: 120.

710 For the surviving archaeological evidence of these mines and miners' camps, see du Plat Taylor 1952, 150–153, 166, Appendix 6, Merrillees 1984, Koucky and Steinberg 1989: 275–288, Kassianidou 1999, Knapp 1999b, and Knapp 2003.

contrast to the Egyptian mining operations at Timna. Here complex interconnected tunnels were needed to follow the veins of mixed oxide nodular ores. The removal of waste rock from the tunnels and access shafts made this method of mining a very labour-intensive process. The gaps in our understanding of the complete end-to-end copper production process in the LBA are filled by using indirect evidence from experimental archaeology, scenes of metal processing in Egyptian tomb paintings, ancient and Classical textual evidence, and archaeological and ethnographic evidence.[711] Modern scientific studies have also increased our knowledge of ancient metal-working processes and the provenance of metals found in the archaeological record.[712]

At Timna, the copper nodules mined and smelted in the LBA were predominantly complex mixtures of copper hydroxyl oxide and copper hydroxycarbonate ores.[713] The copper mineralisation in Cyprus is different from Timna and geologists have named these geological formations 'massive sulphide ore deposits'. They were formed when volcanic molten magma broke through the earth's crust and reacted with seawater on the ocean floor to form principally, deposits of iron pyrite (FeS_2) and chalcopyrite ($CuFeS_2$).[714] The main target for LBA Cypriot miners in these deposits was the secondary enrichment zone where concentrated copper ores (chalcopyrite, bornite, chalcocite, covellite, and pyrite) were formed above and below the old water table (Figure 5.1). The concentrated copper mineralisation around the water table formed under the action of oxygen rich percolating rainwater that reacted with the primary ores ('weathering'). The copper content in the secondary enrichment zone is three times more concentrated than in the non-weathered massive sulphide deposit. The water table changed during the Pleistocene Period due to rapid changes in sea level and after millennia of erosion, the enrichment zone was accessible to LBA miners, without the risk of flooding (Figures 5.2 and 5.3).[715]

Definitions of the technical terminology employed in this chapter can be found in the metallurgical glossary.

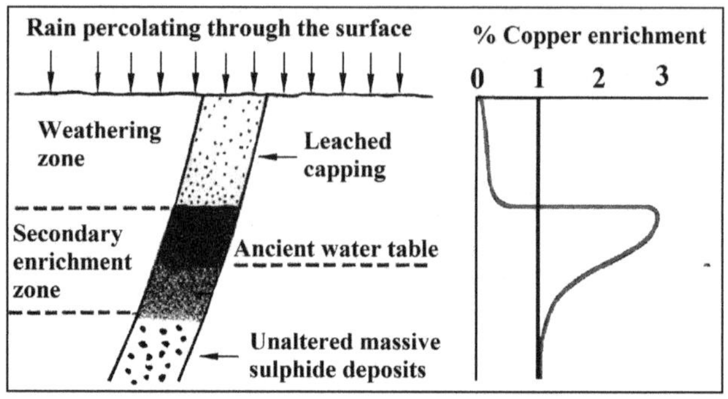

Figure 5.1: The secondary enrichment zone in the Cypriot Troodos mountains.

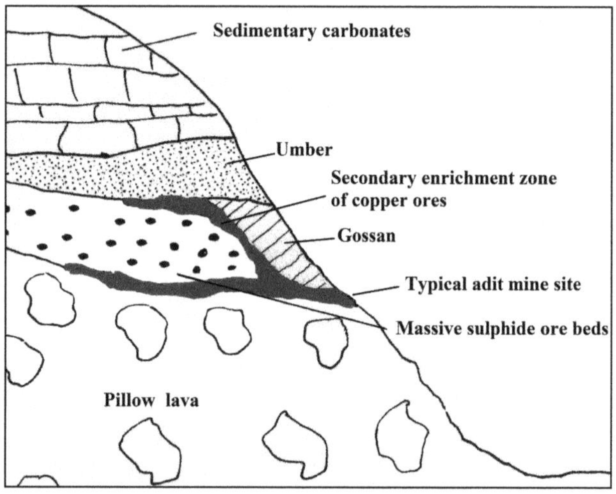

Figure 5.2: Typical position of an adit mine on the pillow lavas of the Troodos mountains.

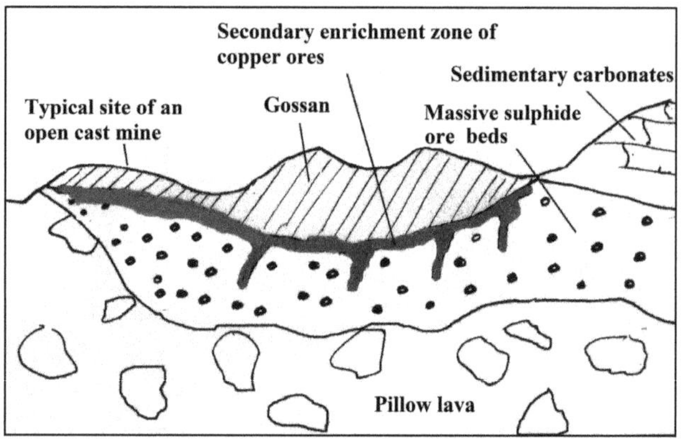

Figure 5.3: Typical position of an open-cast mine on the pillow lavas of the Troodos mountains.

5.2 Labour-rates associated with the LBA bronze production

The main end-to-end process activities for bronze production in the LBA are summarised here, from mining the ores through to alloying the copper and tin. The logical sequence of these activities is shown in Figure 5.4. The processes varied between Cyprus and Timna due to the types of ore found in each location. BRONZECALC is used in this section to calculate the labour-rates associated with:

[711] The evidence from experimental archaeology is taken from Tylecote and Boydell 1978, Merkel 1982: 32–72, Merkel 1983a, Merkel 1983b, Marechal 1985, Merkel 1985, Tylecote and Merkel 1985. Crew 1990: 57, Lewis 1990, Merkel 1990, Earl and Yener 1993, Timberlake 1994, and Py and Ancel 2006. For ethnographic evidence, see Merkel 1982: 141–158.

[712] Of particular importance to this study is lead isotope analysis, which measures four lead isotopes (Pb^{206}, Pb^{207}, Pb^{208}, and Pb^{204}). These are present in all copper based ores and the artefacts made from them. Combinations of these isotopes provide a location-specific isotopic signature that differentiates copper ores both geologically and geographically. This provides the link between the provenance of the mine and the bronze/copper artefacts made from excavated ore (Gale 1999, Gale 2001, Gale 2003, Gale and Stos-Gale 2005, and Gale 2011).

[713] The irregularly shaped copper nodules at Timna are within a sandstone matrix and comprise malachite, azurite, calcite, chalcocite, cuprite, goethite, gypsum, and limonite. The copper mineralization is mixed with quartz and sand gangue (Merkel 1985: 164).

[714] Koucky and Steinberg 1989: 285–286.

[715] Koucky and Steinberg 1989: 287–288, and Footnote 10.

- The quantity of ore to produce one kg of copper or tin.
- Mining the ore.
- The preparation of ores for smelting.
- The smelting of copper and tin.
- Refining copper and alloying with tin to make bronze.
- Charcoal for roasting, smelting ores, refining, alloying, and casting.
- Supplies of food for the workers and fodder for their donkeys.
- The transport of men, materials, and supplies.

The quantity of ore to be mined to produce one kg of copper or tin

In Cypriot adit mines, the volume of sulphide ore that had to be excavated to make one kg of smelted copper is estimated to be 0.0318 m^3.[716] With open cast mining the volume of sulphide ore and overlaying 'gossan' that had to be excavated to make one kg of refined copper is estimated to be 0.0692 m^3.[717] At Timna, the volume of nodule ore and 'gangue' excavated from the tunnels to make one kg of smelted copper, is estimated to be 1.19 m^3.[718] This is greater than Cyprus because additional gangue above and below the undulating nodule vein had to be removed to allow the miner to work at the tunnel face (Figure 5.5). The estimated volume of cassiterite ore (2% tin content) and gangue that had to be mined to produce one kg of tin in the trench mines in Uzbekistan, is 0.0571 m^3.[719]

Mining the ore

The variables involved in the mining process are numerous and each influenced the time taken to extract the ore. They include the width of the ore vein, the depth of the mine, the stability of the surrounding rock, the need for ventilation for the miners, and the depth of the water table. The limitations of LBA mining technology prevented ancient Cypriot miners from extracting ore from the deep massive sulphide ore beds and ventilation and dust problems limited the length and depth of the tunnels at Timna.[720]

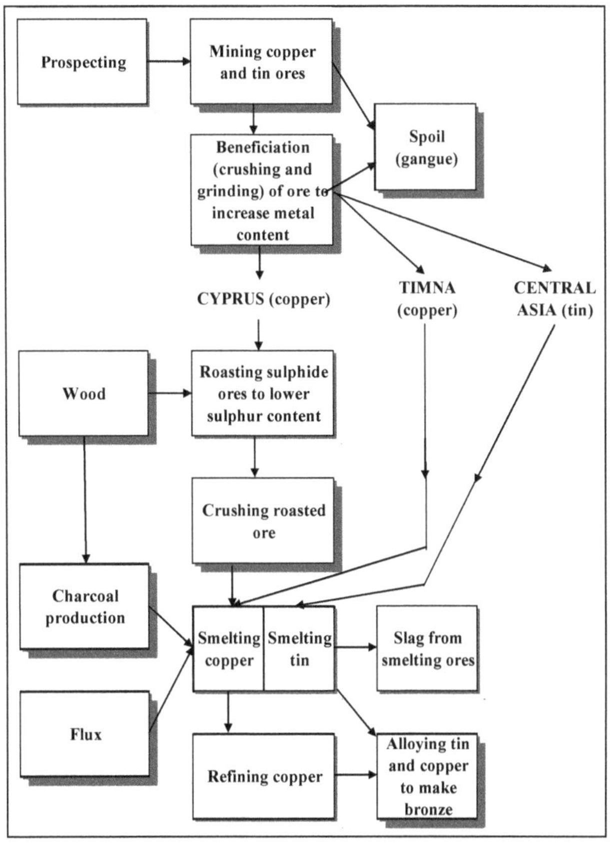

Figure 5.4: Processes from mining copper and tin through to the production of bronze.

The extraction labour-rate for the copper ore at Timna is based on a text that describes the digging of the Egyptian NK tomb of Senenmut (*c.*1473–1458 B.C.).[721] This hieratic ostracon outlines the work record of a day's work carried out by eleven masons excavating his tomb. It shows that in a day the masons progressed one rod in depth (0.65 m), 6 rods in width (3.9 m), and one cubit into the tomb (0.52 m). This means that 1.319 m^3/day of limestone was removed by eleven masons with an extraction rate of 0.1199 m^3/day/worker. Socket chisels fitted to wooden shafts have been found at Timna that were used to form an undercut, triangular in cross-section that made excavation of the ore vein easier for the miner (Figure 5.5).[722]

Most of the limited evidence of mining in the Troodos mountains that has survived suggests that adit mining rather than open cast mining was the most common practice and this study assumes that 60% of the ore removed was from adit mining. The adit mines in Cyprus

[716] The volume/kg of smelted copper is based on assumptions made by Healy 1978: 195, in his analysis of the Roman mines at Rio Tinto. Bear describes the copper ores from the Apliki mining district, a site used in antiquity, as porous and spongy in character with an average density of 2,265 kg/m^3 (Bear 1963: 46, 63). This study assumes the density of Cu/Fe sulphide ores with gangue as 2,320 kg/m^3 and this is the same as that found in the Mavrovouni and Kalavasos mines (Bear 1963: 46). Bear's estimate of the copper content of the Apliki ore was 1.8% (Bear 1963: 40, Table 10).

[717] Gossan is the oxidised and weathered rock above the ore deposit.

[718] Gangue is the worthless matrix of rock that is mixed and integral with the mineral ore. For the tunnel measurements from Site 27 at Timna and the ratios of ore to gangue, see Bartura *et al* 1980: 41–56, particularly Figure 20. The tunnels ranged from 0.5–1.5 m high and 0.3–0.6 m wide. The tunnels of the exhausted veins were backfilled to minimise the quantity of gangue that had to be lifted to the surface. For drawings of the complex tunnels extant in Timna, see Craddock 1995: 70, Figure 2.32.

[719] Cierny and Weisgerber 2003: 26–27. In Uzbekistan the tin ore veins were 0.40 to 1.20 m thickness but the concentrated cassiterite mineralisation in the vein suitable for smelting, ranges between 5 to 10 centimetres (Cierny and Weisgerber 2003: Figures 2–3). With an average thickness of the cassiterite tin ore vein of 0.075 m, a volume of 33.75 m^3 of ore, and gangue weighing 236,250 kg would be removed (Cierny and Weisgerber 2003: 27). With a 2% tin concentration the resulting weight of tin would have been 4,725 kg. The volume of ore and gangue to make one kg of tin would be = 270 ÷ 4,725 = 0.0571 m^3 weighing 50 kg.

[720] Shaw and Durucan 2008 for methods of ventilation in the mines at Timna.

[721] Hayes 1942: 21. Depth here refers to a vertical depth, i.e. height.

[722] Conrad *et al* 1980: 84, Figure 70.

share the same characteristic as Timna where the minimum of gossan and gangue surrounding the ore vein were removed to enable the miner to work. The adit mines were easier to work than Timna because they were shorter with better air supply and there was less distance to remove spoil. The labour-rate of Cypriot adit mining is assumed to be 85% of Timna equal to 0.102 m^3/day/worker. The open cast mining in Cyprus (Figure 5.3) would have been easier than Cypriot adit mines despite the additional gossan that had to be removed to reach the secondary enrichment zones of the copper sulphide ores and a rate of 0.0935 m^3/day/worker is used in BRONZECALC.[723]

The tin ores from Uzbekistan are in narrow veins of cassiterite mineralisation within a granite/quartz rock matrix. It was mined by excavating trenches from the surface down to the ore vein.[724] The extraction rate used in BRONZECALC is based on the analysis by Conophagos of the archaeological survey carried out by Ardaillon, who investigated the Greek silver mines at Laurion.[725] The mineralised ore at Laurion, like Uzbekistan, is surrounded by a hard igneous rock and the Ardaillon analysis is used for estimating the workload for tin ore extraction. The tin ores in Uzbekistan required an additional step in the mining process that Conophagos calls 'firesetting.'[726] This was a technique used to fracture rock by thermal stress. A wood or charcoal fire was lit against the ore-bearing rock face and when the rock was hot, it was doused with cold water. The thermal shock caused by the sudden contraction of the hot rock made the rock crack and fall away and the fragments could then be removed with pickaxes.[727] The firesetting experiments of Py and Ancel have demonstrated that the ratio of rock removed to the weight of wood burnt, is in the ratio 1:0.62.[728] Conophagos estimates that a three man digging team with one man digging at the tunnel face, working in short bursts, while the other two workers removed the surrounding rock at a rate of 0.008 m^3/hr/team. When adjusted for the use of firesetting and the benefits of vertical trenches, which provided fresher air compared with the Laurion tunnels and galleries, this study assumes a 300% improvement in extraction labour-rate for tin ore of 0.002667 m^3/day/worker. The labour-rates for Uzbekistan trench tin mines, Cypriot combined open cast and adit mining, and Egyptian tunnel mining in Timna are 0.205, 0.0125, and 0.2527 man-years/kg of metal smelted and refined ready for smelting.

Figure 5.5: Sketch showing the volume of gangue that had to be extracted to allow access to the vein of copper ore.
Sketch based on Conrad 1980: 84, Figure 70.

The preparation of ores for smelting

Beneficiation

Beneficiation is the process of removing unwanted gangue from the ore to enrich its metal content, maximising the efficiency of smelting, and minimising the quantity of charcoal burnt. The evidence from Timna and other sites shows that the first stage of beneficiation was backfilling previously exhausted tunnels and galleries with gangue that had no or minimal copper ore. The ore was then taken to the surface and hand sorted. The 'tailings' (rejected lumps of discarded gangue) from this hand sort are still to be found in many ancient mining/smelting sites. The remaining, more concentrated ore still mixed with some remaining gangue, was ground and hammered on large heavy stone mortars into small 4–5 mm pieces.[729] The final stage to remove gangue was winnowing, in which the ground ore and gangue were thrown into the wind, letting the heavier ore separate from the lighter gangue. The scale of the beneficiation process carried out at the ancient mine at Agrokipia Kriadis in Cyprus, is clearly seen in a spoil heap, which was 9.5 m high.[730] Koucky and Steinberg and Raber suggest a copper content of 12% as a realistic average of enriched ore after beneficiation.[731] This 12% figure is supported by Doonan's beneficiation experiments, which sorted and crushed 150 kg of chalcopyrite ore and produced 33.4 kg (22.27%) of enriched ore with an average copper content of 11.5%.[732]

Merkel's beneficiation experiments in the laboratory and onsite at Timna show that the average copper content after beneficiation varied between 15–18%. This study has used 15% as an average of the above studies.

[723] This rate is based on the experimental archaeology on West Overton Down (Jewell 1963: 50–64). Jewell's excavation rates were for chalk and have been adjusted for this study proportional to the density of chalk and that of the gossan found on the Troodos mountains (1,795 and 5,700 kg/m^3).

[724] Cierny and Weisgerber 2003: Figure 12, cross-section of the Kanab mine 6–1. The volume removed in a trench mine in Uzbekistan was 270 m^3 (depth 15 m, width of 0.6 m, and a length of 30 m).

[725] Ardaillon 1897: 24–26, Figures 6–8 and Conophagos 1980: 194–198.

[726] For evidence of firesetting, see Cierny and Weisgerber 2003: 26 and Figure 6.

[727] Firesetting gives a characteristic concave shape to the mining tunnel. Lewis 1990: 55 and Timberlake 1990. For textual evidence of firesetting in antiquity, see Pliny, *Naturalis historia*. 33.21.71–73.

[728] Py and Ancel 2006: 78, Figure 4. This ratio is the average of 66 experiments that replicated ancient firesetting practices at the medieval Fournel silver mines in the Hautes-Alpes, France. This figure is used in calculating the additional manpower for lumbering and transporting the wood to the mines.

[729] Rothenberg 1962: Plates VIII-IX, XIV.

[730] Given *et al* 2003: 64–69, Figures 4.3–4.5.

[731] Koucky and Steinberg 1982b: 173 and Raber 1987: 304. Also see the on-site experiments using Timna nodules (Merkel 1985: 166).

[732] Doonan 1994: 86–87.

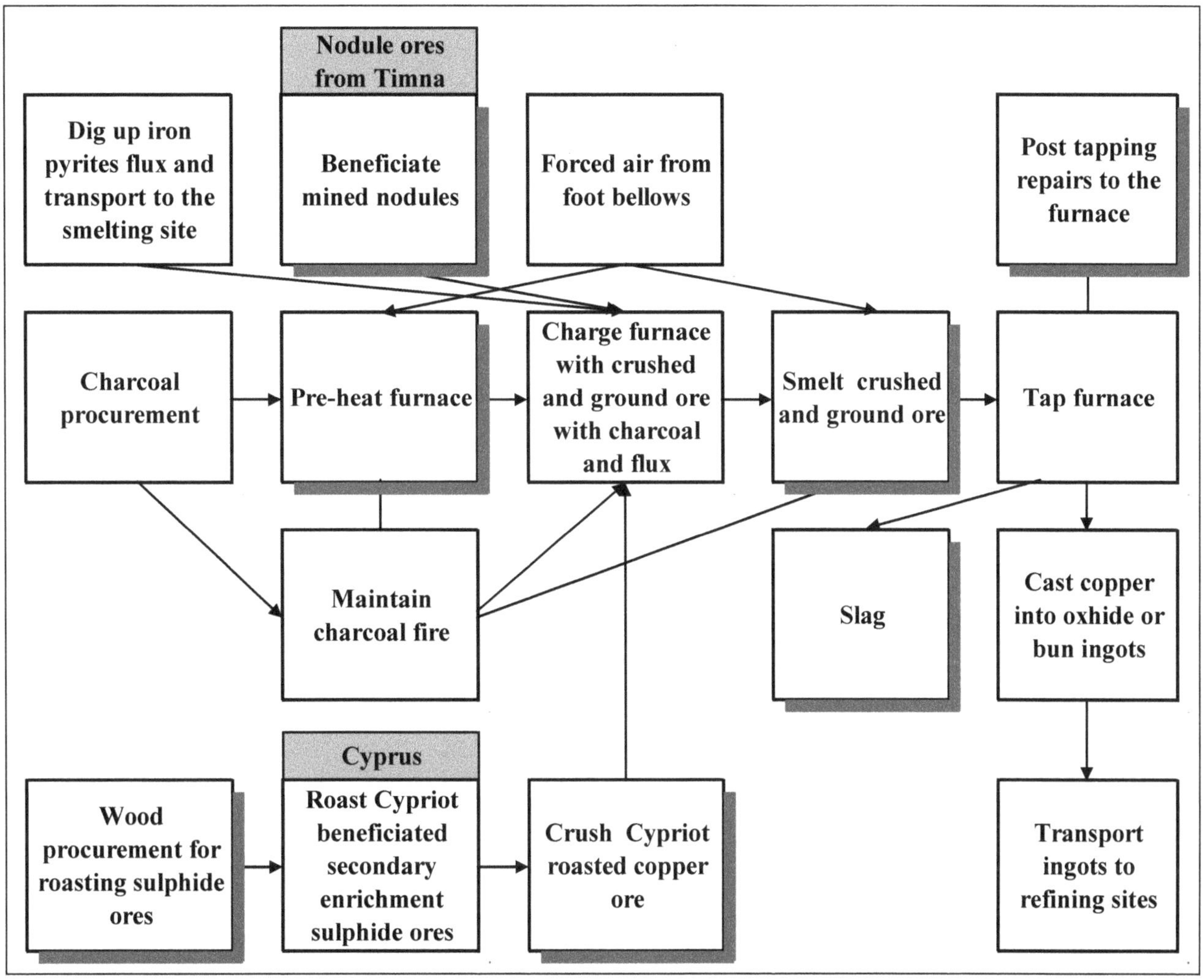

Figure 5.6: The process to smelt copper sulphide ores in Cyprus and nodule ores in Timna.

With a recovery rate of 85% after smelting, the weight of beneficiated ore to make 1 kg of copper = (100 ÷ 15) × (100 ÷ 85) = 7.84 kg.[733] In his work-study analysis using these ores, Merkel demonstrated that the beneficiation process took 42 man-hours, representing an average labour-rate of 0.8 kg/hr enriched ore.[734]

Roasting Cypriot ores

The Cypriot copper sulphide ores found in the Troodos mountain range require roasting to increase the percentage of retrievable copper when it is smelted. The most common copper ore in Cyprus is chalcopyrite ($CuFeS_2$) intermixed with iron pyrites (FeS_2) and the roasting process reduces the level of sulphur and oxidises the iron while retaining the copper in a sulphide form. The resulting copper sulphide called chalcocite (Cu_2S) is reduced to about 7% and can then be smelted.[735] During roasting with burning wood at a temperature of *c.*400 °C, the complex chemical reactions taking place are highly exothermic and if the temperature is not controlled the ore mix sinters and the copper will oxidise making smelting to base copper metal difficult. The copper ores from Timna do not require this preliminary roasting.

The smelting of copper ores

A flow diagram of the smelting process is shown in Figure 5.6. Described simply, smelting is the heating of the ore in a reducing atmosphere until the metal separates from its oxides, gangue, or other undesired metals within the ore. In the process, a slag is formed containing all unwanted material, which can then be removed.[736] The molten copper separates from the slag because copper has a higher specific gravity and a lower viscosity than the slag, thereby falling by gravity to the floor of the furnace.[737] To achieve a successful smelt a flux must be added to remove any gangue remaining from the beneficiation process. This ensures that a free flowing slag forms, which can be tapped from the furnace. The most common fluxes used in the LBA were iron pyrites when the gangue was silica and silica based or manganese if the gangue was iron pyrite based. The labour associated with adding iron pyrite would have been minimal, as iron pyrites would have been available in close proximity to the Cypriot and Timna smelting

[733] Merkel 1985: 166. If 18% is taken, the beneficiation ore requirement = 6.54 kg.

[734] Doonan 1994: Table 3 for the complete analysis of the beneficiation labour-rate.

[735] Kelso 1951.

[736] Charles 1980: 153.

[737] Atzeni 2005: 18.

sites. Experiments indicate that the range of the ratios by weight of iron pyrites to copper ore for a successful smelt varied between 4.5:1 and 6.1:1. The free-flowing nature of the resulting combined molten flux and gangue has the additional benefit of reducing the time taken to tap the furnace and therefore decreasing the total elapse time to smelt a given quantity of ore.[738]

Ancient furnaces

The design of ancient furnaces and smelting crucibles differs from pottery kilns, because the fuel has to be in close contact with the ore in order to produce reducing conditions. In general, pottery kilns have the fire at the entrance or bottom of the kiln in a horizontal firing chamber quite separate from the pots. Consequently, the smelter has less control than the potter, once the furnace is fired. The labour-rates for smelting draw upon the experiments carried out with replicas of LBA furnaces by Merkel and Tylecote.[739]

In his replication of the ancient Egyptian smelting process, Merkel based his design of furnace on the remains of shaft furnaces at Sites 2, 30, and 39 at Timna. One of the problems in determining the design of LBA furnaces is that the top half of the furnaces were destroyed or badly damaged when the smelted products were removed in antiquity. Rothenberg's excavation of LBA furnaces from Site 2 at Timna shows that the furnaces were built on a slope, a practice common at Timna from the second millennium onwards. The furnace shaft and tapping pit encompassed an area 1 x 2 m. The furnace shaft had an inner diameter *c.*0.4–0.45 m with the maximum preserved height of 0.4 m. The tapping point was drilled through the wall just above the furnace bottom, allowing the hot liquid slag to flow quickly into the slag pit while still retaining the molten metallic copper in the furnace bottom.[740] Smelting furnaces of a similar design to those excavated at Timna have been found at Ayia Varara-Almyras (Iron-Age) and Politico Phorades in Cyprus suggesting that the weight of copper per smelt would be of the same order.[741]

Tuyères found in situ were 0.2 m (on the inner wall) above the bottom of the furnace (0.26–0.3 m on the outside of the wall) angled at 25–30° to the horizontal. The LBA tuyère was a pipe of clay that allowed the forced air from the bellows to pass into the furnace. A tuyère typically comprised a 0.1 m clay tube fitted into the back of the furnace, into which was placed a 0.003 m clay tube with a nozzle of clay to minimise the conduction of heat from the furnace along the pipes to the bellows.[742] Two tuyères were fitted, one at the rear and one at the front of the furnace, though there may have been more. In the tomb scenes of Rekhmire (TT 100) the tuyères are shown attached to foot bellows (Figure 5.7).[743] Merkel's field experiments found that three bellow-operated tuyères gave adequate airflow for successful smelting.[744] The total smelting labour-rate to smelt copper is 0.0143 man-years/kg of copper.

Figure 5.7: Workers using foot bellows attached to tuyères.
Sketch of Davies 1943b: Plate LII. The tomb of Rekhmire (TT 100).

The smelting of tin ores

The archaeological evidence suggests that crucible furnaces were used for smelting tin ore rather than shaft furnaces and Timberlake based his experiments on the flat ceramic bowls excavated in Göltepe.[745] Finely ground cassiterite was fed into a hole poked into the centre of a bed of burning charcoal, and a successful smelt was completed in 1.5 hrs after charging the furnace with ore and using clay tuyères to maintain temperature.[746] A small lump of very pure tin with a purity higher than 99% formed on the furnace bottom together with tin 'prills' that had formed within the slag-ash matrix. The prills were easily extracted by grinding and or hammering with a stone on a stone anvil.[747] The theoretical maximum weight of tin that could be smelted from the 0.25 kg of cassiterite ore concentrate with a 60% purity is 0.128 kg.[748] Timberlake achieved a maximum recovery of 0.065

[738] The analysis of ancient slag from Cyprus shows that siliceous flux had been used at Kalavasos, while at Skouriotissa and Lefkara manganese oxides were employed. Manganese oxide has the advantage over siliceous flux in that it removes any iron produced in the smelting process, which would otherwise contaminate the copper smelt (Bachmann 1982: 148–149). On the other hand, if the ores contained an excess of silica through poor beneficiation, iron oxide could be added (Tylecote 1980a: 184).

[739] Tylecote 1974: 54, Tylecote and Boydell 1978, Tylecote 1980b, Merkel 1982: 159–262, Merkel 1983a, and Merkel 1983b.

[740] The slope of the second millennium furnaces excavated at Timna was approximately 1 in 4 (Rothenberg 1972: 73, Figure 19 and Plate 35, VII). For excavation reports of the Timna furnaces see Rothenberg 1990: 4–29.

[741] For Ayia Varara-Almyras see Fasnacht and Kassianidou 1992 and Fasnacht 2008 *et al.* For Politico Phorades see Knapp 1996b, Knapp 1999b: 100, and Knapp 2001: 207-210.

[742] Rothenberg 1972: 72–74 and Rothenberg 1990: 29–36.

[743] The scene portrayed in Rekhmire's tomb could be the refining of copper, alloying tin and copper or casting bronze. (Davies 1943a: 53 and Davies 1943b: Plate LII). For a more detailed discussion on the design and development of the Egyptian combined tuyère and bellow-forced draught systems, see Nibbi 1977: 59–60 and Tylecote 1981: 107–118. For a diagrammatic sketch of the sequence of operations to produce a force draft with bellows and tuyères, which were used across the Near East see Davey 1979: 101, Figure 2.

[744] Merkel 1983a: 176, Plate 2.

[745] Earl and Yener 1993, Muhly 1993, Yener and Vandiver 1993, and Timberlake 1994: 124–125, Figure 5.

[746] Tylecote's experiments indicate that a temperature of 1000°C was necessary for successful smelting of cassiterite ore (Tylecote 1986: 43).

[747] Timberlake 1994: 122–126.

[748] Timberlake 1994: 125.

kg of tin from 0.25 kg of cassiterite ore concentrate. A second experiment using 0.2 kg of cassiterite ore concentrate achieved a maximum recovery of 0.08 kg of tin. The reducing environment was produced by covering the ore charge with charcoal and the smelt was achieved in one smelt using one tuyère, without any need for further refining.

Refining copper

Analyses of LBA copper ingots show a significant level of contaminants such as iron, sulphur, trace metals, residual flux, and slag inclusions. The highest level of contaminant was iron, which entered the copper melt from the iron pyrites flux.[749] As a result, un-refined copper was brittle and porous with poor mechanical properties, making it unsuitable for tools and weapons. It is assumed that refining took place in crucibles allowing contact with air. A crucible excavated at Enkomi is significantly larger that those used at Piramesses and would take longer to reach the required temperature.[750] It is estimated that it would take 1 hour and 0.3 of an hour for the Cypriot and the Egyptian crucibles respectively. Air removes the impurities by oxidisation but the reaction also produces cuprous oxide (Cu_2O) and if too much is created, it leaves the copper overly brittle for hammering or casting. The melt was covered by charcoal to prevented further oxidisation and the excess cuprous oxide was removed by a process called 'poling' in which green branches were pushed through the charcoal into the melt. The branches caught fire and produced hydrocarbon gases which reacted with the cuprous oxide breaking it down and lowering the oxygen content of the metal.[751] Figure 5.8 is a flow diagram of this process. The estimated total labour-rate for refining is 0.0006 and 0.0007 man-years/kg of copper for Cyprus and Egypt respectively.[752]

Alloying copper and tin to make bronze

The quantification of the labour-rate to cast bronze into artefacts is not included in this section because this process is part of the discretionary use of surplus food rations for the production of added-value goods by non-basic workers.[753] The process of alloying was less complex than smelting or refining and could be completed in one cycle. To make bronze, tin is added to copper in either a solid form or a molten state. A high tin content makes bronze easier to cast with fewer defects. A number of factors may have influenced the proportion of tin added to copper to produce bronze such as the relative scarcity of tin, and therefore its cost. Another factor is that the fuel requirement for alloying varies with the content of tin. For example, bronze made with 25% tin requires less charcoal for casting, as it has a melting point of 798 °C, compared with 6% tin, which melts at 1036 °C. Assuming that it took the same furnace pre-heat time and melt time as refining, the labour-rate for alloying copper and tin (ratio 10:1) in both Cyprus and Piramesses would be 0.0003 man-years/kg of bronze.

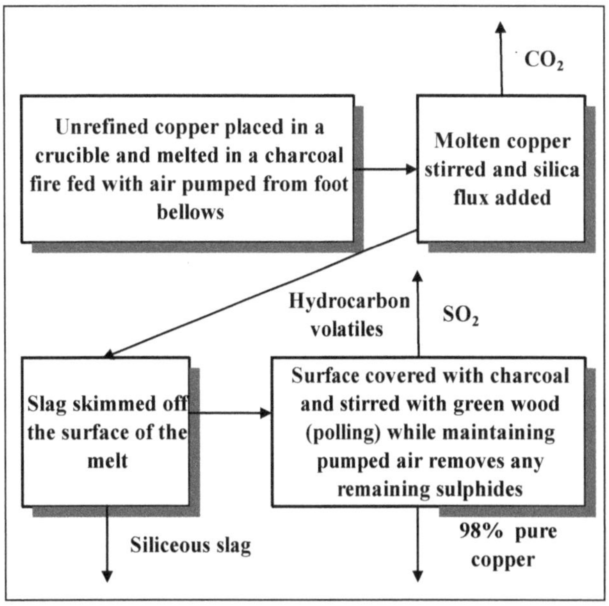

Figure 5.8: The refining process for copper.

5.3 Charcoal for roasting and smelting ores, refining and alloying

Charcoal was used for the smelting, refining, and alloying of copper and tin and it has three main benefits over wood for pyro-metallurgical processes. Charcoal can achieve higher temperatures in furnaces.[754] It produces a reducing environment when burnt with a limited air supply, producing the carbon monoxide essential for smelting, refining, and alloying operations.[755] A higher heat output is achieved with charcoal, as it has higher carbon content than wood per unit weight.[756] Consequently, more precise temperature control can be

749 Merkel's refining experiments using charcoal as fuel in a shallow clay-lined pit, decreased the iron content of impure smelted copper to 6%, (approximately 25% of its original level). A second re-melting experiment decreased the iron to 3%, a third experiment reduced it to 2% (Merkel 1993: 177, Table 1).

750 Tylecote 1982: Figure 5. An LBA Cypriot crucible found at Enkomi (Tylecote 1982: 92) was larger than the Piramesses crucible (30–40 cms vs 15 cms). Also see Pusch 1994: 153, Figure 1.

751 Kelso 1951, Forbes 1972: 20–21, and Atzeni 2005: 21.

752 This analysis has assumed 2 hrs for melting and poling 20 kg of unrefined copper.

753 Figure 1.1 in Chapter 1.

754 Charcoal burns naturally at 900°C but with forced air, temperatures of 1600 °C can be reached within the furnace (Sim and Ridge 2002: 21). Charcoal has a calorific value of 6,500–7,200 kilocalories/kg comparable to bituminous coal (Olson 1991: 412).

755 Wood produces carbon dioxide when burnt within a furnace rather than carbon monoxide, which was necessary to form a reducing atmosphere.

756 The calorific value of charcoal is 7,400 kcal/kg, compared with 3,580 kcal/kg for green wood (FAO. 1985a). Depending on the type of wood used to make it, charcoal has a carbon content ranging from 78–92% compared with 50% carbon content in wood. When charcoal is burnt instead of wood, the thermal efficiency increases because the heat out put of charcoal is higher than wood but the heat losses remain the same irrespective of the fuel. For a schematic of all the heat sources and losses in an ancient furnace used for smelting or refining, see Bamberger and Wincierz 1990: 146, Graph 18.

achieved, because smaller quantities of charcoal than wood can be added at a time for the same energy input.[757]

Charcoal production

Making charcoal is a labour-intensive process and involves cutting down trees, trimming the felled trees, transporting the wood to the charcoal maker, stacking the wood, covering it with earth to inhibit combustion, and breaking the charcoal into pieces suitable for use in furnaces. Figure 5.9 is a flow diagram of these processes. The traditional process of making charcoal, either by an earth-covered mound or in a pit, has not changed essentially from the Bronze Age to today. Charcoal is made from hard woods and produced when the wood is heated with insufficient air for combustion to take place, at a temperature in excess of 480°C. Hard wood was preferred to soft wood for making charcoal, as it has higher carbon content and thus produces higher temperatures in furnaces.

In Egypt, an extensive charcoal industry flourished in both the Sinai and the Eastern Desert.[758] Rothenberg suggests that the sources of wood at Timna for charcoal were acacia trees and brushwood, which grow in the nearby saline marshes near Yotvatah (40 km north of the Red Sea) and along the Wadi Arabah (part of the Great Rift Valley).[759] It is assumed that for both Timna and Cyprus the charcoal makers would have chosen hard wood if available. Therefore, for the assessment of the lumbering workload this study uses 38 kg of charcoal from an average size oak tree.[760] A lower weight of 30 kg reflects a medium-sized Egyptian acacia tree.[761]

Traditional methods of producing charcoal reduce the volume of timber by 25% and its weight by 75%. This means that 1 kg of charcoal can be made from 1.65 kg of wood with a 15% water content, and 2.5 kg of green wood with 60% water content. To improve the efficiency of the charcoal-making process, the cut wood is left to dry or kiln dried, avoiding wasting energy that would otherwise be needed to evaporate the wood sap.[762]

The length of time to prepare wood for charcoal production is based on the Roman army sources. To cut down an average size hard wood tree, cut it into smaller pieces suitable for a charcoal clamp, and then stack them took 6.5 hrs.[763] This equates to a total lumbering and stacking labour-rate of 10 and 12.2 man-days/kg for all the charcoal used in the end-to-end bronze production process.

Weight of charcoal to produce one kg of bronze

Merkel's experiments on smelting demonstrate that a shaft furnace based on those from Site 2 and 30 from Timna and operated with foot bellows, required on average 61.4 kg of charcoal for pre-heating and smelting 1 kg of copper.[764] Extrapolating the results of tin smelting experiments by Earle and Timberlake who used a simple crucible furnace, resulted in an average charcoal consumption rate of 70 kg of charcoal per kg of smelted tin.[765]

The charcoal usage given in Table 5.1 has adjusted Merkel's copper results and Earle and Timberlake's tin smelting to reflect that 1 kg of bronze comprised 0.9 kg of copper and 0.1 kg of tin. For refining, an additional 10% of the charcoal needed for smelting has been allowed.

Charcoal requirements	Weight (kg)
Smelting 0.9 kg of copper = 61.4 × 0.9 =	55.3
Refining 0.9 kg of copper = 10 × 55.3 ÷ 100 =	5.5
Smelting 0.1 kg of tin = 70 × 0.1 =	7
Alloying 0.9 kg of copper and 0.1 kg of tin to make 1 kg of bronze = 1.5 × (55.3 + 7) ÷ 100 =	0.9
Charcoal requirement (kg)	**68.7**
Add 5% for losses in production/transit	**3.4**
Total charcoal requirement (kg)	**72.1**

Table 5.1: Total charcoal requirements for the end-to-end process of producing one kg of bronze.

For alloying, an additional 1.5% of the charcoal needed for smelting copper and tin has been allocated.[766] Charcoal is friable and some losses took place when it was transported by donkey in panniers from the charcoal pits to the metal working sites and when mixed with the ore and flux charge in the furnace.[767] This study uses a charcoal loss rate of 5%. The total charcoal requirement to make 1 kg of bronze is 72.1 kg.[768]

[757] Craddock 1995: 189.

[758] Killen 2000: 353. In Egypt and the Wadi Arabah close to Timna, charcoal was made from a range of tree woods: acacia, juniper, oak, olive, pistachio and the tamarisk. *Pistacia atlantica* grows in the wadi beds close to Timna (Rothenberg 1962: 17–19 and Werker 1988: 232, Table 1).

[759] For a map of the Timna area see Rothenberg 1972: 26, Figure 5.

[760] Allan 1970: 10. Allan's estimate is based on Roman evidence of the copper mines in Rio Tinto and would be typical of trees in Cyprus. Charcoal found in ancient sites shows that it was made from mixed forests of dwarf oak, hawthorn, olive, and pine on the lower slopes of the Troodos mountains, and from the coast, oak and poplar. Cedars and cypresses are also common in all parts of Cyprus (Raber 1987: 303 and Knapp 1999c: 237).

[761] Rothenberg 1978: 9.

[762] Undried hard wood containing 30% of water requires less energy to make charcoal than undried softwood which has 42% water content (Olson 1991: 412).

[763] Shirley 2001: 41. Also see Cleere and Crossley 1985: 133–135.

[764] The average weight of charcoal used to smelt 1 kg of copper in Merkel's experiments 17, 18, 20, 23, 24, 25, 27, 29, and 29 was 20.3 kg for pre-heating and 41.1 kg for smelting, a total of 61.4 kg (Merkel 1990: Table 1).

[765] The charcoal/kg for smelted tin in this analysis is an estimate as some unburnt charcoal was left in the experimental furnace ash/charcoal/tin matrix furnace following the smelt. Timberlake 1994: 123 estimated that the smelt consumed 15–20 kg of charcoal. Earle 1996: 17 records a tin yield of 2.95 g using 0.118 kg of charcoal.

[766] It is assumed that alloying was completed in one cycle compared with refining that could have up to 5 cycles to remove impurities to a satisfactory level (Merkel 1983a: 177, Table 1).

[767] Cleere and Crosby 1985: 135.

[768] Merkel 1983b: Table 31 and Merkel 1990: 87, Table 2.

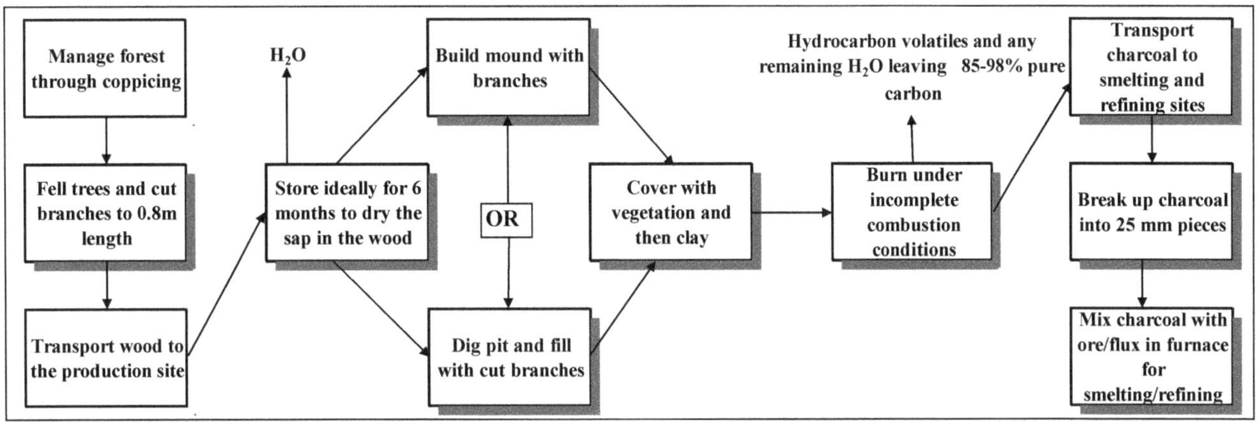

Figure 5.9: The production process for charcoal in the LBA.

The labour-rate to produce the charcoal to make one kg of bronze

Two experimental archaeological studies were carried out by Pleiner to evaluate the yield of charcoal using traditional processes.[769] The first experiment used logs cut to 0.6 m, laid in horizontal layers in a mound 2.5 m in diameter at the bottom and 2 m at the top, and 1.4 m high. The wood was covered with green branches and moist turf and mud to prevent ingress of air through the sides. The mound produced 70 kg of charcoal from 400 kg of chopped wood (17.5%, or 1:5.7, yield). The process took 48 hrs and needed constant monitoring to ensure that the clay covering did not crack, allowing an ingress of air. The second experiment was on a larger scale, producing 100 kg of charcoal from 570 kg of pine (also a 17.5% yield) but this time taking a longer period of 68 hrs. Cleere and Pleiner's studies both suggest a ratio of charcoal to wood of 1:7.[770] Based on Pleiner's charcoal-making experiments, the labour-rate for the production of charcoal is 0.68 hrs/kg of charcoal.[771]

5.4 Transport considerations

By choice, transport in antiquity would have been by river or sea but when this was not feasible, overland journeys utilised donkey caravans.[772] Textual evidence shows that donkeys were the primary beast of burden in the Eastern Mediterranean and the value of a donkey was high in antiquity.[773] Other costs involved in the transport of metals, could include security guards, donkey fodder, and donkey handlers.[774]

Modern cost accounting practices would apportion the cost of transport over the expected life of the boat and for land transport, the life expectancy of the donkey, to produce an indirect cost rate/journey. For simplicity, this study has only included the direct costs for overland transport given above (people, food and supplies, and fodder). For sea transport, a nominal apportioned cost is included (discussed below).

Transporting copper, tin, and bronze

There were many possible routes for the flow of copper, tin and bronze to and from Cyprus and Egypt as shown in Figures 5.10 and 5.11.[775] It has been assumed in this study that in order to minimise the movement of ore, the smelting operation was carried out close to the mines, and that refining copper, alloying with tin, and casting of bronze was carried out close to towns and ports. Piramesses has been chosen for the destination of tin and copper for Egypt as this Ramesside city was a major centre for added-value production of bronze artefacts on an industrial-scale.[776] In order to assess transport workload costs for Cyprus and Egypt, eight combinations of routes have been analysed for the transport of the metal cargo on the Ulu Burun and are represented in Figures 5.10–5.12. For Cyprus, these are:

- The transport of tin from Central Asia to Ugarit (Route 1–*c.*2,300 km).
- The transport of tin to Cyprus from Ugarit Route (2– *c.*950 km). Another route, more difficult in terms of currents and prevailing winds but much shorter, was to ship tin direct from Ugarit to the harbour towns (Route 3–*c.*285 km).
- The transport of un-refined copper from the Cypriot Apliki mines to the refining centres on

[769] Pleiner 2000: Figure 29.

[770] Cleere 1976: 240 and Pleiner 2000: 126.

[771] Pleiner 2000: 126.

[772] Mainly MK evidence attests to large mining expeditions with up to 500 donkeys and 4000 personnel. Shipping played a major role transporting workers and equipment across the Red Sea (Mumford and Parcak 2003: 89–90).

[773] In Ugarit the cost of a donkey ranged between 10–25 shekels of silver (Heltzer 1977: 207–208). Ugaritic text PRU, IV, 17.348 shows 400 donkeys were purchased as caravan-animals in the trade between Ugarit and Karchemish (Heltzer 1978: 75). In Egypt the most frequently quoted price for a donkey from Deir el-Medina was 30 deben of copper (Janssen 2005: 87–88).

[774] AGCALC shows that the manpower effort to grow green fodder for one donkey amounts to 23 man-days per donkey (see again Section 2.7). Veenhof 1972: 86 considers that one handler is required for every 2–3 donkeys.

[775] Astour discusses the many alternative trading routes that criss-crossed the Eastern Mediterranean and their connections with overland trade routes into ancient Central Asia (Astour 1995). For textual sources of the routes for the metals trade with an emphasis on tin, see Muhly 1973: 290–338, Heltzer 1977, and Larsen 1977. For a recent discussion on the sources of tin and the tin trade in south-west Asia, see Pigott 2011. In particular, see Figure 27.2 for a map of tin trading routes from Central Asia to Ugarit and Anatolia. The Amarna letters show that Cyprus provided copper for Egypt, Ḫatti, Anatolia, Babylonia, Ugarit, and other northern Syrian city-states (Knapp 2011).

[776] This site is close to modern Quantir in the Delta. For an overview of the metal working facilities at Piramesses, see Pusch 1990.

the coast of Cyprus (Route 4–*c.*175 km). The most likely route would be along riverbeds that are dry in summer.
- The transport of bronze from the harbour towns on the south-western coast of Cyprus to Ugarit (Route 5–*c.*285 km).

For Egypt, three possible combinations of routes have been analysed:

- The transport of tin from Central Asia to Piramesses via Ugarit using Routes 1 and 6 *c.*2,300 km.
- The transport of unrefined copper from Timna to Piramesses using Route 7 *c.*500 km.
- The transport of unrefined copper from Timna to Piramesses using Route 8 *c.*155 km overland and *c.*425 km by sea.

Overland transport

All assumptions related to transport by donkey associated with the metals industry are as stated in Table 5.2 with references given in the text. In this study, a caravan refers to donkeys carrying goods that are organised into a number of smaller groups. Each group is called a train, controlled by handlers responsible for the donkeys in their charge. Fodder requirements are based on those given in Section 2.7. Transporting tin to Piramesses from Ugarit would have added approximately 900 km to the journey.

Load (kg) carried by donkeys over long distances	75
Daily water requirement for donkeys litres/day	27
Daily water requirement for humans litres/day	3.5
Number of donkeys/train	10
Number of handlers/train	3
Number of rest periods/day	3
Duration of rest period (hrs)	1
Working day (hrs)	9
Effective time (hrs) caravan is on the move	6
Speed of donkey caravan (km/hr)	4.5
Number of soldiers per caravan required for security	20

Table 5.2: Summary of assumptions used for transporting supplies by donkey on mining expeditions.

Sea transport

Cyprus depended on its tin imports being delivered by sea. The archaeological record shows that refining of copper and bronze was particularly active in the harbour towns of Enkomi, Kition, and Hala Sultan Tekke. Tin could be imported and bronze exported by sailing direct from any other harbour towns along the south-west coast of Cyprus to and from Ugarit (Route 2). Alternatively, the ships could have sailed in an anticlockwise direction along the coast of Anatolia, around the west of Cyprus and eventually to Enkomi (Route 3 *c.*950 km).

The movement of smelted copper from Timna may have been overland (Route 7). Duncan-Jones proposes that the ratio of the cost of land transport to sea transport in antiquity was 22.6:1.[777] An alternative, lower cost, route would be a combined land and sea route (Route 8) from Timna, sailing around the Sinai peninsular to Ras Budran and then across the Red Sea to Ayn Sukhna and overland to Piramesses (Figure 5.11). Miners travelling to Timna would take the reverse route. Route 8 would reduce the elapse return journey from Piramesses to Timna from 37 days to 12 days.

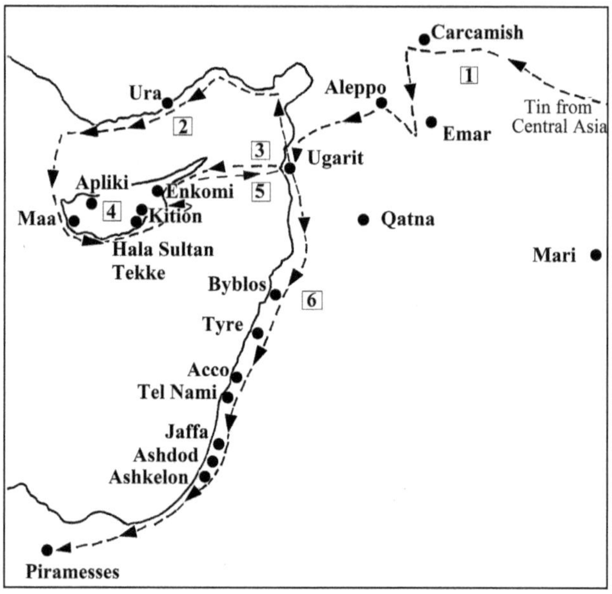

Figure 5.10: Routes taken for the transport of tin from Central Asia to Cyprus and Egypt via Ugarit.

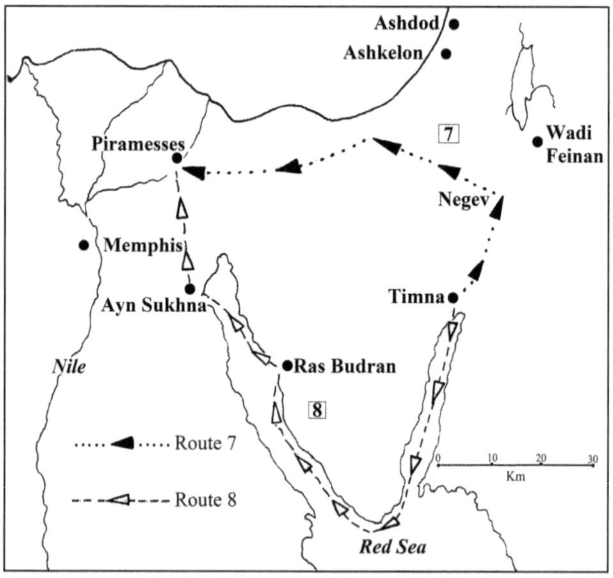

Figure 5.11: Alternative Routes 7 and 8 to transport copper from Timna to Piramesses.

The route chosen by the ship owners probably depended on trading considerations, which favoured mixed loads, which could be exchanged at more than one harbour. All the sea routes are relatively short. As the boat would make many journeys in its life, the apportioned cost of the boat would be minimal and has been set at a nominal 5 man-years (Table 5.14).[778]

[777] Duncan-Jones 1974: 366–369.

[778] This is an example where the cost of an asset can be related to the effort involved in its construction, maintenance, and crewing.

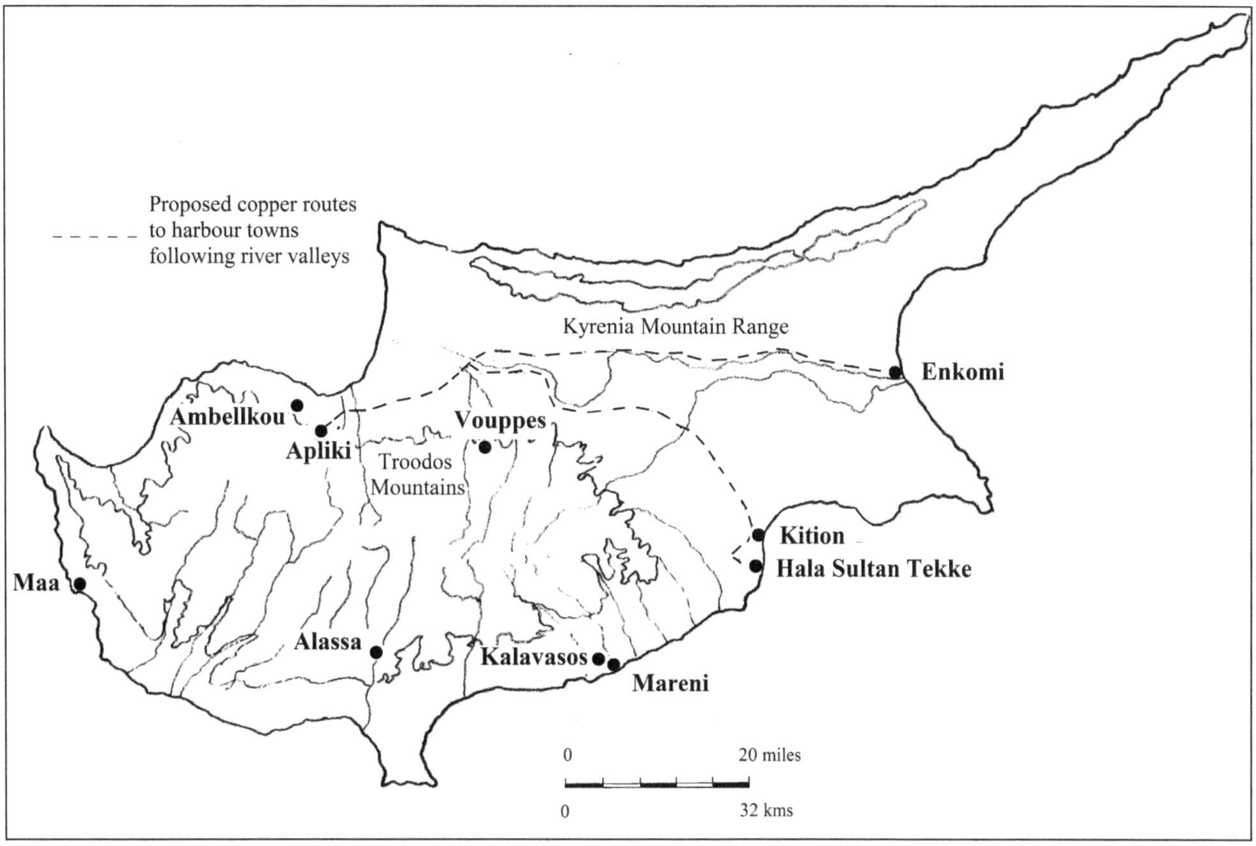

Figure 5.12: Possible routes for the movement of copper mined at Apliki to the LBA harbour towns.

Transport of supplies to Timna

The analysis of the ancient Egyptian diet discussed in Section 2.4 showed that an adult male required 345 kg/yr of grain and 110 kg/yr of pulses in their diet.[779] For the mining community it is assumed that grain was sourced from local settlements during the mining season. Protein in the form of wildfowl could have been sourced from the salt marshes at Yotvatah near Timna. Man-made cisterns may have collected run-off water from infrequent rain showers.[780] For this exercise, it is assumed that the grain was procured from the nearest settlements (average 100 km return journey) and transported by donkey caravans to Timna (Figure 5.13).

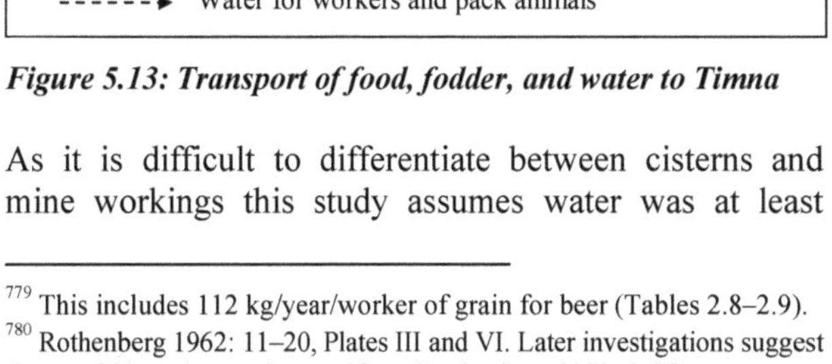

Figure 5.13: Transport of food, fodder, and water to Timna

As it is difficult to differentiate between cisterns and mine workings this study assumes water was at least partially sourced at Ein Radiyan and transported to Timna by donkeys.

Mines in the Cypriot Troodos mountains would have had lower logistical costs than Egypt, as water was available from mountain streams and food supplies from agricultural districts bordering the mountains.[781] Using these assumptions, the transport labour-rate to produce one kg of bronze for Cyprus and Egypt was 0.964 and 1.33 man-years/kg of bronze respectively.[782]

This study has chosen Routes 7 and 8 for movements of men and materials to and from Timna and Piramesses to provide maximum and minimum costs. Egypt maintained hegemony over the Levant in the LBA with an annual expedition to Timna. It is probable that supply centres would have been well established. However, Ward has clearly demonstrated that the Egyptians had the marine capability to sail across the Red Sea, follow the coast around the Sinai peninsular, and then up to the Gulf of Eilat to Timna.[783] If Route 8 had been chosen then the Egyptian transport labour-rate would be reduced from 1.33 to 1.27 man-years/kg bronze.[784]

[779] This includes 112 kg/year/worker of grain for beer (Tables 2.8–2.9).

[780] Rothenberg 1962: 11–20, Plates III and VI. Later investigations suggest they could have been mine workings (Rothenberg 1988: 4,d 8).

[781] Knapp 1997a: 60, Figure 6.

[782] The workload for associated with these labour-rates.

[783] Ward 2004, Ward 2006, and Ward 2010.

[784] These transport labour-rates are used later to calculate the workload associated with the metals for making bronze with the same quantity of copper and tin found on the Ulu Burun shipwreck.

5.5: Comparing the cost of bronze production in Cyprus and Egypt

Although the consensus of scholars is that the Ulu Burun ingots were mined and smelted in Cyprus, it is useful for a comparison of cost to calculate the workload for the production of bronze by Cyprus and Egypt. To illustrate the cost differences, the weights of copper and tin found on the Ulu Burun (10,478 kg and 1000 kg respectively) are used. Conveniently, the weights of copper and tin ingots are in the ratio of 10:1 that is typical for bronze production in the LBA.

It is assumed that:

- Labour-rates of mining, roasting ores, smelting, refining, alloying, and associated transport are as calculated in Section 5.2.
- Tin is imported by both regions from Central Asia.
- Cypriot copper is mined and smelted in the Troodos mountains.
- Egyptian copper is mined and smelted at Timna.
- Cypriot copper is refined and alloyed with tin in the harbour towns along the south-western coast of Cyprus.
- Egyptian copper is refined and alloyed with tin at Piramesses.

Summary tables show the workload (man-years) for each stage of bronze production (Figure 5.4), culminating in the consolidation of workload and manpower.

Mining copper ores in Cyprus and Egypt, and tin in Central Asia

The LBA mining practices of Cyprus and Egypt differ because the geology has different characteristics (Section 5.2). The key assumptions and workload are summarised in Table 5.3.

Activity	Cyprus open cast mine	Cyprus adit mine	Timna
Vol. of ore extracted m^3/kg of copper	0.0692	0.0318	1.19
Rate of ore extracted m^3/day/worker	0.0935	0.102	0.1199
Number of men in the mining team	10	6	8
Labour-rate (man-days/kg)	7	1.86	79.36
Labour-rate (man-years/kg)	0.022	0.006	0.253
Total mining workload (man-years) required to make the Ulu Burun cargo	**234**	**62**	**2,648**
Combined Cypriot mining workload (man-years)	**131**		

Table 5.3: Workload to mine the copper ore in Cyprus and Timna to make the copper ingots on the Ulu Burun.

It is assumed that 40% of the Cypriot ores was obtained from open cast mines and 60% from adit mines. The resulting mining workload to supply the copper ores on the Ulu Burun ship is 131 man-years. This compares with 2,648 man-years for copper mining in Timna. The cost of producing tin in Central Asia has to be included in the analysis of the cost of bronze. The cost of tin for Egypt would be greater for Egypt due to greater cost of transport from Ugarit to Piramesses (Section 5.4).

The assumptions to lumber the wood, prepare wood faggots, transport wood to the mining centre for firesetting followed by dousing with water, are shown in Table 5.4. The workload for these activities is 32 man-years (Reports 5.1–5.2 in the Appendix).[785]

Preparation/transport of wood faggots for firesetting (man-years)	**6**
Arranging faggots and monitoring fire at the mine face (man-days)	4
Moving water to the mine face and pouring on to the fire (man-days)	2
Weight of tin ore (kg) to produce 1 kg of smelted tin	50
Total wt. (kg) of tin ore to make the 1,000 kg of tin on the Ulu Burun	50,000
Number of firesetting cycles required	1,337
Total firesetting workload (man-years)	26
Total lumbering, transport, and firesetting workload (man-years)	**32**

Table 5.4: Total workload associated for lumbering, transport, and firesetting of wood.

The assumptions in Table 5.5 are based on Ardaillon's estimate of the extraction rate in the Laurian silver mines.

Activity	Central Asia
Vol. of ore extracted m^3/kg of copper	0.0571
Rate of ore extracted m^3/day/worker	0.002667
Number of men in the mining team	3
Labour-rate (man-days/kg)	64.2
Labour-rate (man-years/kg)	0.204
Firesetting workload required to make Ulu Burun cargo	32
Extraction workload required to make the Ulu Burun tin	205
Total mining workload (man-years)	**237**

Table 5.5: Workload for the extraction of tin ore required to make the tin ingots on the Ulu Burun.

Using his estimate the extraction workload would be 205 man-years to produce the 1,000 kg of tin on the Ulu Burun.[786] It is assumed that a further three men assisted the digging team to remove soil and carry out a preliminary sort of the ore from the gangue.

Beneficiation of copper ores in Cyprus and Egypt, and tin in Central Asia

As discussed in Section 5.2, the mining operation in Central Asia used vertical trenches following the tin ore veins. This differed markedly from the adit and open cast mines of Cyprus and the deep tunnel mining at Timna.

[785] The analysis is based on the data presented in Cierny and Weisgerber 2003: 25. The average depth of trench mined = 15 m, width 0.6 m, length 30 m. A typical ore vein of 2% tin concentrate was 0.075 m resulting in a need for 0.0571 m^3 ore to be removed weighing 50 kg, to make one kg of tin.

[786] Ardaillon 1987. An earlier estimate by Conophagos gives a lower extraction rate of 0.008 m^3/team of three workers taking turns at the tunnel face/day giving an extraction workload of 136 man-years (Conophagos 1980: 195–196).

The stability of the background rock in Central Asia and the discrete veins of tin ore resulted in a lower ratio of gangue to usable ore, giving significantly lower workloads (Table 5.6).

Activity	Copper mined in Cyprus and Egypt	Tin mined in Central Asia
Weight of ore (kg) to make 1 kg of smelted metal	65.4	50.0
Doonan's experimental beneficiation results kg/hr	0.8	0.8
Days to collect/grind ore charge + crush flux and charcoal	81.75	62.5
Total weight of ore (kg) required to make Ulu Burun ingots	685,261	50,000
Total number of man-days for beneficiation	856,577	62,500
Labour-rate (man-days/kg) of copper and tin	82	63
Workload (man-years)	**2,728**	**199**

Table 5.6: Beneficiation workload (man-years) for the copper and tin found on the Ulu Burun.

Roasting Cypriot sulphide ores

If the copper ingots on the Ulu Burun came from Cyprus, the wood requirement for roasting of the ore would be 228,421 kg.[787] One roast may not have been sufficient as Agricola writes that the roasting process may have been repeated up to nine times to increase the copper to sulphur ratio to a level ready for smelting.[788] To produce the equivalent 10,478 kg of copper ingots found on the Ulu Burun wreck and five roastings were necessary. The workload required for cutting the timber, transporting the wood by donkey to the roasting site, roasting and then grinding the roasted ore, was in total, 133 man-years (Table 5.7).[789]

Roasting workload assuming five cycles	
Workload (man-days) lumbering wood	21,710
Workload (man-days) moving wood to the roasting site	330
Workload for 5 roastings and grinding the ore (man-days)	19,800
Workload for 5 roasting cycles (man-days)	41,840
Workload for 5 roasting cycles (man-years)	**133**

Table 5.7: Total workload (man-years) to roast the Cypriot sulphide ore, lumbering, and transporting wood.

Smelting copper ores in Cyprus and Egypt

Using the workloads derived above for each stage of smelting sufficient copper, assumed to be the same for Cyprus and Egypt, to produce the equivalent of the 10,478 kg of copper ingots on the Ulu Burun wreck would have required up to 150 man-years using a 3 tuyère furnace (Table 5.8).[790]

Smelting copper	
Number of smelting cycles required to produce the copper ingots on the Ulu Burun	6,858
Workload (man-days) to prepare iron oxide flux from the gossan ready for smelting	294
Workload (man-days) to smelt the copper ingots on the Ulu Burun	44,609
Workload (man-days) to rebuild and repair the furnace after each smelting cycle	2,096
Workload (man-days) to smelt the equivalent of the 10,478 kg of copper ingots found on the Ulu Burun	46,999
Weight (kg) of copper ingots on the Ulu Burun	10,478
Smelting labour-rate (man-days/kg) of copper	4.49
Workload (man-years) to smelt the equivalent of the 10,478 kg of copper ingots found on the Ulu Burun	**150**

Table 5.8: Workload (man-years) to smelt the equivalent of the 10,478 kg of copper found on the Ulu Burun.

Smelting tin ores

The workload to smelt the equivalent of the 1,000 kg of tin ingots found on the Ulu Burun wreck is given in Table 5.9.

Smelting tin	
Tin recovery rates %	51
Wt (kg) of recovered tin/smelt (Timberlake 1994: 125)	0.065
No. of smelts required to produce the 1000 kg of tin ingots on the Ulu Burun	15,385
Smelting labour-rate (man-days/kg) of tin	9.4
Workload (man-days) to smelt the 1,000 kg of tin ingots on the Ulu Burun	9,402
Workload (man-years) required to smelt the 1,000 kg of tin ingots on the Ulu Burun	**30**

Table 5.9: Workload to smelt the equivalent of the 1,000 kg cargo of Ulu Burun tin.

Timberlake's experiments show the recovery rate of tin from the crucible furnace ash and unburnt charcoal was 51% of the theoretical maximum. He smelted 0.25 kg of cassiterite ore taking one hour to raise the crucible furnace to temperature.[791] Smelting started after another ten to fifteen minutes and was continued for an additional hour to ensure a full smelt. To this must be added thirty minutes to extract prills of tin from the remains in the post smelt ash/charcoal matrix,

[787] Allan 1970: 10. His estimate for roasting is 21.8 kg for every kg of copper smelted. The total weight of wood required to produce the copper ingots on the Ulu Burun = 10,478 (weight of Ulu Burun ingots) × 21.8 = 228,421 kg. This equates to a volume of 317 m^3, assuming the wood was dwarf oak (*Quercus alnifolia)* with an average density of 720 kg/m^3.

[788] Agricola, *De re metallica.* 8. 350.

[789] The weight of usable wood per tree is taken as 6,012 kg giving a total requirement of 6.5 trees to roast the ore to make the copper ingots in Cyprus. Cleere and Crossley 1985: 133–135 state that on average it would take 4,342 hours/tree for lumbering. For transport calculations it is assumed a donkey could carry 75 kg of wood (Mumford 2006: 48, Footnote 38). Also, the donkeys worked in a caravan train of 10 animals, each train requiring 3 workers for loading, unloading wood, and feeding and watering. After beneficiation it is assumed that the enriched ore was roasted 7.5 days/roasting requiring 3 workers each 24 hours to monitor the roasting process. This equates to 3,600 man-days for a single roast of the copper Ulu Burun. This number is uplifted by 10% for time taken to grind the roasted ore and therefore five roastings = (3600 × 1.1) × 5 = 19,800 man-days.

[790] Based on Merkel's experiments (Merkel 1983b and Merkel 1990) it is assumed that LBA furnaces would smelt/firing between 1.1 and 2.5 kg of unrefined copper. The number of smelting cycles for these limits would be 10,478 ÷ 1.1 and 10,478 ÷ 2.5, giving 9526 and 4191 cycles respectively, with an average of 6,858 cycles.

[791] Two charges each comprising 5 ore balls of cassiterite weighing on average 0.125 kg of concentrate were dropped in the crucible furnace at 25 minute intervals (Timberlake 1994: 123).

giving an elapse time of 2.75 hrs.[792] The total smelting labour-rate to smelt tin is 0.03 man-years/kg of tin. Using these results, the smelting labour-rate would be 9.4 man-days to produce 1 kg of tin.[793] To smelt the 1,000 kg of tin removed from the Ulu Burun would be 30 man-years.[794]

Refining copper

The Cypriot and Egyptian workload would be 6 and 7 man-years respectively to refine the equivalent weight of un-refined copper ingots found on the Ulu Burun wreck, assuming 3 workers per refining cycle (Table 5.10).[795]

Refining copper	Cyprus	Egypt
Minimum number of men/team	3	3
Weight of copper refined/crucible	28	20
No. of cycles to refine 10,478 kg copper	374	524
No. of times the copper is refined/cycle	4	4
Time (hrs) to preheat crucible	1	0.3
Time (hrs) to melt copper, add flux, poling and remove the melt to repair fire	2	1.5
Time (hrs) to maintain crucible temperature	0.3	0.3
Total elapse time (hrs) for one complete refining cycle[796]	9.9	7.2
Total elapse time (hrs) to refine 10,478 kg of copper	3,703	3,773
Total elapse time (man-days) to refine 10,478 kg of copper	1,851	1,886
Workload (man-years) to refine 10,478 kg of copper	**6**	**7**

Table 5.10: Workload (man-years) to refine the 10,478 kg of copper in Cyprus and Egypt.

Alloying tin and copper

Assuming the time to pre-heat the crucible and melt time was the same as for refining, the labour-rate for alloying copper and tin (ratio 10:1) in both Cyprus and Piramesses would be 3 man-years (Table 5.11).[797]

Alloying copper and tin	Cyprus	Egypt
Minimum number of men/team	3	3
Weight of copper and tin alloyed in a crucible	28	20
No. of cycles to alloy 10,478 kg copper + 1,000 kg tin	410	574
Time (hrs) to preheat crucible	1	0.3
Time to alloy copper and tin per cycle	2	1.5
Total elapse time (hrs) for one alloying cycle	3	1.8
Total elapse time (hrs) to alloy 10,478 kg of copper and 1,000 kg of tin	1,230	1,034
Total elapse time (man-days) to alloy 10,478 kg of copper	820	862
Workload (man-years) to alloy 10,478 kg of copper and 1,000 kg of tin	**3**	**3**

Table 5.11: Workload (man-years) to alloy the copper and tin on the Ulu Burun in Cyprus and Egypt.

Charcoal requirement to smelt, refine, and alloy the Ulu Burun metals cargo

It was shown earlier (Table 5.1) that to produce 1 kg of bronze 72.1 kg of charcoal was required. This includes a 5% uplift for losses within the charcoal production cycle. The total charcoal requirement to smelt 10,478 kg of copper and 1000 kg of tin and alloy them together was 827,290 kg (Table 5.12).

Process	Total Wt. (kg) of charcoal required	%
Smelting copper	643,349	81.6
Refining copper	60,260	7.7
Smelting tin	70,000	8.9
Alloying copper and tin	14,010	1.8
Charcoal requirement (kg) for copper and tin on the Ulu Burun	**787,619**	**100**
Add 5% losses in charcoal production/transit	39,381	
Total charcoal requirement (kg) for copper and tin on the Ulu Burun	**827,000**	
Charcoal requirement/kg of bronze	**72.1**[798]	

Table 5.12: Weight (kg) of charcoal required to produce and alloy copper and tin.

Pleiner's experiments in charcoal burning showed that to produce 100 kg of charcoal took 68 hours.[799] In addition, effort would have been required to build up the charcoal clamp and monitor it during charcoal production.[800] In total 20.3 man-days were required to make 100 kg of charcoal and this equates to a workload of 167,940 man-days to produce the 827,290 kg needed to produce the copper and tin cargo on the Ulu Burun and alloy them together. In Cyprus, this would have required 158,443 oak trees with each an average 38 kg of usable wood. Timna required 193,081 acacia trees with each an average 30 kg of usable wood to produce the required charcoal. The lumbering and stacking workload was the 6.5 hours (Section 5.3) giving a grand total of 114,367 man-days. The man-days needed to transport the wood by

[792] Timberlake 1994: 123–124.

[793] Smelting labour-rate = 2.75 × 2 workers ÷ (0.065 kg of tin recovered/smelt) × 9 working hours/day) = 9.4 hours/kg. Although one man was only required for the tuyères in the pre-heating stage, 2 men used the tuyères in the smelting phase. However it was assumed that 2 men were involved throughout the process for ancillary activities such as stoking the fire with charcoal and preparing the concentrate cassiterite ore balls.

[794] Timberlake 1994: 125. A second tin smelting experiment showed that a recovery rate of 78% was achieved which would mean the workload to smelt the 1,000 kg of tin ingots on the Ulu Burun would take 25 man-years (Timberlake 1994: 127).

[795] An LBA Cypriot crucible found at Enkomi (Tylecote 1982: 92) was larger than the Piramesses crucible (30–40 cms vs 15 cms). The Enkomi crucible with a larger thermal capacity would therefore require fewer refining cycles than the Piramesses crucible. For experimental refining results see Merkel 1983b: Table 31.

[796] The total elapse time for the 4 refining cycles = (1 (time (hrs) to pre-heat crucible) × 1 (no. of times carried out/refining cycle)) + (0.3 (Time (hrs) to reheat crucible between refinings) × 3 (no. of times to maintain temperature between refinings)) + (2 (time (hrs) to melt copper, add flux, and poling)× 4 (no. of times carried out/refining cycle)) = 9.9 hrs. A similar calculation is provided for Egypt. It is assumed for the workload analysis that the workers only laboured for 6 hours per day due to the high temperatures of an open crucible furnace.

[797] It is assumed that 3 workers supported the process and for Cyprus and Piramesses 28 and 20 kg of tin and copper respectively, were alloyed per cycle. Each cycle lasted 3 and 1.8 hrs respectively.

[798] The Ulu Burun carried a cargo of 10,478 kg of copper and 1,000 kg of tin. The charcoal required to produce one kg of bronze = 827,000 (total charcoal requirement to produce the Ulu Burun cargo and alloy them together to make bronze) ÷ (10,478 + 1,000) = 72.1 kg.

[799] Pleiner 2000: 126.

[800] This study has assumed that this took 4.5 days with 2 men working 12 hours per burn cycle.

donkey would have been 10,260 and is inclusive of donkey handlers, rest stops for watering and feeding the donkeys, and loading and unloading the wood on the donkeys.[801] The workload required to make charcoal is collated for the end-end bronze production in Table 5.13. Cyprus has a lower workload because the sulphide ores had been roasted (using wood to lower the sulphur content) and this meant they required less charcoal in the smelting process.

Process	Cypriot workload man-years	Egyptian workload man-years
Smelting copper	762	831
Refining copper	71	78
Smelting tin	83	91
Alloying copper and tin	17	18
Total charcoal workload (man-years)	**933**	**1,018**

Table 5.13: Workload to make the charcoal to smelt, refine, and alloy the equivalent of the Ulu Burun copper and tin.

Transport and fodder

Table 5.14 summarises the total transport costs for Cyprus and routes 7 and 8 for Egypt.

Activity	Cyprus	Egypt Route 7	Egypt Route 8
Tin from Uzbekistan to Ugarit (Route 1)	18	18	18
Tin from Ugarit to Piramesses (Route 6)	0	10	10
Transport of tin from Ugarit to Cyprus (Routes 2/3)	5	0	0
Copper mines to refining centres (Routes 4 and 7	2	4	2
Supply of food to the metal workers each season	36	129	129
Transport miners food in/out of Timna (Route 7)	0	128	15
Transport wood and charcoal	34	41	41
Water for donkeys	0	28	28
Water for human consumption	0	144	144
Time expended travelling to and from mining site	28	822	267
Fodder costs	10	96	71
Transport workload	**133**	**1,420**	**725**

Table 5.14: Transport workload (man-years).

The Egyptians favoured mining expeditions rather than permanent settlements at the site.[802] We have limited evidence on the exact routes taken, so for comparison purposes the following analyses calculate the cost of the production of copper, tin, bronze, inclusive and exclusive of transport. The most significant cost of bronze production for Egypt was the expense of supplying the mining expeditions (Table 5.14). Route 7 is 16.8% of the total workload for producing bronze and Route 8 is 9.4% (Figure 5.11).

Workload consolidation

The workload to produce the 1,000 kg of tin and 10,478 kg of copper on the Ulu Burun wreck and then alloy them to make 11,478 kg of bronze would be 4,683 man-years for Cyprus (Table 5.15). For Egypt the workload to produce the 11,478 kg of bronze on the Ulu Burun wreck and then alloy them together would 8,440 man-years and 7,745 man-years for Routes 7 and 8 respectively (Tables 5.16–5.17).

CYPRUS	Tin	Copper	Bronze	Total	%
Extraction of ore	205	131	0	336	7.2
Firesetting	32	0	0	32	0.7
Beneficiation	199	2,728	0	2,927	62.4
Roasting of sulphide ore	0	133	0	133	2.8
Smelting ores	30	150	0	180	3.9
Refining	0	6	0	6	0.1
Alloying	0	0	3	3	0.1
Charcoal production	83	833	17	933	20.0
Transport/fodder costs	23	108	2	133	2.8
Total workload (man-years)	**572**	**4,089**	**22**	**4,683**	**100**

Table 5.15: Total man-years to produce and alloy the copper and tin found on the Ulu Burun to make bronze.

EGYPT (Timna) Route 7	Tin from Central Asia	Copper	Bronze	Total	%
Extraction of ore	205	2,648	0	2,853	33.9
Firesetting in Uzbekistan	32	0	0	32	0.4
Beneficiation	199	2,728	0	2,927	34.6
Roasting of sulphide ore	0	0	0	0	0
Smelting ores	30	150	0	180	2.1
Refining	0	7	0	7	0.1
Alloying	0	0	3	3	0.0
Charcoal production	91	909	18	1,018	12.1
Transport and fodder costs	28	1,388	4	1,420	16.8
Total workload (man-years)	**585**	**7,830**	**25**	**8,440**	**100**

Table 5.16: Workload to produce and alloy the copper and tin on the Ulu Burun to make bronze (Route 7).

Table 5.18 collates the data from Tables 5.15–5.17 into the workloads for the production of copper and tin, and then alloying them to make bronze. This table emphasises that Cyprus was a low cost producer of bronze compared with Egypt irrespective of the route taken by Egypt from Timna. The cost of the end-to-end bronze process for Egypt was 180% and 165% (Routes 7 and 8 respectively) more expensive than Cyprus.

Labour-rate to make one kg of bronze

The labour-rate required to produce one kg of bronze in Cyprus is 0.41 man-years/kg of bronze. For Egypt, using Route 7, it is 0.735 man-years/kg of bronze and for Route 8, 0.675 man-years/kg of bronze.

[801] This analysis assumes that a donkey could carry 75 kg wood for 8 km.

[802] There are many inscriptions that attest to mining expeditions to the Wadi el-Hudi amethyst mines, the Wadi Hammamat siltstone quarries, and the Sinai copper, turquoise, and malachite mines (Rothenberg 1987). See also Hikade 1998 for evidence of NK mining expeditions to Timna.

EGYPT (Timna) Route 8	Tin from Central Asia	Copper	Bronze	Total	%
Extraction of ore	205	2,648	0	2,853	36.8
Firesetting in Uzbekistan	32	0	0	32	0.4
Beneficiation	199	2,728	0	2,927	37.9
Roasting of sulphide ore	0	0	0	0	0
Smelting ores	30	150	0	180	2.3
Refining	0	7	0	7	0.1
Alloying	0	0	3	3	0
Charcoal production	91	909	18	1,018	13.1
Transport and fodder costs	28	695	2	725	9.4
Total workload (man-years)	**585**	**7,137**	**23**	**7,745**	**100**

Table 5.17: Workload to produce and alloy the copper and tin on the Ulu Burun to make bronze (Route 8).

Workload (man-years) inclusive of transport	Cyprus	Egypt (Route 7)	Egypt (Route 8)
Workload required for copper production	4,089	7,830	7,137
Workload required for tin production	572	585	585
Workload required for bronze production	22	25	23
Total	**4,683**	**8,440**	**7,745**

Table 5.18: Workload costs (man-years) inclusive of transport, to produce and alloy the Ulu Burun copper and tin.

Manpower consolidation

In calculating the manpower associated with the manufacture of bronze, it is assumed that the metal workers were fully skilled adults and the competency index of 1.15 reflects an increase in productivity.[803] The resulting manpower requirements for Cyprus would be 5,385 workers. For Egypt using Route 7 the manpower would be 9,705 workers and Route 8 the manpower would be 8,906 workers (Table 5.19).

Manpower inclusive of transport	Cyprus	Egypt (Route 7)	Egypt (Route 8)
Manpower required for copper production	4,702	9,004	8,208
Manpower required for tin production	658	672	672
Manpower required for bronze production	25	29	26
Total	**5,385**	**9,705**	**8,906**

Table 5.19: Manpower costs (competency index of 1.15) to produce and alloy the Ulu Burun copper and tin.

5.6 Observations

For Cyprus, beneficiation and charcoal production dominated production costs, as shown in the able 5.15. For Egypt, as well as the high beneficiation and charcoal production costs, the mining centre at Timna required mining expeditions and this meant that there was a significant additional cost of transport. The summary findings in Tables 5.16–5.17 clearly show this impact on its overall cost.

The scale of the workload and manpower resources expended on the production of the ingots of copper and tin found on Ulu Burun wreck raises a number of interesting points. In Cyprus the cost of copper and therefore bronze was relatively low compared with other regions and this could be the reason why Alašia was courted by other powers in the LBA to procure copper/bronze through gift exchange.[804] It may also explain why exploitation of copper deposits in the Arabah, particularly Timna, has fluctuated from the Bronze Age through to the present day.[805] It is possible that the LBA Egyptian strategy was to only produce copper from the Arabah when military campaigns created peak demands for bronze or when Cyprus was not able to supply sufficient quantities.

One outcome of the growth in the metals industry in the Bronze Age, and later, in the iron industry, was deforestation. This problem was exacerbated by the need for charcoal in other pyro-technological processes such as the casting of metal artefacts, annealing and work-hardening metal objects, and lime and gypsum plaster production.[806] Wood and charcoal was used for pottery kilns, and the production of faience and glass. There was also a demand for fuel for domestic purposes such as cooking and heating that could not be met from burning animal dung. It has been estimated on ethnographic evidence that a family household would require one ton of firewood per year.[807] Agriculture also contributed to deforestation, with increased terracing of land and the widespread practice of allowing the grazing of sheep and goats in woodland areas that discouraged forest re-growth.[808]

Mixed deciduous forests of oak and pine that are felled, take between 50–80 years to grow again. Constantinou has calculated that 200,000 tons of copper have been produced in Cyprus over the last 3,000–4,000 years.[809] To support copper production with charcoal, the entire area of ancient forests of Cyprus would have been replaced 16 times over this period. To minimise deforestation,

[803] Table 2.27 gives a competency index of 1.17 but this includes adolescents.

[804] Knapp 2008: 308–313 for a review of ancient texts relating to exports from Cyprus.

[805] Mumford and Parcak 2003: 86, 89–90, and 98.

[806] For example for each ton of lime plaster, two tons of limestone must be burned and this requires up to two tons of fuel (Miller 1990: 71).

[807] This estimate may be conservative, it is based on the assumption of a sustainable collection rate of 500–1300 kg of usable fuel/ha/year and that each household required up to 3 ha of scrub/woodland to meet their requirements for wood (Shay and Shay 1978: 48, 57).

[808] Wertime 1983: 445–446.

[809] Constantinou estimates that the 20 ancient slag heaps found in Cyprus contain 4 million tons of slag (Constantinou 1982: 19). The largest is the 2 million ton slag heap at Skouriotissa (Bruce 1937: 642). Using this estimate and a copper/slag ratio of 1:20, he deduces that 200,000 tons of copper were smelted up to the modern period (Constantinou 1982: 19).

coppicing of the hardwood trees that grow on the island is likely to have been practiced.[810]

While the ancient forests of Cyprus could perhaps have been sustained, the level of tree felling around Timna would have caused deforestation. A contributory factor for the migration from bronze to iron at the end of the LBA/EIA may have been because the estimated weight of charcoal needed to make 1 kg of bronze was 72.1 kg, whereas iron only required 10.9 kg of charcoal for every kg of iron produced.[811]

[810] The area of ancient forest has been estimated to be 15,000,000 ha (Constantinou 1982: 22).
[811] Cleere 1976: 240. This is based on Roman data for the Weald in Kent (A.D. 12–140 A.D.) where an annual iron production of 550,000 kg (550 metric tonnes) required 6,000,000 kg (6,000 metric tonnes) of charcoal.

Chapter 6: The scale and nature of the LBA economy

6.1 Introduction

This chapter challenges some of the basic tenets of the substantivists who maintain that the LBA economy was minimalist in scale, conservative in nature, and had no characteristics expected of a market economy.[812] The LBA and the transition to the EIA was a period when the ruling élites were faced with rapid changes in interregional politics, economics, and technology. An unprecedented level of contact was taking place between ruling élites with improved communication and diplomatic contact.[813] The archaeological and textual record shows that LBA merchants had interregional weights and measures, which facilitated agreement on the value of goods exchanged.[814] Developments in metal alloying technology resulted in an increasing dependence on bronze, which became the alloy of choice for weapons and tools creating an unparalleled demand for copper and tin. In return for metals, a complex network of trade developed involving added-value products and foodstuffs with a general flow of these goods from west to east.[815] Marine technology had improved both ship design and carrying capacity and harbours around the Mediterranean provided shelter and services for long distance maritime trading missions. These advances resulted in new markets opening up in those regions that before the LBA had minimal contact on a regular basis. All the elements necessary for LBA Eastern Mediterranean regions to become more responsive to market forces were in place but working against this development was a culture of conservative traditional values unresponsive to change. How the ruling élites came to terms with these two conflicting influences is the focus of this chapter on the nature of the LBA economy.

The sections that follow examine the LBA economy of Egypt and Cyprus, drawing on the findings of the previous chapters. They show that in this period the scale of the non-basic sector of the economy enabled the formation of an embryonic formalist market. This argues against the substantive view that in this period the economy was embedded and totally under control of the ruling élites. Nevertheless, in spite of the unprecedented level and diversity of trade much of the economy was still substantive in nature. The evaluation of the scale and nature of the LBA economy is presented by the key factors that lie at the centre of the substantive and formalist debate:

- The scale of the LBA economy of Egypt and Cyprus.
- The validity of Polanyi's redistribution model applied to NK Egypt.
- The evidence for cost accounting.
- The evidence for a private sector with entrepreneurial merchants.
- The evidence for prices that varied with demand profits and trading motivated by profit.

The chapter concludes with four theoretical constructs that are used by scholars to interpret the nature of the ancient economy and discusses whether these constructs apply to the LBA economies of Egypt and Cyprus.

6.2 The scale of the LBA economy

The first topic challenges the substantive view that scale of the LBA economy for the period 1400–1175 B.C. was minimalist in scale. Key factors related to the LBA economies of Egypt and Cyprus are considered, using the workload and manpower analyses from Chapters 2–5.

- The scale of the basic activities (agriculture, cloth production, and shelter).
- The scale of the non-basic activities (added-value production, the élite/administration, and the army).

A significant non-basic workforce would indicate that the LBA economy was not minimalist or primitive. However, the priorities and activities chosen by the élite for this non-basic workforce indicate the degree to which the economy was substantive in nature. Also two of the most important non-basic activities in the LBA are examined in detail:

- The scale of the metals trade.
- The scale of the LBA maritime trade.

Basic, non-basic workers, and their non-productive dependants

In this section, the population profiles of NK Egypt and LBA Cyprus are analysed to determine the proportion of the population that could be dedicated to the non-basic workforce.[816] The population of Egypt and and the normalised population of Cyprus (2.2 million and 100,000 respectively) are categorised into three main groups.[817] The first group is the basic workers who provide the food and the provision of domestic water, shelter, cloth, and the production of pots for domestic use

[812] An overview of the substantive and formalist views of the ancient economy is provided in Section 1.2 in Chapter 1.

[813] We know from the Amarna Letters that communication between ruling élites in Akkadian was possible and commonplace (Liverani 1979b and Zaccagnini 1987).

[814] In the context of this discussion 'value' is defined as the interaction between the desirability of an object and the difficulty of accessing it (van Wijngaarden 1999: 3).

[815] See Sherratt and Sherratt 1991: 385, Figure 1.

[816] See Hopkins's approach to quantify the minimum GDP of the Roman Empire (Hopkins 2000).

[817] The population at the end of the NK is assumed to be 2.2 million in this study as discussed in Section 4.3. The population of Cyprus is uncertain for the LBA and for comparison purposes with Egypt it is assumed to be equal to the 100,000 cohort used throughout this study. However, if the population was for example 50,000 then the absolute calculated results should be halved (Footnote 14 in Chapter 1).

for the total population. The second group comprises the non-basic workers, the élite/administration, the standing army, the producers of added-value goods, and other non-basic state services. The non-basic state sector covers a wide range of activities in addition to added-value workers and includes those workers who provided support and services to the élite administration, such as servants, low ranking scribes, and other categories of worker that would be expected in a hierarchical society.[818] The third consists of those non-productive individuals aged six or under and 60 years and over (29,890), in both the basic and non-basic sectors who, although non-productive, still have to be fed.

Basic workforce

The Hierarchy of Needs dictates that basic needs must be met before non-basic needs. The prime need of the population is the physiological requirements for water and food.[819] To maintain a cohort of 100,000 people of all ages (males and females) in a sufficiently healthy state, 84,684 million kcals/100,000 cohort/yr would be required.[820] However, due to wastage and the need for seed corn, the agricultural sector was required to produce 102,907 and 103,259 million kcals/100,000 cohort/yr for Cyprus and Egypt respectively. Chapter 2 has shown that to produce these calories in Egypt, up to 33,693 agrarian workers/100,000 cohort/yr were required. For a population of 2.2 million the total agrarian workforce of 741,246 would be required. For rain dependant agricultural regions such as Cyprus, the number of agrarian workers would be 43,393 per 100,000 cohort/yr.[821] These resource requirements include the workers required for essential infrastructure investment such as the repair of dykes, canals, and other activities associated with the annual inundation.

Chapter 4 has shown that a small workforce could fulfil the basic need for domestic housing resulting from population growth, requiring only 269 full time workers in Egypt and 13 in Cyprus to support their annual population growth.[822] The workforce required to make traditional hand thrown pots for domestic use in simple kilns fired by dung or wood has been set at a nominal 62 workers per 100,000 cohort/yr in Egypt and in Cyprus.[823] In Egypt with an estimated population of 2.2 million at the end of the NK, the actual pottery requirement would be 22 times larger (1,360).[824] A significant basic need requiring a dedicated workforce was the production of cloth for domestic purposes. For Egypt using flax, and Cyprus using wool, this would require workforces of 16,023 per 100,000 cohort/yr and 15,869 per 100,000 cohort/yr respectively. A summary of the workforce to meet the basic needs of Egypt and Cyprus for their total populations are 2,200,000 and 100,000 respectively shown in Table 6.1. When referring to basic and non-basic workers it should be remembered that they have 29,890 non-contributing dependants/100,000 cohort (see Table 2.3 for children 6 and under, and the elderly, 60 and over).

Number of workers/yr	Egypt	Cyprus
Agrarian workers	741,246	43,393
Cloth workers required to meet domestic need	352,506	15,869
Building workers required to meet the annual population growth	269	13
Potters required to meet the annual demand	1,360	62
Active basic workers	**1,095,381**	**59,337**

Table 6.1: The workforce required/yr to meet the basic needs of the total population of Egypt, and Cyprus.

Non-basic workforce

The non-basic workforce was supported by the harvest surplus produced by the agrarian workforce. The size of the non-basic workforce of NK Egypt is equal to the total population (2.2 million), minus the sum of the basic workforce plus the élite and those members of the population that are either too old or too young to work. The Coale-Demeny Model 3 West demographic model shows that 29,890 individuals/100,000 were aged six or under and aged 60 or over (Table 2.3). However, within this range the number of individuals that required cultivated food is reduced by the number of infants who were breastfed (assumed to be 3.24% of the 100,000 cohort). The number of individuals in these age bands requiring cultivated food to support them = 29,890 – 3,240 = 26,650. It is reasonable to assume that these age groups would not have contributed significantly to manual work. Applying these demographic age groups to the populations of NK Egypt (2,200,000) and LBA Cyprus (100,000), they equate to 657,580 and 29,890 individuals respectively. The size of the Egyptian non-basic workforce = 2,200,000 (NK population) – ((1,095,381 (basic workforce from Table 6.1) + 39,204 (élite from Table 3.1) + 657,580 (number of dependants)) = 407,835 workers for an estimated population of 2,200,000. A similar calculation is used for non-basic workforce of Cyprus (Table 6.2).

Population	Egypt	Cyprus
Élite and their dependants	39,204	1,782
Basic workers	1,095,381	59,337
Non-basic workers	407,835	8,991
Dependants of basic and non-basic workers	657,580	29,890
Total population	**2,200,000**	**100,000**

Table 6.2: The total population collated into élite, non-basic workers, basic sector workers, and dependants.

In order to assess the rations that needed to be stored in granaries for redistribution to the non-basic sector, it is necessary first to allocate the non-productive dependants to both groups. This study treats these demographic

818 This means that when calculating the non-basic workforce the number of workers engaged on added-value utilitarian and conspicuous consumption tasks is lower than the total non-basic sector.

819 It is assumed that by the LBA adequate processes were in place to obtain water for human and farm animal consumption (water sources were known, wells and cisterns had been dug) so that only minimal effort was needed to obtain water.

820 Section 2.3.

821 For Cyprus see Tables 2.62 and 2.64 and for Egypt see Table 2.63 2.65. Within these analyses, it has been assumed that the weight ratio of seed corn to yield was 1:10 and wastage was 15%.

822 Section 4.3.

823 I am grateful for this estimate from traditional potter and sculptor Jacqui Pavlovsky.

824 Rounded to the nearest 10.

groups as an overhead and they are prorated across the non-basic and basic sectors (Table 6.3). For example the proportion of the 657,580 individuals aged 0–6 and over 60 that is required to be added to the non-basic workforce as an overhead = (657,580 × 407,835) ÷ (2,200,000–39,204)) = 124,114. A similar calculation is used for a Cypriot cohort of 100,000 (Table 6.3).

Total population	Egypt	Egypt % of total population	Cyprus	Cyprus % of 100,000 cohort
Élite	39,204		1,782	
Non-basic active workers	407,835		8,991	
Dependants overhead	124,114		2,736	
Non-basic sector	**571,153**	**26**	**13,509**	**13.5**
Basic active workers	1,095,381		59,337	
Dependants overhead	533,466		27,154	
Basic sector	**1,628,847**	**74**	**86,491**	**86.5**
Total population	**2,200,000**	**100**	**100,000**	**100**

Table 6.3: The total populations collated into basic and non-basic sectors with non-productive dependants.

Table 6.3 highlights the fact that in antiquity the majority of the workforce with their dependants were in the basic sector (74% and 86.5% for Egypt and Cyprus respectively). The majority of the basic workers were primarily engaged in agriculture, 67.7% and 73.1% for Egypt and Cyprus respectively.[825] This sector had to produce a surplus of food for any non-basic activity to take place and it explains the economic dominance of Egypt, which had the benefit of high cereal yields. However, it does raise the issue of how Cyprus could be a major producer of copper in the LBA when such a large proportion of a small population were dedicated to the basic workforce and their dependants and this is discussed further in the next section. Figure 6.1 defines the non-basic and basic sectors and their manpower levels for the total population in NK Egypt and LBA Cyprus in the categories of the Hierarchy of Needs.

Whilst it is impossible to know how the élite prioritised the allocation of manpower resources, it is possible to identify the choices that they could make between supporting state and élite needs. In part, this would have been a factor of the absolute size of the population. In Egypt, the élite would have greater choice because it had a much larger population with a non-basic workforce that was 45 times greater than Cyprus.[826] The scale of the Egyptian non-basic workforce clearly demonstrates the underlying strength of the Egyptian economy. As Egypt was a regional superpower, the standing Egyptian army is included within the non-basic sector. In Egypt and Cyprus the conclusion must be drawn that the concept of an *oikos* economy (minimalist in scale) as proposed by Bücher, Weber, and Finley is inappropriate in terms of scale for the economy of the LBA. The sections following support the proposition that the LBA economy was not minimalist in scale.

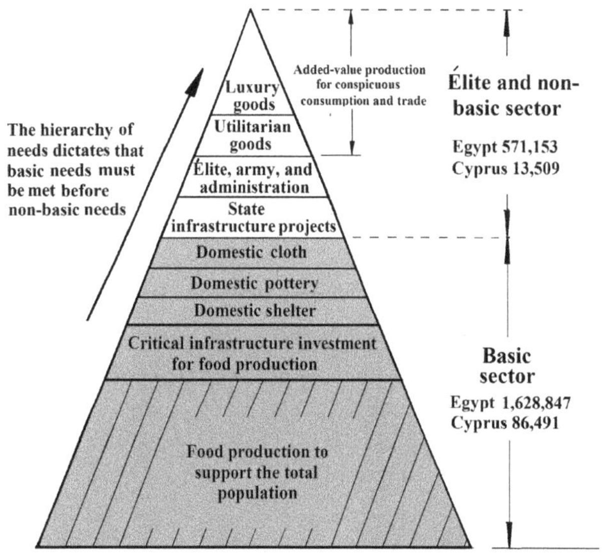

Figure 6.1: Non-basic and basic sector manpower levels (not to scale).

The scale of the metals trade in the LBA Eastern Mediterranean

A defining aspect of the LBA economy was the universal demand for bronze across the Eastern Mediterranean.[827] This commodity has been chosen for analysis from all the other possible added-value activities because it was a critical requirement for the operation of the LBA economy.[828] Without bronze for tools and weapons, the rival power blocks would not have been able to compete in military terms and in the production of added-value goods. The balance of power was maintained by considerable investment in the improved designs of weapons and this resulted in a large demand for bronze.[829]

The evaluation of the scale of the metals trade in LBA Eastern Mediterranean is presented in two stages. The first is a summary of the production costs of bronze in terms of manpower. This is followed by three Case Studies: D–F that evaluate the scale of demand in the LBA for bronze. This allows a comparison of the production costs of Cyprus and Egypt and the effect this would have had on

[825] The total number of agrarian workers in a NK population of 2.2 million = 33,693 (Table 2.63) × 22 = 741,246. The total basic workers = 1,095,381 in a NK population of 2.2 million (Table 6.1). The percentage agricultural to basic workers = 100 × 741,246 ÷ 1,095,381 = 67.7%. A similar calculation is used for LBA Cyprus.

[826] From Table 6.3 the ratio of non-basic workers = 407,835 (Egypt) ÷ 8,991 (Cyprus) = 45. If the Cypriot population was lower than 100,000 (see Footnote 14), say 75,000, then the ratio of non-basic workers = 407,835 (Egypt) ÷ (8,991 × 75,000 ÷ 100,000) (Cyprus) = 61.

[827] Gale 1991.

[828] Knapp 1988: 152 defines a commodity as having both an economic and a utilitarian value whereas a luxury item is related to conspicuous consumption with a social but a non-utilitarian value.

[829] Spalinger 2005 particularly Chapters 10–13. Spalinger provides an overview of the interregional politics of the period 1400–1200 B.C. Using a wide range of evidence and quantitative analyses he discusses the importance of the latest designs of weaponry and mobility in the battlefield using chariots and large cohorts of archers supporting traditional infantry.

the scale of the metals trade, the production source chosen by the trader, and whether this trade of this quantity of metals was state administered or entrepreneurial. A further consideration is the capacity constraints on the production of bronze in Cyprus, due to its small population.

Production cost of bronze

Section 5.5 compared the copper production costs in Cyprus in the Troodos mountains and Timna in the Sinai desert under the control of Egypt. Lead isotope analysis demonstrates that the majority of oxhide ingots in the Eastern Mediterranean have a Cypriot provenance.[830] Textual evidence shows that LBA Cyprus exported copper to Mesopotamia, the Ḫatti, and Egypt either through trade and/or gift exchange.[831] In Chapter 5 the production costs in terms of the workload required to make one kg of copper, tin, and bronze was assessed (Table 6.4). It is assumed that tin was mined in Central Asia (Uzbekistan, Tajikistan, and Afghanistan) and transported by donkey trains to Ugarit before entering the Eastern Mediterranean trading network.[832] Two routes have been analysed for Egyptian copper, Route 7 is overland from Timna to Piramesses and Route 8 is a combined overland and sea route along the Gulf of Eilat (Figure 5.11 in Chapter 5).

Metal	Cypriot workload	Egyptian workload Route 7	Egyptian workload Route 8
Copper	0.39	0.747	0.681
Tin	0.572	0.585	0.585
Bronze	0.408	0.735	0.675

Table 6.4: Cypriot and Egyptian workload (man-years) to make one kg of copper, tin, and bronze.

For copper, the manpower cost of Egyptian copper production at Timna (workers/kg) using Routes 7 and Route 8 compared with Cyprus is 191% and 174% more expensive respectively (Table 6.5). For bronze, the manpower cost of Egyptian bronze (workers/kg) using Routes 7 and Route 8 compared with Cyprus is 180% and 165% respectively (Table 6.5). This emphasises the cost advantage of producing copper in Cyprus.

Metal	Cypriot workers/kg	Egyptian workers/kg Route 7	Egyptian workers/kg Route 8
Copper	0.449	0.859	0.783
Tin	0.658	0.672	0.672
Bronze	0.469	0.846	0.776

Table 6.5: Cypriot and Egyptian manpower to make one kg of copper, tin, and bronze.

Supply constraints

Tables 5.18–5.19 shows that to make the 10,478 kg copper ingots found on the Ulu Burun in Cyprus would require a workload of 4,089 man-years, which equates to a manpower requirement of 4,702 workers with a competency index of 1.15. Table 6.2 shows that the Cypriot non-basic workforce is 8,991 workers/100,000 cohort representing 52.3% of the non-basic workforce who would be dedicated to producing copper. In reality this percentage would be even greater because a significant proportion of non-basic workers were involved in direct support services to the élite/administration and not available for non-basic added-value activities.[833] Assuming that the support non-basic workers could have comprised as much as a third of the added-value workforce, the production of the 10,478 kg of copper ingots on the Ulu Burun would need 78.4% of the added-value non-basic workforce.[834] It is unlikely that such a large proportion of the available non-basic population would have been dedicated full time to this activity. Therefore if the Eastern Mediterranean demand for copper was greater than the cargo found on the Ulu Burun there would be a supply constraint.

The number of workers required by Egypt to make the same quantity of copper has a higher manpower requirement of 9,004 and 8,208 workers for Routes 7 and 8 respectively. However, with an estimated population of 2.2 million, Egypt had a non-basic workforce of 479,115 workers that could easily absorb this manpower requirement even if a significant number were engaged in supporting the élite and administration. This may explain why Egypt continued to mine copper at Timna despite being nearly twice (191%) as expensive in terms of workers as Cyprus. However, if Cyprus wanted to increase its copper production, its first option would have been to increase the productivity of the agrarian workforce so that more food could be grown/ha to support a larger mining workforce. The introduction of bronze axes would have made land clearance easier, adding bronze tips to ploughs and hoes would have lowered ploughing labour-rates, and the increased use of oxen ploughing over hoeing would have all contributing to increased food production.[835] Another option would have been to import grain and other staples in exchange for copper so releasing agricultural workers to support the copper industry. A further option to increase the copper production in Cyprus would have been to import labour, although these workers would have to be fed from imported cereals. As discussed previously, the use of slave labour would not reduce costs significantly, as

[830] Gale 1999, Gale 2001, Gale 2003, Gale and Stos-Gale 1995, Stos-Gale and Gale 2002, Gale and Stos-Gale 2005, and Gale 2011. Contra Budd *et al* 1995a, Budd *et al* 1995b, Budd *et al* 1995c, and Budd *et al* 1995d.

[831] Gifts from the King of Cyprus to the King of Egypt: Amarna letters EA 33 (200 talents of copper and 10 talents of fine copper), EA 34 (100 talents of copper), EA 35 (500 talents of copper), EA36 ([...] + 70 talents remain), EA 37 (5 talents of copper), and EA 40 (14 talents of copper and 3 talents of fine copper). For a full list of gift-exchange correspondence to and from the King of Cyprus see Moran 1992, Knapp 1996a, and Knapp 2008: 309.

[832] Figure 5.10.

[833] If a third of the non-basic workforce was involved in supporting the palace/administration the available number of workers available for non-basic added-value activities = 8991 – (8991 ÷ 3) = 5,995 workers.

[834] The percentage used for producing the equivalent of 10,478 kg of copper of the non-basic workforce available for added-value activities = 100 × 4,702 ÷ 5,995 = 78.4%.

[835] Manning 1993: 43–44, 48–49 and Knapp 2008: 79 discuss increases in agrarian productivity. The increased use of large oxen for ploughing is not without cost because manpower is needed for growing, collecting, and distributing fodder as discussed in Section 2.7.

slaves also require sufficient calories to be effective workers.

Recycling as a response to supply constraints

The evidence of a rapid increase in scrap metal trade at the end of the thirteenth century B.C. may be an indication that there was a constraint in the supply of copper. Alternatively, it could reflect the development of an embryonic metals market where the cost/unit weight of metal influenced exchange patterns as buyers looked for low cost commodities. The cargo of the Gelidonya (*c.*1200 ± 50 years B.C.) contained a large quantity of scrap bronze.[836] During this period scrap metals also appear in workshop sites, many located in sanctuary/temple complexes, where they would have been re-melted and used for the manufacture of added-value goods.[837] The cost-saving re-melting scrap compared with the total cost of producing bronze is very significant. Melting scrap bronze would be of the same order as refining, a mere 0.1% of the total cost of producing bronze (Table 5.17). The archaeological record shows that recycling was active in the harbour towns along the south-western coast of Cyprus such as Hala Sultan Tekke, Kition, and Enkomi.[838] Excavation of Building XI at Kalavasos *Ayios Dhimitrios* revealed large numbers of crucible and or furnace fragments, scrap metal and oxhide ingot fragments that South interprets as a large scale recycling operation.[839] Further evidence of recycling has been found in the harbour towns along the Levantine coast at Tel Akko, Tell Abu Hawam, Tel Dor, Tel Nami, and Tel Qasile.[840] The cost-saving of re-cycling bronze may have opened a new market where the increased affluence of the sub-élites meant they could afford small quantities for their own conspicuous consumption needs.[841]

The demand for bronze

Numerous examples of bronze tools and weapons have been found in the archaeological record but they do not represent the absolute demand for bronze because most are recycled rather than entering the archaeological record. Three Case Studies follow that demonstrate the large scale of the demand for bronze to provide the weapons for the army of Ramesses II, bronze tipped ploughs and hoes for the agrarian sector, and bronze tools for the artisans. Assumptions have been made for all three studies, which examine a range of possible conditions. In each case, the estimates are conservative and therefore the analysis quantifies the minimum demand for bronze.[842] NK Egypt is the region studied in these Case Studies as it is representative of the larger economies in the Eastern Mediterranean.

Case Study D: Bronze for the Egyptian army at the time of Ramesses II

The archaeological record at Timna and Serabit el-Khadim attests to large-scale copper production and mining expeditions during the reign of Ramesses II. It is possible that this was the result of the increase in size of the Egyptian standing army, which took place at this time.[843] To estimate weights of artefacts I have converted two-dimensional scaled images into bar and cylindrical shapes and from these calculated their volume.[844] Multiplying the volume by the density of bronze (8,100 kg/m^3) gives an estimate of their weight.[845] Taking Spalinger's highest estimate that the standing army of Ramesses II was 40,000 men, this analysis estimates that the weight of bronze weaponry was 50,056 kg (Reports 6.1–6.2 in the Appendix).[846] This is equivalent to 4.4 times the weight of the copper and tin ingots on the Ulu Burun shipwreck. However, the actual copper and tin requirement would be higher, which shows that the weight of bronze has to be increased by 16.9% to take into account losses in the total copper, tin, and bronze production processes.[847] This uplift means an increase in the weight of bronze from 50,056 to 58,515 kg. This is 5.1 times all the copper and tin found on the Ulu Burun

[836] The boat had a large quantity of scrap copper and bronze in wicker baskets that held axes, adzes, chisels, pruning hooks, a spade, knives, and casting waste. Bass suggests that a tinker may have been on board because typical metal working tools were found (Bass 1967c and Bass 2010: 800).

[837] Knapp refer to these hoards as 'foundry hoards' that have a utilitarian value whereas votive deposits (non-utilitarian) were never intended to be retrieved (Courtois 1982: 166–167, Karageorghis and Demas 1985: 84, 106, 132, and Knapp 1988: 159, 165 citing Hawkes 1974, 115–116).

[838] Knapp 2000: 45–45.

[839] South 1989: 320.

[840] Artzy 1994: 126–127, Sherratt 1998: 299–300, Artzy 1999, Karageorghis and Kassianidou 1999.

[841] Artzy 2001: 11–12 links this demand for scrap with imports of White Slip pottery as evidence for a thriving sub-élite market.

[842] Objects were still produced in copper but by this period metal production had turned to bronze, which had improved casting and mechanical properties.

[843] I am grateful for discussions on this topic with Dr G. Mumford, University of Alabama (Birmingham), USA when he was at Swansea University 2002–2004. For the size of the army at the time of the battle of Kadesh, I have used the analysis of Spalinger 2005: 202–205, 214–230, Footnote 16 who estimates that in the reign of Ramesses II it was 30,000–40,000 strong. Kitchen 1982: 140 considers that during the NK there was a full time standing army of three to four divisions each 5,000 men. In addition, he suggests that there was an un-quantified home reserve as well as other units stationed in Nubia.

[844] The weights of artefacts are not recorded in most museum collections. Estimations for the weights of the Egyptian weapons have drawn upon the measured weight of weapons from the Ulu Burun and Gelidonya wrecks in the weapons catalogue of Yalçin, Pulak and Slotta 2005: 621–623 and estimates made from drawings of LBA weapons in Bass 1967c: 103–104, Figures 114–115, Babón 2003: 161–200, and McDermott 2004: 129–187).

[845] My estimate of the weight of a thigh length, bronze, scale corselet is 6.1 kg (Report 6.1 in the Appendix).

[846] Darnell and Manassa 2007: 70–83 provide an informative overview of the weaponry at the end of the Eighteenth Dynasty/beginning of the Nineteenth Dynasty. An additional need for bronze in the second half of the NK was a result of the introduction of helmets for officers, archers, and élite non-commissioned troops in the period 1479–1425 B.C. Helmets started to be worn post 1294 B.C. by frontline troops but this is later than the battle of Kadesh (*c.*1274 B.C.) so bronze for helmets has been ignored (McDermott 2004: 138–139).

[847] The evidence of Pettinato 1981: 178 relating to Ebla text TM.75.G.1860 shows that the weight of bronze required has to be increased by 16.9% to take into account this loss. This uplift has been used for Case Studies D–F.

wreck.[848] Even if we assume that some of the bronze was recycled as discussed in Case Study E, the demand for new bronze would be significant.

If the requirement for bronze to fully equip the new standing army is amortised over 30 years, the annual bronze production rate would be a more manageable 1,951 kg/yr.[849] Table 6.5 shows that the number of workers to make 1 kg of bronze in Egypt with copper mined at Timna was 0.846 (Route 7) or 0.776 (Route 8) workers/kg depending on the routes taken. This means the number of workers required/yr would be 1,514 and 1,651 workers/yr for each respective route.[850]

Case Study E: Bronze for the NK Egyptian agrarian sector

This analysis estimates the demand for bronze in the agrarian sector of the Egyptian LBA economy. In the NK bronze tips were fitted to the bottom of the ard plough.[851] The Gelidonya wreck had many examples of designs for bronze heads thought to have been fitted to wooden shafts and used as hoes.[852] Taking a plough head and a hoe head from the Gelidonya as being representative of such items, the estimated weights are 1.18 and 0.51 kg respectively.[853]

In Table 2.65 the total agrarian manpower/100,000 cohort/yr was 33,693 workers. Assuming a family unit of six and that between two-three were males of which at least two were actively engaged as farmers, the total number of farms/100,000 cohort would be 16,847 and for an Egyptian population of 2.2 million would be 370,623. Table 6.6 show the total demand for bronze if 1%, 10%, or 25% of farms had one bronze tip for their ploughing ards and one bronze headed hoe. The weights of bronze for the three percentages are compared with the equivalent weight of copper and tin (11,478 kg) carried on the Ulu Burun. These comparisons give an appreciation of the scale of the demand for bronze in the agrarian sector. These estimates represent the initial setting up cost and not an ongoing demand resulting from loss, wear, and the need to bring more land under cultivation (particularly marginal stony land). In addition, the increasing population levels would add significantly to the quantities of bronze needed for the agrarian sector. The number of equivalent Ulu Burun cargoes of copper and tin as a function of the percentage of farms that had bronze tipped ploughs and hoes is given in Table 6.6, which is a summary of Report 6.3 in the Appendix.

% of farms with one bronze tipped plough	**1**	**10**	**25**
Number of bronze tipped ploughs/100,000 cohort	3,707	37,063	92,656
Weight of bronze plough tip kg	1.18	1.18	1.18
Total weight (kg) of bronze plough tips/2.2 million population	4,374	43,734	109,334
Equivalent Ulu Burun cargoes	0.4	3.8	9.5
Uplifted by 16.8% for losses in production	**0.4**	**4.5**	**11.1**

% of farms with one bronze tipped hoes	**1**	**10**	**25**
Number of bronze tipped hoes	3,707	37,063	92,656
Weight of bronze hoe tip kg	0.51	0.51	0.51
Total weight (kg) of bronze hoe tips/2.2 million population	1,891	18,902	47,255
Equivalent Ulu Burun cargoes	0.2	1.6	4.1
Uplifted by 16.8% for losses in production	**0.2**	**1.9**	**4.8**

Table 6.6: Equivalent number of Ulu Burun cargoes of tin and copper.

Case Study F: Bronze for the tools of Egyptian state craftsmen

The range and diversity of the bronze tools found on the Gelidonya wreck, the intact caches of tools found in tombs, and the numerous depictions of Egyptian artisans with metal tools in tomb art, show that bronze tools were not rare and should be considered as a common commodity. This Case Study estimates the demand for bronze for tools in the Egyptian LBA economy.[854] Table 6.7 summarises the demand for bronze taking into account losses in production, calculated in Report 6.4 in the Appendix. This estimated demand is based on three different percentages (1%, 5%, or 10%) of the working adult male population that could have used bronze tools.

Average weight (kg) of tools used per craftsman	**% of Egyptian adult males who used bronze tools**		
	1	5	10
	Equivalent number of Ulu Burun carrying cargos of copper and tin		
1	0.8	3.6	7.2
2	1.5	7.2	14.5
4	2.9	14.5	29

Table 6.7: The equivalent number of the Ulu Burun tin and copper cargoes.

Table 2.3 shows that the adult male population between 10 and up to 60 years old was 32,255 individuals/100,000 cohort (709,610 for a NK population of 2.2 million). The other variable that influences the demand for bronze is

[848] The copper ingots on the Ulu Burun wreck weighed 10,478 kg and the tin ingots weighed 1,000 kg. The equivalent number of Ulu Burun cargoes = 58,515 ÷ (10,478 + 1,000) = 5.1.

[849] The amortised rate to equip a standing army over 30 years = 58,515 (weight of bronze kg) ÷ 30 = 1,951 kg/yr.

[850] Number of workers (Route 7) = 1,951 × 0.846 = 1,514. A similar calculation pertains to Route 8. For archaeological and textual evidence of expeditions to the copper deposits in the Sinai peninsular, see Rothenberg 1987 and Mumford and Parcak 2003: 89.

[851] Russell 1988: 118, Figure 15.

[852] The archaeological record shows that bronze heads were fitted to both ploughs and hoes (Catling 1964: 79–80 and Bass 1967c: 88–95, Figure 106). Many museum collections have NK bronze plough heads (e.g., British Museum EA 50705 with bronze head attached to the plough). Similar designs are attested in Mycenaean mainland Greece, Cyprus, Palestine, Ugarit, and the Gelidonya wreck (Catling 1964: 79–82 and Bass 1967c: 93).

[853] Bass 1967c: 89, Figure 102. B48 as representative of a plough tip and B47, a hoe tip. My estimates of their weights are given in Report 6.3 in the Appendix.

[854] This assumes that the tools belonged to the élite. The tools were allocated to the artisans when needed and monitored closely by scribes and security staff (McDowell 1999: 209–210, Texts 158–159).

the weight of the tools used, which vary from 1 to 4 kg.[855] The number of equivalent Ulu Burun cargoes of copper and tin as a function of the percentage of adult males who were craftsmen and the average weight of tools used by them for the total population of 2.2 million, is given in Table 6.7.

These three studies suggest that the demand for both copper and tin for making bronze was significant in scale over a range of applications. New uses for bronze developed in every sector of the economy, throughout the NK military, agricultural, craft sectors, and the possession of bronze objects contributed to the conspicuous consumption of the élite.[856] The levels of demand particularly for new uses could not have been satisfied by re-cycling. This section has demonstrated in terms of the scale of domestic and industrial application that the metals trade was not minimalist in scale.

Observations

Neoclassical economics stipulates that a low cost supplier competing in a market would stimulate demand for its own products, provided the quality of the good was comparable to its competitors. As Cyprus produced much cheaper copper than at Timna, it might be expected that Egypt would have sourced all its copper in Cyprus. The fact that Egypt continued large-scale operations in Timna while importing some copper from Cyprus shows that either Cyprus in the LBA could not meet NK Egypt's demand for copper or that market supply and demand forces, as we understand them today, did not influence procurement decisions. The latter would indicate that, at least at a strategic level, external trade was administered between state élites and therefore substantive in nature. However if Egypt had chosen to source some of its copper in Cyprus on expense grounds then this would indicate a rational, formalist approach. Matters such as security of supply or even the wish not to be beholden to another region would be indicative of a conservative consideration more in keeping again with a substantive approach to the economy.

It is notable that the Ulu Burun shipwreck carried approximately 1,000 kg of tin ingots and this is almost exactly the ratio 1:10 of copper required to make tin-bronze. Although this may have been a coincidence, we can speculate that this cargo was a complete consignment of these metals to a customer without indigenous supplies of copper and tin. Assuming that the Ulu Burun was not a singleton but part of a fleet of other vessels with similar cargoes that traded across the Eastern Mediterranean then the quantity of metals on this ship indicates the very large scale of the bronze industry. If so, the scale of the shipment is likely to have represented administered trade between the ruling élites from two regions and beyond the private trade from a sponsored or self-funded entrepreneur.

[855] The full analysis is given in Report 6.3 in the Appendix.

[856] For example, the tomb of Kha (TT 8) contained many bronze items (Schiaparelli 1927). They included bronze vase stands, a bronze razor, and several bronze bowls.

6.3 The scale of LBA maritime trade

Substantivists argue that maritime trade in the LBA was minimal in scale because marine technology was primitive, and vessels could not withstand the fierce storms in the Mediterranean.[857] However, some scholars consider that in the LBA, competing empires became economically interdependent, driven by the need of some regions for copper and the pan-Eastern Mediterranean need for tin. This interdependency led to the exchange of significant quantities of metals and other goods over long distances by sea, requiring well designed boats.[858] Three aspects that indicate of the scale of maritime trade are examined here: the improvements in ship design that increased the reliability of sea transport, improvements in the marine infrastructure, and the relative cost of sea to land transport. This section also considers whether there is sufficient evidence to counter the substantive argument that maritime trade was minimal and ship technology primitive.

Improvements in LBA ship design

By the LBA, ship design had improved and the increased reliability reduced the financial risk taken by the merchants. Commodities and manufactured products could be transported more safely and with greater regularity.[859]

Keel and hull

A key development in sea-going ships was the development of a sturdy keel, which is thought to have been introduced in the fifteenth century B.C.[860] A keel minimises longitudinal differential movement of hull planks from hogging and bending stresses generated by the combination of cargo and waves. The Ulu Burun wreck shows that instead of the keel projecting mainly below the bottom planks of the hull, it extended upward into the hull.[861] The weight of this keel increased stability by lowering the centre of gravity of the ship. This robust design would have given immense longitudinal strength as well as protecting the hull when the boat was beached.[862] However, the keel only projected

[857] Humphreys 1969: 187, 194, Finley 1985, and Snodgrass 1991.

[858] Sherratt and Sherratt 1991, Sherratt and Sherratt 1993, Zaccagnini 2000, and Monroe 2010: 19.

[859] This is not to say long distance trade did not occur in earlier periods. Even in the Neolithic Period sea craft had developed sufficiently to move communities and their cattle to Crete (Broodbank and Strasser 1991). The significant shift in the LBA was the improvement in marine technology which led to the increased certainty of supply. This enabled embryonic industries to raise their scale of production to a level not seen before.

[860] Monroe 2009: 10.

[861] Detailed drawings for three possible designs of the Ulu Burun can be found in Lin 2003.

[862] Lin 2003: 13. Lin has analysed the surviving pieces of the hull and keel and the distribution of the cargo on the sea floor. Using naval architectural principles and computer modelling techniques, he has proposed a hull design for the Ulu Burun wreck. A part of the keel survived so that the cross section could be measured. Combining these parameters and knowing the density of Lebanese cedar wood (560 kg/m^3) the weight of the keel and end posts is estimated to be 952 kg (Lin 2003: 62).

approximately 2 cms below the hull and unlike modern keels could not assist in maintaining course in adverse weather conditions.[863] The Egyptian seagoing ships did not have a keel like that of the Ulu Burun, instead they used a truss attached to the stern and bow, which ran over uprights set along the length of the vessel and could be tightened to minimise the effects of hogging.[864] In addition, the Egyptian shipwrights used a central plank from which they used strong mortise-and-tenon joints and rope stitching to fasten together the planks of the hull.[865] Egyptian cargo boats designed specifically to carry heavy weights such as quarried stone blocks, minimised longitudinal and bending stresses in the deck with a long centreline timber (carling) running under the deck beams.[866] The use of mortise and tenon joints to join the longitudinal planks of the hull was a method used up to and including the Classical Period by Greek and Roman shipbuilders.[867] This type of planking was found on the Gelidonya, Ulu Burun, and Point Iria wrecks.[868] Recent excavations at Mersa/Wadi Gawasis on the Red Sea have found hull planks of an Egyptian boat made of imported cedar up to 0.293 m long, 0.046 m wide, and 0.015 m thick, with a single transverse structural member, possibly a proto-keel, and a complete deck-level beam.[869]

Mast

The mast of the Ulu Burun, possibly following Theran practice, may have been set just forward of the centre as this allowed a ship to sail close to the wind and provided more stability in downwind situations.[870]

Increased visibility

The ships portrayed in the tombs of Iniwia and Kenamun TT 162 show that the boats (perhaps of Syrian origin) had lookout platforms (crow's-nest) attached to the top of the masts (Figure 6.2).[871] The visibility from these positions would have helped to overcome the effects of the curvature of the earth, enabling high landmarks such as headlands and islands out of sight from deck level, to remain in view.[872]

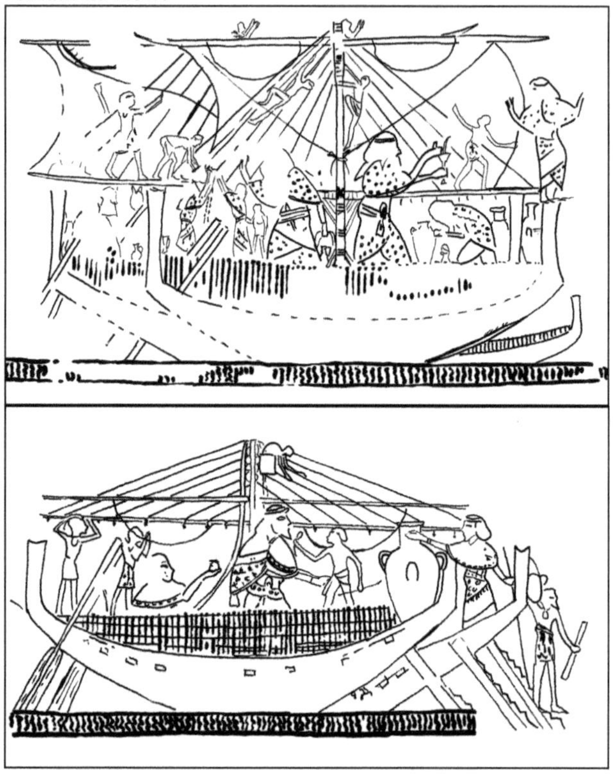

Figure 6.2: NK tomb scenes of ships that may be Syrian.
Adapted sketch from Wachsmann 1998: Figures 3.29–3.30.

Increased size of LBA ships

The improvements in ship design meant that large vessels could be built and safely sailed long distances carrying significant volumes of cargo.[873] We know from the large stone anchors found across the Eastern Mediterranean that large ships were built in the LBA.[874] The autobiography of Ineni states that a Nile river boat 120 cubits (62.4 m) in length and 40 cubits in width (20.8 m) was used to transport the obelisks of Tuthmosis I to Karnak.[875] Although this craft was a river boat it is an example of how in the NK, Egyptian boat building had reached a technological level at which large heavy cargoes could be carried. Large boats such as the Ulu Burun (length 15 m and beam width 5 m) and the Gelidonya (length 8–9 m) were capable of sailing across open sea, decreasing the transit time between ports while

[863] Pulak 1999: 216.

[864] Casson 1995: 20–21.

[865] Ward 2004: Figure 2.6. Ethnographic evidence shows that this technique is still successfully used today in Madras (Casson 1994: 12, Figure 8). Egyptian rope stitch techniques are discussed in Casson 1994: 17 and Figure 14, Ward 2000a: 20–21 and Figure 5.4; Ward 2000b: 47–54 and Ward 2004.

[866] Ward 2004: 20–21, 23 and Figure 2.3, Wachsmann 1998, 241–242, and Pulak 1999: 223–224.

[867] Pulak 1999: 213. For the Gelidonya wreck, see Bass 1967a: 48–50.

[868] Bass 1961: 270–271; Figures 11, 13, Pulak 1998: 210–213, Pulak 1999, and Pulak 2000a. The tenons on the Ulu Burun were made of oak and measured 0.3 m in length, 0.061 m in width, and 0.016 m thick (Pulak 2000a: 29). Only one small piece of wood from the Point Iria has been recovered; a fragment with a 6 mm hole, the same diameter as the dowel holes found on the Gelidonya wreck suggesting a similar hull design (Bass 1967a: Figures 46 and 51 and Vichos 1999: 78–79).

[869] Ward and Zazzaro 2007: 138. For comparisons with measurements from the Dashur boat in the Carnegie Museum of History, see Ward and Zazzaro 2007: 144.

[870] Georgiou 1991: 66 citing personal communication with G. Bass.

[871] Relief from the tomb of Iniwia (Nineteenth/Twentieth Dynasty) in Wachsmann 1998: Figure 3.24 and TT 162, the tomb of Kenamun (Davies and Faulkner 1947: Plate VIII). Wachsmann suggests that the depictions could have been hybrid constructions rather than accurate representations and attempts to reconstruct an actual ship from them are not valid (Wachsmann 1998: 60). Nevertheless, even if the crow's-nest is a figment of the artist's imagination, sailors can clearly be seen on the top yard-arm from which they could see into the distance (Wachsmann 1998: 58–59, Figures 3.29 and 3.30).

[872] Morton 2001: 180–193 and Vella 2004: 42–48. See Artzy 1994: 7 for navigational landmarks for locating Tel Nami.

[873] See Artzy 1985b: 138–139 for optimising cargo space. Artzy proposed that in the LBA mixed cargoes were carried, heavy but low volume copper, large volume but low weight ceramics, and a minimum of dunnage for packing. The most common form of dunnage was brushwood (Bass 1967a: 51, Figure 53) but in the Ulu Burun large pithoi containing Cypriot pottery gave greater protection than brushwood dunnage alone while still maintaining a low space weight ratio (Pulak 2010: 864).

[874] For archaeological evidence of anchors, see Frost 1969a, Frost 1969b, Frost 1979, Frost 1986, and Wachsmann and Haldane 1997.

[875] Breasted 1906b: Text 105.

smaller boats like the Point Iria (length 7 m minimum and beam 1.7 m minimum) took longer because they probably hugged the coast (tramping), taking refuge at night and beaching overnight on the shore.[876] The sailing season was normally from the end of May to the end of September/early October.[877] While sailing in open water was comparatively safe in summer, coastal navigation was not possible in winter when the adverse weather could cause small vessels to be wrecked on shore reefs or to founder from water intake.[878] The larger robust LBA boats could travel across open water routes because they were less vulnerable to the winter conditions and with the possible exception of January could sail all year, so increasing the level of trade.[879]

Improvement in sails

Fabric

LBA sails had improved dramatically in design and operation.[880] The sails were made of linen with a 2 x 2 twill weave, which was strong, resistant to tearing, and therefore particularly suitable for sails.[881] A reconstructed boat 20 m long and 5 m wide, based on the reliefs of Hatshepsut's expedition to Punt, had a linen square sail measuring 14.25 m × 5 m. The ship could sail at 6 knots in winds up to 25 knots.[882]

Brailing

One of the most important innovations in the LBA was the invention of rope brails. Each brail was attached at intervals of 0.3–0.45 m to the bottom of the sail, passing up to the yard through metal rings that were sewn into the sail. They then passed over the yard and down to the deck where they could be controlled. By adjusting the brails, the shape of the sail could be changed and the sails could be furled by pulling on all the brails at once.[883] Altering the shape and size of the sails helped a ship to maintain course when the wind changed direction (reefing) enabling it to sail close to the wind.[884] Empirical tests show that replicas of Classical Period ships rigged with brails could sail at an angle as small as 50 degrees off the wind.[885]

The LBA maritime infrastructure

Evidence of LBA harbours is found around the Eastern Mediterranean facilitating both coastal tramping and direct port-to-port sailings. The increased investment in safe harbour facilities contributed to the lowering of maritime costs by providing safe anchorage, storage for traded goods, and loading and unloading facilities, as well as contact points for buyers and sellers.[886]

In tidal waters, boats can approach the shore when the tide is high and use the outgoing tide to settle on the shore. The tides of the Eastern Mediterranean are minimal and this makes the beaching of a heavily loaded ship such as the Ulu Burun a problem, particularly along the Levantine coast, which has prevailing onshore winds that create waves.[887] Lin's estimate of the weight of the Ulu Burun shipwreck is 8 tonnes, with cargo/ballast/anchors of 20.4 tonnes, plus 6 passengers weighing 0.4 tonnes giving a gross tare tonnage of 28.8 tonnes. The estimated draft was 1.29 m and this would have restricted the number of places that the boat could unload heavy cargoes.[888] It seems more likely then that the Ulu Burun boat used sheltered harbours such as Enkomi, Kition, Sidon, Hala Sultan Tekke, Tel Nami, Tyre, and Mahadu that had sufficient depth of water at low tide to enable the boat to float for transhipment to the coast via smaller vessels or at a quay. In the LBA Levant, technical knowledge and expertise existed to build artificial harbours on the sea coast. The geo-archaeological evidence suggest these proto-harbours were in operation in the Middle Bronze Age with Sidon's Northern Harbour dated to 1700–1450 B.C. Both harbours had the facility for small boats to be pulled up on sandy beaches and for larger vessels to anchor in the deeper water of the bay.[889]

[876] For sizes of LBA boats see Bass 1961: 271, Vichos 1999: 98, Figure 16, Lin 2003: 34, and Ward 2004.

[877] Casson 1995: 270–271, Footnote 2. In the Classical Period typical sailing speeds varied between 1.5–5.5 knots depending on the amount of tacking required (Casson 1995: 286–296 and Tables 3–6 in particular).

[878] See Morton 2001: 156–159 for the factors influencing choices made by ancient mariners between coastal routes with risks of submerged reefs and rocks, versus open-sea routes with attendant risks of storms and pirates. For sea routes and navigation in the LBA see Agouridis 1997.

[879] Tammuz 2005: 155–156. His analysis of pre-Roman texts indicates that four open-sea routes operated all year round: Greece and Asia Minor to Egypt, Egypt to Greece and Asia Minor, Phoenicia to Egypt, and Egypt to Phoenicia.

[880] The organic nature of linen sails means that none have survived from antiquity. Seal iconography and Egyptian tomb paintings give evidence for the designs of Aegean, Syrian, and Egyptian sail designs. It can be assumed that sails were made from several pieces stitched together with ropes and double stitching to strengthen the edges. Minoan seals depict sails with a form of hatching that might represent leather strips applied along the stitched seams for additional strength (Tzachili 1999: 858). Sails were stitched in a way that made them slightly concave to catch the wind (Tzachili 1999: 859).

[881] Tiboni 2005.

[882] Ward 2010: 47.

[883] Vinson 1993. See also Georgiou 1991: 67.

[884] Roberts 1991, and Casson 1994: 39–46. Vinson 1993: 133 shows that the Egyptians had brail technology at least since the Amarna Period.

[885] Vinson 1993: 145.

[886] For anchorage systems along the Levantine and Canaanite coast in the second millennium B.C., see Raban 1991 and Frost 1993. For Tel Nami (Carmel coast) see Artzy 1995. For Cyprus, see Knapp 1997b: 156–159, Gifford 1985 and Raban 1995. For details of an Egyptian MK harbour on the Red Sea at Mersa/Wadi Gawasis, see Bard and Fattovich 2010. An example of a safe haven, a victualling centre, as well as an export centre for regional goods was Bates's Island on the eastern Marmarican, north-west coast of Egypt (White 2003, and White *et al* 2002).

[887] The Israeli Oceanographic and Limnological Research centre have plotted the range of the tides off the coast of Israel and the difference between high and low tide is 0.36 m (Israel Oceanographic and Limnological Research 2008).

[888] Lin 2003: 68, Table 7.1.

[889] Marriner *et al* 2005: 1319. The MBA site of Yavne-Yam in Israel has boulder piles on a submerged ridge suggesting they were placed to improve the quality of the ancient anchorage (Marriner *et al* 2005: 1319). There is evidence that a form of stone quay was built in the sheltered harbour of Tel Dor (Israel) in the latter part of the fourteenth and early thirteenth centuries B.C. (Rabin 1995: 147 and Figures 6–7, 9–12). Raban believes that structures excavated in the harbour level at Kition (Cyprus) resemble the quays found at Tel Dor as well as the ashlar paved basins at Hala Sultan Tekke (Raban 1995: 148 and Figures 14–15). For evidence of harbours at Tel Nami, see Artzy and Marcus 1991.

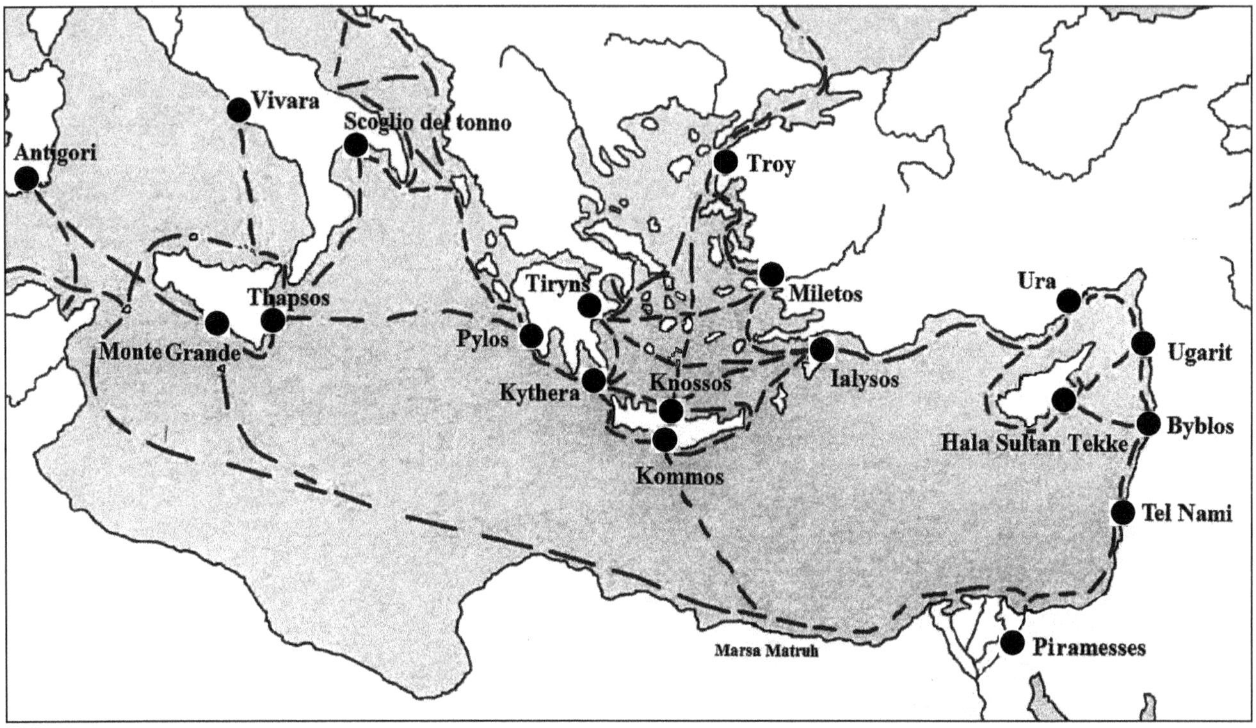

Figure 6.3: Proposed coastal hubs in the Central and Eastern Mediterranean.

All these factors indicate that ships similar to the Ulu Burun vessel were able to carry significant quantities of high value goods to many ports along the coast of the Mediterranean, sailing directly across open sea.[890]

Sherratt suggests that harbour towns such as those along the south-western coast of Cyprus were actively involved in a maritime trade network for metals, added-value metal artefacts, textiles, olive oil, and the acquisition of silver, which was used throughout the Eastern Mediterranean as a standard of exchange.[891] The number of these harbour towns suggests that the local élites allowed traders to seek new markets and opportunities without the burden of a centralised or 'tight palatial' forms of economic and political control.[892] The entrepreneurial recycling activity (Section 6.2) was supplemented by an increase in pottery exports such as Cypriot White Slip and wheel based pottery.[893] These items are quite different from the products normally associated with ruling élite gift exchange and administered trade. The wide range of added-value metal goods and pottery types found in the archaeological record of these sites is what would be expected from an embryonic market economy.

Much of this trade was probably 'opportunist' and exploited by sailors as their boats tramped around the Eastern Mediterranean.[894] Artzy suggests that this entrepreneurial activity was loosely controlled by an oligarchy of local élites and merchants, supported by an independent shipping sector that she refers to as the 'Nomads of the Sea.'[895]

The cargoes of LBA ships were not limited to added-value goods. The large Canaanite jars and the pithoi found on the Ulu Burun shipwreck could have carried staples safely without the risk of contamination by salt water.[896] The capability to carry grain and other foodstuffs by sea has a significant implication for assessing the level of LBA trade. Staples, now invisible in the archaeological record, could have augmented the total scale of trade in the value of the staples traded and the increased opportunity for regions that imported grain and pulses to divert manpower to added-value activities.

The cost of sea transport

Improvements in marine technology, which led to the transportation of large cargoes, reduced the cost of transport, which on land, was limited to the speed of a donkey or an oxen which had to be fed. Duncan-Jones has analysed land versus sea transport costs from the Edict of Diocletian that shows land transport was 34–42

[890] Monroe 2010.

[891] Sherratt 1998: 305.

[892] Sherratt 1998: 306. Bureaucratic administrative texts normally associated with a substantive palace administrations were absent in the ports lining the south-western coast of Cyprus (Sherratt 1998: 297). Merrillees 1992: 320–324 comments on the lack of evidence to draw any firm conclusions on the nature of Cypriot LBA government structures. Despite the wealth found in some Cypriot tombs, Merrillees questions whether the term 'élite' is appropriate and he concludes that there is no evidence that the harbour towns were 'prompted, co-ordinated or supervised by a single ruler, kingdom or city. Quite the opposite. Each urban entity was probably independent and autonomous.'

[893] Artzy 1985a and Hatcher 2007: 74–81.

[894] Gill 1991: 29–30 uses the term 'space fillers' or 'profitable ballast.'

[895] Artzy 1998.

[896] For evidence of grain transport on the Nile in the LBA, see Janssen 2004. For containers that could have transported perishables see Sherratt and Sherratt 1991: 364 and Crewe 2007: 13. The Ulu Burun carried organic crops such as olives (one Canaanite jar contained at least 2,500 olives), pomegranates, grapes, figs, nuts, almonds, pine, pistachio, acorns, coriander, cumin, sumac seed, grain, and pulses (Haldane 1990, Haldane 1993, and Pulak 2001: 36–37).

times more expensive.[897] The scale of the cost of transport between land and sea was probably of the same order in the LBA because ship designs were similar with comparable construction costs.[898] In the LBA, interconnected trading networks linked the Eastern Mediterranean to the Aegean, and the Central Mediterranean trading networks and beyond by long distance sea routes taking advantage of prevailing winds and currents.[899] Each trading network had sea hubs that were in turn linked to important overland trade routes as well as local sea or land networks.[900] The major trading networks (Eastern Mediterranean, Aegean, and Western Mediterranean) may have been linked through gateways such as Mahadu (Ugarit), Hala Sultan Tekke (Cyprus), Ialysos (Rhodes), Komos (Crete), Monte Grande (Sicily), and Antigori (Sardinia). The locations of the hubs occur at points that optimised transport costs between the regional trading blocks (Figure 6.3) making sea transport significantly less costly than land transport.

The cost and efficiency of sea transport was further improved by optimising the design of storage vessels and metal and glass ingots. Canaanite jars were similar in shape and capacity and this meant they were easier to stack in the boats and it was easier to monitor loading and unloading at the ports of call.[901] Increasingly in the LBA, oxhide copper ingots became standardised in shape and weight and this enabled them to be carried by one man from the boat to the quay.[902] Similarly, glass ingots found on the Ulu Burun wreck appear to have some degree of standardisation as they are of a similar shape to those found in Amarna and Qantir Piramesses.[903]

Observations

During the LBA significant improvements were made in ship design and there was a network of sea hubs and gateways between trading networks that facilitated marine transport. The evidence suggests that the Ulu Burun, Gelidonya, and Point Iria vessels were capable of circumnavigating the Central and Eastern Mediterranean using the prevailing circular patterns of wind and currents. Experimental archaeology has shown they were able to sail directly between sea hubs without having to follow the coast. Ships such of these were capable of carrying large volumes of cargo at a lower cost than land transport and encouraged economic interdependence between Eastern Mediterranean regions. They are an indication that trading between these regions took place on a large scale.

When improved ship technology is linked to the demand for bronze, the scale of copper production on Cyprus, and the relatively low-cost of sea transport, it suggests that the Ulu Burun, Gelidonya, and Point Iria wrecks were not isolated, high risk trading enterprises. Instead, they should be seen as a part of a major maritime trade system regularly connecting all parts of the Eastern Mediterranean and possibly beyond to the Central Mediterranean. The marine archaeological record for this period shows that seagoing ship design had evolved so that investment in fleets of ships rather than singletons made economic sense. Examination of the shipwrecks' hulls of the Ulu Burun, Gelidonya, and Point Iria shows a commonality of design that was too sophisticated and too similar to be three independent, parallel, and isolated examples; they are more likely to be representative of fleets of boats supported by an infrastructure of skilled boat builders.[904]

Despite the improvements in the effectiveness of LBA ships and the associated marine infrastructure, the financing of maritime trade would have required significant investment. Monroe has estimated that the sunk-cost (ship and cargo) of the Ulu Burun wreck was 12,000 shekels.[905] Ugaritic texts show that four wealthy merchant entrepreneurs operated without palace endowments and wealthy enough to finance their trading expeditions.[906] The evidence counters the argument that trade with large-scale transport of goods by sea was minimal because marine technology was primitive.

[897] As a check, he compared the Roman road and sea cost ratios with eighteenth century A.D. road and sea cost ratios. The result shows a land to sea ratio of 22.6:1 (Duncan-Jones 1974: 368).

[898] Pulak 1999: 213.

[899] The Eastern Mediterranean sea currents and prevailing winds were seasonally dependent. In summer, the prevailing winds favour an anticlockwise direction for sailing boats assisted by the prevailing currents. In winter, sailing is more difficult in the Eastern Mediterranean due to the 'northerlies' (Boreas and associated winds) and the 'southwesterlies' (the Sirocco and associated winds). See Morton 2001: Figure 23.

[900] The Carmel coastal anchorages of Tel Nami, Tel Abu Hawan, and Tel Akko are good examples of sea hubs. They provided LBA routes to Megiddo and Beth Shean that joined a trans-Jordan north-south route connecting Arabia, Syria and inner Anatolia (Artzy 2006: 51 and Figures 1 and 5).

[901] The capacity of the Canaanite jar for storage and shipping (small mouth and small foot) was 45.3 litres (Grace 1956: 83–84, Figure 5 and Parr 1973: 180) and for transport containers in general see Sherratt and Sherratt 1991: 363.

[902] See Buchholz 1959 for the standardised shape and weights of copper oxhide ingots. The heaviest ingot weighed 29.5 and the lightest 20.1 kg. The average of the 165 ingots measured was 23.9 kg but some allowance has to be made for corrosion (Pulak 2000c: 141 and Figure 7). For the 121 smaller plano-convex bun shaped ingots found on the Ulu Burun with an average weight of 6.2 kg (Pulak 2002c: 143–144 and Figure 9). Variations in moulds used in the casting process and the inclusions of gas in unrefined raw (blister) copper would mean they could not be accurate standards of weight. However, Pulak 2001: 18 considers that, '... they were not intended to contain a standardized quantity of metal. Rather, they would have constituted a quantity of raw (blister) copper subject to weighing and evaluation during each commercial transaction.'

[903] The blue cobalt glass ingots found on the Ulu Burun wreck are almost identical in size to those found at Amarna (Nicholson *et al* 1997: 147).

[904] There is possibly another LBA shipwreck site at Kfar Samir off the Carmel Coast in Northern Israel (Galili *et al* 1986 and Galili and Rosen 2007).

[905] Monroe 2010.

[906] One was Yabinu who was a probably the last resident in the Southern Palace at Ugarit and who was closely involved in the copper trade between Cyprus and Ugarit (Singer 1999: 677 and Bell 2005: 130–133).

6.4 The nature of the LBA economy

To determine whether NK Egypt and LBA Cyprus were formalist or substantive in nature, the following aspects are examined:

- The validity of the Polanyi's redistribution model.
- The evidence for cost accounting in NK Egypt.
- The emergence of a private sector in NK Egypt.
- Whether LBA merchants understood the inter-relationship between cost, price, and profit.
- Whether trade was state administered or carried out by entrepreneurial merchants.

Polanyi's redistribution model challenged

Polanyi, in his analysis of the ancient economy believed that the material wants of ancient societies were satisfied through the redistribution of food and other basic requirements, administered by a central ruling élite. He associated 'redistribution' in a society with the flow of the great majority of the population's agrarian produce passing into centralised storage under élite control who subsequently allocated rations back into the community. 'Centricity' is the core concept that underpins much of Polanyi's economic thinking, both ancient and modern.[907]

The archaeological record shows that large granaries were built in Egypt indicating that some degree of centralised redistribution did take place. This section evaluates the practical realities of collecting, storing, and redistributing harvest produce. Whether this redistribution of rations was total or only for some sectors of society of NK Egypt, is examined next in two further Case Studies:

- Case Study G: The storage and redistribution of rations for the total population.
- Case Study H: The storage and redistribution of rations to satisfy the non-basic workforce, élite, and administration.

In each study, the number of granaries that would be required and the manpower to build the granaries is examined. Only NK Egypt is considered because the Ramesseum on the west bank of the Nile at Thebes is mainly intact and the volume of the silos can be estimated with a reasonable degree of accuracy. Kemp has estimated that the Ramesseum held 16,522,000 litres (16,522 m^3) of grain making this size of granary a convenient comparative measure.[908] For each of the two Case Studies it is assumed that fresh horticultural produce for non-basic workers and dependants (45,831,632 kg with a volume of 91,663 m^3) was stored locally in small centres so that they were fresh when issued to the populace. Wine because of its value and storability, is assumed to have been kept in the granary store-rooms as attested by wine labels found in the Ramesseum.[909]

Case Study G: Storage and redistribution of rations for the population of NK Egypt

Table 6.8 gives the food storage requirements (excluding horticultural produce) for the total population of Egypt at the end of the NK (2.2 million). This amounts to 694,405,602 kg of food with a volume of 1,096,645 m^3, which would have to be distributed from the granaries. Using Kemp's estimate of the capacity of the Ramesseum as 16,522 m^3, it would require 66 granaries of the same size to store the produce for the total population.

Table 4.9 shows that a minimum of 1,938 workers would be required to build one granary the size of the Ramesseum. To build the 66 granaries would require 127,908 man-years of effort. Although this large investment could be spread over many years, it would be a significant state infrastructure investment of manpower. Taking into account, the cost of building, maintaining the granaries, collecting and storing the food, and then redistributing the food as rations back to the people makes Polanyi's proposal of total centralised redistribution, is in the author's opinion, impractical.[910]

Food storage requirements excluding horticultural produce for the total population of Egypt at the end of the NK (2.2 million)		
Crop	**Weight of crops (kg) to feed total population/yr**	**Volume of crops (m^3) to feed total population/yr**
Barley	394,257,226	647,385
Emmer wheat	206,292,328	268,261
Pulses	87,143,672	174,287
Wine	6,712,376	6,712
Sub total	**694,405,602**	**1,096,645**

Table 6.8: Egyptian storage requirements for grain, pulses, and wine to feed a total population of 2.2 million.

Case Study H: Storage and redistribution of rations to satisfy the non-basic sector

This study examines the granary storage needed to support the 648,320 élite, non-basic workers, and their dependants (given in row (A) in Table 6.9).

Non-basic and basic sectors	NK Egypt
Élite/senior officials/professional class	39,204
Non-basic workers	479,115
Non-basic sector dependants	130,001
(A) Élite, non-basic workers and their dependants	**648,320**
Basic sector workers	1,095,381
Basic dependants	456,299
(B) Total non-basic	**1,551,680**
Total population (a + b)	**2,200,000**

Table 6.9: The non-basic and basic sectors of NK Egypt and their dependants.

[907] Polanyi 1977: 40–42.
[908] Kemp 2006: 259, Figure 94.
[909] Kitchen 1992: 119.
[910] This study has not included the logistical cost of moving the harvest from the fields to the Nile and the transport cost of taking grain by boat to the nearest state granary. See Janssen 1994b for his estimate of the cost of transporting grain in boats along the Nile.

The weight of crops and the volume of storage required in state granaries to supply the rations for the non-basic sector of NK Egypt including their dependants are prorated from Table 6.8 and given in Table 6.10.[911]

Crop	Weight kg	Volume m^3
Barley	116,184,020	190,778
Emmer wheat	60,792,474	79,054
Pulses	25,680,448	51,361
Wine	1,978,076	1,978
Sub total	**204,635,018**	**323,171**

Table 6.10: Food storage requirements for Egyptian non-basic workers and their dependants.

The weight and the volume of crops required to be stored would be 204,635,018 kg and 323,171 m^3. The number of granaries required, each the size of the Ramesseum holding 16,522 m^3 of agrarian produce, would be 20 and would require 38,760 man-years of effort to build them. Although this is a large number over the period of the NK (*c.*500 years), it is within the capability of the Egyptian state but the NK archaeological record does not support this number. A more likely solution would be a few granaries the size of the Ramesseum and a larger number of smaller granaries, as attested in Amarna, sourced with staples from royal, nobles, and temple estates.[912]

This case illustrates that the élite and non-basic workers with their dependants, which numbered 648,320 people (Table 6.9) could be supported through redistribution. For redistribution to work effectively granaries would be located in areas where there was concentration of non-basic workers, the élite, and the administration, and their dependants. This would minimise the collection, storage, and redistribution costs. The archaeological record attests to large granaries sited near or in temples, industrial complexes, military establishments, and capital cities such as Amarna and Thebes.[913] As before, horticultural produce is assumed to have been sourced and stored locally.

Observations

The findings of these two case studies challenges Polanyi's assertion that the material wants in terms of the basic need for food for the total population of NK Egypt could be satisfied through redistribution. The analyses show that total redistribution would be impractical (Case Study G). Any benefits for the élite of maintaining complete control of a region through control of the material wants of region would have been offset by the inefficiency and the cost of distribution and administration involved. In addition, there is no evidence in the archaeological record of enough granaries to store the volume of food required. The most viable option is that the redistribution process supported non-basic workers, the élite, and the administration that predominantly lived and worked in the urban and temple centres (Case Study H). The basic workers living in rural areas, who were the majority of the population, would have been supported by food stored and redistributed locally.

Evidence for cost accounting in the LBA

Weber considered that ancient societies had no concept of profit and cost as understood in modern market economies and that sophisticated cost accounting processes did not develop. He also emphasised the difficulty in ancient societies of apportioning the costs of labour, particularly slave labour.[914] This section examines ancient Egyptian evidence to ascertain whether cost accounting processes existed, how they were they used, and whether they could have supported an embryonic market economy. Substantive economies limited the use of cost accounting methods to the monitoring and control of resources, the flow of goods through administered trade, and planning and control of redistribution processes. Market economies in contrast are proactive to changes in the market and use cost accounting methods to forecast the cost of a product, to measure the actual cost of a product against planned cost (plan versus actual), and to improve the efficiency of the processes involved in order to minimise cost and maximise profit.[915] Optimising cost does not necessarily indicate a reaction to market forces but the ability to minimise cost is an essential building block on which an embryonic market could develop. A number of examples follow that illustrate the use of sophisticated and complex accounting processes in NK Egypt, which monitored a wide range of economic factors.

Accounting algorithms are attested in Egypt and would have enabled the administration to plan for and redistribute rations, taking into account different wage structures based on rank and profession.[916] The Egyptians understood the arithmetic concept of fractions (Horus Eye fractions) and they were used for the issue of rations and

[911] For example, the weight of barley for the non-basic sector is calculated by the ratio of the total non-basic workforce (648,320) to the total population of Egypt (2,200,000) and would = 394,257,226 × 648,320 ÷ 2,200,000 = 116,184,032. The rest of the calculations in Table 6.10 use the same ratio.

[912] The smaller granaries were tall, circular mud-brick silos with an average diameter of 2.5 m. They are thought to have had domed tops with an opening for pouring in the grain and a trap door at the bottom to remove the stored grain (Kemp 1991: 296). For examples of granaries at Amarna see Kemp 1991: Plate 11, Waki 2002, and Kemp 2006: Figures 109 and 115.

[913] Kemp 2006: 257–260, 312.

[914] Weber 1976 [1896]: 54, 66. For the purposes of this study, the difference between the rations of a slave and any other manual worker is not significant, as both have to be fed if they are to work effectively.

[915] 'Cost' in neoclassical economics is a concept that refers to those factors, both variable and fixed, that are incurred in the production of the good, for which revenue must be used in payment. The difference between such payments and total revenue determines profit (Schneider 1974: 231). Direct costs are those costs that can be attributed directly to the production of the good. The two main direct costs are labour costs and material costs. Variable costs, sometimes referred to as indirect costs, are those that are apportioned as an overhead to the direct cost. For example, the overhead cost of the supervisor of a team of workers producing a range of products would be the proportion of the time the supervisor spends on each product.

[916] Mueller 1975.

materials in units less than one.[917] In the Rhind Mathematical Papyrus, Problem 65 was set for scribes learning how to calculate the correct quantity of rations for redistribution. This problem asks the scribes to distribute 100 loaves between ten men on single rations, and a sailor, a foreman, and the doorkeeper on double rations. The solution, also provided, was to divide the hundred loaves into 13 portions using the Egyptian system of multiplication and division by remainders. The result is a single ration of 7 + 9/13 for the manual workers and 15 + 5/13 for the officials.[918]

The Reisner I and Reisner III Papyri show that the labour requirements were planned before the start of a project. Papyrus Reisner I reveals that scribes used conversion factors to calculate the man-days required to move different materials for a given volume of material.[919] These rates reflected a wide range of activities and showed the sophistication of their control processes.[920] Kadish shows that the administration used the concept of man-day rates to determine the manpower requirements and materials for a wide range of construction projects.[921] Knowing the man-days required for any project gave the administration the information it needed to calculate the rations required to support the workmen. Records of a MK expedition sent to the Wadi Hammamat in the reign of Sesostris I show that the wage rate of a common manual worker was a single ration of ten bread loaves and ⅓ unit of beer and a craftsman received a double ration of 20 loaves and ½ unit of beer.[922] Such data when linked to the size of the harvest surplus in the current year and the grain stored in the state granaries enabled rational decision-making on the investment in state projects based on affordability. An additional benefit for accurate manpower planning is that it gave the administrators of state projects early warning that additional rations would be needed to complete the task if the project was falling behind time. This 'plan versus actual' forms the basis of modern cost accounting practices.[923] With the benefits gained from the use of labour-rates in accounting practices it would be surprising if the administration did not apply manpower and materials planning to at least some non-basic state investment activities.

There is evidence of cost accounting practices in the production of bread rations for non-basic state workers. The baking records dated to Seti I, stipulated the type of grain, fineness of the flour, and the quantities of the ingredients in the recipes for baking bread and brewing beer, ensuring they were consistent across Egypt.[924] Loaves were of a standard size and there was a standard unit for beer. This meant that ration allocation could be planned, monitored, and controlled because each man's ration for any given rank or profession varied only in quantity, not in its nutritional value.[925] Standardised recipes enabled an end-to-end audit of the bakeries, reconciling the planned number of loaves and the number and weight of loaves produced. They took into account the quality of the materials used, the water retention rate of the flour, the dough produced from them, and any losses in the cooking process.[926] Spalinger suggests that the accounting process for bakeries and breweries was possibly an early form of double entry bookkeeping.[927] Having an audit process that reconciled the accounts also minimised corruption. Scribes tracked the whole process from forecasting demand to the issuing of loaves and beer as rations. These baking accounts show that demand could be forecast, ingredients could be ordered, sufficient bakeries built, and the necessary manpower sourced. The result was an optimised and known cost per loaf (unit cost).

Observations

The Egyptians had a sophisticated method of cost accounting that gave them the means to calculate the manpower effort required to produce products and provide services. They were also able to apportion costs to a production process. The cost accounting processes in Egypt provided the administration with information so that they could plan, forecast, and control large scale projects and manage the logistics entailed in ration distribution. The textual evidence for the use of these processes counters the substantive view that the ancients did not have cost accounting processes of sufficient sophistication to enable the ancient economy to reach its full potential.

However, it is not proven that these cost accounting processes had the profit motive that is inherent in a

[917] The Horus eye fractions arranges fractions into an ordered, descending geometric series 1/2, 1/4, 1/8 ... 1/64 (Ezzamel 2009: 356).

[918] The stages of the calculation are given in Robins and Shute 1987: 41.

[919] Simpson 1969: 13–14. The Egyptian man-day was based on a ten hour working day (Simpson 1969: 14). This study accepts an elapse working day equal to the ten hours of daylight. However, within this period an hour is allowed for meal breaks reducing the effective working day to nine hours. Even as early as the Sixth Dynasty in the OK, the term 'man-day' was used to plan state projects (Berlev 1965: 264).

[920] The conversion ratios of man-days to the volume of material moved are given in Section K of Reisner I for following activities: 1:10 for rubble and earth, 2:9 for builder's materials (not specified), 5:1 for hauling stone, 2:3 for sand movement, 1:65 for moving mud-bricks, and 1:10 for loosening earth. These conversion ratios are used in Reisner II to calculate the man-days to move the sand and stone in the construction of the royal dockyard. This was a project in the MK reign of Senwosret I that amounted to 101½ man-days to move the sand and 715 man-days to move the stone (Simpson 1969: 15 and Kadish 1996: 443).

[921] Kadish notes that 'man-day' was used as a labour planning unit as well as a worker compensation basis. Complex projects would have numerous man-day rates. Egyptian workload planning defined the tasks, remuneration, the allocation of labour and materials, and the time constraints to complete the task (Kadish 1996: 444).

[922] Mueller 1975: 253.

[923] Another example of the plan versus actual approach, is demonstrated in the third millennium B.C. Mesopotamian accounting texts, which show that the accounting practice monitored the actual outcome of a process versus a pre-determined plan. Any discrepancy was recorded in the form of a 'balancing' entry (Mattessich 1998: 18). See Carmona and Ezzamel 2007 for a full review of this topic and the work in particular of Mattessich 1989, 1991, and 1998 and Nissen *et al* 1993.

[924] Bibliographic references for the Seti I baking accounts are given in Spalinger 1986: 307, Footnote 1.

[925] Using the same recipe to make a loaf or a unit of beer ensured rations had a consistent uniform size or volume that gave the same nutritional content to the consumer. The Egyptians referred to this as *pefsu* meaning 'baking value' (Bleiberg 2007: 182).

[926] Spalinger 1986: 340.

[927] Spalinger 1986: 324.

modern market economy. The examples do not necessarily demonstrate that the Egyptians used accounting procedures to increase the efficiency of a process, a trait common in market economies that focus on cost reduction to maximise profit. There is also no evidence for the use of cost-benefit analysis to choose between alternative investment strategies. In fact, Egyptian cost accounting did not extend beyond process control to ensure that food and material arrived at the right place, at the right time to complete the project, and to reduce corruption. The accounting process had most of the elemental building blocks that could have been easily been adapted in the right circumstances to support an embryonic market economy. However, the evidence from Egypt suggests that the motivation for cost accounting was control rather than maximising market opportunity.

The development of a private sector in the LBA

The rations paid to NK state non-basic workers varied by their rank and profession and many were allocated more rations than they needed to feed themselves and their families. Skilled manual workers from Deir el-Medina in the Nineteenth Dynasty received an annual wage of 48 *khar* of emmer wheat with an additional 16 *khar* of barley. The chief workman received 66 *khar* of emmer wheat with an additional 22 *khar* of barley. For a guard, the emmer ration was 24 *khar* of emmer wheat and 8 *khar* of barley and for a porter, as low as 12 *khar* of emmer wheat and 4 *khar* of barley.[928] The surplus rations could be bartered for non-staples and luxury items, possibly via local marketplaces. I propose that if the demand for goods that could be exchanged for this surplus was not satisfied by traditional methods, then private entrepreneurs could have filled the gap. This would have created a private decentralised market outside the control of the ruling élite that may have had some characteristics of a formalist economy.

An example of an interaction between the state/temple economy and an embryonic private sector is revealed in a late NK administrative papyrus. A ship belonging to a temple dispensed clothing and honey to women on the riverbank who exchanged their own goods in return.[929] Another example comes from the letters of Heqanakht of the Twelfth Dynasty that reveal how he planned to maximise his income through astute deals with neighbours and others. It is clear that he did this without any involvement or control by an outside authority.[930] The opportunity for an embryonic private sector would increase in the years of harvest gluts that gave a grain surplus over and above the tax due to the state (or rent to the temples if working on temple estates).[931] The decentralised market based on surplus rations (hereafter called informal market) circulated outside of the control of the administration and could have stimulated an embryonic formalist market.

The volume of grain required to feed an average size family for a year was 1,638 kg (2.5 m^3). This exercise assumes that two-thirds of the grain by weight was barley and one third was emmer wheat.[932] As discussed in Section 2.4 the diet was supplemented with the quantities of protein, pulses, and dairy products.[933] Table 6.11 shows that all ranks at Deir el-Medina, with the exception of a porter, would have a significant grain surplus per annum.[934] Although Deir el-Medina workers may have been paid more than the average wage of state non-basic workers, due to the importance of their work in building the Royal tombs, comparisons with other ration texts show that a significant quantity of other rations may have flowed into a decentralised informal market. For example, NK archaeological evidence shows that state bakeries produced large quantities of baked loaves of bread and fermented beer, which were distributed to workers engaged on state projects.[935]

Rank within crew at Deir el-Medina	Weight (khar) of grain ration	Weight (kg) of grain ration	Surplus weight (kg) of grain ration	Surplus volume (m^3) of grain ration
Chief foreman	88	4,930	3,292	5.02
Skilled worker	64	3,586	1,948	2.97
Guard	32	1,793	155	0.24
Porter	16	896	–741	-1.13

Table 6.11: Weight and volume of the grain rations of an average family at Deir el-Medina.

Textual evidence shows that rations were paid according to rank and profession and that the lowest paid workers received ten loaves of bread and two full jugs of beer per day.[936] An inscription in the sixth regnal year of Seti I shows that royal quarry workers at Silsila, on the east bank opposite Kom Ombo, received 4 lbs (1.82 kg) of

[928] Janssen 1975b: 460–466 and Janssen 1979a: 512. In addition, they received rations of fish, firewood, garments, water and unspecified quantities of vegetables. Papyrus Greg records the day-to-day supply of rations of loaves, grain, beer, fish, plaster, wood, lamps, wicks, and lamps (see Warburton 1997: 152–158, 219–220 for translation and commentary). The fish ration in the reign of Ramesses III was 8.4 kg of fish per month (McDowell 1999: 232). Occasionally some royal tomb workers received luxuries, as attested by the stele, British Museum 588, translated by Janssen 1963. Inherkhau received from Ramesses III, fine cloth, bronze *kebu*-jars, silver *tjebu*-vases, sweet *ben*-oil, honey, fat, cream, incense, olives, papyrus, *sety*-fruit, and olives. For a complete list see McDowell 1999: 234.

[929] Baines and Yoffee 1998: 230, Eyre 1998: 181, and Janssen 1980a.

[930] Kemp 2006: 323.

[931] The Wilbour Papyrus shows that the tax rate was 1.5 *khar*/aroura (Katary 1999: 65 and Katary 2007: 192–197).

[932] Using the dry densities of 609 and 769 kg/m^3 for barley and wheat respectivel, the weight of surplus barley would be 1,081 kg and of wheat 557 kg. The volume of this combined barley and wheat surplus = (1,081 ÷ 609) + (557 ÷ 769) = 1.775 (m^3 of barley) + 0.725 (m^3 of wheat) = 2.5 m^3.

[933] It is assumed that the family size on average was 6, making the number of families/100,000 cohort = 100,000 ÷ 6 = 16,667 families. The total combined weight of barley and emmer consumed/100,000 cohort = 27,297,707 kg (Table 2.23). The annual ration/family = 27,297,707 ÷ 16,667 = 1,638 kg/family/year.

[934] The porter needed to have a second job or members of his family would be required to work to make up the shortfall of –741 kg/yr of grain.

[935] For the evidence for Egyptian baking and brewing processes, see Samuel 2000: 537–576.

[936] Bleiberg 2007: 182.

bread daily, a bundle of vegetables, a portion of roast meat, and 2 sacks of grain monthly.[937] This would have equated to an annual surplus of 296 kg and would be available for exchange for other goods and services (Table 6.12). Another text shows that higher ranked workers such as a captain of a boat, received 38.33 loaves but the lowest crewmember received only 1.33 loaves.[938] The priests were more affluent because in addition to their standard allocation of food rations they received a commission on the tax and rental dues paid to the temple from tenant farmers.[939]

Rations	kg
Annual requirement (kg) /family of 6	1,638
Av. weight (kg)/sack (emmer + barley)	53
4 lbs bread ration/day	1.81
2 sacks of grain/month	106
Rations/yr	1,934
Annual surplus rations	**296**

Table 6.12: Surplus rations given to quarry workers at Silsila in the reign of Seti I.

Surplus rations could not easily be stored, as they needed significant space and the right conditions to prevent deterioration and damage from vermin. The quantity of surplus grain earned by the workers at Deir el-Medina is beyond the storage capacity of most houses in the village particularly as the grain would be stored in pots taking up additional space.[940] It is also known that some of the grain entered the local economy to be exchange for other goods such as pottery, clothing, and sandals.[941]

Storage of surplus rations was even more of a problem for state workers who were paid in loaves and beer instead of grain. In antiquity, bread and beer had a short storage life compared with their modern equivalents. This means that it was imperative that the surplus was utilised as quickly as possible and one solution would have been to send it to the local market place. It is reasonable to assume that there would be a demand for additional grain in local markets because workers earned, for their rank, the same rations regardless of the size of the family. Family size varied considerably in antiquity and large families would be seeking additional grain from the local markets.

Independent or semi-independent artisans using the market place as an outlet for their goods would have further stimulated the informal market. Cooney asserts that there is sufficient textual evidence to conclude there were artisans building and decorating private tombs on the west bank at Thebes who were working independently or semi-independently of the state.[942] Cooney divided the workforce into three main categories: unattached labour systems (artisans in rural villages), fully attached state labour systems (workers employed on state infrastructure, expeditions, and royal/temple building projects), and semi-attached labour systems (entrepreneurial artisans as attested in Deir el-Medina).[943] Helk considers that the textual evidence from Deir el-Medina demonstrates that the workers used grain and other commodities to purchase funerary goods and to pay for their own decorated private tombs.[944] Cooney's analysis however, suggests that the cost of decorating a tomb (240–300 *deben*) would still be too high for an average Deir el-Medina artisan even if they were working privately, and this investment in their mortuary cult would be restricted to the highest ranking village scribes, crew leaders, and draftsmen.[945]

The lowest paid state workers such as the porters working on the construction of the royal necropolis at Deir el-Medina were near or below the subsistence level. To supplement their rations they could have worked part time in cottage industries producing the goods to be exchanged for grain in the market place, which in turn increased the scale of the decentralised informal market. Surplus grain entering the informal economy from higher ranked state non-basic workers could have stimulated the demand for luxury goods normally associated with the élite.[946] This commercial activity would have contributed to the size of the informal market.[947]

The potential size of this informal market taken together with the high level of interregional trade in the LBA is another key indicator that the LBA economy was not minimalist in scale. The fact that higher ranked workers and skilled workers were paid more than others meant that some workers became wealthy, giving them the opportunity to acquire luxury goods to fulfil their desire for conspicuous consumption, and perhaps leading to the formation of a sub-élite sector.

The emerging spending power of the sub-élite

The next consideration is whether this emerging sub-élite sector in the LBA economy may have led to the

[937] Kitchen 1982: 26.

[938] Bleiberg 1995: 1380.

[939] For example at the MK temple of Wepwawet, priests received a commission on the taxed goods arriving to fill up the temple granaries as well other tax goods received in kind and the commission reflected rank. According to the grain tax receipts, high priests received 4/360th of the grain received that day and the regular priest received 2/360th of the daily quantity arriving at the temple. The unit of reckoning equated to one temple day (Kemp 2006: 177). We do not have direct textual evidence for this practice in the NK but it is probable that it continued.

[940] At the back of the Deir el Medina houses were small rooms between 3-6 m^2 thought to be used for cooking and processing and it is in this area that food would be stored (Meskell 2002: 41).

[941] For examples, see Janssen 1975a: 158–161, 172.

[942] Helk 1993, Cooney 2007a: 172–173, and Cooney 2008.

[943] Cooney 2007a: 164–173. For the role of slaves, servants, and prisoners of war in the Egyptian labour force, see Allam 2001.

[944] Helk 1993.

[945] Cooney 2008: 91. For details of recompense for private work carried out by Deir el-Medina workmen see Cooney 2008: 92ff.

[946] The evidence that the workers at Deir el-Medina were given rations above a subsistence level of rations is shown by the fact that the more affluent could afford goods made by other artisans. This is attested in many ostraca and was probably typical of most villages throughout Egypt. This diverse informal market is illustrated by the payment of 1½ sacks of grain for construction work in the house of Paneb, clothing, food, sandals, and baskets worth 6½ 'silver units', given in payment by a workman for his tomb decoration, and the production of a headrest for Qenherkhepishef's tomb (McDowell 1999: 66, 69, and 71).

[947] Cooney 2007b.

formation of an embryonic formalist economy. All wealth and resources in Egypt nominally belonged to the Pharaoh. Even so, in the NK, land and valuable goods were given to individuals for services to him and it is clear from the tombs at Deir el-Medina that this sector of society could accumulate considerable quantities of goods acquired during their lifetime.[948]

Several scholars have proposed that the increased wealth moving down the social scale of LBA society formed a 'sub-élite' (middle class). This created a demand for objects that emulated the conspicuous consumption of the ruling élite and gave them prestige in the eyes of their contemporaries.[949] S. Sherratt proposes that the Cypriot pottery in the pithoi on the Ulu Burun wreck was destined for a sub-élite market.[950] The cargoes from the Ulu Burun, Gelidonya, and Point Iria shipwrecks included some relatively low value manufactured goods and raw materials, such as Cypriot pottery, foodstuffs, faience beads, exotica (ostrich, ivory, tortoise shells), and scrap gold and jewellery.[951] The main cargo of the Ulu Burun wreck was 10 tons of copper, one ton of tin, one ton of pistacia (mastic) resin, and 175 lapis lazuli, turquoise, purple, and amber coloured glass ingots weighing *c.*350 kg, and these probably represented state administered trade.[952] However, it seems likely that the ship's crew traded the lower value items for speculative exchange as the boat moved from port to port.

Modern scholarship is moving away from interpreting imported pottery as being exclusively pieces of fine ware destined for the ruling élite. Increasingly pottery is seen as entrepreneurial space fillers between the commodity cargoes as proposed by Artzy and Gill.[953] Of interest to the period under study are Cypriot pottery, particularly White Slip ware, Base-ring bowls, and large storage jars that are found extensively across both Central and Eastern Mediterranean.[954] White Slip II, predominantly WS II Late, was a lower quality than White Slip I.[955] Yon considers that, 'Another striking feature is the vulgarisation of White Slip which became a utilitarian ware at the end of the Late Bronze Age. ... White Slip was no longer the merchandise of a luxury trade [for the ruling élite], but rather a mass-produced ordinary type of pottery which was no doubt sold at a moderate price.'[956]

Mass production techniques were introduced to lower production costs of White Slip ware and increase production rates.[957] This led to deterioration in slip preparation and the quality of the materials used.[958] The designs were simplified and to save time paint was applied with a multiple tipped brush.[959] The resulting availability at a lower cost led to a fashion for this pottery among the sub-élite sector. The widespread finds of White Slip ware outside of ruling élite contexts led to Artzy's ironic comment, 'White Slip ware was but one more element in this new or newer type of trade. It probably became a prestige object for the new "sub-élite", and one could not survive the neighbours' stare without at least one White Slip bowl covering the store jar.'[960] Bennet suggests that by the LBA the demand for 'international style' goods was no longer an exclusive élite phenomenon and had broadened to at least a sub-élite.[961]

Not all the pottery found in non-ruling élite contexts are necessarily poor quality. Fine ware Mycenaean amphoroid kraters have been found in five tombs in Ugarit that belonged to wealthy traders yet they are rare even within royal palace contexts. Van Wijngaarden proposes that these traders wished to enhance their status by distinguishing themselves from members of the royal court with ceramics obtained through their international relationships.[962]

This section has argued that an informal economy had developed in the latter part of the NK Egypt that was sufficiently large for wealth to have aggregated amongst a new sub-élite sector who sought goods to display their rising social position. However, outside of this embryonic formalist niche sector, the economy remained essentially substantive in nature. In itself, the evidence for imported goods across the Near East and Egypt does not prove that a formalist market had developed. However, by the end of the twelfth millennium B.C., maritime trade had become increasingly decentralised from state control, and had enlarged in scale to satisfy the growing sub-élite market that had characteristics of an embryonic market

[948] McDowell 1999: 69.

[949] Merrillees 1968: 195 and Hulin 2009: 40 and 45. The term sub-élite has been used in preference to 'middle class' to avoid placing a modern worldview onto the past (Grajetski 2010: 180–181). Richards 2005: 179–180 uses the term 'middle class' to define and distinguish an identifiable social group, a small but wealthy and influential group of court officials and provincial élites.

[950] Sherratt 1994: 67 and Sherratt 2000: 83. Pithoi on the Ulu Burun wreck contained Cypriot Base-ring and White Slip bowls, White Shaved juglets, Bucchero jugs, clay oil lamps, and wall brackets (Pulak 2001: 40–42, Figures 2–4).

[951] Bass 1967a, Lolos 1999, and Pulak 2001. In a large pithoi, almonds, pine nuts, fig seeds, grape pips, pomegranate seeds, and fruit fragments have been identified indicating the possible LBA trade in foodstuffs. In a number of smaller Canaanite jars olive stones, charred barley and wheat were probably stores for the crew rather than cargo (Pulak 2001: 37).

[952] Pulak 2001: 25. The blue glass ingots found at Amarna were made with cobalt oxide and other associated minerals (Nicholson and Jackson 1997: 147, Footnote 23 and Shortland and Tite 2000).

[953] Artzy 1985b: 137 and Gill 1991. Also see Artzy 2001 who demonstrates that large clusters of White Slip ware have been found close to ports along the Carmel coast of Israel. Similar findings along the Northern Levantine coast support the same argument.

[954] Bergoffen 1991, Yon 2001, van Wijngaarden 2002, White 2003: 71–83, Artzy 2001, Vagnetti 2001, and Hatcher 2007.

[955] Artzy 1985a: 98–99 and Artzy 1985b: 136.

[956] Yon 2001: 123.

[957] Artzy 1985a: 98.

[958] Artzy 2001: 112.

[959] Artzy 1985a: 96–98 and Sherratt 1991: 191, Footnote 9.

[960] Artzy 2001: 114.

[961] Barrett 2009: 225–226. Feldman 2006: 64 considers that merchants amassed substantial personal wealth and rank. This fostered a demand for a more individualistic style of luxury goods supplied by a thriving entrepreneurial, seaborne, mercantile trade network.

[962] Van Wijngaarden 1999: 22.

economy.[963] The response to a demand for non-essential goods further down the social scale, running in parallel with administered commodity trade, could have been the first steps in the formation of a true market.

Price formation

A number of factors influence the price of a good, principally its value, supply and demand, and the exchange process. Polanyi considered that, 'Prices are originally set by tradition or authority, and their alternation, when it occurs, is again brought about by institutional, not by market methods.'[964] Some scholars believe that the term 'price' is only relevant to the period following the introduction of coinage. There are however other scholars who consider that the concept of price did exist in antiquity. Nevertheless, when considering the evidence, the randomness of the survival of texts in the archaeological record, and whether the term 'price' had the same meaning in the LBA as it does in modern market economies, must be taken into account.[965]

Value

S. Sherratt proposes that several characteristics of value were in play in the LBA. She suggests that precious and base metals (gold, silver, copper, and tin) had a prime or convertible value in the exchange systems of the Eastern Mediterranean, an example of this being the silver shekel.[966] Rare metals and other materials such as lapis lazuli as well as objects such as fine pottery and jewellery had a preciosity value, gained from their perceived status as rare or exotic. When made into metal artefacts such as tools and weapons they have an added-value, which is the value added by a craft or manufacturing process. Her fourth characteristic is 'cultural value' where a good or goods '...acquire a universally recognised social or ideological significance.[967] Gregory considers that base metals, staples, and oil have a 'use-value.'[968] Tin for example has a use-value because it is combined with copper to make bronze tools. Similarly, grain has a use-value because of its nutritional properties. Adam Smith, David Ricardo, and Karl Marx proposed that labour should be the measure of value.[969] Janssen has also shown in his analysis of the price of beds at Deir el-Medina that in some invoices the cost of labour and materials were listed in terms of value equivalences.[970] Menger proposed that 'marginal utility' (a measure of relative satisfaction) is the best determinant of value.[971]

In the marketplace as apposed to the market, the price could vary depending on the skill of the buyer and seller. Evidence from Deir el-Medina shows that in the bartering process both parties used equivalences to assess the value of goods exchanged. The value equivalents attested were copper weights (*deben*), grain (*khar*, sack, and *oipe*), oil (*hin*), and quantities of silver, originally called *šʿty,* in the Twentieth Dynasty texts *sniw*.[972] For example, an ox was bartered for goods that had the equivalent value of 60 *deben* of copper: a jar of fat, 2 linen pieces, copper/bronze scraps, and 10 *hin* of oil with equivalent values of 30, 10, 5, 5 *deben* respectively.[973] In this example the sum of the value of the goods, expressed in *deben*, can be considered to be the price of the ox.

In the pursuit of trade in the LBA some objective method of determining and agreeing the value of goods traded must have been present, particularly in the trade of commodities and staples across regional borders. The archaeological record has a rich source of evidence showing that a wide range standardised weights were used in the pursuit of trade.[974] The evidence shows convincingly that there was a rational mathematical progression within each region's system of weights.[975] It is this rational attribute that facilitated a common understanding of the inter-regional relationship of standardised weights that enabled a consensus to be reached for the value of the good traded.[976] It is not surprising therefore that the

---

963 Sherratt 1998: 294–301. In Egypt, this was all part of a growing democratisation of religion and social position (Baines 1987, and Finnestad 1988).

964 Polanyi 1977: lii.

965 Monroe 2009 has made a comprehensive analysis of Hittite, Ugaritic, Assyrian, and Egyptian texts related to trade, price, and profit. See also Silver's interpretation of Ugaritic, Mesopotamian, and Egyptian texts from his formalist stance (Silver 1985: 73–79, 95–123, 133–135, 158, 165–166). For Ugaritic evidence, see Heltzer 1977: 203–211. The texts show the exchange rates of the following metals: silver to tin 1:227, silver to copper (or bronze as the texts are not clear on this point) is within the range 1:200 to 1: 235, and gold to silver was between 1:3 and 1:4 (Heltzer 1977: 204).

966 Sherratt 2000: 83.

967 Sherratt 1994: 62–64.

968 Gregory 1982: 10. Use-value rather than exchange value was the important criterion (Janssen 1988: 14–16).

969 Smith 1880 [1723–1790], Marx 1971 [1859], Ricardo 1971 [1867].

970 These included combinations of the cost of wood (including type of wood particularly if rare woods were used such as ebony), shaping of the wood, stringing the mattress, and any decoration and recompense for making the bed (Janssen 1975b: 180–184, Table 18).

971 Menger 1950 [1871].

972 See Kemp 2006: 319–326 and Janssen 1988: 13–14. In the NK, the copper *deben* weighed 91g divided into 10 *qdt*. In the NK, a *khar* of grain had a volume of 76.8 litres. The use of the *deben* was preferable to grain for large exchange transactions or exchanges involving large distances (Snell 1995: 1492).

973 Janssen 1975b: 9. Another example on Ostracon Deir el-Medina 73, verso, shows that a coffin notionally valued by buyer and seller at 25.5 copper *deben* was exchanged for 2 pieces of scrap copper with an equivalent value of 13.5 *deben* + two goats with an equivalent value of 6 *deben* + two sycamore logs with an equivalent value of 2 *deben* + one pig with an equivalent value of 5 *deben*. Resulting in 25.5 *deben* (Janssen 1975b: 10 and Kemp 2006: 321, Figure 113).

974 Bass 1967d, Powell 1979, Young 1979, Petruso 1984, Michailidou 1999, Lassen 2000, Pulak 2000b, Michailidou 2003, Petruso 2003, Mederos and Lamberg-Karlovsky 2004, Alberti and Parise 2005, Hafford 2005, Michailidou 2010, and Rahmstorf 2010.

975 For example, Hafford 2005 demonstrates that the shekel measured 8.4 grams of silver the mathematical progression of weights was based on 1/60 of a shekel and followed a modified Fibonacci sequence (starting from 3, 3 + 6 = 9, 6 + 9 = 15, 9 + 15 = 24). Using 1/20 of a shekel, a true Fibonacci sequence is derived 1, 2, 3, 5, 8 where the next in the series is the sum of the preceding two numbers. As Hafford 2005: 36 points out this sequence has a practical benefit when using hand balances, because 'Increasing the load by the next higher weight reaches the next in the sequence, and so forth. With several weights of each denomination, any amount could be assessed quickly and easily.'

976 The Hittites, Ugaritarians, and merchants from Ebla (Syria) all had a common unit of a talent (28.2 kg) and a mina that was 1/60th of a talent (0.47 kg). They each had a different shekel equivalent to 1/40th (11.75 g), 1/50th (9.4 g), and 1/60th (7.9 g) of a mina respectively (Lassen 2000:

Gelidonya wreck had at least seven different weight standards and the Ulu Burun wreck had three, indicating that the ship's captain understood the relationship between weight and value across a range of cultures, enabling them to trade in many regions.[977]

Supply and demand

Neoclassical economics dictate that supply and demand pressures set the level of prices and for a given cost of production and overheads, the level of profit. This means that if the demand for a good exceeds supply, prices will rise and if supply of a good exceeds demand, prices will fall. Formalists believe that in post hunter-gatherer societies this law is universal, irrespective of culture or time-period. Most formalist interpretations do however concede that in antiquity, the relationship between price, supply, and demand was not the same as the neoclassical supply and demand curve.[978] Communications were slow in antiquity so that it was difficult for suppliers to know what shortfall or glut opportunities existed in the market. In addition, the level of technology in the production of food and added-value goods, was not conducive to rapid changes in demand. These inhibitors would minimise the scale of opportunist trade but would not preclude it.

S. Sherratt proposes that if production had met the demand, the increased quantities of the metal flowing around the Eastern Mediterranean would have devalued the exchange rate of bronze. She suggests that to compensate for the devaluation, the Cypriots diversified in the twelfth and eleventh centuries B.C. from exclusively making bronze into the production of iron to make iron knives/daggers for export.[979] This response to market conditions with new products is an indicator that by the end of the LBA/EIA transition an embryonic formalist market was in place.

Polanyi recognised that events such as harvest failures would affect prices but considered that in times of crisis, the institutions of the state still controlled underlying value equivalents. He states, 'The rationale of the procedure is, of course, to keep the equivalents unchanged; if they must adjust to actual supply situations, as in an emergency, this is phrased as trading two to one or two and one-half to one …'.[980] In other words, state adjustments were in distinct multiples and not incremental as seen in a market economy. Polanyi did accept however, it was not possible to control prices of staples in the local marketplace but traditional cultural values and social considerations ensured local suppliers did not exploit the situation for personal profit.[981]

Kemp takes a mid-way position between the substantivists and formalists and believes that prices fixed themselves but not solely through the mechanism of supply and demand. He suggests that the personal concept of value is multifaceted, '… do I think that something is worth a particular price?' … It is a relationship that basically reflects a general human preference for buying cheaply, coupled with thresholds of resistance against prices which seem to be high as measured against an intuitive appreciation of the 'value' of a thing.'[982]

The exchange rates for commodities and goods remained reasonably stable in antiquity.[983] This may have been influenced through state control of wages and the use of granaries to minimise fluctuations in harvest yields. An exception in Egypt was when the ratio of copper/silver/gold changed from 1:100:200 to 1:60:120 in the Twentieth Dynasty.[984] Kemp suggests that this decline in the value of silver and gold to bronze was the result of large quantities of circulating precious metals from the extensive tomb robbing that took place at that time.[985]

Proto-currencies

According to Janssen, the Egyptian practice of comparing the values of goods exchanged in terms of the equivalents (copper *deben*, grain, oil or silver) was not a monetary system in a neoclassical sense but an intermediate stage between bartering and a monetary system.[986]

The LBA Ugaritic and earlier Mesopotamian texts show that weighed silver (shekels) was a practical and non-ceremonial method of computing values in the exchange of dissimilar goods. Morris Silver proposes that the silver weights carried in the first half of the second millennium in official, sealed and labelled purses (*kaspum kankum*) acted as proto-currency.[987] Veenhof notes that Polanyi admitted that silver functioned as standard of value and as means of payment, but not as an 'indirect means of exchange.'[988] Polanyi defines the latter as 'acquiring units of quantifiable objects for indirect exchange through

235). For further discussion on the use of the mina across the Near East, see Parise 1989.

977 Bass 1967d and Pulak 2000b.

978 Schneider 1974: 32–34 and Figure 2.3. From UR III texts Snell analysed a range of commodities to see whether more of a product was bought when it was cheap and less when it was expensive. With the exception of raisins, no commodity followed the neoclassical supply and demand curve (Snell 1982: 190, Table 34).

979 Sherratt 2003: 43–51.

980 Polanyi 1977: 95.

981 Polanyi 1977: 41–42. Zingarelli emphasises the importance of fair play in exchange transactions between interested parties in the NK community of Deir el-Medina. In a dispute, third party mediators and or the town council provided arbitration (Zingarelli 2010: 64). For ethnographic evidence from West Africa of fair play in exchange transactions to prevent instability in the market by unscrupulous price cutting, see Humphreys 1969: 188 citing Bauer 1954: 191.

982 Kemp 2006: 322.

983 Haring 2009: 6. Also see Snell's study of merchants' silver balanced UR III accounts shows that prices were relatively stable across that period or they hovered around a central point (Snell 1982: 1890).

984 Janssen 1988: 17.

985 Kemp 2006: 319.

986 Janssen 1975b: 545.

987 True coinage did not appear in the Eastern Mediterranean until the seventh century B.C. in the Anatolian Kingdom of Lydia. This was followed in 630 B.C. by the Greek city-state of Aegina (Silver 1985b: 87–88, 126–130).

988 Veenhof 1972: 348.

direct exchange, in order to acquire the desired objects through a further act of exchange.'[989] An example of indirect exchange in an LBA context would be to exchange grain in Egypt for silver, travel to Ugarit with the silver, and exchange this for tin, which Egypt required to make bronze. The benefit of travelling with shekels rather than moving grain in bulk over a long distance is self-evident. In this sense, the silver shekel acted as a form of proto-currency that facilitated commercial exchange but lacked the ceremonial prestige of silver in gift exchange between ruling élites.[990] One problem in the use of precious metals as 'money' in antiquity was the difficulty of accurately determining metal purity.[991]

Vickers and Gill suggest we should broaden our view of what was proto-currency to include precious metals in the form of scrap, bullion, and even damaged fine art metal objects.[992] Sherratt and Sherratt suggest that the lack of silver objects found in the archaeological record resulted from their use as proto-currency.[993] Commodities such as copper ingots could also act as a form of proto-currency because they fulfilled four essential attributes. They were a means of exchange, could fulfil certain tax liabilities and ceremonial obligations, could compare values of different commodities, and were a means to store accumulated wealth.[994] In Mesopotamia, Powell argues that commodities acted as money, with barley used as cheap money and silver used for more expensive transactions.[995]

Powell argues that the mina and the shekel were originally Mesopotamian weights that evolved into monetary units that spread across the Near East to become monetary units in other cultures.[996] His analyses of the weights of silver rings and coils found in the Mesopotamian archaeological record demonstrate that they have an underlying metrological statistical relationship.[997] The interregional nature of contact between merchants is clearly demonstrated by the range of weights found in the archaeological record on shipwrecks, at ancient ports, and along caravan routes.

The merchant: profiteer or agent of the state

This section discusses the evidence for a profit motive in LBA trading and whether the pursuit of profit created a niche opportunity for entrepreneurial merchants that led to an embryonic formalist market.

Profit in the LBA: reality or myth

The prime motivation underpinning any enterprise in a modern market economy is the desire to make a net profit. Formalists believe that this profit motive was, for whatever period, a universal characteristic of merchants and traders. Substantivists believe that prices were based on cultural values and administered by the state through its control of redistribution that satisfied material wants. As a result, merchants were fundamentally different from their modern counterparts and were embedded within the needs and operation of the state economy.[998]

There is little hard evidence for the concept of profit in Egyptian texts. There is no word for 'profit' in the ancient Egyptian vocabulary and Kemp considers that this indicates that they did not have this concept.[999] Janssen concludes from the textual evidence found at Deir el-Medina that there is little evidence of the profit-making motive in the local marketplace.[1000] He believes that to the Egyptian mind, the use of value comparators in exchange transactions was perfectly rational and what was important was that no party knowingly lost out in the transaction.[1001] However, Janssen points out that textual evidence for Egypt-wide internal trade may be unrepresentative as it is dominated by the Deir el-Medina corpus. The merchants are presented as being in the service of institutions receiving rations or fields for their services and if a profit is made then this is an outcome that was unintentional.[1002] The 'Instruction of Any' however, a text dated to the Twenty-First or Twenty-Second Dynasty of Egypt may allude to profit with the

[989] Veenhof 1972: 348 citing Polanyi 1968: 167–168 and 192.

[990] Liverani 1979b: 28–29 uses the term 'silver money' in exchange situations but not in the exchange of prestige objects among kings of equal rank. An exception is the king of Alašia who asks the Pharaoh for 'silver in large quantities' in return for copper, emphasising the commercial nature of this exchange (EA 35, 19–22, and 43–44). In Egypt the use of the *deben* was preferable to grain as a form of proto-currency for large exchange transactions or exchanges involving large distances (Snell 1995: 1492).

[991] Powell 1999: 19–23. Some of the scrap silver from the Ulu Burun was significantly debased with copper contents varying from 14.3–26.3%. Two silver bars had copper contents of 70.6% and 73.4% (Pulak 2001: 25). The problem of determining the purity of precious metals was not resolved until Archimedes (287–*c*.212 B.C.).

[992] Vickers and Gill 1994: 40–42 and Gill 2008: 336–344.

[993] Sherratt and Sherratt 1991: 360 Kassianidou does observe however that scarcity of silver in the archaeological record may be due to chlorides in the soil reacting with the silver to form silver chloride (Kassianidou 2009: 49).

[994] Goddeeris 2002: 390 based on Renger 1995: 271–274, 282–283.

[995] Powell lists the commodities that acted as proto-currencies in ascending order of value: barley, lead, copper or bronze, tin, and silver. These were used as indices or standards of value and were stockpiled as storable wealth (Powell 1996: 227–228). Ancient scales were inaccurate for weighing small quantities of valuable metals such as silver. Powell suggests that barley, with its high volume to weight ratios, overcame these problems and could be was used in settlement of low value transactions (Powell 1996: 229).

[996] Powell 1990 and Powell 1996. Also, see Sherratt 2000: 83 and the importance of mutual understanding of 'embedded equivalences' between ruling élites in the gift–exchange process.

[997] Some Egyptologists suggest that *šʿty* meant 'rings'. Powell, using evidence primarily from the Old Babylonian Period in Mesopotamia, concludes that rings or coils of metal were used as money for the purposes of payment (Powell 1978: 213–222). Some of the coils have been snipped and Powell proposes that they were used as payment of goods and services (Powell 1978: 228–230, Plate IIC). For Cypriot evidence of gold earrings, spirals, and armlets which might be related to balance weights that were excavated at Kalavasos-Ayios Dhimitrios, see Goring 1989, South 1989, and Lassen 2000: 241-242, Figures 16.2–16.3.

[998] Finley warns against interpreting ancient economic texts from the perspective of neoclassical 'economizing' accounting practices as the 'ancients' lacked the concept of an 'economy' (Finley 1973: 21).

[999] Kemp 2006: 323. Also see earlier discussion in Kemp 2006: 302–303.

[1000] Janssen 1975b: 561 and Janssen 1988: 15–16, 20–21.

[1001] Janssen 1988: 15.

[1002] Janssen 1988: 20–21.

advice, 'If wealth is placed where it bears interest, it comes back to you redoubled.'[1003]

Near Eastern and Mesopotamian texts appear at face value to indirectly, and in some scholars' opinions explicitly, demonstrate the intention of merchants and their sponsors to make a profit as well as recording the profit in economic accounts. In Artzy's study of cargoes flowing from Cyprus to the Levantine Littoral, she concludes that the profit element was at least as important in shaping the patterns of trade as changes in power and power bases.[1004] Book keeping records from Larsa were 'balanced accounts' in a formulaic style that presented a statement of receipts and expenses of a business transaction. Line 1 of the text begins with the balance of the proceeding account, this is followed by an itemised list of receipts and its sub-total and then a list of itemised expenditures. The next line has the balance between receipts and expenditures that is transferred to the next account.[1005] Sumerian merchants' balanced accounts were similar in format, starting with the merchant's value of assets at the start of the trading period in silver shekels. Receipts are itemised in silver equivalents with the respective sub-total in silver. Expenditures follow, also in silver equivalents, by a statement of credit balance (LAL.NI = positive difference) or overdraft (dirig = negative difference). In the best traditions of good accountancy practice, the text includes a dated statement of responsibility usually phrased, 'balanced account of PN, the merchant' (NÍG.ŠID.AK PN dam-gàr).[1006] Powell concludes from his analysis of Sumerian merchants' UR III accounts that the merchant operated primarily on the basis of profit and loss and that the state or temple did not systematically underwrite his losses.[1007] It is this personal accountability for profit and loss and the merchant's degree of independent action, which suggests the balanced account records do reflect formalist entrepreneurship. Powell also considers that the term 'balance' in UR III accounts was interpreted by the administration as profit.[1008] He does however, emphasise that while maximising profit was an important motive it does not imply their sole motive.[1009]

If neoclassical accounting rules are applied to the merchants' texts for the tin and textile caravan trade in the Old-Assyrian Period, they show that gross profits could be as high as 100% for tin, and 200% for textiles.[1010] Net profit levels of 30–35% could be expected for tin and higher levels for textiles after taking into account taxes and travel costs.[1011] Both Larsen and Silver propose that the word *nēmulum* used in the texts is equivalent in sense to the modern day equivalent for net profit.[1012]

The silver balanced accounts were laid out in such a manner that not only could the profit on an exchange could have been deduced, it was explicitly stated.[1013] Formalists would argue that the transactions were profitable because the difference between expenses and receipts (net balance) on trading accounts show a profit or loss. The substantivists would counter with the argument that the texts were simply a record of the expenses and receipts incurred as well as providing the sponsors of the trading expedition with an audit of the trading transactions.

The evidence that profit was an important motivation for merchants is not conclusive. Although we can see that the merchants made a profit or loss, we cannot tell whether making a profit was their primary motive for trading or whether the concept of profit had a different nuance from its modern meaning.

Evidence for entrepreneurial merchants

There are three criteria against which the nature of merchants and trade is assessed, the existence of a private sector, the degree of independence of the merchants from state control, and the financing of trading missions. This section examines the evidence from three areas: Egypt, the Levantine littoral, and Assyria.

Egypt

Evidence of the presence of private merchants from Egypt is silent. Low status traders (*šwtyw*) moved goods up and down the Nile and were probably agents of the state/temples with few opportunities for private entrepreneurial activities.[1014] A problem specific to Egyptian sources is that decorum dictated that the dependence on the Pharaoh had to be emphasised and claims to independent wealth was not acceptable.[1015] Nevertheless, a number of Egyptologists propose that some land was in private ownership.[1016] In addition, Castle concludes that fishermen used their boats to transport

[1003] Lichtheim 1976a: 138.
[1004] Artzy 1985b: 136.
[1005] Leemans 1954: 49–51.
[1006] Young 1979: 195–207.
[1007] Powell 1977: 27–28.
[1008] Powell 1977: 25–27.
[1009] Powell 1977: 24.
[1010] Veenhof 1972: 85.
[1011] Larsen 1967: 4 and Larsen 1977: 136–137. For tax levels and expenses related to operating caravan expeditions see Veenhof 1972: 85–87.
[1012] Larsen 1987: 139 and Silver 1985: 88.
[1013] UR III silver balance accounts show that the difference between receipts and expenditures was recorded; the positive or negative balance was carried forward to the next account and entered as 'remainder' (Powell 1977: 27). The term remainder can only be interpreted as profit or loss. However, Snell 1982 suggests that the comparison of prices for different volumes of the same commodity in UR III accounts shows that the agency was not interested in maximizing return and the money spent but was only interested in making sure that the bureaux were properly supplied.
[1014] See Bleiberg 2007: 178–180 for a summary of the alternative substantive and formalist interpretations for this riverine trade.
[1015] Kemp *et al* 1994: 134.
[1016] Castle 1992: 247–248 and Baer 1962. The main source of evidence being the Wilbour Papyrus (Gardiner 1948b). Gardiner proposed the status of the owners of the smallholdings, '… either was, or else closely resembled, that of private owners.' (Gardiner 1948b: 75). Baer considers that the Wilbour Papyrus was, '… a register of rents due to various institutions for land to which they held complete or partial ownership rights.' (Baer 1962: 32).

grain along the Nile as a private enterprise.[1017] Cooney argues that there was a thriving private group of artisans supporting the demand for funerary equipment, tomb building, and tomb decoration.[1018]

The Amarna letters do show that Egyptian diplomats of the Pharaohs were involved in gift exchange and perhaps administered trade between ruling élites. Their role was to facilitate the gift exchange process; monitoring the gifts to ensure they were equitable in value, asking for specific items, criticising inadequate gifts, and stressing the need for reciprocity. Any personal rewards for services rendered were presented to them solely as servants of the Pharaoh and not as independent merchants. On the back of this activity, they may also have facilitated trade in commodities such as un-refined copper and tin. Texts from Ugarit show that Egyptians along with merchants from Canaan, Assyria, and Ḫatti, operated in Ugarit.[1019]

Another factor that may explain the lack of evidence of NK merchants is that there may not have been a need to seek many goods from outside Egypt's sphere of control. Egypt had access to a wide range of natural resources within its borders, the land was fertile, and tribute was received from all parts of its empire.[1020] This made its economy significantly more self-sufficient than those in other parts of the Near East and Mesopotamia. High-ranking diplomats may have engaged in administered trade on behalf of the king but there is no evidence of entrepreneurship or a desire to maximise profit. It was the custom of Egyptian Pharaohs to award services rendered with high status gifts such as the 'Gold of Honour'.[1021] This tends to support Polanyi's view that merchants did not make their living from profit.[1022] Janssen supports this view and considers that the ancient Egyptians lacked the individualism of the traders of Mesopotamia.[1023]

Levantine littoral

The extensive corpus of LBA economic texts from Ugarit shows that despite its small size it was a major centre of trade/exchange of the Eastern Mediterranean in the LBA.[1024] Even so, it is not easy to establish whether merchants were members of the private sector or whether they operated in the state sector.[1025] Ugaritic texts are generally vague when it comes to clarifying social positions and the large numbers of foreign merchants living in Ugarit make it difficult to decipher the hierarchy of the merchant community as a whole.[1026] Heltzer believed that LBA foreign trade in Ugarit was a royal monopoly and merchants were 'royal service-people' (*tamkār ša šepīšū*).[1027] On the other hand, we do know of at least four wealthy high status entrepreneurial Ugaritic merchants: Rapanu, Rašap-abu, Yabinu, and Urtenu, who had large houses in Ras Shamra, and who were closely involved in the copper trade with Cyprus.[1028] They were independent of the state in the sense that they received no endowments from the King but they still had intermittent dealings and administrative links to the Royal Palace.[1029] This means that to finance long distance trade expeditions they would have to raise finance through their own lines of credit, allow other associates to join them in a consortium, or fund themselves from their own accumulated profits accrued in previous trading ventures.[1030] In the transitional period from the LBA to the EIA there is evidence of increased separation of merchants' personal interests and their links to the state.[1031] Ugaritic merchants, particularly maritime traders, were free to trade with whomever they wished, and could accumulate considerable wealth, provided they paid appropriate taxes.[1032] Liverani considers that the Ugaritic *tamkāru* had adopted a strategy of disengagement from the Royal Palace by the fourteenth-thirteenth centuries B.C., obtaining exemptions from service in exchange for silver payments.[1033]

Other evidence of independent trading in the LBA is the 'fill in' cargoes carried by sailors from port to port. These

[1017] Castle 1992: 248–49, 270, Janssen 1961: 99, Gardiner 1941 based on evidence from Papyrus Turin 1895 + 2006.

[1018] Cooney 2008.

[1019] Rainey 1963a: 43 citing texts UT 311: 1, 7,8; UT 1089: 7, 10; and UT 1090: 4, 9. They lived in a separate quarter in the immediate vicinity of Ugarit's main harbour Minet el-Beida under the supervision of an *akil kar-ri*, 'overseer of the merchant colony' (Rainey 1963b: 319). Mesopotamian merchants were set apart from the urban élite, working, and possibly living, in a walled-off 'harbour' outside of the city walls. These harbours were centres of foreign trade and provided lodgings and safety for visiting merchants (Trigger 2003: 350).

[1020] However, it is possible that Egyptian texts that describe the bringing of tribute may in fact be disguising that they are in part, trading missions (Janssen 1988: 18).

[1021] Binder 2008. As well as one or more golden necklaces, the officials were rewarded with other prestigious goods.

[1022] Polanyi 1977: 139.

[1023] Janssen 1975a: 138–139.

[1024] Ugarit had a land area of at least 2,000 km^2 with an estimated population of 20,000–25,000 (Yon 2003: 41). Heltzer 1996b: 177 suggests an area of 3,000 km^2. The estimated population of Ras Shamra ranges between 6,000–8,000 (Yon 2003: 41 and Calvet 2007: 108).

[1025] Diakonoff, Liverani, and Heltzer have proposed that many states of the Eastern Mediterranean including Ugarit had both a private and a state sector, which has become known as the two-state model (Diakonoff 1982; 1991, Heltzer 1976; 1978; 1979; 1982; 1984; 1987; 1996; and 1999, and Liverani 2003: 120–123). Discussion of this model is returned to in the next section.

[1026] Part of the confusion is that the Ugaritic language used two terms for merchants, the general West Semitic *mkrm* the other being *bdlm* (Astour 1972: 11). Administration records reveal the cosmopolitan nature of merchants working in and out of Ugarit, who comprised Canaanites, Egyptians, Ashdodites, Assyrians, and Hittites (Rainey 1963a: 43). Merchants from Ura made frequent visits to Ugarit, some under the direction of the King of the Hittites (Astour 1972: 24). The Egyptian merchants formed a distinct corporate group with a juridical personality and collective responsibility, whose interests were protected by the king (Astour 1981: 24–26).

[1027] Heltzer 1996b: 177. Taking a similar view, Schloen 2001: 222 agrees that merchants were palace dependants. Monroe 2009: 107–108 refers to merchants sponsored by the palace for trade as 'endowed merchants'.

[1028] Yon 1999: 113–119 and Bell 2006: 65–67. In each merchant's house Cypro-Minoan texts were found that indicated their links with copper imports from Cyprus.

[1029] Bell 2006: 65. For details of endowed state merchants from Ugarit see Monroe 2009: 105–108.

[1030] Monroe 2009: 108–117. See also the evidence of the close trading relationship between Cyprus and Ugarit in Knapp 1983.

[1031] Bell 2006: 109.

[1032] Monroe 2009: 283.

[1033] Liverani 2003: 129.

sailors are unlikely to have been under the control of the ruling élites and this informal 'sailors' trade' points to another dimension to private profitable entrepreneurship. There is no direct textual evidence to support this 'piggy back' trade in Ugaritic texts but we can speculate that these fill in goods could have passed unofficially through the hands of the foreign resident merchants working in the immediate vicinity of the harbour. Barrett suggests that Minoan and Mycenaean pottery came into Ugarit and was then re-exported down the Levantine littoral to meet the demand of from growing LBA Egyptian sub-élite.[1034] Artzy proposes that LBA merchants based along the Levantine littoral in the LBA demonstrated their independence, entrepreneurial initiative and a desire to maximise profit when they founded Tel Nami to avoid paying harbour taxes at the larger port cities such as Tell Abu Hawam.[1035]

Assyria

Previous scholarship has long established the importance of the private sector in Assyria in the Old Assyrian Period (2000–1740 B.C.).[1036] Although this is outside of the period under study, the evidence from the entrepreneurial profit- seeking Assyrian merchants is indicative that if the opportunity exists, formalist characteristics come to the fore. The merchants were mainly involved in the long-distance trade of tin and textiles, back and forth between the mother city of Assur on the Tigris and trading colonies (*kārū*) at Kültepe in Anatolia.[1037] Entrepreneurial merchants within family firms were a fundamental unit in the Old Assyrian socio-economic system. The terms and conditions for the financing for the trade between Assur and Kültepe were clearly stated in formal contracts (*naruqqum*).[1038] The merchants formed joint-banking partnerships to raise capital and were adept at exploiting the lack of strong centralised governments in the areas they operated.[1039] In every aspect, these merchants were true opportunity seeking, profit seeking, and profit maximising entrepreneurs.

The evidence presented for Egypt, Levantine littoral, and Assyria emphasises the regional differences in the status of merchants, the degree to which they operated independently from the control of the state, and the motivation to maximise profit in exchange situations. The evidence for profit seeking merchants in Assyria is clear. In Ugarit, merchant entrepreneurial activity was more qualified as they still had to work periodically for the Royal Palace and were at a stage of development between the examples of Egypt and Assyria. The merchants based in the harbour towns along the southern Levantine coast show more independence. Egypt in contrast, follows most closely Polanyi's postulate that trading officials were embedded within the institutions of the state and merchants did not make their living from the difference between the buying and selling price.[1040] He proposed that the livelihood of the merchants, '... was not dependent on the commercial transaction in hand; it was secured by status revenue, mostly through landed property or at least through the claim to maintenance according to his rank from the royal or temple store.'[1041]

Taking a pan-Mediterranean view, it would not have been practical for a state controlled process based on gift exchange to manage the type and volume of goods found in the archaeological record. It is likely then that a semi-independent or possibly a totally independent merchant class did operate in the LBA.

6.5 Four theoretical socio-economic frameworks applied to the LBA Eastern Mediterranean

There are four conceptual frameworks which can be used to interpret the evidence covered in Chapters 2–5: Marx's 'Asiatic model of production', Diakonoff's 'two-sector' model, Weber/Schloen's 'patrimonial model', and Wallenstein's core/periphery 'world-systems'.[1042] No single construct can reflect all the cultural differences and the historic development of the LBA Eastern Mediterranean economies. Earle discusses how such models are not actual reflections of ancient societies but they can help to identify how wealth is distributed within the state, their socio-economic organisation, and the political/economic interconnections between regions.[1043]

The Asiatic mode of production

Marx first used the term 'Asiatic mode of production' (hereafter AMP) to define pre-capitalist cultures that developed outside of Western Europe.[1044] His writings on the topic were contributory to his critique of political economy and his analysis of the capitalist mode of production. Marx never achieved a full systematic exposition of the theory of AMP but published the key elements over a period of 30 years: property, the division of labour, surplus appropriation, exchange, and commodity production.[1045]

1034 Barrett 2009: 213, 225–226. For Mycenaean pottery entering Ugarit, see van Wijngaarden 1999.

1035 Artzy 1995: 17.

1036 Veenhof 1972, 1977, Larsen 1976, 1977, 1987, and Baines and Yoffee 1998: 227–228.

1037 Larsen 1977: 121. These firms also had representatives, partners, and agents, who worked for the business interests of the family.

1038 Larsen 1977: 124–125. These consisted of the quantity of cash (silver or gold) invested, the period of the contract, the profit level retained by the investor (one third), and the gold/silver exchange rate of 1:4. They specified that if funds were withdrawn prematurely or the investor pulled out of the contract, the merchant would forgo the accrued profits to date.

1039 Baines and Yoffee 1998: 228.

1040 Polanyi 1977: 139.

1041 Polanyi 1977: 87.

1042 For a wide-ranging discussion on the application of the theory of the Asiatic mode of production, see Bailey and Llobera 1981. For the two-sector model, see Diakonoff 1982. For the patrimonial model see Weber 1976 [1922] and Schloen 2001. For world-systems, see Wallerstein 1974a and Wallerstein 1974b, Rowlands 1987, and Hall 1997.

1043 Earle 2011: 237.

1044 Marx did not intend his theory to be applied to just the geographical area of Asia. He used the word 'Asiatic' to refer to any despotic culture.

1045 Bailey and Llobera 1981: 23.

AMP categorises society into two segments, the rural 'village' community and the centralised state élite. Marx believed that the latter controlled production processes through its organisation of labour and resources and from this, the inevitable exploitation of workers. Marxists generally do not accept the argument that the agrarian sector was feudal in nature as the agrarian workers did not have tenure of the land that would give them the means of production. In this respect, they consider that the ancient Near East was more akin to a slave society.[1046] Marx was convinced that there was a fundamental difference between a slave society and one in which free workers sold their labour power to capitalists even though they were cheated of part of the value created.[1047] The emphasis that Marx placed in his writings on production, exploitation, class dynamics, and social change is referred to as 'historical materialism' by his followers.[1048] The Marxist expression 'mode of production' explains these changing relationships between rulers and producers ('exploiters' and 'exploited' classes), the ownership or lack of ownership of the means of production, and the flow of products from one class to another.[1049] Marx defined the mode of production as all the aspects of production that contribute to everything necessary for life. It has two main components 'forces of production' (such as labour time, raw material, technology, tools, industrial complexes) and 'relations of production' (the interpersonal connections of the people who use these forces in the production of material goods). Fundamental to Marxist thinking is that society has evolved through five progressive stages of social evolution: the first being communal kin-based hunter-gatherers and early farmers, then slavery, followed by feudalism, then capitalism, and finally the collapse of capitalism through class conflict and revolution from which communism would arise.

There is no evidence in Egypt of deliberate state exploitation of the workers. The Turin Strike texts show that if the royal tomb workers rights for rations were not upheld, strikes could arise. These workers in the reign of Ramesses III (regnal year 29) withdrew their labour when they were not supplied with their rations.[1050] A Twentieth Dynasty ostracon also shows that royal tomb workers went on strike for late payment of rations at Deir el-Medina in the reign of Ramesses V (possibly Ramesses VI).[1051] These examples appear to be more a case of genuine shortage than deliberate exploitation of the necropolis workers by the royal palace.

In summary, the Marxist AMP is useful in emphasising the importance of the owner of the means of production and the interrelationship between the owners and the peasants who worked on the land.[1052] Superficially, Egypt fits Marx's AMP with agrarian and added-value production under the central control of the state and temples.[1053] However, the textual evidence fails to demonstrate that Pharaonic Egypt was despotic.[1054] On the contrary, Egypt may have been authoritarian but it was not tyrannical. As discussed earlier, state workers' rations were generally in excess of that required to feed themselves and their families. The role of the Pharaoh as a priest king with the prime obligation of maintaining *maat*, remained unchanged and ensured the economic well-being, and ordered life of the people. In return, the people owed the king absolute obedience.[1055] This made the ancient Egyptians conservative in nature and resistant to change. Even in the Intermediate Periods and the Late Period where the authority of kingship waned, the emphasis of the importance of *maat* was still central to the psyche of Egyptians. The autobiographical inscriptions found in élite tombs emphasised the tomb owners' adherence to traditional social and ethical values.[1056] These inscriptions described how they fulfilled their responsibility to feed the poor in times of harvest failures.[1057] Although it is accepted that no evidence is not evidence, the textual evidence remains silent for major class conflicts between Egypt's non-élite (predominantly agrarian) and the controlling élite. Strikes by the royal tomb workers at Deir el-Medina are far from Marx's key element in the AMP treatise that maintains the exploitation of workers would inevitably lead to the uprising of workers against a despotic regime resulting in economic change.

The two-sector model

Marx's ideas generated many interpretations of socio-economic history.[1058] Of these, Diakonoff's 'two-sector model, which strongly influenced the work of Heltzer,

[1046] Cole 2004: 35.

[1047] Morley 2004: 36. Chase-Dunn and Hall prefer the term 'mode of accumulation' as this broadens discussion beyond production processes to include distribution, exchange, and all forms of accumulation (Chase-Dunn and Hall 1997: 29). This could include kin-based, tributary, capitalist, and socialist modes as defined in Chase-Dunn and Hall 1997: 30.

[1048] Marx 1988 [1848]: 24–25. The conventional Marxist definition of 'class' is a group sharing a relationship to the means of production (Monroe 2009: 250).

[1049] Şaul 2005: 505 and Schloen 2001 187–188.

[1050] Janssen 1979b discussing Ostracon Turin 57072, formerly No. 6365 and Gardiner's publication of the Turin Strike Papyrus (Gardiner 1948b). For further discussion see Eyre 1979 and Janssen 1994a.

[1051] Griffiths Institute archives (Černý Mss 17.49.66 (3)). Eyre 1979: 80 made restorations to this translation of which the part relevant to strikes follows, '... the crew having gone out, being hungry, [saying] "We have gone out because we are hungry; there is no wood, (nor) vegetables, (nor) fish, ...".'

[1052] Jursa 2010: 18.

[1053] This is not to dismiss the evidence of farmers such as Heqanakht who rented land but to emphasis that the bulk of land capable of growing crops for the period under study still belonged to the state or temples.

[1054] In Egypt the king could command his subjects to work on large state projects. However the state paid rations so that those affected were recompensed for their service. Kemp differentiates slavery from this conscription service (corvée labour) as he defines slavery as 'outright ownership of the person as a piece of property ... as distinct from a temporary claim to total service' (Kemp 2006: 180).

[1055] Tobin 1978: 77–102, Lloyd 1983: 288, and Assmann 2002: 127–134. Assmann defines *maat* as 'connective justice' that, '... forms individuals into communities and that gives their actions meaning and direction by ensuring that good is rewarded and evil punished.' (Assmann 1962: 128).

[1056] Baines 1982: 33–34, 36.

[1057] For example, the stele of Tjia (Cairo JE 89624) states, 'I gave bread to the hungry, water to the thirsty, clothes to the naked ...' (KRI III 367.13–15).

[1058] Bailey and Llobera 1981.

and Liverani, is the most notable.[1059] Diakonoff adapted the Marxist AMP model to develop his two-sector model and proposed that Near Eastern society, between the rise of urbanism and the end of the second millennium B.C., comprised a royal redistributive 'state-sector' and a larger agrarian based 'private-sector', which was linked to the king through taxation and conscription.[1060] Diakonoff considered that the inhabitants of 'free villages' who owned the means of production, unlike AMP, were not an exploited class.[1061] The relative size of these two sectors has been estimated by Liverani as 20% of the population living in or near the capital city and 80% living in the agrarian private sector.[1062] In any pre-industrial society with its dependence on agriculture, understanding who owns the land, whether communal, private or institutional is important. The major difference between the two-sector model and Marx's AMP model is that Diakonoff maintains that the agrarian private sector owns the means of production and is not an exploited class.[1063]

The subsequent development of Diakonoff's two-sector model by Heltzer was based on Ugaritic texts that identified the socio-economic organisation of the state and private sectors.[1064] Royal dependants in the state sector (*bnš mlk*) were organised into professional groups: specialised crafts, administration, and trade.[1065] All were dependent on the king for their livelihood and were supervised by royally appointed managers (*rbm*).[1066] They were supplied with land allotments and received the benefits of managing the land on the condition they gave service (*pilku* = *ubdy*) to the king.[1067] This placed them under the patriarchal authority of the king.[1068] There were exceptions and there is textual evidence that some state officials from Ugarit did own, sell, and purchase land.[1069] Royal Ugaritic commercial agents (*tamkars*) also received land into conditional holding for the whole time they were carrying out trade or collecting taxes for the king.[1070] Foreign merchants however, were not allowed to own land in Ugarit.[1071] Craft skills identified from the texts included shipbuilders, builders, textile workers, bakers, millers, but the most numerous were metalworkers.[1072] The palace/temple supplied craft workers with raw materials from royal storehouses, rations, and/or land allotments under tenure.[1073] At the bottom of the social scale peasants working on royal state farms gave all their harvest produce to the state storehouses and in return for their labour received subsistence level rations.[1074]

In the private sector, Diakonoff's two-sector model assumed that the land was privately owned.[1075] In Heltzer's interpretation of these private sector family 'communes' (extended families) he designated them as villages or rural communities, who paid homage to the King as their sovereign.[1076] Community members had the right to own property and to take part in self-government, as well as sharing all the incomes, material, and non-material benefits accruing from the land owned by the community.[1077] The whole commune was collectively responsible for the taxes due to the king either in produce from the land, in silver, or through the supply of corvée workers.[1078] The rural communities were conscripted to provide warriors and bowmen for service to the king as required.[1079] In legal texts, the use of a different naming convention for the heads of these communes differentiates them from royal men.[1080] Unlike the king's men, 'citizens' of the private sector had the right to 'full property in land'.[1081] In the rural private sector, day-to-day

---

[1059] Diakonoff 1982; 1991, Heltzer 1976; 1978; 1979; 1982; 1984; 1987; 1996; and 1999, and Liverani 2003: 120–123.

[1060] Schloen 2001: 187–188, 190–191 and for Ugarit specifically, see Heltzer 1996b.

[1061] Cole 2004: 37.

[1062] Liverani 2003: 120, Footnote 6.

[1063] Diakonoff first proposed the concept of the two-sector model in 1963 stating, 'Alongside slave production, there always existed small-scale subsistence production by independent free producers.' (Diakonoff 1963: 33). For a critical view of Diakonoff's model, see Schloen 2001: 193–194.

[1064] Heltzer 1976, 1978, 1979, 1982, 1984, 1987, 1996b, and 1999.

[1065] Heltzer 1982: 36. The main groups of 'service men' (royal dependants) noted in the texts were, starting with the highest rank, high status 'friends of the king' (*md (m)*/*mūdū*), military servicemen, royal agricultural professionals, professional artisans, priests and other temple personnel, administrative personnel, and finally 'overseers of workers of ten' (*ʿšrm =rb ʿšrt*).

[1066] Heltzer 1996b: 177.

[1067] Heltzer 1982: 22–37 and Diakonoff 1982: 71, Footnotes 227–229.

[1068] Diakonoff 1982: 33.

[1069] Diakonoff 1982: 25, Footnote 43 gives details of the deeds of sale. In Ugarit, we know of 37 documents related to sale and purchase of land and two pertaining to house purchase. The average price of land was 37.5 shekels of land per *ikû* (Heltzer 1996b: 178). Using the conversion 1 *ikû* = 3,500 m^2 = 0.35 ha (Heltzer 1996a: 78). This made the price = 107 shekels/ha.

[1070] Heltzer 1978: 124. For the role *tamkars* in tax collection, see Heltzer 1978: 135–136.

[1071] Heltzer 1996b: 180–181.

[1072] Heltzer 1982: 99.

[1073] Heltzer 1979: 495 and Footnote 250 details the supply of raw materials to artisans. This practice was the same in ancient Egypt.

[1074] Diakonoff 1982: 68–69, Footnotes 216–220 uses evidence from the rural estates in the Kingdom of Sumer and Akkad in which male and female farm workers were in effect slaves receiving starvation level rations.

[1075] Heltzer 1976 and Liverani 2003: 120.

[1076] Ugaritic villages as collective units were obliged to meet all taxes and duties placed upon them by the royal government, demonstrating the communal character of these rural communities. However, these obligations, with the possible exception of military conscription, were not necessarily distributed equally among all the villagers and may have been apportioned based on the amount of property owned or on size of the family (Heltzer 1976: 47 and Heltzer 1982: 179).

[1077] Diakonoff 1982: 32.

[1078] In Ugarit taxes could be in kind and included grain, wine, olive oil, and cattle (Heltzer 1976: 35–44). Artefacts such as utensils and weapons made by craft workers in the villages could also be used to pay tax (Heltzer 1976: 44–46). For labour obligations (corvée labour) see Heltzer 1976: 24–30.

[1079] Heltzer: 1976 18–21. In Ugarit, the king was in overall control of the military including the conscription and mobilisation of both sectors (Heltzer 1982: 105–113). Peasants from coastal villages were obliged to serve in the fleet (Heltzer 1976: 21–23).

[1080] Men from ancient western Asia who were in royal service were called by their name and their profession. A member of a rural community was called by his name, patronymic, and the name of his community. Only on a few occasions was the profession added (Diakonoff 1982: 28).

[1081] This means the owner had to be a person *sui juris,* and not subject to anyone's patriarchal authority, with all the rights to which a freeman is entitled (Diakonoff 1982: 33).

administration of infrastructure, maintenance projects, and the responsibility for local defence were devolved to the heads of the communal farms acting through local councils ('house of assembly').[1082] Related and unrelated family communes were normally organised into territorial communities under a collective government of a council of elders.[1083]

Some scholars are critical of the urban/rural divide of the two-sector model. Schloen argues that the archaeological and textual evidence indicates that craft workers and city state workers (traders, priests, administrators, and soldiers) both worked to a greater or lesser degree on the land to provide their food requirements. Kemp recognises this blurring between a rural and urban division at Amarna where the lack of town planning gives the impression of a series of joined villages, and he observes that the larger houses look like little farms.[1084] Craft workers in an *oikos* economy set up production centres in their own homes as well as growing their own food, supplying goods, not only for their own needs but also to their own settlements and perhaps beyond.[1085] The 'urban-rural dichotomy' with its strict separation between royal service men and those living in the rural communities led Schloen to support the 'patrimonial household model' discussed below.[1086]

In Egypt, the king owned all the land and resources of Egypt and there was no direct equivalent of the private sector in Ugarit.[1087] The king made gifts of land to the temples and those members of the administration and military that had served him well.[1088] In return, taxes collected by the treasury, were paid in kind to the king.[1089] Over time, temples became increasingly wealthy and from the MK, temple land was allocated to workers who in return paid taxes in grain and other commodities.[1090] The Wilbour Papyrus, indicates that this tax varied from 1.5 sacks/aroura for non-apportioned land to 5 sacks/aroura for ordinary land (apportioned land).[1091] As Katary points out, the terminology we possess for describing the status of smallholders, '... is abysmally inadequate.'[1092] As the NK progressed, kingship weakened and the independence of the temples increased, the rights to work specific plots of land remained within the family from generation to generation. Katary considers these smallholders were 'virtual owners' or 'private possessors'. Their land-tenure may have been, for all practical purposes, the same as private ownership even though the land technically belonged to the state.[1093]

In summary, Egypt does not fit comfortably into the two-centre model as developed by Diakonoff, Liverani, and Heltzer. They based their ideas on the economic structures of city-states such as Ugarit that had a single strong bureaucratic state urban centre (palace) supported by an agrarian 'communal-private' village based sector.[1094] In contrast, Egypt's unique topography with the long narrow Nile Valley was atypical of the other 'hydraulic civilisations'.[1095] Egypt's unification in *c.*2950 B.C. meant that without the threat of civil war, it had no need to develop fortified independent city-states. Instead, the country was divided into nomes each with its own provincial capital that was small compared with the population they administered. These centres were supported by the agrarian output of dispersed hamlets and villages along the Nile.[1096] Equally, the textual evidence of private ownership of land although limited suggests that it is inappropriate to classify Egypt with a private sector and a state sector as envisaged by Diakonoff. The two-centre model therefore oversimplifies the complexity of the state/religious/social/economic structure of NK Egypt.

The patrimonial household model (PHM)

The German sociologist Max Weber, dissatisfied with the ideas of Marx, regarded the various states of the ancient Near East and Pharaonic Egypt, as 'patrimonial' rather than bureaucratic.[1097] Schloen built on the work of Weber and developed his own patrimonial household model.[1098]

[1082] Diakonoff 1982: 32–33 and Heltzer 1976: 63–65, 73–74, 77–79.

[1083] Diakonoff 1982: 46–47 from evidence based on Old Babylonian textual evidence. Heltzer 1976: 79, though accepting that councils of elders existed in Ugarit, he notes that textual evidence is limited and he has a cautious view on their exact role.

[1084] Kemp 2006: 329.

[1085] Heltzer 1996b: 183 and Schloen 2001: 105.

[1086] Weber 1978: 1217ff, Finley 1977, and Schloen 2001: 101–104.

[1087] Katary 2007: 185.

[1088] Kemp 2006: 254–256.

[1089] See Málek 1986 for the OK bequests but the same pattern followed throughout the Pharaonic Period.

[1090] Papyrus Harris I demonstrates the wealth of the temples of Amun, Ra, Ptah, and other smaller temples that had accrued 295,000 ha equivalent to up to 18% of all available cultivable land (Katary 1989 193–194). Also see Janssen 1979a for the role of the temple in the NK economy.

[1091] Eyre 1994a: 120. The Wilbour Papyrus, dated to immediately after the reign of Ramesses III, is in two parts. Text A relates to 2,800 plots in Middle Egypt and Text B to crown land. Each plot identifies the institution owner and revenues due (Katary 1999: 62–65). Eyre describes how in the papyrus, temple holdings were registered under either 'ordinary' or 'apportioned' (*pš*) land. One temple was responsible for apportioned land that they did not own and they managed it on a share basis with another institution. They sub-contracted its cultivation to *rwḏw* 'representatives/managers/agents' who managed it but were not necessarily cultivators themselves. The income generated was as low as 7.5% of the standard assessment of ordinary land. The temple's other *pš* land (commonly plots of 3, 5 or 10 aroura) were allocated to tenants or beneficiaries comprising, 'minor officials, soldiers, craftsmen, specialists or their women and heirs', implying that the plots were transferable or heritable'. Larger plots belonged to high-ranking individuals who employed cultivators to work the land on their behalf. The tenure involved a share or partnership between the temple and the land-holder, based on a division of harvest. The assessment of dues for these lands was very low: only 1.5 *khar* per aroura, against 5 *khar* for ordinary land, in addition only a fraction of the size of each plot was assessed (Eyre 1994a: 119–122).

[1092] Katary 1999: 66–67, Footnotes 8–10.

[1093] Katary 1999: 66.

[1094] Diakonoff 1972: 43, Heltzer 1976, and Liverani 1989.

[1095] Butzer 1976 clearly demonstrates the differences between the basin irrigation agriculture of the ancient Egyptians driven by the inundation and the canal irrigation agriculture practiced by the city-states along the Euphrates and the Tigris.

[1096] Trigger 1985: 347–348. Egypt became united under the kingship of the ruler of Tjeni, more commonly known as Narmer (Wilkinson 2010: 25–27).

[1097] Weber 1978 [1922]: 1006–1110 and Schloen 2001: 51, Footnote 5.

[1098] Schloen: 50–53, 255–316.

Weber and Schloen rejected Marx's assertion that the political interests of Marx's 'classes' were derived from their relationship to production.[1099] Schloen, used the concept of the 'house of the father', which he considers was and still is today a 'root metaphor' common across the Near East.[1100] Schloen's patrimonial household model, differs from the two-sector model because he rejects polarised structural divisions between town and country, 'there is no "free" sector of independent proprietors who enjoy a separate conceptual and legal status from that of "nonfree" palace dependents,' as proposed by Diakonoff in his two-sector model.[1101] He saw no fundamental differences between state taxation and smaller-scale reciprocal and redistributive economic exchanges that were rooted in personal social relationships. This is because he believed that governmental administration was effected through personal relationships based on a household model rather than through an impersonal bureaucracy.[1102] The main characteristics of patrimonialism are that the head of the 'clan' would hierarchically divide his land between clan members as a father would divide assets within a family household. In return, there was a collective obligation by the 'dependants' to satisfy his material and political needs.[1103]

A patrimonial government therefore is one where the relationship between the ruler and his officials is dependent on paternal authority and filial dependence.[1104] Schloen's model has the ruler at the apex of an integrated hierarchical socio-economic system with his subjects whose, '... "household" domains are smaller in scale but similar in structure ...' to the king's domain.[1105] Fleming defines this structure as a pyramidal matrix of 'nested' households loyal to the king.[1106] These household domains are commonly located in one geographic area but can spread across both town and country.[1107] Central to Schloen's thinking is that in a 'kin' based society there is no conflict of interest between rural and urban sectors because the household extends across all boundaries. The patrimonial head of the 'household' is unencumbered by rules created and administered by bureaucrats and his power is limited only by tradition or competing powers.[1108] The patrimonial household model is essentially substantive in nature and fits well into Karl Polanyi's vision of the ancient economy. In a patrimonial society, the law exhibits 'substantive' values based on traditional precedents rather than a formally rationalised legal code.[1109] Laws reflected the traditional value of obedience of the family to the patriarch and his reciprocal obligation to care for his 'household'.[1110] Schloen sees no requirement for formal markets in a patrimonial society as the flow of commodities circulated via redistribution and reciprocity.[1111]

The hierarchical administrative structure of Egypt is well suited to the patrimonial household model. Weber described Egypt as a, 'single tremendous *oikos* ruled patrimonially by the Pharaoh.'[1112] The housing in Amarna graduated in size according to status and this hierarchical structure had many different levels of economic and social dependence, possibly indicative of a patrimonial society. Its suburbs show signs of contiguous groups of workers houses, which Kemp suggests belonged to a family network.[1113] Excavations of the larger houses in Amarna show a clustering of workers' houses around those of the nobles probably sharing the wells and grain silos.[1114] The MK Heqanakht letters gives an example of how a powerful patrimonial head of a household managed his assets and dependants. It demonstrates that his farms were run as a single-family economic entity under his leadership as the 'household father'.[1115]

In the NK, the king had a dual role. He was the divine son of the supreme solar deity Amun-Ra and the ruler who provided the authority and stability to overcome conflicting interests between the state and temple organisations.[1116] Egyptian religion reinforced the authority of the father-son relationship. The king maintained the divine cult of his father Amun-Ra and in all non-royal families the oldest son had the responsibility of maintaining his father's mortuary cult. The ancestral *ka* was passed down from father to son and on death each family member rejoined the ancestral *ka* showing a continuity through the generations of the father-son relationship that applied to both the king and his non-royal subjects.[1117]

[1099] Schloen 2001. Schloen's criticism of orthodox Marxism is that it minimises the importance of social relationships, and associated religious and political symbols, and over emphasises the importance of economic factors and production (Weber 1978 [1922]: 515–517, 1091 and Schloen 2001: 49–50, and 66. For a critical review of Schloen's PHM model and in particular Schloen's criticism of Marx AMP, see Monroe 2002: 904–907.

[1100] Schloen 2001: 51. Lehner 2000: 275–353 similarly applied the PHM to ancient Egypt, attempting to verify it with textual and archaeological sources.

[1101] Schloen 2001: 65 referring to Diakonoff 1982.

[1102] Schloen 2001: 64–65.

[1103] Weber 1978 [1922]: 1022.

[1104] Bendix 1977: 360.

[1105] Schloen 2001: 65.

[1106] Fleming 2002: 75–76.

[1107] Schloen 2001: 108–116, 136–141 reviews Islamic and Israeli ethnographic town and country planning in his interpretation of LBA Ugarit.

[1108] Weber 1978 [1922]: 1006–1007.

[1109] Schloen 2001: 76 citing Weber 1978 [1922]: 641 asserted that patrimonial societies approached all legal questions either from the viewpoint of political expediency [practical rationality] or substantive [value-rational] justice.

[1110] Schloen 2001: 65, 77.

[1111] Schloen 2001: 79.

[1112] Weber 1978 [1922]: 1013.

[1113] Kemp 1991: 308.

[1114] For example, the residence of the high priest Panehesy is surrounded by a 'village' of small houses (Kemp 2008: 36).

[1115] Allen 2002.

[1116] His supreme authority had weakened by the Third Intermediate Period (*c.*1069 B.C.) with a changing relationship with civil government, the army, and the increasing economic and political power of the temples (O'Connor: 1983: 229-242). However in the Late Period much of royal authority was regained (Lloyd 1983).

[1117] The *kȝ*, which had no physical form, had connotations of reproduction and it was passed from father to child at the moment of conception and represented a continuous link with past generations (Taylor 2001: 18–20).

Egyptian laws were not an extension of state bureaucracy but were guided by custom and tradition following patrimonial values and codes of behaviour based on the concept of *maat*.[1118] There was no specialist body responsible for the administration of law and it seems that anyone with authority could be called upon to make legal decisions. For minor offences and disputes, judgement was made by local courts (*kenbet*) whose members, called magistrates, came from the town or village.[1119] Although there were administrative centres along the Nile and a prime religious centre at Thebes, city-states as found across the Near East did not develop in Egypt.

In summary, the economy of Egypt in the NK remained essentially substantive in nature with material wants satisfied through reciprocity, redistribution, and administered trade based on the authority of 'the father'. All these characteristics are relevant to Weber and Schloen's concept of patrimonialism. The patrimonial household model is useful when examining and interpreting the socio-economic processes of LBA Egypt.

A world-systems perspective of the LBA Eastern Mediterranean

Wallerstein proposes that there is a world-system interconnected by a nexus of relationships based on economic exchange. The economic strength of the participants defines their position within the world-system. Wallerstein developed this approach to explain the position of the third world in the twentieth century A.D.[1120] His model has been adapted by scholars to interpret the economic relationship of ancient cultures. In this section, the 'world-systems' perspective is employed to analyse the quantitative data for Egypt and Cyprus from Chapters 2–5 in order to determine patterns of core/periphery relationships within the LBA Eastern Mediterranean. For this period, interregional connectivity was high, driven principally by the widespread demand for tin and copper, with goods moving in the opposite direction to pay for them. Also traded were luxury goods, symbols of status for the élite and the emerging 'sub-élite.'

In Wallerstein's model the core exploits the periphery states for raw materials and goods making them passive and dependent satellites.[1121] In this relationship, the ruling élites of the cores become net consumers of the resources from the rest of the world-system.[1122] The peripheries that supply resources to the core are politically weak, with a small ruling élite and a large peasant class.[1123] Semi-periphery states have economic relationships that lie between a core and a periphery. In this role, they moderate the cores by acting as political and geographical buffers that integrate the core and periphery into a single world-system.[1124] Wallerstein used a range of criteria to identify the relationship of certain factors within a world-system, such as the complexity of economic activities, the strength of the state machinery, and cultural integrity. The relationship between them was not static but reflected the changing nature of the trade itself and the social changes of the societies engaged in that trade.[1125] Wallerstein believed peripheral élites had less flexibility to choose trading partners, as economic forces would force them to trade with the core.[1126] He observed that periphery and semi periphery areas might have previously been cores and some may have been former peripheral areas that were, 'later promoted, so to speak, as a result of the changing geopolitics of an expanding world-economy.' The boundaries of a world-system are also fluid as they are a function of, '… the state of technology, and in particular of the possibilities of transport and communication within its bounds.'[1127]

Wallerstein specifically excluded pre-capitalist societies from his 'world-systems' approach to interregional relations. He classified pre-capitalist societies as 'world-empires' rather than world-systems because they were based on hegemony to a ruling state. He followed Polanyi's 'centricity' theme and considered that goods moved to the political centre.[1128] Fundamental to his model is that a world-system has to be capitalist in nature because its structure of exploitation and dominance is, unlike earlier imperial systems, economic and not political.[1129] He believed that common economic interests bound together the component regions of a capitalist world-system. New technologies enabled capitalist world systems to develop and operate with a sphere of influence beyond the capabilities of an ancient world empire. Ancient empires employed wasteful, cumbersome, and primitive methods of economic domination.[1130]

[1118] Wisdom texts such as the Maxims of Ptahhotep and the Teaching of Merikare laid out the acceptable forms of behaviour including how to act as a good magistrate (Simpson 1973: 159–176, 180–192).

[1119] Kemp 1983: 83–85 and McDowell 2001: 168–169. There were two other legal bodies. The vizier on behalf of the king judged offences involving the state. For some other offences, the guilt or innocence of the suspect could be decided by divine oracles through consultation with the statues of deities such as the deified Amenhotep I and the god Amun -Ra.

[1120] Wallerstein 1974a and Wallerstein 1974b.

[1121] Kardulias 2007: 55.

[1122] Rowlands 1987: 5.

[1123] Hall 1997: 498.

[1124] Champion 1989: 6.

[1125] Edens 1992: 121.

[1126] Wallerstein 1974a: 349 states, '… the creation of a strong state machinery coupled with a national culture, a phenomenon often referred to as integration, serves both as a mechanism to protect disparities that have arisen within the world-system, and as an ideological mask and justification for the maintenance of these disparities.'

[1127] Wallerstein 1974a: 349.

[1128] Kohl 1996: 145. See earlier discussion on 'centralised redistribution' in Section 6.4.

[1129] Wallerstein 1974b: 391.

[1130] Wallerstein states that in the late fifteenth and early sixteenth century [A.D.], '… there came into existence what we may call a European world-economy. It was not an empire yet it was as spacious as a grand empire and shared some features with it. But it was different, and new. It was a kind of social system the world has not really known before and which is the distinctive feature of the modern world-system. It is an economic but not a political entity, unlike empires, city-states and nation-states … it is a "world-economy" because the basic linkage between the parts of the system is economic.' (Wallerstein 1974a: 15).

Despite Wallerstein's reticence to apply his theory to pre-capitalist societies many historians, archaeologists, and social scientists have applied and modified his world-systems perspective to those societies.[1131] In their view, a world-system approach encourages a wider perspective of chronological and spatial boundaries. For example, Sherratt adds another interpretive dimension to our understanding of the past by linking the Near East (core) with Europe (periphery) over a time horizon of the Neolithic to the Iron Age.[1132] A world-systems perspective of the past helps to identify how long-distance relationships between societies change because of the evolving nature of political and/or trading interconnections.

The core-periphery interrelationship between Egypt, Cyprus, Ugarit, and Central Asia is examined here as they all played pivotal roles in the operation of the LBA Eastern Mediterranean economy.[1133] The following discussion focuses on whether Egypt with its dominant economic strength derived from large harvest surpluses and tribute received from its vassal states, exploited the rest of the Eastern Mediterranean region. Cyprus had three commodities that were in universal demand: copper, wood, and olive oil. Ugarit was a major sea hub and with its maritime strength acted as a conduit for tin and other commodities from Central Asia into the Eastern Mediterranean arena.

The economic strength of Egypt

The scale of the non-basic workforce in the LBA economy of Egypt clearly demonstrates that from a world-systems perspective it was a core. Cores could maximise their wealth as they had the flexibility to choose the location of production sites and maximise their return on investment.[1134] Egypt was in this fortunate position as it could procure copper from Timna in the Sinai that was within its own sphere of influence, or it could import copper via trade, gift exchange, or tribute.[1135] The annual inundation of the Nile ensured that in most years there was a harvest surplus that could be used to support non-basic added-value production of goods and services. The absolute size of the non-basic workforce that could be used for added-value production and state infrastructure investment was approximately 39 times larger than Cyprus (assuming the Egyptian population was 2.2 million and the normalised Cypriot population was 100,000). The larger size of Egypt's non-basic workforce was primarily due to its larger population supported by the size of its harvest surplus.

Section 6.2 demonstrates that the LBA economy for the period 1400–1200 B.C. was not minimalist in scale. On the contrary, Table 6.3 shows that the sum of the basic and non-basic active workers was 1,503,216 and 68,328 for Egypt and Cyprus respectively. The percentage of active non-basic workers to total active workers is 27.1 and 13.2% respectively.[1136] The absolute number of workers dedicated to the non-basic sector shows that the Egyptian economy was 45 times bigger than that of Cyprus and significantly bigger than the other powers of the Eastern Mediterranean.[1137] If the LBA Eastern Mediterranean economy was a fully developed formalist economy, then Egypt would have had such a competitive edge they would have been able, like Wallerstein's capitalist cores, to exploit their size and stifle fair trade. However, this study concludes that the economy of Egypt was essentially substantive in nature and met its exchange needs through gift exchange, tribute, and administered trade, observing the appropriate diplomatic protocols of the day. The only exception to this was the small embryonic market that had developed to support the needs of a small but growing sub-élite sector of the economy.[1138] Although Egypt used its military power to control its vassal states and extracted tribute from them, there is no evidence of economic exploitation as described in Wallerstein's definition of a capitalist core. On the other hand, in terms of economic and political relationships, Egypt can be considered a pre-capitalist core state.

Cyprus and Ugarit in the LBA, semi-peripheries or peripheries?

Cyprus was an island with safe harbours on the west and south-west coasts and was well positioned to take part in trading activities, being only 72 km from Ugarit. The prevailing winds for seven months of the year and favourable currents made Cyprus an ideal interface between the Central and Eastern Mediterranean world-systems (Figure 6.3). At the same time, it was sufficiently remote from the mainland to be isolated from the political and military posturing between Egypt and Ḫatti. The insularity of Cyprus enabled it to maintain its neutrality and at the same time exploit its commercial maritime connectivity.[1139] This made Cyprus an important participant in the interregional trade of the period.[1140] The archaeological record of Cyprus shows that conspicuous consumption in both tomb goods and monumental ashlar

---

[1131] Reynolds 1987, Champion 1989, Chase-Dunn and Hall 1991; 1997, Gills and Frank 1991, and Sherratt 1993. Sceptics include Stein 1998: 220–255, and Schloen 2001.

[1132] Sherratt 1993: 1–57.

[1133] The trading patterns of the LBA suggest that two other world-systems bordered the Eastern Mediterranean. One being the Central Mediterranean, which extended from Sardinia in the West to Crete in the East and encompassed Mainland Greece, Italy and the Adriatic to the North. The other world-system extended from Mesopotamia, Central Asia, south-eastern Arabia, and the Indus (Edens 1992: 118–139).

[1134] Rowlands 1987: 5.

[1135] As demonstrated by the Amarna Letters. The Egyptians also had gold mines in the Eastern Desert stretching from Qena-Qusier to the current Sudanese border (Ogden 2000: 161).

[1136] The percentage of Egyptian non-basic workers to total active workers = 100 × 407,835 ÷ (407,835 + 1,095,381) = 27.1%. For Cyprus this percentage = 100 × 8,991 ÷ (8,991 + 59,337) = 13.2%.

[1137] Ratio active non-basic Egypt workers to Cypriot active non-basic workers = 407,835 ÷ 8,991 = 45

[1138] Covered in Section 6.4.

[1139] Cyprus was not totally immune from periods of social unrest caused by war as illustrated in EA 35 when the king of Alašia complains, '... he has slain all the men of my country, and there is not a (single) copper-worker.' (Morran 1992: 107, Text BM 29788: 10–15). For a discussion on the location of Alašia see Merrillees 1987 and Merrillees 1995.

[1140] Knapp 2008: 24.

buildings increased significantly in the transition between the LBA and EIA (1250–1150 B.C.). This seems at odds with world-systems theory that proposes peripheries are exploited for raw materials. However, the widespread demand for copper and its island status that gave it protection from land states, suggest that the island had a position of economic strength greater than its small population would suggest. This would indicate that the economy had grown to the status of a semi-periphery with the potential to grow into a core.[1141] The events of the widespread destruction by the 'Sea Peoples' combined with internal collapse of LBA palace civilisation in the first part the twelfth century B.C., created an Eastern Mediterranean wide economic depression.[1142] This curtailed any progress that Cyprus might have made to become a core in its own right. On balance, in the LBA, Cyprus should be considered a semi-periphery.

Ugarit may also have been a semi-periphery as it held a unique, strategic, geographic, and political position in the Eastern Mediterranean. Hegemony passed from Egypt to Ḫatti *c.*1365 B.C. and Ugarit, capitalising on the relative peace of the period provided a strategically important semi-autonomous buffer zone between the two states, Egypt and Ḫatti, and the rising power of the Assyrians to the east.[1143] Ugarit became a focus of trade by becoming the main conduit of tin, copper, and other commodities into the wider Mediterranean arena.[1144] It had a good geographic position with well-protected harbours and Ugarit's large merchant fleet was capable of travelling to any part of the Central and Eastern Mediterranean. Texts, and artefacts found in the harbour warehouses indicate a wide range of other goods imported and exported through the port of Mahadou.[1145] Ugarit's wealth was not limited to maritime trade; it was located on the intersection of two major trade routes through which it operated a lucrative 'caravan' trade with the Mesopotamian and Anatolian markets.[1146] The east-west route carried tin from Central Asia and the north-south route provided direct land access to the kingdom of Ḫatti; both gave Ugarit considerable trading advantage over other ports along the Levantine coast.[1147] Ugaritic-Hittite trade was financed through a 'commercial bank' in Ḫattušas, the capital city of Ḫatti.[1148] Ugarit's strategic location with land and sea access, evidence of the trade with the whole of the Eastern Mediterranean, and the importance of the goods traded, mean that Ugarit like Cyprus was a semi-periphery.

Multiple cores in the Near East LBA world-system

Although Egypt was by far the largest economy in the Eastern Mediterranean world-system and remained so until the end of Roman-Egypt, other cores rose and fell throughout the LBA. The most significant of these was the kingdom of Ḫatti, which was at its height of military and economic power between 1400–1350 B.C. Ḫatti's wealth was based on the rich farming land of the central high plateau of Anatolia. With adequate rainfall in the spring growing season, harvests were large. Central Anatolia also had dense forests that provided timber for shipping and building. The Anatolian plateau provided rich metal resources of copper, iron, tin, gold, and silver. Although landlocked, Ḫatti did have access to imported goods through the port of Ura on the coast of Cilicia and from the coastal ports of Ugarit. Hittite and Ugaritic sources show that the port of Ura was a major commercial outlet for goods from central Anatolia.[1149]

As Wallerstein observed, the core/periphery relationship between states can change. By 1300 B.C. the Mitanni (southern Anatolia and Northern Syria) was a waning power and had lost its economic and political influence in the Near East and although it was once a core it lost

[1141] See Keswani 2004 for her findings on the significance of Cypriot funerary evidence for changes in élite conspicuous consumption in this period.

[1142] Younger 2007: 140–142.

[1143] The king of Ugarit (Niqmaddu) under the hegemony of the Hittites, paid annual tribute of 20 (Hittite) minas and 20 shekels of gold to the Hittite king (Ŝuppiluliumaš). In addition, he supplied a number of gold and silver vessels, pieces of clothing, and quantities of red and blue purple wool (Astour 1981: 20). However, texts show that the kings of Ugarit had a high degree of autonomy. An edict of Ŝuppiluliumaš increased Ugarit's kingdom by *c.*1000 sq. km to *c.*3225 sq. km, mainly at the expense of the vanquished Mukiŝ. The newly acquired land comprised valuable forests (1000 sq. km) with the rest of the land being rich farmland (Astour 1981: 21).

[1144] Tin is mentioned in six texts from Ugarit (Heltzer 1977: 203). Also see Linder 1981: 37 for textual evidence of requests for imports of copper by sea.

[1145] Yon 1994: 421–427. Ugarit in the LBA had maritime trading relationships with Byblos, Tyre, and Akko (Heltzer 1977: 209). For a comprehensive review of the texts relating to the flow of commodities and luxury goods into and out of Ugarit in the thirteenth century B.C. see Singer 1999: 653–678. Main exports were dyed wool, linen garments, oil, *alun*-stone, lead, copper, and added-value bronze objects. Some of these products were probably imported and then sold on with a increase in price (Singer 1992: 657–658). Texts show male and female slaves, horses, fabrics, textiles and oil were imported (Yon 1994: 426).

[1146] Ugarit commanded the caravan route from the coast, through the Amuq plain to Aleppo, which connected to the caravan route to Carchemish via Emar. Carchemish trade moved up and down the Euphrates to Babylon or by another caravan route eastwards to Assyria through the Upper Khabur region. A major caravan route ran north to central Anatolia taking advantage of north-south alignment of the Syrian mountains and principal rivers. It crossed the Orontes at the site of Antioch, bypassing the eastern side of Mount Casius, over the Beilān pass in south-east Turkey before traversing the Taurus mountains using the Old Assyrian caravan route through the Eyerbel Pass (Astour 1995). Also see Ökse 2007 for ancient mountain routes connecting central Anatolia to the Upper Euphrates Region.

[1147] Ugarit had its main harbour, Mahadou, 1.5 km. from Ras Shamra and a number of smaller harbours north and south. Ugarit had 10 ports in total attested by a range of evidence: textual, archaeological, surviving Ugarit place names, and patterns of Ugarit settlements (Astour 1970: 113–115). One of these, Rešu close to Ras Shamra, was a major centre for the production of purple dye made from murex shells (Astour 1970: 115–116 and van Soldt 1990: 345–347). For the relationship of Rešu to Ras Shamra see van Soldt 2005: 142–144.

[1148] Astour 1981: 22, Footnote 106.

[1149] The Hittite capital Ḫattušas was landlocked making it vulnerable to siege but its empire created a buffer zone with access to the Mediterranean at Ugarit. It is thought that Ura provided an alternative outlet to the Mediterranean (Heltzer 1977: 209 and De Martino 1999). The site of the port of Ura has not been conclusively identified. Albright 1961: 44, Footnote 42 suggests that its location is at or near Silifke (classical Seleucia) in the delta of the Calycadnus River in western Cilicia. Beal 1992: 69 proposes that the port was on the Cilician coast perhaps close to modern Gilindere (classical Kelenderis) on the southern coast of Turkey.

this position. On the other hand, the rising power of Assyria (modern day Iraq) is an example of a state progressing economically and militarily into a future core in the EIA.

LBA world-systems interactions

I consider that from a world-systems perspective the LBA Eastern Mediterranean world-system had two cores, Egypt and Ḫatti. Wallerstein paints a bleak picture of 'cores' ruthlessly exploiting peripheries. This does not seem to be so in the LBA, where political and trading alliances were made between peripheries, semi-peripheries, and a number of overlapping core regions, not necessarily through the threat of force, but through mutual benefit to both parties.[1150] In modern world-systems, the peripheries suffer from a technology gap in military, agrarian, and industrial terms compared with the affluent cores. In contrast, in antiquity this was not the case because technology was in an early stage of development and processes were still dependent on manual labour. Peripheries in the LBA had well established craft skills in metallurgy, shipbuilding, weapons production, mining, textiles, ceramics, and irrigation. The Amarna letters show that vassal states were able to write critical and demanding letters to the rulers of the cores indicating a degree of independence rather than one of exploitation. Kohl is correct in preferring the term 'interdependencies' rather than 'dependencies' when referring to pre-capitalist components of a world-system.[1151]

Cyprus was a semi-periphery due to the demand for its natural resources, which gave it an economic ranking considerably above that expected from an area with a low population. By the end of the LBA, Ugarit fulfilled Wallerstein's criteria for a semi-periphery, being wealthy from trade by land and sea. The vassal states of Egypt and those of Ḫatti were peripheries and they were the main providers of tribute to the two cores.

The world-systems theory is flexible enough to cater for overlapping world-systems. If a periphery was the source of a commodity required by two world-systems then its bargaining power and influence would increase. For example, Central Asia provided tin to the Eastern Mediterranean and another world-system incorporating Mesopotamia, Southern Arabia, and the Indus and as such should be considered as a semi-periphery.

In summary, the contribution that a world-systems approach adds to our understanding of the LBA is that by definition, if a dominant economic core existed, its economy could not be minimalist in scale. However, demonstrating that a core existed does not mean that its economy was formalist. It does show however that the minimalist *oikos* model is inappropriate for the LBA Eastern Mediterranean.

[1150] Kohl 1996: 148.

[1151] Kohl 1996: 149.

6.6 *Final observations*

Economy

Chapters 2–5 of this study have quantified the manpower required to support the basic needs of Egypt and Cyprus in the LBA. The results show that both Egypt and Cyprus had a significant proportion of their population involved in agrarian activities and any non-basic activity was dependant on the harvest surplus. Egypt had a lower percentage of agrarian workers than Cyprus, principally due to the higher grain yields grown on fertile basin land. Consequently, the workforce available for the production of added-value goods for trade, the conspicuous consumption of the élite or for investment in state infrastructure projects, was significantly greater in Egypt.

Cost

It is often considered that the concept of cost could not exist in ancient economies without a fully developed monetary and cost accounting systems. However, this study has shown that all processes have a cost in terms of the people involved and the need for them to be fed. This applies to the use of slaves, as they also needed food. Relating everything to food consumed by worker and his family is an effective measure of cost. Using this simple measure allows an assessment of value across a range of goods by relating them to the amount of the food to feed the worker. Across the LBA Eastern Mediterranean equivalences developed for added-value goods, metals, animals, and foodstuffs that could be related to basic staples, principally grain. The quantity of food required to be supplied as rations for a worker producing the good and his family is the cost of that good.

Modelling

It is possible to estimate the cost of ancient production processes in terms of the resources required, using process modelling that is complementary and symbiotic with traditional disciplines. When combined with archaeological, ethnographic, experimental, archaeo-scientific, epigraphic, and textual evidence, it provides a powerful analytical tool. This can challenge established thinking of ancient processes and give insight into the reality of what outcomes were achievable.

The LBA economy can be modelled in terms of the manpower required to support the major economic sectors that make up a regions economy: agriculture, cloth, building, bronze, and added-value manufacturing. Examining the economy from the perspective of satisfying unlimited needs with finite manpower resources that have to be supported by the harvest surplus, identifies the decision-making constraints within which the ruling LBA élites operated.

Trade

In the LBA there was a significant increase in trade, and this accelerated in the LBA/EIA transition in response to several factors. As bronze became the metal of choice, those regions without indigenous copper and tin reserves had to acquire them from other sources. This meant that they had to develop other products and services to exchange for the metals. Support services such as boat builders, the provision of safe harbours, secure warehousing, and the sailors themselves, all facilitated an increase in the scale of the economy through increased interregional trade.

Marine technology developed to an extent that enabled fleets of boats to sail on open sea rather than singletons tramping around dangerous rocky coasts. Improvements in storage containers enabled the transport of organic goods and delicate pottery. With these improvements in sea vessels, portage, and reliability, a merchant class developed with differing degrees of independence from state control. Trading between merchants from different regions was facilitated by metrology systems that could be related to each other because they were based on rational mathematical progressions. This meant that a merchant from one region could mutually agree values with a merchant from another region. In the LBA there was a growing sub-élite, socio-economic group who wanted to show their wealth through the ownership of their own 'brands' of luxury goods. This demand was met by entrepreneurial sailors trading on the back of élite-administered trade.

The importance of LBA Cyprus

Cyprus had unlimited supplies of copper that in the LBA could be easily exploited from the secondary enrichment zones in the Troodos mountains. This copper had significantly lower production costs than the deep mining carried out in the Egyptian Timna mines. Textual evidence and scientific tests on the provenance of copper oxhide ingots around the Central and East Mediterranean confirm that Cyprus was the major exporter of copper at the end of the LBA. Kassianidou argues that the two LBA tin ingots found in Haifa with Cypro-Minoan scripts could indicate that Cyprus administered and distributed tin ingots within the Eastern Mediterranean trading network, centred in the harbour towns of south-west Cyprus.[1152]

Cyprus was ideally positioned, making it pivotal in Eastern and Western Mediterranean trading; it was an island, which gave it some protection from invasion and it was surrounded with favourable currents and winds. It had commercial connections with entrepreneurial merchants from Ugarit and other city-states along the Levantine littoral.[1153] As a result, in spite of its small population it 'punched above its weight' in economic terms and held a strategic position in the metals trade that gave it considerable influence.[1154] It is however not clear how Cyprus was able to meet the demand for copper with such a low population, most of whom were required to produce agricultural and domestic supplies. One possibility is that it used migrant miners and smelters who were fed with grain imports acquired in exchanged for the copper. If this were so then the transport of grain by sea would have made the level of goods circulating the Eastern Mediterranean even greater in the LBA than previously thought.

[1152] Kassianidou 2003.

[1153] Karageorghis 1996, Kassianidou 2003, and Kassianidou 2005.

[1154] As discussed, for this study the population of LBA Cyprus has been normalised to 100,000 to enable direct comparisons to be made with NK Egypt. It is likely but unknown, that the actual population was less than a cohort of 100,000.

The scale and nature of the LBA economy

This study does not support Polanyi's assertion that in ancient societies all workers were supported by rations from centrally controlled granaries. It would be impractical in both the number of granaries required and the logistics of moving crops from the fields to the granaries and then redistributing them back. In Egypt, it is more likely that only the rations for the non-basic workers and their families were stored and redistributed.

The findings of this study clearly show that the scale of production in LBA Eastern Mediterranean in staples, metals, and added-value goods was not 'minimalist' in scale as proposed by Bücher, Weber, and Finley. They also demonstrate that the '*oikos* model' is not appropriate for LBA Eastern Mediterranean. On balance, this study supports the assertion of S. Sherratt that we should view the LBA as a period that was a '... short-lived flowering of international trade as a late second millennium B.C. version of globalisation.'[1155]

NK Egypt was essentially substantive in nature with some characteristics of an embryonic formalist economy satisfying the demand for sub-élite goods. The size of Egypt's population as well as the high agriculture yields made it the largest economic power in the Eastern Mediterranean. As a result, it could afford to satisfy its needs for tin and luxury goods without needing to develop a market economy. Its élite sector was immune from the pressures of 'cost' and could remain aloof from the 'market' and remain autonomous and semi-isolated. These factors and the reliability of surplus food supplies for most years, meant that Egypt retained its traditional administrative processes. In contrast, by the LBA/EIA transition Cyprus, Ugarit, and other city-states along the Levantine littoral had pockets of independent embryonic pockets of private enterprise. Market opportunities were identified, small in scale admittedly, but entrepreneurs found solutions to fill them. This demonstrates a fundamental characteristic of homo sapiens which is to challenge the status quo in pursuit of self interest.

The existence of certain aspects of a market economy operating within an otherwise substantive world shows there is a need to go beyond the terminology and arguments used by committed substantivists and formalists to explain the complexities of the transition period when a society is in the first stages of market development. It is too limiting to use a rigid set of definitions for ancient economies that were fluid, complex, and diverse.

[1155] Sherratt 2000: 89 and Sherratt 2003.

Appendix

AGCLAC summaries of yield rates and references used in this study
Reports 2.1–2.8

Reference	Area	Barley kg/ha	Wheat kg/ha	Pulses kg/ha	Lentils kg/ha
Gallant 1991: 77, Table 4.7	Achaia	695.5	642.7	743.5	594.5
Gallant 1991: 77, Table 4.7	Aitolia	666.9	666.4	650.9	537.2
Gallant 1991: 77, Table 4.7	Argolid	733.4	624.5	542.7	498.1
Gallant 1991: 77, Table 4.7	Arkadia	598.7	470	657.2	410.9
Gallant 1991: 77, Table 4.7	Athens	793.7	629.1	630.9	539.9
Gallant 1991: 77, Table 4.7	Evros	990.3	871.9	638.4	611.2
Gallant 1991: 77, Table 4.7	Evvoia	552.7	540	602.7	444.5
Gallant 1991: 77, Table 4.7	Crete	902.6	748.1	624.7	578.8
Gallant 1991: 77, Table 4.7	Epiros	563.6	536.4	478.7	589.1
Gallant 1991: 77, Table 4.7	Kalamata	650.9	571.8	659.1	482.7
Gallant 1991: 77, Table 4.7	Kavala	907	903.2	976	608.1
Gallant 1991: 77, Table 4.7	Kefalonia	698.1	754.8	876.4	718.8
Gallant 1991: 77, Table 4.7	Kerkyra	529.1	581	521.9	547.7
Gallant 1991: 77, Table 4.7	Korinth	708.8	611	537.2	484.6
Gallant 1991: 77, Table 4.7	Kozani	899	720	691.4	449.4
Gallant 1991: 77, Table 4.7	Lakonia	627.7	646.4	621.8	453.6
Gallant 1991: 77, Table 4.7	Lesbos	689.2	662.6	539.6	465.1
Gallant 1991: 77, Table 4.7	Phthiotis	650	668.2	460.9	370
Gallant 1991: 77, Table 4.7	Thessaly	1097.1	889.5	886.9	504
Gallant 1991: 77, Table 4.7	Zakynthos	689.1	733.6	1098.2	924.6
Garnsey 1988: 95, fn 19.	Athens/Boeotia	789	697		
Hopkins 1983: 91 data 1922-38	Greece 1922-1928	620	620		
Tsouderos 1919: 132	Mainland Greece		742		
Gomme 1933: 31	Attica-Boeotia	650	350		
Gomme 1933: 31	Attica-Boeotia	660	290		
Gomme 1933: 31	Laconia	590	560		
Gomme 1933: 31	Laconia	700	770		
Gomme 1933: 31	Messenia	690	710		
Gomme 1933: 31	Messenia	770	730		
Gomme 1933: 31	Larissa	640	400		
Gomme 1933: 31	Larissa	520	400		
Gomme 1933: 31	Trikkala	270	350		
Gomme 1933: 31	Trikkala	610	560		

Report 2.1: Yield rates (kg/ha) for crops grown on Greek farms using traditional farming practices.

Reference	Area	Barley kg/ha	Wheat kg/ha	Pulses kg/ha	Lentils kg/ha
Simms and Russell 1997: Table 1	Petra L. Wadi Beida		900		900
Simms and Russell 1997: Table 1	Petra L. Wadi Beida		1,580		1580
Simms and Russell 1997: Table 1	Petra L. Wadi Beida		660		660
Simms and Russell 1997: Table 1	Petra L. Wadi Beida		400		400
Simms and Russell 1997: Table 1	Petra L. Wadi Beida		330		330
Simms and Russell 1997: Table 1	Petra L. Wadi Beida		2,480		
Simms and Russell 1997: Table 1	S. Petra Valley		950		950
Simms and Russell 1997: Table 1	S. Petra Valley		640		640
Adams 1928: Table 13	Palestine 1926		720		720
Steitieh and Smadi 1974: 13, Table 2	Jordan East Bank		690		690
Steitieh and Smadi 1974: 10, Table 1	Tot. Jordan 1957-66		520		520
Zohary 1969: 56	Eastern Galilee		1,000		1000
Gallant 1991: 48	Lebanon		1,460		1460
Gallant 1991: 48	Lebanon		1,520		1520
Gallant 1991: 48	Lebanon		1,560		1560
Mayerson 1955: 55; 1960: 18	Negeb	600	500	600	500
Simpson 1930: 185, Appendix 24	Mandate Palestine	480	630	480	630
Simpson 1930: 177	Israel	600	500	600	500
Avitsur 1972: 214	Iretze (Israel)	600	550	600	550
Weitz 1950: 35	Negeb	250	275	250	
Weitz 1950: 35	Negeb	1,670	1,630	1,670	1,630
Weitz 1950: 35	Negeb	80	870		870
Webley 1972: 173, 175	Tell Gezer, Israel	595		595	
Helms 1981: 187	Northern Jordon	500		500	
Simms and Russell 1997: Table 1	Ras Mu'aesrah	720		720	
Simms and Russell 1997: Table 1	Ras Mu'aesrah	600		600	
Simms and Russell 1997: Table 1	S. Petra Valley	440		440	
Simms and Russell 1997: Table 1	S. Petra Valley	1,350			
Simms and Russell 1997: Table 1	S. Petra Valley	670		670	
Simms and Russell 1997: Table 1	S. Petra Valley	500		500	

Report 2.2: Yield rates (kg/ha) for crops grown on Levantine farms using traditional farming practices.

Reference	Ref	Period	Barley kg/ha
James and Gunn 1962: 115.	Hekenakhte P.	MK	750
James and Gunn 1962: 115.	Hekenakhte P.	MK	1250
Gardiner 1941: 64-66; 1948: 198.	Wilbour P.	*c.*1150 B.C.	1067
Gardiner 1948: 198.	Wilbour P.	*c.*1150 B.C.	534
Rathbone 1991: 242-243.	Middle Egypt	3rd c. A.D.	1242
Rathbone 1991: 242-243.	Middle Egypt	3rd c. A.D.	877
Rathbone 1991: 242-243.	Theadelphia	3rd c. A.D.	1728

Report 2.3: Textual evidence for ancient Egyptian yield rates.

Reference	Year	Barley yield		Wheat yield		Horse bean yield	
		Ardeb per feddan	Kg/ha	Ardeb per feddan	Kg/ha	Ardeb per feddan	Kg/ha
Ross 1889: xix.	19th c. AD		2,088		1,827		
Allbaugh 1953: 267, Table 48	1934-38		1,622				
Adams 1965: 17	1958		1,396		1,132		
Adams 1965: 17	1958		1,025		764		
Hopkins 1983: 91	1925-34				1,710		
Richards 1982: Table 5.2, 145	1920	5.78	1,651	5.02	1,793	4.46	1,646
Richards 1982: Table 5.2, 145	1921	5.71	1,631	4.78	1,707	4.46	1,646
Richards 1982: Table 5.2, 145	1922	5.68	1,623	4.55	1,625	4.44	1,639
Richards 1982: Table 5.2, 145	1923	5.64	1,611	4.98	1,779	4.43	1,635
Richards 1982: Table 5.2, 145	1924	5.44	1,554	4.55	1,625	3.95	1,458
Richards 1982: Table 5.2, 145	1925	5.72	1,634	4.94	1,764	4.45	1,642
Richards 1982: Table 5.2, 145	1926	5.71	1,631	4.57	1,632	3.87	1,428
Richards 1982: Table 5.2, 145	1927	6.0	1,714	5.05	1,804	4.65	1,716
Richards 1982: Table 5.2, 145	1928	5.55	1,586	4.42	1,579	3.8	1,402
Richards 1982: Table 5.2, 145	1929	5.95	1,700	5.28	1,886	4.56	1,683
Richards 1982: Table 5.2, 145	1930	5.74	1,640	4.92	1,757	4.31	1,591
Richards 1982: Table 5.2, 145	1931	5.97	1,706	5.26	1,879	4.17	1,539
Richards 1982: Table 5.2, 145	1932	6.21	1,774	5.62	2,007	4.87	1,797
Richards 1982: Table 5.2, 145	1933	5.95	1,700	5.28	1,886	4.47	1,650
Richards 1982: Table 5.2, 145	1934	5.98	1,709	4.87	1,739	4.09	1,509
Richards 1982: Table 5.2, 145	1935	7.01	2,003	5.56	1,986	4.55	1,679
Richards 1982: Table 5.2, 145	1936	7.22	2,063	5.88	2,100	4.89	1,805
Richards 1982: Table 5.2, 145	1937	7.35	2,100	6.01	2,146	4.94	1,823
Richards 1982: Table 5.2, 145	1938	7.35	2,100	5.88	2,100	4.78	1,764
Richards 1982: Table 5.2, 145	1939	7.55	2,157	6.15	2,196		
Scheidel 2001: 224 citing with full references the 19th c. A.D. yields given in O'Brien 1968, Owen 1969, Rivlin 1961	1844	3.6	1,016	2.77	990		
	1844	4	1,143	3	1,071		
	1872	2.02	577	2.21	789		
	1881/85	2.21	631	3.36	1,201		
	1886/90	3.33	951	3.82	1,364		
Average			**1,764**		**1,850**		**1,634**
95% confidence level			**87**		**82**		**55**
Av. - 95% confidence level			**1,677**		**1,768**		**1,579**
Av. + 95% confidence level			**1,851**		**1,932**		**1,689**
Maximum			**2,157**		**2,196**		**1,823**
Minimum			**1,554**		**1,579**		**1,402**
Standard deviation			**198**		**186**		**123**
Average deviation			**161**		**154**		**93**

Report 2.4: Egyptian crop yield rates from using traditional farming practices textual or basin agriculture records.

Reference	Country/polis	Barley bushels/acre	Wheat bushels/acre	Pulses bushels/acre	Barley kg/ha	Wheat kg/ha	Beans kg/ha
Allbaugh 1953: 267, Table 267	Crete	15	12.8		816	871	0
Allbaugh 1953: 267, Table 267	Albania	19.3	15.6		1,050	1,061	0
Allbaugh 1953: 267, Table 267	Greece	17.6	13.4	9.6	958	912	653
Allbaugh 1953: 267, Table 267	Turkey	20.4	14.7	12.5	1,110	1,000	680
Hillman 1973: 226-227, Appendix 1	Aşvan Turkey				410	630	
Allbaugh 1953: 267, Table 267	Yugoslavia	17.8	16.9	14.7	969	1,150	800
Allbaugh 1953: 267, Table 267	Bulgaria	25	18.8	8.2	1,361	1,279	446
Allbaugh 1953: 267, Table 267	Rumania	12.2	14.4	8.6	664	980	468
Allbaugh 1953: 267, Table 267	Italy	20.2	21.4	4.9	1,099	1,456	267

Report 2.5: Yield rates (kg/ha) for crops grown on north-eastern Mediterranean, Italian, and Balkan farms using traditional farming practices.

Reference	Area	Period	Olives kg/ha	% oil extraction	Olive oil kg/ha	Olive oil litres/ha
Mattingly 1988b: 41.	Southern Spain	2nd Century A.D.	2,500	16	400	465
Melena 1986: 105.	Knossos palace	Linear B Tablets	1,700	16	250	291
Osborn 1987: 45-46.	Greece	Classical period	1,719	16	275	320
Mattingly 1988b: 45.	Tunisia (Sahel)	1970-1980 A.D.	1,700	16	272	316
Mattingly 1988b: 45.	Tunisia (Sfax)	1970-1980 A.D.	2,750	16	440	512
Amouretti 1986: 204.	North Med.	Post 1960 A.D.	2,000	15	300	349
Brun 1987: 208 footnote 30.	Italy	1st Century B.C.	1,000	16	160	186
Rosen 1996: 28, Table 2.	Israel	1930-1940 A.D.	1,875	16	300	349
Allbaugh 1953: 269.	Crete	1930-1940 A.D.	1,375	16	220	256
Allbaugh 1953: 269.	Crete	1930-1940 A.D.	1,563	16	250	291
Allbaugh 1953: 269.	Crete (Hierapetra)	1948-1949 A.D.	2,125	16	340	395
Aschenbrenner: 1972, Table 4.2.	Greece Messenia	1940-1950 A.D.	1,563	16	250	291
Moreno 2007: 65.	Greece (Euonymon)	1940-1950 A.D.	2,120	16	250	291
Hutchinson 1968: 41.	Greece	1930-1940 A.D.	1,125	16	180	209
Hutchinson 1968: 41.	Italy and Turkey	1940-1950 A.D.	938	16	150	174
Bintliff 1974: 634.	Italy and Aegean	1930-1950 A.D.	1,875	16	300	349
Zertal 1996: 310 citing Lavi 1976: 207.	Southern Levant	1970-1980 A.D.	2,500	16	400	465
Heltzer: 1996: 79.	Israel	1940-1950 A.D.	1,200	16	192	223
Heltzer: 1996: 79.	Israel	1940-1950 A.D.	2,550	16	408	474

Report 2.6: Yield rates (kg/ha and litres/ha) for olives and olive oil from textual sources or farms using traditional practices.

Date	ha	Olives production kg	Yield of olives	% Extraction rate olive oil	Olive Oil kg/ha
1985	6,288	11,500,000	1,829	16	293
1986	6,287	12,000,000	1,909	16	250
1987	6,287	8,000,000	1,272	16	275
1988	6,300	18,000,000	2,857	16	457
1989	6,300	9,000,000	1,429	16	229
1990	6,300	10,500,000	1,667	16	267
1991	6,300	7,000,000	1,111	16	178
1992	6,100	19,000,000	3,115	16	498
Average	**6,270**	**11,875,000**	**1,899**	**N/A**	**306**

Report 2.7: Olive oil production in Cyprus for 1985/1988. European Community - International Olive Oil Council project (see Gregoriou, C. 2008 available from http://www.olivebusiness.com/articles/OBGuest/Oth/olives_and_olive_oil_in_cyprus.htm. Nicosia: Agricultural Research Institute) and Charis, G. 1979. The olive tree. Department of Agriculture, Nicosia, Cyprus, Publ. 19/1979.

Agrarian sector/100,088 cohort (Tables 6.1–6.3)	
Size of basic sector	59,337
Number of dependants	12,231
Number of agrarian workers	43,395
Number of agrarian dependants	8,945
Total agrarian workers and dependants	**52,340**
Number of adolescents/adults/farm	6
Number of farms	8,723
Basin inundation labour-rate (man-days/farm)	95
Total man-days expended/100,000 cohort/yr	828,685
Total man-years expended/100,000/cohort/yr	**2,656**

Report 2.8: Workload (man-years) associated with the control of the inundation in basin agriculture.

SHELTER analyses for mud-brick production and construction of domestic and state granaries

Reports 4.1–4.6

Type 1a workers house		
Total length of walls	26.2	m
Wall thickness	0.1575	m
Height of wall	2.5	m
Total volume of mud-brick walls	10.4	m^3
Number of bricks required	2,161	
Man-days to make bricks	57.3	man-days
Man-days to mix mortar, move bricks + mortar, and lay bricks	41.6	man-days
Total man-days to make and lay bricks	98.9	man-days
Man-yrs to build house uplifted for roof, fittings, foundations	0.32	

Type 1b house workers house		
Total length of walls	33.5	m
Wall thickness	0.1575	m
Height of wall	2.5	m
Total volume of mud-brick walls	13.2	m^3
Number of bricks required	2,743	
Man-days to make bricks	72.7	man-days
Man-days to mix mortar, move bricks + mortar, and lay bricks	54.3	man-days
Total man-days to make and lay bricks	127.0	man-days
Man-yrs to build house uplifted for roof, fittings, foundations	0.41	

Type 1c workers house		
Wall thickness of inner walls of type 1c house at Amarna inner walls	0.1575	m
Wall thickness of outer walls of type 1c house at Amarna inner walls	0.1575	m
Total length of inner walls	23.5	m
Height of inner walls	3.5	m
Total length of outer walls	16.5	m
Height of outer walls	2.5	m
Surface area of ancillary brickwork on roof	38.28	m^2
Volume of inner wall	13	m^3
Volume of outhouses' walls and single thick mud-brick walls	6.5	m^3
Volume of ancillary brickwork on the roof	6	m^3
Total volume of mud-brick walls	25.5	m^3
Number of bricks required	5,298	
Man-days to make bricks alone	140.4	man-days
Man-days to mix mortar, move bricks + mortar, and lay bricks	108.9	man-days
Man-days to make and lay bricks	249.2	man-days
Man-yrs to build house uplifted for roof, fittings, foundations	0.8	

Type 1d workers house		
Wall thickness of inner walls of type 1c house at Amarna inner walls	0.1575	m
Wall thickness of outer walls of type 1c house at Amarna inner walls	0.1575	m
Total length of inner walls	23.5	m
Height of inner walls	3.5	m
Total length of outer walls houses	34.5	m
Height of outer walls	2.5	m
Surface area of ancillary brickwork on roof	38.28	m^2
Volume of inner wall	13	m^3
Volume of outhouses' walls and single thick mud-brick walls	13.6	m^3
Volume of ancillary brickwork on the roof	10	m^3
Total volume of mud-brick walls	36.6	m^3
Number of bricks required	7,605	
Man-days to make bricks alone	201.5	man-days
Man-days to mix mortar, move bricks + mortar, and lay bricks	160.4	man-days
Man-days to make and lay bricks	361.9	man-days
Man-yrs to build house uplifted for roof, fittings, foundations	1.16	

Type 2c house: Middle class house		
Wall thickness of inner walls of type 2d house at Amarna outer walls	0.1574	m
Wall thickness of outer walls of type 2d house at Amarna inner walls	0.34	m
Tot. length of inner walls + butressed enclosure wall 2 bricks thick	21.5	m
Height of inner walls	3	m
Total length of outer walls/out houses	27	m
Height of outer walls Kemp 2000: 296.	3	m
Surface area of ancillary brickwork on roof	39	m^2
Volume of inner wall	10.2	m^3
Volume of outhouses' walls and single thick mud-brick walls	27.5	m^3
Volume of ancillary brickwork on the roof	13.3	m^3
Total volume of mud-brick walls	51	m^3
Number of bricks required	10,597	
Man-days to make bricks alone	280.8	man-days
Man-days to mix mortar, move bricks + mortar, and lay bricks	233.3	man-days
Man-days to make/lay bricks uplifted for roof, fittings, foundations etc	514.0	man-days
Man-years to build house uplifted for roof, fittings, foundations	1.64	

Type 2d house: Middle class house		
Wall thickness of inner walls of type 2d house at Amarna outer walls	0.34	m
Wall thickness of outer walls of type 2d house at Amarna inner walls	0.34	m
Tot. length of inner walls + butressed enclosure wall 2 bricks thick	46	m
Height of inner walls	3	m
Total length of outer walls/out houses	38.5	m
Height of outer walls Kemp 2000: 296.	3	m
Surface area of ancillary brickwork on roof	40.14	m^2
Volume of inner wall	46.9	m^3
Volume of outhouses' walls and single thick mud-brick walls	39.3	m^3
Volume of ancillary brickwork on the roof	13.6	m^3
Total volume of mud-brick walls	99.8	m^3
Number of bricks required	20,737	
Man-days to make bricks alone	549.4	man-days
Man-days to mix mortar, move bricks + mortar, and lay bricks	475.5	man-days
Man-days to make/lay bricks uplifted for roof, fittings, foundations etc	1,024.9	man-days
Man-years to build house uplifted for roof, fittings, foundations	3.27	

Report 4.1: Tietze Amarna house designs 1a–2d.

Type 2e house: Senior official house		
Wall thickness of inner walls of type 2e house at Amarna outer walls	0.34	m
Wall thickness of outer walls of type 2e house at Amarna inner walls	0.34	m
Thickness of perimeter walls/outhouses of type 2e house at Amarna	0.1575	m
Tot. length of inner walls + butressed enclosure wall 2 bricks thick	53	m
Height of inner walls	3	m
Total length of outer walls	52.0	m
Height of outer walls Kemp 2000: 296.	3	m
Total length of perimeter walls and outhouses	33.0	m
Height of perimeter walls/out houses	2.5	m
Surface area of ancillary brickwork on roof	65	m^2
Volume of inner wall	54.1	m^3
Volume of outer walls of house	53	m^3
Volume of ancillary brickwork on the roof	10.2	m^3
Total volume of mud-brick for perimeter walls and out buildings	13.0	m^3
Total volume of mud-brick walls	130.3	m^3
Number of bricks required	37,904	
Man-days to make bricks alone	716.4	man-days
Man-days to mix mortar, move bricks + mortar, and lay bricks	903.9	man-days
Man-days to make/lay bricks uplifted for roof, fittings, foundations etc	1,620.2	man-days
Man-years to build house uplifted for roof, fittings, foundations	**5.17**	

Competency index	1.17

Type 3e Palace style		
Total thickness of outer palace walls	0.8	m
Thickness of internal walls of palace excluding central high status room	1.02	m
Wall thickness of high status room	1.02	m
Wall thickness of outhouses	0.34	m
Thickness of enclosure wall	0.4	m
Thickness of ancilliary buildings on the roof	0.3	m
Tot. length of outer palace walls	84.3	m
Total length of internals excluding central high status room	71.1	m
Total length of high status room	27.4	m
Total length of the walls of the out houses	105.7	m
Total length of butressed outer walls	144	m
Total length of all walls	432.5	m
Height of outer palace walls	4	m
Height of palace internal walls excluding central high status room	4	m
Height of high status room	5.4	m
Height of out house walls	2.5	m
Height of butressed outer walls	4	m
Area of ancilliary fixtures on the roofs	92.25	m^2
Volume of outer palace walls	269.8	m^3
Volume of palace internal walls excluding central high status room	290.1	m^3
Volume of high status room	151	m^3
Volume of out house walls	89.9	m^3
Volume of butressed outer walls	230.4	m^3
Volume of ancillary rooms on the roofs	27.7	m^3
Total volume of mud-brick walls	**1058.9**	m^3
Number of bricks required	220,020	
Man-days to make bricks alone	5,829.6	man-days
Man-days to mix mortar, move bricks + mortar, and lay bricks	6,255.6	man-days
Man-days to make and lay bricks	12,085.3	man-days
Man-yrs to build house uplifted for roof, fittings, foundations	**38.49**	man-years

Report 4.2: Tietze Amarna house designs 2e–3e.

Tieze's typology	SEG	100,000 cohort	No. of families = houses	Total population 2,200,000 at	No. of families = houses	Population compound annual growth	No. of families = houses
1a	**5**	66,159	11,027	1,455,498	242,583	1,713	286
1b	**5**	22,053	3,676	485,166	80,861	571	96
1c	**4**	7,500	1,250	165,000	27,500	194	32
1d	**4**	2,500	278	55,000	9,167	65	11
2c	**3**	1,143	191	25,146	4,191	30	5
2d	**3**	381	64	8,382	1,397	10	2
2e	**2**	187	31	4,114	686	5	1
3e	**1**	77	13	1,694	282	2	1
		100,000	**16,528**	**2,200,000**	**366,667**	**2,589**	**434**

Report 4.3: Annual growth of 2,589 individuals in population at the end of the NK and the additional housing required collated by Tietze and SEG groupings.

Social Economic Group (SEG) classification	5b	5a	4b	4a	3	3	2	1	
House design typology (Tietze 1985)	1a	1b	1c	1d	2c	2d	2e	3e	**Total**
Population growth at the end of the NK	1,713	571	194	65	30	10	5	2	**2,590**
Number of families/houses	286	96	32	11	5	2	1	1	**434**
Number of bricks required	618,025	263,301	171,470	82,037	52,264	41,473	37,904	220,020	**1,486,493**
Man-days to make bricks alone	16,375	6,976	4,543	2,174	1,385	1,099	716	5,830	**39,098**
Man-days to mix mortar,and lay bricks	11,903	5,216	3,523	1,731	1,150	951	904	6,256	**31,634**
Total workload (man-days)	28,279	12,193	8,066	3,904	2,535	2,050	1,620	12,085	**70,732**
Total workload (man-years)	**91**	**39**	**26**	**13**	**9**	**7**	**6**	**39**	**230**
Manpower to build domestic housing	**106**	**46**	**30**	**15**	**11**	**8**	**7**	**46**	**269**

Report 4.4: Domestic housing required to support population growth at the end of the NK.

Amarna domestic housing (Kemp 2008: 34 population estimate = 18,240)						
Brick assumptions	Length m	Width m	Height m	Volume m^3	Man-days to make 1000 bricks	No. of bricks laid per day
Amarna domestic North Suburb mean	0.345	0.155	0.09	0.00481275	26.50	368

Social Economic Group (SEG) classification	**5b**	**5a**	**4b**	**4a**	**3**	**3**	**2**	**1**	
House design typology (Tietzy 1985)	1a	1b	1c	1d	2c	2d	2e	3e	Total
Number of families	773	515	258	172	809	270	182	61	3,040
Number of bricks required	1,670,396	1,412,498	1,366,994	1,308,026	8,572,853	5,598,878	6,898,462	13,421,204	40,249,311
Man-days to make bricks alone	44,259	37,425	36,220	34,657	227,146	148,348	130,381	355,607	1,014,043
Man-days to mix mortar,and lay bricks	32,173	27,983	28,084	27,593	188,706	128,378	164,503	381,594	979,013
Total workload (man-days)	76,431	65,408	64,304	62,250	415,852	276,725	294,884	737,202	1,993,056
Total workload (man-years)	**243**	**208**	**205**	**198**	**1,324**	**881**	**939**	**2,348**	6,347
Manpower to build domestic housing	**285**	**244**	**240**	**232**	**1,550**	**1,031**	**1,099**	**2,747**	7,426

Ramesseum external walls	
Thickness m enclosure walls 1	3.1
Thickness main walls 2	2.2
Length m enclosure walls 1	689
Length m main walls 2	268
Height m enclosure walls 1	0.7
Height m main walls 2	5.2
Combined volume of enclosure + walls 2	17,376
Number. of bricks for main walls	2,784,615
Man-days to make 1000 NK Ramesseum wall bricks	34.4
Man-days to make bricks of main walls	95,791
Number of granary wall bricks laid per day	284
A. Man-years to make bricks for the main granary walls	306
B. Man-years to build main walls + uplift for height	297
Total man-years A+B	**603**

Brick assumptions	Length m	Width m	Height m	Volume m^3	Man-days to make 1000	No. of bricks laid per day
Granary walls	0.4	0.12	0.13	**0.00624**	**34.4**	**284**
Vaulted ceilings	0.35	0.21	0.065	**0.0047775**	**26.3**	**371**

Ranesseum granary compartments	
Width m of compartments inside span	3.8
Width m of compartments inside span + one wall hickness	5.7

o. of granary wall bricks laid per day adjusted when working at the top of the w	**142**

Compartment section	A	B	C	D	E	F	G	H
No. of compartments	15	15	6	6	13	9	17	13
Length of compartments m	30	30	54	54	28.5	28.5	19	12
Thickness m	1.3	1.3	1.3	1.3	1.3	1.3	1.3	1.3
Ht. of vertical wall in compartment, 22 bricks high with brick ht 0.0864 m	2.4	2.4	2.4	2.4	2.4	2.4	2.4	2.4
Volume of vertical walls	1322	1322	850	850	1076	718	957	454
Length of span 2.3 times height of vertical walls	5.52	5.52	5.52	5.52	5.52	5.52	5.52	5.52
Volume of spans m^3	3229.2	3229.2	2325	2325	2658.7	1840.6	2317.8	1119.5
Number of bricks in vertical walls of the grain compartments	211,859	211,859	136,218	136,218	172,436	115,065	153,366	72,757
Number of bricks in vault ceilings of the grain compartments	675,919	675,919	486,657	486,657	556,505	385,265	485,150	234,328
Total number of bricks for walls+vaulted ceilings	**887,778**	**887,778**	**622,875**	**622,875**	**728,941**	**500,330**	**638,516**	**307,085**

Total number of compartment wall bricks	1,209,778
Number of compartment vault bricks bricks	3,986,400
Total bricks required	**5,196,178**

Compartment vertical walls	
Total man-days to make bricks for compartment vertical walls	41,617
Total man-years to make bricks for compartment vertical walls	133
Total man-years to build walls +scaffolding uplift	97
Total man-years	**230**
Vault ceiling	
Total man-days required to make bricks	104,843
Total man-years required to make bricks	334
Total man-years to build vaults	489
Total man-years to make bricks, build vault ceiling	**823**
Total man-years to make bricks for main walls + compartments	773
Total man-years to lay bricks for main walls + compartments	883
Workload (man-yrs) to make/lay bricks for main walls+compartments	**1,656**

Man-days required to make 1000 NK Ramesseum wall bricks	34.4	man-days
Number of granary wall bricks laid per day	284	man-days
Man-days required to make 1000 NK Ramesseum wall bricks	26.3	man-days
Number of granary vault bricks laid per day	370.7	man-days

Competency index	**1.17**
Manpower	**1,938**

Report 4.6: The Ramesseum granary at Thebes.

BRONZECALC analyses for bronze demand
Reports 5.1–5.2 and 6.1–6.4

Weight of wood burnt	59.7	kg
Weight of rock extracted	37.4	kg
Weight of wood per kg of tin ore extracted	1.6	kg
Weight of tin ore per kg of tin smelted	50	kg
Weight of wood burnt per kg of tin smelted	80	kg
Total weight of wood required for firesetting to extract sufficient ore to smelt the 1,000 kg of tin on the Ulu Burun	80,000	kg
Weight of usable branches on a tree	38	kg
Number of trees required	2,106	
Number of hours to cut and stack wood	6.5	hrs
Number of man-days to cut wood	1,521	man-days
Workload for lumbering wood required for firesetting	**5**	**man-years**
Carrying capacity of a donkey	75	
Number of donkeys required	1,067	
Number of donkeys in a train	10	
Number of return trips required to carry sufficient wood for firesetting to extract sufficient ore to smelt the 1,000 kg cargo of tin on the Ulu Burun	107	
Speed of donkey train	4.48	
Assume average return distance from the forest to the mine	15	
Time taken for a single return journey plus loading time and feeding/watering donkeys	6.7	
Number of donkey handlers per train	3	
Workload to transport the wood required for firesetting	**1**	**man-year**
Total lumbering and transport workload	**6**	**man-years**

Report 5.1: Workload associated with preparing faggots of wood.

Number of daysa required for arranging faggots and monitoring the fire	4	man-days
Workload carrying water to the firesetting site and pouring water on the heated rock	2	man-days
Total man-days	6	man-days
Weight of tin ore with 2% tin content to smelt 1 kg of tin	50	
Total weight of ore excavated to make the 1,000 kg of tin cargo on the Ulu Burun	50,000	kg
Number of firesetting cycles required	1,337	
Total man-days	8,022	man-days
Firesetting workload	26	man-years
Lumbering and transport workload from Report 5.1	6	man-days
Total workload for firesetting required to extract the ore to produce the 1,000 kg of tin on the Ulu Burun	**32**	**man-years**

Report 5.2: Total workload associated with preparing faggots and firesetting.

	Large	Medium	Small	
Number of bronze plates on a charioteer's corslet	270	44	34	m
	0.001	0.001	0.001	m
	0.071	0.008	0.003	m
	0.03925263	0.0024	0.002	m^3
	0.00075	0.000000845	0.0000002	kg/m^3
	Total weight		**0.61**	**kg**

Report 6.1: Estimated weight (kg) of bronze LBA corselet based on a drawing of a relief in the Mortuary Temple of Ramesses II (Reference Partridge 2002: 55).

CASE STUDY D

Example - Army of Rameses II Numbers deduced from the analysis of the army of Ramesses II by Spalinger 2005: 202-205, 214-230,	Number of soldiers at Kadesh	Border soldiers	Total
Chariot drivers	2,500	500	3,000
Chariot archers	2,500	500	3,000
Archers	5,000	1,500	6,500
Infantry	20,000	7,500	27,500
Total	**30,000**	**10,000**	**40,000**

Ref. Pettinato 1981: 178 relating to Ebla text TM.75.G.1860	%
% loss of metal throughout the manufacturing process	16.8
Assumed % recycling rate	33

Bronze Required kg - High Case	No. of weapons to support army	Unit weight of bronze kg	No. of weapons	Wt. of bronze required kg	Wt. of bronze required with 16.8% lost in the prod'n processs	
Cheekpieces, rings and bits on chariot horses	3,000	1	1	3,000	3,507	Azzaroli 1985. Estimate from drawings in Littauer 1979
Chariot arrow heads	3,000	0.00605	80	1,452	1,697	Yalçin et al 2005: 623 and Wernick 2004
Charioteers' mail corselet	3,000	6.1	1	18,300	21,393	Estimate from drawing in Partridge 2002: 55
Archers' arrow heads	7,500	0.00605	80	3,630	4,243	Yalçin et al 2005: 623
Archers, officers and élite infantry headgear	9,500	0.5	1	4,750	5,553	Estimate using McDermott 2004: 138-139 & Partridge 2002: 57
Spear heads	27,500	0.132	1	3,630	4,243	Yalçin et al 2005: 622
Nails in infantry shields	30,500	0.007	1	214	250	McDermott 2004: 145-146
Battle axes	10,000	1	1	10,000	11,690	Beit-Arieh 1985: 96
Chariot officers' khepesh Swords	2,500	2	1	5,000	5,845	Wernick 2004: 151, Photograph 86.[1]
Officers' daggers	400	0.2	1	80	94	Yalçin et al 2005: 620-621
				50,056	**58,515**	
Ratio estimate of bronze required vis a vis the wt. of copper and tin on the Ulu Burun wreck				**4.4**	**5.1**	
Ratio estimate assuming recycling rate				**2.9**	**3.4**	
Wt. of copper and tin (kg) required assuming recycling				**33,538**		

Annual bronze production rate (kg/yr) amortised over 30 yrs	**1,951**
Egyptian workload (man-yrs) to produce 1 kg of bronze	**0.75**
Amortised annual workload man-yrs	**1,463**

Bronze Required kg - Low Case	No. of weapons to support army of 40,000	Unit weight of bronze kg	No of weapons	Wt. of bronze required kg	Wt. of bronze required with 16.8% lost in the prod'n processs
		Assumed % recycling rate		33	
Cheekpieces, rings and bits on chariot horses	2,500	1	1	2,500	2,923
Chariot arrow heads	2,500	0.00605	80	1,210	1,414
Charioteers' mail corselet	2,500	6.1	1	15,250	17,827
Archers' arrow heads	7,500	0.00605	80	3,630	4,243
Archers, officers and élite infantry headgear	7,500	0.5	1	3,750	4,384
Spear heads	20,000	0.132	1	2,640	3,086
Nails in infantry shields	20,000	0.007	1	140	164
Battle axes	6750	1	1	6,750	7,891
Chariot officers' khepesh Swords	300	2	1	600	701
Officers' Daggers	300	0.2	1	60	70
				36,530	**42,704**
Ratio estimate of bronze required vis a vis the wt. of copper and tin on the Ulu Burun wreck				**3.2**	**3.8**
Ratio estimate assuming 50% recycling rate				**2.144**	**2.5**

[1] Note, as Wernick points out khepesh swords have only been found in burial contexts. The general purpose issue swords would be based on this design but would have been re-cycled.

Report 6.2: Case Study D: Bronze requirement for the standing army of Ramesses II.

CASE STUDY E

Total weight (kg) of copper and tin ingots on the Ulu Burun wreck	11478
% loss of metal throughout the manufacturing process	16.9
Reference Pettinato 1981: 178 relating to Ebla text TM.75.G.1860	

Estimate of the weight of a bronze tips on ploughing ards and hoes						
Percentage farms with a plough	1	5	10	15	20	25
No. of farms per 100,000 population	16,667	16,667	16,667	16,667	16,667	16,667
Population of Egypt in the LBA	2,200,000	2,200,000	2,200,000	2,200,000	2,200,000	2,200,000
Total number of farms in Egypt	366,667	366,667	366,667	366,667	366,667	366,667
Number of ploughs	3,667	18,334	36,667	55,000	73,334	91,667
Wt of bronze plough tip kg	1.18	1.18	1.18	1.18	1.18	1.18
Total weight of bronze plough tips kg	4,327	21,634	43,267	64,900	86,534	108,167
Equivalent. No. of Uluburuns	0.4	1.9	3.8	5.7	7.6	9.5
Equiv. no. uplifted for losses in production	**0.5**	**2.2**	**4.4**	**6.7**	**8.9**	**11.1**

Percentage farms with bronze tip hoe	1	5	10	15	20	25
No. of farms per 100,000 population	16,667	16,667	16,667	16,667	16,667	16,667
Population of Egypt in the LBA	2,200,000	2,200,000	2,200,000	2,200,000	2,200,000	2,200,000
Total number of farms in Egypt	366,667	366,667	366,667	366,667	366,667	366,667
Number of hoes	3,667	18,334	36,667	55,000	73,334	91,667
Wt of bronze plough tip kg	0.51	0.51	0.51	0.51	0.51	0.51
Total weight of bronze plough tips kg	1,870	9,350	18,700	28,050	37,400	46,750
Equivalent. No. of Ulu Buruns	0.17	0.9	1.7	2.5	3.3	4.1
Equiv. no. uplifted for losses in production	**0.2**	**1.1**	**2.0**	**2.9**	**3.9**	**4.8**

Dimensions taken from Bass 1967: 89, figure 102.		
Length of plough tip B48	0.22	m
Width main blade	0.05	m
Mean length socket sections	0.05	m
Mean width	0.022	m
Mean thickness	0.011	m
Volume	0.0001452	m^3
Density of bronze	8100	kg/m^3
Weight of plough tip	1.18	kg
Length of hoe tip B47	0.14	m
Width main blade	0.045	m
Mean length socket sections	0.035	m
Mean width	0.022	m
Mean thickness	0.008	m
Volume	0.00006272	m^3
Density of bronze	8100	kg/m^3
Weight of plough tip	0.51	kg

Report 6.3: Case Study E: Estimated weight of bronze tips on ploughing ards and hoes.

CASE STUDY F

Assumed population of Egypt	2.2	million

Bronze requirement to support craftsmen in LBA Egypt					
Percentage adult males with tools	1	2.5	5	7	10
Number of males aged 16-50	709,610	709,610	709,610	709,610	709,610
Number of craftsmen	7,097	17,741	35,481	49,673	70,961
Assume av. weight of tools kg	1	1	1	1	1
Total weight of tools kg	7,097	17,741	35,481	49,673	70,961
No. of equiv. Ulu Burun cargoes	0.7	1.6	3.1	4.4	6.2
Uplifted for production losses	**0.8**	**1.9**	**3.6**	**5.1**	**7.2**

Assume average weight of tools kg	2	2	2	2	2
Total weight of tools kg	14,194	35,482	70,962	99,346	141,922
No. of equiv. Ulu Burun cargoes	1.3	3.1	6.2	8.7	12.4
Uplifted for production losses	**1.5**	**3.6**	**7.2**	**10.2**	**14.5**

Assume average weight of tools kg	4	4	4	4	4
Total weight of tools kg	28,388	70,964	141,924	198,692	283,844
No. of equiv. Ulu Burun cargoes	2.5	6.2	12.4	17.4	24.8
Uplifted for production losses	**2.9**	**7.2**	**14.5**	**20.3**	**29.0**

Metallurgical glossary

Annealing: Heating the metal object to a suitable temperature before allowing it to slowly cool. In this process, the grains of the metal are re-aligned and grow larger. This relieves stresses built up when artefacts are hammered or rolled into shape.

Alloying: Deliberate chemical combination of two or more metals.

Azurite: Blue copper carbonate ore ($Cu(OH)_2 . 2CuCO_3$).

Beneficiation: The process where extracted ore from mining is broken down by hammering or grinding into smaller particles that can be separated into pure ore and gangue, the former suitable for further processing and the latter rejected.

Black copper: The name given to impure copper after smelting.

Bloomery Iron: The first product of smelting iron ore in charcoal. It is relatively pure iron with only small amounts of slag inclusions.

Calorific value: Amount of heat produced by the complete combustion of a unit weight of fuel. Calorific value is usually expressed in kcals/kg for solid fuels or MJ/m^3 for gas.

Cassiterite: The main ore used to produce sin (SnO_2). It is usually yellow, brown, or black in colour, depending on the amount of iron within the ore.

Chalcocite: A black or gray lustrous copper sulphide ore (Cu_2S).

Chalcopyrite: The most common naturally-occurring copper sulphide ore and is yellow in colour ($CuFeS_2$).

Cold working: Any process that alters the shape or size of a metal by plastic deformation when carried out below the recrystallisation point usually at room temprature. Processes include hammering, rolling, drawing, pressing, spinning, and extruding. Hardness and tensile strength are increased with the degree of cold work whilst ductility and impact values are lowered.

Copper matte: The product of roasting dry concentrated sulphide ores to drive off excess sulphur prior to smelting.

Crysocolla: Copper silicate ore ($CuSiO_3 . 2H_2O$).

Cuprite: A natural red secondary ore of copper, essentially cuprous oxide Cu_2O that forms as a result of weathering.

Endothermic reaction:
A reaction that absorbs heat from its surrounding as the reaction proceeds.

Exothermic reaction:
A reaction that produces heat as the reaction proceeds.

Flux: A substance added in the smelting process to combine with impurities to form a molten mixture. This mixture, being lighter than the smelted metal, enables it to be easily removed from the furnace of crucible.

Gas porosities: Pits, holes, and blisters found on the surface of copper ingots caused by the escape of gasses in the cooling process.

Gangue: The valueless rock component of metal ores.

Goethite: Iron oxyhydroxide ($FeO(OH)$) formed by the weathering of iron rich minerals.

Gossan: A weathered iron-rich product overlying exposed sulphide deposit mix, formed by the oxidation of the sulphides of copper by the percolation of rainwater through the veins of minerals.

Grade: The concentration by weight of a metal in a mineral deposit or ore.

Hydrothermal: The action of the passage of hot water through rocks. Important in mineral exploration because hot, often superheated, water can dissolve and carry metals, and later precipitate them to form mineral deposits.

Isotope: A characteristic of an element that differentiates from other isotopes of the same metal by the number of neutrons in the nucleus.

LIA (Lead Isotope Analysis):
The measurement of the stable isotopes of lead using a mass spectrometer in order to characterise particular ores or artefacts and associate them with known lead sources. The four common isotopes measured are Pb^{206}, Pb^{207}, Pb^{208}, and Pb^{204}

Liquidus temperature:
The temperature at which the molten flux and gangue become a low viscous fluid.

Lode deposit: A discrete mineral deposit found within a consolidated host rock (see placer deposit below).

Magmatism: The formation of igneous rock from magma.

Malachite: Green copper carbonate ore ($Cu_2CO_3(OH)_2$.

Matte: An unfinished metallic product of copper and iron formed in the smelting process of copper sulphide ores and made up of copper, sulphur, and iron.

Melt: The liquid phase of smelted metal and molten slag. The slag, being lighter than the molten metal, floats to the top and can be removed through a tap hole in the side of the furnace.

Petrography: The study of rocks by means of microscopic examination of thin sections using a polarisation microscope.

Petrology: The geological and chemical study of rocks

pH: A measure of alkalinity or acidity of a solution. A neutral solution would have a pH of 7, and a pH of 1 would be the strongest acid solution and 15 the strongest alkaline solution.

Pillow lava: Lava that forms from an underwater eruption and is characterised by pillow-shaped masses.

Placer deposit: A placer or stream deposit is formed when the original deposit of ore has been eroded, carried away by water and laid down as an alluvial deposit, most frequently in the sands and gravels of river valleys.

ppm: Parts per million by weight.

Prills: Prills are small inclusions of copper trapped in the slag formed in the smelting process.

Pyrite: An iron disulphide mineral (FeS_2), sometimes called 'fools gold' owing to its brass-yellow colour.

Refining: Removes any remaining gangue and other impurities in smelted black copper. In antiquity this was carried out by melting the black copper in a reducing charcoal fire, which oxidised the impurities.

Refractory: A refractory material is one that can withstand very high temperatures without changes to its basic physical or chemical structure.

Reduction: A reduction process occurs when oxygen is absent and elements are reduced by gaining electrons. Under anaerobic conditions sulphur ores are reduced to produce hydrogen sulphide (H_2S).

Roasting: The process of heating copper sulphide and chalcopyrite ores to produce and remove sulphur dioxide from the ore.

Sintering: A solid-state process where bonds are developed in high-temperature conditions between grains of materials that have been brought into contact.

Shear zone: A linear zone of fracturing and tearing of the rocks, which can provide passage for hydrothermal mineralising fluids.

Slag: A furnace product formed in the smelting process by the fusion of waste material (gangue) with flux formed after the separation of the metal phase. Tap slag is the free-flowing liquid state in the smelting process. The term furnace slag, used by archaeologists, is a viscous form of slag where there has been an incomplete separation of gangue and metal.

Smelting: A pyro-technology where metals are separated from the other components of its ore. The process normally includes a liquid metal phase followed by a liquid slag phase.

Specific heat: The ratio of thermal energy required to raise the temperature of a body by 1°C to the thermal energy required to raise an equal mass of water by 1°C.

Tailings: Gangue left after the beneficiation process.

Tap a furnace: The removal of slag or metal from a furnace through a tap hole in the side of a furnace.

Tonne: A metric tonne of 1,000 kilograms.

Tuyère: An air tube made of clay, connecting the bellows and the furnace.

Viscosity: The material property that measures a fluid's resistance to flowing.

Vitrification: The change in the fabric of the ceramic through the action of heat in a reducing atmosphere.

Work hardening: The process where metal is made harder by rolling or hammering, owing to a reduction of the size of grains in the metal's polycrystalline material.

Chemical glossary

As: Arsenic
Au: Gold
C: Carbon
CO: Carbon monoxide
CO_2: Carbon dioxide
Cu: Copper
CuO_2: Cuprous oxide
Fe: Iron
H_2SO_4: Sulphuric acid
Mn: Manganese
Pb: lead
O: Oxygen
S: Sulphur
Si: Silica
Sn: Tin
SO_2: Sulphur dioxide

Bibliography

Adams, F. 1928. 'Summary of Economic Data Relating to Jewish Agricultural Colonies in Palestine.' In eds. Lord Melchett, L.K. Frankel, F.M. Warburg, *Wassermann Reports of the Experts Submitted to the Joint Palestine Survey Commission*: 67-142. Boston: Daniels Printing.

Agouridis, C. 1997. 'Sea Routes and Navigation in the Third Millennium Aegean.' *Oxford Journal of Archaeology* 16: 1–24.

Agricola. *De re metallica*. Translated by H.C. Hoover and L.H Hoover. 1950. *De re metallica. Translated from the First Latin Edition of 1556*. Reprint. New York: Dover.

Alberti, M.E. and N. Parise. 2005. 'Unification of Mass-Units in the Aegean and the Levant.' In eds. R. Laffineur and E. Greco, *Emporia: Aegeans in the Central and Eastern Mediterranean: Proceedings of the 10th International Aegean Conference/10e rencontre égéene internationale, Athens, Italian School of Archaeology, 14-18 April 2004*. Aegaeum; 25: 384–395. Liège: Université de Liège.

Albright, W.F. 1936–1937. *The Excavation of Tell Beit Mirsim: The Bronze Age*. Annual of the American Schools of Oriental Research; 17. New Haven: American Schools of Oriental Research, Under the Jane Dows Nies Publication Fund.

Albright, W.F. 1961. 'Abram the Hebrew: A New Archaeological Interpretation.' *Bulletin of the American Schools of Oriental Research* 163: 44–54.

Allam, S. 2001. 'Slavery.' In ed. D.B. Redford, *The Oxford Encyclopedia of Ancient Egypt,* Vol. 3: 293–296. Oxford: Oxford University Press.

Allan, J.C. 1970. *Considerations on the Antiquity of Mining in the Iberian Peninsula*. Royal Anthropological Institute of Great Britain and Ireland Occasional Paper; 27. London: Royal Anthropological Institute.

Allan, W. 1965. *The African Husbandman*. Edinburgh: Oliver and Boyd.

Allbaugh, L.G. 1953. *Crete. A Case Study of an Undeveloped Area*. Princeton: Princeton University Press.

Allen, J.P. 1999. *Middle Egyptian: An Introduction to the Language and Culture of Hieroglyphs*. Cambridge: Cambridge University Press.

Allen, J.P. 2002. *The Heqanakht Papyri*. New York: The Metropolitan Museum of Art.

Allen, P.S. 1989. 'Dhali: A Traditional Community in Transition.' In eds. L.E. Stager and A.M. Walker. *American Expedition to Idalion, Cyprus 1973–1980,* Oriental Institute Communications; 24: 425–446. Chicago: Oriental Institute of the University of Chicago.

Allgrove-McDowell, J. 2003. 'Industries of the Near East and Europe in Prehistory. Ancient Egypt, 5000–332 B.C.' In ed. D.T. Jenkins, *The Cambridge History of Western Textiles*: 30–38. Cambridge: Cambridge University Press.

Amouretti, M-C. 1986. *Le pain et l'huile dans la Grèce antique: de l'araire au Moulin.* Paris: Belles Lettres.

Anderson, P.C. 1999. 'Experimental Cultivation, Harvest, and Threshing of Wild Cereals: Their Relevance for Interpreting the Use of Epipaleolithic and Neolithic Artifacts.' In ed. P.C. Anderson. *Prehistory of Agriculture: New Experimental and Ethnographic Approaches,* Monograph, Institute of Archaeology, University of California Los Angeles; 40: 118–144. Los Angeles: Institute of Archaeology, University of California.

Ardaillon, É. 1897. *Les Mines du Laurion dans l'antiquité*. Bibliothèque des écoles françaises d'Athènes et de Rome; 77. Paris: Thorin et fils, 1897.

Arnon, I. 1972a. *Crop Production in Dry Regions. Background and Principles*. Vol. 1. Plant Science Monographs; 1. London: Leonard Hill.

Arnon, I. 1972b. *Crop Production in Dry Regions. Systematic Treatments of the Principal Crops*. Vol. 2. Plant Science Monographs; 1. London: Leonard Hill.

Artzy, M. 1985a. 'Supply and Demand: A Study of Second Millennium Cypriote Pottery in the Levant.' In eds. A.B. Knapp and T. Stech, *Prehistoric Production and Exchange: The Aegean and the Eastern Mediterranean.* Monograph, Institute of Archaeology, University of California Los Angeles; 25: 93–99. Los Angeles: Institute of Archaeology, University of California.

Artzy, M. 1985b. 'Merchandise and Merchantmen: On Ships and Shipping in the Late Bronze Age Levant.' In eds. Th. Papadopoulos and S.A. Hadjistyllis, *Acts of the Second International Cyprological Congress,* Vol. 1: 135–140. Nicosia: Society of Cypriot Studies.

Artzy, M. 1994. 'Incense, Camels and Collared Rim Jars: Desert Trade Routes and Maritime Outlets in the 2nd Millennium.' *Oxford Journal of Archaeology* 13: 121–147.

Artzy, M. 1995. 'Anchorage Systems of the Second Millennium B.C. at Tel Nami.' In ed. H.E. Tzalas, *Tropis III: 3rd International Symposium on Ship Construction in Antiquity: Proceedings Athens, 24–27th August, 1989*: 23–30. Athens: Hellenic Institute for the Preservation of Nautical Tradition.

Artzy, M. 1999. 'Cult and Recycling of Metal at the End of the Late Bronze Age.' In eds. P. Åström and D. Sürenhagen, *Periplus*. Studies in Mediterranean Archaeology; 127: 27–31. Jonsered: P. Åströms Förlag.

Artzy, M. 2001. 'White Slip Ware for Export? The Economics of Production.' In ed. V. Karageorghis, *The White Slip Ware of Late Bronze Age Cyprus: Proceedings of an*

International Conference Organized by the Anastasios G. Leventis Foundation, Nicosia in Honour of Malcolm Wiener, Nicosia 29th–30th October 1998: 107–116. Vienna: Verlag der Österreichischen Akademie der Wissenschaften.

Artzy, M. 2006. 'The Carmel Coast During the Second Part of the Late Bronze Age: A Center for Eastern Mediterranean Transshipping.' *Bulletin of the American Schools of Oriental Research* 343: 45–64.

Artzy, M. and E. Marcus. 1991. The MB IIa Coastal Settlement at Tel Nami. *Michmanim* 5: 5–16.

Asael, D., A. Matthews, M.B. Miryam Bar-Matthews, and L. Halicz. 2007. 'Copper Isotope Fractionation in Sedimentary Copper Mineralization (Timna Valley, Israel).' *Chemical Geology* 243: 238–254.

Aschenbrenner, S. 1972. 'A Contemporary Community.' In eds. W.A. McDonald and G.R. Rapp, *The Minnesota Messenia Expedition: Reconstructing a Bronze Age Regional Environment*: 47–63. Minneapolis; London: University of Minnesota Press: Oxford University Press.

Assmann, J. 2002. *The Mind of Egypt. History and Meaning in the Time of the Pharaohs.* Translated by Andrew Jenkins. New York: Metropolitan Books.

Astour, M.C. 1965. 'New Evidence on the Last Days of Ugarit.' *American Journal of Archaeology* 69: 253–258.

Astour, M.C. 1970. 'Ma'hadu, the Harbour of Ugarit.' *Journal of the Economic and Social History of the Orient* 13: 113–127.

Astour, M.C. 1972. 'The Merchant Class of Ugarit.' In ed. D.O. Edzard. *Gesellschaftsklassen im Alten Zweistromland und in den angrenzenden Gebieten*; 75: 11–26. Munich: Verlag der Bayerischen Akademie der Wissenschaften.

Astour, M.C. 1981. 'Ugarit and the Great Powers.' In eds. G.D. Young and C.F.A. Schaeffer, *Ugarit in Retrospect: 50 Years of Ugarit and Ugaritic*: 3–29. Winona Lake, Ind.: Eisenbrauns.

Astour, M.C. 1995. 'Overland Trade Routes in Ancient Western Asia.' In ed. J.M. Sasson. *Civilizations of the Ancient Near East,* Vol. 3: 1401–1420. New York: Scribner.

Åström, P. 1982. 'The Bronzes of Hala Sultan Tekke.' In eds. J.D. Muhly, R. Maddin, and V. Karageorghis, *Acta of the International Archaeological Symposium: Early Metallurgy in Cyprus, 4000–500 B.C.: Larnaca, Cyprus, 1–6 June 1981*: 177–181. Nicosia: The Foundation.

Åström, P. 1984. 'Aegyptiaca at Hala Sultan Tekke.' *Opuscula Atheniensia* 14: 17–24.

Åström, P. 1986. 'Hala Sultan Tekke – An International Harbour Town of the Late Cypriote Bronze Age.' *Opuscula Atheniensia* 16: 7–17.

Åström, P. 1991. 'Canaanite Jars from Hala Sultan Tekke.' In ed. N.H. Gale, *Bronze Age Trade in the Mediterranean: Papers Presented at the Conference Held at Rewley House, Oxford, in December 1989.* Studies in Mediterranean Archaeology; 90: 149–151. Jonsered: P. Åströms Förlag.

Åström, P. 1996. 'Hala Sultan Tekke: A Late Cypriot Harbour Town.' In eds. P. Åström, and E. Herscher, *Bronze Age Settlement in Cyprus: Function and Relationship.* Studies in Mediterranean Archaeology; 126: 9–14. Jonsered: P. Åströms Förlag.

Ataman, K. 1999. 'Threshing Sledges.' In ed. P.C. Anderson, *Prehistory of Agriculture: New Experimental and Ethnographic Approaches.* Monograph, Institute of Archaeology University of California Los Angeles; 40: 211–220. Los Angeles: Institute of Archaeology, University of California.

Atzeni, C. 2005. 'Aspects of Ancient Metallurgy.' In eds. F. Lo Schiavo and C. Atzeni, *Archaeometallurgy in Sardinia: From the Origins to the Beginning of the Early Iron Age.* Monographies Instrumentum; 30: 17–30. Montagnac: M. Mergoil.

Audouze. F. 1999. 'New Advances in French Prehistory.' *Antiquity* 73: 167–175.

Avitsur, S. 1972. *Daily life in Eretz Israel in the XIX Century.* Tel-Aviv: ʿAm Ha-Sefer.

Azzaroli, A. 1985. *An Early History of Horsemanship.* Leiden: E.J. Brill.

Babón, J.M. 2003. *Historia militar de Egipto durante la Dinastía XVIII.* Barcelona: Fundació Arqueològica Clos-Museu Egipci.

Bachmann, H.G. 1982. 'Copper Smelting Slags from Cyprus: Review and Classification of Analytical Data.' In eds. J.D. Muhly, R. Maddin and V. Karageorghis, *Acta of the International Archaeological Symposium: Early Metallurgy in Cyprus, 4000-500 B.C.: Larnaca, Cyprus, 1-6 June 1981*: 143-151. Nicosia: Department of Antiquities of Cyprus.

Badawy, A. 1956. 'Philological Evidence about Methods of Construction in Ancient Egypt.' *Annales du Service des antiquités de l'Égypte* 54: 51–74.

Baer, K. 1962. 'The Low Price of Land in Ancient Egypt.' *Journal of the American Research Center in Egypt* 1: 25–45.

Baer, K. 1963. 'An Eleventh Dynasty Farmer's Letters to His Family.' *Journal of the American Oriental Society* 83: 1–19.

Bagnall, R.S. and B.W. Frier. 1994. *The Demography of Roman Egypt.* Cambridge Studies in Population, Economy, and Society in Past Time; 23. Cambridge: Cambridge University Press.

Bailey, A.M. and J.R. Llobera. 1981. 'The AMP: Sources and Formation of the Concept.' In eds. A.M. Bailey and J.R. Llobera, *The Asiatic Mode of Production: Science and Politics*: 13–45. London: Routledge and Kegan Paul Ltd.

Baines, J. 1982. 'Interpreting Sinuhe.' *Journal of Egyptian Archaeology* 68: 31–44.

Baines, J. 1983. 'Literacy and Ancient Egyptian Society.' (The Curl Lecture for 1981) *Man, New Series*; 18: 572–599.

Baines, J. 1987. 'Practical Religion and Piety.' *Journal of*

Egyptian Archaeology 73: 79–97.

Baines, J. 2007. *Visual and Written Culture in Ancient Egypt*. Oxford: Oxford University Press.

Baines, J. and C. Eyre. 1983. 'Four Notes on Literacy.' *Göttinger Miszellen* 61: 65–96.

Baines, J. and J. Málek. 1980. *Atlas of Ancient Egypt*. Oxford: Phaidon Press Ltd.

Baines, J. and N. Yoffee. 1998. 'Order, Legitimacy, and Wealth.' In eds. G.M. Feinman and J. Marcus, *Archaic States*: 199–260. Santa Fe: School of American Research Press.

Baines, J. and N. Yoffee. 2000. 'Order, Legitimacy, and Wealth: Setting the Terms.' In eds. J. Richards and M. Van Buren, *Order, Legitimacy, and Wealth in Ancient States*: 13–17. Cambridge: Cambridge University Press.

Bamberger, M. and P. Wincierzt. 1990. 'Ancient Smelting of Oxide Copper Ore.' In eds. B. Rothenberg and H.G. Bachmann, *The Ancient Metallurgy of Copper: Archaeology-Experiment-Theory*: 123–157. London: Institute for Archaeo-Metallurgical Studies, Institute of Archaeology, University College, London.

Barber, E.J.W. 1982. 'New Kingdom Egyptian Textiles: Embroidery vs. Weaving.' *American Journal of Archaeology* 86: 442–445.

Barber, E.J.W. 1991. *Prehistoric Textiles. The Development of Cloth in the Neolithic and Bronze Ages*. Princeton: Princeton University Press.

Bard, K.A. and R. Fattovich. 2010. 'Spatial Use of the Twelfth Dynasty Harbor at Mersa/WadiGawasis for the Seafaring Expeditions to Punt.' *Journal of Ancient Egyptian Interconnections* 2: 1–13.

Barrett, C.E. 2009. 'The Perceived Value of Minoan and Minoanizing Pottery in Egypt.' *Journal of Mediterranean Archaeology* 22: 211–234.

Bartosiewicz, L., W. van Neer, and An. Lentacker. 1997. *Draught Cattle: Their Osteological Identification and History*. Koninklijk Museum voor Midden-Afrika, Annalen, Zoologische Wetenschappen; 281. Tervuren: Musée royal de l'Afrique centrale.

Bartura, Y., A. Hauptmann, and G. Schöne-Warnefeld. 1980. 'Zur Mineralogie und Geologie der antik genutzten Kupferlagerstätte in Timna-Tel.' In eds. H.G. Conrad and B. Rothenberg, *Antikes Kupfer im Timna-Tal: 4000 Jahre Bergbau und Verhüttung in der Arabah*. Der Anschnitt; 1. Veröffentlichungen aus dem deutschen Bergbau-Museum Bochum; 20: 41–56. Bochum: Deutsches Bergbau-Museum.

Basler, F. 1981. 'Weeds and their Control.' In eds. C. Webb, and G. Hawton, *Lentils*: 143–152. London: Commonwealth Agricultural Bureau and the International Centre for Agricultural Research in the Dry Areas.

Bass, G.F. 1961. 'The Cape Gelidonya Wreck: Preliminary Report.' *American Journal of Archaeology* 65: 267–276.

Bass, G.F. 1967a. 'The Ship and Its Lading.' In ed. G.F. Bass, *Cape Gelidonya: A Bronze Age Shipwreck*. Transactions of the American Philosophical Society; 57, Part 8: 44–51. Philadelphia: The American Philosophical Society.

Bass, G.F. 1967b. 'The Ingots.' In ed. G.F. Bass, *Cape Gelidonya: A Bronze Age Shipwreck*. Transactions of the American Philosophical Society; 57, Part 8: 52–83. Philadelphia: The American Philosophical Society.

Bass, G.F. 1967c. 'The Bronzes.' In ed. G.F. Bass, *Cape Gelidonya: A Bronze Age Shipwreck*. Transactions of the American Philosophical Society; 57, Part 8: 84–121. Philadelphia: The American Philosophical Society.

Bass, G.F. 1967d. 'The Weights.' In ed. G.F. Bass, *Cape Gelidonya: A Bronze Age Shipwreck*. Transactions of the American Philosophical Society; 57, Part 8: 135–142. Philadelphia: The American Philosophical Society.

Bass, G.F. 1972. 'The Earliest Seafarers in the Mediterranean and the Near East.' In ed. G.F. Bass, *A History of Seafaring Based on Underwater Archaeology*: 12–36. London: Thames and Hudson.

Bass, G.F. 1973. 'Cape Gelidonya and Bronze Age Mediterranean Trade: Essays Presented to Cyrus H. Gordon on the Occasion of His Sixty-Fifth Birthday.' In ed. H.A. Hoffner, *Orient and Occident*: 29–38. Kevelaer: Butzon and Bercker.

Bass, G.F. 1986. 'A Bronze Age Shipwreck at Ulu Burun (Kas): 1984 Campaign.' *American Journal of Archaeology* 90: 269–296.

Bass, G.F. 1991. 'Evidence of Trade from Bronze Age Shipwrecks.' In ed. N.H. Gale, *Bronze Age Trade in the Mediterranean: Papers Presented at the Conference Held at Rewley House, Oxford, in December 1989*. Studies in Mediterranean Archaeology; 90: 69–82. Jonsered: P. Åströms Förlag.

Bass, G.F. 1997. 'Prolegomena to a Study of Maritime Traffic in Raw Materials to the Aegean During the Fourteenth and Thirteenth Centuries B.C.' In eds. R. Laffineur and P.P. Betancourt, *Techne: Craftsmen, Craftswomen, and Craftsmanship in the Aegean Bronze Age: Proceedings of the 6th International Aegean Conference/6e Rencontre égéenne internationale, Philadelphia, Temple University, 18–21 April 1996*. Aegaeum; 16: 153–170. Liège: Université de Liège.

Bass, G.F., C. Pulak, D. Collon, and J. Weinstein. 1989. 'The Bronze Age Shipwreck at Ulu Burun: 1986 Campaign.' *American Journal of Archaeology* 93: 1–29.

Bauer, A.A. 1998. 'Cities of the Sea: Maritime Trade and the Origin of Philistine Settlement in the Early Iron Age Southern Levant.' *Oxford Journal of Archaeology* 17: 149–168.

Bauer, P.T. 1954. *West African Trade: A Study of Competition, Oligopoly and Monopoly in a Changing Economy*. Cambridge: Cambridge University Press.

Beal, R.H. 1992. 'The Location of Cilician Ura.' *Anatolian Studies* 42: 65–73.

Bear, L.M. 1963. *The Mineral Resources and Mining*

Industry of Cyprus. Bulletin of the Geological Survey Department; 1. Nicosia: Geological Survey Department.

Beaumont, P. 1993. 'Climate and Hydrology.' In ed. G.M. Craig, *The Agriculture of Egypt*: 16–38. Oxford: Oxford University Press.

Beit-Arieh, I. 1985. 'Serabit el-Khadim: New Metallurgical and Chronological Aspects.' *Levant* 17: 89-116.

Bell, C. 2006. *The Evolution of Long Distance Trading Relationships across the LBA/Iron Age Transition on the Northern Levantine Coast: Crisis, Continuity and Change; a Study Based on Imported Ceramics, Bronze and Its Constituent Metals*. BAR International Series; 1574. Oxford: BAR Publishing.

Bell, L., J.H. Johnson, and D. Whitcomb. 1984. 'The Eastern Desert of Egypt: Routes and Inscriptions.' *Journal of Near Eastern Studies* 43: 27–46.

Bellinger, L. 1959. 'Craft Habits, Part 1: Loom Types Suggested by Weaving Details.' *Textile Museum Workshop Notes* 19: 1–4. Washington, D.C.: Textile Museum.

Bendix, R. 1977. *Max Weber: An Intellectual Portrait* [1960]. Berkely: University of California Press.

Bergoffen, C.J. 1991. 'Overland Trade in Northern Sinai: The Evidence of the Late Cypriot Pottery.' *Bulletin of the American Schools of Oriental Research* 286: 59–76.

Berlev, O.D. 1965. 'Review of "William Kelly Simpson, Reisner Papyri I. The Records of a Building Project in the Reign of Sesostris I."' *Bibliotheca Orientalis* 22: 263–268.

Betancourt, P.P. and R.H. Simpson. 1992. 'The Agricultural System of Bronze Age Pseira.' *Cretan Studies* 3: 47–54. Amsterdam: Adolf M. Hakkert.

Binder, S. 2008. *The Gold of Honour in New Kingdom Egypt*. Studies (Australian Centre for Egyptology); 8. Oxford: Aris and Phillips.

Binford, L.R. 1968. 'Some Comments on Historical versus Processual Archaeology.' *Southwestern Journal of Anthropology* 24: 267–275.

Binford, L.R. 1981. *Bones: Ancient Men and Modern Myths*. Studies in Archaeology. New York; London: Academic Press.

Binford, L.R. and J. Sabloff. 1982. Paradigms, Systematics, and Archaeology. *Journal of Anthropological Research* 38: 137–153.

Binford, S.R. and L.R. Binford. 1968. *New Perspectives in Archaeology*. Chicago: Aldine Publishing Company.

Blackmann, D.J. 1982. 'Ancient Harbours in the Mediterranean.' *The International Journal of Nautical Archaeology and Underwater Exploration* 11: 79–104.

Blake, R.C., E.A. Shute, and G.T. Howard. 1994. 'Solubilization of Minerals by Bacteria: Electrophoretic Mobility of Thiobacillus Ferrooxidans in the Presence of Iron, Pyrite, and Sulfur.' *Applied Environmental Microbiology* 60: 3349–3357.

Bleeker, C.J. 1973. *Hathor and Thoth. Two Key Figures of the Ancient Egyptian Religion.* Studies in the History of Religions; 26. Leiden: Brill.

Bleiberg, E. 1988. 'The Redistributive Economy in New Kingdom Egypt.' *Journal of the American Research Center in Egypt* 25: 157–168.

Bleiberg, E. 1995. 'The Economy of Egypt.' In ed. J.M. Sasson, *Civilizations of the Ancient Near East.* Vol. 3: 1373–1386. New York: Scribner.

Bleiberg, E. 1996. *The Official Gift in Ancient Egypt.* Norman: University of Oaklahoma Press.

Bleiberg, E. 2007. 'State and Private Enterprise.' In ed. T.A.H. Wilkinson, *The Egyptian World*: 175–184. London: Routledge.

Bloch, M. 1942. 'Chiefs and Villagers.' In eds. J.H. Clapham and E. Power, *The Cambridge Economic History of Europe from the Decline of the Roman Empire.* Vol. 1: 260–270. Cambridge: Cambridge University Press.

Borowski, O. 1987. *Agriculture in Iron Age Israel.* Winona Lake: Eisenbrauns.

Bourdieu, P. 1977. *Outline of a Theory of Practice.* Cambridge Studies in Social Anthropology; 16. Cambridge: Cambridge University Press.

Bowman, A.K. and E.L. Rogan. 1999. 'Agriculture in Egypt from Pharaonic to Modern Times.' In eds. A.K. Bowman and E.L. Rogan, *Agriculture in Egypt*. Proceedings of the British Academy; 96: 1–29. Oxford: Oxford University Press.

Bradbury, F. 1920. *Flax, Culture and Preparation.* Pitman's Textile Industries Series. London: Pitman.

Braudel, F. 1972. *The Mediterranean and the Mediterranean World in the Age of Philip II.* Vol. 1. New York: Harper & Row.

Breasted, J.H. 1906a. *Ancient Records of Egypt: The First Through the Seventeenth Dynasties.* Vol. 1. Chicago: University of Chicago Press.

Breasted, J.H. 1906b. *Ancient Records of Egypt: The Eighteenth Dynasty.* Vol. 2. Chicago: University of Chicago Press.

Breasted, J.H. 1906c. *Ancient Records of Egypt: The Nineteenth Dynasty.* Vol. 3. Chicago: University of Chicago Press.

Breasted, J.H. 1906d. *Ancient Records of Egypt: The Twentieth Through the Twenty-Sixth Dynasties.* Vol. 4. Chicago: University of Chicago Press.

Breasted, J.H. 1906e. *Ancient Records of Egypt: Supplementary Bibliographies and Indices.* Vol. 5. Chicago: University of Chicago Press.

Brengle, K.G. 1982. *Principles and Practices of Dryland Farming.* Boulder: Associated Universities Press.

Brewer, D.J. 2007. 'Agriculture and Animal Husbandry.' In ed. T.A.H. Wilkinson, *The Egyptian World*: 131–145. London: Routledge.

Brewer, D.J. and E. Teeter. 2007. *Egypt and the Egyptians.* Second Edition. Cambridge: Cambridge University Press.

Brewer, D.J. and R.F. Friedman. 1989. *Fish and Fishing in Ancient Egypt.* Natural History of Egypt; 2. Warminster: Aris and Phillips.

Brewer, D.J., D.B. Redford and S. Redford, 1994. *Domestic Plants and Animals: The Egyptian*

Origins. Warminster: Aris and Phillips Ltd.

Broodbank, C. 2000. *An Island Archaeology of the Early Cyclades*. Cambridge: Cambridge University Press.

Broodbank, C. and T.F. Strasser. 1991. 'Migrant Farmers and the Neolithic Colonization of Crete.' *Antiquity* 65: 233–245.

Brothwell, D. and P. Brothwell 1998. *Food in Antiquity: A Survey of the Diet of Early Peoples*. Baltimore; London: Johns Hopkins University Press.

Brownson, R. 2000. 'Beef Cattle Feed Management During a Drought.' *Cattle Producer's Library*. Second Edition. Cattle Producers Library; CL 1130: 1–3. Montana State University.<http://drought. wsu.edu/ 1100/1130.pdf>, accessed 14/01/2013.

Bruce, J.L. 1937. 'Antiquities in the Mines of Cyprus. Appendix V.' In eds. E. Gjerstad, J. Lindos, E. Sjöqvist, and A. Westholm, *The Swedish Cyprus Expedition. Finds and Results of the Excavations in Cyprus 1927–1931*: 637–671. Stockholm: The Swedish Cyprus Expedition.

Brun, J.-P. 1987. *L'Oléiculture antique en Provence. Les huileries du département du Var*. Paris: Éditions du Centre national de la Recherche scientifique.

Brun, T. 1992. 'The Assessment of Total Energy Expenditure of Female Farmers Under Field Conditions.' *Journal of Biosocial Science* 24: 325–333.

Bruyère, B. 1926. *Rapport sur les fouilles de Deir el Médineh (1924–25)*. Fouilles de l'Institut français du Caire; 3. Cairo: Imprimerie de l'Institut français d'archéologie orientale.

Bruyère, B. 1930. *Rapport sur les fouilles de Deir el Médineh (1929)*. Fouilles de l'Institut français du Caire; 7. Cairo: Imprimerie de l'Institut français d'archéologie orientale.

Bruyère, B. 1937. *Rapport sur les fouilles de Deir el Médineh (1934–1935). Deuxièm partie: la nécropole de l'est*. Fouilles de l'Institut français du Caire; 15. Cairo: Imprimerie de l'Institut orientale.

Bruyère, B. 1939. *Rapport sur les fouilles de Deir el Médineh (1934–1935). Troisièm partie: le village, les décharges publiques, la station de repos du col de la vallée des rois*. Fouilles de l'Institut français du Caire; 16. Cairo: Imprimerie de l'Institut français d'archéologie orientale.

Bücher, K. 1893 [1847–1930]. *Die Entstehung der Volkswirtschaft: Vorträge und Versuche*. Tübingen: H. Laupp'schen Buchhandlung.

Bücher, K. 1901 [1847–1930]. *Industrial Evolution*. Translation of Third Edition: Entstehung der Volkswirtschaft by S.M. Wickett. London: Bell.

Buchholz, H. 1959. 'Keftiubarren und Erzhandel im zweiten vorchristlichen Jahrtausend.' *Prähistorische Zeitschrift* 37: 1–40.

Budd, P. and B.S. Ottaway. 1995. 'Eneolithic Arsenical Copper: Chance or Choice.' In ed. P. Petrovic, *Ancient Mining and Metallurgy in Southeast Europe: International Symposium, Donji Milanovac, May 20–25, 1990*: 95–102. Belgrade: Archaeological Institute: Museum of Mining and Metallurgy.

Budd, P., A.M. Pollard, B. Scaife, and R.G. Thomas. 1995a. 'Rethinking the Quest for Provenance.' *Antiquity* 70: 168–174.

Budd, P., A.M. Pollard, B. Scaife, and R.G. Thomas. 1995b. 'Oxhide Ingots, Recycling and the Mediterranean Metals Trade.' *Journal of Mediterranean Archaeology* 8: 1–32.

Budd, P., A.M. Pollard, B. Scaife, and R.G. Thomas. 1995c. 'Lead Isotope Analysis and Oxhide Ingots: A Final Comment.' *Journal of Mediterranean Archaeology* 8: 70–75.

Budd, P., A.M. Pollard, B. Scaife, and R.G. Thomas. 1995d. 'The Possible Fractionation of Lead Isotopes in Ancient Metallurgical Processes. *Archaeometry* 37: 143–150.

Burleigh, R. and B.J. Southgate 1975. 'Insect Infestation of Stored Egyptian Lentils in Antiquity.' *Journal of Archaeological Science* 2: 391–392.

Burnet, J.E. 2004. *Forest Bioresource Utilisation in the Eastern Mediterranean Since Antiquity: A Case Study of the Makheras, Cyprus*. BAR International Series; 1243. Oxford: BAR Publishing.

Butzer, K.W. 1976. *Early Hydraulic Civilization in Egypt: A Study in Cultural Ecology*. Prehistoric Archaeology and Ecology. Chicago; London: University of Chicago Press.

Butzer, K.W. 1996. 'Ecology in the Long View: Settlement Histories, Agrosystemic Strategies, and Ecological Performance.' *Journal of Field Archaeology* 23: 141–150.

Butzer, K.W. 1997. 'Sociopolitical Discontinuity in the Near East *c.*2200 B.C.E.: Scenarios from Palestine and Egypt.' In eds. H.N. Dalfes, G. Kukla, and H. Weiss, *Third Millennium BC Climate Change and Old World Collapse*: 245–296. London: Springer.

Butzer, K.W. 2001. 'Irrigation.' In ed. D.B. Redford, *The Oxford Encyclopedia of Ancient Egypt*. Vol. 2: 400–412. Oxford: Oxford University Press.

Caldwell, S.A.D. 1931. *The Preparation and Spinning of Flax Fibre*. London: Emmott and Company Ltd.

Callot, O. 1987. 'Les Huileries du bronze Récent à Ougarit: premiers éléments pour une étude.' In ed. M. Yon, *Le Centre de la ville, Ras Shamra: 38e-44e Campagnes (1978–1984)*. Ras Shamra-Ougarit; 3: 197–212. Paris: Éditions Recherche sur les Civilisations.

Callot, O. 1994. *La Tranchée 'Ville Sud': études d'architecture domestique*. Ras Shamra-Ougarit; 10. Paris: Editions Recherche sur les Civilisations.

Calvet, Y. 2007. 'The Kingdom and the City-Urban Features.' In ed. K.L. Younger, *Ugarit at Seventy-Five*: 101–111. Winona Lake, Indiana: Eisenbrauns.

Caminos, R.A. 1963. 'Papyrus Berlin 10463.' *Journal of Egyptian Archaeology* 49: 29–37.

Carmona S. and M. Ezzamel 2007. 'Accounting and Accountability in Ancient Civilizations: Mesopotamia and Ancient Egypt.' *Accounting,*

Auditing and Accountability Journal 20: 177–209.

Carr, M. and M. Hartl. 2010. *Lightening the Load. Labour-saving Technologies and Practices for Rural Women.* Bourton on Dunsmore: International Fund for Agricultural Development.

Casson, L. 1994. *Ships and Seafaring in Ancient Times.* London: British Museum Press.

Casson, L. 1995. *Ships and Seamanship in the Ancient World.* Baltimore; London: Johns Hopkins University Press.

Castle, E.W. 1992. 'Shipping and Trade in Ramesside Egypt.' *Journal of the Economic and Social History of the Orient* 35: 239–277.

Catling, H.W. 1964. *Cypriot Bronzework in the Mycenaean World.* Oxford Monographs on Classical Archaeology. Oxford: Clarendon Press.

Caton-Thompson, G. and E.W. Gardner. 1934. *The Desert Fayum.* London: The Royal Anthropological Institute of Great Britain and Ireland.

Černý, J. 1975. 'Workmen of the King's Tomb.' In eds. I.E.S. Edwards, C.J. Gadd, N.G.L. Hammond, and E. Sollberger, *Cambridge Ancient History.* Vol. 2: 620–625. Cambridge: Cambridge University Press.

Chadwick, J. 1972. 'The Mycenaean Documents.' In eds. W.A. McDonald and G.R. Rapp, *The Minnesota Messenia Expedition: Reconstructing a Bronze Age Regional Environment*: 100–116. Minneapolis; London: University of Minnesota Press: Oxford University Press.

Champion, T.C. 1989. 'Introduction.' In ed. T.C. Champion, *Core and Periphery*: 1–21. London: Unwin Hyman.

Charles, J.A. 1978. 'The Development of the Usage of Tin and Tin Bronze.' In eds. A.D. Franklin, J.S. Olin, and A. Wertime, *The Search for Ancient Tin*: 25–32. Washington: U.S. Government Printing Office.

Charles, J.A. 1980. 'The Coming of Copper and Copper-Base Alloys and Iron.' In eds. T.A. Wertime, J.D. Muhly, and J.A. Charles, *The Coming of the Age of Iron*: 151–181. New Haven; London: Yale University Press.

Charles, M.P. 1988. 'Irrigation in Lowland Mesopotamia.' *Bulletin on Sumerian Agriculture* 4: 1–39.

Chase-Dunn, C. and T. Hall 1991. 'Conceptualizing Core/Periphery Hierarchies for Comparative Study.' In eds. C. Chase-Dunn and T. Hall, *Core/Periphery Relations in Precapitalist Worlds*: 5–44. Boulder: Westview Press.

Chase-Dunn, C. and T. Hall. 1997. *Rise and Demise: Comparing World-Systems.* New Perspectives in Sociology. Boulder: Westview Press.

Chmyriov, V. M. 1975. 'The Main Features of Tin Mineralization in Afghanistan. Theses of Reports.' *Bulletin of the Third Scientific Conference Held in Ku and Kpi*: 74–75. Kabul.

Chmyriov, V.M., K.F. Stazhilo-Alekseev, and N. Azimi. 1976. 'Ore Formations of Afghanistan.' *Bulletin of the Fourth Scientific Conference Held in Ku and Kpi*: 62–63. Kabul.

Christodoulou, D., R.R. Rowson, and K.R. Sealy. 1959. *The Evolution of the Rural Land Use Pattern in Cyprus.* World Land Use Survey. Regional Monographs; 2. Bude: Geographical Publications.

Christophe, L-A. 1965. 'Le Ravitaillement en poissons des artisans de la nécropole thébaine à la fin du règne de Ramsès III.' *Bulletin de l'Institut français d'archéologie orientale* 65: 177–199.

Cierny, J. and G. Weisgerber. 2003. 'Bronze Age Tin Mines in Central Asia.' In eds. A. Giumlia-Mair and F. Lo Schiavo, *The Problem of Early Tin.* BAR International Series; 1199: 23–31. Oxford: BAR Publishing.

Clapham, A. and Rowley-Conwy. 2006. 'Qasr Ibrim's Archaeobotany.' *Egyptian Archaeology: The Bulletin of the Egypt Exploration Society* 29: 6–7.

Clarke, S. 1908. 'The Use of Mud-Brick in Egypt.' *Cairo Scientific Journal* 2: 211–220.

Clarke, S. and R. Engelbach. 1990. *Ancient Egyptian Construction and Architecture.* Dover Books on Architecture. New York: Dover Publications.

Clarysse, W. and D.J. Thompson. 2006. *Counting the People in Hellenistic Egypt.* Cambridge Classical Studies. Cambridge: Cambridge University Press.

Cleere, H. 1976. 'Operating Parameters for Roman Iron Works.' *Bulletin of the Institute of Archaeology* 13: 233–246.

Cleere, H. and D.W. Crossley. 1985. *The Iron Industry of the Weald.* Leicester: Leicester University Press.

Cleuziou, S. and T. Berthoud. 1982. 'Tin in the Ancient Near East: A Reassessment in the Light of New Evidence from Western Afghanistan.' *Expedition* 25: 14–19.

Cline, E. 1999. 'Coals to Newcastle, Wallbrackets to Tiryns: Irrationality, Gift Exchange, and Distance Value.' In eds. P.P. Betancourt and M.H. Wiener, *Meletemata: Studies in Aegean Archaeology Presented to Malcolm H. Wiener as He Enters His 65th Year.* Aegaeum; 20: 119–124. Liège: Université de Liège.

Cline, E. 2005. 'Multivalent Nature of Imported Objects.' In eds. R. Laffineur and E. Greco, *Emporia: Aegeans in the Central and Eastern Mediterranean: Proceedings of the 10th International Aegean Conference/10e rencontre égéene internationale, Athens, Italian School of Archaeology, 14–18 April 2004.* Aegaeum; 25: 45–51. Liège: Université de Liège.

Coale, A.J., P.G. Demeny, and B. Vaughan. 1983. *Regional Model Life Tables and Stable Populations.* New York; London: Academic Press.

Collier, M. and S. Quirke. 2006. *The UCL Lahun Papyri: Accounts.* BAR International Series; 1471. Oxford: BAR Publishing.

Colonial Office and F.W. Barry. 1884. *Report on the Census of Cyprus with Appendix. 1881.* London: Eyre and Spottiswoode.

Columella. *Res rustica.* Translated by H.B. Ash. 1948. *On Agriculture.* The Loeb Classical Library. Cambridge Mass.: Harvard University.

Conophagos, C.E. 1980. *Le Laurium antique et la*

technique grecque de la production de l'argent. Athenes: Ekdotike Hellados.

Conrad, H.G. and B. Rothenberg, eds. 1980. *Antikes Kupfer im Timna-Tal: 4000 Jahre Bergbau und Verhüttung in der Arabah.* Der Anschnitt; 1. Veröffentlichungen aus dem deutschen Bergbau-Museum Bochum; 20. Bochum: Deutsches Bergbau-Museum.

Conrad, H.G., L. Fober, A. Hauptmann, I. Ordentlich, and G. Weisgerber. 1980. 'Untersuchungen zur Bergbautechnik und ihre Interpretation.' In eds. H.G. Conrad and B. Rothenberg, *Antikes Kupfer im Timna-Tal: 4000 Jahre Bergbau und Verhüttung in der Arabah.* Der Anschnitt; 1. Veröffentlichungen aus dem deutschen Bergbau-Museum Bochum; 20: 69–94. Bochum: Deutsches Bergbau-Museum.

Constantinou, G. 1982. 'Geological Features and Ancient Exploitation of the Cupriferous Sulphide Orebodies of Cyprus.' In eds. J.D. Muhly, R. Maddin, and V. Karageorghis, *Acta of the International Archaeological Symposium: Early Metallurgy in Cyprus, 4000–500 B.C.: Larnaca, Cyprus, 1–6 June L981*: 13–24. Nicosia: Department of Antiquities of Cyprus.

Constantinou, G. 1992. 'Ancient Copper Mining in Cyprus.' In eds. A. Marangou and K. Psillides, *Cyprus, Copper, and the Sea*: 43–76. Nicosia: Government of Cyprus.

Cook, S. 1966. 'The Obsolete "Anti-Market" Mentality: A Critique of the Substantive Approach to Economic Anthropology.' *American Anthropologist* 68: 323–345.

Cook, S. 1968. 'Review of Primitive, Archaic, and Modern Economies: Essays of Karl Polanyi, edited by George Dalton.' *American Anthropologist* 70: 966–969.

Cook, S. 1969. 'The "Anti-Market" Mentality Re-Examined: A Further Critique of the Substantive Approach to Economic Anthropology.' *South Western Journal of Anthropology* 25: 378–406.

Cooney, K.M. 2007a. 'Labour.' In ed. T.A.H. Wilkinson, *The Egyptian World*: 160–174. London: Routledge.

Cooney, K.M. 2007b. *The Cost of Death: The Social and Economic Value of Ancient Egyptian Funerary Art in the Ramesside Period.* Egyptologische Uitgaven; 22. Leiden: Nederlands Instituut voor het Nabije Oosten.

Cooney, K.M. 2008. 'Profit or Exploitation? The Production of Ramesside Tombs Within the West Theban Funerary Economy.' *Journal of Egyptian History* 1: 79–115.

Courtois, J.C. 1982: 'L'Activité métallurgique des bronzes d'Enkomi au Bronze Récent (1650–1100 avant J.-C.).' In eds. J.D. Muhly, R. Maddin, and V. Karageorghis, *Early Metallurgy in Cyprus, 4000–500 BC*: 155–174. Nicosia: Pierides Foundation.

Craddock, P.T. 1980. 'The Composition of Copper Produced at the Ancient Smelting Camps in the Wadi Timna.' In ed. P.T. Craddock, *Scientific Studies in Early Mining and Extractive Metallurgy*. British Museum Occasional Paper; 20: 165–173. London: British Museum.

Craddock, P.T. 1986: 'Report on the Composition of Bronzes Excavated from a Middle Cypriot Site at Episkopi Phaneromeni and Some Comparative Cypriot Bronze Age Metalwork.' In eds. S. Swiny, G. Rapp, and E. Hersher, *The Kent State University Expedition to Episkopi Phaneromeni, Part 2.* Studies in Mediterranean Archaeology; 74: 153–158. Nicosia: P. Åströms Förlag.

Craddock, P.T. 1989. 'The Scientific Analysis of Early Mining and Smelting Technology.' In ed. J. Henderson, *Scientific Analysis in Archaeology and Its Interpretation.* Archaeological Research Tools; 5: 178–212. Oxford: Oxford University Committee for Archaeology, Institute of Archaeology.

Craddock, P.T. 1995. *Early Metal Mining and Production.* Edinburgh: Edinburgh University Press.

Crane, E. 1983. *The Archaeology of Beekeeping.* London: Duckworth.

Crane, E. 1999. *The World History of Beekeeping and Honey Hunting.* London: Duckworth.

Crane, E. and A.J. Graham. 1985. 'Bee Hives of the Ancient World.' *Bee World* 66: 25–41, 148–170.

Crawford, D.J. 1979. 'Food: Tradition and Change in Hellenistic Egypt World Archaeology.' *World Archaeology* 11: 136–146.

Crew, P. 1990. 'Firesetting Experiment at Rhiw Goch, 1989.' In eds. P. Crew and S. Crew, *Early Mining in the British Isles: Proceedings of the Early Mining Workshop at Plas Tan Y Bwlch, Snowdonia National Park Study Centre, 17–19 November, 1989.* Plas Tan Y Bwlch Occasional Paper; 1: 57. Tan y Bwlch, Gwynedd: Plas Tan y Bwlch, Snowdonia National Park Study Centre.

Crewe, L. 1998. *Spindle Whorls: A Study of Form, Function and Decoration in Prehistoric Bronze Age Cyprus.* Studies in Mediterranean Archaeology and Literature; 149. Jonsered, Sweden: P. Åströms Förlag.

Crewe, L. 2007. *Early Enkomi: Regionalism, Trade and Society at the Beginning of the Late Bronze Age on Cyprus.* BAR International Series; 1706. Oxford: BAR Publishing.

Crewe, L. and I. Hill. 2012. 'Finding Beer in the Archaeological Record: A Case Study from Kissonerga-Skalia on Bronze Age Cyprus.' *Levant: The Journal of the Council for British Research in the Levant* 44: 205–237.

Crowfoot, G.M.H. 1931. *Methods of Hand Spinning in Egypt and the Sudan.* County Borough of Halifax, Bankfield Museum Notes. Second Series; 12. Halifax: F. King and Sons.

Crowfoot, G.M.H. 1954. 'Textiles, Basketry, and Mats.' In eds. C.J. Singer, T.I. Williams, and R. Raper, *A History of Technology.* Vol. 1: 413–417. Oxford: Clarendon Press.

Curtis, R.I. 2001. *Ancient Food Technology.* Leiden: Brill.

Dalton, G. 1961. 'Economic Theory and Primitive

Society.' *American Anthropologist* 63: 1–25.

Dalton, G. 1971. *Economic Anthropology and Development.* London: Basic Books.

Dalton, G. and J. Köcke. 1983. 'The Work of the Polanyi Group: Past, Present, and Future.' In ed. S. Ortiz, *Economic Anthropology: Topics and Theories*: 21–50. Lanham: University Press of America.

Darby, W.J., P. Ghalioungui, and L. Grivetti. 1977. *Food: The Gift of Osiris.* 2 Vols. London; New York: Academic Press.

Darnell, J.C. and C. Manassa. 2007. *Tutankhamun's Armies: Battle and Conquest During Ancient Egypt's Late Eighteenth Dynasty.* Hoboken: John Wiley and Sons.

Davey, C.J. 1979. 'Some Ancient Near Eastern Pot Bellows.' *Levant: Journal of the British School of Archaeology in Jerusalem* 11: 101–111.

David, A.R., A. Kershaw, and A. Heagerty. 2010. 'Atherosclerosis and Diet in Ancient Egypt.' *Lancet* 375: 718–719.

Davies, N. de G. 1901. *The Rock Tombs of Sheikh Saïd.* Memoir of the Archaeological Survey of Egypt; 10. London: Offices of the Egypt Exploration Fund.

Davies, N. de G. 1903. *The Rock Tombs of El-'Amarna. The Tomb of Meryra.* Vol. 1. Memoir of the Archaeological Survey of Egypt; 13. London: Egypt Exploration Fund.

Davies, N. de G. 1913. *Five Theban Tombs.* Memoir of the Archaeological Survey of Egypt; 21. London: The Egypt Exploration Society.

Davies, N. de G. 1917. *The Tomb of Nakht at Thebes by Norman de Garis Davies; With Plates in Color by L. Crane, N. de Garis Davies, and F. S. Unwin, of the Egyptian Expedition, and Nina de Garis Davies.* Publications of the Metropolitan Museum of Art Egyptian Expedition. Robb de Peyster Tytus Memorial Series; 1. New York: Metropolitan Museum of Art.

Davies, N. de G. 1927. *Two Ramesside Tombs at Thebes by N. de Garis Davies; With Plates in Color by N. de Garis Davies, H. R. Hopgood, C. K. Wilkinson, the Late N. Hardy and Nina de Garis Davies of the Egyptian Expedition.* Publications of the Metropolitan Museum of Art Egyptian Expedition. Robb de Peyster Tytus Memorial Series; 5. New York: Metropolitan Museum of Art.

Davies, N. de G. 1929: 'The Town House in Ancient Egypt.' *Metropolitan Museum Studies* 1: 233–255.

Davies, N. de G. 1933. *The Tomb of Nefer-Hotep at Thebes: Plates in Folio by N. de Garis Davies, with Plates in Color by Nina de Garis Davies.* Vol. 1. Publications of the Metropolitan Museum of Art Egyptian Expedition; 9. New York: Metropolitan Museum of Art.

Davies, N. de G. 1943a. *The Tomb of Rekh-mi-Re at Thebes.* Vol. 1. Publications of the Metropolitan Museum of Art Egyptian Expedition; 11. New York: Plantin Press.

Davies, N. de G. 1943b. *The Tomb of Rekh-mi-Re at Thebes.* Vol 2. Publications of the Metropolitan Museum of Art Egyptian Expedition; 11. New York: Plantin Press.

Davies, N. de G. and A.H. Gardiner. 1920. *The Tomb of Antefoker, Vizier of Sesostris I, and of His Wife, Senet (No. 60). Illustrated by Six Plates in Colour by Nina de G. Davies and by Forty-two Plates in Line and Collotype.* Published Under the Auspices of the Egypt Exploration Society. London: Alan and Unwin.

Davies, N. de G. and R.O. Faulkner. 1947. 'A Syrian Trading Venture to Egypt.' *Journal of Egyptian Archaeology* 33: 40–46.

Davies, N. de G. and T.E. Peet. 1941. *The Tomb of the Vizier Ramose.* Mond Excavations at Thebes; 1. London: Egypt Exploration Society

Davies, N.M. and A.H.S. Gardiner. 1926. *The Tomb of Huy, Viceroy of Nubia in the Reign of Tutankhamun (No.40). Copied in Line and Colour by Nina de Garis Davies and with Explanatory Text by Alan H. Gardiner.* The Theban Tombs Series; 4th Memoir. London: The Egypt Exploration Society.

Davies, N.M. and A.H. Gardiner. 1936. *Ancient Egyptian Paintings Selected, Copied, and Described by Nina M. Davies with the Editorial Assistance of Alan H. Gardiner.* Vol. 1. Special Publication of the Oriental Institute of the University of Chicago. Chicago: The University of Chicago Press.

Dayton, J.E. and A. Dayton. 1986. 'Uses and Limitations of Lead Isotopes in Archaeology.' In eds. J.S. Olin and M.J. Blackman, *Proceedings of the 24th International Archaeometry Symposium*: 13–37. Washington D.C.: Smithsonian Institution Press.

de Jesus, P.S. 1980. *The Development of Prehistoric Mining and Metallurgy in Anatolia.* Vol. 1. BAR International Series; 74. Oxford: BAR Publishing.

de Martino, S. 1999. 'Ura and the Boundaries of Tarhuntašša.' *Altorientalische Forschungen* 26: 291–300.

de Vartavan, C.V. and A. Amorós. 1997. *Codex of Ancient Egyptian Plant Remains.* London: Triade Exploration.

Degen, A.A. 2007. 'Sheep and Goat Milk in Pastoral Societies.' *Small Ruminant Research* 68: 7–19.

Dennell, R.W. 1979. 'Prehistoric Diet and Nutrition: Some Food for Thought.' *World Archaeology* 11: 121–135.

Dercksen, J.G. 1996. *The Old Assyrian Copper Trade in Anatolia*, Nederlands Historisch-Archaeologisch Instituut Te Istanbul 75. Istanbul.

Deshayes, J. 1960. *Les Outils de bronze, de l'Indus au Danube (IVe au IIe Millénaire).* Vol. 1. Institut français d'archéologie de Beyrouth, Bibliothèque archéologique et historique. Paris: Librairie orientaliste Paul Geuthner.

Dharmalingam A. 2004. 'Reproductivity.' In eds. D.A. Swanson and J.S. Seigel, *The Methods and Materials of Demography,* Second Edition: 429–453. Amsterdam: Elsevier Press.

Diakonoff, I.M. 1963. 'The Commune in the Ancient East as Treated in the Works of Soviet Researchers.' *Soviet Anthropology and Archeology* 2: 32–46.

Diakonoff, I.M. 1972. 'Socio-economic Classes in Babylonia and the Babylonian Concept of Social Stratification.' In ed. D.O. Edzard, *Gesellschaftsklassen im Alten Zweistromland und in den angrenzenden Gebieten: XVIII. Rencontre assyriologique internationale, München, 29. Juni bis 3. Juli 1970*: 41–52. Munich: Verlag der Bayerischen Akademie der Wissenschaften.

Diakonoff, I.M. 1975. 'The Rural Community in the Ancient Near East.' *Journal of the Economic and Social History of the Orient* 18: 121–133.

Diakonoff, I.M. 1982. 'The Structure of Near Eastern Society Before the Middle of the Second Millennium B.C.' *Oikumene* 3: 7–100.

Diakonoff, I.M. and P.L. Kohl. 1991. *Early Antiquity.* Chicago: University of Chicago.

Dijkman, J.T. and P.R. Lawrence. 1997. 'The Energy Expenditure of Cattle and Buffaloes Walking and Working in Different Soil Conditions.' *The Journal of Agricultural Science* 128: 95–103.

Dixon, D.M. 1969. 'A Note on Cereals in Ancient Egypt.' In eds. P.J. Ucko and G.W. Dimbleby, *The Domestication and Exploitation of Plants and Animals*: 131–142. London: Duckworth.

Doe, B. and R.B. Serjeant. 1975. 'A Fortified Tower-House in Wadi Jirdan.' *Bulletin of the School of Oriental and African Studies, University of London* 38: 1–23.

Doonan, R.C.P. 1994. 'Sweat, Fire and Brimstone: Pre-Treatment of Copper Ore and the Effects on Smelting Technology.' *The Journal of the Historical Metallurgy Society* 28: 84–97.

Dossin, G. 1952. *Correspondance de Iasmaḫ-Addu* Transcribed and translated by Georges Dossin. *Archives royales de Mari*; 5. Paris: Imprimerie nationale.

Dothan, T.K. 1963. 'Spinning Bowls.' *Israel Exploration Journal* 13: 97–112.

Dovring, F. 'Unemployment in Traditional Agriculture.' *Economic Development and Cultural Change* 15: 163–173.

Drenka, A. 2003. 'New Excavations in the Chalcolithic Mine T of Timna. Preliminary Report of the Excavations March-May 2001.' *Institute for Archaeo-Metallurgical Studies* 23: 21–26.

Drew, J.S. 1947. 'Manorial Accounts of St. Swithun's Priory, Winchester.' *The English Historical Review* 62: 20–41.

Drews, R. 1993. *The End of the Bronze Age.* Princeton: Princeton University Press.

du Plat Taylor, J. 1952. 'A Late Bronze Age Settlement at Apliki, Cyprus.' *The Antiquaries Journal* 32: 133–167.

Duncan-Jones, R. 1974. *The Economy of the Roman Empire: Quantitative Studies.* London: Cambridge University Press.

Duncan-Jones, R. 1976. 'The Price of Wheat in Roman Egypt Under the Principate.' *Chiron* 6: 241–262.

Dziobek, E. 1992. *Das Grab des Ineni. Theben Nr. 81.* Archäologische Veröffentlichungen. Deutsches Archäologisches Institut. Abteilung Kairo; 63. Mainz: Philipp von Zabern.

Earl B. 1996. 'Melting Tin in the West of England: Part 2.' *The Journal of the Historical Metallurgy Society* 20: 17–32.

Earl, B. and K.A. Yener. 1993. 'Replication Experiments of Tin Using Crucibles.' *Arkeometri Sonuçları Toplantısı* 9: 163–175.

Earle T. 2011. 'Redistribution in Aegean Palatial Societies. Redistribution and the Political Economy: The Evolution of an Idea.' *American Journal of Archaeology* 115: 237–244.

Earle, T. 1977. 'A Reappraisal of Redistribution.' In eds. T. Earle and J.E. Ericson, *Exchange Systems in Prehistory*: 213–219. London: Academic Press.

Eastwood, G.M. 1985. 'Preliminary Report on the Textiles.' In ed. B.J. Kemp, *Amarna Reports II.* London: Egypt Exploration Society.

Ebeling, J.R. and M.R. Yorke. 2004. 'The Archaeology of the Daily Grind: Ground Stone Tools and Food Production in the Southern Levant.' *Near Eastern Archaeology* 67: 108–117.

Edens, C. 1992. 'Dynamics of Trade in the Ancient Mesopotamian "World System".' *American Anthropologist* 94: 118–139.

Edmonds, M. 1990. 'Description, Understanding and the Chaînes Opératoire.' *Archaeological Review from Cambridge* 9: 55–81.

Ellis, R.S. 1976. 'Mesopotamian Crafts in Modern and Ancient Times: Ancient Near East Weaving.' *American Journal of Archaeology* 80: 76–77.

Ellison, R. 1982. 'The Agriculture of Mesopotamia c.3000–600 B.C.' *Tools and Tillage* 4: 173–184.

Emery, W.B. 1962. *A Funerary Repast in an Egyptian Tomb of the Archaic Period.* Scholae Adriani de Buck memoriae dicatae; 1: Leiden: Nederlands Instituut voor het Nabije Oosten.

Emery, W.B., H.S. Smith, and A. Millard 1979. *The Fortress of Buhen: The Archaeological Report.* Excavations at Buhen; 1. London: Egypt Exploration Society.

Endesfelder, E. 1979: 'Zur Frage der Bewässerung im pharaonischen Ägypten.' *Zeitschrift für ägyptische Sprache und Altertumskunde* 106: 37–51.

Engel, T. 1993. 'Charcoal Remains from an Iron Age Copper Smelting Slag Heap at Feinan, Wadi Arabah, Jordan.' *Vegetation History and Archaeobotany* 2: 205–211.

Erman, A and H. Grapow, eds. 1971. *Wörterbuch der aegyptischen Sprache: im Auftrage der deutschen Akademien.* 7 Vols. Unchanged Reprint. Berlin: Akademie-Verlag.

Evans-Pritchard, E.E. 1969. 'Introduction.' In M. Mauss, *The Gift: Forms and Functions of Exchange in Archaic Societies*: *i-x*. Translated by I. Cunnison. London: Routledge and Kegan Paul.

Evershed, R.P., C. Heron, S. Charters and L.J. Goad. 1992. 'The Survival of Food Residues: New Methods of Analysis, Interpretation and Application.' In ed. A.M. Pollard, *New Developments in Archaeological Science. A Joint Symposium of the Royal Society and the British Academy, February 1991*: 187–208.

Oxford: Oxford University Press.

Eyre, C. 1979. 'A "Strike" Text from the Theban Necropolis.' In eds. J. Ruffle, J.G.A. Gaballa, and K.A. Kitchen, *Orbis Aegyptiorum Speculum: Glimpses of Ancient Egypt. Studies in Honour of H. W. Fairman*: 80–91. Warminster: Aris and Phillips Ltd.

Eyre, C. 1987a. 'Work and the Organisation of Work in the Old Kingdom.' In ed. M.A. Powell, *Labor in the Ancient Near East*. American Oriental Series; 68: 5–47. New Haven: American Oriental Society.

Eyre, C. 1987b. 'Work and the Organisation of Work in the New Kingdom.' In ed. M.A. Powell, *Labor in the Ancient Near East*. American Oriental Series; 68: 167–221. New Haven: American Oriental Society.

Eyre, C. 1987c. 'The Use of Data from Deir el-Medina.' *Bibliotheca Orientalis* 44: 21–32.

Eyre, C. 1994a. 'Feudal Tenure and Absentee Landlords.' In ed. S. Allam, *Grund und Boden in Altägypten (rechtliche und sozio-ökonomische Verhältnisse): Akten des internationalen Symposions, Tübingen 18.-20. Juni 1990*. Untersuchungen zum Rechtsleben im alten Ägypten; 2: 107–133. Tübingen: Im Selbstverlag des Herausgebers.

Eyre, C. 1994b. 'The Water Regime for Orchards and Plantations in Pharaonic Egypt.' *Journal of Egyptian Archaeology* 80: 57–80.

Eyre, C. 1995a. 'The Agricultural Cycle, Farming, and Water Management in the Ancient Near East.' In ed. J.M. Sasson, *Civilizations of the Ancient Near East*. Vol. 1: 175–190. New York: Scribner.

Eyre, C. 1995b. 'The Village Economy in Pharaonic Egypt.' In eds. A.K. Bowman and E.L. Rogan, *Agriculture in Egypt*. Proceedings of the British Academy; 96: 33–60. Oxford: Oxford University Press.

Eyre, C. 1998. 'The Market Women of Pharaonic Egypt.' In eds. N.-C. Grimal and B. Menu, *Le Commerce en Égypte ancienne*: 173–191. Cairo: Institut français d'archéologie orientale.

Eyre, C. 1999. 'Village Economy in Pharaonic Egypt.' In eds. A.K. Bowman and E.L. Rogan, *Agriculture in Egypt from Pharaonic to Modern Times*: 33–60. Oxford: Published for the British Academy by Oxford University Press.

Eyre, C. 2010. 'The Economy: Pharaonic.' In ed. A.B. Lloyd, *A Companion to Ancient Egypt*: 291–308. Oxford: Blackwell Publishing Ltd.

Ezzamel, M. 1997. 'Accounting, Control, and Accountability: Preliminary Evidence from Ancient Egypt.' *Critical Perspectives on Accounting* 8: 563–601.

Ezzamel, M. 2002. 'Accounting and Redistribution: The Palace and Mortuary Cult in the Middle Kingdom, Ancient Egypt.' *Accounting Historians Journal* 29: 1–27.

Ezzamel, M. 2009. 'Order and Accounting as a Performative Ritual: Evidence from Ancient Egypt.' *Accounting, Organizations and Society* 34: 348–380.

Ezzamel, M. and K. Hoskin. 'Retheorizing the Relationship Between Accounting, Writing and Money with Evidence from Mesopotamia and Ancient Egypt.' *Critical Perspectives on Accounting* 13: 333–367.

Fabre, D. 2005. *Seafaring in Ancient Egypt*. London: Periplus Publishing London Ltd.

FAO. 1969. *Farm Implements for Arid and Tropical Regions*. FAO Agricultural Development Paper; 91 prepared by H.J. Hopfen. Agricultural Series; 13. Rome: Food and Agriculture Organization of the United Nations.

FAO. 1973. *Energy and Protein Requirements*. FAO Nutrition Meetings Report Series; 52 and WHO 1973. Technical Report Series; 522. Rome: Food and Agriculture Organization of the United Nations.

FAO. 1985a. *Industrial Charcoal Making: Useful Coversion Factors*. FAO Forestry Paper 63. Rome: Food and Agriculture Organization of the United Nations.

FAO. 1985b. *Prevention of Post-Harvest Food Losses:A Training Manual*. Rome: Food and Agriculture Organization of the United Nations. [Online Publication]. <http://www.fao.org/docrep/x0039e/x0039e00.htm>, accessed 15/10/2010.

FAO. 1987. *Simple Technologies for Charcoal Making: Earth Pits for Charcoal Making*. FAO Forestry Paper 41. Rome: Food and Agriculture.

FAO. 1994. *Production Year Book 1993*. Vol. 47. FAO Statistics Series; 117. Rome: Food and Agriculture Organization of the United Nations.

FAO. 1995. *Harvesting of Textile Animal Fibres*. FAO Agricultural Services Bulletin 122. Rome: Food and Agriculture Organization of the United Nations.

FAO. 1999. *Fermenting Cereals. A Global Perspective*. FAO Agricultural Services Bulletin 138. Rome: Food and Agriculture Organization of the United Nations.

FAO. 2007. *Improved Use of Hoes for Land Preparation, Planting and Weeding*. Rural Infrastructure and Agro-industries Division (Agricultural Machinery and Infrastructure) in FAO. Published Online by TECA (Technologies and Practices for Small Agricultural Producers). Updated 2013. <http://teca.fao.org/technology/labour-saving-technologies-and-practices-improved-use-hoes-land-preparation-planting-and>, accessed 15/10/2012.

Fasnacht, W. and V. Kassianidou. 1992. 'Copper at Almyras. A Mining and Smelting Site in Cyprus.' In eds. A. Marangou and K. Psillides, *Cyprus, Copper and the Sea*: 78–90. Nicosia: Government of Cyprus.

Fasnacht, W., D. Rechenmacher, and E. Hack. 2008. 'A Complete Iron Age Copper Smelting Furnace from Cyprus – Reconstructed, Digitised, and Virtualised.' In eds. Ü. Yalçın, H. Özbal, and A.G. Pasamehmetoglu, *Ancient Mining in Turkey and the Eastern Mediterranean:*

International Conference AMITEM 2008, June 15–22: 465–473. Ankara: Atılım University.

Fathy, H. 1973. *Architecture for the Poor: An Experiment in Rural Egypt*. Chicago: University of Chicago Press.

Faulkner, R.O. 1940. 'Egyptian Seagoing Ships.' *Journal of Egyptian Archaeology* 26: 3–9.

Feldman, M. 1976. 'Wheats.' In ed. N.W. Simmonds, *Evolution of Crop Plants*: 120–128. Reprint 1986. Harlow: Longman Scientific and Technical.

Feldman, M.H. 2006. *Diplomacy by Design*. Chicago: University of Chicago Press.

Fielding, D. and P. Krause. 1998. *Donkeys*. London: Macmillan Education.

Finley, M.I. 1956. *The World of Odysseus*. London: Chatto and Windus Ltd.

Finley, M.I. 1977. 'The Ancient City: From Fustel de Coulanges to Max Weber and Beyond.' *Comparative Studies in Society and History* 19: 305–327.

Finley, M.I. 1985. *Ancient Economy*. Second Edition. London: Hogarth.

Finnestad, R.B. 1988. 'The Pharoah and the Democratisation of Post-Mortem Life.' In ed. G. Englund, *The Religion of the Ancient Egyptians: Cognitive Structures and Popular Expressions: Proceedings of Symposia in Uppsala and Bergen, 1987 and 1988*. Acta Universitatis Upsaliensis. Boreas; 20: 89–93. Uppsala: S. Academiae Ubsaliensis; Stockholm: Almqvist & Wiksell International.

Firth, R.W. 1950. *Primitive Polenesian Economy*. New York: Humanities Press.

Firth, R.W. 1959. *Economics of the New Zealand Maori*. Second Edition. Wellington: R.E. Owen.

Firth, R.W. 1964. 'Editors' Preface.' In eds. R.W. Firth and B.S. Yamey, *Capital, Saving, and Credit in Peasant Societies: Studies from Asia, Oceania, the Caribbean, and Middle America*: 7–10. London: Allen and Unwin.

Firth, R.W. 1967. 'Themes in Economic Anthropology: A General Comment.' In ed. R.W. Firth, *Themes in Economic Anthropology*: 1–27. London: Tavistock Publications.

Fleming, D.E. 2002. Review of David Schloen, *Patrimonial Pyramid: Explaining Bronze Age Society* in *Bulletin of the American Schools of Oriental Research* 328: 73–80.

Foaden, G.P. and F. Fletcher. 1908. *Text Book of Egyptian Agriculture*. Vol. 1. Cairo: National Printing Department.

Foaden, G.P. and F. Fletcher. 1910. *Text Book of Egyptian Agriculture*. Vol. 2. Cairo: F. Eimer.

Forbes, H. 1992. 'The Ethnoarchaeological Approach to Ancient Greek Agriculture.' In ed. B. Wells, *Agriculture in Ancient Greece: Proceedings of the Seventh International Symposium at the Swedish Institute of Athens, 16–17 May 1990*. Skrifter Utgivna av Svenska institutet i Athen; 42: 87–104. Stockholm: Svenska institutet i Athen.

Forbes, R.J. 1964. *Studies in Ancient Technology*. Vol. 4. Second Edition. Leiden: Brill.

Forbes, R.J. 1972. *Studies in Ancient Technology*. Vol. 9. Second Edition. Leiden: Brill.

Forbes, R.J. 1993. *Studies in Ancient Technology*. Vol. 2. Third Edition. Leiden: Brill.

Foxhall, L. and H.A. Forbes. 1982. 'Sitometreia: The Role of Grain as a Staple Food in Classical Antiquity.' *Chiron* 12: 41–90.

Frier, B. 1982. 'Roman Life Expectancy: Ulpian's Evidence.' *Harvard Studies in Classical Philology* 86: 213–251.

Frier, B. 2000. 'Demography.' In eds. A.K. Bowman, P. Garnsey and D. Rathbone, *Cambridge Ancient History. The High Empire, A.D. 70–192*. Vol. 11. Second Edition: 787–816. Cambridge: Cambridge University Press.

Frost, H. 1969a. 'The Stone Anchors of Ugarit.' *Ugaritica* 6: 235–245.

Frost, H. 1969b. 'The Stone Anchors of Byblos.' *Mélanges de l'Université Saint-Joseph* 45: 425–442.

Frost, H. 1979. 'Egypt and Stone Anchors: Some Recent Discoveries.' *Mariner's Mirror* 65: 137–161.

Frost, H. 1986. 'Anchors Sacred and Profane: Ugarit-Ras Shamra, 1986, the Stone Anchors Revised and Compared.' In ed. M. Yon, *Arts et industries de la Pierre*.Publicatio ns de la Mission archéologique française de Ras Shamra-Ougarit; 6: 355–410. Paris: Maison de L'Orient.

Frost, H. 1993. 'Harbours and Proto-Harbours; Early Levantine Engineering.' In eds. V. Karageorghis and D. Michaelides, *Proceedings of the International Symposium, Cyprus and the Sea. Nicosia 25th-26th September, 1993*: 1–22. Nicosia: University of Cyprus.

Gale, N.H. 1991. 'Copper Ingots: Their Origin and their Place in the Bronze Age Metals Trade in the Mediterranean.' In ed. N.H. Gale, *Bronze Age Trade in the Mediterranean: Papers Presented at the Conference Held at Rewley House, Oxford, in December 1989*. Studies in Mediterranean Archaeology; 90: 197–239. Jonsered: P. Åströms Förlag.

Gale, N.H. 1999. 'Lead Isotope Characterisation of the Ore Deposits of Cyprus and Sardinia and Its Application to the Discovery of the Sources of Copper for Late Bronze Age Oxhide Ingots.' In eds. S.M.M. Young, A.M. Pollard, P. Budd, and R.A. Ixer, *Metals in Antiquity*, BAR International Series; 792: 110–121. Oxford: BAR Publishing.

Gale, N.H. 2001. 'Archaeology, Science-Based Archaeology, and the Mediterranean Bronze Age Metals Trade: A Contribution to the Debate.' *European Journal of Archaeology* 4: 113–130.

Gale, N.H. 2003. 'Disciplinary Fault Lines: Science and Social Archaeology - another View.' *Mediterranean Archaeology and Archaeometry* 3: 55–62.

Gale, N.H. 2011. 'Copper Oxhide Ingots and Lead Isotope Provenancing.' In eds. P. Betancourt and S.C. Ferrence, *Metallurgy: Understanding How, Learning Why; Studies in Honor of James D.*

Muhly: 213–229. Philadelphia: INSTAP Academic Press.

Gale, N.H. and Z.A. Stos-Gale. 1995. 'Comments on 'Oxhide Ingots, Recycling, and the Mediterranean Metals Trade.' *Journal of Mediterranean Archaeology* 8: 33–41.

Gale, N.H. and Z.A. Stos-Gale. 2005. Zur Herkunft der Kupferbarren aus dem Schiffswrack von Uluburun und der spätbronzezeitliche Metallhandel im Mittelmeerraum.' In eds. Ü. Yalçin, C. Pulak, und R. Slotta, *Das Schiff von Uluburun: Welthandel vor 3000 Jahren: Katalog der Ausstellung des Deutschen Bergbau-Museums Bochum vom 15. Juli 2005 bis 16. Juli 2006.* Veröffentlichungen aus dem Deutschen Bergbau-Museum Bochum; 138: 117–131. Bochum: Deutsches Bergbau-Museum.

Galili, E. and B. Rosen. 2011. 'Ancient Underwater and Coastal Settlements of Israel: An Endangered Cultural Resource.' In eds. H. Oniz and E. Aslan, *SOMA 2009: Proceedings of the XIII Symposium on Mediterranean Archaeology, Selcuk University of Konya, Turkey 23–24 April 2009.* BAR International Series; 2200. Oxford: BAR Publishing.

Galili, E., N. Shmueli, and M. Artzy. 1986. 'Bronze Age Ship's Cargo of Copper and Tin.' *International Journal of Nautical Archaeology and Underwater Exploration* 15: 25–37.

Gallant, T.W. 1991. *Risk and Survival in Ancient Greece.* Cambridge: Cambridge University Press.

Gardiner, A.H. 1941. 'Ramesside Texts Relating to Taxation and Transport of Corn.' *Journal of Egyptian Archaeology* 27: 19–73.

Gardiner, A.H. 1947a. *Ancient Egyptian Onomastica.* Vol. 1. Oxford: Oxford University Press.

Gardiner, A.H. 1947b. *Ancient Egyptian Onomastica.* Vol. 2. Oxford: Oxford University Press.

Gardiner, A.H. 1948. *The Wilbour Papyrus: Commentary.* Vol. 2. London: Published for the Brooklyn Museum at the Oxford University Press.

Garnsey, P. 1988. *Famine and Food Supply in the Graeco-Roman World. Responses to Risk and Crisis.* Cambridge: Cambridge University Press.

Garnsey, P. 1992. 'Yield of the Land.' In ed. B. Wells, *Agriculture in Ancient Greece: Proceedings of the Seventh International Symposium at the Swedish Institute of Athens, 16–17 May 1990.* Skrifter Utgivna av Svenska institutet i Athen; 42: 147–153. Stockholm: Svenska institutet i Athen.

Garnsey, P. 1998. *Cities, Peasants and Food in Classical Antiquity: Essays in Social and Economic History.* Cambridge: Cambridge University Press.

Gelb, I.J. 1965. 'The Ancient Mesopotamian Ration System.' *Journal of Near Eastern Studies* 24: 230–243.

Geller, J.R. 1992. 'From Prehistory to History: Beer in Egypt.' In eds. R. Friedman and B. Adams, *The Followers of Horus.* Egyptian Studies Association Publication; 2: 19–26. Oxford: Oxbow Books.

Georgiou, H.S. 1991. 'Bronze Age Ships and Rigging.' In eds. R. Laffineur and L. Basch, *Thalassa: l'Égée préhistorique et la mer:* actes *de la troisième Rencontre égéenne internationale de l'Université de Liège, Station de recherches sous-marines et océanographiques, Calvi, Corse, 23–25 avril 1990.* Aegaeum; 7: 61–72. Liège: Université de Liège.

Germer, R. 1992. *Die Textilfärberei und die Verwendung gefärbter Textilien im alten Ägypten.* Wiesbaden: Harrassowitz.

Giardino, C., G.E. Gigante, and S. Ridolfi. 2003. 'Appendix 8.1: Archaeometallurgical Studies.' In eds. S. Swiny, G. Rapp, and E. Herscher, *Sotira Kaminoudhia. An Early Bronze Age Site in Cyprus.* Cyprus American Archaeological Research Institute Monograph Series; 8: 385–396. Boston: American Schools of Oriental Research.

Gibson. M. 1974. 'Violation of Fallow: An Engineered Disaster in Mesopotamian Civilisation.' In eds. T.E. Downing and M. Gibson, *Irrigation's Impact on Society.* Anthropological Papers of the University of Arizona; 25: 7–19. Tucson, Arizona: The University of Arizona Press.

Gifford, J.A. 1985. 'Paleogeography of the Ancient Harbour Sites of the Larnaca Lolands, Southeastern Cyprus.' In ed. A. Raban, *Harbour Archaeology: Proceedings of the First International Workshop on Ancient Mediterranean Harbours, Caesarea Maritima, 24–28.6.83.* BAR International Series; 257: 45–48. Oxford: B.A.R.

Gilbert, R.I. and J.H. Mielke. 1985. 'Preface.' In eds. R.I. Gilbert and J.H. Mielke, *The Analysis of Prehistoric Diets.* Studies in Archaeology: i-xiv. Orlando: Academic Press.

Gilbreth, F.B. 1949. *Cheaper by the Dozen.* London: Heinemann.

Gill, D.W.J. 1991. 'Pots and Trade: Spacefillers or Objects d'Art.' *Journal of Hellenic Studies* 111: 29–47.

Gill, D.W.J. 2008. 'Inscribed Silver Plate from Tomb II at Vergina.' *Hesperia* 77: 335–358.

Gillis, C., R. Clayton, E. Pernicka, and N.H. Gale. 2003. 'Tin in the Bronze Age.' In eds. R. Laffineur and K.P. Foster, *Metron: Measuring the Aegean Bronze Age. Proceedings of the 9th International Aegean Conference/9e Rencontre égéenne internationale, New Haven, Yale University, 18–21 April 2002.* Aegaeum; 24: 103–110. Liège: Université de Liège.

Gills, K. and A.G. Frank. 1991. '5000 Years of World System History: The Cumulation of Accumulation.' In eds. C. Chase-Dunn and T. Hall, *Core/Periphery Relations in Precapitalist Worlds*: 67–112. Boulder: Westview Press.

Given, M., A.B. Knapp, and D. Coleman. 2003. *The Sydney Cyprus Survey Project: Social Approaches to Regional Archaeological Survey.*

Monumenta Archaeologica; 21. Los Angeles: Cotsen Institute of Archaeology, University of California.

Given, M., A.B. Knapp, N. Meyer, T.E. Gregory, V. Kassianidou, J.S. Noller, L. Wells, N. Urwin, and H. Wright. 1999. 'The Sydney Cyprus Survey Project: An Interdisciplinary Investigation of Long-Term Change in the North Central Troodos, Cyprus.' *Journal of Field Archaeology* 26: 19–39.

Goddeeris, A. 2002. *Economy and Society in Northern Babylonia in the Early Old Babylonian Period (ca. 2000–1800 B.C.)*. Orientalia Lovaniensia Analecta; 109. Leuven: Peeters.

Goe, M.R. 1982. 'Tillage with the Traditional Maresha in the Ethiopian Highlands.' *Tools and Tillage* 6: 127–175.

Goedicke, H. 1984. *Studies in the Hekanakte Papers.* Baltimore: Halgo.

Gomme, A.W. 1933. *The Population of Athens in the Fifth and Fourth Centuries BC.* Oxford: Oxford Blackwell.

Good, I. 2001. 'Archaeological Textiles: A Review of Current Research.' *Annual Review of Anthropology* 30: 209–226.

Goring, E. 1989. 'Death in Every-day Life: Aspects of Burial Practice in the Late Bronze Age.' In ed. E.J. Peltenburg, *Early Society in Cyprus*: 95-106. Edinburgh: Edinburgh University Press.

Grace, V. 1956. 'The Canaanite Jar.' In ed. S. Weinberg, *The Aegean and the Near East: Studies Presented to Hetty Goldman*: 80–109. Locust Valley: J.J. Augustin Publisher.

Grajetski, W. 2010. 'Class and Society: Position and Possessions.' In ed. W. Wendrich, *Egyptian Archaeology*: 180–199. Oxford: Wiley-Blackwell.

Grattan, J., S. Huxley, L.A. Karaki, L.H. Toland, D. Gilbertson, B. Pyatt, and Z. Saad. 2002. '"Death ... More Desirable Than Life?" The Human Skeletal Record and Toxicological Implications of Ancient Copper Mining and Smelting in Wadi Faynan, Southwestern Jordan.' *Toxicology and Industrial Health* 18: 297–307.

Greenough, H. 1947. *Form and Function: Remarks on Art, Design, and Architecture.* Berkeley: University of California Press.

Grégoire, J-P. 1999. 'Major Units for the Transformation of Grain.' In ed. P.C. Anderson, *Prehistory of Agriculture: New Experimental and Ethnographic Approaches*. Monograph, Institute of Archaeology, University of California Los Angeles; 40: 223–237. Los Angeles: Institute of Archaeology, University of California.

Gregory, C.A. 1982. *Gifts and Commodities*. London: Academic Press.

Griffith, F.L. 1898. *The Petrie Papyri: Hieratic Papyri from Kahun and Gurob (Principally of the Middle Kingdom)*. Vol. 2. London: Bernard Quaritch.

Grigg, D.B. 1974. *The Agricultural Systems of the World: An Evolutionary Approach.* Cambridge: Cambride University Press.

Guasch-Jané M.R., C. Andrés-Lacueva, O. Jáuregui, and R.M. Lamuela-Raventós. 2006. 'First Evidence of White Wine in Ancient Egypt from Tutankhamun's Tomb.' *Journal of Archaeological Science* 33: 1075–1080.

Hadfield, J.W. 1953. *Linen Flax Fibre Production in New Zealand.* [s.l]: Published Jointly by the Linen Corporation of N.Z. and the N.Z. Department of Agriculture.

Hadjisavvas, S. 1992. *An Introduction to Olive Oil Processing in Cyprus*. Studies in Mediterranean Archaeology; 99. Jonsered: P. Åströms Förlag.

Hadjisavvas, S. 1996. 'An Introduction to Olive Oil Production in Cyprus.' In eds. M. Heltzer and D. Eitam, *Olive Oil in Antiquity: Israel and Neighbouring Countries from the Neolithic to the Early Arab Period.* History of the Ancient Near East Studies; 7: 63–75. Haifa: University of Haifa.

Hafford, W.B. 2005. 'Research Notes: Hanging in the Balance: Precision Weighing in Antiquity.' *Expedition* 47: 35–37.

Haldane, C.W. 1990. 'Shipwreck Plant Remains.' *The Biblical Archaeologist* 53: 55–60.

Haldane, C.W. 1993. 'Direct Evidence for Organic Cargoes in the Late Bronze Age.' *World Archaeology* 24: 348–360.

Hall, M.E. and S.R. Steadman. 1991. 'Tin and Anatolia: Another Look.' *Journal of Mediterranean Archaeology* 4: 217–234.

Hall, R. 1981. 'The Pharaonic *mss* Tunic as a Smock.' *Göttinger Miszellen* 43: 29–37.

Hall, R. 1985. 'The Cast-Off Garment of Yesterday: Dresses Reversed in Life and Death.' *Bulletin de l'Institut français d'archéologie orientale* 85: 235–245.

Hall, R. 1986. *Egyptian Textiles.* Shire Egyptology Series; 4. Princess Risborough: Shire Publications Ltd.

Hall, T.D. 1997. 'World-system Theory.' In ed. T. Barfield, *The Dictionary of Anthropology*: 498–499. Oxford: Blackwell Publishing Ltd.

Hallager, B.P. 1993. 'Mycenaean Pottery in Crete.' In eds. C. Zerner, P. Zerner, J. Winder, A.J.B. Wace, and C.W. Blegen, *Wace and Blegen: Pottery as Evidence for Trade in the Aegean Bronze Age, 1939–1989: Proceedings of the International Conference, Held at the American School of Classical Studies at Athens, December 2–3, 1989*: 263–269. Amsterdam: J.C. Gieben.

Halstead, P. 1987. 'Traditional and Ancient Rural Economy in Mediterranean Europe: Plus ça Change?' *Journal of Hellenic Studies* 107: 77–87.

Halstead, P. 1989. 'The Economy Has Normal Surplus: Economic Stability and Social Change Among Early Farming Communities of Thessaly, Greece.' In eds. P. Halstead and J. O'Shea, *Bad Year Economics: Cultural Responses to Risk and Uncertainty.* New Directions in Archaeology: 68–80. Cambridge: Cambridge University Press.

Halstead, P. 1992. 'Agriculture in the Bronze Age Aegean: Towards a Model of Palatial Economy.' In ed. B. Wells, *Agriculture in Ancient Greece:*

Proceedings of the Seventh International Symposium at the Swedish Institute of Athens, 16–17 May 1990. Skrifter Utgivna av Svenska institutet i Athen; 42: 105–117. Stockholm: Svenska institutet i Athen.

Halstead, P. 1993. 'Banking on Livestock: Indirect Storage in Greek Agriculture.' *Bulletin on Sumerian Agriculture* 7: 63–75.

Halstead, P. 1994. 'The North-South Divide: Regional Paths to Complexity in Prehistoric Greece.' In eds. C. Mathers and S. Stoddart, *Development and Decline in the Mediterranean Bronze Age.* Sheffield Archaeological Monographs; 8: 195–219. Sheffield: J.R. Collis Publications.

Halstead, P. 1995. 'Plough and Power. The Economic and Social Significance of Cultivation with the Ox-Drawn Ard in the Mediterranean.' *Bulletin on Sumerian Agriculture* 8: 11–22.

Halstead, P. 1996. 'Pastoralism or Household Herding? Problems of Scale and Specialisation in Greek Animal Husbandry.' *World Archaeology* 28: 20–42.

Halstead, P. and G. Jones. 1997. 'Agrarian Ecology in the Greek Islands: Time Stress, Scale and Risk.' In eds. P.N. Kardulias and M.T. Shutes, *Aegean Strategies: Studies of Culture and Environment on the European Fringe*: 271–294. Lanham: Rowman and Littlefield.

Halstead, P. and J.C. Barrett. 2005. *Food, Cuisine and Society in Prehistoric Greece.* Sheffield Studies in Aegean Archaeology; 5. Oxford: Oxbow Books.

Halstead, Paul. 2011. 'Redistribution in Aegean Palatial Societies: Terminology, Scale, and Significance.' *American Journal of Archaeology* 115: 229–35.

Hankey, V. 1995. 'Stirrup Jars at El-Amarna.' In eds. W.V. Davies and L. Schofield, *Egypt, the Aegean, and the Levant: Interconnections in the Second Millennium B.C.*: 116–126. London: British Museum Press.

Haring, B. 2003. 'From Oral Practice to Written Record in Ramesside Deir El-Medina.' *Journal of the Economic and Social History of the Orient* 46: 249–272.

Haring, B. 2009. 'Economy.' In eds. E. Frood and W. Wendrich, *UCLA Encyclopedia of Egyptology.* Los Angeles. <http://digital2.library.ucla.edu/ viewItem.do? ark=21198/zz001nf64c>, accessed 29/07/2012.

Harpur, Y. 1987. *Decoration in Egyptian Tombs of the Old Kingdom: Studies in Orientation and Scene Content.* Studies in Egyptology. London: KPI.

Hartwig, M.K. 2004. *Tomb Painting and Identity in Ancient Thebes, 1419–1372 BCE.* Monumenta Aegyptiaca. Série imago; 10. Brussels: Fondation égyptologique reine Élisabeth; Turnhout: Brepols.

Hassan, F. 1994. 'Population Ecology and Civilization in Ancient Egypt.' In ed. C.L. Crumley, *Historical Ecology: Cultural Knowledge and Changing Landscapes.* School of American Research Advanced Seminar Series: 83–89. Santa Fe: School of American Research Press.

Hassan, F. 1997a. 'Nile Floods and Political Disorder in Early Egypt.' In eds. H.N. Dalfes, G. Kukla, and H. Weiss, *Third Millennium BC Climate Change and Old World Collapse*: 1–23. London: Springer.

Hassan, F. 1997b. 'The Dynamics of the Riverine Civilization: A Geoarchaeological Perspective on the Nile Valley, Egypt.' *World Archaeology* 29: 51–74.

Hassan, F. 2005. 'A River Runs Through Egypt: Nile Floods and Civilsation.' *Geotimes* 50: 22–25.

Haswell, M.R. 1953. *Economics of Agriculture in a Savannah Village: Report on Three Years' Study in Genieri Village and Its Lands, the Gambia.* Colonial Research Studies; 8. London: H.M.S.O. for the Colonial Office.

Hatcher, H. 2007. 'A Provenance Study on White Slip Wares from Late Bronze Age Cyprus and the Levant.' Unpublished Ph.D. Thesis, University of Reading. Reading.

Hauptmann, A. 2007. 'Problems and Methods of Archaeometallurgy.' In ed. Andreas Hauptmann, *The Archaeometallurgy of Copper. Evidence from Faynan, Jordan,* Natural Science in Archaeology: 7–38. Bochum: Deutsches Bergbau-Museum.

Hauptmann, A., R. Maddin, and M. Prange. 2002. 'On the Structure and Composition of Copper and Tin Ingots Excavated from the Shipwreck of Uluburun.' *Bulletin of the American Schools of Oriental Research* 328: 1–30.

Hawkes, C.F.C. 1974. 'Bronze Age Hungary, a Review of Recent Work.' *Proceedings of the Prehistoric Society* 40: 113–117.

Hayes, W.C. 1942. *Ostraka and Name Stones from the Tomb of Sen-Mut (No. 71) at Thebes.* Publications of the Metropolitan Museum of Art Egyptian Expedition; 15. New York: Metropolitan Museum of Art.

Healy, J.F. 1978. *Mining and Metallurgy in the Greek and Roman World.* Aspects of Greek and Roman Life. London: Thames and Hudson.

Helbaek, H. 1960. 'The Paleoethnobotany of the Near East and Europe.' In eds. R.J. Braidwood and B. Howe, *Prehistoric Investigations in Iraqi Kurdistan.* Studies in Ancient Oriental Civilization; 31: 99–118. Chicago: University of Chicago Press.

Helck, W. 1993. 'Wer konnte sich ein Begräbnis in Theben-West Leisten?' *Göttinger Miszellen* 135: 39–40.

Hellbing, L. 1979. *Alasia Problems.* Studies in Mediterranean Archaeology; 57. Gothenburg: P. Åström.

Helms, S.W. 1981 *Jawa: Lost City of the Black Desert.* London: Methuen.

Heltzer, M. 1976. *The Rural Community in Ancient Ugarit.* Wiesbaden: Reichert.

Heltzer, M. 1977. 'The Metal Trade of Ugarit and the Problem of Transportation of Commercial Goods.' *Iraq* 39: 203–211.

Heltzer, M. 1978. *Goods, Prices and the Organization of Trade in Ugarit: Marketing and Transportation in the Eastern Mediterranean in the Second Half of the Second Millennium B.C.E.* Wiesbaden: Reichert.

Heltzer, M. 1979. 'Royal Economy in Ugarit.' In ed. E. Lipinski, *State and Temple Economy in the Ancient Near East: Proceedings of the International Conference Organised by the Katholieke Universiteit Leuven from 10th to 14th April 1978*. Orientalia Lovaniensia Analecta; 5–6: 459–496. Leuven: Departement Oriëntalistiek.

Heltzer, M. 1982. *The Internal Organization of the Kingdom of Ugarit*. Wiesbaden: Reichert.

Heltzer, M. 1984. 'Private Property in Ugarit.' In ed. A. Archi, *Circulation of Goods in Non-Palatial Context in the Ancient Near East*. Incunabula Graeca; 82: 161–194. Rome: Edizioni dell'Ateneo.

Heltzer, M. 1996a. 'Olive Growing and Olive Oil in Ugarit.' In eds. M. Heltzer and D. Eitam, *Olive Oil in Antiquity: Israel and Neighbouring Countries from the Neolithic to the Early Arab Period*: History of the Ancient Near East Studies; 7: 77–89. Haifa: University of Haifa.

Heltzer, M. 1996b. 'The Symbiosis of Public and Private Sectors in Ugarit, Phoenicia, and Palestine.' In eds. B.A. Levene and M. Hudson, *Privatization in the Ancient Near East and Classical World.* Peabody Museum Bulletin; 1: 177–196. Cambridge, Mass.: Peabody Museum of Archaeology and Ethnology.

Heltzer, M. 1999. 'The Economy of Ugarit.' In eds. W.G.E. Watson and N. Wyatt, *Handbook of Ugaritic Studies*. Handbuch der Orientalistik. Erste Abteilung, Nahe und der Mittlere Osten; 39: 423–454. Leiden: Brill.

Henfaes Research Centre. 2004–2005. 'Guidelines for Growing Flax.' Flax and Hemp Project 2004–2005 [Online PDF]. Bangor: University of Wales. <http://www.flaxandhemp.bangor.ac.uk/pdfs/GuidelinesForGrowingFlax.pdf>, accessed 09/05/2013.

Hepper, F.N. 2009. *Pharaoh's Flowers: The Botanical Treasures of Tutankhamun*, Second Edition. Royal Botanic Gardens, Kew: HMSO.

Hermanson, R.E. and P.K. Kalita. 2012, 'Animal Manure Data Sheet.' *American Society of Agricultural Engineers.* D384.1. <http://cru.cahe.wsu.edu/CEPublications/eb1719/eb1719.html>, accessed 05/11/2012.

Herodotus. *Histories.* Translated by G.C. Macaulay. 1890. *The History of Herodotus.* London: Macmillan.

Herskovits, M.J. 1940. *The Economic Life of Primitive Peoples*. New York: A.A. Knopf.

Herskovits, M.J. 1952. *Economic Anthropology: A Study of Comparative Economics*. New York: A.A. Knopf.

Herskovits, M.J. 1959. 'Before the Machine.' In ed. M.H. Fried, *Readings in Anthropology.* Vol. 2: 147–160. New York: Thomas Y. Crowell Company.

Herskovits, M.J. 1968 [*c.*1952: 3–24]. 'Economizing and Rational Behavior.' Reprint in eds. E.E. LeClair and H.K. Schneider 1968, *Economic Anthropology: Readings in Theory and Analysis*: 40–55. New York; London: Holt, Rinehart, and Winston.

Hikade, T. 1998. 'Economic Aspects of the New Kingdom: The Mining Expeditions of the New Kingdom.' *The Bulletin of the Australian Centre for Egyptology* 9: 43–52.

Hillier, J.K., J.M. Bunbury, and A. Graham. 2007. 'Monuments on a Migrating Nile.' *Journal of Archaeological Science* 34: 1011–1015.

Hillman, G.C. 1973. 'Agricultural Productivity and Past Population Potential at Aqvan: An Exercise in the Calculation of Carrying Capacities.' *Anatolian Studies* 23: 225-240.

Hillman, G.C. 1984. 'Traditional Husbandry and Processing of Archaic Cereals in Recent Times: The Operations, Products and Equipment Which Might Feature in Sumerian Texts. Part I: The Glume Wheats.' *Bulletin on Sumerian Agriculture* 1: 114–152.

Hodder, I. 1977. 'Toward a Contextual Approach to Prehistoric Exchange.' In eds. T.K. Earle and J.E. Ericson, *Exchange Systems in Prehistory:* 199–211. London: Academic Press.

Hodder, I. 1991a. 'The Decoration of Containers: An Ethnographic and Historical Study.' In ed. W. Longacre, *Ceramic Ethnoarchaeology*: 71–94. Tucson: University of Arizona Press.

Hodder, I. 1991b. *Reading the Past: Current Approaches to Interpretation in Archaeology,* Second Edition. Cambridge: Cambridge University Press.

Hodel-Hoenes, S. 2000. *Life and Death in Ancient Egypt. Scenes from Private Tombs in New Kingdom Thebes*. Ithaca: Cornell University Press.

Hoffner, H.A. 1969. 'A Hittite Text in Epic Style about Merchants.' *Journal of Cuneiform Studies* 22: 34–45.

Hofmann, E. and K.L. Hofmann. 2004. *Bilder im Wandel: die Kunst der ramessidischen Privatgräber*. Theben; 17. Mainz: Philipp von Zabern.

Hood, A.D. 2003. *The Weaver's Craft: Cloth, Commerce, and Industry in Early Pennsylvania.* Philadelphia: University of Pennsylvania Press.

Hopkins, K. 1980. 'Taxes and Trade in the Roman Empire (200 B.C. - A.D. 400).' *Journal of Roman Studies* 70: 101–125.

Hopkins, K. 1983. Death and Renewal: Sociological Studies in Roman History. Vol. 2. Cambridge: Cambridge University Press.

Hopkins, K. 2002. 'Rome, Taxes, Rents and Trade.' In eds. W. Scheidel and S. Von Reden, *The Ancient Economy*: 190–230. Edinburgh: Edinburgh University Press.

Hopper, R.J. 1968. 'The Laurion Mines: A Reconsideration.' *The Annual of the British School at Athens* 63: 293–326.

Horne, L. 1982. 'Fuel for the Metal Worker.' *Expedition* 25: 6–13.

Hornell, J. 1930. 'The Cypriot Threshing Sledge.' *Man* 30: 135–139.

Houston, M.G.B. 1954. *Ancient Egyptian, Mesopotamian and Persian Costume and Decoration.* A Technical History of Costume; 1. London: A. Black and C. Black.

Huckle, G.M. 2005. 'The Local Dimension in the Late Bronze Age Southern Levant.' In ed. J. Clarke, *Archaeological Perspectives on the Transmission and Transformation of Culture in the Eastern Mediterranean*: 59–65. Oxford: Oxbow Books.

Hughes, F. 1911. 'Note on the Amount of Silt Carried by the Nile During the Floods of 1908 and 1910.' *Cairo Scientific Journal* 5: 29–36.

Hulin, L. 1986. 'Building 300: A Set of Animal Pens.' In ed. B.J. Kemp, *Amarna Reports III*: 50–59. London: Egypt Exploration Society.

Hulin, L. 2009. 'Embracing the New: the Perception of Cypriot Pottery in Egypt.' In eds. D. Michaēlidēs, V. Kassianidou, and R.S. Merrillees, *Proceedings of the International Conference 'Egypt and Cyprus in Antiquity', Nicosia, 3–6 April 2003*: 40–47. Oxford: Oxbow Books.

Humphreys, S.C. 1969. 'History, Economics, and Anthropology: The Work of Karl Polanyi.' *History and Theory* 8: 165–212.

Hutchinson, R.W. 1968. *Prehistoric Crete.* Harmondsworth: Penguin.

Ikram, S. 1995. *Choice Cuts: Meat Production in Ancient Egypt*. Orientalia Lovaniensia Analecta; 69. Leuven: Peeters: Departement Oosterse Studies.

Ikram, S. 2000. 'Meat Processing.' In eds. P.T. Nicholson and I. Shaw, *Ancient Egyptian Materials and Technology*: 656–671. Cambridge: Cambridge University Press.

Ilani, S., A. Flexer, and J. Kronfeld. 1987. 'Copper Mineralization in Sedimentary Cover Associated with Tectonic Elements and Volcanism in Israel.' *Mineralium Deposita* 22: 269–277.

Interweave Press LLC. 2007. 'Master Yarn Chart.' *Handwoven Magazine*. <http://www.interweave.com/weave/handwoven_magazine/files/yarn_chart.pdf>, accessed 21/07/2009.

Isaac, B.L. 2005. 'Karl Polanyi.' In ed. J.G. Carrier, *A Handbook of Economic Anthropology*: 14–25. Edward Elgar Publishing Ltd.

Isager, S. and J.E. Skydsgaard. 1992. *Ancient Greek Agriculture*. London: Routledge.

Israel Oceanographic and Limnological Research 2008. *Tide Map at the Israeli Mediterranean Coastline.* Israel Oceanographic and Limnological Research. Israel Marine Data Center (ISRAMAR). < http://isramar.ocean.org.il/TideHadera/default.aspx>, accessed 21/09/2009.

Jacobsen, T. 1970. 'On the Textile Industry of Ur Under Ibbī Sîn.' In ed. W.L. Moran, *Toward the Image of Tammuz, and Other Essays on Mesopotamian History and Culture.* Harvard Semitic Series; 21: 216–219. Cambridge, Mass.: Harvard University Press.

James T.G.H. and B.G. Gunn. 1962. *The Ḥeḳanakhte Papers and Other Early Middle Kingdom Documents*. New York: Metropolitan Museum of Art.

Jameson, M. 1983. 'Famine in the Greek World.' In eds. P. Garnsey and C.R. Whittaker, *Trade and Famine in Classical Antiquity*: 6–16. Cambridge: Cambridge Philological Society.

Janssen, J.J. 1961. *Two Ancient Egyptian Ship's Logs: Papyrus Leiden I 350 Verso, and Papyrus Turin 2008 + 2016*. Leiden: Brill.

Janssen, J.J. 1963. 'An Unusual Donation Stela of the Twentieth Dynasty.' *Journal of Egyptian Archaeology* 49: 64–70.

Janssen, J.J. 1975a. 'Prolegomena to the Study of Egypt's Economic History During the New Kingdom.' In eds. H. Altenmüller and D. Wildung, *Studien zur altägyptischen Kultur*; 3: 127–185. Hamburg: H. Buske Verlag.

Janssen, J.J. 1975b. *Commodity Prices from the Ramessid Period. An Economic Study of the Village of Necropolis Workmen at Thebes*. Leiden: Brill.

Janssen, J.J. 1976. 'The Economic System of a Single Village.' *Royal Anthropological Institute News* 15: 17–19.

Janssen, J.J. 1979a. 'The Role of the Temple in the Egyptian Economy During the New Kingdom.' In ed. E. Lipinski, *State and Temple Economy in the Ancient Near East: Proceedings of the International Conference Organised by the Katholieke Universiteit Leuven from 10th to 14th April 1978*. Orientalia Lovaniensia Analecta; 5–6: 505–515. Leuven: Departement Oriëntalistiek.

Janssen, J.J. 1979b: 'Background Information on the Strikes of Year 29 of Ramesses III.' *Oriens Antiquus* 18: 301–308.

Janssen, J.J. 1980a. *De Markt op de Oever:Rede uitgesproken bij de aanvaarding van het ambt van Gewoon Hoogleraar in de Egyptologie aan de Rijksuniversiteit te Leiden op vrijdag 10 Oktober 1980.* Leiden: Brill.

Janssen, J.J. 1980b. 'Absence from Work by the Necropolis Workmen of Thebes.' *Studien zur altägyptischen Kultur* 8: 127–152.

Janssen, J.J. 1988. 'On Prices and Wages in Ancient Egypt.' *Altorientalische Forschungen* 15: 10–23.

Janssen, J.J. 1994a. 'The Year of the Strikes.' *Bulletin de la Société d'égyptologie Genève* 16, 41–49.

Janssen, J.J. 1994b. 'The Cost of Nile-transport.' *Bulletin de la Société d'égyptologie Genève* 18, 41–47.

Janssen, J.J. 1994c. 'Debts and Credits in the New Kingdom.' *Journal of Egyptian Archaeology* 80: 129–136.

Janssen, J.J. 1997. *Village Varia: Ten Studies on the History and Administration of Deir el-Medina.* Leiden: Nederlands Intituut voor het Nabije Oosten.

Janssen, J.J. 2004. *Grain Transport in the Ramesside Period: Papyrus Baldwin (BM EA 10061) and Papyrus Amiens*. Hieratic Papyri in the British Museum; 8. London: British Museum Press.

Janssen, J.J. 2005. *Donkeys at Deir El-Medina*. Leiden: Nederlands Instituut Voor Het Nabije Oosten.

Janssen, J.J. 2008. *Daily Dress at Deir el-Medina: Words for Clothing*. London: Golden House Publications.

Jeffreys, D. 2007. 'The Nile Valley.' In ed. T.A.H. Wilkinson, *The Egyptian World*: 7–14. London: Routledge.

Jennings, J., K.L. Antrobus, S.J. Atencio, E. Glavich, R. Johnson, G. Loffler, and C. Luu. 2005. '"Drinking Beer in a Blissful Mood": Alcohol Production, Operational Chains, and Feasting in the Ancient World.' *Current Anthropology* 46: 275–304.

Jewell, P.A. 1963. *The Experimental Earthwork on Overton Down Wiltshire 1960: An Account of the Construction of an Earthwork to Investigate by Experiment the Way in which Archaeological Structures are Denuded and Buried*. London: The British Association for the Advancement of Science.

Jones, M.K. 1992. 'Food Remains, Food Webs and Ecosystem.' In ed. A.M. Pollard, *New Developments in Archaeological Science. A Joint Symposium of the Royal Society and the British Academy, February 1991*: 209–222. Oxford: Oxford University Press.

Jongman, W.M. 2007. 'The Early Roman Empire: Consumption.' In eds. W. Scheidel, I. Morris and R.P. Saller, *The Cambridge Economic History of the Greco-Roman World*: 592–618. Cambridge: Cambridge University Press.

Jovanovic, B. 1980. 'Primary Copper Mining and the Production of Copper.' In ed. P.T. Craddock, *Scientific Studies in Early Mining and Extractive Metallurgy*. British Museum Occasional Paper; 20: 31–40. London: British Museum.

Jursa. M. 2010. *Aspects of the Economic History of Babylonia in the First Millennium BC: Economic Geography, Economic Mentalities, Agriculture, the Use of Money and the Problem of Economic Growth*. Münster: Ugarit-Verlag.

Kadish, G.E. 1996. 'Observations on Time and Work-Discipline in Ancient Egypt.' In eds. P. Manuelian and R.E. Freed, *Studies in Honor of William Kelly Simpson*. Vol. 2: 439–448. Boston: Department of Ancient Egyptian, Nubian and Near Eastern Art, Museum of Fine Arts.

Kanawati, N. 1985. *The Rock Tombs of El-Hawawish, the Cemetery of Akhmim*. Vol. 5. Sydney: Macquarie Ancient History Association.

Kanawati, N. 2001. *The Tomb and Beyond: Burial Customs of Egyptian Officials*. Warminster: Aris and Phillips.

Karageorghis, V. 1981. *Ancient Cyprus: 7,000 Years of Art and Archaeology*. Baton Rouge: Louisiana State University Press.

Karageorghis, V. 1996. 'Some Aspects of the Maritime Trade of Cyprus.' In eds. V. Karageorghis and D. Michaelides, *The Development of the Cypriot Economy: From the Prehistoric Period to the Present Day*: 61–70. Nicosia: University of Cyprus.

Karageorghis, V. and M. Demas. 1985. *Excavations at Kition: The Pre-Phoenician Levels*. Vol. 5. Nicosia: Published for the Republic of Cyprus by the Deptartment of Antiquities, Cyprus.

Karageorghis, V. and V. Kassianidou. 1999. 'Metalworking and Recycling in Late Bronze Age Cyprus. The Evidence from Kition.' *Oxford Journal of Archaeology* 18: 171–188.

Kardulias, P.N. 2007. 'Negotiations and Incorporation on the Margins of World-Systems: Examples from Cyprus and North America.' *Journal of World-Systems Research* 13: 55–82.

Kassianidou, V. 1999. 'Bronze Age Copper Smelting Technology in Cyprus–the Evidence from Politico Phorades.' In eds. S.M.M. Young, A.M. Pollard, P. Budd, and R.A. Ixer, *Metals in Antiquity*. BAR International Series; 792: 91–97. Oxford: BAR Publishing.

Kassianidou, V. 2003. 'The Trade of Tin and the Island of Cyprus.' In eds. A. Giumlia-Mair and F. Lo Schiavo, *The Problem of Early Tin*. BAR International Series; 1199: 109–119. Oxford: BAR Publishing.

Kassianidou, V. 2004. 'Recording Cyprus's Mining History Through Archaeological Survey.' In ed. M. Iakovou, *Archaeological Field Survey in Cyprus: Past History, Future Potentials: Proceedings of a Conference Held by the Archaeological Research Unit of the University of Cyprus, 1–2 December 2000*. British School at Athens Studies; 11: 95–104. London: British School at Athens.

Kassianidou, V. 2005. 'Cypriot Copper in Sardinia. Yet Another Case of Bringing Coals to Newcastle.' In eds. F. Lo Schiavo and C. Atzeni, *Archaeometallurgy in Sardinia: From the Origins to the Beginning of the Early Iron Age*. Monographies Instrumentum; 30: 333–341. Montagnac: Éditions Monique Mergoil.

Kassianidou, V. 2009. '"May He Send Me Silver in Very Great Quantities" EA 35.' In eds. D. Michaelides, V. Kassianidou, and R.S. Merrillees, *Proceedings of the International Conference Egypt and Cyprus in Antiquity, Nicosia, 3–6 April 2003*: 48–57. Oxford: Oxbow Books.

Katary, S.L.D. 1989. *Land Tenure in the Ramesside Period*. London: Kegan Paul International.

Katary, S.L.D. 1999. 'Land-Tenure in the New Kingdom: The Role of Women Smallholders and the Military.' In eds. A.K. Bowman and E.L. Rogan, *Agriculture in Egypt*. Proceedings of the British Academy; 96: 61-82. Oxford: Oxford University Press.

Katary, S.L.D. 2007. 'Land Tenure and Taxation.' In ed. T.A.H. Wilkinson, *The Egyptian World*: 185–201. London: Routledge.

Kelso, J.L. 1951. 'Ancient Copper Refining.' *Bulletin of the American Schools of Oriental Research* 122: 26–28.

Kemp, B.J. 1972. 'Temple and Town in Ancient Egypt.' In eds. P.J. Ucko, R. Tringham, and G.W.

Dimbleby, *Man, Settlement and Urbanism. Proceedings of a Meeting of the Research Seminar in Archaeology and Related Subjects Held at the Institute of Archaeology, London University*: 657–680. London: Duckworth.

Kemp, B.J. 1983. 'Old Kingdom, Middle Kingdom and Second Intermediate Period *c.*2686–1552 BC.' In B.G. Trigger, B.J. Kemp, D. O'Connor and A.B. Lloyd. *Ancient Egypt: A Social History*: 71–182. Cambridge: Cambridge University Press.

Kemp, B.J. 1986. 'Large Middle Kingdom Granary Buildings.' *Zeitschrift für ägyptische Sprache und Altertumskunde* 113: 120–136.

Kemp, B.J. 1991. *Ancient Egypt: Anatomy of a Civilization.* First Edition. London, New York, Routledge.

Kemp, B.J. 1994. 'Food for an Egyptian City.' In eds. R.M. Luff and P. Rowley-Conwy, *Whither Environmental Archaeology?* Oxbow Monograph; 38: 133–153. Oxford: Oxbow.

Kemp, B.J. 2000. 'Soil (Including Mud-Brick Architecture).' In eds. P.T. Nicholson and I. Shaw, *Ancient Egyptian Materials and Technology*: 78–103. Cambridge: Cambridge University Press.

Kemp, B.J. 2006. *Ancient Egypt: Anatomy of a Civilization.* Second Edition. London; New York: Routledge.

Kemp, B.J. 2008. 'The People of Amarna.' *Ancient Egypt* 8: 33–38.

Kemp, B.J. 2013. *Amarna Project: Workmens' Village Textiles.* <http://www. amarnaproject.com/pages/ recent_projects/material_culture/workmans.shtml>, accessed 03/01/2012.

Kemp, B.J. and G. Vogelsang-Eastwood. 2001. *The Ancient Textile Industry at Amarna.* Excavation Memoir; 68. London: Egypt Exploration Society.

Keswani, P.S. 1992. 'Gas Chromatography Analyses of Pithoi from Kalavasos-Ayios Dhimitrios: A Preliminary Report.' In *Report of the Director of the Department of Antiquities Cyprus, 1992*: 141–145. Nicosia: Department of Antiquities and Zavallis Press Ltd.

Keswani, P.S. 1993. 'Models of Local Exchange in Late Bronze Age Cyprus.' *Bulletin of the American Schools of Oriental Research* 292: 73–83.

Keswani, P.S. 2004. *Mortuary Ritual and Society in Bronze Age Cyprus.* Monographs in Mediterranean Archaeology. London: Equinox Publishing Ltd.

Keswani, P.S. and A.B. Knapp 2003: 'Bronze Age Boundaries and Social Exchange in North-West Cyprus.' *Oxford Journal of Archaeology* 22: 213–223.

Killen, G. 2000. 'Wood: Procurement and Primary Processing.' In eds. P.T. Nicholson and I. Shaw, *Ancient Egyptian Materials and Technology*: 353–371. Cambridge: Cambridge University Press.

Killen, J.T. 1964. 'The Wool Industry of Crete in the Late Bronze Age.' *The Annual of the British School at Athens* 59: 13–15.

Killen, J.T. 2007. 'Cloth Production in Late Bronze Age Greece. The Documentary Evidence.' In eds. C. Gillis and M. Nosch, *Ancient Textiles: Production, Craft and Society; Proceedings of the First International Conference on Ancient Textiles, Held at Lund, Sweden, and Copenhagen, Denmark, on March 19–23, 2003*: 50–58. Oxford: Oxbow Books.

Kitchen, K.A. 1982. *Pharaoh Triumphant: The Life and Times of Ramesses II, King of Egypt.* Warminster: Aris and Phillips.

Kitchen, K.A. 1992. 'The Vintage of the Ramesseum.' In ed. A.B. Lloyd, *Studies in Pharaonic Religion and Society in Honour of J. Gwyn Griffiths.* Egypt Exploration Society Occasional Publications; 8: 115–123. London: Egypt Exploration Society.

Kitchen, K.A. 2000. *Ramesside Inscriptions. Translated and Annotated. Translations: Ramesses II, His Contemporaries.* Vol. 3. Oxford: Blackwell Publishers.

Kitchen, K.A. 2009. 'Alas(h)i(y)a (Irs) and Asiya (Isy) in Ancient Egyptian Sources.' In eds. D. Michaelides, V. Kassianidou, and R.S. Merrillees, *Proceedings of the International Conference Egypt and Cyprus in Antiquity, Nicosia, 3–6 April 2003*: 2–8. Oxford: Oxbow Books.

Knapp, A.B. 1983. 'An Alashiyan Merchant at Ugarit.' *Tel-Aviv: Journal of the Institute of Archaeology of Tel Aviv University* 10: 38–45.

Knapp, A.B. 1985. 'Alayshiya, Caphtor/Keftiu, and Eastern Mediterranean Trade: Recent Studies in Cypriote Archaeology and History.' *Journal of Field Archaeology* 12: 231–250.

Knapp, A.B. 1986. *Copper Production and Divine Protection: Archaeology, Ideology and Social Complexity on Bronze Age Cyprus.* Studies in Mediterranean Archaeology; 42. Gothenburg: P. Aström Förlag.

Knapp, A.B. 1988. 'Hoards d'oeuvres: Metals and Men on Bronze Age Cyprus.' *Oxford Journal of Archaeology* 7: 147–176.

Knapp, A.B. 1990. 'Production, Location, and Integration in Bronze Age Cyprus.' *Current Anthropology* 31: 147–176.

Knapp, A.B. 1991. 'Spice, Drugs, Grain and Grog: Organic Goods in Bronze Age East Mediterranean Trade.' In N.H. Gale, *Bronze Age Trade in the Mediterranean: Papers Presented at the Conference Held at Rewley House, Oxford, in December 1989.* Studies in Mediterranean Archaeology; 90: 21–68. Jonsered: P. Aström Förlag.

Knapp, A.B. 1995. 'Lead Isotope and the Archaeologist.' *Journal of Mediterranean Archaeology* 8: 54–58.

Knapp, A.B. 1996a. *Near Eastern and Aegean Texts from the Third to the First Millennia B.C.* Vol. 2. Sources for the History of Cyprus. Albany: Institute of Cypriot Studies, University at Albany, State University of New York; Nicosia: Cyprus College.

Knapp, A.B. 1996b. 'Settlement and Society on Late Bronze Age Cyprus: Dynamics and Development.' In eds. P. Åström and E.C. Herscher, *Late Bronze Age Settlement in Cyprus: Function and Relationship.* Studies in Mediterranean Archaeology; 126: 54–80. Jonsered: P. Åströms Förlag.

Knapp, A.B. 1997a. *The Archaeology of Late Bronze Age Cypriot Society: The Study of Settlement, Survey and Landscape.* Occasional Paper Series; 4. Glasgow: Cruithne Press.

Knapp, A.B. 1997b. 'Mediterranean Maritime Landscapes: Transport, Trade, and Society on Late Bronze Age Cyprus.' In eds. S. Swiny, R.L. Hohlfelder, and H. Wylde Swiny, *Res maritimae: Cyprus and the Eastern Mediterranean from Prehistory to Late Antiquity. Proceedings of the Second International Symposium "Cities on the Sea", Nicosia, Cyprus, October 18–22, 1994*: 153–162. Atlanta: Scholars Press.

Knapp, A.B. 1998. 'Mediterranean Bronze Age Trade: Distance, Power and Place.' In eds. E.H. Cline and D. Harris-Cline, *The Aegean and the Orient in the Second Millennium. Proceedings of the 50th Anniversary Symposium Cincinnati, 18–20th April 1997.* Aegaeum; 18: 193–207. Liège: Université de Liège.

Knapp, A.B. 1999a. 'Social Complexity: Incipience, Emergence, and Development on Prehistoric Cyprus.' *Bulletin of the American Schools of Oriental Research* 292: 85–106.

Knapp, A.B. 1999b. 'The Archaeology of Mining: Fieldwork Perspectives from the Sydney Cyprus Survey Project.' In eds. S.M. Young, A.M. Pollard, P. Budd, and R.A. Ixer, *Metals in Antiquity*, BAR International Series; 792: 98–109. Oxford: BAR Publishing.

Knapp, A.B. 1999c. 'Ideational and Industrial Landscape on Prehistoric Cyprus.' In eds. W. Ashmore and A.B. Knapp, *Archaeologies of Landscape: Contemporary Perspectives*: 229–252. Malden, Mass.: Blackwell Publishers.

Knapp, A.B. 2000. 'Archaeology, Science-Based Archaeology and the Mediterranean Bronze Age Metals Trade.' *European Journal of Archaeology* 3: 31–56.

Knapp, A.B. 2001. 'Copper Smelting in Late Bronze Age Cyprus: The Excavations at Politiko Phorades.' *Journal of Near Eastern Archaeology* 64: 204–210.

Knapp, A.B. 2003. 'The Archaeology of Community on Cyprus: Politiko-Phorades in Context.' *American Journal of Archaeology* 107: 559–580.

Knapp, A.B. 2008. *Prehistoric and Protohistoric Cyprus: Identity, Insularity, and Connectivity.* Oxford; New York: Oxford University Press.

Knapp, A.B. and J.F. Cherry. 1994. *Provenience Studies and Bronze Age Cyprus: Production, Exchange and Politico-Economic Change.* Monographs in World Archaeology; 21. Madison: Prehistory Press.

Knapp, A.B., S. Held and S. Manning. 1994. "The Prehistory of Cyprus: Problems and Prospects," *Journal of World Prehistory* 377: 377-453.

Knapp, A.B., V. Kassianidou, and M. Donnelly. 1999. 'Excavations at Politiko Phorades 1998.' In *Report of the Director of the Department of Antiquities Cyprus, 1999*: 125–146. Nicosia: Department of Antiquities and Zavallis Press Ltd.

Kohl, P.L. 1996. 'The Ancient Economy, Transferable Technologies and the Bronze Age World-system: A View from the Northeastern Frontier of the Ancient Near East.' In eds. R. Preucel and I. Hodder, *Contemporary Archaeology in Theory.* Social Archaeology: 143–164. Oxford: Blackwell Publishing.

Korobkova, G.F. 1981. 'Ancient Reaping Tools and their Productivity in Light of Experimental Traceware Analysis.' In ed. P.L. Kohl, *The Bronze Age Civilization of Central Asia: Recent Soviet Discoveries*: 325–349. New York: M.E. Sharpe.

Koucky, F. and A. Steinberg. 1982a. 'The Ancient Slags of Cyprus.' In eds. J.D. Muhly, R. Maddin, and V. Karageorghis, *Early Metallurgy in Cyprus, 4000–500 B.C.*: 117–142. Nicosia, Cyprus: Department of Antiquities.

Koucky, F. and A. Steinberg. 1982b. 'Ancient Mining and Mineral Dressing on Cyprus.' In eds. T.A. Wertime and S.F. Wertime, *Early Pyrotechnology: The Evolution of the First Fire-Using Industries*: 149–180. Washington, D.C.: Smithsonian Institution Press.

Koucky, F. and A. Steinberg. 1989. 'Ancient Mining and Mineral Dressing on Cyprus.' In eds. L.E. Stager and A.M. Walker, *American Expedition to Idalion, Cyprus 1973-1980.* Oriental Institute Communications; 24: 275–320. Chicago: Oriental Institute of the University of Chicago.

Koura, B. 1995. Ist *b3ḳ* Moringanöl oder Olivenöl? *Göttinger Miszellen*: 145: 79–82.

Kuhrt, A. 1995. *The Ancient Near East: c.3000–330 B.C.* Vol. 1. London; New York: Routledge.

Lamberg-Karlovsky, C.C. 1996. 'The Archaeological Evidence for International Commerce: Public and/or Private Enterprise in Mesopotamia?' In eds. B.A. Levene and M. Hudson, *Privatization in the Ancient Near East and Classical World.* Peabody Museum Bulletin; 1: 177–196. Cambridge, MA.: Peabody Museum of Archaeology and Ethnology.

Landi, S. and R.M. Hall. 1979. 'The Discovery and Conservation of an Ancient Egyptian Linen Tunic.' *Studies in Conservation* 24: 141–152.

Landström, B. 1970. *Ships of the Pharaohs: 4000 Years of Egyptian Shipbuilding. Architectura Navalis.* London: Allen and Unwin.

Larsen, M. 1967. *Old Assyrian Caravan Procedures.* Uitgaven van het Nederlands Historisch-Archaeologisch Instituut te İstanbul; 22. Istanbul: Nederlands Historisch-Archaeologisch Instituut in het Nabije Oosten.

Larsen, M. 1976. *The Old Assyrian City-State and Its Colonies.* Mesopotamia; 4. Copenhagen: Akademisk Forlag.

Larsen, M. 1977. 'Partnerships in Old Assyrian Trade.' *Iraq* 39: 119–145.

Larsen, M. 1987. 'Commercial Networks in the Ancient Near East.' In eds. M. Rowlands, M. Larsen, and K. Kristiansen, *Commercial Networks in the Ancient Near East*: 47–56. Cambridge: Cambridge University Press.

Lassen, H. 2000. 'Introduction to Weight Systems in the Bronze Age East Mediterranean: The Case of Kalavasos-Ayios Dhimitrios.' In ed. C.F.E. Pare, *Metals Make the World Go Round: Proceedings of a Conference Held at the University of Birmingham in June 1997*: 233–246. Oxford: Oxbow Books.

Laurence, R. 1998. 'Land Transport in Roman Italy: Costs, Practice and the Economy.' In eds. H.M. Parkins and C.J. Smith, *Trade, Traders and the Ancient City*: 129–148. London; New York: Routledge.

Lavi, S. 1976. 'Olive.' In ed. C. Halpern, *Encyclopaedia of Agriculture.* Vol. 3: 201-208. Jerusalem: [s.n.].

Layton, R. and P.J. Ucko. 1999. 'Introduction: Gazing on the Landscape and Encountering the Environment.' In eds. P.J. Ucko and R. Layton, *The Archaeology and Anthropology of Landscape: Shaping your Landscape*: 1–20. London: Routledge.

Leadbeater, E. 1976. *Handspinning.* London: Studio Vista.

LeClair, E.E. 1962. 'Economic Theory and Anthropology.' *American Anthropologist* 64: 1179–1203.

LeClair, E.E. and H.K. Schneider 1968. 'Introduction.' In eds. E.E. LeClair, and H.K. Schneider, *Economic Anthropology: Readings in Theory and Analysis*: 3–13. New York; London: Holt, Rinehart and Winston.

Leemans, W.F. 1954. *Legal and Economic Records from the Kingdom of Larsa.* Studia ad tabulas cuneiformes collectas ab F.M.Th. de Liagre Böhl pertinentia; 2. Leiden: Brill.

Lehner, M. 2000. 'The Fractal House of Pharaoh.' In eds. T.A. Kohler and G.J. Gumerman, *Dynamics in Human and Primate Societies: Agent-based Modelling of Social and Spatial Processes*: 275–353. Oxford: Oxford University Press.

Lejeune, M. 1961. 'Les Forgerons de Pylos.' *Historia* 10: 409–434.

Lemonnier, P. 1976. 'La Description des chaînes opératoires: contribution a l'analyse des systemes techniques.' *Techniques et culture* 1: 100–151.

Leonard, A. 1994. *An Index to the Late Bronze Age Aegean Pottery from Syria-Palestine.* Studies in Mediterranean Archaeology; 114. Jonsered: P. Åströms Förlag.

Leonard, A. 1995. '"Canaanite Jars" and the Late Bronze Age Aegeo-Levantine Wine Trade.' In eds. P.E. McGovern, S. Fleming, and S. Katz. *The Origins and Ancient History of Wine*: 233–254. New York: Gordon and Breach Publishers.

Lerche, G. 1968. 'Observations on Harvesting with Sickles in Iran.' *Tools and Tillage* 1: 33–49.

Leroi-Gourhan, A. 1943. *L'Homme et la matiere.* Paris: Albin Mitchel.

Lesko, L.H. 1995. 'Egyptian Wine Production During the New Kingdom.' In eds. P.E. McGovern, S.J. Fleming, and S.H. Katz, *The Origins and Ancient History of Wine*: 215–230. Luxembourg: Gordon and Breach Publishers.

Levinson, H. and A. Levinson. 1994. 'Origin of Grain Storage and Insect Species Consuming Desiccated Food.' *Anzeiger für Schädlingskunde, Pflanzenschutz, Umweltschutz* 67: 47–59.

Lewartowski, K. 2000. *Late Helladic Simple Graves: A Study of Mycenaean Burial Customs.* BAR International Series; 878. Oxford: BAR Publishing.

Lewis, A. 1990. 'Firesetting Experiments on the Great Orme, 1989.' In eds. P. Crew and S. Crew, *Early Mining in the British Isles: Proceedings of the Early Mining Workshop at Plas Tan Y Bwlch, Snowdonia National Park Study Centre, 17–19 November, 1989.* Plas Tan Y Bwlch Occasional Paper; 1: 55–56. Tan y Bwlch, Gwynedd: Plas Tan y Bwlch, Snowdonia National Park Study Centre.

Lewis, O. 1951. *Life in a Mexican Village: Tepozlán Restudied.* Urbana: University of Illinois Press.

Lichtheim, M. 1973: *Ancient Egyptian Literature.* Vol. 1. Berkley: University of California Press.

Lichtheim, M. 1976a: *Ancient Egyptian Literature.* Vol. 2. Berkley: University of California Press.

Lichtheim, M. 1976b: *Ancient Egyptian Literature.* Vol. 3. Berkley: University of California Press.

Lin, S.S. 2003. 'Lading of the Late Bronze Age Ship at Uluburun.' Unpublished M.A. Thesis. Texas A&M University. Austin.

Linder, E. 1981. 'Ugarit: A Canaanite Thalassocracy.' In ed. G.D. Young, *Ugarit in Retrospect: 50 Years of Ugarit and Ugaritic*: 31–42. Winona Lake, Ind.: Eisenbrauns.

Lipschitz, N. 1996. 'Olives in Ancient Israel in View of Dendroarchaeological Investigations.' In eds. D. Eitam and M. Heltzer, *Olive Oil in Antiquity: Israel and Neighbouring Countries from the Neolithic to the Early Arab Period.* History of the Ancient Near East Studies; 7: 7–13. Padova: Sargon.

Littlejohn, L. 1946. 'Some Aspects of Soil Fertility in Cyprus.' *Empire Journal of Experimental Agriculture* 14: 123–134.

Liverani, M. 1979a. 'Economia della fattorie palatine ugaritiche.' *Dialoghi di Archeologia* 1: 57–72.

Liverani, M. 1979b, '"Irrational" Elements in the Amarna Trade.' In *Three Amarna Essays.* Translated by M.L. Jaffe. Monographs on the Ancient Near East. Vol. 1: Fasc. 5, 21–34. Malibu: Undena Publications.

Liverani, M. 1984. 'Land Tenure and Inheritance in the Ancient Near East.' In ed. T. Khalidi, *Land Tenure and Social Transformation in the Middle*

East: 33–44. Beirut: American University of Beirut.

Liverani, M. 1987. 'The Collapse of the Near Eastern Regional System at the End of the Bronze Age: the Case of Syria.' In eds. M. Rowlands, M. Larsen and K. Kristiansen, *Centre and Periphery in the Ancient World*: 66–73. Cambridge: Cambridge University Press.

Liverani, M. 1989. 'Economy of Ugaritic Royal Farms.' In ed. C. Zaccagnini, *Production and Consumption in the Ancient Near East*: 127–168. Budapest: Chaire d'Égyptologie de l'Université Loránd Eötvös.

Liverani, M. 2003. 'The Influence of Political Institutions on Trade in the Ancient Near East (Late Bronze to Early Iron Age).' In ed. C. Zaccagnini, *Mercanti e politica nel mondo antico*. Saggi di storia antica; 21: 119–137. Rome: L'Erma di Bretschneider.

Lloyd, A.B. 1976. *Herodotus Book II. Commentary 1–98*. Etudes préliminaires aux religions orientales dans l'Empire romain. Leiden: Brill.

Lloyd, A.B. 1983. 'The Late Period: 664–323 B.C.' In eds. B.G. Trigger, B.J. Kemp, D.B. O'Connor, and A.B. Lloyd, *Ancient Egypt: A Social History*: 279–364. Cambridge: Cambridge University Press.

Loizides, P.A. 1949. 'The Cereal-Fallow Rotation in Cyprus.' *Proceedings of the First Commonwealth Conference on Tropical and Sub-Tropical Soils*. Technical Communication; 46: 210–217. Harpenden: Commonwealth Bureau of Soil Science.

Lolos, Y.G. 1999. 'The Cargo of Pottery from the Point Iria Wreck: Character and Implications.' In eds. W.W. Phelps, Y.G. Lolos and G. Vechos, *The Point Iria Wreck: Interconnections in the Mediterranean, Ca. 1200 B.C.: Proceedings of the International Conference, Island of Spetses, 19 September 1998*: 43–58. Athens: Hellenic Institute of Marine Archaeology.

Lucas, A. and J.R. Harris. 1962. *Ancient Egyptian Materials and Industries*. Fourth Edition. London: E. Arnold.

Lukermann, F.E. 1972. Settlement and Circulation: Pattern and Systems. In eds. W.A. McDonald and G.R. Rapp, *The Minnesota Messenia Expedition: Reconstructing a Bronze Age Regional Environment*: 148–170. Minneapolis: University of Minnesota Press.

Ludington, S.D. and S. Peters. 2007. 'Tin and Tungsten Deposits.' *Preliminary Non-Fuel Mineral Resource Assessment of Afghanistan 2007*: 106–114. <http://pubs.usgs.gov/of/2007/1214/PDF/4.0–felsic-intrusives-FINAL.pdf>, accessed 21/09/2009.

Luff, R. 1994. 'Butchery at the Workmen's Village (WV), Tell-el-Amarna, Egypt.' In eds. R.M. Luff and P. Rowley-Conwy, *Whither Environmental Archaeology?* Oxbow Monograph; 38: 158–170. Oxford: Oxbow.

Lyman, R.L. 1979. 'Available Meat from Faunal Remains: A Consideration of Techniques.' *American Antiquity* 44: 536–546.

Macdonald, M. 1920. *Nile Control: A Statement of the Necessity for Further Control of the Nile to Complete the Development of Egypt and Develop a Certain Area in the Sudan, with Particulars of the Physical Conditions to Be Considered and a Programme of the Engineering Works Involved.* Cairo: Government Press.

McCorriston, J. 1997. 'The Fiber Revolution: Textile Extensification, Alienation and Social Stratification in Ancient Mesopotamia.' *Current Anthropology* 38: 517–549.

McDermott, B. 2004. *Warfare in Ancient Egypt*. Stroud: Sutton Publishing Ltd.

McDowell, A.G. 1999. *Village Life in Ancient Egypt: Laundry Lists and Love Songs*. New York: Clarendon Press.

McGovern, P.E. 1997. 'Wine of Egypt's Golden Age: An Archaeochemical Perspective.' *Journal of Egyptian Archaeology* 83: 69–108.

McGovern, P.E. 2003. *Ancient Wine: The Search for the Origins of Viniculture*. Princeton: Princeton University Press.

McGovern, P.E., U. Hartung, V.R. Badler, R.L. Glusker, and L.J. Exner. 1997. 'The Beginnings of Winemaking and Viniculture in the Ancient Near East and Egypt.' *Expedition* 39: 3–21.

McGrail, S. 1983. 'Cross-Channel Seamanship and Navigation in the Late First Millennium B.C.' *Oxford Journal of Archaeology* 2: 353–8.

McLeod, B.H. 1962. 'The Metallurgy of King Solomon's Copper Smelters.' *Palestine Exploration Quarterly* 94: 68–71.

McMillan, D. 1988. 'Seasonality, Planned Settlements, and River Blindness Control in Burkina Faso.' In ed. R. Huss-Ashmore, *Coping with Seasonal Constraints*. MASCA Research Papers in Science and Archaeology; 5: 97–120. Philidelphia: University of Pennsylvania Museum of Archaeology.

Maddin, R., T.S. Wheeler and J.D. Muhly. 1977. 'Tin in the Ancient Near East: Old Questions and New Finds.' *Expedition* 19: 35–47.

Maher-Taha, M. 2002. *Le Tombeau de Menna*. Cairo: Ministere de la culture, Conseil suprême des antiquites.

Málek, J. 1986. *In the Shadow of the Pyramids: Egypt During the Old Kingdom*. Norman: University of Oklahoma Press.

Mancourant, J. 2002. 'Polanyi on Institutions and Money: An Interpretation Suggested by a Reading of Commons, Mitchell and Veblen.' In eds. F. Adaman and P. Devine, *Economy and Society: Money, Capitalism and Transition*: 150–172. Montreal: Black Rose Books.

Manniche, L. 1999. *Sacred Luxuries: Fragrance, Aromatherapy and Cosmetics in Ancient Egypt*. London: Opus.

Manning, S.W. 1993. 'Prestige, Distinction, and Competition: The Anatomy of Socioeconomic Complexity in Fourth to Second Millennium

B.C.E.' *Bulletin of the American Schools of Oriental Research* 292: 35–58.

Manning, S.W. and L. Hulin. 2005. 'Maritime Commerce and Geographies of Mobility in the Late Bronze Age of the Eastern Mediterranean: Problematisations.' In eds. E. Blake and A.B. Knapp, *The Archaeology of Mediterranean Prehistory*. Blackwell Studies in Global Archaeology; 6: 270–302. Oxford: Blackwell Publishing.

Mansinghka, S.S. 2002. 'Bi-Products of Cattle, Organic Manure and Cow Urine, Medicines, Gas, and Electricity.' *Report of the National Commission on Cattle, July 2002*. Department of Animal Husbandry and Dairying, Ministry of Agriculture, Government of India.

Marechal, J.R. 1985. 'Method of Ore Roasting and the Furnaces Used.' In eds. P.T. Craddock and M.J. Hughes, *Furnaces and Smelting Technology in Antiquity*. British Museum Occasional Paper; 48: 29–41. London: British Museum.

Marriner, N., C. Morhange, M. Boudagher-Fadel, M. Bourcier, and P. Carbonel. 2005. 'Geoarchaeology of Tyre's Ancient Northern Harbour, Phoenicia.' *Journal of Archaeological Science* 32: 1302–1327.

Martlew, H. 1999. 'What Did They Drink?' In eds. Y. Tzedakis and H. Martlew, *Minoans and Mycenaeans: Flavours of Their Time*: 144–179. Athens: Kapon.

Martlew, H. 2004. 'Minoan and Mycenaean Technology as Revealed Through Organic Residue Analysis.' In eds. J. Bourriau and J.S. Phillips, *Invention and Innovation: The Social Context of Technological Change 2: Egypt, the Aegean and the Near East, 1650–1150 B.C.: Proceedings of a Conference Held at the Mcdonald Institute for Archaeological Research, Cambridge, 4–6th September 2002*: 121–148. Oxford: Oxbow Books.

Martlew, H., C.W. Beck and P.E. McGovern. 1999. 'Introduction to Organic Residue Analysis.' In eds. Y. Tzedakis and H. Martlew, *Minoans and Mycenaeans: Flavours of Their Time*: 17–29. Athens: Kapon.

Marx, K. 1971 [1859]. *A Contribution to the Critique of Political Economy*. Translated from the German by S.W. Ryazanskaya. Edited with an introduction by M. Dobb. London: Lawrence and Wishart.

Marx, K. 1988 [1848]. *The Communist Manifesto*. In ed. F.L. Bender, with prefaces by Marx and Engels. New York; London: W.W. Norton.

Maslow, A.H. 1970. *Motivation and Personality*. New York; London: Harper and Row.

Mattessich, R. 1989. 'Accounting and the Input-Output Principle in the Ancient and Prehistoric World.' *Abacus* 25: 74–84.

Mattessich, R. 1991. 'Counting, Accounting, and the Input-Output Principle: Recent Archaeological Evidence Revising Our View on the Evolution of Early Record Keeping. In ed. O.F. Graves, *The Costing Heritage – Studies in Honor of S. Paul Garner*; 6: 25–49. Harrisonburg: Academy of Accounting Historians.

Mattessich, R. 1998. 'Recent Insights into Mesopotamian Accounting of the 3rd Millennium BC – Successor to Token Accounting.' *Accounting Historians Journal* 25: 1–27.

Matthäus, H. 2005. 'Kulturaustausch, Handel und Seefahrt im Mittelmeerraum während der Späten Bronzezeit.' In eds. Ü. Yalçin, C. Pulak, und R. Slotta, *Das Schiff von Uluburun: Welthandel vor 3000 Jahren: Katalog der Ausstellung des Deutschen Bergbau-Museums Bochum vom 15. Juli 2005 bis 16. Juli 2006.* Veröffentlichungen aus dem Deutschen Bergbau-Museum Bochum; 138: 333–366. Bochum: Deutsches Bergbau-Museum.

Mattingly, D.J. 1988. 'Megalithic Madness and Measurement. Or How Many Olives Could an Olive Press Press?' *Oxford Journal of Archaeology* 7: 177–195.

Mattingly, D.J. 1996. 'First Fruit? The Olive in the Roman World.' In eds. G. Shipley and J. Salmon, *Human Landscapes in Classical Antiquity*: 213–253. London: Routledge.

Mauss, M. 1969 [1872–1950]. *The Gift: Forms and Functions of Exchange in Archaic Societies.* Translated by Ian Cunnison. London: Routledge and Kegan Paul.

Mayerson, P. 1955. 'Arid Zone Farming in Antiquity: A Study of Ancient Agriculture and Related Hydrological Practices in Southern Palestine.' Ph.D. Dissertation, New York University. University Microfilms, Ann Arbor.

Mayerson, P. 1960. *The Ancient Agricultural Regime of Nessana and the Central Negeb*. London: Colt Archaeological Institute.

Mays, L.W. 2010. 'Water Technology in Ancient Egypt.' In ed. L.W. Mays, *Ancient Water Technologies*: 53–66. Dordrecht: Springer.

Mederos, A. and C.C. Lamberg-Karlovsky. 2004. 'Weight Systems and Trade Networks.' In eds. M. Hudson and C. Wunsch, *Creating Economic Order: Record-Keeping, Standardization, and the Development of Accounting in the Ancient Near East*: 199–214. Bethesda: CDL Press.

Meiggs, R. 1982. *Trees and Timber in the Ancient Mediterranean World*. Oxford: Clarendon Press.

Melena, J.L. 1983. 'Olive Oil and Other Sorts of Oil in Mycenaean Tablets.' *Minos* 18: 89–123.

Mellor, G.E.M 1928. 'Beekeeping in Egypt: Part 1. An Account of the Beladi Craft, That Is to Say the Craft Native to the Country; With Observations Made upon it from September 1926–January 1928.' *Bulletin de la Société Royale Entomologique d'Égypte* 12.

Menger, K. 1950 [1871]. *Principles of Economics.* Glencoe: Free Press.

Merkel, J.F. 1983a. 'Summary of Experimental Results for Late Bronze Age Copper Smelting and Refining.' *MASCA Journal* 2: 173–178.

Merkel, J.F. 1983b. 'Reconstruction of Bronze Age Copper Smelting: Experiments Based on Archaeological Evidence from Timna, Israel.'

Unpublished Ph.D Dissertation, University of London. London.

Merkel, J.F. 1985. 'Ore Beneficiation During the Late Bronze Age/Early Iron Age at Timna, Israel.' *MASCA Journal* 3: 164–169.

Merkel, J.F. 1989. 'Experience with Refractories in Reconstruction Copper Smelting: Archaeo-Metallurgical Evidence from Timna Israel.' In eds. P.E. McGovern and M.D. Notis, *Cross-Craft and Cross-Cultural Interactions in Ceramics.* Ceramics and Civilization; 4: 217–234. Westerville: American Ceramic Society.

Merkel, J.F. 1990. 'Experimental Reconstruction of Bronze Age Copper Smelting Based on Archaeological Evidence from Timna.' In eds. B. Rothenberg and H.G. Bachmann, *The Ancient Metallurgy of Copper, Researches in the Arabah, 1959–1984.* Vol. 2: 78–122. London: Institute for Archaeo-Metallurgical Studies, Institute of Archaeology, University College, London.

Moreno, A. 2007. *Feeding the Democracy: The Athenian Grain Supply in the Fifth and Fourth Centuries BC.* Oxford: Oxford University Press.

Merrillees, R.S. 1968. *The Cypriote Bronze Age Pottery Found in Egypt.* London: University of London.

Merrillees, R.S. 1984. *Ambelikou-Aletri: A Preliminary Report.* Report of the Director of the Department of Antiquities, Cyprus, 1984: 1–13. Nicosia: Department of Antiquities and Zavallis Press Ltd.

Merrillees, R.S. 1987. *Alashia Revisited.* Cahiers de la Revue biblique; 22. Paris: Gabalda.

Merrillees, R.S. 1992. 'The Government of Cyprus in the Late Bronze Age.' In ed. P. Åström, *Acta Cypria: Acts of an International Congress on Cypriote Archaeology Held in Göteborg on 22–24 August, 1991*: 310–328. Jonsered: P. Åström.

Merrillees, R.S. 1995. 'Alashia Revisited Again.' *Cahier Centre d'études chypriotes* 23: 17–22.

Meskell, L. 1998. 'Intimate Archaeologies: The Case of Kha and Merit.' *World Archaeology* 29: 363–379.

Meskell, L. 1999. *Archaeologies of Social Life: Age, Sex, Class et cetera in Ancient Egypt.* Oxford: Blackwell Publishers.

Meskell, L. 2002. *Private Life in New Kingdom Egypt.* Princeton: Princeton University Press.

Meunier-Goddik, L. and H. Nashnush. 2006. 'Producing Sheep Milk Cheese.' Oregan State University. <http://extension.oregonstate.edu/catalog/pdf/em/em8908.pdf>, accessed 28/06/2013.

Meyer, E. 1922 [1910]. *Kleine Schriften zur Geschichtstheorie und zur Wirtschaftlichen und politischen Geschichte des Altertums.* Halle: M. Niemeyer.

Meyer, E. 1924. 'Die wirtschaftliche Entwicklung des Altertums.' In ed. E. Meyer, *Kleine Schriften zur Geschichtstheorie und zur Wirtschaftlichen und Politischen Geschichte des Altertums.* Vol. 1. Second Edition: 79–168. Halle: M. Niemeyer.

Michailidou, A. 1999. 'Systems of Weights and Social Relations of "Private" Production in the Late Bronze Aegean.' In ed. A. Chaniotis, *From Minoan Farmers to Roman Traders: Sidelights on the Economy of Ancient Crete.* Heidelberger althistorische Beiträge und epigraphische Studien; 29: 87–113. Stuttgart: F. Steiner.

Michailidou, A. 2003. 'Measuring Weight and Value in Bronze Age Economies in the Aegean and the Near East: A Discussion on Metal Axes of No Practical Use.' In eds. R. Laffineur and K.P. Foster, *Metron: Measuring the Aegean Bronze Age. Proceedings of the 9th International Aegean Conference/9e Rencontre égéenne internationale, New Haven, Yale University, 18–21 April 2002.* Aegaeum; 24: 301–316. Liège: Université de Liège.

Michailidou, A. 2005. *Weight and Value in Pre-Coinage Societies.* Meletēmata; 42. Athens: Diffusion de Boccard.

Michailidou, A. 2010. 'The Concept of Weighing During the Bronze Age in the Aegean, the Near East and Europe.' In eds. I. Morley and C. Renfrew, *The Archaeology of Measurement*: 71–87. Cambridge: Cambridge University Press.

Midgley, W.W. 1911. 'Linen of the Third Dynasty.' In eds. W.M.F. Petrie, E.B. Knobel, W.W. Midgley, J.G. Milne and M.A. Murray, *Historical Studies*: 37–39. London: British School of Archaeology in Egypt.

Midgley, W.W. 1978. 'An Examination of Fifteen Specimens of Mummy Wrapping.' In ed. H.L. Roth, *Ancient Egyptian and Greek Looms*: 26–29. Bedford: Ruth Bean.

Miller, N.F. 1984. 'The Use of Dung as Fuel: An Ethnographic Example and an Archaeological Application.' *Paleorient* 10: 71–79.

Miller, N.F. 1990. 'Clearing Land for Farmland and Fuel: Archaeobotanical Studies of the Ancient Near East.' In ed. N.F. Miller, *Economy and Settlement in the Near East: Analyses of Ancient Sites and Materials.* MASCA Research Papers in Science and Archaeology; Supplement to Vol. 7: 71–78. Philidelphia: University of Pennsylvania Museum of Archaeology.

Miller, R.L. 1987. 'Appendix: Ash as an Insecticide.' In ed. B.J. Kemp, *Amarna Reports IV.* London: Egypt Exploration Society: 14–16.

Miller, R.L. 1991. 'Counting Calories in Egyptian Ration Texts.' *Journal of the Economic and Social History of the Orient* 34: 257–269.

Mills, J.S. and R. White 1999. *The Organic Chemistry of Museum Objects.* Second Edition. Oxford: Butterworth-Heinemann.

Mitchell, S. 2005. 'Olive Cultivation in the Economy of Roman Asia Minor.' In eds. S. Mitchell and C. Katsari, *Patterns in the Economy of Roman Asia Minor*: 83–113. Swansea: Classical Press of Wales.

Moens, M-F and W. Wetterstrom. 1988. 'The Agricultural Economy of an Old Kingdom Town in Egypt's West Delta: Insights from the Plant Remains.' *Journal of Near Eastern Studies* 47: 159–173.

Möller, A. 2000. *Naukratis: Trade in Archaic Greece.* Oxford: Oxford University Press.

Monroe, C. 2002. Review of David Schloen, *The House of the Father as Fact and Symbol: Patrimonialism in Ugarit and the Ancient Near East* in *Journal of the American Oriental Society* 122: 904–907.

Monroe, C. 2009. *Scales of Fate: Trade, Tradition and Transformation in the Eastern Mediterranean ca. 1350–1175.* Münster: Ugarit-Verlag.

Moorey, P.R.S. 1999. *Ancient Mesopotamian Materials and Industries: The Archaeological Evidence.* Winona Lake: Eisenbrauns.

Moorey, P.R.S. 2001. 'The Mobility of Artisans and Opportunities for Technology Transfer.' In ed. A.J. Shortland, *The Social Context of Technological Change: Egypt and the Near East, 1650–1550 B.C.: Proceedings of a Conference Held at St. Edmund Hall, Oxford 12–14th September 2000*: 1–14. Oxford: Oxbow Books.

Moran, W.L. 1992. *The Amarna Letters.* Baltimore; London: Johns Hopkins University Press.

Morcos, S.R., S.M. Hegazi, and S.T. El-Damhougy. 1973. 'Fermented Foods in Common Use in Egypt II. The Chemical Composition of Bouza and Its Ingredients.' *Journal of the Science of Food and Agriculture* 24: 1157–1161.

Moreland J. 2000. 'Concepts in the Early Medieval Economy.' In eds. I.L. Hansen and C. Wickham, *The Long Eighth Century*: 1–34. Leiden: Brill.

Moreno, A. 2007. *Feeding the Democracy: The Athenian Grain Supply in the Fifth and Fourth Centuries BC.* Oxford: Oxford University Press.

Moritz, L.A. 1958. *Grain-Mills and Flour in Classical Antiquity.* Oxford: Clarendon Press.

Morley, N. 2004. *Theories, Models, and Concepts in Ancient History. Approaching the Ancient World.* London: Routledge.

Morley, N. 2007. *Trade in Classical Antiquity. Key Themes in Ancient History.* Cambridge: Cambridge University Press.

Morris, I. 1994. 'The Athenian Economy Twenty Years After *The Ancient Economy*.' *Classical Philology* 89: 351–366.

Morton, J. 2001. *The Role of the Physical Environment in Ancient Greek Seafaring.* Leiden: Brill.

Mueller, D. 1975. 'Some Remarks on Wage Rates in the Middle Kingdom.' *Journal of Near Eastern Studies* 34: 249–263.

Muehlbauer, F.J., R.J. Summerfield, W.J. Kaiser, S.L. Clement, C.M. Boerboom, M.M. Welsh-Maddux, and R.W. Short. 2002. *Principles and Practice of Lentil Production.* USDA-United States Department of Agriculture, Agricultural Research Service. <http://www.ars.usda.gov/is/np/lentils/lentils.htm>, accessed 12/12/2012.

Muhly, J.D. 1973. *Copper and Tin: The Distribution of Mineral Resources and the Nature of the Metals Trade in the Bronze Age.* Transactions of the Connecticut Academy of Arts and Sciences; 43: 155–535. Hamden: Archon Books.

Muhly, J.D. 1985: 'Sources of Tin and the Beginnings of Bronze Metallurgy.' *American Journal of Archaeology* 89: 275-291.

Muhly, J.D. 1993. 'Early Bronze Age Tin and the Taurus.' *American Journal of Archaeology* 97: 239–253.

Muhly, J.D., F. Begemann, Ö. Öztunali, E. Pernicka, S. Scmitt-Stecker, and G.A. Wagner. 1991. 'The Bronze Metallurgy of Anatolia and the Question of Local Tin Sources.' In eds. E. Pernicka and G.A. Wagner, *Proceedings of the 27th International Symposium on Archaeometry Held in Heidelberg Apr. 2–6, 1990.* Archaeometry; 90: 209–220. Basel; Boston: Birkhauser Verlag.

Mumford, G. 2006. 'Tel Ras Budran (Site 345): Defining Egypt's Eastern Frontier and Mining Operations in South Sinai During the Late Old Kingdom.' *Bulletin of the American Schools of Oriental Research* 342: 13–67.

Mumford, G. and S. Parcak. 2003. 'Pharaonic Ventures into South Sinai: el-Markha Plain Site 346.' *Journal of Egyptian Archaeology*; 89: 83–116.

Murray, M.A. 1993. 'Recent Archaeobotanic Research at the Site of Memphis.' In eds. V. Davies, W.V. Davies, and R. Walker, *Biological Anthropology and the Study of Ancient Egypt*: 165–168. London: British Museum Press.

Murray, M.A. 2000a. 'Cereal Production and Processing.' In eds. P.T. Nicholson and I. Shaw, *Ancient Egyptian Materials and Technology*: 505–536. Cambridge: Cambridge University Press.

Murray, M.A. 2000b. 'Viticulture and Wine Production.' In eds. P.T. Nicholson and I. Shaw, *Ancient Egyptian Materials and Technology*: 577–599. Cambridge: Cambridge University Press.

Murray, M.A. 2000c. 'Fruits, Vegetables, Pulses and Condiments.' In eds. P.T. Nicholson and I. Shaw, *Ancient Egyptian Materials and Technology*: 609–655. Cambridge: Cambridge University Press.

Mylonas, G. 1959. *Aghios Kosmas: An Early Bronze Age Settlement and Cemetery of Attica.* Princeton: Princeton University.

Myres, J.L. 1931. 'The Distribution of the Threshing Sledge.' *Man* 31: 32.

National Oceanic and Atmospheric Administration. 2007 'Egypt Climatological Data.' (Updated 7/01/2008) NOAA Central Library, National Oceanogrphic Data Center. U.S.A Governmentd Department of Commerce. <http://docs.lib.noaa.gov/rescue/data_rescue_egypt.html>, accessed 02/07/2013.

Neale, W.C. 1957. 'The Economy as an Instituted Process.' In eds. K. Polanyi, C.M. Arsensberg, and H.W. Pearson, *Trade and Market in the Early Empires: Economies in History and Theory*: 357–372. Glencoe: Free Press.

Negbi, O. 1986. 'The Climax of Urban Development in Bronze Age Cyprus.' *Report of the Director of the Department of Antiquities Cyprus, 1986*: 97–121. Nicosia: Department of Antiquities and Zavallis Press Ltd.

Negbi, O. 2005. 'Urbanism on Late Bronze Age Cyprus: LC II in Retrospect.' *Bulletin of the American Schools of Oriental Research* 337: 1–45.

Nesheim, M.C. 1993. 'Human Nutrition Needs and Parasitic Infections.' *Parasitology* 107: 7–18.

Newberry, P.E. 1928. 'The Pig and the Cult-Animal of Set.' *Journal of Egyptian Archaeology* 14: 211–225.

Newberry, P.E. 1983. *Beni Hasan.* Vol. 1. Memoir of the Archaeological Survey of Egypt; 1–2, 5, 7. London: Egypt Exploration Fund (1893–1900).

Newman, E.I. 1997. 'Phosphorus Balance of Contrasting Farming Systems, Past and Present. Can Food Production Be Sustainable?' *Journal of Applied Ecology* 34: 1334–1347.

Nicholson, P. T., C. M. Jackson, and K.M. Trott. 1997. 'The Ulu Burun Glass Ingots, Cylindrical Vessels and Egyptian Glass.' *Journal of Egyptian Archaeology* 83: 143–153.

Nissen, H.J., P. Damerow, and R.K. Englund 1993. *Archaic Bookkeeping: Early Writing and Techniques of the Economic Administration in the Ancient Near East.* Translation of: *Frühe Schrift und Techniken der Wirtschaftsverwaltung im alten Vorderen Orient: Informationsspeicherung und–verarbeitung vor 5000 Jahren.* Translated by P. Larsen. Chicago: The University of Chicago Press.

Nørgaard, A. and E. Östergaard. 1994. 'A Reconstruction of a Blanket of the Migration Period Made by Anna Nørgaard.' *Archaeological Textiles Newsletter* 18/19: 17–19.

North, D.C. 1977. 'Markets and Other Allocation Systems in History: The Challenge of Karl Polanyi.' *The Journal of European Economic History* 6: 703–716.

North, D.C. 1981. *Structure and Change in Economic History.* New York: W.W. Norton.

North, D.C. 1984. 'Government and the Cost of Exchange in History.' *Journal of Economic History* 44: 255–264.

North, D.C. 1991. 'Institutions.' *The Journal of Economic Perspectives* 5: 97–112.

Nougayrol, J. 1956. *Le Palais royal d'Ugarit. VI. Textes en cunéiformes Babyloniens des archives du grand palais et du palais sud d'Ugarit.* Mission de Ras Shamra; 12. Paris: Imprimerie Nationale.

Nougayrol, J. 1968. *Ugaritica. V, Nouveaux textes accadiens, hourrites et ugaritiques des archives et bibliothèques privées d'Ugarit: commentaires des textes historiques (première partie).* Mission de Ras Shamra; 16. Paris: Imprimerie Nationale.

Nunn, J.F. 1996. *Ancient Egyptian Medicine.* London: British Museum Press.

Oates, D. 1990. 'Innovations in Mud-Brick: Decorative and Structural Techniques in Ancient Mesopotamia.' *World Archaeology* 21: 388–406.

O'Connor, D.B. 1983. 'New Kingdom and Third Intermediate Period.' In eds. B.G. Trigger, B.J. Kemp, D.B. O'Connor, and A.B. Lloyd, *Ancient Egypt: A Social History*: 183–278. Cambridge: Cambridge University Press.

O'Connor, D.B. 1995. 'The Social and Economic Organization of Ancient Egyptian Temples.' In ed. J.M. Sasson, *Civilizations of the Ancient Near East.* Vol. 1: 319–329. New York: Scribner.

Ogden, J. 2000. 'Metals.' In eds. P.T. Nicholson and I. Shaw, *Ancient Egyptian Materials and Technology*: 148–176. Cambridge: Cambridge University Press.

Ökse, A.T. 2007. 'Ancient Mountain Routes Connecting Central Anatolia to the Upper Euphrates Region.' *Anatolian Studies* 57: 35–45.

Oller, G.H. 1995. 'Messengers and Ambassadors in Ancient Western Asia.' In ed. J.M. Sasson, *Civilizations of the Ancient Near East.* Vol. 3: 1465–1473. New York: Scribner.

Olson, S.D. 1991. 'Firewood and Charcoal in Classical Athens.' *Hesperia* 60: 411–420.

Oppenheim, A.L. 1970. 'Trade in the Ancient Near East.' In *5th International Congress of Economic History*: 1–37. Moscow: Nauka Publishing.

Osborn, D.J. 1968. 'Notes on Medicinal and Other Uses of Plants in Egypt.' *Economic Botany* 22: 165–177.

Osborne, R. 1987. *Classical Landscape With Figures: The Ancient Greek City and Its Countryside.* London: George Philip.

Padgham, K. 2007. 'The Nature and Scale of the Late Bronze Age Economy in the Eastern Mediterranean for the Period 1400–1175 B.C.' Unpublished Ph.D. Thesis. Swansea University: Swansea.

Palmer, R. 1989. 'Subsistance Rations at Pylos and Knossos.' *Minos* 24: 89–124.

Panagiotakopulu, E. 1998. 'An Insect Study from Egyptian Stored Products in the Liverpool Museum.' *Journal of Egyptian Archaeology* 84, 231–234.

Panagiotakopulu, E. 2001. 'New Records for Ancient Pests: Archaeoentomology in Egypt.' *Journal of Archaeological Science* 28: 1235–1246.

Panagiotakopulu, E. and P.C. Buckland 1991. 'Insect Pests of Stored Products from Late Bronze Age Santorini, Greece.' *Journal of Stored Product Research* 27: 179–184.

Panagiotakopulu, E., P.C. Buckland, P. Day, A. Sarpaki, and C. Doumas. 1995. 'Natural Insecticides and Insect Repellents in Antiquity: A Review of the Evidence.' *Journal of Archaeological Science* 22: 705–710.

Papachristodoulou, S. 1976. *Norm Input-Output Data of the Main Crops of Cyprus.* Nicosia: Agricultural Research Institute, Ministry of Agriculture and Natural Resources.

Papadopoulos, I., C. Metochis, and D. Chimonidou. 2005. 'Irrigation Systems Performance: Case Study of Cyprus.' In eds. N. Lamaddalena, F. Lebdi, M. Todorovic, and C. Bogliotti, *Irrigation Systems Performance. Proceedings of 2nd Water Saving in Mediterranean Agriculture*

Workshop. Options Méditerranéennes; Séries B, N. 52: 80–85. Bari: CIHEAM.

Pare, C.F.E. 2000. 'Bronze and the Bronze Age.' In ed. C.F.E. Pare, *Metals Make the World Go Round: Proceedings of a Conference Held at the University of Birmingham in June 1997*: 1–38. Oxford: Oxbow Books.

Parise, N. 1989. 'The Mina of Ugarit, the Mina of Karkemish, the Mina of Khatti.' In ed. C. Zaccagnini, *Production and Consumption in the Ancient Near East*: 333–341. Budapest: Chaire d'Égyptologie de l'Université Loránd Eötvös.

Parkin, T.G. 1992. *Demography and Roman Society*. Ancient Society and History. Baltimore; London: Johns Hopkins University Press.

Parkin, T.G. 2003. *Old Age in the Roman World*. Baltimore: The Johns Hopkins University Press.

Parkinson, R.B. 1991. *Voices from Ancient Egypt: An Anthology of Middle Kingdom Writings*. Oklahoma Series in Classical Culture; 9. London: British Museum.

Parr, P.J. 1973. 'The Origin of the Canaanite Jar.' In ed. D. Strong, *Archaeological Theory and Practice*: 173–181. London: Seminar Press.

Parsons, T. and Neil J. Smelser. 1956. *Economy and Society: A Study in the Integration of Economic and Social Theory*. London: Routledge and Kegan Paul.

Partridge, R.B. 2002. *Fighting Pharaohs: Weapons and Warfare in Ancient Egypt*. Manchester: Peartree Publishing.

Peacock, E. 2001. 'The Contribution of Experimental Archaeology to the Reseach of Ancient Textiles.' In eds. P.W. Rogers, L.B. Jorgensen, A. Rast-Eicher, and J.P. Wild, *The Roman Textile Industry and Its Influence: A Birthday Tribute to John Peter Wild*: 181–192. Oxford: Oxbow.

Pearce, L.E. 1995. 'The Scribes and Scholars of Ancient Mesopotamia.' In ed. J.M. Sasson, *Civilizations of the Ancient Near East*. Vol. 4: 2265–2278. New York: Scribner.

Pearson, L.E. 1977. 'Editor's Introduction.' In K. Polanyi, 1977. *The Livelihood of Man*: *xxv-xxxvi*. New York; London: Academic Press.

Peet, T.E. and C.L. Woolley. 1923. *The City of Akhenaten. Part I. Excavations of 1921 and 1922 at El-'Amarneh*. Memoir of the Egypt Exploration Society; 38. London: Egypt Exploration Society.

Peltenburg, E.J. 1985 *Lemba Archaeological Project: Excavations at Lemba Lakkous, 1976–1983*. Vol. 1. Studies in Mediterranean Archaeology; 70. Lemba Archaeological Project; 1. Gothenburg: P. Åströms Förlag.

Peña-Chocarro, L. and L. Zapata 2003. 'Post-Harvest Processing of Hulled Wheats.' In eds. P.C. Anderson, L.S. Cummings, T.K. Schippers, and B. Simonel, *Le Traitement des récoltes: un regard sur la diversité du Néolithique au present*: 99–113. Antibes: APDCA.

Pendlebury, J.D.S. 1951a. *The City of Akhenaten. Part III: The Central City and the Official Quarters. The Excavations at Tell-El-Amarna During the Seasons 1926–1927 and 1931–1936: Texts*. Vol. 1. Memoir of the Egypt Exploration Society; 44. London: Egypt Exploration Society.

Pendlebury, J.D.S. 1951b. *The City of Akhenaten. Part III: The Central City and the Official Quarters. The Excavations at Tell-El-Amarna During the Seasons 1926–1927 and 1931–1936: Plates*. Vol. 2. Memoir of the Egypt Exploration Society; 44. London: Egypt Exploration Society.

Percival, J. 1976. *The Roman Villa: An Historical Introduction*. London: Batsford.

Perkins, J.A. 1976. 'Harvest Technology: Labour Supply.' *Tools and Tillage* 4: 173–184.

Pernicka, E. 1995. 'Crisis or Catharsis in Lead Isotope Analysis?' *Journal of Mediterranean Archaeology* 8: 59–64.

Pernicka, E. 1999. 'Trace Element Fingerprinting of Ancient Copper: A Guide to Technology or Provenance.' In eds. S. Young, A.M. Pollard, P. Budd, and R.A. Ixer, *Metals in Antiquity*. BAR International Series; 792: 163–186. Oxford: BAR Publishing.

Petrie, W.M.F. 1894. *Tell El Amarna*. London: Methuen and Co.

Petrie, W.M.F. 1898. *Deshasheh*. Memoir of the Egypt Exploration Fund; 15. London: Egypt Exploration Fund.

Petrie, W.M.F. 1917. *Tools and Weapons Illustrated by the Egyptian Collection in University College, London*. London: British School of Archaeology in Egypt.

Petrie, W.M.F. 1938. *Egyptian Architecture*. London: British School of Archaeology in Egypt; Bernard Quaritch Ltd.

Petrie, W.M.F., F.L. Griffith, and P.E. Newberry. 1890. *Kahun, Gurob, and Hawara*. London: K. Paul, Trench, Trübner and Co.

Petrini, M. 2012. *Calculations of Take-up and Shrinkage*. Handweavers Guild of America Inc. <http://www.weavespindye.org/html/rfts-doc.html>, accessed 08/01/2012.

Petruso, K.M. 1984. 'Prolegomena to Late Cypriot Weight Metrology.' *American Journal of Archaeology* 88: 293–304.

Petruso, K.M. 2003. 'Quantal Analysis of Some Mycenaean Balance Weights.' In eds. R. Laffineur and K.P. Foster, *Metron: Measuring the Aegean Bronze Age. Proceedings of the 9th International Aegean Conference/9e Rencontre égéenne internationale, New Haven, Yale University, 18–21 April 2002*. Aegaeum; 24: 285–292. Liège: Université de Liège.

Pettinato, G. 1981. *The Archives of Ebla: An Empire Inscribed in Clay*. Garden City, N.Y.: Doubleday.

Petzel, F.E. 1987. *Textiles of Ancient Mesopotamia, Persia, and Egypt*. Corvallis, Oregon: Cascade Printing Company.

Phelps, W.W, Y.G. Lolos and G. Vechos. 1999. *The Point Iria Wreck: Interconnections in the Mediterranean, Ca. 1200 B.C.: Proceedings of the International Conference, Island of Spetses, 19 September 1998*. Athens: Hellenic Institute of Marine Archaeology.

Pickles, S. and E.J. Peltenberg. 1998. 'Metallurgy, Society and the Bronze/Iron Transition in the East Mediterranean and the Near East.' *Report of the Director of the Department of Antiquities Cyprus, 1998*: 67–100. Nicosia: Department of Antiquities and Zavallis Press Ltd.

Pigott, V.C. 2011. 'Sources of Tin and the Tin Trade in Southwest Asia: Recent Research and Its Relevance to Current Understanding.' In eds. P.P. Betancourt and S.C. Ferrence, *Metallurgy: Understanding How, Learning Why: Studies in Honor of James D. Muhly*: Prehistory Monographs; 29: 273–291. Philadelphia: INSTAP Academic Press.

Pilides, D. 1996. 'Storage Jars as Evidence of the Economy in the Late Bronze Age.' In eds. V. Karageorghis and D. Michaelides, *The Development of the Cypriot Economy: From the Prehistoric Period to the Present Day*: 107–127. Nicosia: University of Cyprus: Bank of Cyprus.

Pleiner, R. 2000. 'Charcoal Burning.' In ed. R. Pleiner, *Iron in Archaeology: The European Bloomery Smelters*: 115–130. Praha: Archeologický ústav AVČR.

Pliny. *Naturalis historia*. Translated by W.H.S. Jones. 1951. *Natural History*. Loeb Classical Library. Cambridge, Mass.: Harvard University Press.

Polanyi, K. 1944. *The Great Transformation*. Boston: Beacon Press.

Polanyi, K. 1947. 'Our Obsolete Market Mentality.' *Commentary* 3: 109–117.

Polanyi, K. 1957. 'Marketless Trading in Hammurabi's Time.' In ed. K. Polanyi, *Trade and Market in the Early Empires: Economies in History and Theory*: 12–26. Glencoe: Free Press.

Polanyi, K. 1960. 'On the Comparative Treatment of Economic Institutions in Antiquity with Illustrations from Athens, Mycenae and Alalakh.' In eds. C.H. Kraeling and R.M. Adams, *City Invincible: A Symposium on Urbanization and Cultural Development in the Ancient Near East Held at the Oriental Institute of the University of Chicago, December 4–7, 1958*: 329–350. Chicago: University of Chicago Press.

Polanyi, K. 1963. 'Ports of Trade in Early Societies.' *Journal of Economic History* 23: 38–63.

Polanyi, K. 1968. 'Our Obsolete Market Mentality.' In ed. G. Dalton, *Primitive, Archaic, and Modern Economics: Essays of Karl Polanyi*. Garden City, New York: Anchor Books.

Polanyi, K. 1977. *The Livelihood of Man*. H.W. Pearson ed. Studies in Social Discontinuity. New York; London: Academic Press.

Polanyi, K., C.M. Arensberg and H.W. Pearson. 1957. 'The Place of Economics in Societies.' In ed. K. Polanyi, *Trade and Market in the Early Empires: Economies in History and Theory*: 239–242. Glencoe: Free Press.

Porter, B., and R. Moss. 1994. *Topographical Bibliography of Ancient Egyptian Hieroglyphic Texts, Reliefs, and Paintings*. Vol. 1. *The Theban Necropolis*, Part 1. *Private Tombs*. Second Edition, revised and augmented. Oxford: Clarendon.

Postgate, J.N. 1985. 'The Oil Plant in Assyria.' *Bulletin on Sumerian Agriculture* 2: 145–152.

Powell, M.A. 1977. 'Sumerian Merchants and the Problem of Profit.' *Iraq* 39: 23–29.

Powell, M.A. 1978. 'A Contribution to the History of Money in Mesopotamia Prior to the Invention of Coinage.' In eds. L. Matous and G. Komoróczy, *Festschrift Lubor Matouš*. Vol. 1. Assyriologia; 4–5: 211–243. Budapest: Eötvös Loránd Tudományegyetem.

Powell, M.A. 1979. 'Ancient Mesopotamian Weight Metrology: Methods, Problems and Perspectives.' In eds. T.B. Jones and R.H. Sack, *Studies in Honor of Tom B. Jones*. Alter Orient und Altes Testament; 203: 71–89. Kevelaer; Neukirchen-Vluyn: Butzon and Bercker: Neukirchener Verlag.

Powell, M.A. 1990. 'Masse und Gewichte.' *Reallexikon der Assyriologie* 7: 457–517.

Powell, M.A. 1995. 'Wine and the Vine in Ancient Mesopotamia: The Cuneiform Evidence.' In eds. P.E. McGovern, S.J. Fleming, and S.H. Katz, *The Origins and Ancient History of Wine*: 97–122. Luxembourg: Gordon and Breach Publishers.

Powell, M.A. 1996. 'Money in Mesopotamia.' *Journal of the Economic and Social History of the Orient* 39: 224–242.

Powell, M.A. 1999. 'Monies, Motives, and Methods.' In ed. J.G. Derckson, *Trade and Finance in Ancient Mesopotamia: Proceedings of the First MOS Symposium (Lieden 1997)*: 5–23. Leiden: Nederlands Instituut voor het Nabije Oosten.

Pritchard, J. 1955. *Ancient Near Eastern Texts Relating to the Old Testament*. Second Edition with Supplement. Princeton: Princeton University Press.

Pryce, T.O., Y. Bassiakos, M. Catapotis, and R.C. Doonan. '"De Caerimoniae" Technology Choices in Copper Smelting Furnace Design at Early Bronze Age Chrysokamino, Crete.' *Archaeometry* 49: 543–557.

Pulak, C. 1988. 'The Bronze Age Shipwreck at Ulu Burun, Turkey: 1985 Campaign.' *American Journal of Archaeology* 92: 1–37.

Pulak, C. 1997. 'The Ulu Burun Shipwreck.' In eds. S. Stuart, R.L. Hohlfelder, and H.W. Swiny, *Res Maritimae: Cyprus and the Eastern Mediterranean from Prehistory to Late Antiquity: Proceedings of the Second International Symposium "Cities on the Sea". Nicosia, Cyprus, October 18–22, 1994*: 233–262. Atlanta: Scholars Press.

Pulak, C. 1998. 'The Uluburun Shipwreck: An Overview.' *International Journal of Nautical Archaeology and Underwater Exploration* 27: 188–224.

Pulak, C. 1999. 'The Late Bronze Age Shipwreck at Ulu Burun: Aspects of Hull Construction.' In eds. W.W. Phelps, Y.G. Lólos, and G. Vechos, *The Point Iria Wreck: Interconnections in the Mediterranean, ca. 1200 B.C.: Proceedings of the International Conference, Island of Spetses, 19 September 1998*: 209–238. Athens: Hellenic Institute of Marine Archaeology.

Pulak, C. 2000a. 'Mortice-and-Tenon Joints of Bronze Age Seagoing Ships.' In ed. C. Beltrame, *Boats, Ships and Shipyards: Proceedings of the Ninth International Symposium on Boat and Ship Archaeology, Venice 2000*: 28–34. Oxford: Oxbow.

Pulak, C. 2000b. 'The Balance Weights from the Late Bronze Age Shipwreck at Ulu Burun.' In ed. C.F.E. Pare, *Metals Make the World Go Round: Proceedings of a Conference Held at the University of Birmingham in June 1997*: 247–266. Oxford: Oxbow Books.

Pulak, C. 2000c. 'The Copper and Tin Ingots from the Late Bronze Age Wreck at Uluburun.' In ed. U. Yalçin, *Anatolian Metal*, Vol. 1. Der Anschnitt 15: 137–157. Bochum: Deutsches Bergbau-Museum.

Pulak, C. 2001. 'The Cargo of the Uluburun Ship and Evidence of Trade with the Aegean.' In eds. L. Bonfante and V. Karageorghis, *Italy and Cyprus in Antiquity, 1500–450 B.C.: Proceedings of an International Symposium Held at the Italian Academy for Advanced Studies in America at Columbia University, November 16–18, 2000*: 13–60. Nicosia: Costakis and Leto Severies Foundation.

Pulak, C. 2010. 'Uluburun Shipwreck.' In ed. E.H. Cline, *The Oxford Handbook of the Bronze Age Aegean*: 862–876. Oxford: Oxford University Press.

Pullen, D.J. 1992. 'Ox and Plough in the Early Bronze Age Aegean.' *American Journal of Archaeology* 96: 45–54.

Pusch, E.B. 1990. 'Metallverarbeitende Werkstätten der frühen Ramessidenzeit in Quantir-Piramesse/Nord.' In ed. M. Bietak, *Ägypten und Levante: Zeitschrift für ägyptische Archäologie und deren Nachbargebiete* 1: 75–113. Vienna: Verlag der Österreichischen Akademie der Wissenschaften.

Pusch, E.B. 1994. 'Divergierende Verfahren der Metallverarbeitung in Theben und Qantir? Bemerkungen zu Konstruktion und Technik.' In ed. M. Bietak, *Ägypten und Levante: Zeitschrift für ägyptische Archäologie und deren Nachbargebiete* 4: 145–170. Vienna: Verlag der Österreichischen Akademie der Wissenschaften.

Pusch, Edgar B. 2005. 'Hittite and Mycenaean Remains at Qantir and their Implications for the Understanding of International Relations.' Conference Paper Presented at the British Museum, London 14th July 2005, *Egypt and the Hittites: Contacts, Conflict and Diplomacy in the Late Bronze Age*.

Py, V. and B. Ancel. 2006. 'Archaeological Experiments in Fire-Setting: Protocol, Fuel and Anthracological Approach.' In ed. A. Dufraise, *Charcoal Analysis: New Analytical Tools and Methods for Archaeology*: 71–82. Oxford: BAR Publishing.

Quack, J.F. 'Ein ägyptisches Handbuch des Tempels und seine griechische Übersetzung.' *Zeitschrift für Papyrologie und Epigraphik* 119: 297–300.

Quibell, J.E. 1898. *The Ramesseum by J.E. Quibell, with Translation and Comments by W. Spiegelberg, and The Tomb of Ptah-hetep, Copied by R.F.E. Paget and A.A. Pirie, with Comments by F.Ll. Griffith.* Egyptian Research Account 1896. London: Willian Clowes and Sons.

Quirke, S. 2004. *Egyptian Literature: 1800 B.C. Questions and Readings.* London: Golden House Publications.

Raban, A. 1991. 'Minoan and Canaanite Harbours.' In eds. R. Laffineur and L. Basch, *Thalassa: l'Égée préhistorique et la mer*. Aegaeum; 7: 129–154. Liège: Université de Liège.

Raban, A. 1995. 'The Heritage of Ancient Harbour Engineering in Cyprus and the Levant.' In eds. V. Karageorghis and D. Michaelides, *Proceedings of the International Symposium, Cyprus and the Sea.* Nicosia 25th-26th September, 1993: 139–190. Nicosia: University of Cyprus.

Raber, P. 1987. 'Early Copper Production in the Polis Region, Western Cyprus.' *Journal of Field Archaeology* 14: 297–312.

Rabino, J. 1884. 'Some Statistics of Egypt.' *Journal of the Statistical Society of London* 47: 415–467.

Rahmstorf, L. 2010. 'The Concept of Weighing During the Bronze Age in the Aegean, the Near East and Europe.' In eds. I. Morley and C. Renfrew, *The Archaeology of Measurement*: 88–105. Cambridge: Cambridge University Press.

Rainey, A.F. 1963a. 'A Canaanite at Ugarit.' *Israel Exploration Journal* 13: 43–45.

Rainey, A.F. 1963b. 'Business Agents at Ugarit.' *Israel Exploration Journal* 13: 313–321.

Ransome, H.M. 1937. *The Sacred Bee in Ancient Times and Folklore,* London: George Allen and Unwin.

Rathbone, D. 1990. 'Villages, Land and Population in Graeco-Roman Egypt.' In eds. E.J. Kenny and M.M. Mackenzie, *Proceedings of the Cambridge Philological Society.* Vol. 36: 103–142. Cambridge: Cambridge University Press.

Rathbone, D. 1991. *Economic Rationalism and Rural Society in Third-Century A.D. Egypt.* Cambridge: Cambridge University Press.

Rehder, J.E. 1999. 'High Temperature Technology in Antiquity. A Sourcebook on the Design and Operation of Ancient Furnaces.' In eds. E. Pernicka, Ü. Yalçin, T. Rehren, and A. Hauptmann, *The Beginnings of Metallurgy: Proceedings of the International Conference*

'The Beginnings of Metallurgy', Bochum 1995. Der Anschnitt; 9: 305–315. Bochum: Deutsches Bergbau-Museum.

Renfrew, C. 1972. *The Emergence of Civilisation: The Cyclades and the Aegean in the Third Millennium B.C.* London: Methuen.

Renfrew, C. 1993. 'Trade Beyond the Material.' In eds. C. Scarre and F. Healy, *Trade and Exchange in Prehistoric Europe*: 5–16. Oxford: Oxbow Books.

Renfrew, C. and Bahn, P. 1996. *Archaeology: Theories, Methods and Practice*. Second Edition. London: Thames and Hudson.

Renfrew, J.M. 1973. *Palaeoethnobotany: The Prehistoric Food Plants of the Near East and Europe.* London: Butler and Tanner Ltd.

Renfrew, J.M. 1984. 'Cereals Cultivated in Ancient Iraq.' *Bulletin on Sumerian Agriculture* 1: 32–44.

Renfrew, J.M. 1985. 'Preliminary Report on the Botanical Remains.' In ed. B.J. Kemp, *Amarna Reports II*: 175–190. London: Egypt Exploration Society.

Renfrew, J.M. 1995. 'Palaeoethnobotanical Finds of Vitus from Greece.' In ed. P.E. McGovern, *The Origins and Ancient History of Wine*: 255–267. New York: Gordon and Breach Publishers.

Renger, J. 1994. 'On Economical Structures in Ancient Mesopotamia.' *Orientalia* 63: 157–208.

Renger, J. 1995. 'Subsistenzproduktion und redistributive Palastwirtschaft: Wo bleibt die Nische für das Geld? Grenzen und Möglichkeiten für die Verwendung von Geld im alten Mesopotamien.' In eds. W. Schelkle and M. Nitsch, *Rätsel Geld: Annäherungen aus ökonomischer, soziologischer und historischer Sicht*: 271–324. Marburg: Metropolis-Verlag.

Revere, R.B. 1957. '"No Man's Coast": Ports of Trade in the Eastern Mediterranean.' In ed. K. Polanyi, *Trade and Market in the Early Empires: Economies in History and Theory*: 38–63. Glencoe: Free Press.

Reynolds, P.J. 1981. 'Deadstock and Livestock.' In ed. R. Mercer, *Farming Practice in British Prehistory*: 97–122. Edinburgh: Edinburgh University Press.

Reynolds, P.J. 1992. 'Crop Yields of the Prehistoric Cereal Types Emmer and Spelt: The Worst Option. A Discussion of the Data Achieved from 15 Years of Research at the Butser Ancient Farm.' In ed. P. Anderson, *Préhistoire de l'agriculture nouvelles approaches éxperimentales et ethnographiques.* Monographie du Centre de Researches Archaéologiques; 6: 383–393. Paris: Editions du Centre de Researches Archaéologiques.

Reynolds, P.J. 1999. 'The Nature of Experiment in Archaeology.' In ed. A.F. Harding, *Experiment and Design: Archaeological Studies in Honor of John Coles*: 156–162. Oxford: Oxbow Books.

Ricardo, D. 1821 [1772–1823]. *On the Principles of Political Economy, and Taxation.* Third Edition. London: John Murray.

Richards, A. 1982. *Egypt's Agricultural Development, 1800–1900.* Boulder: Westview Press.

Richards, J.E. 2005. *Society and Death in Ancient Egypt: Mortuary Landscapes of the Middle Kingdom.* Cambridge: Cambridge University Press.

Riley, F.R. 1999. *The Role of the Traditional Mediterranean Diet in the Development of Minoan Crete.* Oxford: BAR Publishing.

Riley, F.R. 2002. 'Olive Oil Production on Bronze Age Crete: Nutritional Properties, Processing Methods and Storage Life of Minoan Olive Oil.' *Oxford Journal of Archaeology* 21: 63–75.

Roaf, M. 1990. *Cultural Atlas of Mesopotamia and the Ancient Near East.* Oxford: Facts on File Ltd.

Roberts, O.T.P. 1991. 'The Developments of the Brail into a Viable Sail Control for Aegean Boats of the Bronze Age.' In eds. R. Laffineur and L. Basch, *Thalassa: l'Égée préhistorique et la mer.* Aegaeum; 7: 55–60. Liège: Université de Liège.

Robins, G. 1993. *Women in Ancient Egypt.* London: British Museum Press.

Robins, G. and C. Shute. 1987. *The Rhind Mathematical Papyrus.* London: Published for the Trustees of the British Museum by British Museum Publications.

Roehrig, C.H. 1996. 'Women's Work: Some Occupations of Nonroyal Women as Depicted in Ancient Egyptian Art.' In eds. A.K. Carpel and G.E. Markoe, *Mistress of the House, Mistress of Heaven*: 13–24. New York: Hudson Hills Press.

Ross, J.C. 1889. 'Introduction.' In W. Willcocks, *Egyptian Irrigation*: v-xxii. London: E. and F.N. Spon.

Rostovtzeff, M.I. 1941. *The Social and Economic History of the Hellenistic World.* Vol. 2. Oxford: Clarendon Press

Roth, H.L. 1978. *Ancient Egyptian and Greek Looms.* Second Edition. Bedford: Ruth Bean.

Rothenberg, B. 1962. 'Ancient Copper Industries in the Western Arabah.' *Palestine Exploration Quarterly* 94: 5–67.

Rothenberg, B. 1972. *Timna: Valley of the Biblical Copper Mines.* London: Thames and Hudson.

Rothenberg, B. 1978. 'Excavations at Timna Site 39. A Chalcolithic Copper Smelting Site and Furnace and Its Metallurgy.' In ed. B. Rothenberg, *Chalcolithic Copper Smelting.* Archaeo-Metallurgy; 1: 1–15. London: Institute for Archaeo-Metallurgical Studies.

Rothenberg, B. 1985. 'Copper Smelting Furnaces in the Arabah, Israel: The Archaeological Evidence.' In eds. P.T. Craddock and M.J. Hughes, *Furnaces and Smelting Tecnology in Antiquity.* British Museum Occasional Paper; 48: 123–150. London: British Museum.

Rothenberg, B. 1987. 'Pharaonic Copper Mines in South Sinai.' *Institute of Archaeo-Metallurgical Studies Newsletter* 10/11: 1–7.

Rothenberg, B. 1988. *The Egyptian Mining Temple at Timna.* Researches in the Arabah, 1959-1984. Vol. 1. London: Institute for Archaeo-Metallurgical Studies.

Rothenberg, B. 1990. 'Copper Smelting Furnaces, Tuyères, Slags, Ingot-moulds and Ingots in the Arabah: The Archaeological Data.' In eds. B. Rothenberg and H.G. Bachmann, *The Ancient Metallurgy of Copper, Researches in the Arabah, 1959–1984*, Vol. 2: 1–77. London: Institute for Archaeo-Metallurgical Studies, Institute of Archaeology, University College, London.

Rothenberg, B. 1999. Archaeo-Metallurgical Researches in the Southern Arabah 1959–1990: 2. Egyptian New Kingdom (Ramesside) to Early Islam. *Palestine Exploration Quarterly* 131: 149–175.

Roucek, T.S. 1935. 'Economic Geography of Greece.' *Economic Geography* 11: 91–104.

Rowlands, M. 1987. 'Centre and Periphery.' In eds. M. Rowlands, M. Larsen, and K. Kristiansen, *Centre and Periphery in the Ancient World. New Directions in Archaeology*: 1–12. Cambridge: Cambridge University Press.

Rowlands, M.J. 1976. *The Production and Distribution of Metalwork in the Middle Bronze Age in Southern Britain*. BAR International Series; 31. Oxford: BAR Publishing.

Ruf, T. 1993. 'The History of Agricultural Development.' In ed. G.M. Craig, *The Agriculture of Egypt*: 188–208. Oxford: Oxford University Press.

Runnels, C.N. and J.M. Hansen. 1986. 'The Olive in the Prehistoric Aegean: The Evidence for Domestication in the Early Bronze Age.' *Oxford Journal of Archaeology* 5: 299–307.

Rupp, D.W., L.W. Sørensen, R.H. King, and W.A. Fox. 1984. 'Canadian Palaipaphos (Cyprus) Survey Project: Second Preliminary Report, 1980–1982.' *Journal of Field Archaeology* 11: 133–154.

Russell, K.W. 1988. *After Eden: The Behavioural Ecology of Early Food Production in the Near East and North Africa*. BAR International Series; 391. Oxford: BAR Publishing.

Ryder, M.L. 1983. *Sheep and Man*. London: Duckworth.

Sabet, A. H., V. B. Tsogoev, S.P. Shibanin, M.B. Kadi, and S. Awad. 1976. 'The Placer Deposits of Igla, Aby Dabbab and Nuweib.' *Annals of the Geological Survey of Egypt* 6: 169–180.

Sahlins, M.D. 1972. *Stone Age Economics*. Chicago: Aldine Atherton.

Samuel, D. 1989. 'Their Staff of Life: Initial Investigations on Ancient Egyptian Bread Baking.' In ed. B.J. Kemp, *Amarna Reports V*: 253–290. London: Egypt Exploration Society

Samuel, D. 1996. 'Archaeology of Ancient Egyptian Beer.' *Journal of the American Society of Brewing Chemists* 54: 3–12.

Samuel, D. 1999. 'Bread Making and Social Interactions at the Amarna Workmen's Village, Egypt.' *World Archaeology* 31: 121–144.

Samuel, D. 2000. 'Brewing and Baking.' In eds. P.T. Nicholson and I. Shaw, *Ancient Egyptian Materials and Technology*: 537–577. Cambridge: Cambridge University Press.

Samuel, D. 2010. 'Experimental Grinding and Ancient Egyptian Flour Production.' In eds. S. Ikram and A. Dodson, *Beyond the Horizon: Studies in Egyptian Art, Archaeology and History in Honour of Barry J. Kemp*: 456–477. Cairo: Supreme Council of Antiquities Press.

Sarpaki, A. 1992. 'The Palaeoethnobotanical Approach. The Mediterranean Triad or is it Quartet?' In ed. B. Wells, *Agriculture in Ancient Greece: Proceedings of the Seventh International Symposium at the Swedish Institute of Athens, 16–17 May 1990.* Skrifter Utgivna av Svenska institutet i Athen; 42: 61–76. Stockholm: Svenska institutet i Athen.

Şaul, M. 2005. 'Africa South of the Sahara. ' In ed. J.G. Carrier, *A Handbook of Economic Anthropology*: 500–513. Cheltenham: Edward Elgar.

Sauneron, S. 2000: *The Priests of Ancient Egypt.* Translated by D. Lorton. Ithaca; London: Cornell University Press.

Sauvage, C. 2008. 'Trade and Exchange in the Late Bronze Age: An Adaption to the Envionmental Milieu.' In eds. H. Kühne, R.M. Czichon, and F.J. Kreppner, *Proceedings of the 4th International Congress of the Archaeology of the Ancient Near East, 29 March–3 April 2004, Freie Universität Berlin.* Vol. 1: 209–217. Wiesbaden: Harrassowitz.

Savage, G. 1968. *A Concise History of Bronzes.* London: Thames and Hudson.

Säve-Söderbergh, T. 1957. *Four Eighteenth Dynasty Tombs.* Private Tombs at Thebes; 1. Oxford: Printed for the Griffith Institute at the University Press by C. Batey.

Scheidel, W. 1982. 'Roman Age Structure: Evidence and Models.' *Journal of Roman Studies* 86: 1–26.

Scheidel, W. 1996. *Measuring Sex, Age and Death in the Roman Empire: Explorations in Ancient Demography.* Journal of Roman Archaeology Supplementary Series; 21. Ann Arbor: Journal of Roman Archaeology.

Scheidel, W. 2001a. *Death on the Nile: Disease and the Demography of Roman Egypt.* Mnemosyne, Bibliotheca Classica Batava. Supplementum; 228. Leiden: Brill.

Scheidel, W. 2001b. 'Roman Age Structure: Evidence and Models.' *Journal of Roman Studies* 91: 1–26.

Scheidel, W. 2007. 'Demography.' In eds. W. Scheidel, I. Morris, and R.P. Saller, *The Cambridge Economic History of the Greco-Roman World*: 38–86. Cambridge: Cambridge University Press.

Schenkel, W. 1978. *Die Bewässerungsrevolution im alten Ägypten.* Mainz: Philipp von Zabern.

Schiaparelli, E. 1927. *La tomba intatta dell'architetto cha nella necropoli di tebe (relazione sui lavori della missione archeologica italiana in egitto, anni 1903–1920).* Vol. 2. Torino: Museo di antichità.

Schiaparelli, E. 2008. *The Intact Tomb of the Architect Kha in the Necropolis of Thebes.* First English Edition. Turin: AdArte.

Schick, T. 1998. 'Red Ochre: The Material and Its Cultural Background.' In eds. T. Schick and D. Barshad, *The Cave of the Warrior: A Fourth*

Millennium Burial in the Judean Desert. Israel Antiquities Authority Reports; 5: 63–64. Jerusalem: Israel Antiquities Authority.

Schlabow, K. 1974. 'Vor-und frühgeschichtliche Textilfunde aus den nördlichen Niederlanden.' *Palaeohistoria* 16: 171–221.

Schlanger, N. 1990. 'Technique as Human Action.' *Archaeological Revue from Cambridge* 9: 18–26.

Schloen, D. 2001. *The House of the Father as Fact and Symbol: Patrimonialism in Ugarit and the Ancient Near East.* Winona Lake: Eisenbrauns.

Schneider, H.K. 1974: *Economic Man: The Anthropology of Economics.* New York: Free Press.

Schneider, J. 1991. 'Was there a Precapitalist World-System?' In eds. C. Chase-Dunn and T. Hall. *Core/Periphery Relations in Precapitalist Worlds*: 45–66. Boulder: Westview Press.

Shortland, A.J. and M.S. Tite 2000. 'Raw Materials of Glass from Amarna and Implications for the Origins of Egyptian Glass.' *Archaeometry* 42: 141–151.

Schortman, E.M. and P.A. Urban. 1992. 'The Ancient World System.' In eds. E.M. Schortman and P.A. Urban, *Resources, Power, and Interregional Interaction. Interdisciplinary Contributions to Archaeology*: 17–21. New York; London: Plenum Press.

Serpico, M. 2003. 'Quantifying Resin Trade in the Eastern Mediterranean During the Late Bronze Age.' In eds. R. Laffineur and K.P. Foster, *Metron: Measuring the Aegean Bronze Age. Proceedings of the 9th International Aegean Conference/9e Rencontre égéenne internationale, New Haven, Yale University, 18–21 April 2002.* Aegaeum; 24: 223–232. Liège: Université de Liège.

Serpico, M. 2004. 'Natural Product Technology in New Kingdom Egypt.' In eds. J. Bourriau and J.S. Phillips, *Invention and Innovation: The Social Context of Technological Change 2: Egypt, the Aegean and the Near East, 1650–1150 B.C.: Proceedings of a Conference Held at the Mcdonald Institute for Archaeological Research, Cambridge, 4–6th September 2002*: 96–120. Oxford: Oxbow Books.

Serpico, M. and R. White. 2000. 'Oil, Fat and Wax.' In eds. P.T. Nicholson and I. Shaw, *Ancient Egyptian Materials and Technology*: 390–429. Cambridge: Cambridge University Press.

Sethe, K. (ed). 1933. *Urkunden des Alten Reichs.* Vol 1. Urkunden des aegyptischen Altertums. Liepzig: J.C. Hinrichs.

Sharman, J. 2009. 'Infant Feeding and Weaning Practices as Data for Fertility Estimates of a Roman-Period Population Sample from Kellis 2, Dakhleh Oasis, Egypt.' In eds. S. Baker, A. Ray, K. Lakin, R. Madgwick, K. Poole, and M. Sandias, *Food and Drink in Archaeology 2: University of Nottingham Postgraduate Conference 2008*: 81–89. Totnes: Prospect.

Shaw. C.T. and Ş. Durucan. 2008. 'A Study of Mining Methods and Ventilation During the Egyptian Period at the Mines of Timna.' In eds. Ü. Yalçın, H. Özbal, and A.G. Pasamehmetoglu, *Ancient Mining in Turkey and the Eastern Mediterranean: International Conference AMITEM 2008, June 15–22*: 435–464. Ankara: Atılım University.

Shay, J.M. and C.T. Shay. 1978, 'Modern Vegetation and Fossil Plant Remains.' In eds. G. Rapp and S. Aschenbrenner, *Excavations at Nichoria in Southwest Greece.* Vol. 1: 48. University of Minnesota: Minneapolis.

Shedid, A.G. and M. Seidel. 1996. *The Tomb of Nakht: The Art and History of an Eighteenth Dynasty Official's Tomb at Western Thebes.* Mainz: Philipp von Zabern.

Sherratt, A.G. 1993. What Would a Bronze Age World System Look Like? Relations Between Temperate Europe and the Mediterranean in Later Prehistory. *Journal of European Archaeology* 1: 1–57.

Sherratt, A.G. and S. Sherratt. 1991. 'From Luxuries to Commodities: The Nature of Mediterranean Bronze Age Trading Systems.' In ed. N.H. Gale, *Bronze Age Trade in the Mediterranean: Papers Presented at the Conference Held at Rewley House, Oxford, in December 1989.* Studies in Mediterranean Archaeology; 90: 351–386. Jonsered: P. Åströms Förlag.

Sherratt, A.G. and S. Sherratt. 1993. 'The Growth of the Mediterranean Economy in the Early First Millennium BC.' *World Archaeology* 24: 361–378.

Sherratt, A.G. and S. Sherratt. 1998. 'Small Worlds: Interaction and Identity in the Ancient Mediterranean.' In eds. E.H. Cline and D. Harris-Cline, *The Aegean and the Orient in the Second Millennium: Proceedings of the 50th Anniversary Symposium Cincinnati, 18–20th April 1997.* Aegaeum; 18: 329–342. Liège: Université de Liège.

Sherratt, S. 1991. 'Cypriot Pottery of Aegean Type in LC II-III: Problems of Classification. Chronology and Interpretation.' In eds. J.A. Barlow, D.R. Bolger, and B. Kling, *Cypriot Ceramics: Reading the Prehistoric Record.* Philadelphia: University Museum of Archaeology and Anthropology, University of Pennsylvania

Sherratt, S. 1994. 'Commerce, Iron, and Ideology: Metallurgical Innovation in 12th-11th Century Cyprus.' In ed. V. Karageorghis, *Cyprus in the 11th Century B.C.: Proceedings of the International Archaeological Symposium Held in Nicosia, Oct. 30–31, 1993*: 59–108. Athens: A.G. Leventis Foundation University of Cyprus.

Sherratt, S. 1998. '"Sea Peoples" and the Economic Structure of the Late Second Millennium in the Eastern Mediterranean.' In eds. T.K. Dothan, S. Gitin, A. Mazar, and E. Stern, *Mediterranean Peoples in Transition: Thirteenth to Early Tenth*

Centuries B.C.E.: 292–313. Jerusalem: Israel Exploration Society.

Sherratt, S. 1999. 'E pur si muove: Pots, Markets and Values in the Second Millennium Mediterranean.' In eds. J.P. Crielaard, V. Stissi, and G.J. van Wijngaarden, *The Complex Past of Pottery: Production, Circulation and Consumption of Mycenaean and Greek Pottery (Sixteenth to Early Fifth Centuries B.C.): Proceedings of the Archon International Conference, Held in Amsterdam, 8–9 November 1996*: 163–211. Amsterdam: J. C. Gieben.

Sherratt, S. 2000. 'Circulation of Metals and the End of the Bronze Age in the Eastern Mediterranean.' In ed. C.F.E. Pare, *Metals Make the World Go Round: Proceedings of a Conference Held at the University of Birmingham in June 1997*: 82–98. Oxford: Oxbow Books.

Sherratt, S. 2003. 'The Mediterranean Economy: "Globalisation" at the End of the Second Millennium B.C.E.' In eds. W.G. Dever and S. Gitin, *Symbiosis, Symbolism, and the Power of the Past: Canaan, Ancient Israel, and Their Neighbors from the Late Bronze Age Through Roman Palaestina. Proceedings of the Centennial Symposium, W.F. Albright Institute of Archaeological Research and American Schools of Oriental Research, Jerusalem, May 29–31, 2000*: 214–238. Winona Lake: Eisenbrauns.

Shirley, E.A.M. 2001. *Building a Roman Legionary Fortress*. Stroud: Tempus.

Shore, A.F. 1990. 'Smash Not Sieve: Heqanakhte II, rt. 30.' *Journal of Egyptian Archaeology* 76: 164–166.

Sibella, P. 1996. 'The Copper Oxide and Bun Ingots.' *The International Journal of Nautical Archaeology and Underwater Exploration* 23: 9–11.

Siegelová, J. 2008. 'Wind-powered Copper Smelting Technology from the 3rd Millennium BC at Feinan/Jordan.' In eds. Ü. Yalçın, H. Özbal, and A.G. Pasamehmetoglu, *Ancient Mining in Turkey and the Eastern Mediterranean: International Conference AMITEM 2008, June 15–22*: 43–56. Ankara: Atılım University.

Sievertsen, U. 2007. 'Wine Drinking at HK6.' *Nekhen News* 19: 13.

Silver, M. 1983. 'Karl Polanyi and Markets in the Ancient Near East: The Challenge of the Evidence.' *Journal of Economic History* 2: 795–829.

Silver, M. 1985. *Economic Structures of the Ancient Near East*. London: Croom Helm.

Silver, M. 2004. 'Modern Ancients.' In eds. R. Rollinger, C. Ulf, and K. Schnegg, *Commerce and Monetary Systems in the Ancient World: Means of Transmission and Cultural Interaction. Proceedings of the Fifth Annual Symposium of the Assyrian and Babylonian Intellectual Heritage Project, Held in Innsbruck, Austria, October 3rd–8th 2002*: 65–87. Stuttgart: Franz Steiner.

Sim, D. and I. Ridge. 2002. *Iron for Eagles: The Iron Industry of Roman Britain*. Stroud: Tempus Publishing Ltd.

Simms, S.R. and K.W. Russell. 1997. 'Bedouin Hand Harvesting of Wheat and Barley: Implications for Early Cultivation in Southwestern Asia.' *Current Anthropology* 38: 696–702.

Simpson, W.K. 1963. *Papyrus Reisner I. The Records of a Building Project in the Reign of Sesostris I*. Boston: Museum of Fine Arts.

Simpson, W.K. 1965. *Papyrus Reisner II. The Accounts of the Dockyard Workshop in the Reign of Sesostris I*. Boston: Museum of Fine Arts.

Simpson, W.K. 1969. *Papyrus Reisner III. The Records of a Building Project in the Early Twelfth Dynasty*. Boston: Museum of Fine Arts.

Simpson, W.K. 1973. *The Literature of Ancient Egypt: An Anthology of Stories, Instructions, and Poetry*. New Haven and London: Yale University Press.

Simpson, W.K. 1986. *Papyrus Reisner IV. Personal Accounts of the Early Twelfth Dynasty*. Boston: Museum of Fine Arts.

Singer, I. 1999. 'A Political History of Ugarit.' In eds. W.G.E. Watson and N. Wyatt, *Handbook of Ugaritic Studies*. Handbuch der Orientalistik. Erste Abteilung, Nahe und der Mittlere Osten; 39: 603–733. Leiden: Brill.

Skakun, N.N. 1999. 'Evolution of Agricultural Techniques in Eneolithic (Chalcolithic) Bulgaria.' In ed. P.C. Anderson, *Prehistory of Agriculture: New Experimental and Ethnographic Approaches*. Monograph, Institute of Archaeology, University of California Los Angeles; 40: 199–210. Los Angeles: Institute of Archaeology, University of California.

Snell, D.C. 1982. *Ledgers and Prices: Early Mesopotamian Merchant Accounts*. Yale Near Eastern Researches; 8. New Haven; London: Yale University Press.

Snell, D.C. 1991. 'Marketless Trading in Our Time.' *Journal of the Economic and Social History of the Orient* 34: 129–141.

Snell, D.C. 1995. *Life in the Ancient Near East, 3100–332 B.C.E.* New Haven: Yale University Press.

Snell, D.C. 1995. 'Methods of Exchange in Ancient Western Asia.' In ed. J.M. Sasson, *Civilizations of the Ancient Near East*. Vol. 3: 1487–1497. New York: Scribner.

Snodgrass, A.M. 1991. 'Bronze Age Exchange: A Minimalist Position.' In ed. N.H. Gale, *Bronze Age Trade in the Mediterranean: Papers Presented at the Conference Held at Rewley House, Oxford, in December 1989*. Studies in Mediterranean Archaeology; 90: 15–20. Jonsered: P. Åströms Förlag.

Sokona, Y. 1988. 'Food, Energy and the Daily Chores of Women in West Africa.' In ed. T.K. Moulik, *Food-Energy Nexus and Ecosystem; Proceedings of the Second International Symposium on Food-Energy Nexus in New Delhi, India, 12–14 February 1986*: 68–89. Oxford: Indian Institute for Management. Centre for Management in Agriculture.

South, A.K. 1989. 'From Copper to Kingship: Aspects of Bronze Age Society Viewed from the Vasilikos Valley.' In ed. E.J. Peltenburg, *Early Society in Cyprus:* 315–324. Edinburgh: Edinburgh University Press.

South, A.K. 1992. 'Kalavasos-Ayios Dhimitrios 1991.' *Report of the Director of the Department of Antiquities Cyprus, 1992*: 133–141. Nicosia: Department of Antiquities and Zavallis Press Ltd.

South, A.K. 1995. 'Urbanism and Trade in the Vasilikos Valley in the Late Bronze Age.' In eds. S. Bourke and J-P Descœudres, *Trade, Contact, and the Movement of Peoples in the Eastern Mediterranean: Studies in Honour of J. Basil Hennessy*: 187–197. Sydney: Meditarch.

South, A.K. 1997. 'Late Bronze Age Society in Cyprus.' *Minerva* 8: 28–34.

Spalinger, A. 1986. 'Baking During the Reign of Seti I.' *Bulletin de l'Institut français d'archéologie orientale* 86: 307–352.

Spalinger, A.J. 2005. *War in Ancient Egypt*. Oxford: Blackwell Publishing.

Speiser, E.A. 1954. 'The Alalakh Tablets.' *Journal of the American Oriental Society* 74: 18–25.

Spencer, A.J. 1979. *Brick Architecture in Ancient Egypt*. Warminster: Aris and Phillips.

Spencer, A.J. 1982. *Death in Ancient Egypt*. London: Penguin Books Ltd.

Spurr, M.S. 1986. *Arable Cultivation in Roman Italy c.200 B.C.-c.A.D.100*. Journal of Roman Studies Monograph; 3. London: Society for the Promotion of Roman Studies.

Steel, L. 1998. 'The Social Impact of Mycenean Imported Pottery in Cyprus.' *The Annual of the British School at Athens* 93: 285-296.

Steel, L. 2004. 'Goodly Feast… a Cup of Mellow Wine: Feasting in Bronze Age Cyprus.' In ed. J. Wright, *The Mycenaean Feast*: 161–180. Princeton: American School of Classical Studies at Athens.

Steel, L. and S. Janes. 2005. 'Survey at Aredhiou Vouppes, Cyprus.' *Report of the Department of Antiquities, Cyprus*: 231–244.

Steensberg, A. 1943. *Ancient Harvesting Implements: A Study in Archaeology and Human Geography*. Dissertation Copenhagen. Nationalmuseets Skrifter. Arkæologisk-Historisk Række; 1. København: I Komission hos Gyldendalske Boghandel, Nordisk Forlag, 1943.

Steensberg, A. 1957. 'Parallel Ploughing with Alternatively Sloping and Upright Ard in Columella.' *Folk-Liv* 21: 157–162.

Steensberg, A. 1976. 'Virgil's Wheel-Ard and the Two Mouldstrokers.' In ed. C. Ó Danachair, *Folk and Farm: Essays in Honour of A.T. Lucas*. Dublin: Royal Society of Antiquaries of Ireland.

Stein, G.J. 1998. 'World System Theory and Alternative Modes of Interaction in the Archaeology of Culture Contact.' In ed. J.G. Cusick, *Studies in Culture Contact: Interaction, Culture Change, and Archaeology*. Southern Illinois University at Carbondale. Center for Archaeological Investigations Occasional Paper; 25: 220–255. Carbondale: Center for Archaeological Investigations, Southern Illinois University.

Steinkeller, P. 1995. 'Sheep and Goat Terminology in Ur III Sources from Drehem.' *Bulletin on Sumerian Agriculture* 8: 49–70.

Steitieh, A.M. and M.A. Smadi. 1974. *Wheat in Jordan: Demand and Supply Estimations and Projections*. Amman: Ministry of Agriculture.

Stevenson Smith, W.M. 1951. 'Paintings of the Egyptian Middle Kingdom at Bersheh.' *American Journal of Archaeology* 55: 321–332.

Stewart, R.G. 1962. 'A Solvent-Soluble Fraction of the Fleece of Sheep Associated with Suint.' *Nature* 195: 907.

Stewart, R.T. 1974. 'Paleobotanic Investigation: 1972 Season.' In eds. L.E. Stager, A.M. Walker, and E.G. Wright, *American Expedition to Idalion, First Preliminary Report: Seasons of 1971 and 1972*. Bulletin of the American Schools of Oriental Research. Supplemental Studies; 18: 123–129. Chicago: Oriental Institute of the University of Chicago.

Stieglitz, R.R. 1979. 'Commodity Prices at Ugarit.' *Journal of the American Oriental Society* 99: 15–23.

Stol, M. 1993. 'Milk, Butter and Cheese.' *Bulletin on Sumerian Agriculture* 7: 99–113.

Stoll, M. and D. Fengel. 1988. 'Chemical and Structual Studies on Ancient Ancient Egyptian Linen.' *Berliner Beiträge zur Archäometrie* 10: 151–172.

Stos-Gale, Z.A. and N.H. Gale. 2002. 'The Characterisation by Lead Isotopes of the Ore Deposits of Cyprus and Sardinia and Its Bearing on the Possibility of the Lead Isotope Provencing of Copper Alloys.' In eds. E. Jerem and K. T. Biró, *Archaeometry 98: Proceedings of the 31st International Archaeometry Symposium, April 26–May 3 1998*. Vol. 2. BAR International Series; 1043: 359–362. Oxford: BAR Publishing.

Strand, E.A. 2010. 'The Basics of Textile Tools and Textile Technology: From Fibre to Fabric.' In eds. C. Michel and M.-L. Nosch, *Textile Terminologies: in the Ancient Near East and the Mediterranean Area from the Third to the First Millennia BC*: 10–22. Oxford: Oxbow.

Sullivan, L.H. 1896. 'The Tall Office Building Artistically Considered.' *Lippincott's Monthly Magazine*: 403–409.

Sweeney, D. 2006. 'Women Growing Older in Deir el-Medina.' In eds. A. Dorn and T. Hofmann, *Living and Writing in Deir el-Medina: Socio-Historical Embodiment of Deir el-Medina Texts*. Ægyptiaca Helvetica: 19: 135–153. Basel: Schwabe.

Sweet-Escott, B. 1954. *Greece: A Political and Economic Survey 1939–1953*. London: Royal Institute of International Affairs.

Szpakowska, K.M. 2008. *Daily Life in Ancient Egypt:*

Recreating Lahun. Malden, Mass.; Oxford: Blackwell.

Takács, L. 1982. 'Grubbing by Swine as a Means of Preparing the Soil on Swampy Ground.' *Tools and Tillage* 4: 155–157.

Tammuz, O. 2005. 'Mare clasum? Sailing Seasons in the Mediterranean in Early Antiquity.' *Mediterranean Historical Review* 20: 145–162.

Taylor, J.H. 2001. *Death and the Afterlife in Ancient Egypt*. London: British Museum Press.

Thomas, A.P. 1981. *Gurob: A New Kingdom Town*. Egyptology Today; 5. Warminster: Aris and Phillips.

Thureau-Dangin, F. 1931. 'Vocabulaire de Ras Shamra.' *Syria* 12: 228–230.

Tiboni, F. 2005. 'Weaving and Ancient Sails: Structural Changes to Ships as a Consequence of New Weaving Technology in the Mediterranean Late Bronze Age.' *The International Journal of Nautical Archaeology and Underwater Exploration* 34: 127–130.

Tiedeman, J., B. Boulanouar, S. Christiansen, and M. Derkaoui. 1998. 'Sheep Production on Medic and Weedy Pasture in Semi-Arid Morocco.' *The Journal of Range Management* 51: 288–292.

Tiedemann, E.J. and J.A. Jakes. 2006. 'An Exploration of Prehistoric Spinning Technology: Spinning Efficiency and Technology Transition.' *Archaeometry* 48: 293–307.

Tietze, C. 1985. 'Amarna. Analyse der Wohnhäuser und soziale Struktur der Stadtbewohner.' *Zeitschrift für ägyptische Sprache und Altertumskunde* 112: 48–84.

Timberlake, S. 1990. 'Review of the Historical Evidence for the Use of Firesetting.' In eds. P. Crew and S. Crew, *Early Mining in the British Isles: Proceedings of the Early Mining Workshop at Plas Tan Y Bwlch, Snowdonia National Park Study Centre, 17–19 November, 1989*. Plas Tan Y Bwlch Occasional Paper; 1. Tan y Bwlch, Gwynedd: Plas Tan y Bwlch, Snowdonia National Park Study Centre.

Timberlake, S. 1994. 'An Experimental Tin Smelt at Flag Fen.' *The Journal of the Historical Metallurgy Society* 28: 121–130.

Timberlake, S. 2009. 'The Use of Experimental Archaeology/Archaeometallurgy for the Understanding and Reconstruction of Early Bronze Age Mining and Smelting Experiments.' In eds. S. La Niece, D. Hook, and P. Craddock, *Metals and Mines: Studies in Archaeometallurgy*: 27–36. London: Archetype Publications Ltd.

Tobin, V.A. 1989. *Theological Principles of Egyptian Religion*. New York: Lang.

Todd, I.A. 1979. 'Vasilikos Valley Project: Third Preliminary Report, 1978.' *Journal of Field Archaeology* 6: 265–300.

Trigger, B.G. 1985. 'The Evolution of Pre-Industrialised Cities: A Multilinear Perspective.' In eds. F. Geus, J. Vercoutter, W.Y. Adams, and F. Thill, *Mélanges offerts à Jean Vercoutter*: 343–354. Paris: Éditions Recherche sur les Civilisations.

Trigger, B.G. 2003. *Understanding Early Civilizations: A Comparative Study*. Cambridge: Cambridge University Press.

Tylecote, R.F. 1974. 'Can Copper Be Smelted in a Crucible.' *The Journal of the Historical Metallurgy Society* 8: 1–6.

Tylecote, R.F. 1980a. 'Furnaces, Crucibles, and Slags.' In eds. T.A. Wertime, J.D. Muhly, and J.A. Charles, *The Coming of the Age of Iron*: 183–228. New Haven; London: Yale University Press.

Tylecote, R.F. 1980b. 'Summary of Results of Experimental Work on Early Copper Smelting.' In ed. W.A. Oddy, *Aspects of Early Metallurgy*. British Museum Research Laboratory Occasional Paper; 17: 5–12. London: Department of Scientific Research, British Museum.

Tylecote, R.F. 1981. 'From Pot Bellows to Tuyéres.' *Levant: Journal of the British School of Archaeology in Jerusalem* 11: 107–118.

Tylecote, R.F. 1982. 'The Late Bronze Age: Copper and Bronze Metallurgy at Enkomi and Kition.' In eds. J.D. Muhly, R. Maddin, and V. Karageorghis, *Acta of the International Archaeological Symposium: Early Metallurgy in Cyprus, 4000–500 B.C.: Larnaca, Cyprus, 1–6 June 1981*: 81–103. Nicosia: Department of Antiquities of Cyprus.

Tylecote, R.F. 1986. *The Prehistory of Metallurgy in the British Isles*. Institute of Metals; 319. London: Institute of Metals.

Tylecote, R.F. and J.F. Merkel. 1985. 'Experimental Smelting Techniques: Achievements and Future.' In eds. P.T. Craddock and M.J. Hughes, *Furnaces and Smelting Technology in Antiquity*. British Museum Occasional Paper; 48: 3–20. London: British Museum.

Tylecote, R.F. and P.J. Boydell. 1978. 'Experiments on Copper Smelting Based on Early Furnaces Found at Timna.' In ed. B. Rothenberg, *Chalcolithic Copper Smelting*. Archaeo-Metallurgy; 1: 27–51. London: Institute for Archaeo-Metallurgical Studies.

Tylor, J.J. 1895. *Tomb of Paheri*. Wall Drawings and Monuments of El Kab. London: The Egypt Exploration Society.

Tzachili, I. 1999. 'The Making of Sails in the Second Millennium B.C.' In eds. P.P. Betancourt and M.H. Wiener, *Meletemata: Studies in Aegean Archaeology Presented to Malcolm H. Wiener as He Enters His 65th Year*. Vol. 3. Aegaeum; 20: 857–865. Liège: Université de Liège.

United States Department of Labor. 1899. *Thirteenth Annual Report of the Commissioner of Labor, 1898: Hand and Machine Labor*. Washington D.C.: U.S. Government Printing Office.

Vagnetti, L. 2001. 'How Far Did White Slip Pottery Travel? Some Evidence from Italy and from the Libyan Coast.' In ed. V. Karageorghis, *The White Slip Ware of Late Bronze Age Cyprus:*

Proceedings of an International Conference Organized by the Anastasios G. Leventis Foundation, Nicosia in Honour of Malcolm Wiener, Nicosia 29th-30th October 1997: 101–106. Vienna: Verlag der Österreichischen Akademie der Wissenschaften.

Van Oosterom, E.J., S. Ceccarelli, and J.M. Peacock. 1993. 'Yield Response of Barley to Rainfall and Temperature in Mediterranean Environments.' *Journal of Agricultural Science* 121: 307–313.

van Soldt, W.H. 1990. 'Fabrics and Dyes in Ugarit.' In eds. K. Bergerhof, M. Dietrich, and O. Loretz *Ugarit-Forschungen: Internationales Jahrbuch für die Altertumskunde Syrien-Palästinas* 22: 321–357. Kevelaer: Verlag Butzon and Bercker.

van Soldt, W.H. 1995. 'Ugarit.' In ed. J.M. Sasson, *Civilizations of the Ancient Near East.* Vol. 2: 1255–1266. New York: Scribner.

van Soldt, W.H. 2005. *The Topography of the City-State of Ugarit.* Alter Orient und Altes Testament; 324. Münster: Ugarit-Verlag.

van Wijngaarden, G.J. 1999. 'An Archaeological Approach to the Concept of Value.' *Archaeological Dialogues* 6: 2–23.

van Wijngaarden, G.J. 2002. *Use and Appreciation of Mycenaean Pottery in the Levant, Cyprus and Italy (1600–1200 B.C.).* Amsterdam Archaeological Studies; 8. Amsterdam: Amsterdam University Press.

Vargyas, P. 1986 'Trade and Prices in Ugarit.' *Oikumene* 5: 103–116.

Varisco, D.M. 1982. 'The Ard in Highland Yemeni Agriculture.' *Tools and Tillage* 4: 158–172.

Veenhof, K.R. 1972. *Aspects of Old Assyrian Trade and Its Terminology.* Leiden: Brill.

Veenhof, K.R. 1977. 'Some Social Effects of Old Assyrian Trade.' *Iraq* 39: 109–118.

Vella, N.C. 2004. 'A Maritime Perspective: Looking for Hermes in an Ancient Seascape.' In eds. J. Chrysostomides, C. Dendrinos, and J. Harris, *The Greek Islands and the Sea: Proceedings of the First International Colloquium Held at the Hellenic Institute, Royal Holloway, University of London, 21–22 September 2001*: 33–58. Camberley: Porphyrogenitus.

Ventris, M. and J. Chadwick. 1973. *Documents in Mycenaean Greek.* Cambridge: Cambridge University Press.

Vichos, Y. 1999. 'The Point Iria Wreck: The Nautical Dimension.' In eds. W.W. Phelps, Y.G. Lolos, and G. Vechos, *The Point Iria Wreck: Interconnections in the Mediterranean, ca. 1200 B.C.: Proceedings of the International Conference, Island of Spetses, 19 September 1998*: 77–98. Athens: Hellenic Institute of Marine Archaeology.

Vickers, M. and D. Gill. 1994. *Artful Crafts: Ancient Greek Silverware and Pottery.* Oxford: Clarendon Press.

Vinson, S. 1993. 'The Earliest Representations of Brailed Sails.' *Journal of the American Research Center in Egypt* 30: 133–150.

Virolleaud, C. 1953. 'Les Nouveaux textes alphabétiques de Ras-Shamra (XVIe Campagne 1952).' *Syria*: 187–195.

Vogelsang-Eastwood, G. 1992a. *Patterns for Ancient Egyptian Clothing.* Leiden: Stitching Textile Research Centre.

Vogelsang-Eastwood, G. 1992b. *The Production of Linen in Pharaonic Egypt.* Leiden: Stitching Textile Research Centre.

Vogelsang-Eastwood, G. 1993. *Pharaonic Egyptian Clothing.* Studies in Textile and Costume History; 2. Leiden; New York: Brill.

Vogelsang-Eastwood, G. 1994. *De Kleren van de Farao.* Amsterdam: Bataafsche Leeuw.

Vogelsang-Eastwood, G. 2000. 'Textiles.' In eds. P.T. Nicholson and I. Shaw, *Ancient Egyptian Materials and Technology*: 268–298. Cambridge: Cambridge University Press.

von Mises, L. 1949. *Human Action: A Treatise on Economics.* London: W. Hodge.

Wachsmann, S. 1998. *Seagoing Ships and Seamanship in the Bronze Age Levant.* London: Chatham Publishing.

Wachsmann, S. and D. Haldane. 1997. 'Anchors.' In ed. E.M. Meyers, *The Oxford Encyclopedia of Archaeology in the Near East.* Vol. 1: 137–140. Oxford: Oxford University Press.

Waetzoldt, H. 1972. *'Untersuchungen zur neusumerischen Textilindustrie.'* Studi Economici e Tecnologici; 1: Rome: [s.n.].

Waetzoldt, H. 1980–1983a. 'Clothing.' In eds. E. Ebeling, B. Meisner, and D.O. Edzard, *Reallexikon der Assyriologie* 6: 18–31. Berlin: Walter de Gruyer.

Waetzoldt, H. 1980–1983b. 'Leinen (Flachs).' In eds. E. Ebeling, B. Meisner, and D.O. Edzard, *Reallexikon der Assyriologie* 6: 583–594. Berlin: de Gruyer.

Waetzoldt, H. 1987. 'Compensation of Craft Workers and Officials in the UR II Period.' In ed. M.A. Powell, *Labor in the Ancient Near East.* American Oriental Series; 68: 117–142. New Haven: American Oriental Society.

Waki, M. 2002. 'Storage in Ancient Egyptian Towns and Cities (with a Focus on Amarna).' *Göttinger Miszellen* 190: 103–112.

Wallerstein, I.M. 1974a. *The Modern World System: Capitalist Agriculture and the Origins of the European World-Economy in the Sixteenth Century.* Vol. 1. New York: Academic Press.

Wallerstein, I.M. 1974b. 'The Rise and Future Demise of the World Capitalist System: Concepts for Comparative Analysis.' *Comparative Studies in Society and History* 16: 387–415.

Wallerstein, I.M. 1979. 'A World System Perspective on the Social Sciences.' *The Capitalist World-Economy.* Cambridge: Cambridge University Press: 152–154.

Warburton, D.A. 1997. *State and Economy in Ancient Egypt: Fiscal Vocabulary of the New Kingdom.* Orbis Biblicus et Orientalis; 151. Fribourg: Vandenhoeck and Ruprecht Göttingen.

Warburton, D.A. 2007. 'Work and Compensation in Ancient Egypt.' *Journal of Egyptian Archaeology* 93: 175–194.

Ward, C.A. 2000a. 'Sewn Planked Boats from Early Dynastic Abydos, Egypt.' In ed. C. Beltrame, *Boats, Ships and Shipyards: Proceedings of the Ninth International Symposium on Boat and Ship Archaeology, Venice 2000*: 19–23. Oxford: Oxbow.

Ward, C.A. 2000b. *Sacred and Secular: Ancient Egyptian Ships and Boats*. Monographs, Archaeological Institute of America; 5. Philadelphia: Published for the Archaeological Institute of America by the University Museum, University of Pennsylvania; Dubuque: Kendall/Hunt.

Ward, C.A. 2004. 'Boatbuilding in Ancient Egypt.' In eds. F.M. Hocker and C.A. Ward, *The Philosophy of Shipbuilding: Conceptual Approaches to the Study of Wooden Ships*: 15–24. College Station, Texas: Texas A&M University Press.

Ward, C.A. 2010. 'Seafaring in the Bronze Age Aegean: Evidence and Speculation.' In ed. D.J. Pullen, *Political Economies of the Aegean Bronze Age*: 149–160. Oxford: Oxbow Books.

Ward, C.A. and C. Zazzaro. 2007. 'Synthesis.' In eds. K.A. Bard, and R. Fattovich, *Harbor of the Pharaohs to the Land of Punt: Archaeological Investigations at Mersa/Wadi Gawasis, Egypt, 2001–2005*: 135–160. Naples: Università degli Studi di Napoli "L'Orientale".

Warnock, P. 2007. *Identification of Ancient Olive Oil Processing Methods Based on Olive Remains.* BAR International Series; 1635. Oxford: BAR Publishing.

Watrous, L.V. 1985. 'Late Bronze Age Kommos: Imported Pottery as Evidence of Foreign Contact.' In ed. A. Percival, *A Great Minoan Triangle in Southcentral Crete: Kommos, Hagia Triadha, Phaistos. Proceedings of the Kommos Symposium Royal York Hotel, Toronto, Canada Held on December 29th, 1984.* Vol. 6: 7–30. Mississauga, Ontario: Benben.

Watson, E.R., P. Lapins, and R.J.W. Barron. 1976. 'Effect of Waterlogging on the Growth, Grain and Straw Yield of Wheat and Oats.' *Australian Journal of Experimental Agriculture and Husbandry* 16: 114–122.

Watson, P.J. 1979. *Archaeology Ethnography in Western Iran.* Viking Fund Publications in Anthropology; 57. Tucson: University of Arizona Press.

Webb, J. and D. Frankel. 2004. 'Intensive Site Survey. Implications for Estimating Settlement Size, Population and Duration in Prehistoric Bronze Age Cyprus.' British School at Athens Studies 11: 125-137.

Weber, M. 1976 [1896]. *The Agrarian Sociology of Ancient Civilizations.* Translated by R.I. Frank. Foundations of History Library. First published as Agrarverhältnisse im Altertum, in Handwörterbuch der Staatwissenschaften, 1909; and Die sozialen Gründe des Untergangs der antiken Kultur, in Die Wahrheit, May 1896. London: NLB.

Weber, M. 1978 [1922]. *Economy and Society: an Outline of Interpretive Sociology.* Eds. G. Roth and C. Wittich. Translated from *Wirtschaft und Gesellschaft*, Fourth German Edition. Berkeley: University of California Press.

Weber, M. 2009 [1905]. *The Protestant Ethic and the Spirit of Capitalism.* Translated from *Die protestantische Ethik und der Geist des Kapitalismus,* Fourth Edition, introduced by Stephen Kalberg. Oxford: Oxford University Press.

Webley, D. 1972. 'Soils and Site Location in Prehistoric Palestine.' In ed. E.S. Higgs, *Papers in Economic Prehistory*: 169-180. Cambridge: Cambridge University Press.

Weisgerber, G. 1982. 'Towards a History of Copper Mining in Cyprus and the Near East: Possibilities of Mining Archaeology.' In eds. J.D. Muhly, R. Maddin, and V. Karageorghis, *Acta of the International Archaeological Symposium: Early Metallurgy in Cyprus, 4000–500 B.C.: Larnaca, Cyprus, 1–6 June 1981*: 25–32. Nicosia: The Foundation.

Weisgerber, G. 2006. 'The Mineral Wealth of Ancient Arabia and Its Use: Copper Mining and Smelting at Feinan and Timna – Comparison and Evaluation of Techniques, Production, and Strategies.' *Arabian Archaeology and Epigraphy* 17: 1–30.

Weisgerber, G. and E. Pernicka 1995. 'Ore Mining in Prehistoric Europe.' In eds. G. Morteani and J.P. Northover, *Prehistoric Gold in Europe*: 159–182. Amsterdam: Klewer Academic Publishers.

Weisgerber, G. and J. Cierny. 2002. 'Tin for Ancient Anatolia.' In ed. Ü. Yalçin, *Anatolian Metal.* Vol. 2. Der Anschnitt, Beiheft; 15: 179–186. Bochum: Deutsches Bergbau-Museum.

Weiss, H. 1997. 'Late Third Millennium Abrupt Climate Change and Social Collapse in West Asia and Egypt.' In eds. H.N. Dalfes, G. Kukla, and H. Weiss, *Third Millennium BC Climate Change and Old World Collapse*: 711–724. London: Springer.

Werker, E. 1988. 'The Finds: Wood.' In ed. B. Rothenberg, *The Mining Temple at Timna. Researches in the Arabah 1959–1984*: 232–235. London: Institute for Archaeo-Metallurgical Studies.

Wernick, N. 2004. 'A Khepesh Sword in the University of Liverpool Museum.' *Journal of the Society for the Study of Egyptian Antiquities* 31: 151–155.

Wertime, T.A. 1982. 'Cypriot Metallurgy Against the Backdrop of Mediterranean Pyrotechnology: Energy Reconsidered.' In eds. J.D. Muhly, R. Maddin, and V. Karageorghis, *Acta of the International Archaeological Symposium: Early Metallurgy in Cyprus, 4000–500 B.C.: Larnaca, Cyprus, 1–6 June 1981*: 351–361. Nicosia: The Foundation.

Wertime, T.A. 1983. 'The Furnace versus the Goat: The Pyrotechnologic Industries and Mediterranean Deforestation in Antiquity.' *The Journal of Field Archaeology* 10: 445–452.

White, D. 1999. 'Water, Wood, Dung and Eggs: Reciprocity in Trade Along the LBA Marmarican Coast.' In eds. P.P. Betancourt and M.H. Wiener, *Meletemata: Studies in Aegean Archaeology Presented to Malcolm H. Wiener as He Enters His 65th Year*. Vol. 3. Aegaeum; 20: 931–937. Liège: Université de Liège.

White, D. 2003. 'Multim in Parvo: Bate's Island on the NW Coast of Egypt.' In eds. N.C. Stampolis and V. Karageorghis, *Sea Routes: Interconnections in the Mediterranean 16th - 6th C. B.C.: Proceedings of the International Symposium Held at Rethymnon, Crete. September 29th–October 2nd 2002*: 71–82. Athens: University of Crete and the A.G. Leventis Foundation.

White, D., R. Gardner and L. Hulin. 2002. *Marsa Matruh: The University of Pennsylvania Museum of Archaeology and Anthropology's Excavations on Bates's Island, Marsa Matruh, Egypt, 1985–1989.* Prehistory Monographs; 1–2. Philadelphia: Institute for Aegean Prehistory Academic Press.

Whittaker, J.C. 2000. 'The Ethnoarchaeology of Threshing in Cyprus.' *Near Eastern Archaeology* 63: 62–69.

Whittaker, J.C. 2003. 'Threshing Sledges and Threshing Floors in Cyprus.' In eds. P.C. Anderson, L.S. Cummings, T.K. Schippers, and B. Simonel, *Le Traitement des récoltes: un regard sur la diversité du Néolithique au present*: 375–387. Antibes: APDCA.

Widtsoe, A.M. 1913. *Dry-Farming: A System of Agriculture for Countries Under Low Rainfall.* New York: Macmillan.

Wild, J.P. 2002. 'The Textile Industries of Roman Britain.' *Britannia* 33: 1–42.

Wilke, T. 2000. 'Ancient Egypt: An Economist's View.' *Göttinger Miszellen* 178: 81–95.

Wilkinson, T.J. 1994. 'The Structure and Dynamics of Dry-Farming States in Upper Mesopotamia.' *Current Anthropology* 35: 483–505.

Wilkinson, T.J. 1997. 'Environmental Fluctuations, Agricultural Production and Collapse. A View from Bronze Age Mesopotamia.' In eds. H.N. Dalfes, G. Kukla, and H. Weiss, *Third Millennium BC Climate Change and Old World Collapse*: 67–106. London: Springer.

Willcocks, W. 1889. *Egyptian Irrigation.* London: E. and F.N. Spon.

Willcocks, W. 1904. *The Assuân Reservoir and Lake Moeris*. London; New York: E. and F.N. Spon Ltd.

Willcocks, W. and H.J.L. Beadnell. 1904. *The Nile in 1904*. London: E. and F.N. Spon.

Willcox G.H. 1974. 'A History of Deforestation as Indicated by Charcoal Analysis of Four Sites in Eastern Anatolia.' *Anatolian Studies* 24: 117–133.

Williams-Thorpe, O., R.S. Thorpe, C. Elliott, and C. Xenophontos. 1991. 'Archaeology, Geochemistry, and Trade of Igneous Rock Millstones in Cyprus During the Late Bronze Age to Roman Periods.' *Geoarchaeology* 6; 27-60.

World Bank, FAO, and IFAD. 2008. *Missing Food: The Case of Postharvest Grain Losses in Sub-Saharan Africa*. Washington, DC: World Bank, Report Number 60371–AFR.

Worrall, G.A. 1958. 'Deposition of Silt by the Irrigation Waters of the Nile at Khartoum.' *The Geographical Journal* 124: 219–222.

Wright, G.R.H. 1992. *Ancient Building in Cyprus*. Vol. 1. Handbuch der Orientalistik. Siebente Abteilung, Kunst und Archäologie; 1. Leiden: Brill.

Yalçin, Ü., C. Pulak and R. Slotta. 2005. *Das Schiff von Uluburun: Welthandel vor 3000 Jahren: Katalog der Ausstellung des Deutschen Bergbau-Museums Bochum vom 15. Juli 2005 bis 16. Juli 2006*, Veröffentlichungen aus dem Deutschen Bergbau-Museum Bochum; 138. Bochum: Deutsches Bergbau-Museum.

Yener, K.A. and P.B. Vandiver. 1993. 'Tin Processing at Goltepe, an Early Bronze Age Site in Anatolia.' *American Journal of Archaeology* 97: 207–238.

Yener, K.A., P.B. Vandiver, and L. Willies. 1993. 'Reply to J.D. Muhly, "Early Bronze Age Tin and the Taurus."' *American Journal of Archaeology* 97: 255–264.

Yerks, R.W. 2000. 'Ethnoarchaeology in Central Cyprus: Interdisciplinary Studies of Ancient Population and Agriculture by the Athienou Archaeological Project.' *Near Eastern Archaeology* 63: 20–34.

Yon, M. 1994. 'Ougarit et ses relations avec les régions maritimes voisines (d'après travaux récents).' In eds. G.J. Brooke, A. Curtis, and J.F. Healy, *Ugarit and the Bible: Proceedings of the International Symposium on Ugarit and the Bible, Manchester, September 1992*: 421–439. Münster: Ugarit-Verlag.

Yon, M. 1999. 'Chypre et Ougarit à la fin du Bronze Récent.' *Report of the Department of Antiquities Cyprus*: 113–119.

Yon, M. 2001. 'White Slip Ware in the Northern Levant.' In ed. V. Karageorghis, *The White Slip Ware of Late Bronze Age Cyprus: Proceedings of an International Conference Organized by the Anastasios G. Leventis Foundation, Nicosia in Honour of Malcolm Wiener, Nicosia 29th-30th October 1998*: 117–125. Vienna: Verlag der Österreichischen Akademie der Wissenschaften.

Yon, M. 2003. 'The Foreign Relations of Ugarit.' In: eds. N.C. Stampolidis and V. Karageorghis, *Sea Routes: Interconnections in the Mediterranean, 16th-6th c. BC: Proceedings of the International Symposium Held at Rethymnon, Crete, September 29th–October 2nd, 2002*: 41–52. Athens: Published by the University of Crete and the A.G. Leventis Foundation 2003.

Yon, M. 2006. *The City of Ugarit at Tell Ras Shamra.* Winona Lake: Eisenbrauns.

Young, G.D. 1979. 'A Merchant's Balanced Account and Neosumerian Gold.' In eds. T.B. Jones and R.H. Sack, *Studies in Honor of Tom B. Jones*. Alter Orient und Altes Testament; 203: 195–217. Kevelaer; Neukirchen-Vluyn: Butzon and Bercker: Neukirchener Verlag.

Younger K.L. 2007. 'The Late Bronze Age/Iron Age Transition and the Origins of the Arameans.' In ed. K.L. Younger, *Ugarit at Seventy-Five*: 131–175. Winona Lake: Eisenbrauns.

Zaccagnini, C. 1975. 'The Yield of Fields at Nuzi.' *Oriens Antiquus* 14: 181–225.

Zaccagnini, C. 1987. 'Aspects of Ceremonial Exchange in the Near East During the Late Second Millennium BC.' In eds. M. Rowlands, M. Larsen, and K. Kristiansen, *Centre and Periphery in the Ancient World. New Directions in Archaeology*: 57–65. Cambridge: Cambridge University Press.

Zaccagnini, C. 1989. 'Asiatic Mode of Production and Ancient Near East: Notes Towards a Discussion.' In ed. C. Zaccagnini, *Production and Consumption in the Ancient Near East*: 1–126. Budapest: University of Budapest.

Zaccagnini, C. 2000. 'The Interdependence of the Great Powers.' In eds. R. Cohen and R. Westbrook, *Amarna Diplomacy: The Beginning of International Relations*: 141–153. Baltimore: Johns Hopkins University.

Zahran, M.A. and A.J. Willis. 1992. *The Vegetation of Egypt*. London; New York: Chapman and Hall.

Zaky, A. 1942. 'Ancient Egyptian Cheese.' *Annales du Service des antiquités de l'Égypte* 41: 295–313.

Zangger, E. 1992. 'Prehistoric and Historic Soils in Greece: Assessing the Natural Resources for Agriculture.' In ed. B. Wells, *Agriculture in Ancient Greece: Proceedings of the Seventh International Symposium at the Swedish Institute of Athens, 16–17 May 1990.* Skrifter Utgivna av Svenska institutet i Athen; 42: 13–19. Stockholm: Svenska institutet i Athen.

Zertal, A. 1996. 'The Cultivation and the Economy of Olives During the Iron Age in the Hill-Country of Manasseh.' *Olive Oil in Antiquity: Israel and Neighbouring Countries from the Neolithic to the Early Arab Period.* History of the Ancient Near East Studies; 7: 307–314. Padova: Sargon.

Zohary, D. and M. Hopf. 1994. *Domestication of Plants in the Old World. The Origin and Spread of Cultivated Plants in West Asia, Europe and the Nile Valley.* Second Edition. Oxford: Clarendon Press.